PROFESSIONAL ETHICS AND INSIGNIA

by

JANE CLAPP

The Scarecrow Press, Inc.
Metuchen, N.J.   1974

Library of Congress Cataloging in Publication Data

Clapp, Jane.
    Professional ethics and insignia.

    Bibliography: p.
    1. Trade and professional associations--United States
--Directories. 2. Trade and professional associations--
United States--Handbooks, manuals, etc. I. Title.
HD6504.A194   061'.3   74-10501
ISBN 0-8108-0735-1

CONTENTS

v

vii

ix

INTRODUCTION

Professional Ethics and Insignia brings together the codes of conduct and the emblems of major professional organizations in the
United States.   Each of the 205 organizations listed has one or
more of the following:
  (1) A code of ethics; code of conduct, standards, or rules;
       or other document or procedure for the self-regulation
       of actions of members;
  (2) An emblem;
  (3) An accreditation program, in which sequential awards
       in the form of professional designations (letters or title)
       are granted.   These accreditations--which have prolif-
       erated within the past twenty-five years--are described
       because they represent a voluntary indication of com-
       petence (through certification, registration, or chartering)
       by occupational groups.   These awards are directed to
       providing the public with an indication of members, or
       other individuals, judged competent on the basis of pre-
       scribed education, experience, examinations, or other
       qualifications.

The groups described are major national organizations in all occupational areas--the biological and physical sciences; social sciences;
fine arts and humanities; and technology.   Most are professional
associations, but certain additional groups considered to be of current public interest and a sampling of other types of occupational
organizations are described.   These include:

   Trade Associations: American Advertising Federation; Inde-
      pendent Garage Owners of America; Associated General
      Contractors of America; National Hearing Aid Society;
      National Association of Manufacturers; and--in the "mass
      media"--American Newspaper Publishers Association;
      Motion Picture Association of America; National Associa-
      tion of Broadcasters; and Comics Magazine Association
      of America.

   Labor Unions and Workers in Trades: American Federation
      of Labor and Congress of Industrial Organizations;

1

National Automotive Technicians Certification Board;
The Newspaper Guild.

Businesses: American Society of Composers, Authors, and
     Publishers; New York Stock Exchange.

United States Government Employees: In addition to two gen-
     eral occupational headings (Government Employees--
     Civilian, and Government Employees--Military) includes
     Federal Mediation and Conciliation Service (under ARBI-
     TRATORS); National Archives and Records Service (under
     ARCHIVISTS); United States Department of Commerce
     (under BUSINESSMEN); and Judicial Conference of the
     United States (under JUDGES).

While most of the organizations are located in the United States,
with membership drawn from this area, a few international associations are listed, including the International Bar Association,
London; World Medical Association, New York; International Commission on Zoological Nomenclature, London; and one foreign group
--The Heraldry Society, London.

The groups described are a sampling only of the great number of
occupational organizations in the United States that have published
codes of ethics, adopted an insignia, or that award professional
designations.   Information about each organization was obtained from
the organization and in all but a few instances the information was
reviewed in draft form by the organization, for factual correctness.

Groups are listed under 173 general occupations, alphabetically
ranging from ACCOUNTANTS to ZOOLOGISTS, and are then (if
there is more than one organization) arranged alphabetically under
the occupation.   Information about each group is given in a standardized format (varying in completeness with information provided):

ASSOCIATION NAME, address, and corresponding officer.

Membership: Date group founded, changes in association
     name; categories and qualifications for membership; pro-
     fessional designations awarded in the form of titles and
     initials, as an organizational control of competence; quali-
     fications for professional designation--education; experi-
     ence; written, oral or performance tests; published re-
     search or other reports or publications.

Code of Ethics: Information about conduct guide--standards or
     ideals of professional (or occupational) conduct or per-
     formance--"formulated to guarantee competence and honour
     of professional practitioners" (Carr-Saunders:302).   These
     rules and traditions--voluntarily promulgated and sub-
     scribed to--are alternative to or in addition to statutory
     regulation.   They may vary from a brief hortatory state-

ment to a detailed conduct guide. Periodic revision of
the code to accommodate social or professional changes.
Interpretation of code provisions. Implementation pro-
cedure--who receives and investigates complaints of unprofessional conduct, holds hearings, appeals. Disciplinary action for infractions of code of conduct, or unprofessional conduct.
　　The actual text of each code of ethics will be given
at the end of the whole entry for each association.

Other Guides to Professional Conduct: In addition to the code
of ethics, an oath, pledge, or other rules for specific or
special occupational activity.

Professional Insignia: The emblem associated with the or-
ganization--its seal, insignia, monogram, or logotype.
Described verbally and pictured (in black and white).
Official or unofficial color of the emblem is given. Significance of emblem or its symbols is included. Motto
of the organization is shown, with translation if in language other than English. No attempt has been made to
describe the insignia in technical (heraldic) form. The
only emblem blazoned in conventional heraldic style is
that of The Heraldry Society (under HERALDS).

Other Identification of Professional Status: Includes professional designations--titles, letters, insignia authorized
by the organization; may describe and picture insignia
denoting grade of membership or of designation. Additional forms of emblems may be described and pictured--
as a banner, a flag, a coat of arms.

Bibliography: An annotated list of printed sources of information, furnished by the organization described. Includes
general informational brochures; history of organization;
accreditation procedure; code of ethics, and other conduct
guide, interpretations of ethical code; insignia, with history
and symbolism; description of accreditation, or other,
examinations, with a list of suggested readings and outline of examination form and content; basic documents of
group's organization--Constitution and Bylaws.

At the end of the entry for each association is given the full
text of its "code of ethics"--often called just that and
sometimes "standards" or "rules" of conduct, and the
like.

The other sections of this book are:

BIBLIOGRAPHY--A brief, selected list of recent (last five
years) or especially significant older publications in English about occupational organizations; professions, pro-

fessional associations, professional ethics; professional
accrediting programs.

INDEX--A detailed listing to provide immediate reference to
    occupational group, association name, professional desig-
    nations and titles, abbreviations of association names and
    professional designations, and subjects--including, code of
    ethics texts, and other conduct guides, as pledge, credos,
    oaths.

Appreciation is expressed to the organizations and their employees
who provided information and reviewed drafts, and who allowed the
printing of their codes of ethics, or other conduct guides, and the
reproduction of their emblems or insignia--which are registered or
copyrighted, and may be used only by the organizations or their
designated members.

ACCOUNTANTS

AMERICAN INSTITUTE OF CERTIFIED PUBLIC ACCOUNTANTS
(AICPA)
666 Fifth Avenue, New York, N.Y. 10019
John Lawler, Administrative Vice President

Membership: The American Institute of Certified Public Accountants, founded in 1887 and with a present (1973) membership of about 81,000, is a professional association of accountants, certified by state authorities as professionally competent. The Institute requires for full professional membership:
(1) Possession of a certified public accountant certificate issued by a State of the United States;
(2) Passing "an examination in accounting and related subjects satisfactory to the committee on admissions";
(3) Experience of two years in public accounting practice, as an independent accountant or in the employ of a practicing public accountant, or equivalent.

Code of Ethics: One of the purposes of the Institute--"To promote and maintain high professional and moral standards within the accountancy profession" (By-Laws I)--is carried out in part by the issuance and enforcement of a code of ethics, which has been in force since the inception of the organization. The present code of ethics--Rules of Conduct--of the AICPA, effective March 1, 1973, sets forth guides to the professional conduct of public accountants in five sections:
Independence, Integrity and Objectivity;
Competence and Technical Standards;
Responsibility to Clients;
Responsibility to Colleagues;
Other Responsibilities and Practices.

5

The Rules of Conduct, subject to amendments only by vote of
the Institute membership, is enforced through two permanent AICPA
committees:

> Professional Ethics Division--which receives and investigates
> complaints of infractions of the Rules;
> Trial Board--which conducts disciplinary hearings, which
> may result in censure, suspension, or revocation of member-
> ship.   Interpretive Opinions of the Ethical Division are
> printed as a section in the Restatement of the Code of Pro-
> fessional Ethics.   Prior to the current Rules of Conduct
> (effective March 1, 1973), 22 Ethical Opinions were printed,
> dealing with such questions as "Advertising," "Prohibited
> Self-Incrimination," "Data Processing Services," "Indepen-
> dence," "Tax Practice," "Specialization," and "Participation
> in Educational Seminars."

Professional Insignia: The AICPA seal is the Institute's official
emblem: a round design showing an eagle with out-stretched wings

beneath a balance scale, a shield
--symbolic of the United States--
on its chest (six colored vertical
bars alternate with seven white
bars), with a wide horizontal top
bar bearing two rows of stars
(7 and 6); the eagle perches on an
arched scroll carrying the motto
of the Institute, "Custos Fidelitatis"
("Faithful Guardian"), and the
border of the seal shows the organization name, "American Institute of Certified Public Accountants."

Other Identification of Professional Status: Upon election to the
Institute, a professional member is issued a "Certificate of Membership," and may hold himself out on letterheads, cards, as a
member.   A firm or partnership of accountants, all of whose partners are members of the Institute, may describe itself as "Members
of the American Institute of Certified Public Accountants" (Rules of
Conduct, Rule 505).   Members of AICPA are expressly prohibited
from describing themselves as "Tax Consultant" or "Tax Specialist"
(Interpretations of Rules of Conduct, 502.9), which follows the rules
promulgated in 1951 by the National Conference of Lawyers and
Certified Public Accountants (Statement of Principles Relating to
Practice in the Field of Federal Income Taxation).

Bibliography:
> American Institute of Certified Public Accountants.   By-Laws,
>   as amended to February 20, 1969.   Pamphlet.   42 pages.
>   Includes qualifications for membership and issuance of Cer-
>   tificate of Membership, and procedures for enforcement of
>   the Rules of Conduct.
> _____.   Restatement of the Code of Professional Ethics,

effective March 1, 1973. 1972. 43 pages.
Three parts are: Concepts of Professional Ethics; Rules of
Conduct; Interpretations of Rules of Conduct.
_____. Summaries of Ethics Rulings. New York, The Insti-
tute, 1970. 196 pages. paperbound. $4.50.
Question-and-answer format summary "of more than 350 of
the most interesting and significant rulings" on professional
ethics of the AICPA.

Cary, John L. The CPA Plans for the Future. New York,
The Institute, 1965. 559 pages. $6.
"Ethics" is one of the topics discussed in the chapter,
"Foundations of Professional Status."
_____, and William O. Doherty. Ethical Standards of the
Accounting Profession. New York, The Institute, 1966.
330 pages. $6.
"Expert explanation and analysis of the ethical rules which
govern the CPA's practice of accountancy," with index.
_____. The Rise of the Accountancy Profession. New York,
The Institute, 1970. 2 vols. vol. 1, 387 pages, $9.50;
vol. 2, 545 pages, $11.50.
Chapters in volume 1 consider "Ethics and Self Discipline"
and "Development of Standards of Competence"; in volume 2
"Ethical Responsibilities" are discussed.

"Rules of Conduct"*

DEFINITIONS

The following definitions of terminology are applicable wherever such terminology is used in the rules and interpretations.
Client. The person(s) or entity which retains a member or
his firm, engaged in the practice of public accounting, for the performance of professional services.
Council. The Council of the American Institute of Certified
Public Accountants.
Enterprise. Any person(s) or entity, whether organized for
profit or not, for which a CPA provides services.

---

*In the numbered notes below (presented at the end), the references
to specific rules or numbered Opinions indicate that revised sections
are derived therefrom; where modifications have been made to the
present rule or Opinion, it is noted. The reference to "prior rulings" indicates a position previously taken by the ethics division in
response to a specific complaint or inquiry, but not previously published. The reference to "new" indicates a recommendation of the
Code restatement committee not found in the present Code or prior
rulings of the ethics division. References in the notes and in the
text ["(See Interpretation...)"] are to Restatement of the Code...,
the second item of the Bibliography.

Firm. A proprietorship, partnership or professional corporation or association engaged in the practice of public accounting,
including individual partners or shareholders thereof.

Financial statements. Statements and footnotes related
thereto that purport to show financial position which relates to a
point in time or changes in financial position which relate to a period of time, and statements which use a cash or other incomplete
basis of accounting. Balance sheets, statements of income, statements of retained earnings, statements of changes in financial position and statements of changes in owners' equity are financial statements.

Incidental financial data included in management advisory
services reports to support recommendations to a client, and tax
returns and supporting schedules do not, for this purpose, constitute
financial statements; and the statement, affidavit or signature of
preparers required on tax returns neither constitutes an opinion
on financial statements nor requires a disclaimer of such opinion.

Institute. The American Institute of Certified Public Accountants.

Interpretations of Rules of Conduct. Pronouncements issued
by the Division of Professional Ethics to provide guidelines as to
the scope and application of the Rules of Conduct.

Member. A member, associate member or international
associate of the American Institute of Certified Public Accountants.

Practice of public accounting. Holding out to be a CPA or
public accountant and at the same time performing for a client one
or more types of services rendered by public accountants. The
term shall not be limited by more restrictive definition which might
be found in the accountancy law under which a member practices.

Professional services. One or more types of services performed in the practice of public accounting.

APPLICABILITY OF RULES

The Institute's Code of Professional Ethics derives its authority from the bylaws of the Institute which provide that the Trial
Board may, after a hearing, admonish, suspend or expel a member who is found guilty of infringing any of the bylaws or any provisions of the Rules of Conduct. [1]

The Rules of Conduct which follow apply to all services performed in the practice of public accounting including tax[2] and
management advisory services[3] except (a) where the wording of
the rule indicates otherwise and (b) that a member who is practicing
outside the United States will not be subject to discipline for departing from any of the rules stated herein so long as his conduct
is in accord with the rules of the organized accounting profession in
the country in which he is practicing. [4] However, where a member's
name is associated with financial statements in such a manner as

to imply that he is acting as an independent public accountant and under circumstances that would entitle the reader to assume that United States practices were followed, he must comply with the requirements of Rules 202 and 203. [5]

A member may be held responsible for compliance with the Rules of Conduct by all persons associated with him in the practice of public accounting who are either under his supervision or are his partners or shareholders in the practice. [6]

A member engaged in the practice of public accounting must observe all the Rules of Conduct. A member not engaged in the practice of public accounting must observe only Rules 102 and 501 since all other Rules of Conduct relate solely to the practice of public accounting. [7]

A member shall not permit others to carry out on his behalf, either with or without compensation, acts which, if carried out by the member, would place him in violation of the Rules of Conduct. [8]

INDEPENDENCE, INTEGRITY AND OBJECTIVITY

Rule 101--Independence. A member or a firm of which he is a partner or shareholder shall not express an opinion on financial statements of an enterprise unless he and his firm are independent with respect to such enterprise. [9] Independence will be considered to be impaired if, for example:

    A.   During the period of his professional engagement, or at the time of expressing his opinion, he or his firm
1. Had or was committed to acquire any direct or material indirect financial interest in the enterprise;[10] or
2. Had any joint closely held business investment with the enterprise or any officer, director or principal stockholder thereof which was material in relation to his or his firm's net worth;[11] or
3. Had any loan to or from the enterprise or any officer, director or principal stockholder thereof. [12] This latter proscription does not apply to the following loans from a financial institution when made under normal lending procedures, terms and requirements:
   (a)   Loans obtained by a member or his firm which are not material in relation to the net worth of such borrower.
   (b)   Home mortgages.
   (c)   Other secured loans, except loans guaranteed by a member's firm which are otherwise unsecured. [13]

    B.   During the period covered by the financial statements, during the period of the professional engagement or at the time of expressing an opinion, he or his firm

1. Was connected with the enterprise as a promoter, underwriter or voting trustee, a director or officer or in any
   capacity equivalent to that of a member of management or
   of an employee;[14] or
2. Was a trustee of any trust or executor or administrator
   of any estate if such trust or estate had a direct or
   material indirect financial interest in the enterprise; or
   was a trustee for any pension or profit-sharing trust of
   the enterprise. [15]

The above examples are not intended to be all-inclusive.
(See Interpretations 101-1, 101-2, and 101-3, pages 32-3 of the
Code.)

Rule 102--Integrity and objectivity. A member shall not
knowingly misrepresent facts, and when engaged in the practice of
public accounting, including the rendering of tax and management
advisory services, shall not subordinate his judgment to others. [16]
In tax practice, a member may resolve doubt in favor of his client
as long as there is reasonable support for his position. [17]

COMPETENCE AND TECHNICAL STANDARDS

Rule 201--Competence. A member shall not undertake any
engagement which he or his firm cannot reasonably expect to complete with professional competence. [18] (See Interpretation 201-1,
page 34 of the Code.)

Rule 202--Auditing standards. A member shall not permit
his name to be associated with financial statements in such a manner as to imply that he is acting as an independent public accountant
unless he has complied with the applicable generally accepted auditing
standards [ten such are listed in Appendix A, page 26 of the Code]
promulgated by the Institute. Statements on Auditing Procedure
issued by the Institute's committee on auditing procedure are, for
purposes of this rule, considered to be interpretations of the generally accepted auditing standards, and departures, from such statements must be justified by those who do not follow them. [19]

Rule 203--Accounting principles. A member shall not express an opinion that financial statements are presented in conformity with generally accepted accounting principles if such statements
contain any departure from an accounting principle promulgated by
the body designated by Council to establish such principles which
has a material effect on the statements taken as a whole, unless
the member can demonstrate that due to unusual circumstances the
financial statements would otherwise have been misleading. In such
cases his report must describe the departure, the approximate
effects thereof, if practicable, and the reasons why compliance
with the principle would result in a misleading statement. [20] (See
Interpretation 203-1, page 35 of the Code.-)

Rule 204--Forecasts. A member shall not permit his name to be used in conjunction with any forecast of future transactions in a manner which may lead to the belief that the member vouches for the achievability of the forecast. [21] (See Interpretation 204-1, page 36 of the Code.)

RESPONSIBILITIES TO CLIENTS

Rule 301--Confidential client information. A member shall not disclose any confidential information obtained in the course of a professional engagement except with the consent of the client. [22]

This rule shall not be construed (a) to relieve a member of his obligation under Rules 202 and 203, (b) to affect in any way his compliance with a validly issued subpoena or summons enforceable by order of a court, (c) to prohibit review of a member's professional practices as a part of voluntary quality review under Institute authorization or (d) to preclude a member from responding to any inquiry made by the ethics division or Trial Board of the Institute, by a duly constituted investigative or disciplinary body of a state CPA society, or under state statutes. [23]

Members of the ethics division and Trial Board of the Institute and professional practice reviewers under Institute authorization shall not disclose any confidential client information which comes to their attention from members in disciplinary proceedings or otherwise in carrying out their official responsibilities. However, this prohibition shall not restrict the exchange of information with an aforementioned duly constituted investigative or disciplinary body. [24] (See Interpretation 301-1, page 36 of the Code.)

Rule 302--Contingent fees. [25] Professional services shall not be offered or rendered under an arrangement whereby no fee will be charged unless a specified finding or result is attained, or where the fee is otherwise contingent upon the findings or results of such services. However, a member's fees may vary depending, for example, on the complexity of the service rendered. [26]

Fees are not regarded as being contingent if fixed by courts or other public authorities or, in tax matters, if determined based on the results of judicial proceedings or the findings of governmental agencies. [27]

RESPONSIBILITIES TO COLLEAGUES

Rule 401--Encroachment. [28] A member shall not endeavor to provide a person or entity with a professional service which is currently provided by another public accountant except:

1. He may respond to a request for a proposal to render services and may furnish service to those who request it. [29] However, if an audit client of another independent public accountant requests a member to provide professional advice on accounting or auditing matters in connection with an expression of opinion on financial statements, the member must first consult with the other

accountant to ascertain that the member is aware of all the available relevant facts. [30]

2. Where a member is required to express an opinion on combined or consolidated financial statements which include a subsidiary, branch or other component audited by another independent public accountant, he may insist on auditing any such component which in his judgment is necessary to warrant the expression of his opinion. [31]

A member who receives an engagement for services by referral from another public accountant shall not accept the client's request to extend his service beyond the specific engagement without first notifying the referring accountant, nor shall he seek to obtain any additional engagement from the client. [32] (See Interpretations 401-1 and 401-2, page 37 or the Code.)

Rule 402--Offers of employment. A member in public practice shall not make a direct or indirect offer of employment to an employee of another public accountant on his own behalf or that of his client without first informing such accountant. This rule shall not apply if the employee of his own initiative or in response to a public advertisement applies for employment. [33]

OTHER RESPONSIBILITIES AND PRACTICES

Rule 501--Acts discreditable. A member shall not commit an act discreditable to the profession. [34]

Rule 502--Solicitation and advertising. A member shall not seek to obtain clients by solicitation. [35] Advertising is a form of solicitation and is prohibited. [36] (See Interpretations 502-1 to -14, pages 37-42 of the Code.)

Rule 503--Commissions. A member shall not pay a commission to obtain a client, nor shall he accept a commission for a referral to a client of products or services of others. [37] This rule shall not prohibit payments for the purchase of an accounting practice[38] or retirement payments to individuals formerly engaged in the practice of public accounting or payments to their heirs or estates. [39] (See Interpretation 503-1, page 42 of the Code.)

Rule 504--Incompatible occupations. A member who is engaged in the practice of public accounting shall not concurrently engaged in any business or occupation which impairs his objectivity in rendering professional services or serves as a feeder to his practice. [40]

Rule 505--Form of practice and name. A member may practice public accounting, whether as an owner or employee, only in the form of a proprietorship, a partnership or a professional corporation whose characteristics conform to resolutions of Council. [41] (See Appendix B, page 28 of the Code.)

A member shall not practice under a firm name which includes any fictitious name, indicates specialization or is misleading as to the type of organization (proprietorship, partnership or corporation). [42] However, names of one or more past partners or shareholders may be included in the firm name of a successor partnership or corporation. [43] Also, a partner surviving the death or withdrawal of all other partners may continue to practice under the partnership name for up to two years after becoming a sole practitioner. [44]

A firm may not designate itself as "Members of the American Institute of Certified Public Accountants" unless all of its partners or shareholders are members of the Institute. [45] (See Interpretation 505-1, page 43 of the Code.)

[1] Bylaw Section 7.4.
[2] Opinion No. 13.
[3] Opinion No. 14.
[4] Prior ruling.
[5] Rules 2.01, 2.02, 2.03 and prior rulings.
[6] New.
[7] New.
[8] Opinion No. 2.
[9] Rule 1.01 ("shareholder" added to recognize corporate practice).
[10] Rule 1.01.
[11] Prior rulings.
[12] Prior rulings.
[13] Opinion No. 19.
[14] Rule 1.01 (present Rule 1.01 uses the phrase "key employee").
[15] Prior rulings. In order that a member may arrange an orderly transition of his relationship with clients, section B2 or Rule 101 relating to trusteeships and executorships will not become effective until two years following the adoption of these Rules of Conduct.
[16] New.
[17] Opinion No. 13.
[18] New.

[19] New (replaces Rules 2.01-2.03).
[20] New (replaces Rules 2.01-2.03).
[21] Restatement of Rule 2.04.
[22] Restatement of Rule 1.03.
[23] Prior rulings.
[24] New.
[25] Restatement of Rule 1.04.
[26] New.
[27] Rule 1.04.
[28] Restatement of Rule 5.01.
[29] Rule 5.01.
[30] New.
[31] Opinion No. 20.
[32] Rule 5.02 restated to include prior rulings.
[33] Rule 5.03, "or that of his client" added.
[34] Rule 1.02.
[35] Rule 3.02
[36] Rule 3.01.
[37] Restatement of Rule 3.04.
[38] Prior rulings.
[39] Opinion No. 6.
[40] Restatement of Rule 4.04.
[41] Rule 4.06.
[42] Prior rulings.
[43] Rule 4.02.
[44] Prior rulings.
[45] Rule 4.01.

NATIONAL SOCIETY OF PUBLIC ACCOUNTANTS (NSPA)
1717 Pennsylvania Ave., N.W., Washington, D.C. 20006
Stanley Stearman, Executive Director

<u>Membership</u>: The National Society of Public Accountants, founded
in 1945 and with a present (1973) membership of over 13,000, is
a professional association of accountants in public practice. NSPA
"Active Members"--the fully professional membership category--
must be:
 "Certified Public Accountants;
 Licensed or Registered Public Accountants;
 Other practitioners who have had at least 3 years of public
 accounting experience or the equivalent, who hold themselves
 out to the public, and who maintain an office for the rendition of accounting, tax, or related services."
 Members are organized in affiliated societies throughout the
United States.

<u>Code of Ethics</u>: The guide to professional conduct of the NSPA--
carrying out one of the objectives of the group: "elevating and
maintaining among its members a high standard of proficiency and
integrity" (<u>Constitution,</u> Article III)--is its <u>Code of Ethics</u> and
<u>Rules of Professional Conduct</u>. These guides, adopted by the NSPA
Board of Governors upon recommendation of the Committee on
Ethics and Grievances, serve "as a hallmark of the practicing accountant who renders the highest level of professional services and
who observes a strict standard of ethics." The Code gives in six-
teen paragraphs a condensation of the principles of conduct in the
<u>Rules of Professional Conduct and Official Interpretations</u>, including
standards to be observed in private interest and professional practice, confidentiality of information, and promotional activities--
which are defined in some detail in the Rules, with guidelines for
acceptable letterheads, directory listings, signs. Official interpretations of the Rules cover justification, explanations and specific
examples of professional conduct standards pertaining to relation
with client and public, operating practices, technical standards,
promotional practices, and relations with other members.

 Enforcement of the Code and Rules is generally at the local
level--in one of the affiliated societies--and disciplinary action may
include suspension of expulsion from membership. Complaints of
unprofessional conduct of a member are filed in writing with the
Executive Director of the NSPA, the charges are considered by a
local (or national) Committee on Ethics and Grievances, and a
formal hearing may be held before a specially appointed Trial Board
of the National Society, with the Board of Governors acting as an
appeal Board.

<u>Other Standards of Professional Conduct</u>: The NSPA <u>Guide to Pro-
fessional Ethics</u> contains--in addition to the Code of Ethics--the
<u>Rules of Professional Conduct</u>, and the <u>Official Interpretation</u> of
these Rules.

Professional Insignia: The official emblem of the NSPA is the seal, designed by Marcus L. Deal, NSPA member of Greensboro, North Carolina, and adopted by the Society in 1953--a circular emblem with a centered open book--symbolizing the records used by the practicing accountant in preparing financial statements and income tax returns; two crossed quills above the book represent the accountant's chief tools--the pen and the pencil. The Latin motto "Integritas Professionis," inscribed across the face of the book is translated "Professional Integrity." Beneath the book is the date of

organization of the NSPA, "Organized 1945," and a bordering band bears the association name, "National Society of Public Accountants."

This emblem is used on letterheads, documents and publications of the National Society and affiliated State societies, and is authorized for use by members on stationery, business cards and as jewelry to be worn.

Other Identification of Professional Status: Another emblem of the NSPA is its official flag, the banner presented to the Society by the Washington Institute of Public Accountants in August 1957, during the 12th annual NSPA convention, in Washington, D.C. The rectangular flag shows the seal of the Society in the area nearest the staff, and is decorated with frange and two tasseled cords. The color of the banner is purple, with gold seal and decorations.

Bibliography:

National Society of Public Accountants. "Come On In." Folder.
Membership brochure includes NSPA purposes and membership requirements.

_____. Constitution and Bylaws. November 1970. 31 pages.
Provisions for permanent Ethics and Grievances Committee,
and publication of Code of Ethics and Rules of Professional
Conduct, with procedures for enforcement of these conduct
standards.

_____. Guide to Professional Ethics. 15 pages. Pamphlet.
Includes Code of Ethics, Rules of Professional Conduct with
Official Interpretations, and detailed guide to use of promo-
tional materials.

_____. 25 Years of Progress, 1945-1970. 1970. 75 pages.
Pamphlet.
Illustrated history of the National Society of Public Account-
ants.

"Code of Ethics"

A member of this society shall not violate the confidential
relationship between himself and his client or former client.

A member of this society shall not offer or render professional services the fee for which shall be contingent upon the findings or results of such services, except in those cases involving
federal, state or other taxes in which the findings are those of the
tax authorities and not those of the member, or in cases where
fees are fixed by courts or other public authorities.

A member of this society shall not express an opinion on
financial statements of an enterprise financed in whole or in part
by public distribution of securities if he or a member of his immediate family owns or is committed to acquire a substantial financial interest in the enterprise, or if during the period covered by
the examination, he has been a director, officer or employee of
the enterprise, unless such interest or relationship is disclosed in
the report.

A member of this society shall not allow any person to practice in his name who is not in partnership with him or in his employ.

A member of this society shall not engage simultaneously in
any business or occupation with that of the practice of public accounting which is incompatible or inconsistent therewith.

A member of this society shall not advertise his professional
attainments or services.

A member of this society shall be diligent, thorough and
completely candid in expressing an opinion on representations in
financial statements which he has examined.

A member of this society shall not sign a report purporting to express his opinion as the result of an examination of financial statements, unless they have been examined by him, or by a member or employee of his firm.

A member of this society shall not permit his name to be used in conjunction with any special purpose statement prepared for his clients that anticipates results of future operations, unless he discloses the source of the information used and what assumptions he has made, and unless he indicates he does not vouch for the accuracy of the forecast.

A member of this society shall not allow or pay, directly or indirectly, commissions, brokerage or other participation in the fees or profits of professional work to any person not in the public accounting profession.

A member of this society shall not directly or indirectly solicit clients nor encroach upon the practice of another accountant in public practice.

A member of this society shall not make a competitive bid for professional engagements except to those clients who are required by law to secure more than one bid.

A member of this society in practice as an individual shall not use a firm name or plural term, as "and company" or "and associates" or any other designation indicating anything other than individual ownership, unless such member shall file a statement of ownership, or statement of doing business under an assumed name with the proper authorities.

A member of this society who receives an engagement for services by referral from another member shall not discuss or accept an extension of his services beyond the specific engagement without first consulting with the referring member.

A member of this society shall not criticize another accountant in public practice in a degrading manner in the presence of anyone other than the accountant being criticized.

A member of this society shall not offer employment, directly or indirectly, to any employee of another accountant in public practice without first informing such accountant.

ACTUARIES

CASUALTY ACTUARIAL SOCIETY (CAS)
    200 E. 42nd St., New York, N.Y. 10017
    Ronald L. Bornhuetter, Secretary-Treasurer

Membership: The Casualty Actuarial Society, founded in 1914 and with a present (1973) membership of about 500, is a professional association of insurance actuaries in the casualty, fire and social insurance fields. Originally titled the Casualty Actuarial and

Statistical Society of America, the organization adopted its present
name on May 14, 1921.
   Members are engaged in the application of actuarial knowledge
to insurance areas other than life insurance--primarily in workman's
compensation, sickness, disability and casualty insurance, and--
since the specialty was added in November 1950--fire insurance.
Each of the two classes of membership of CAS--Associateship and
Fellowship--requires the passing of a series of examinations.
These qualifying examinations are held twice a year, in May and
November, in various cities of the United States and Canada.   The
Society distributes Recommendations for Study, a pamphlet outlining
the course of study recommended for the examinations that Associate Members (five examinations) and Fellows (four additional
examinations) must complete successfully before they are admitted
to membership.

>   ASSOCIATESHIP--Required Examinations
>   1.   General Mathematics (jointly sponsored with the Society
>   of Actuaries),
>   2.   Probability and Statistics (jointly sponsored with the
>   Society of Actuaries),
>   3.   Compound Interest and Life Contingencies,
>   4.   (a) Principles of Economics: Theory of Risk and In-
>   surance,
>   (b) Insurance Coverages and Policy Forms,
>   5.   (a) Principles of Ratemaking,
>   (b) Insurance Statistics and Data Processing.
>   FELLOWSHIP--Examinations required--in addition to above,
>   6.   (a) Insurance Law; Supervision, Regulations and Taxa-
>   tion,
>   (b) Statutory Insurances,
>   7.   (a) Insurance Accounting and Expense Analysis,
>   (b) Premium, Loss, and Expense Reserves,
>   8.   Individual Risk Taking,
>   9.   Advanced Insurance Problems.

Each examination has a time allowance of three hours, except Part
3 and Part 8, which have a time allowance of two hours each.
The examinations are written and the form of questions is multiple
choice, problems in completion or free-answer form, or essay.

Code of Ethics: The CAS has issued an ethical code, Guides to
Professional Conduct, as one of the steps in carrying out an objective of the Society: "to promote and maintain high standards of
conduct and competence within the actuarial profession" (Constitution, Article II).   This code sets forth principles of conduct in
seven sections: Professional Duty; Relationship of Actuary to his
Client or Employer; Nature of the Actuary's Responsibility to his
Client or Employer; Calculations and Recommendations; Advertising
and Relations with Other Members; Remuneration.

   Revision and enforcement of the Guides are carried out by a
Committee on Professional Conduct, which recommends changes

(revision, repeal, or addition) to the Guides, answers inquiries
about professional conduct in general and specific situations, and
assists the President and Council of CAS in evaluating alleged
breaches of ethics. Procedures are specified for investigation,
prosecution, hearings of charges or unethical conduct (Bylaws,
Article IV), and the Council may discipline a member (Constitution,
Article X), after investigation and a hearing before the Council or
a disciplinary board, by warning, admonishment, reprimand, suspension, or expulsion.

Professional Insignia: The Casualty Actuarial Society reports no
professional emblem.

Other Identification of Professional Status: As described above under
"Membership," members passing the qualifying examinations are
authorized to use the designation indicating professional competence:
        "ACAS"--Associate, Casualty Actuarial Society;
        "FCAS"--Fellow, Casualty Actuarial Society
An additional professional organization of actuaries is the American
Academy of Actuaries, organized on October 25, 1968, and sponsored by the Casualty Actuarial Society and the Society of Actuaries
--as well as by two other specialized actuarial groups, Conference
of Actuaries in Public Practice and Fraternal Actuarial Association.
Fellows of the CAS are eligible for membership in the Academy
provided they have had five years of experience in "responsible
actuarial work," and Associates of the CAS are eligible for membership in the Academy if they have had seven years of experience and
have passed a comprehensive subject examination.   Membership in
the American Academy of Actuaries is an additional indication of
professional competence.

Bibliography:
        Casualty Actuarial Society.   Guides to Professional Conduct.
            3 pages.
        Rules of conduct for actuaries.
            _____.   Guides to Professional Conduct--Interpretative
            Opinions.
        Applications and explanations of the Guides to Professional
        Conduct.
            _____.   Recommendations for Study.   Pamphlet.
        Outlines course of study recommended for qualifying examina-
        tions for Associateship or Fellowship in the CAS.   Sent free
        upon request.
            _____.   Year Book.   Annual, each January.
        Includes CAS Constitution and Bylaws, Guides to Professional
        Conduct, and Guides for the Submission of Papers.

                    "Guides to Professional Conduct"
                        (As revised May 24, 1970)

        Professional conduct involves the actuary's own sense of in-
tegrity and his professional relationship with those to whom he

renders service, with his employer, with other members of the profession, and with the world at large. In all these relationships every member of the profession is concerned with his own behavior and, as the good name of the profession is the concern of all its members, with the behavior of his colleagues.

In order to assist the Council and the Society in achieving the objectives of the Constitution and, more importantly, to guide members of the Society when they encounter questions of professional conduct as actuaries, the following "Guides to Professional Conduct" have been prepared by order of, and approved by, the Council. As is true of codes of ethics generally, these Guides deal with precepts and principles only. They are not precise rules and are subject to interpretations in relation to the variety of circumstances that occur in practice. Any member wishing advice regarding the application of these Guides to a particular set of facts is urged to consult the Chairman of the Committee on Professional Conduct.

1.   Professional Duty

A.   The member will act in a manner to uphold the dignity of the actuarial profession and to fulfill its responsibility to the public.

B.   The member will bear in mind that the actuary acts as an expert when he gives actuarial advice, and he will give such advice only when he is qualified to do so.

C.   The member will not provide actuarial service for or associate professionally with any person or organization where there is an evident possibility that his service may be used in a manner that is contrary to the public interest or the interest of his profession or in a manner to evade the law.

2.   Relationship of the Actuary to His Client or Employer

A.   Matters will be so ordered that all concerned are clear as to who is the member's client or employer and in what capacity the member is serving his client or employer.

B.   The member will act for each client or employer with scrupulous attention to the trust and confidence that the relationship implies and will have due regard for the confidential nature of his work.

C.   The member will recognize his ethical responsibilities to the person or organization whose actions may be influenced by his actuarial opinions or findings. When it is not feasible for the member to render his opinions or findings directly to such person or organization, he will act in such a manner as to leave no doubt that he is the source of the opinions or findings and to indicate clearly his personal availability to provide supplemental advice and explanation. If such opinions or findings are submitted to another actuary for review, either he or the other actuary will be available for supplemental advice and explanation.

3. Nature of the Actuary's Responsibility to His Client or Employer

In any situation in which there is or may be a conflict of interest involving the member's actuarial service, whether one or more clients or employers are involved, the member will not perform such actuarial service if the conflict makes or is likely to make it difficult for him to act independently. Even if there is no question as to his ability to act independently, he will not act unless there has been a full disclosure of the situation to all parties involved and the parties have expressly agreed to his performance of the service.

4. Calculations and Recommendations

A. The member will customarily include in any report or certificate quoting actuarial costs, reserves, or liabilities a statement or reference describing or clearly identifying the data and the actuarial methods and assumptions employed.

B. The member will exercise his best judgment to ensure that any calculations or recommendations made by him or under his direction are based on sufficient and reliable data, that any assumptions made are adequate and appropriate, and that the methods employed are consistent with the sound principles established by precedents or common usage within the profession.

C. If, nevertheless, a client or employer requests the member to prepare a study which in his opinion deviates from this practice, any resulting report, recommendation, or certificate submitted by him will include an appropriate and explicit qualification of his findings.

5. Advertising and Relations with Other Members

A. The member will neither engage in nor condone any advertising or other activity which can reasonably be regarded as being likely to attract professional work unfairly, or where the tone, form and content are not strictly professional.

B. The member will conduct his professional activities on a high plane. He will avoid unjustifiable or improper criticism of others and will not attempt to injure maliciously the professional reputation of any other actuary. He will recognize that there is substantial room for honest differences of opinion on many matters.

6. Remuneration

The member will make full and timely disclosure to a client as to all direct and indirect compensation that he or his firm may receive from all sources in relation to any assignment the member or his firm undertakes for the client.

7. Titles

The member will use a designation dependent upon elective or appointive qualifications within the Society, such as "President, "

"Member of the Council," or "Member of the Education and Examination Committee," only when he is acting in such capacity on behalf of the Society.

[Copies of interpretative opinions for these Guides may be obtained
from the Secretary-Treasurer of the Society.]

SOCIETY OF ACTUARIES (SA)
    208 South LaSalle St., Chicago, Ill. 60604
    Charles B. Watson, Executive Director

Membership: The Society of Actuaries, founded in 1949 with a
merger of two predecessor actuarial organizations--Actuarial
Society of America, and American Institute of Actuaries--and with
a present (1973) membership of 4000, is a professional association
of executives "professionally trained in the science of mathematical
probabilities."

    Admission to the Society is by written examinations. Comple-
tion of all ten examinations (taken at six-month intervals) qualifies
an applicant as: "Fellow, Society of Actuaries," with privilege of
using the designation: "F.S.A.," to indicate his professional competence. An applicant who completes the first five examinations
is admitted to the Society as: "Associate, Society of Actuaries,"
and is entitled to use with his name the professional designation:
"A.S.A."

    The examinations are begun with "general mathematics through
calculus, and then move upward through such specialized mathematics fields as probability and statistics, mathematics of finance,
numerical analysis, and mathematics of life contingencies." The
last five examinations--required to qualify as "Fellow"--cover all
areas of life insurance, health insurance and pension plans, including such subjects as construction of mortality tables, selection
of risks, calculation of premiums and dividends, insurance law,
social insurance, accounting, and investments. In the final two
examinations, applicants may elect to take the specialized Fellowship examinations in either:
            (1) Group Life and Health Insurance, Pensions and Social
                Insurance; or
            (2) Individual Life and Health Insurance and Annuities.

Code of Ethics: As a step in carrying out one of its basic pur-
poses--"to promote the maintenance of high standards of competence
and conduct within the actuarial profession" (Constitution, Article
II)--the Society of Actuaries has issued its code of ethics, Guides
to Professional Conduct. This code, which provided the model for
the code of ethics of the Casualty Actuarial Society, sets forth

principles of conduct in seven sections: Professional Duty; Relationship of Actuary to his Client or Employer; Nature of the Actuary's Responsibility to his Client or Employer; Calculations and Recommendations; Advertising and Relations with Other Members; Remuneration; and Use of Titles.

Enforcement of the Guides is provided for in the Society's Constitution (Article VII), with procedures for the appointment of investigating committees, and disciplinary boards, prosecuting committees to consider complaints as to a member's unprofessional conduct. When alleged unethical conduct is substantiated, a member may be reprimanded, suspended or expelled from the Society.

Applications and explanations of the Guide to Professional Conduct are given in Interpretive Opinions issued by the Committee on Professional Conduct, which also recommends repeal and revision of specific guides, and suggests new guides.

Professional Insignia: The official emblem of the Society of Actuaries is its seal--a circular design, adopted in 1949, with a centered shield divided by a diagonal of four lines from upper left to lower right; in the upper right is the designation, "ASA," (initials of the predecessor society, Actuarial Society of America) and the date of its founding, "1889," and in the lower left, the designation, "AIA," (initials of the second predecessor organization, American Institute of Actuaries) and the date it was organized, "1909"; a bordering band bears the association name, "Society of Actuaries" at the top, date of its founding, "1949," at the bottom, a maple leaf at left of this date, and an eagle at the right of the date represent Society members in Canada and in the United States.  The color of the emblem is shown variously--black on light green; navy blue on turquoise. The emblem is shown on CAS publications and is available to members for display on plaques and paperweights.

Other Identification of Professional Status: As described above under "Membership," designations are authorized for members as an indication of professional competence:

"ASA"--Associate, Society of Actuaries;
"FSA"--Fellow, Society of Actuaries.

The motto of the Society of Actuaries is a quotation from John Ruskin: "The work of science is to substitute facts for appearances and demonstrations for impressions."

Bibliography:
     Society of Actuaries. The Actuarial Profession. 1971. Pam-
       phlet.
     Defines profession, and gives syllabus of qualifying examina-
     tions, and a list of professional actuarial associations.
     _____. Constitution and By-Laws. Pamphlet.
     Includes enforcement procedure for code of ethics through
     disciplinary action (Article VII).
     _____. Guide to Professional Conduct and Interpretive
       Opinions. January 13, 1971. 13 pages. Pamphlet.
     Principles to be followed in rendering professional actuarial
     services, and working with clients, employers, and fellow
     actuaries.
     _____. Preliminary Actuarial Examinations. Pamphlet.
     Detailed description of Examination Parts 1 and 2 (General
     Mathematics; Probability and Statistics), with sample ques-
     tions. Sent free upon request.
     _____. So You're Good at Math ... Then Consider a Career
       as an Actuary.
     Informational folder outlining opportunities, qualifications,
     and professional examination for actuaries.

"Guides to Professional Conduct"
(Issued by Authority of the Board of Governors, November, 1969)

Professional conduct involves the actuary's own sense of integrity and his professional relationship with those to whom he renders services, with his employer, with other members of the profession, and with the world at large. In all these relationships
every member of the profession is concerned with his own behavior
and, as the good name of the profession is the concern of all its
members, with the behavior of his colleagues.

In order to assist the Board of Governors and the Society in
achieving the objectives of the Constitution and, more importantly,
to guide members of the Society when they encounter questions of
professional conduct as actuaries, the following "Guides to Professional Conduct" have been prepared by order of, and approved by,
the Board. As is true of codes of ethics generally, these Guides
deal with precepts and principles only. They are not precise rules
and are subject to interpretations in relation to the variety of circumstances that occur in practice. Any member wishing advice regarding the application of these Guides to a particular set of facts is
urged to consult the Chairman of the Committee on Professional
Conduct.

1.   Professional Duty.

     a)   The member will act in a manner to uphold the dignity of
          the actuarial profession and to fulfill its responsibility to
          the public.
     b)   The member will bear in mind that the actuary acts as an

expert when he gives actuarial advice, and he will give
such advice only when he is qualified to do so.

c) The member will not provide actuarial service for or associate professionally with any person or organization where
there is an evident possibility that his service may be used
in a manner that is contrary to the public interest or the
interest of his profession or in a manner to evade the law.

2. <u>Relationship of the Actuary to His Client or Employer.</u>

a) Matters will be so ordered that all concerned are clear as
to who is the member's client or employer and in what
capacity the member is serving his client or employer.

b) The member will act for each client or employer with
scrupulous attention to the trust and confidence that the
relationship implies and will have due regard for the confidential nature of his work.

c) The member will recognize his ethical responsibilities to
the person or organization whose actions may be influenced
by his actuarial opinions or findings. When it is not feasible for the member to render his opinions or findings directly to such person or organization, he will act in such
a manner as to leave no doubt that he is the source of
the opinions or findings and to indicate clearly his personal
availability to provide supplemental advice and explanation.
If such opinions or findings are submitted to another actuary
for review, either he or the other actuary will be available
for supplemental advice and explanation.

3. <u>Nature of the Actuary's Responsibility to His Client of Employer.</u>

In any situation in which there is or may be a conflict of interest involving the member's actuarial service, whether one
or more clients or employers are involved, the member will
not perform such actuarial service if the conflict makes or is
likely to make it difficult for him to act independently. Even
if there is no question as to his ability to act independently, he
will not act unless there has been a full disclosure of the situation to all parties involved and the parties have expressly agreed
to his performance of the service.

4. <u>Calculations and Recommendations.</u>

a) The member will customarily include in any report or certificate quoting actuarial costs, reserves, or liabilities a
statement or reference describing or clearly identifying
the data and the actuarial methods and assumptions employed.

b) The member will exercise his best judgment to ensure that
any calculations or recommendations made by him or under
his direction are based on sufficient and reliable data, that
any assumptions made are adequate and appropriate, and
that the methods employed are consistent with the sound
principles established by precedents or common usage
within the profession.

   c) If, nevertheless, a client or employer requests the member to prepare a study which in his opinion deviates from this practice, any resulting report, recommendation, or certificate submitted by him will include an appropriate and explicit qualification of his findings.

5. Advertising and Relations with Other Members.

   a) The member will neither engage in nor condone any advertising or other activity which can reasonably be regarded as being likely to attract professional work unfairly, or where the tone, form, and content are not strictly professional.

   b) The member will conduct his professional activities on a high plane. He will avoid unjustifiable or improper criticism of others and will not attempt to injure maliciously the professional reputation of any other actuary. He will recognize that there is substantial room for honest differences of opinion on many matters.

6. Remuneration.

The member will make full and timely disclosure to a client as to all direct and indirect compensation that he or his firm may receive from all sources in relation to any assignment the member or his firm undertakes for the client.

7. Titles.

The member will use a designation dependent upon elective or appointive qualification within the Society, such as "President," "Member of the Board of Governors," or "Member of the Education and Examination Committee," only when he is acting in such capacity on behalf of the Society.

ADVERTISING WORKERS

AMERICAN ADVERTISING FEDERATION (AAF)
   1225 Connecticut Ave., N.W., Washington, D.C. 20036
   Joseph Gitlitz, Executive Vice President

Membership: The American Advertising Federation, founded in 1967 (with the merger of two predecessor organizations established in 1905: Advertising Federation of America and Advertising Association of the West) and with a present (1973) membership of approximately 40,000, is a trade association in the field of advertising.
   Membership is open to any interested individual or group, and

members are organized in 181 advertising clubs throughout the United States.   There are 450 company members (advertisers, advertising agencies, media and advertising services) and 32 affiliated associations.

Code of Ethics: The guide to conduct developed by the American Advertising Federation--in cooperation with the Association of Better Business Bureaus International--is the Advertising Code of American Business.   This Code sets forth nine general principles governing ethical content of advertisements: Truth, Responsibility, Taste and Decency, Disparagement, Bait Advertising, Guarantees and Warranties, Price Claims, Testimonials.   No provisions for enforcement of this Code are reported.

Since 1970 the AAF has been active in a new "program of self-regulation to deal with problems of truth and accuracy in national consumer advertising." Applications of standards are carried out by the National Advertising Review Board and the National Advertising Division of the Council of Better Business Bureaus.
    The AAF national ethics committee--now known as the Advertising Standards Committee--acts in enforcing conduct standards in advertising, and local advertising clubs can act, with Better Business Bureaus, "to handle consumer complaints using as a base the Advertising Code of American Business..."

Professional Insignia: The emblem of the Federation is its logotype--the organization initials "AAF" enclosed in a line-bordered rectangle.   Color of this insignia is shown variously-- blue initials in blue rectangle (letterhead); black initials in black rectangle (envelope); blue initials in red rectangle (Code).

Bibliography:
    American Advertising Federation.   Annual Report.
        Reviews activities of the Federation, including ethical standards, committee, and self-regulatory.
        .   Ten Questions and Answers About the American Federation.   4 pages.
    Purposes, history, services of AAF.
        and Association of Better Business Bureaus International.   The Advertising Code of American Business.   Single sheet.
    Principles defining ethical content of advertising.

"The Advertising Code
of American Business"*

1 -- TRUTH... Advertising shall tell the truth, and shall
reveal significant facts, the concealment of which would mislead the
public. 2 -- RESPONSIBILITY... Advertising agencies and advertisers shall be willing to provide substantiation of claims made.
3 -- TASTE AND DECENCY... Advertising shall be free of statements, illustrations or implications which are offensive to good
taste or public decency. 4 -- DISPARAGEMENT... Advertising
shall offer merchandise or service on its merits, and refrain
from attacking competitors unfairly or disparaging their products,
services or methods of doing business. 5 -- BAIT ADVERTISING...
Advertising shall offer only merchandise or services which are
readily available for purchase at the advertised price. 6 -- GUAR-
ANTEES AND WARRANTIES... Advertising of guarantees and warranties shall be explicit. Advertising of any guarantee or warranty
shall clearly and conspicuously disclose its nature and extent, the
manner in which the guarantor or warrantor will perform and the
identity of the guarantor or warrantor. 7 -- PRICE CLAIMS...
Advertising shall avoid price or savings claims which are false or
misleading, or which do not offer provable bargains or savings.
8 -- UNPROVABLE CLAIMS... Advertising shall avoid the use of
exaggerated or unprovable claims. 9 -- TESTIMONIALS... Advertising containing testimonials shall be limited to those of competent witnesses who are reflecting a real and honest choice.

AGRICULTURAL CONSULTANTS

AMERICAN SOCIETY OF AGRICULTURAL CONSULTANTS (ASAC)
        Salisbury, Missouri 65281
        W. W. Leatherwood, D. V. M., Secretary Treasurer

Membership: The American Society of Agricultural Consultants,
founded in 1963 and with a present (1973) membership of approximately 100, is a professional organization of agricultural consultants
in the United States and Canada. To carry out one of its objectives
--"To establish high standards of technical competence" for agricultural consultants--ASAC has established requirements for Full
Member that include:
        Education--Four-year college degree in an appropriate field,
        or equivalent; plus
        Experience--Four years experience in agricultural consulta-

---

*Developed by the American Advertising Federation and the Associa-
tion of Better Business Bureaus International.

tion.   A master's degree may substitute for one year, and a Ph. D. for two years of this required experience.

Because of the diversity of modern agribusiness, each member has training and experience in one or more agricultural specialties. Specialization of members in farm and ranch management and in plant and animal sciences--as listed in the membership directory of ASAC--includes:

Livestock (Beef Cattle, Dairy Cattle, Swine) and Poultry
Nutrition and Physiology--feedlot ingredients, formulations, evaluation, management; milling and handling systems, such as dehydration; ruminant research.
Breeding and Health--Genetics, pharmaceutical formulations; microbiological research.
Plant Crops
Timber Management, Grain Management, Crop handling and storage, Fertilizers, Pesticides, Tropical Agriculture.
Soil and Water
Land Selection, reclamation, development; Land Management; Irrigation; Aquiculture.
Agronomics (Agricultural Economics)
Feasibility studies; Least cost formulations; Agri-damage causes and valuation; Agricultural Marketing.
Farm Machinery and Structures
Confinement Housing; Environmental Control.

Code of Ethics: The professional conduct guide for agricultural consultants is the ASAC Code of Ethics, adopted in its present form in September 1970.   These Standards of Practice, developed by a committee of the society, enumerate ten principles that include relationships with clients and colleagues.   Two committees of the society are concerned with the Code of Ethics:

Ethics Committee--Reviews the Code and suggests revisions to the Executive Board;
Grievance Committee--Enforces the Code by receiving complaints of violations of standards of professional practice; investigating complaints and holding hearings and recommending disciplinary action to the Executive Board.

Professional Insignia: The ASAC emblem is its official seal--a circular design with a centered shield, bearing in five sections symbols of the subjects and techniques of agricultural consultation--from upper left: animal science (beef); plant science (corn plant); tools for learning and research (microscope, open book, chemical flask and retort); the association name, "American Society of Agricultural Consultants, " is

shown around the design in a bordering band. The color of the emblem is shown variously--red on white (stationery); brown on buff, blue on pink, black on blue (publications). The official color of the ASAC is blue.

Bibliography:

American Society of Agricultural Consultants. Constitution and By-Laws. Revised edition, October 1970. 16 pages. Pamphlet.
Gives membership qualifications; Code of Ethics; and procedures for enforcement of the Code (By-Laws, Article VII).

_____. The Professional Consultant in Today's Agriculture. Brochure.
Includes ASAC purpose, organization, membership qualifications.

["Professional Standards of Practice"]

"Code of Ethics"

Membership in the American Society of Agricultural Consultants is characterized by experience, competence, responsibility and honor in the profession. These basic qualifications are extended in the following principles of ethical practice to which members of the Society as professional agricultural consultants fully subscribe:

1. A member is distinguished by the independence, objectivity and moral concern by which his business affairs are conducted.
2. A member will accept only those engagements he is qualified to undertake and which in the light of his knowledge and experience, are in the best interests of clients.
3. A member can be depended upon to serve his clients with true professional honesty; he will refuse to serve under terms or conditions that may impair his independence, objectivity or integrity.
4. A member will respect and guard as confidential any information obtained from clients which is of a sensitive and confidential nature.
5. A member will serve two or more competing clients at the same time on problems of conflicting nature only with their full knowledge.
6. A member shall not accept or pay fees for referral of clients, nor will he accept compensation, financial or otherwise, from persons or companies whose products, equipment or services he may recommend to clients during the course of an engagement without full disclosure to the client.
7. A member shall always respect the rights of his fellow consultants in negotiating for professional work or advancement;

he may use all honorable means in competition for an assignment, but shall not attempt to supplant a fellow consultant once
engaged.
8. A member will condemn unethical or illegal conduct by other
consultants and shall report any infraction of these principles
to the Society for proper investigation and action.
9. A member shall promote his services in a professionally dignified and proper manner, being careful to avoid inaccuracies
or misleading statements.
10. A member recognizes that the Society's code of professional
ethics signifies a voluntary assumption of the obligation of self-
discipline above and beyond the requirements of law. By it he
strives to uphold the honor and maintain the dignity of his profession.

AGRICULTURAL ECONOMISTS

AMERICAN AGRICULTURAL ECONOMICS ASSOCIATION (AAEA)
    Department of Agricultural Economics
    University of Kentucky, Lexington, Ky. 40506
    John C. Redman, Secretary-Treasurer

Membership: The American Agricultural Economics Association,
founded in 1910 (as the American Farm Management Association,
becoming the Farm Economics Association in 1918, and adopting
its present name in 1968) and with a present (1973) membership of
4500, is a professional association of teachers, research workers,
and consultants in the business aspects of all phases of agriculture.
    Membership is "open to those having a professional interest in
agricultural economics. " While no educational requirements are
necessary for membership the AAEA recommends graduate study
in agricultural economics or agricultural business, available at a
number of colleges and universities.

Code of Ethics: No formal
written code of ethics has
been issued.

Professional Insignia: The
official emblem of the AAEA
is its seal--a circular design
with a centered vertically-
striped shield surmounted by
an eagle with outstretched
wings, facing left; a plow is
shown on the shield, which
has six dark stripes

alternating with six lighter stripes; the organization name, "American Agricultural Economics Association," is shown around the design in a bordering band. The colors of this insignia are maroon on white, but the design is also shown in other colors--brown on white (publication).

Bibliography:
> American Agricultural Economics Association. American Agricultural Economics Association. Single sheet.
> AAEA purposes, activities, membership requirements; emblem, without bordering name, in color.
> _____. Economists in Agriculture, Business, Government... and Rural Affairs. 4 pages.
> Illustrated brochure defining duties of agricultural economists, and describing academic courses available for training.

AIR POLLUTION CONTROL WORKERS

AIR POLLUTION CONTROL ASSOCIATION (APCA)
   4400 Fifth Ave., Pittsburgh, Pa. 15213
   Lewis H. Rogers, Executive Vice President

Membership: The Air Pollution Control Association, founded in 1907 and with a present (1973) membership of approximately 6500, is a professional association of engineers and physical scientists active in teaching, research and practice of bettering the air environment. Any person--individual, company, or government agency-- interested in the purposes of the Association (primarily abatement and prevention of atmospheric pollution) is eligible for membership.

Code of Ethics: The guide to professional conduct for members of the Air Pollution Control Association is its Code of Ethics (By-Laws, Article XIV--Professional Practice, Section 1). These general principles to professional practice in air pollution control concern honorable work methods, confidentiality of information, client and employer relations, and concern with public welfare.
   The Code is enforced by the APCA Board of Directors, which receives complaints of violations of the conduct guide (submitted in writing and signed by "not less than three members of the Association"), acts as a Hearing Board, and may expel a member charged with unprofessional conduct when the complaint is justified (By-Laws, Article XIV, Section 3).

Professional Insignia: The official emblem of the Air Pollution Control Association shows a quartered square on a dotted ground, enclosed in a loop--
   "The loop around the outside stands for purification. The

'window' in the center is one of the symbols for air. And
the surrounding dots signify dust, ashes, and other forms of
particulate matter--by extension, air contaminants. The
symbols are taken from alchemy."
A scroll below the insignia bears the date of organization establishment, "Founded 1907."

The emblem is shown in black on white, in black on white with
gold loop and scroll (letterhead), but the colors of the insignia are
officially described:
"Our colors have been chosen from those representing
academic interests. Scarlet represents 'humanity,' orange
represents 'engineering,' and yellow (gold) represents 'science.' These are most apropos since they represent engineering and science working in behalf of humanity for its
general welfare, through the control of Air Pollution."

Bibliography:
Air Pollution Control Association. APCA Directory. Annual.
Includes By-Laws with text of Code of Ethics, and procedures
for Code enforcement.

"Code of Ethics"

Section 1. That the duty of his chosen profession be maintained, it is the duty of every member:

(a) To carry on his work in a spirit of fairness to all those with
whom he comes in professional contact. This includes his employees and contractors, fidelity to clients and employers, and devotion
to high ideals of personal honor.
(b) To refrain from associating himself with or allow the use of
his name by any enterprise of questionable character.
(c) To treat as confidential his knowledge of the business affairs or
technical processes of clients or employers when their interests require secrecy.
(d) To inform a client or employer of any business connections,
interests, or affiliations which might influence his judgment or

impair the disinterested quality of his services.

(e) To accept financial or other compensation for a particular service from one source only, except with the full knowledge and consent of all interested parties.

(f) To advertise only in a dignified manner, to refrain from using improper or questionable methods for promoting professional work, and to decline to pay or to accept commissions for work secured by improper or questionable methods.

(g) To refrain from using unfair means to win professional advancement, and to avoid unfairly injuring another person's chances to secure and hold employment.

(h) To co-operate in building up the profession of air pollution control by the interchange of general information and experience with his fellow members; and by contributing to the work of other associations, schools of applied science, and the technical press.

(i) To interest himself in the public welfare and to be ready to apply his special knowledge, skill, and training in the public behalf for the use and benefit of mankind.

Section 2. In all professional or business relations the membership of the Association shall be governed by the Code of Ethics above and by these By-Laws.

Section 3. Charges that any member has been guilty of violation of the By-Laws of the Association or of conduct unbecoming to a member shall be detailed in a letter addressed to the Board of Directors and signed by not less than three (3) members. Any member who has been so charged or accused shall be entitled to a hearing before the Board of Directors, where he may testify in his own defense. If two-thirds (2/3) of the Board vote that he is guilty as charged, he shall be expelled from the membership.

AIR TRAFFIC CONTROLLERS

AIR TRAFFIC CONTROL ASSOCIATION (ATCA)
     525 School Street, S. W.
     Suite 409, ARBA Building, Washington, D. C.
     Donald E. Francke, Executive Director

Membership: The Air Traffic Control Association, founded in 1956 and with a present (1973) membership of approximately 2000, is a professional association of civilian and military air traffic controllers. Professional members, qualified to hold office in the Association, are air traffic control specialists with at least five years experience in air traffic control. At least two years of this experience must have been in the actual control of air traffic, and completion of a professional course in air traffic control recognized by the ATCA may be substituted for three years of the required general experience.

Other membership categories include any person or corporation with interests or activity in air traffic control, such as pilots, private plane owners and operators, aircraft and electronics engineers, and individuals and organizations concerned with aviation.

Code of Ethics: The ATCA guide for professional conduct is its Code of Ethics (By-Laws, Article IX), adopted in 1956 and amended in its present form on August 25, 1970.   Eight general principles of the Code give standards of accomplishment in air traffic control, and relationship with fellow members.
Revision and enforcement of the Code are assigned to the standing Committee on Professional Ethics and Standards.   This Committee recommends changes or amendments in the Code, and receives complaints of violations of the Code, conducts investigations and hearings as required, and recommends disciplinary measures for members found guilty of unprofessional conduct, to the ATCA National Council for action.

Professional Insignia: The emblem of the ATCA is an oval direction finder (viewed obliquely from the right), with compass radials marked "N" at the top of the design, "S" at the bottom, and "W" at the left--symbolizing "that the air traffic control program guides the safety of aircraft through the national airspace system in all quadrants of the country"; the initials of the organization, "ATCA," are shown in the quadrants of the direction indicator, reading from left to right in upper and lower quadrants; the design is surmounted by a wing, symbolizing flight.
The color of the insignia is shown variously--black on white (publications); white on a rectangular background of different colors--such as red, green, yellow, etc. (publication); or white on a rectangular background of blue (letterhead).

Bibliography:
        Air Traffic Control Association.   Air Traffic Control Association.
                Pamphlet.
        Informational brochure giving objectives, types of members,

publications, and meetings.
_____. Constitution and By-Laws.   Amended to August 25,
1970.
Includes membership requirements, and Code of Ethics (By-
Laws, Article IX).

"Code of Ethics"

In order that the dignity and honor of the Air Traffic Control Profession may be upheld, that its sphere of usefulness and
its benefits may be extended and that members of this Association
may be guided by the highest standards of integrity and fair dealing whether as individuals or in association with others in the aviation industry, the Council of the Air Traffic Control Association has
adopted the following Code of Ethics and Conduct for the guidance
of the Association's membership:

1. Each member will endeavor to keep abreast of scientific
and technical development within the Profession, and will constantly
strive for improvement.
2. Each member will endeavor to contribute new knowledge
to the Air Traffic Control Service by making known to the aviation
world any significant work, improvements or research accomplished.
3. A member will not engage in unfair competition with other
members of his profession.
4. A member will not take credit for research or technical
work done by others; and in publications or meetings, will attempt
to give credit where due.
5. A member will, to the best of his ability, render instructions, advice and other assistance to his fellow members in
the discharge of their professional services.
6. A member will base his professional practice on safe
and sound principles.
7. A member will refuse to engage in practices which are
generally recognized as being detrimental to the public welfare.
8. A member will make every effort to discourage sensationalism, exaggeration and unwarranted statements concerning the
field of his profession, and will refrain from making extravagant
claims.

AIRPLANE PILOTS

PILOTS INTERNATIONAL ASSOCIATION (PIA)
     2649 Park Ave., Minneapolis, Minn. 55407
     Eugene C. Roeckers, Executive Secretary

<u>Membership</u>:   Pilots International Association, founded in 1965 and
with a present (1973) membership of 12,000, is a professional and
recreational association among whose members are professional
commercial and military airplane pilots, as well as student pilots,
private airplane pilots, and all others interested in aircraft flying.

<u>Code of Ethics</u>:   The qualifications and performance standards for
airplane pilots are given in the state and federal laws, and by the
regulations of the Federal Aviation Administration and the Civil
Aeronautics Board.   The Pilots International Association has issued
no formal code of ethics.

<u>Other Standards of Professional Conduct</u>:   Purposes of the Associa-
tion are set forth in the <u>PIA Creed,</u> which gives ten points of the
goals of the Association, such as promotion of the use of the airplane for pleasure, for commerce and for defense; striving for aircraft safety; and cooperation with other private and public organizations in the best interest of flyers and flying.

<u>Professional Insignia</u>:   The official emblem of PIA--adopted when
the organization was formed in 1965--was designed by Eugene
Roeckers, Executive Secretary of the organization, and George
Glotzbach, the Association's Vice President.   The design shows the
silhouette of an airplane--similar to that found on the instruments
in aircraft--superimposed on a
globe (symbolizing the "international appeal" of the Association); which is placed within
stylized wings (signifying "flight");
the organization initials, "PIA,"
appear above the globe.

    The color of the insignia
varies--wings are blue, and
the globe may be blue (letterhead), or black (logotype); and
the "PIA" may be shown in red
(letterhead, publications) or
black (logotype).   This emblem
is available to members for
wear and display as jewelry--
tie-clip, lapel-pin, money-clip; as an embroidered cloth patch; a
decal; and on a PIA blazer.   Jewelry is silver; the color of the
cloth patch is blue on white.

<u>Other Identification of Professional Status</u>:   The motto of the Pilots
International Association is: "Good Luck and Good Flying."

<u>Bibliography</u>:
       Pilots International Association.   <u>Benefits.</u>   Single sheet.
       Includes PIA Creed and the official emblem.

"PIA Creed"

The Pilots International Association is dedicated to promote the best interests of flyers and/or flying around the world. Its major objectives cover, but are not limited to the following:

1. To promote the use of the airplane for pleasure, for commerce, and for defense.
2. To strive for aircraft safety, via education, economic influence, and legislation as required.
3. To cooperate with government agencies in serving the general good of the flying and non-flying public.
4. To provide a free forum for the exchange of information, ideas, and attitudes of interest to aviators.
5. To offer services needed and wanted by flyers, at reasonable costs which will make flying safer, more efficient, and just plain fun.
6. To offer welfare benefits needed and wanted by flyers, at reasonable cost.
7. To encourage the development and use of convenient landing and service facilities throughout the world.
8. To search for international understanding through travel and by common approaches to problems involving aircraft.
9. To encourage the application of aircraft and fuel taxes for development of aviation.
10. To cooperate with other private and public organizations in the best interest of flyers and/or flying.

AIRPORT MANAGERS

AMERICAN ASSOCIATION OF AIRPORT EXECUTIVES (AAAE)
    2029 K St., N.W., Washington, D.C. 20006
    F. Russell Hoyt, Executive Vice President

Membership: The American Association of Airport Executives, founded in 1928 as a unit of Aero Chamber and an independent association since 1939, and with a present (1973) membership of over 1000, is a professional association of managers of airports, ranging in size "from multi-million-dollar terminals to smaller general air fields."

Since 1954, the fully professional members of AAAE have been awarded the professional designation: "A.A.E."--"Accredited Airport Executive," and qualify as "Executive Members" of the

Association. To become an Accredited Airport Executive and an Executive Member, an AAAE member must pass a written examination, administered by the Association's Board of Examiners. Only members who are practicing airport managers with three years of experience in airport management are eligible to take the examination.

Code of Ethics: Carrying out one of the purposes of the AAAE--the establishment of professional codes and standards--the Association has issued a Code of Ethical Conduct. This Code is a statement of the general responsibilities and goals of airport executives. The Ethics Committee reviews the Code periodically for possible revision, and--as required--investigates alleged violations of the rules of professional conduct received by the President of AAAE (Bylaws, Article II, Section 12). The Board of Directors enforces the Code, after receiving a report of investigation and recommendation of the Ethics Committee in instances of reported unethical conduct of an Association member, and may censure, suspend, or expel a member, and hear appeals from its disciplinary decisions.

Professional Insignia: The official emblem of the AAAE is its seal--a circular device with centered outline of wings (symbolizing "flight"); the association initials "AA of AE," are spaced within the upper half of the circle border; five stars are spaced around the lower half of the circle border. The color of the emblem is shown variously--light blue on a dark blue ground (publications, membership pins); white on dark blue (publication).

Other Identification of Professional Status: As described above under "Membership," the professional designation authorized by the AAAE to members qualifying with experience and passing a written examination is: "A. A. E."--"Accredited Airport Executive."

Bibliography:
    American Association of Airport Executives. A Code of Ethical
        Conduct. Single sheet.
    Conduct guide for members of the Association.
        . Rules of Procedure and Practice for Investigation by
        Ethics Committee. 3 pages. Processed.
    Procedures for enforcement of the AAAE code of ethics
    (from Bylaws, Article II, Section 12).

"A Code of Ethical Conduct"

We, the members of the American Association of Airport Executives, recognize that we have a special and particular responsibility to Aviation and the Air Transportation System. We realize that this applies not only to those who manage its affairs but to the present and future citizens who utilize it, to those who produce it, and to those who govern it locally, nationally, as well as internationally; for it has no known boundaries.

It is our purpose to respond to this challenge in man's great adventure by acknowledging and practicing through our voluntary thoughts, actions, and words a system of Ethical Human Behavior. We understand this means we have the privilege to remain engaged in the search for truth and understanding, moral ideals, and good conduct. We will do our share in making daily judgements between RIGHT and WRONG and placing a premium on RIGHT. Nothing will appear too minute or loom too great to forsake this effort.

In this science and system of correct living we, the members of the American Association of Airport Executives, pledge our devotion to achieving three prime goals both individually and collectively, for only its members can make it good or bad. These goals are:
1. To so conduct ourselves that SELF-RESPECT is our bounty.
2. To earn and keep the TRUST of our fellow men.
3. To faithfully OBEY the commands of our GOD.

ALLERGISTS

AMERICAN ACADEMY OF ALLERGY (AAA)
225 E. Michigan St., Milwaukee, Wis. 53202
James O. Kelley, Executive Director

Membership: The American Academy of Allergy, founded in 1943 with the merger of two parent societies, the American Association for the Study of Allergy (the "Western Society," established in 1923) and the Association for the Study of Asthma and Allied Conditions (the "Eastern Society," organized in 1924), has a present (1973) membership of about 2200. The Academy is a professional association of doctors of medicine or philosophy or persons with equivalent foreign degrees who specialize in the treatment of asthma, hay fever, eczema, and other allergies. Members, including physicians specializing in research and teaching, as well as diagnosis and treatment of allergies, are located in the United States, Canada, and a number of other countries throughout the world.

After a minimum of five years from the time of graduation

from medical school and three years from the date of election, Members and Corresponding members of AAA are eligible to apply for advancement to Fellowship.   The requirements for Fellowship are proficiency in research or practice in the field of allergy.   This is determined by at least two of the following criteria:

A) Superior training and experience in allergy and in related branches of medicine at clinics, hospitals or under the guidance of recognized experts in the field.

B) Publication of meritorious articles on allergy or on allied subjects which present original experimental research, sound clinical investigation or important discussion of the work of others which advances or extends their conclusions.

C) Certification by specialty boards acceptable to the American Academy of Allergy.

Code of Ethics: Allergists, as doctors of medicine, subscribe to the American Medical Association's Principles of Medical Ethics. This code of ethics is enforced by the Committee on Ethics of the Academy, "which is charged with the investigation of unethical conduct" (Constitution, Article II, Section 10).   Based upon its investigation, the Committee may recommend to the Executive Committee of the AAA "that the accused: 1) be cleared of the charges, 2) be reprimanded, 3) be censured, 4) be expelled from the Academy" (By-Laws, 6, 1).

Professional Insignia: The emblem of the Academy is its official seal, with the name of the organization in a banding border, "American Academy of Allergy," with the founding date, "1943," at the bottom of the border; the initials of the group, "AAA," are shown in a horizontally striped centered circle.   The color of this emblem is blue on white.

Bibliography:
American Academy of Allergy. Membership Directory. Biennial, odd years.
    Includes the Academy Constitution and By-Laws, with membership requirements and procedures for enforcement of the code of ethics.

"Code of Ethics"

see page 564

ANESTHETISTS

AMERICAN ASSOCIATION OF NURSE ANESTHETISTS (AANA)
    111 E. Wacker Dr., Suite 929, Chicago, Ill. 60601
    Bernice O. Baum, C. R. N. A., Executive Director

Membership: The American Association of Nurse Anesthetists,
founded in 1931 and with a present (1973) membership of over
15, 000, is a professional association that requires its "Active Members" be graduate professional nurses, registered in the state in
which they are employed, have completed an approved course in
anesthesia, have passed the Association's qualifying written examination.

The length of the special training course in anesthesia has increased from the four months originally required in 1931 to the
present 18-month course offered in more than 200 Approved Schools
of Anesthesia in the United States, with specified hours of clinical
and class instruction. The qualifying examination--administered
since 1945--is given twice each year (Second Saturday in May and
second Saturday in November) in 32 testing centers throughout the
United States. Examination questions are prepared by the nurse
directors and instructors of the accredited schools of anesthesia,
and are scored by the Psychometry Department of the Roosevelt
University in Chicago.

The AANA "certifies that its members have met the minimum
requirements at the time of admission to membership," and authorizes members to use the professional designation: "C. R. N. A. "
("Certified Registered Nurse Anesthetist").

Code of Ethics: The guide to professional conduct of the Association
is its Code of Ethics, adopted in 1955, and revised several times--
most recently in 1961. The Code gives the general principles
governing the nurse anesthetist in professional relationships with
patients, doctors, and other hospital personnel, and with employer;
standards of remuneration; legal restrictions; public relations; and
other professional obligations and responsibilities.

The conduct guide, prepared by a Planning Committee of members of AANA over a two-year period prior to adoption, is enforced
by the Board of Trustees (Bylaws, Article XIV), who by a two-
thirds vote, after written notice of charges and hearing opportunity,
may expel or suspend a member for unprofessional conduct.

Other Guides to Professional Conduct: The Personnel Policy of
the Association, printed with its Code of Ethics, was prepared by
a special committee of the organization and adopted in 1952. These

policies set forth standards governing the employment of nurse anesthetists, including channels of authority in employing hospitals, work schedules, hours, salaries, resignations, vacations, health programs, and living quarters.

Professional Insignia: The official emblem of the Association is its corporate seal. The design, selected as the best emblem in a contest open to members, was the joint work of Dr. W. W. Bowen, Dean of the Medical Group of Fort Dodge, Iowa; Mrs. Lennie Dearing, Flagstaff, Arizona; artists Hugh Mosher, and Louis Schwarting of Fort Dodge, Iowa. This insignia, adopted in 1940, pictures the theme: "Watchful Care of the Sleeper by the Light of the Lamp of Learning." The circular design shows Hypnos, God of Sleep, asleep in the Cave of Night with poppies in his right hand; Morpheus, God of Dreams, watches over the sleeper Hypnos, and lights his vigil with

the Lamp of Learning, held aloft in his right hand. The organization name, "American Association of Nurse Anesthetists," forms a border within the seal outline; the group's date of establishment, "Founded 1931," is at the bottom of the border. This seal appears on the official pin, worn by members of the Association.

Other Designations of Professional Status: A design used as a sleeve emblem for members, since 1945, and a car emblem, since 1952, is a lozenge with the lamp of learning, organization initials, "AANA," and a caduceus with the entwined double serpent, symbolic of healing, from top to bottom in a centered diamond, inside a dark border; with the group name, "American Association of Nurse Anesthetists," printed around the design within the border.

Blue and silver have been the official Association colors since 1944. The professional designation: "C. R. N. A. " ("Certified Registered Nurse Anesthetist"),

is used by members with their names to indicate competence, as
described above under "Membership."

Bibliography:
    American Association of Nurse Anesthetists.   Bylaws.   1971.
        19 pages.
    Folder gives membership requirements and disciplinary pro-
    cedures.
    _____. Code of Ethics and Personnel Policies.   1953, re-
        vised edition 1961.   11 pages.
    Guide to professional conduct; employment standards.
    _____. Notes on the History and Organization of the Ameri-
        can Association of Nurse Anesthetists.   1969.   31 pages.
    Includes information about founding and development of the
    Association, education and examination qualifications for
    membership, design and significance of insignia.

"Code of Ethics"

Introduction

A code of ethics for the nurse anesthetist is chiefly concerned
with her relationship to all people with whom she comes in contact.
The establishment of a reputation for professional ability and fidelity
is based on the same principles as that of an individual.   It cannot
be attained without the elements of character and good conduct.

Personal Ethics

The right of a nurse anesthetist to professional status rests
in the knowledge, skill, and experience with which she serves the
patient.   Every nurse anesthetist has the obligation to keep this
knowledge and skill refreshed by continued education throughout the
professional life.
The nurse anesthetist can sympathetically appreciate the position of others and shall endeavor to avoid professional or personal
criticism of co-workers.

Professional Relationships

Toward the Patient:
The nurse anesthetist is responsible for giving competent
anesthesia and must refrain from the use of drugs or from any
other acts that will affect her competence.
The nurse anesthetist shows respect and consideration for
the patient, regardless of race, religion, nationality or economic
status.
The nurse anesthetist holds in confidence all information of
a professional, or private nature.

Toward the Doctor:
The nurse anesthetist is responsible for competently and

efficiently administering the anesthetic prescribed.

The nurse anesthetist is obliged to provide the surgeon with intelligent and alert service, and carry out instructions in a reasonable and intelligent manner.

The nurse anesthetist follows the dictates of conscience, giving consideration to the immediate needs of the situation in controversial problems, and may withdraw from participation in what is deemed unethical practice when such withdrawal can be done without jeopardy to the patient.

Toward Hospital Personnel and Employer:

The nurse anesthetist regards contracts with an employer (written or oral) as ethical and legal obligations to be fulfilled in letter and in spirit; however, changed conditions may justify seeking mutual modification of such agreements from proper authority.

The nurse anesthetist will be cognizant of and adhere to the channels of authority; will cooperate and accept the decisions of consultations and discussions concerning hospital policies.

Standard of Remuneration

General rules and standards regarding remuneration may be adopted by the profession in each locale. It should be deemed a point of honor to adhere to these standards with as much uniformity as conditions permit.

The nurse anesthetist has a right to a just remuneration for services, but acceptance of additional compensation by way of bribes or tips is unethical.

The nurse anesthetist is free to render gratuitous service.

The nurse anesthetist, institutionally employed, receives remuneration in accordance with the contract of employment. The nurse anesthetist practicing private anesthesia may submit a statement to the patient or to the surgeon, depending on the policy and the laws of the locale.

Responsibilities Toward Professional Organizations

The nurse anesthetist shall uphold the principles and comply with the By-laws of the American Association of Nurse Anesthetists. The nurse anesthetist shall participate actively, as much as possible, in local, state, and national planning to improve the quality of anesthesia service to the patient.

The nurse anesthetist shall share the responsibilities of the Association and thus contribute time, energy, and means to represent the ideals of the profession.

Special Responsibilities as a Citizen

The nurse anesthetist, as a citizen, should understand and uphold the laws; as a professional worker, she is especially concerned with those laws governing the practice of medicine and

nursing. The nurse anesthetist should participate and share responsibilities with other citizens and public health organizations in promoting efforts to meet the health needs of the public.

Legal Restrictions

The physician has the right to select the anesthetic agent
and pre-operative sedation.
The nurse anesthetist may make suggestions or state a
preference, but she may not administer any drug without approval
of a physician.   Only in cases of emergency and in the absence of
a physician may a nurse anesthetist recommend or administer
emergency care.   This occurring, the nurse anesthetist is obliged
to report the incident to the attending physician at the earliest possible time.

Public Relations

The nurse anesthetist should maintain a true spirit of concern
for the public welfare and community health planning.
The nurse anesthetist should exhibit in herself, and instill
in others, confidence in the medical and nursing professions.
The nurse anesthetist should never criticize nor comment
adversely against a member of the medical or nursing profession
or a medical institution to the general public or to the patient but
should confine such criticism to the proper authorities along constructive lines.
The nurse anesthetist may suggest a professional person or
institution, if requested, but it is preferable to recommend several
as being equally competent.
The nurse anesthetist will not participate in any act in which
the patient may be deceived about the identity of the person or persons administering the anesthesia.
Members shall not solicit funds, gifts, or social functions
from companies or individuals, nor accept such contributions without the right to publicly recognize the contributor.

ANTHROPOLOGISTS

AMERICAN ANTHROPOLOGICAL ASSOCIATION (AAA)
1703 New Hampshire Ave., N.W., Washington, D.C. 20009
Edward J. Lehman, Executive Director

Membership: The American Anthropological Association, founded
in 1902 and with a present (1973) membership of approximately
8000, is the professional association of workers in the science of
anthropology in all of its branches.   "Any person having a demon-

strable professional or scholarly interest in the science of anthropology is eligible to become a member" (Constitution, Article IV,
Section 2) of the organization.

To qualify as "Fellow" of the Association, the fully professional
class of member qualified to vote and hold office, an AAA member
must have graduate education or experience in anthropology:
- a. Doctorate or equivalent degree in anthropology; or
- b. Doctorate or equivalent degree in an allied field, and
  demonstrated professional or scholarly interest in anthropology; or
- c. Master's degree in anthropology or in an allied field,
  and significant contributions to anthropology in teaching
  or research, and active engagement professionally in
  anthropology for at least five years.

Code of Ethics: The guide to professional conduct of the American
Anthropological Association is its Principles of Professional Responsibility, adopted by the association Council May 1971. "This statement of principles is not intended to supersede previous statements
and resolutions of the Association. Its intent is to clarify professional responsibilities in the chief areas of professional concern to
anthropologists." In the statement, "Principles deemed fundamental
to the anthropologists responsible, ethical pursuit of his profession,"
are grouped under six headings, reflecting the complex relationships
with peoples and situations studied in anthropology:
1. Relations with those studied;
2. Responsibility to the public;
3. Responsibility to the discipline;
4. Responsibility to the students;
5. Responsibility to the sponsors;
6. Responsibilities to one's own government and to the host
   government.
No enforcement procedures of the Principles are reported.

Other Guides to Professional Conduct: Among statements and resolutions of the Association, adopted prior to the Principles, is the
Statement on Problems of Anthropological Research and Ethics, issued by the Fellows in 1967. The professional statement on "freedom of publication and protection of the interests of the persons and
groups studied" is given in three sections: (I) Freedom of Research,
(II) Support and Sponsorship, (III) Anthropologists in United States
Government Service.

Professional Insignia: None reported.

Bibliography:
American Anthropological Association. Constitution and By-Laws.
Amended May 1971. 4 pages.
Includes qualification requirements for membership categories.
_____. Principles of Professional Responsibility. May 1971.
Single sheet.

Principles clarifying professional responsibilities of anthropologists in the chief areas of their professional concern.
            . Statement on Problems of Anthropological Research
      and Ethics. 1967. Single sheet.
Fellows of the Association reaffirm and extend the anthropologists' standards for Freedom of Research; Support and
Sponsorship for field and other research; and professional
responsibilities of anthropologists employed by the United
States Government Service.

"Principles of Professional Responsibility"*
Adopted by the Council of the American Anthropological
Association May 1971

Preamble:

        Anthropologists work in many parts of the world in close
personal association with the peoples and situations they study.
Their professional situation is, therefore, uniquely varied and complex. They are involved with their discipline, their colleagues,
their students, their sponsors, their subjects, their own and host
governments, the particular individuals and groups with whom they
do their field work, other populations and interest groups in the
nations within which they work, and the study of processes and issues affecting general human welfare. In a field of such complex
involvements, misunderstandings, conflicts and the necessity to
make choices among conflicting values are bound to arise and to
generate ethical dilemmas. It is a prime responsibility of anthropologists to anticipate these and to plan to resolve them in such a
way as to damage neither to those whom they study nor, in so far
as possible, to their scholarly community. Where these conditions
cannot be met, the anthropologist would be well-advised not to pursue the particular piece of research.
        The following principles are deemed fundamental to the anthro-
pologist's responsible, ethical pursuit of his profession.

1.   Relations with those studied:

        In research, an anthropologist's paramount responsibility is
to those he studies. When there is a conflict of interest, these
individuals must come first. The anthropologist must do everything
within his power to protect their physical, social and psychological
welfare and to honor their dignity and privacy.

_____

*This statement of principles is not intended to supersede previous
statements and resolutions of the Association. Its intent is to clarify
professional responsibilities in the chief areas of professional concern to anthropologists.

a. Where research involves the acquisition of material and information transferred on the assumption of trust between persons, it is axiomatic that the rights, interests, and sensitivities of those studied must be safeguarded.

b. The aims of the investigation should be communicated as well as possible to the informant.

c. Informants have a right to remain anonymous. This right should be respected both where it has been promised explicitly and where no clear understanding to the contrary has been reached. These strictures apply to the collection of data by means of cameras, tape recorders, and other data-gathering devices, as well as to data collected in face-to-face interviews or in participant observation. Those being studied should understand the capacities of such devices; they should be free to reject them if they wish; and if they accept them, the results obtained should be consonant with the informant's right to welfare, dignity and privacy.

d. There should be no exploitation of individual informants for personal gain. Fair return should be given them for all services.

e. There is an obligation to reflect on the foreseeable repercussions of research and publication on the general population being studied.

f. The anticipated consequences of research should be communicated as fully as possible to the individuals and groups likely to be affected.

g. In accordance with the Association's general position on clandestine and secret research, no reports should be provided to sponsors that are not also available to the general public and, where practicable, to the population studied.

h. Every effort should be exerted to cooperate with members of the host society in the planning and execution of research projects.

i. All of the above points should be acted upon in full recognition of the social and cultural pluralism of host societies and the consequent plurality of values, interests and demands in those societies. This diversity complicates choice-making in research, but ignoring it leads to irresponsible decisions.

2. Responsibility to the public:

The anthropologist is also responsible to the public--all presumed consumers of his professional efforts. To them he owes a commitment to candor and to truth in the dissemination of his research results and in the statement of his opinions as a student of man.

a. He should not communicate his findings secretly to some and withhold them from others.

b. He should not knowingly falsify or color his findings.

c. In providing professional opinions, he is responsible not only

for their content but also for integrity in explaining both these
opinions and their bases.

d. As people who devote their professional lives to understanding
man, anthropologists bear a positive responsibility to speak out
publicly, both individually and collectively, on what they know
and what they believe as a result of their professional expertise
gained in the study of human beings. That is, they bear a
professional responsibility to contribute to an "adequate definition of reality" upon which public opinion and public policy may
be based.

e. In public discourse, the anthropologist should be honest about
his qualifications and cognizant of the limitations of anthropological expertise.

3. Responsibility to the discipline:

An anthropologist bears responsibility for the good reputation
of his discipline and its practitioners.

a. He should undertake no secret research or any research whose
results cannot be freely derived and publicly reported.

b. He should avoid even the appearance of engaging in clandestine
research, by fully and freely disclosing the aims and sponsorship of all his research.

c. He should attempt to maintain a level of integrity and rapport
in the field such that by his behavior and example he will not
jeopardize future research there. The responsibility is not to
analyze and report so as to offend no one, but to conduct research in a way consistent with a commitment to honesty, open
inquiry, clear communication of sponsorship and research aims,
and concern for the welfare and privacy of informants.

4. Responsibility to students:

In relations with students an anthropologist should be candid,
fair, nonexploitative and committed to their welfare and academic
progress.

As Robert Lekachman has suggested, honesty is the essential
quality of a good teacher, neutrality is not. Beyond honest teaching,
the anthropologist as a teacher has ethical responsibilities in selection, instruction in ethics, career counseling, academic supervision,
evaluation, compensation and placement.

a. He should select students in such a way as to preclude discrimination on the basis of sex, race, ethnic group, social class
and other categories of people indistinguishable by their intellectual potential.

b. He should alert students to the ethical problems of research and
discourage them from participating in projects employing questionable ethical standards. This should include providing them
with information and discussions to protect them from unethical

pressures and enticements emanating from possible sponsors, as well as helping them to find acceptable alternatives (see point i below).

c. He should be receptive and seriously responsive to students' interests, opinions and desires in all aspects of their academic work and relationships.

d. He should realistically counsel students regarding career opportunities.

e. He should conscientiously supervise, encourage and support students in their anthropological and other academic endeavors.

f. He should inform students of what is expected of them in their course of study. He should be fair in the evaluation of their performance. He should communicate evaluations to the students concerned.

g. He should acknowledge in print the student assistance he uses in his own publications, give appropriate credit (including co-authorship) when student research is used in publication, encourage and assist in publication of worthy student papers, and compensate students justly for the use of their time, energy and intelligence in research and teaching.

h. He should energetically assist students in securing legitimate research support and the necessary permissions to pursue research.

i. He should energetically assist students in securing professional employment upon completion of their studies.

j. He should strive to improve both our techniques of teaching and our techniques for evaluating the effectiveness of our methods of teaching.

5.   Responsibility to sponsors:

     In his relations with sponsors of research, an anthropologist should be honest about his qualifications, capabilities and aims. He thus faces the obligation, prior to entering any commitment for research, to reflect sincerely upon the purposes of his sponsors in terms of their past behavior. He should be especially careful not to promise or imply acceptance of conditions contrary to his professional ethics or competing commitments. This requires that he require of the sponsor full disclosure of the sources of funds, personnel, aims of the institution and the research project, disposition of research results. He must retain the right to make all ethical decisions in his research. He should enter into no secret agreement with the sponsor regarding the research, results or reports.

6.   Responsibilities to one's own government
and to host governments:

     In his relation with his own government and with host governments, the research anthropologist should be honest and candid. He should demand assurance that he will not be required to compromise his professional responsibilities and ethics as a condition of his permission to pursue the research.   Specifically, no secret research, no secret reports or debriefings of any kind should be agreed to or given.   If these matters are clearly understood in advance, serious complications and misunderstandings can generally be avoided.

Epilogue:

In the final analysis, anthropological research is a human undertaking, dependent upon choices for which the individual bears ethical as well as scientific responsibility.   That responsibility is a human, not superhuman responsibility.   To err is human, to forgive humane.   This statement of principles of professional responsibility is not designed to punish, but to provide guidelines which can minimize the occasions upon which there is a need to forgive. When an anthropologist, by his actions, jeopardizes peoples studied, professional colleagues, students or others, or if he otherwise betrays his professional commitments, his colleagues may legitimately inquire into the propriety of those actions, and take such measures as lie within the legitimate powers of their Association as the membership of the Association deems appropriate.

"Statement on Problems of Anthropological Research and Ethics"

by the Fellows of the American Anthropological Association, 1967

The human condition, past and present, is the concern of anthropologists throughout the world.   The study of mankind in varying social, cultural, and ecological situations is essential to our understanding of human nature, of culture, and of society.

Our present knowledge of the range of human behavior is admittedly incomplete.   Expansion and refinement of this knowledge depend heavily on international understanding and cooperation in scientific and scholarly inquiry.   To maintain the independence and integrity of anthropology as a science, it is necessary that scholars have full opportunity to study peoples and their culture, to publish, disseminate, and openly discuss the results of their research, and to continue their responsibility of protecting the personal privacy of those being studied and assisting in their research.

Constraint, deception, and secrecy have no place in science. Actions which compromise the intellectual integrity and autonomy of research scholars and institutions not only weaken those international understandings essential to our discipline, but in so doing they also threaten any contribution anthropology might make to our own society and to the general interests of human welfare.

The situations which jeopardize research differ from year to year, from country to country, and from discipline to discipline. We are concerned here with problems that affect all the fields of anthropology and which, in varying ways, are shared by the social and behavioral sciences.

I. FREEDOM OF RESEARCH

1. The Fellows of the American Anthropological Association reaffirm their resolution of 1948 on freedom of publication and protection of the interests of the persons and groups studied:

Be it resolved: (1) that the American Anthropological Association strongly urge all sponsoring institutions to guarantee their research scientists complete freedom to interpret and publish their findings without censorship or interference; provided that
(2) the interests of the persons and communities or other groups studied are protected; and that
(3) in the event that the sponsoring institution does not wish to publish the results nor be identified with the publication, it permit publication of the results, without use of its name as sponsoring agency, through other channels.
--American Anthropologist 51:370 (1949)

To extend and strengthen this resolution, the Fellows of the American Anthropological Association endorse the following:

2. Except in the event of a declaration of war by the Congress, academic institutions should not undertake activities or accept contracts in anthropology that are not related to their normal functions of teaching, research, and public service. They should not lend themselves to clandestine activities. We deplore unnecessary restrictive classifications of research reports prepared under contract for the Government, and excessive security regulations imposed on participating academic personnel.

3. The best interests of scientific research are not served by the imposition of external restrictions. The review procedures instituted for foreign area research contracts by the Foreign Affairs Research Council of the Department of State (following a Presidential directive of July, 1965) offer a dangerous potential for censorship of research. Additional demands by some United States agencies for clearance, and for excessively detailed itineraries and field plans from responsible scholars whose research has been approved by their professional peers or academic institutions, are contrary to assurances given by Mr. Thomas L. Hughes, Director of the Bureau of Intelligence and Research, Department of State, to the President of the American Anthropological Association on November 9, 1965, and are incompatible with effective anthropological research.

4. Anthropologists employed or supported by the Government

should be given the greatest possible opportunities to participate in planning research projects, to carry them out, and to publish their findings.

II. SUPPORT AND SPONSORSHIP

1. The most useful and effective governmental support of anthropology in recent years has come through such agencies as the National Science Foundation, the National Institutes of Health, and the Smithsonian Institution. We welcome support for basic research and training through these and similar institutions.

2. The Fellows take this occasion to express their gratitude to these members of Congress, especially Senator Harris and Representative Fascell, who have so clearly demonstrated their interest in the social sciences, not only through enlarging governmental support for them, but also in establishing channels for social scientists to communicate their opinions to the Government regarding policies that affect the future of the social sciences and their utilization by Government.

3. When queried by individuals representing either host countries or groups being studied, anthropologists should willingly supply evidence of their professional qualifications and associations, their sponsorship and source of funds, and the nature and objectives of the research being undertaken.

4. Anthropologists engaged in research in foreign areas should be especially concerned with the possible effects of their sponsorship and sources of financial support. Although the Department of Defense and other mission-oriented branches of the Government support some basic research in the social sciences, their sponsorship may nevertheless create an extra hazard in the conduct of fieldwork and jeopardize future access to research opportunities in the areas studied.

5. Anthropologists who are considering financial support from independent research organizations should ascertain the full nature of the proposed investigations, including sponsorship and arrangements for publication. It is the responsibility of anthropologists to maintain the highest professional standards and to decline to participate in or to accept support from organizations that permit misrepresentation of technical competence, excessive costs, or concealed sponsorship of activities. Such considerations are especially significant where grants or fellowships are offered by foundations or other organizations which do not publish balance sheets showing their sources of funds.

6. The international reputation of anthropology has been damaged by the activities of unqualified individuals who have falsely claimed to be anthropologists, or who have pretended to be engaged in anthropological research while in fact pursuing other ends. There

also is good reason to believe that some anthropologists have used their professional standing and the names of their academic institutions as cloaks for the collection of intelligence information and for intelligence operations. Academic institutions and individual members of the academic community, including students, should scrupulously avoid both involvement in clandestine intelligence activities and the use of the name of anthropology, or the title of anthropologist, as a cover for intelligence activities.

III. ANTHROPOLOGISTS IN UNITED STATES GOVERNMENT SERVICE

1. It is desirable that social science advice be made more readily available to the Executive Office of the President.

2. Where the services of anthropologists are needed in agencies of the Government it is most desirable that professional anthropologists be involved at the project planning stage and in the actual recruitment of necessary personnel. Only in this manner is it possible to provide skilled and effective technical advice.

3. Anthropologists contemplating or accepting employment in governmental agencies in other than policy-making positions should recognize that they will be committed to agency missions and policies. They should seek in advance the clearest possible definition of their expected roles as well as the possibilities for maintaining professional contacts, for continuing to contribute to the profession through publication, and for maintaining professional standards in protecting the privacy of individuals and groups they may study.

APPRAISERS

AMERICAN SOCIETY OF APPRAISERS (ASA)
Dulles International Airport
P. O. Box 17265, Washington, D. C. 20041
Dexter D. MacBride, A. S. A. , Executive Vice President

Membership: The American Society of Appraisers, incorporated in 1952 and with a present (1973) membership of 3600, is a professional association of appraisers of all classes of property--real, personal, tangible, intangible--including those active in Appraisal Administration, Intangible Property, Legal, Machinery and Equipment, Personal Property, Real Property, and Technical Valuation. ASA, formed by a merger of the American Society of Technical Appraisers (organized in 1936) and the Technical Valuation Society (established in 1939), groups its members into five specialty classifications:
    Real Property--urban, rural, natural resources;
    Personal Property--collectors items, fine arts, gems and

jewelry, household furnishings, chattels (special);
Intangible Property--equities, future potentials, personal
    subjectives;
Machinery and Equipment--basic industry, fabricating and
    processing, equipment valuations, special services;
Technical Valuation--cost surveys, public utilities, industries.

Requirements for two professional grades of membership of the
Society include specified length of appraisal experience, written
examination, and submission of two representative appraisal reports:
    Member--"minimum five years of collateral and full-time
        appraisal experience."
    Senior Member--"at least five full years of appraisal ex-
        perience."
Membership as "Fellow" may be bestowed upon those Senior Members of ASA "in recognition of outstanding services to the appraisal
profession or to the Society."

The association authorizes professional members to use the following professional designations:
    Member--"Member of the American Society of Appraisers."
    Senior Member--"A. S. A."
    Fellow--"F. A. S. A."
The Professional Appraisal Services Director, issued each year, indicates the Certified Members and the valuation specialization for
each such member.

Code of Ethics: Carrying out one of the purposes of the Society--
to "establish and maintain the principles of appraisal practice and
code of ethics"--a conduct guide, The Principles of Appraisal Practice and Code of Ethics, has been issued by the organization to
serve as a guide to members in their professional work, and to
inform those who use appraisal services of the standards of competent and ethical appraisal practice.

The guide sets forth in detail the objectives of professional
appraisal and valuation work, giving the appraiser's primary duty
and responsibilities, and his obligations to clients and other appraisers. Enforcement of the Principles and Code is carried out
by the International President, the International Ethics Committee,
and the Board of Governors of the Society. A member found in
violation of the standards, after investigation, may be censured,
suspended, or expelled from the Society (Principles...and Code...,
7. 8)

Professional Insignia: The official
emblem of the ASA is an equilateral
triangle, containing in its central
portion a balance scale within a
smaller triangle--symbolizing the
objectivity and equity of the appraisal
process; the initials of the organization,
"ASA," appear at the base of the

smaller triangle. The colors of this emblem are shown variously--
dark blue on white (letterhead), black on white, white on black,
green on yellow (publications).

Other Identification of Professional Status: The Society authorizes
its professional members to use an appropriate professional designation to indicate class of membership, as described above under
"Membership."

Bibliography:
American Society of Appraisers. American Society of Appraisers,
the Multi-Disciplinary Professional Appraisal Society.
Pamphlet.
Informational brochure giving ASA purpose, brief description
of Principles and Code of Ethics, classes of membership and
professional designation.
_____. The Appraisal and Valuation Manual, vols. 1-9,
1955-1971.
_____. The Principles of Appraisal Practice and Code of
Ethics. October 1970. 24 pages. Folder. (Reprint
Series #10).
Principles authorized June 30, 1968 to cover all classes of
property and specialized appraisal procedures; includes pro-
fessional designation authorized, and enforcement of principles
and code (7. 8).

"The Principles of Appraisal Practice and Code
of Ethics of the American Society of Appraisers"

1 INTRODUCTION

1.1 Membership Composition of the American Society of Appraisers

The American Society of Appraisers is a professional organization of individuals. Each of its members who has demonstrated,
to the satisfaction of the Society, that he is qualified to appraise
one or more of the existing kinds of property, has been granted the
right to use the professional designation "A. S. A."

1.2 Definition of "Appraisal Practice" and "Property"

1.21 The term appraisal practice, as defined by the Society,
applies to any of the four following operations, singly or in combination, these operations being executed within a framework of general principles of technical procedure and personal conduct:

(1) Determination of the value of property (the transitive verb "determine" having the meaning: "to come to a decision concerning,
as the result of investigation, reasoning, etc.");
(2) Forecasting of the earning power of property;
(3) Estimation of the cost of

(a) Production of a new property ("production" having the meaning: "brought into being by assembly of elements, fabrication, construction, manufacture, or natural growth of living things");

(b) Replacement of an existing property by purchase or production of an equivalent property;

(c) Reproduction of an existing property by purchase or production of an identical property.

(4) Determining non-monetary benefits or characteristics that contribute to value. The rendering of judgments as to age, remaining life, condition, quality, or authenticity of physical property, amenities; an estimate of the amount of a natural resource, population increase, nature of market, rate of absorption, etc.

1.22   In a valuation and in a forecast of earning power, the word "property" is used to describe the rights to the future benefits of something owned or possessed to the exclusion of other persons. The "something owned" may be tangible, intangible, or both.

In a cost estimation, the word "property" is used to describe the "something owned" without regard to its ownership.

1.3   Purpose of Promulgating the Principles of Appraisal Practice and Code of Ethics

The principles of Appraisal Practice and Code of Ethics of the American Society of Appraisers are promulgated to:

1.31   Inform those who use the services of appraisers what, in the opinion of the Society, constitutes competent and ethical appraisal practice;

1.32   Serve as a guide to its own members in achieving competency in appraisal practice and in adhering to ethical standards;

1.33   Aid in the accomplishment of the purposes of the Society, which include:

(a) Fosterage of appraisal education,

(b) Improvement and development of appraisal techniques,

(c) Encouragement of sound professional practices,

(d) Establishment of criteria of sound performance for the use of employers of staff appraisers,

(e) Enforcement of ethical conduct and practice by its members;

1.34   Provide means, auxiliary to those used in examining applicants for admission to the grades of Member and Senior Member of the Society, for judging their skill, competence, and understanding of ethical principles;

1.35   Epitomize those appraisal practices that experience has found to be effective in protecting the public against exploitation.

2 OBJECTIVES OF APPRAISAL WORK

2.1 Various Kinds of Objectives of Appraisal Work

An appraisal is undertaken for one or more of several objectives, namely: to determine the value of a property; to estimate the cost of producing, acquiring, altering, or completing a property; to estimate the monetary amount of damages to a property; and to forecast the monetary earning power of a property. In specific instances, the work may have additional objectives, such as: the formulation of conclusions and recommendations or the presentation of alternatives (and their consequences) for the client's actions.

2.2 Objective Character of the Results of an Appraisal Undertaking

The primary objective of a monetary appraisal, is the determination of a numerical result, either as a range or most probable point magnitude--the dollar amount of a value, the dollar amount of an estimated cost, the dollar amount of an estimated earning power. This numerical result is objective and unrelated to the desires, wishes, or needs of the client who engaged the appraiser to perform the work. The amount of this figure is as independent of what someone desires it to be as a physicist's measurement of the melting point of lead or an accountant's statement of the amount of net profits of a corporation. All the principles of appraisal ethics stem from this central fact.

3 APPRAISER'S PRIMARY DUTY AND RESPONSIBILITY

The appraiser's duty and responsibility, in each subject case, is twofold.

3.1 Appraiser's Obligation to Determine and Describe the Apposite Kind of Value or Estimated Cost

First, because there are several kinds of value and several kinds of cost estimates, each of which has a legitimate place as the end point of some class of appraisal engagement, it is the appraiser's obligation to ascertain which one of these is pertinent to the particular undertaking. In meeting this obligation, the appraiser may consider his client's instructions and/or may obtain legal or other professional advice, but the selection of the apposite kind of value or estimated cost is the appraiser's sole responsibility. Also, it is his obligation, in this connection, fully to explain and describe what is meant by the particular value or cost estimate which he has determined, in order to obviate misunderstanding and to prevent unwitting or deliberate misapplication. For example, an appraisal engagement which calls for the determination of the replacement cost of a merchant's inventory of goods, for insurance purposes, would not be properly discharged by an appraisal of its retail market value; and an engagement which calls for the determination of the current market value of a multitenant office building leasehold estate would not be properly discharged by a determination of the depreciated new cost of replacement of the improvements.

3.2 Appraiser's Obligation to Determine Numerical Results with Whatever Degree of Accuracy the Particular Objectives of the Appraisal Necessitate

Second, it is the appraiser's obligation to determine the appropriate and applicable numerical results with as high a degree of accuracy as the particular objectives of the appraisal necessitate.

3.3 Appraiser's Obligation to Avoid Giving a False Numerical Result

Obviously, the appraiser has every obligation to avoid giving a false figure. The numerical result of an appraisal could be false for one of two reasons: it could be false because it is a grossly inaccurate estimate of the apposite kind of value or cost estimate, or it could be false, even though numerically accurate, because it is an estimate of an inapposite kind of value or cost estimate.

3.4 Appraiser's Obligation to Attain Competency and to Practice Ethically

In order to meet his obligations, the appraiser must be competent in his field. This competency he attains by education, training, study, practice, and experience. He must also recognize, understand, and abide by those ethical principles that are interwoven with and are an essential part of truly professional practice.

3.5 Professional Character of Appraisal Practice

The members of the Society are engaged in a professional activity. A profession is based on an organized body of specific knowledge--knowledge not possessed by laymen. It is of such a character that it requires a high degree of intelligence and a considerable expenditure of time and effort to acquire it and to become adept in its application. An appraiser's client, because he does not have the necessary specialized knowledge himself, puts his trust in the appraiser and relies on him to use his professional knowledge and abilities to whatever extent may be necessary to accomplish the objectives of the work. There is no caveat emptor principle involved in the relationship between a professional appraiser and his client. Members of the Society recognize this fiduciary relationship.

3.6 Appraiser's Fiduciary Relationship to Third Parties

It frequently happens that an appraisal report is given by the client to third parties for their use. These third parties may or may not be known to the appraiser but, regardless of this fact, they have as much right to rely on the validity and objectivity of the appraiser's findings as does the client. Members of the Society recognize their fiduciary responsibility to those parties, other than the client, who make use of their reports.

3. 7 Appraiser's Fiduciary Relationship to the Public

Since the general public welfare is often involved in the execution of valuation assignments, the appraiser has an obligation and responsibility to the general public that supersedes the appraiser's obligation to his client.

This fiduciary relationship to the public is the same as his fiduciary relationship to third parties (3. 6). It applies to assignments involving depositors in a financial institution making loans, to taxpayers in a school district whose board is acquiring a new schoolsite, to taxpayers represented by government agencies who are acquiring property under eminent domain proceedings, and to publicly displayed values of real or personal property that is offered for sale to the public.

4 APPRAISER'S OBLIGATIONS TO HIS CLIENT

The appraiser's primary obligation to his client is to reach complete, accurate, and pertinent conclusions and numerical results regardless of the client's wishes or instructions in this regard. The relationship between client and appraiser is not one of principal and agent. However, the appraiser's obligations to his client go somewhat beyond this primary obligation. These secondary obligations are set forth in the following sections.

4. 1 Confidential Character of an Appraisal Engagement

The fact that an appraiser has been employed to make an appraisal is a confidential matter. In some instances, the very fact of employment may be information that a client, whether private or a public agency, prefers for valid reasons to keep confidential. Knowledge by outsiders of the fact of employment of an appraiser may jeopardize a client's proposed enterprise or transaction. Consequently, it is improper for the appraiser to disclose the fact of his engagement, unless the client approves of the disclosure or clearly has no interest in keeping the fact of the engagement confidential, or unless the appraiser is required by due process of law to disclose the fact of his engagement.

It is not proper for an appraiser to reveal to any third party the amount of his valuation of a property without the permission of his client or his employer, unless required to do so by due process of law.

In the absence of an express agreement to the contrary, the identifiable contents of an appraisal report are the property of the appraiser's client or employer and, ethically, cannot be submitted

to any professional Society as evidence of professional qualifications,
and cannot be published in any identifiable form without the client's
or employer's consent.

4.2 Appraiser's Obligation to Give Competent Service

It is not proper for an appraiser to accept an engagement to
make an appraisal of property of a type he is not qualified to appraise or in a field outside his Society membership classification,
unless (a) he fully acquaints the client with the limitations of his
qualifications or (b) he associates himself with another appraiser
or appraisers who possess the required qualifications.

As a corollary to the above principle, the Society declares
that it is unethical for an appraiser to claim or imply that he has
professional qualifications which he does not possess or to state his
qualifications in a form which may be subject to erroneous interpretation. (See Sec. 7.7)

4.3 Appraiser's Obligation Relative to Giving Testimony

When an appraiser is engaged by one of the parties in a
controversy, it is unethical for the appraiser to suppress any facts,
data, or opinions which are adverse to the case his client is trying
to establish; or to over-emphasize any facts, data, or opinions
which are favorable to his client's case; or in any other particulars
to become an advocate. It is the appraiser's obligation to present
the data, analysis, and value without bias, regardless of the effect
of such unbiased presentation on his client's case. (Also, see Sec.
7.4)

4.4 Appraiser's Obligation Relative to Serving More Than One Client in the Same Matter

When two or more potential clients seek an appraiser's
services with respect to the same property or with respect
to the same legal action, the appraiser may not properly
serve more than one, except with the consent of all
parties.

4.5 Agreements and Contracts for Appraisal Services

It is good practice to have a written contract, or at least a
clear oral agreement, between appraiser and client, covering objectives and scope of work, time of delivery of report, and amount
of fees. In certain circumstances, it may be desirable to include
in the appraisal-service contract a statement covering the objective
character of appraisal findings and a statement that the appraiser
cannot act as an advocate or negotiator.

5 APPRAISER'S OBLIGATIONS TO OTHER APPRAISERS AND TO THE SOCIETY

5.1 Protection of Professional Reputation of Other Appraisers

The appraiser has an obligation to protect the professional reputation of all appraisers (whether members of the Society or not) who subscribe to and practice in accord with the Principles of Appraisal Practice of the Society. The Society declares that it is unethical for an appraiser to injure, or attempt to injure, by false or malicious statements or by innuendo the professional reputation or prospects of any appraiser.

5.2 Unethical Competitive Conduct

The Society declares that it is unethical conduct for an appraiser to reduce a fee which he has already quoted to a client or a prospective client for a specified appraisal service, in order to supplant another appraiser after the latter's quotation has been made known to him.

The Society declares that it is unethical conduct for an appraiser to supplant, or attempt to supplant, another appraiser after the latter has been engaged to perform a specified appraisal service.

5.3 Appraiser's Obligations Relative to Society's Disciplinary Actions

A member of the Society, having knowledge of an act by another member which, in his opinion, is in violation of the ethical principles incorporated in the Principles of Appraisal Practice and Code of Ethics of the Society, has the obligation to report the matter in accordance with the procedure specified in the Constitution and By-Laws.

It is the appraiser's obligation to cooperate with the Society and its officers in all matters, including investigation, censure, discipline, or dismissal of members who are charged with violation of the Principles of Appraisal Practice and Code of Ethics of the Society.

SOCIETY OF REAL ESTATE APPRAISERS (SREA)
7 S. Dearborn St., Chicago, Ill. 60603
James V. Morgan, Executive Vice President

Membership: The Society of Real Estate Appraisers, one of several national associations that test and accredit professional appraisers, was founded in 1935 and has currently (1973) 18,000 members. Its members--distributed in 180 chapters in the United States and Canada--are employed in real estate businesses, various types of banking and loan organizations, and in the government service as

full-time professional real estate appraisers and analysts, using
skills to evaluate residential and income properties in accordance
with accepted definitions of "market value."

Membership categories, with authorization of professional designation to indicate competence which are currently awarded by SREA,
are:

SREA--Senior Real Estate Analyst--The highest designation
awarded by the Society, "a professional member who has
extensive technical training and long and varied experience
... competent to appraise all types of real estate interests
and ownerships in accordance with accepted definitions of
market value. An SREA has further demonstrated his
ability to extend the appraisal analysis beyond a current
market value to provide a basis for decision-making to
clients responsible for committing funds or assets in the
sale, financing, purchase, lease, trade, renovation, development, demolition or division of real property." SREA
designation awarded for five year period, requiring re-
application for certification at end of five years.

SRA--Senior Realty Appraiser--Designation awarded to indicate competence to appraise residential and income properties in accordance with accepted definitions of market
value.

Education and experience requirements for the two types of
certification include three courses offered through the Society in
various universities (course length one or two weeks):

Course 101:   An Introduction to Appraising Real Property.
Course 201:   Principles of Income Property Appraising.
Course 301:   Special Application of Appraisal Analysis.

The Society offers additional training in the form of one-day clinics
and seminars covering all types of appraisal problems from agriculture to urban renewal, and to writing narrative appraisal reports.
The two classes of professional SREA membership require:

Senior Real Estate Analyst--A Senior Realty Appraiser member who has:
a.   at least 8 years experience in income property appraising;
b.   completed one basic introduction appraisal course and one
advanced course covering the use of capitalization tables,
lease-hold interests, residual techniques and cash flow
analysis;
c.   (if born in 1945 or after) a college degree, or equivalent.

Senior Realty Appraiser--Within a ten-year period as an
Associate Member of the Society, have
a.   completed the SREA professional training and development program, including the two required courses, and
the Narrative Report Income Seminar;
b.   submitted a satisfactory demonstration report on income property;

c. (if born in 1945 or after) a college degree, or equivalent.
d. several years of concentrated appraisal experience or
    appraisal and real estate experience.

Certification as SREA (Senior Real Estate Analyst) requires
passing oral and written examinations as well as review of appraisals
made by applicant, and other investigation to insure competency and
integrity.   A Directory of Designated Members, issued each year in
March, shows professional designation authorized for members, arranged alphabetically under geographical headings.

Code of Ethics: In accordance with one of the purposes of its
founding--"to elevate the standards of the appraisal profession"--
the Society adopted in 1968 as part of its By-Laws a guide to professional conduct: Standards of Professional Practice and Conduct,
which include a newly-revised Code of Ethics.   These standards--
amended in 1970, effective January 1, 1971--set forth general
principles of appraisal conduct, with two specific guides to responsibilities and obligations--
        Standards of Professional Practice; and
        Standards of Professional Conduct.
These conduct standards are enforced by the International Professional Practice Committee of the Society, which generally delegates
enforcement to chapter Professional Practice Committees.   After
investigation and hearing of an alleged code violation, a member may
be expelled, have his professional designation and membership suspended or revoked (Regulation No. 5. Disciplinary Rules and Procedures).

Other Guides to Professional Conduct: To clarify and expand the
section of the Standards of Professional Conduct dealing with forms
of advertising or soliciting business in a professionally acceptable
manner (Rule VI), Standards of Professional Advertising Practice
(amended 1970, and effective January 1, 1971) give form and practice
acceptable for soliciting business, including use of professional
designation.

Professional Insignia: The insignia of the SREA is seen in the emblems identifying the categories of Society members:
        Associate--bronze pin, skyscrapers with a house outline super-
            imposed at the base, with the designation, "Associate,"
            printed on the house.
        Senior Residential Appraiser--silver pin, similar in design,
            except designation "SRA" is printed on the house (this
            designation no longer awarded).

Senior Realty Appraiser--silver and blue pin, same design,
   but "SRA" centered on tall buildings.
Senior Real Estate Analyst--yellow gold pin, same design,
   but the professional designation "SREA" centered on the
   tall buildings.

Bibliography:
   The Real Estate Appraiser 37:1-64 January 1, 1971. Society
      of Real Estate Appraisers. Single issue: $2.50.
   This issue of the bi-monthly publication of the Society gives
   the International By-Laws, Standards of Professional Practice
   and Conduct, Standards of Professional Advertising Practice,
   and Regulations No. 1 through No. 5, including "Admission
   to Membership" (No. 1), and "Disciplinary Rules and Procedures" (No. 5).
   Society of Real Estate Appraisers. Programs and Services of
      the Society of Real Estate Appraisers. 27 pages. Pam-
      phlet.
   Informational pamphlet giving membership qualifications, required education offered, professional standards required,
   and professional designations authorized.
   _____. Progress in Appraising Through Cooperative Action.
      Folder.
   Brief statement of the qualifications for membership and
   professional designations awarded, to indicate professional
   endorsement by the SREA.

"Standards of Professional
Practice and Conduct"

PREAMBLE

The Society of Real Estate Appraisers was founded to elevate the
standards of the appraisal profession, to aid in the solution of the
many problems of the profession in appraising real estate, and to
designate certain members as having attained certain skills and
knowledge. The members are pledged to maintain a high level of
trust and integrity in their practice.

CODE OF ETHICS

This Code of Ethics is a set of dynamic principles guiding the appraiser's conduct and way of life. It is the appraiser's duty to
practice his profession according to this Code of Ethics.
      Each member agrees that he shall:

   I.   Conduct his activities in a manner that will reflect credit
        upon himself, other real estate appraisers, and the Society
        of Real Estate Appraisers.
   II. Cooperate with the Society of Real Estate Appraisers and
        its officers in all matters, including, but not limited to

the investigation, censure, discipline, or dismissal of members, who by their conduct prejudice their professional status or the reputation of the Society of Real Estate Appraisers.

III. Obtain appraisal assignments, prepare appraisals and accept compensation in a professional manner in accordance with the provisions of the Standards of Professional Practice and Conduct of the Society of Real Estate Appraisers.

IV. Accept only those appraisal assignments for which he has adequate time, facilities, and technical ability to complete in a competent professional manner, and in which he has no current or unrevealed interest.

V. Render properly developed, unbiased and objective value opinions.

VI. Prepare an adequate written appraisal for each real estate appraisal assignment accepted.

VII. Reveal his value conclusions and opinions to no one other than his client, except with the permission of the client or by due process of law, and except when required to do so to comply with the rules of the Society of Real Estate Appraisers.

VIII. Conform in all respects to this Code of Ethics, the Standards of Professional Practice and Conduct, and the By-Laws of the Society of Real Estate Appraisers as the same may be amended from time to time.

STANDARDS OF PROFESSIONAL PRACTICE

I. Valuation Practices

A. Prudent and logical appraisal practice suggests these recommended steps in reaching a supportable conclusion of value:

1. The description or identification of the subject property:
   a. The appraiser should include a legal description, street address or other means of specifically and adequately locating the property being appraised.
   b. The appraiser should consider matters relating to title that may affect the final value conclusions, such as:
      1) The nature of the ownership, i. e., fee simple, or an explanation of other division or ownership interest.
      2) Easements, restriction, encumbrances, leases, reservations, convenants, contracts, declarations, special assessments, ordinances, or other items of a similar nature.
   c. Each appraisal should be predicated upon a valuation of the land for its highest and best use as though unimproved and capable of development to its most profitable legal use. The highest and best use of the property as presently improved may or may not result in a

value conclusion exceeding the value of the land alone.
The appraiser should support his estimates of highest
and best use.

d. The appraiser should include an accurate and adequate
description of the political, social and economic factors affecting the property including the effect on both
the land and the physical improvement on and to the
land.

e. The appraiser should consider all physical, functional
and economic factors as they may affect the value conclusion.

2. Purpose of the appraisal and definition of the value estimated:

a. The appraiser should state the purpose of the appraisal
and clearly define the value estimated.

3. Effective date of the appraisal:

a. The date of the value estimate ordinarily should be the
date of the last property inspection except when the appraisal requires a prior date.

4. Data collection, analysis and interpretation:

a. The appraiser should recognize that each of the approaches to value are functions of market phenomena.

b. The appraiser should consider appropriate units of comparison and also whenever possible, practical and appropriate adjustments should be made for all factors of
dissimilarity.

c. The comparable sales approach (when applicable):

1) The appraiser should collect, inspect, verify,
analyze and correlate such comparable sales as
are available to indicate a value conclusion. No
pertinent information shall be withheld. The pertinent comparable sales should be identified by
address and incorporated into the appraisal report
itself.

d. The income approach (when applicable):

1) When applicable to income producing properties, the
appraiser should collect, inspect, verify, analyze
and correlate such comparable rentals as are available to indicate an appropriate estimate of the economic rental value of the property being appraised.
No pertinent information shall be withheld.

2) When applicable to income producing properties,
the appraiser should collect, verify, analyze and
correlate such data on comparable operating expenses as are available to support an appropriate
estimate of all operating expenses of the property
being appraised. No pertinent information shall be
withheld.

3) When applicable to income producing properties, the
appraiser should collect, verify, analyze and correlate such comparable data relating to an appropriate

capitalization rate or rates to be applied to the estimated net income to indicate a proper value conclusion. No pertinent information shall be withheld.

4) When applicable to income producing properties, the method, process and technique of capitalization used should be appropriate to the type and characteristics of the property being appraised.

5) In the case of single-family dwellings, the appraiser should collect, inspect, verify, analyze and correlate such data on comparable sales and rentals as are available to indicate a value conclusion by use of the gross rent multiplier technique. No pertinent information shall be withheld.

e. The cost approach (when applicable):

1) The appraiser should collect, verify, analyze and correlate such comparable cost data as are available for use in estimating the cost new of the subject property.

2) The appraiser should collect, verify, analyze and correlate such comparable data as are available to support and explain the difference between cost new present worth of the improvements (accrued depreciation), reflecting items of deterioration and obsolescence. No pertinent information shall be withheld. The appraiser should qualify the data sources and cost methodology used in his cost estimate.

5. Correlation and final value estimate:

a. In the final value estimate, the appraiser should consider the purpose which the appraisal serves, the type of property being appraised and the relative weights which typical users or investors would accord to the quality and quantity of data available and analyzed within the approaches used.

6. Special and limiting conditions:

a. It should be the duty of the appraiser to support the validity and feasibility of any special and limiting conditions or assumptions under which his appraisal is made. Unquestioning acceptance of an opinion motivated by advocacy, such as an attorney's, does not relieve the appraiser of his responsibility to provide valid support for such conditions and assumptions.

7. Appraiser's certification:

a. The appraiser should certify that he has personally inspected the subject property; that to the best of his knowledge and belief the statements and opinions contained in the resulting report are correct; that no pertinent information has knowingly been withheld; that he has no present or contemplated future interest in the

   property appraised; and that the amount of his fee is
   not contingent upon reporting a predetermined value or
   upon the amount of the value estimate. Any exceptions
   should be clearly stated.

  b. While the appraiser is ultimately responsible for any
   report to which he has affixed his signature, he should
   acknowledge those phases of the appraisal process performed by others under his supervision, and when appropriate they should become signatories to the report.

B. It is unethical for an appraiser to estimate fractional parts of a
property so that the reported value exceeds the value that would
be derived if the property were considered separately as a whole.

C. It is unethical for an appraiser to base his value conclusion upon
the assumed completion of public or private improvements unless
he clearly defines the conditions, extent and effects of such assumption. Any such assumption must be predicated upon sound
valuation principles.

II. Reporting Practices

A. An adequate written appraisal containing a supported value shall
be prepared for each appraisal assignment accepted, and shall
include the following as minimum requirements:

  1. An adequate and definite description of the property being
   appraised.
  2. The purpose of the appraisal and a definition of the value
   estimated.
  3. The effective date of the appraisal.
  4. The data and reasoning supporting the value conclusion
   which may include the comparable sales approach, the income approach and the cost approach. The exclusions of
   any of the usual three approaches must be explained and
   supported.
  5. The final estimate of value.
  6. Special and limiting conditions, if any.
  7. The appraiser's certification and signature.

B. A true copy of each appraisal shall be prepared and retained by the appraiser, and shall be sent on request to
a duly constituted Professional Practice Committee of the
local chapter or of the international Society of Real Estate
Appraisers.

C. It is unethical to issue a separate appraisal report on only a
part of a whole property without stating that it is a fractional
appraisal and as such subject to use in a manner consistent with
such limitation.

D. It is unethical to issue a separate appraisal report when another
appraiser assigned to appraise the same property has had a
part in the formation of the opinion of value.

E. It is unethical for an appraiser to reveal in any way the substance of any appraisal without permission of the client except

under due process of law, or when required to do so in compliance with the rules and regulations of the Society of Real Estate Appraisers.

STANDARDS OF PROFESSIONAL CONDUCT

I. It is unethical for an appraiser to become an advocate of any opinion other than his unbiased and objective value conclusion.

II. It is unethical for an appraiser to conduct himself in any manner which will prejudice his professional status or the reputation of any appraisal organization or any other appraiser.

III. It is unethical to accept an assignment to appraise a property of a type with which he has had no previous experience unless, in making the appraisal, he associates with an appraiser who has had experience with the type of property under appraisement, or makes full disclosure of the degree of his experience, background, and training to the client.

IV. It is unethical for an appraiser to:

A. Contract for or accept compensation for appraisal services in the form of a commission, rebate, division of brokerage commissions, or any similar forms;

B. Receive or pay finder's or referral fees;

C. Compete for any appraisal engagement on the basis of bids when the amount of the fee is the basis for awarding the assignment, but this is not to be construed as precluding the submission of a proposal for services;

D. Accept an assignment to appraise a property for which his employment or fee is contingent upon his reporting a predetermined conclusion;

E. Make his compensation on any basis other than a fair professional fee for the responsibility entailed and the work and expense involved.

V. It is unethical for an appraiser to attempt to supplant another appraiser after definite steps have been taken toward the employment of such other appraiser.

VI. It is unethical for an appraiser to advertise or solicit appraisal business in any manner not consonant with accepted professional practice. (See Interpretation: Standards of Professional Advertising Practices.)

VII. It is unethical for an appraiser to claim professional qualifications which may be subject to erroneous interpretation or to state professional qualifications which he does not possess. Specifically, Associates of the Society of Real Estate Appraisers do not have the Society's professional endorsement and cannot refer to their membership in any way which might imply professional endorsement by the Society.

VIII. It is unethical to fail to report to the Society the actions of any member who, in the opinion of the reporting member, has violated this Standards of Professional Practice and Conduct.

"Standards of Professional
Advertising Practices"
(Adopted July 25, 1968 By the Board of Governors;
Amended October 24, 1970; Effective January 1, 1971)

Interpretation of Rule VI of the Standards of Professional Conduct:
It is Unethical For an Appraiser to Advertise or Solicit
Appraisal Business in Any Manner Not Consonant
With Accepted Professional Practice

DIRECT SOLICITATION

Direct solicitation is not condoned in any profession, nor is it in the Society.   Direct solicitation by a member for appraisal assignments is unethical and shall be considered a violation of Rule VI of the Standards of Professional Conduct.

ADVERTISING

By conducting himself and his professional practice at all times at the highest standards, a member will earn a reputation of trust and ability with his colleagues and the public.   No other form of advertising can be more effective.

The appraisal profession is young and the general public is not fully aware of the importance of the role of the professional appraiser.   The Society has instituted an international and chapter public relations program to correct this and thereby inform the public.   However, until this public awareness and recognition comes into being, the Society realizes that in many instances it is essential for its members to advertise their professional attainment and services within certain limitations.   The Society has therefore established the following provisions as the standards of professional advertising practices for all classifications of membership:

A.   Associate Members

It is unethical for an Associate Member--Applicant Senior Realty Appraiser to refer to his membership in the Society of Real Estate Appraisers in advertisements or in any manner which might imply professional endorsment by the Society.

This shall not be construed to relieve Associate Members of the obligations and responsibilities placed on all members elsewhere in this interpretation.

B.   Designated Members

It is ethical for a designated member to advertise his professional attainment or services, and refer to his designation and membership in the Society of Real Estate Appraisers in accordance with the following only:

   1.   Amount of Advertising
        The amount of advertising utilized within these provisions

should be governed by the member's need for recognition for the purpose of building his professional practice. The amount of advertising utilized should diminish as the member's professional practice becomes established.

The member who is just establishing an appraisal practice and is relatively unknown to the users of appraisals perhaps would have the need to make use of several of the allowable advertising provisions. On the other hand, the member who has earned a trusted reputation and has an established clientele should have little, if any, reason to advertise other than perhaps a listing in a telephone directory.

2. Designations

The member's designation or reference to membership in the Society of Real Estate Appraisers shall be used only following or immediately in connection with the member's name, so that there will be no misinterpretation that the membership refers to a corporate entity or partnership, or anyone other than the individual member.

a. SRA Members

A member holding the SRA designation may advertise within these provisions, and may refer to his membership in the Society of Real Estate Appraisers only if he indicates his designation "SRA," or "Senior Residential Appraiser," or "Senior Realty Appraiser."

b. SREA Members

A member holding the SREA designation may advertise within these provisions and indicate his designation "SREA," or "Senior Real Estate Analyst," or refer to his membership in the Society of Real Estate Appraisers as "Member, Society of Real Estate Appraisers."

3. Listing in a Directory Under "Real Estate Appraiser"

A listing may be placed in a directory under the heading "Real Estate Appraiser" in accordance with the following only:

a. Content

The listing may contain member's name, designation, and reference to membership in the Society of Real Estate Appraisers; company name; address; telephone number; and area of appraisal specialization, i. e., residential, commercial, etc.

This listing shall not contain promotional, qualifying, or self-laudatory words or phrases, photographs; design material; or the Society's emblem.

b. Size of Type and Listing

The maximum size of type utilized shall be 10 point. The maximum size of listing shall be two columns in width and three inches in depth. In any event, the size shall be no larger than that which is typical of the media in which the listing is being placed.

c. Media
    The media utilized shall be:
    1) A directory--a book which lists names and addresses
    of a specific group of persons, such as a telephone di-
    rectory.
    2) A directory within a publication--such publication
    shall concern a related field and/or shall service the
    users of appraisals, such as real estate trade maga-
    zines, law journals, etc.
    The listing shall not be placed in public media such
    as in magazines, newspapers or publications of gen-
    eral circulation.

A typical listing considered appropriate under these provisions:

REAL ESTATE APPRAISERS		
DOE, JOHN, SRA		
Commercial and Industrial		
12345 Main Street 444-4444		

or

DOE APPRAISAL COMPANY	
Commercial and Industrial	
12345 Main Street 444-4444	
John Doe, SRA	William Doe, SREA

Note: To eliminate the need for members to carry individual, more costly listings, chapters are encouraged to
use Yellow Page Directory listing prepared by the Public
Relations Department followed by a listing of designated
members with addresses, telephone numbers, etc.

4. Announcement of Change of Address, Opening of New Office,
    or Change of Business Affiliation
    An announcement of a member's change of address, opening
    of new office, or change of business affiliation may be pre-
    pared and sent out in accordance with the following only:
    a. Contents
        The announcement may contain member's name, desig-
        nation, and reference to membership in the Society of
        Real Estate Appraisers, company name, address, tele-
        phone number, area of appraisal specialization, i.e.,
        residential, commercial, etc., the Society's emblem,
        and a brief statement of the fact for the announcement.
            The announcement shall not contain promotional,
        qualifying, or self-laudatory words or phrases, photo-
        graphs, or design material.
    b. Mailing and Distribution
        The announcement shall be sent only to member's own
        clients or personal affiliates by individually addressed
        cards or correspondence. The announcement shall not
        be sent out in a mass mailing or be given mass dis-
        tribution. A typical announcement considered appro-
        priate under these provisions is shown on page 75.

5. Brochures and Circulars
   A brochure or circular may be published in accordance
   with the following only:
   a. Content
      The brochure or circular may contain reference to a
      member's designation and membership in the Society of
      Real Estate Appraisers, and a personal qualification
      statement. It shall contain honest and accurate in-
      formation, and shall be dignified and conservative in
      keeping with high professional standards.

JOHN DOE, SRA

REAL ESTATE APPRAISER

ANNOUNCES THE OPENING

OF OFFICES

AT

12345 Main Street
Chicago, Illinois
444-4444

The brochure or circular shall not contain exaggerated
promotional statements, or the Society's emblem.
   b. Mailing and Distribution
      The brochure or circular shall only be sent in response
      to inquiries from prospective clients, and/or to in-
      dividuals with whom prior contact has been made.
         The brochure or circular shall not be sent to parties
      with whom no prior contact has been made, or be ad-
      dressed to a company, firm, institution, or "occupant."
   Note: The Society's Public Relations Department encourages
   chapters to distribute the brochure "What Is An Appraisal?"
   with chapter identification imprinted on it.

6. Signs
   A sign may appear at a member's place of business in
   accordance with the following only:
   a. Content
      The sign may contain member's name, designation and
      membership in the Society of Real Estate Appraisers;
      company name; address; telephone number; and area of
      specialization, i.e. residential, commercial, etc.
         The sign shall not contain promotional, qualifying
      or self-laudatory words or phrases; photographs; design
      material; or the Society's emblem.
   b. Size
      The size shall be in keeping with high professional
      standards, shall not be ostentatious, and shall not ex-
      ceed 6" x 18".

C. It is unethical

for a designated member to advertise his professional attainment
or services, and refer to his designation and membership in the
Society in any manner not provided under Paragraph B of this interpretation, and a few of these specifically are as follows:

1. General Advertisements or Public Notices
   General advertisements or public notices shall not be placed
   in publications, except as provided for under a directory
   listing.
   Note: The Society's Public Relations Department has a
   series of general advertisements (public notices) available
   for use by the chapters in their local news media. The
   theme of these ads is to tell the public what an appraisal
   is, what an appraiser does, how to select a qualified appraiser, and where a list of qualified appraisers may be
   obtained.
2. Radio and Television Media
   Advertisements shall not be carried on radio or television.
3. Billboards
   Advertisements shall not be carried on billboards or signs,
   except a sign as provided for at a member's place of
   business.
4. Miscellaneous Imprinted Items--Calendars, Appointment
      Books, Etc.
   Novelty items such as calendars, appointment books, etc.
   shall not be imprinted and distributed.
5. Free or Discounted Appraisals
   Professional services are rendered on a fee basis only.
   Free or discounted appraisals shall not be provided nor
   advertised.

ARBITRATORS

AMERICAN ARBITRATION ASSOCIATION (AAA)
      140 W. 51st St., New York, N.Y. 10020
      Robert Coulson, President

Membership: The American Arbitration Association, founded in
1926, is a non-profit organization that "encourages arbitration as
a method of dispute settlement under the law, and administers
arbitration proceedings. The AAA does not act as an arbitrator
itself," but does "provide impartial administration" and maintains
"a panel of Arbitrators competent to make a determination of the
particular controversy involved."

Any individual, association or corporation interested in the settlement of disputes by arbitration may be a member of the AAA, and among its members are experts in Labor Arbitration, Commercial Arbitration, Legal Arbitration, International Arbitration, and such newer areas of resolving disagreements as family arbitration, consumer arbitration, and campus arbitration. The arbitrators, who perform a quasi-judicial function of resolving differences in a final, non-appealable decision, may be lawyers or laymen.

Code of Ethics: In the field of labor disputes a conduct guide for arbitrators is issued by the American Arbitration Association, and the National Academy of Arbitrators (NAA), and approved by the Federal Mediation and Conciliation Service of the United States. This guide, Code of Ethics and Procedural Standards for Labor-Management Arbitration, was drafted by representatives of these three organizations, first issued in 1951, and most recently republished in 1962. The Code discusses the character of the office of arbitrator, the arbitrator's qualifications, essential conduct, duties and oath of office, and the privacy of arbitration. No procedures for enforcement of the Code are reported.

Other Standards of Professional Conduct: Another guide to conduct for the arbitrator, the "Oath of Office," is required in some states and optional in others with the parties of the dispute. In either event, arbitrators must observe standards that the formal swearing requires, and the form of the oath--approved by arbitrators as "encouraging an attitude of truth-seeking and adding to the dignity of the office of the arbitrator"--is:
> "Do you solemnly swear that you will faithfully and fairly
> hear and examine the matters in controversy and that you
> will make a just award to the best of your understanding."

Professional Insignia: The Association's official insignia (which the By-Laws provide must contain the initials, "AAA"--Article I, Section 2), is a round design with the required monogram of the organization in a stylized form, below a balance scale--signifying the impartiality of the arbitration process. The color of the emblem is gray on white (letterhead).

Bibliography:
American Arbitration Association. By-Laws. 1962. 8 pages. Processed.
    Mentions insignia; gives membership requirements.
        . Code of Ethics and Procedural Standards for Labor-Management Arbitration. 1951, reprinted 1962. 11 pages. Pamphlet.

Three parts are: Code of Ethics for Arbitrators; Procedural
Standards for Arbitrators; Conduct and Behavior of Parties.
_____. A Manual for Commercial Arbitrators. 1970. 31
pages. Pamphlet.
Gives text of arbitrator's oath of office (p. 27).

"Code of Ethics for Arbitrators"

1. Character of the Office

The function of an arbitrator is to decide disputes. He
should, therefore, adhere to such general standards of adjudicatory
bodies as require a full, impartial and orderly consideration of
evidence and argument, in accordance with applicable arbitration
law and the rules or general understandings or practices of the
parties.
The parties in dispute, in referring a matter to arbitration,
have indicated their desire not to resort to litigation or to economic conflict. They have delegated to the arbitrator power to settle their differences. It follows that the assumption of the office of
arbitrator places upon the incumbent solemn duties and responsibilities. Every person who acts in this capacity should uphold the
traditional honor, dignity, integrity and prestige of the office.

2. The Tri-Partite Board

Where tri-partite boards serve in labor arbitrations, it is
the duty of the parties' nominees to make every reasonable effort
to promote fair and objective conduct of the proceedings, to aid the
arbitration board in its deliberations and to bring about a just and
harmonious disposition of the controversy. It is recognized, however, that the parties frequently expect their appointees to serve
also as representatives of their respective points of view. In such
cases, the rules of ethics in this Code, insofar as they relate to
the obligations of strict impartiality, are to be taken as applying
only to the third or neutral arbitrator.
Such representatives, however, unless the parties agree
otherwise, should refrain from conveying to the parties who appointed them, the discussions which take place in executive session
and any information concerning the deliberations of the board. No
information concerning the decision should be given in advance of
its delivery simultaneously to both parties.

3. Qualification for Office

Any person whom the parties or the appointing agency choose
to regard as qualified to determine their dispute is entitled to act
as their arbitrator. It is, however, incumbent upon the arbitrator
at the time of his selection to disclose to the parties any circumstances, associations or relationships that might reasonably raise
any doubt as to his impartiality or his technical qualification for
the particular case.

4. Essential Conduct

a) The arbitrator should be conscientious, considerate and patient in the discharge of his functions. There should be no doubt as to his complete impartiality. He should be fearless of public clamor and indifferent to private, political or partisan influences.

b) The arbitrator should not undertake or incur obligations to either party which may interfere with his impartial determination of the issue submitted to him.

5. Duty to the Parties

The arbitrator's duty is to determine the matters in dispute, which may involve differences over the interpretation of existing provisions or terms and conditions of a new contract. In either event, the arbitrator shall be governed by the wishes of the parties, which may be expressed in their agreement, arbitration submission or in any other form of understanding. He should not undertake to induce a settlement of the dispute against the wishes of either party. If, however, an atmosphere is created or the issues are so simplified or reduced as to lead to a voluntary settlement by the parties, a function of his office has been fulfilled.

6. Acceptance, Refusal or Withdrawal from Office

The arbitrator, being appointed by voluntary act of the parties, may accept or decline the appointment. When he accepts he should continue in office until the matter submitted to him is finally determined. When there are circumstances which, in his judgment, compel his withdrawal, the parties are entitled to prompt notice and explanation.

7. Oath of Office

When an oath of office is taken it should serve as the arbitrator's guide. When an oath is not required or is waived by the parties, the arbitrator should nevertheless observe the standards which the oath imposes.

8. Privacy of the Arbitration

a) An arbitrator should not, without the approval of the parties, disclose to third persons any evidence, argument or discussions pertaining to the arbitration.

b) There should be no disclosure of the terms of an award by any arbitrator until after it is delivered simultaneously to all of the parties and publication or public disclosure should be only with the parties' consent.

Discussions within an arbitration board should be held in confidence. Dissenting opinions may be filed, however, but they should be based on the arbitrators' views on the evidence and controlling principles, and not on the discussions which took place in the executive sessions of the board.

9. Advertising and Solicitation

     Advertising by an arbitrator and soliciting of cases is im-
proper and not in accordance with the dignity of the office. No
arbitrator should suggest to any party that future cases be referred
to him.

FEDERAL MEDIATION AND CONCILIATION SERVICE (FMCS)
    Washington, D. C. 20427
    J. Curtis Counts, Director

Membership: The United States Federal Mediation and Conciliation
Service is the agency of the government that assists labor and management in the resolution of collective bargaining controversies.
The FMCS acted with the Association of Labor Mediation Agencies
in drafting a conduct guide for arbitrators. The Association is
composed of mediation agencies in 29 states of the United States
and of 8 Canadian and United States Cities, Canadian Provinces,
and Puerto Rico.

Code of Ethics: Representatives of the Federal Mediation and Conciliation Service and of the Association of Labor Mediation Agencies
(ALMA) undertook the writing of "a set of canons embodying the
moral and professional duties and responsibilities of mediators," in
November 1963. The Liaison Committee representing the two organizations drafted the Code of Professional Conduct for Labor
Mediators, which was jointly adopted by the FMCS and the ALMA
in September 1964.

    The Code, which was directed to the establishment of "principles
applicable to all professional mediators employed by city, state or
federal agencies and to mediators privately retained by parties" in

labor controversies, has provided a guide to conduct in
collective bargaining mediation
for labor and management, and
for collective bargaining.
Problems developing under the
Code are considered by the
Liaison Committee of the FMCS
and the ALMA at their periodic
meetings. No procedures for
enforcement of the Code are
reported.

Professional Insignia: The
official emblem of the Federal
Mediation and Conciliation Service is its seal--a circular

design, with a centered American eagle, wings outstretched and
looking left, perched on two clasped hands; the name of the agency,
"Federal Mediation and Conciliation Service," forms an unbanded
border around the design; "U.S.A." is shown at the bottom of the
border, separated from the agency name on each side, by a star.
This insignia appears in black on white, white on black; and--in an
alternate form, with eagle of different design, and legend in a
banded border.

Bibliography:
U.S. Federal Mediation and Conciliation Service. Code of
Professional Conduct for Labor Mediators. Adopted jointly
by the Federal Mediation and Conciliation Service ... and
the several state agencies represented by the Association
of Labor Mediation Agencies. 8 pages. Washington,
D.C., Government Printing Office, October 1971.
Gives the responsibility of the mediator toward the parties
involved in controversy, other mediators, his agency and
profession, the public, and the mediation process.

"Code of Professional Conduct
for Labor Mediators"

Preamble

The practice of mediation is a profession with ethical responsibilities and duties. Those who engage in the practice of mediation
must be dedicated to the principles of free and responsible collective bargaining. They must be aware that their duties and obligations relate to the parties who engage in collective bargaining, to
every other mediator, to the agencies which administer the practice
of mediation, and to the general public.
Recognition is given to the varying statutory duties and responsibilities of the city, State and Federal agencies. This code,
however, is not intended in any way to define or adjust any of
these duties and responsibilities nor is it intended to define when
and in what situations mediators from more than one agency should
participate. It is, rather, a personal code relating to the conduct
of the individual mediator.
This code is intended to establish principles applicable to all
professional mediators employed by city, state or federal agencies
and to mediators privately retained by parties.

1 The Responsibility of the Mediator toward the Parties

The primary responsibility for the resolution of a labor dispute rests upon the parties themselves. The mediator at all times
should recognize that the agreements reached in collective bargaining
are voluntarily made by the parties. It is the mediator's responsibility to assist the parties in reaching a settlement.
It is desirable that agreement be reached by collective

bargaining without mediation assistance. However, public policy and
applicable statutes recognize that mediation is the appropriate form
of governmental participation in cases where it is required. Whether
and when a mediator should intercede will normally be influenced by
the desires of the parties.   Intercession by a mediator on his own
motion should be limited to exceptional cases.

The mediator must not consider himself limited to keeping
peace at the bargaining table.   His role should be one of being a
resource upon which the parties may draw and, when appropriate,
he should be prepared to provide both procedural and substantive
suggestions and alternatives which will assist the parties in successful negotiations.

Since mediation is essentially a voluntary process, the acceptability of the mediator by the parties as a person of integrity,
objectivity and fairness is absolutely essential to the effective performance of the duties of the mediator.   The manner in which the
mediator carries out his professional duties and responsibilities will
measure his usefulness as a mediator.   The quality of his character
as well as his intellectual, emotional, social and technical attributes
will reveal themselves by the conduct of the mediator and his oral
and written communications with the parties, other mediators and
the public.

2   The Responsibility of the Mediator Toward Other Mediators

A mediator should not enter any dispute which is being medi-
ated by another mediator or mediators without first conferring with
the person or persons conducting such mediation.   The mediator
should not intercede in a dispute merely because another mediator
may also be participating.   Conversely, it should not be assumed
that the lack of mediation participation by one mediator indicates a
need for participation by another mediator.

In those situations where more than one mediator is participating in a particular case, each mediator has a responsibility to
keep the others informed of developments essential to a cooperative
effort and should extend every possible courtesy to his fellow mediator.

The mediator should carefully avoid any appearance of disagreement with or criticism of his fellow mediator.   Discussions
as to what positions and actions mediators should take in particular
cases should be carried on solely between or among the mediators.

3   The Responsibility of the Mediator Toward His Agency and
His Profession

Agencies responsible for providing mediation assistance to
parties engaged in collective bargaining are a part of government.
The mediator must recognize that, as such, he is part of government.   The mediator should constantly bear in mind that he and
his work are not judged solely on an individual basis but that he is

also judged as a representative of his agency. Any improper conduct
or professional shortcoming, therefore, reflects not only on the individual mediator but upon his employer and, as such, jeopardizes
the effectiveness of his agency, other government agencies and the
acceptability of the mediation process.

The mediator should not use his position for private gain
or advantage, nor should he engage in any employment, activity,
or enterprise which will conflict with his work as a mediator, nor
should he accept any money or thing of value for the performance
of his duties--other than his regular salary--or incur obligations
to any party which might interfere with the impartial performance
of his duties.

4   The Responsibility of the Mediator Toward the Public

Collective bargaining is in essence a private, voluntary process.   The primary purpose of mediation is to assist the parties
to achieve a settlement.   Such assistance does not abrogate the
rights of the parties to resort to economic and legal sanctions.
However, the mediation process may include a responsibility to
assert the interest of the public that a particular dispute be settled;
that a work stoppage be ended; and that normal operations be re-
sumed.   It should be understood, however, that the mediator does
not regulate or control any of the content of a collective bargaining
agreement.

It is conceivable that a mediator might find it necessary to
withdraw from a negotiation, if it is patently clear that the parties
intend to use his presence as implied governmental sanction for an
agreement obviously contrary to public policy.

It is recognized that labor disputes are settled at the bargaining table; however, the mediator may release appropriate information with due regard (1) to the desires of the parties, (2) to
whether that information will assist or impede the settlement of
the dispute and (3) to the needs of an informed public.

Publicity shall not be used by a mediator to enhance his own
position or that of his agency.   Where two or more mediators are
mediating a dispute, public information should be handled through a
mutually agreeable procedure.

5   The Responsibility of the Mediator Toward the Mediation Process

Collective bargaining is an established institution in our economic way of life.   The practice of mediation requires the development of alternatives which the parties will voluntarily accept as a
basis for settling their problems.   Improper pressures which
jeopardize voluntary action by the parties should not be a part of
mediation.

Since the status, experience, and ability of the mediator
lend weight to his suggestions and recommendations, he should
evaluate carefully the effect of his suggestions and recommendations

and accept full responsibility for their honesty and merit.

The mediator has a continuing responsibility to study industrial relations to improve his skills and upgrade his abilities.

Suggestions by individual mediators or agencies to parties, which give the implication that transfer of a case from one mediation "forum" to another will produce better results, are unprofessional and are to be condemned.

Confidential information acquired by the mediator should not be disclosed to others for any purpose or in a legal proceeding or be used directly or indirectly for the personal benefit or profit of the mediator.

Bargaining positions, proposals, or suggestions given to the mediator in confidence during the course of bargaining for his sole information should not be disclosed to the other party without first securing permission from the party or person who gave it to him.

ARCHAEOLOGISTS

SOCIETY FOR AMERICAN ARCHAEOLOGY (SAA)
    Dept. of Anthropology, University of Texas at Austin
    4242 Piedras Drive East, Suite 250, San Antonio, Texas 72882
    Richard E. Adams, Secretary

Membership: The Society of American Archaeology, founded in 1935 and with a present (1973) membership of over 3000, is an association of professionals and interested amateurs in archaeology. The Society defines "Archaeology" as that

> "branch of the science of anthropology ... that area of scholarship concerned with the reconstruction of past human life and culture."

Membership in the SAA is open to anyone with an interest in archaeology who is willing to sign the application form subscribing to the ideals and objects of the Society, which include standards for collection of archaeological materials (Constitution, Article 2, Section 2):

> "The practice of collecting, hoarding, exchanging, buying, or selling archaeological materials with the sole purpose of personal satisfaction or financial gain, and the indiscriminate excavation of archaeological sites are declared contrary to the ideals and objects of the society."

Code of Ethics: Although the SAA has never adopted a formal code of ethics, its Constitution (section cited above), various Statements and Resolutions of the organization are directed to "the primary ethical question for archaeologists ... the problem of appropriate use and conservation of archaeological resources." "Ethics for

Archaeology, " part of "Four Statements for Archaeology, " in the
Report of the Committee on Ethics and Standards of SAA in 1961,
concerns such aspects of archaeologists' professional conduct as
obligation to make collections of archaeological materials available,
and relevant supporting data; reporting findings in recognized scientific media, or in manuscript; refraining from buying or selling arti-
facts; professional courtesy in site study; prohibition of "willfull
destruction, distortion, or concealment of the data of archaeology. "
Disregard of these ethical standards "provides grounds for expulsion from the Society. "

Other Guide to Professional Conduct: A series of four Resolutions
passed by the SAA membership at the annual meeting in 1971 were
directed against the illegal traffic in antiquities, including Museum
acquisition, or Society members' "acquiring, authenticating or
evaluating objects of artistic or scientific significance in contravention of the terms of the UNESCO Convention, " on the Means of
Prohibiting and Preventing the Illicit Import, Export and Transfer
of Ownership of Cultural Property.

Professional Insignia: None adopted.

Bibliography:
    Society for American Archaeology.   "Ethics for Archaeology, "
        in Committee on Ethics and Standards.   "Four Statements
        for Archaeology. "   American Antiquity 27:137-138 October
        1961.
    The archaeologist's professional obligations in the collection
    and disposition of artifacts and data, publication and site
    excavation, published in the SAA quarterly journal.
        _____.   Resolutions Passed by the Membership of the Society.
        Annual Meeting, 1971.   Resolutions 1 through 4:   "Dis-
        couraging Illegal Traffic In Antiquities. "   4 pages.   Pro-
        cessed.   In American Antiquity 36:509-510 April 1971.
    Role of the SAA and its members in discouraging the illicit
    import, export, and transfer of ownership of cultural proper-
    ty, including cooperation with the American Museum Associa-
    tion and UNESCO on this problem.

"Ethics for Archaeology"

        Collections made by competent archaeologists must be avail-
able for examination by qualified scholars; relevant supporting data
must also be accessible for study whether the collection is in a
museum or other institution or in private hands.
        It is the scholarly obligation of the archaeologist to report his
findings in a recognized scientific medium.   In the event that significance of the collection does not warrant publication, a manuscript
report should be prepared and be available.
        Inasmuch as the buying and selling of artifacts usually results
in the loss of context and cultural associations, the practice is censured.

An archaeological site presents problems which must be handled by the excavator according to a plan. Therefore, members of the Society for American Archaeology do not undertake excavations on any site being studied by someone without the prior knowledge and consent of that person.

Willful destruction, distortion, or concealment of the data of archaeology is censured, and provides grounds for explusion from the Society for American Archaeology, at the discretion of the Executive Committee.

"Resolutions Discouraging Illegal Traffic in Antiquities, 1971"

Resolution 1.

Be it resolved:

That in order to discourage illegal traffic in antiquities the SAA will initiate action with the American Museum Association committee on accreditation to consider the mechanics of withholding or withdrawing accreditation from those museums that purchase, certify or authenticate unethically acquired objects of scientific or artistic significance.

Resolution 2.

Be it resolved:

That all archaeologists must be concerned over the destructive illegal traffic in antiquities which is damaging objects of scientific and artistic significance and undermining international professional relationships.

That UNESCO through its formal resolution (Convention) on the Means of Prohibiting and Preventing the Illicit Import, Export and Transfer of Ownership of Cultural Property has made an important first step in attempting to bring an end to this illegal traffic in antiquities. The essence of this resolution (Convention) is that the country of origin accepts the burden of obligation to preserve and protect its own cultural heritage through the establishment of appropriate national services and the maintenance of export controls. While the importing countries would support these measures through certain important areas of cooperation. These measures include:

1. The obligation of each country to prohibit the import of cultural property stolen from a museum, public monument or similar institution in another country and upon request, to recover and return such stolen property.

2. Any country whose cultural heritage is put in jeopardy by pillage of archaeological or ethnological materials may call upon other affected countries to participate in a concerted international effort to determine and to carry out the necessary concrete measures including the control of exports and imports and international commerce in the specific materials concerned. Participant countries would take measures to prevent injury to the cultural heritage of the requesting country.

3. The countries agree to provide for legal actions for the
recovery of cultural property by or on behalf of the rightful owner.
4. The countries would take the necessary measures to prevent institutions from acquiring cultural property illegally exported
from another country.
That the Society for American Archaeology supports the
UNESCO Convention and urges prompt action on the Convention by
all governments at the earliest practical moment.

Resolution 3.

Be it resolved:
That the membership here presents requests that the Executive Committee of the Society for American Archaeology continue
to explore all possible routes of action, including legal action,
against offending parties including museums, archaeologists or any
traffickers in illegal goods as defined by the UNESCO Convention.

Resolution 4.

Be it resolved:
That the Society for American Archaeology calls upon its
members and all archaeologists to refrain from acquiring, authenticating or evaluating objects of artistic or scientific significance
in contravention to the terms of the UNESCO Convention.

ARCHITECTS

AMERICAN INSTITUTE OF ARCHITECTS (AIA)
    1785 Massachusetts Ave., N.W., Washington, D.C. 20036
    William L. Slaton, Executive Vice President

Membership: The American Institute of Architects, incorporated
in 1857, is one of the oldest professional associations in the United
States. Currently (1973) there are over 23,000 members, who
have qualified for membership by licensure in the state of practice--
which, in turn, requires graduation from an approved School of
Architecture, and completion of a specified number of years of
supervised architectural experience.

The Institute authorizes use of two professional designations
as an indication of competence, with member's practice and works,
and an initial suffix to a member's name (Bylaws, Chapter II,
Article 1, Section 10A):
        "Member of the American Institute of Architects"--"A.I.A."--
        authorized for a member's use upon admission to member-
        ship in the Institute.

"Fellow, the American Institute of Architects"--"F.A.I.A."--
authorized for use by a Fellow of the Institute, required
to have at least 10 years as a member of the Institute,
and notable contribution "to the advancement of the profession of architecture in the design, or in the science of
construction, or by literature or educational service, or
by service to the profession, or by public service."

Code of Ethics: The current guide to professional conduct of the
AIA is its Standards of Ethical Practice, most recently revised
January 3, 1972. This code of ethics, developed through the years,
was first devised by the Judiciary Committee and adopted in 1909
as A Circular to Advise Relative to Principles of Professional
Practice. After several revisions, this document was replaced in
1927 by the Principles of Professional Practice, which--after 20
years of use--was superseded by the Standards of Ethical Practice.
The Standards now observed set forth in twelve general principles
the architect's obligation to the public, to the client or employer,
and to the profession and the building industry.

Enforcement of the guide to professional conduct, follows
specified procedures (Bylaws, Chapter XIV, "Architectural Practice"),
with regard to definition and charges of unprofessional conduct,
hearing and review of charges, and disciplinary action in the form
of penalties for violations of the Standards.

Other Guides to Professional Conduct: The AIA has also issued a
Code for Architectural Competitions, as a guide to the architect
serving in a design competition as professional advisor or juror.

Professional Insignia: The emblem of the Institute is its official
seal, adopted in 1912 (revised in 1913), from the design of N. Van
Buren Magonigle. In an oval, an eagle--symbolic of the United

States--perches on a branching tree, before a Greek Doric column--
signifying Architecture--against a horizontally barred background;
two bands set off this oval, which is framed in an unbordered band
made by the name of the organization, "Seal of the American Institute of Architects," with the date of founding in Roman numerals,
"MDCCCLVII," at the bottom of the band. An alternate design
shows the central oval in white and black, with no bands or bordering legend. The insignia may be shown in any size and color, with
or without the full name of the Institute.

The official seal "is reserved exclusively for the official Institute and component use," but an emblem, showing the eagle before
the Doric column may be used by members on business cards and
letterheads, provided all members of a firm using the emblem are
members of the Institute.

Other Designations of Professional Status: As described above under
"Membership," two professional designations are authorized by the
Institute:
> "Member of the American Institute of Architects"--"A. I. A. ";
> "Fellow, the American Institute of Architects"--"F. A. I. A. "

Bibliography:
> American Institute of Architects. The AIA. 1970. 15 pages.
> Informational brochure describing work of the architect,
> Standards of Professional Practice, professional designations.
> _____. Bylaws, 1970-1971. 36 pages.
> Includes qualifications for membership, and procedures for
> enforcement of the code of Ethics (Chapter XIV, "Architec-
> tural Practice").
> _____. Code for Architectural Competitions. 1963, with
> amendments through December 1969. 12 pages.
> Standards to be followed by an architect acting as professional
> advisor or juror in a design competition.
> _____. Description of Memberships. September 1970. 7
> pages.
> Membership qualifications for the AIA, its chapters, and
> state organizations.
> _____. Proceedings. 46th Annual Convention, December 10-
> 12, 1912.
> Description and history of the development of the official
> AIA seal.
> _____. The Standards of Ethical Practice. Revised Decem-
> ber 8, 1972.
> Enumerates broad obligations of the architect, cites Bylaws
> providing implementation of these Standards.
> Saylor, Henry H. The AIA's First Hundred Years. Washington,
> D. C. The Institute, 1957. (Also issued as Part 2 of AIA
> Journal, May 1957). 184 pages.
> Discusses "Competitions and Ethics" (Chapter 9, pages 98-
> 108).

"The Standards of Ethical Practice"
(AIA Document J330; Revised December 8, 1972)

Introduction

These Standards are statements of ethical principles having broad applicability to professional persons. Accordingly, the enumeration of particular duties and the proscription of certain conduct does not negate the existence of other obligations logically flowing from such principles. Conduct proscribed as unethical must be construed to include lesser offenses, such as attempts and aiding-and-abetting. Deviation from these Standards shall be subject to discipline in proportion to the seriousness of the violation.

The Board of Directors of The American Institute of Architects, or its delegated authority, shall have sole power of interpreting these Standards of Ethical Practice, and its decisions shall be final, subject to the provisions of the Bylaws.

The following provisions of the Bylaws of The Institute form the basis for all disciplinary actions taken under the Standards of Ethical Practice.

Implementation

Bylaws: Chapter 14, Article 1, Section 1(c):
Any deviation by a corporate or associate member from any of the Standards of Ethical Practice of The Institute or from any of the Rules of The Board supplemental thereto, or any action by him that is detrimental to the best interests of the profession and The Institute shall be deemed to be unprofessional conduct on his part, and ipso facto he shall be subject to discipline by The Institute.

Charges Privileged

Bylaws: Chapter 14, Article 5, Section 1:
Every formal charge of unprofessional conduct shall be privileged. Except as noted in this Article, all charges, proceedings, evidence, data, notices, transcripts and any other matters relating to the charges shall be confidential. The same qualifications shall apply to any material coming before a chapter governing body or committee in any matter, formal or informal, of alleged unprofessional conduct.

In unusual situations when the President of The Institute (or the Secretary in his absence) determines, after consideration of all the circumstances, that the best interests of the profession, or The Institute, or one of its component bodies so require, he may authorize the release of sufficient information concerning a case to meet the situation.

Preamble

Bylaws: Chapter 1, Article 1, Section 2:
The objects of The American Institute of Architects shall be

to organize and unite in fellowship the architects of the United States of America; to combine their efforts so as to promote the aesthetic, scientific, and practical efficiency of the profession; to advance the science and art of planning and building by advancing the standards of architectural education, training, and practice; to coordinate the building industry and the profession of architecture to insure the advancement of the living standards of our people through their improved environment; and to make the profession of ever-increasing service to society.

Obligations to the Public

1. An architect shall above all serve and promote the public interest in the effort to improve human environment, and he shall act in a manner to bring honor and dignity to the profession of architecture. He shall conform to the registration laws governing the practice of architecture in any jurisdiction in which he practices.
2. An architect shall practice in a manner that will support the human rights of all mankind and shall not discriminate against any employee or applicant because of sex, race, creed, or national origin.
3. An architect shall not use paid advertising; indulge in self-laudatory, exaggerated, misleading, or false publicity; or solicit, or permit others to solicit in his name, advertisements for any publication presenting his work.

Interpretation by The Board of Directors, December 1972:
The above prohibition against paid advertising does not prohibit architects or architectural firms from being included in lists which are compiled and distributed by a client group, and for which a nominal fee is charged to offset the cost of compilation and distribution; provided that such lists and the conditio⸱s of their preparation and use are specifically approved by The Board of Directors. Nor does this prohibition apply to architectural exhibitions sponsored, co-sponsored or specifically approved by The Institute, for which a nominal charge is made to offset wholly or partially the cost of processing and arranging such an exhibition and/or subsequent publication.

4. An architect shall not publicly endorse a product, system, or service, or permit the use of his name or photograph to imply such endorsement. However, he may be identified with any product, system, or service designed or developed by him.

Obligations to the Client or Employer

5. An architect shall preserve the confidences of his client or employer.
6. An architect shall represent truthfully and clearly to his prospective client or employer his qualifications and capabilities to perform services.

Statement in compliance with Consent Judgment entered June 19, 1972:

Under the Standards of Ethical Practice of The American Institute of Architects the submission of price quotations for architectural services is not unethical. An architect is free to state a fee in offering his services. In so doing, however, he must be careful not to violate any law, ordinance, rule, or regulation of any government or agency, official or instrumentality thereof. He must never subordinate the quality and adequacy of his services to any consideration which would tend to impugn the integrity of his professional practice or to jeopardize the professional standards which should at all times guide the practice of his profession.

7. An architect shall not undertake any activity or employment, have any significant financial or other interest, or accept any contribution, if it would reasonably appear that such activity, employment, interest or contribution could compromise his professional judgment or prevent him from serving the best interest of his client or employer.

Interpretation by The Board of Directors, June 1971:

This Standard provides that the architect must avoid any activity which would put, or which could reasonably be construed to put, his financial interest in competition with that of his client; activities during the construction phase are particularly sensitive to such conflicts.

He may not engage in building contracting where compensation, direct or indirect, is derived from profit on labor and materials furnished in the building process.

He may engage in construction management as a professional for professional compensation only.

As a participating owner of a project, he may perform in any role legally consistent with the position of ownership.

A real or apparent conflict of interest must be resolved in the best interest of the client.

The Institute holds that the Standards of Ethical Practice are compromised when a member is employed by individuals or organizations offering to the public architectural services which are in any manner inconsistent with these Standards.

8. An architect may make contributions of service or anything of value to those endeavors which he deems worthy, but not for the purpose of securing a commission or influencing his engagement or employment.

Obligations to the Profession and the Building Industry

9. An architect shall not attempt to obtain, offer to undertake or accept a commission for which he knows another legally qualified individual or firm has been selected or employed, until he has evidence that the latter's agreement has been terminated and he gives the latter written notice that he is so doing.

10. An architect shall recognize the contribution of others engaged in the design and construction of the physical environment and shall not knowingly make false statements about the professional work, or maliciously injure or attempt to injure the prospects, practice, or employment position of those so engaged.
11. An architect shall encourage education and research, and the development and dissemination of useful technical information relating to the design and construction of the physical environment.
12. An architect shall not offer his services in a design competition except as provided in the competition code of The American Institute of Architects.

ARCHIVISTS

NATIONAL ARCHIVES AND RECORDS SERVICE
General Services Administration, Washington, D. C. 20408
James B. Rhoads, Archivist of the United States

Membership: The purpose of archivists working in the National Archives is to preserve, organize, and make available to students, scholars, and the public, the permanently valuable Federal records of the United States Government. The National Archives and Records Service administers six presidential libraries, from Hoover through Johnson, and 15 Federal Records Centers in addition to the National Archives Building. The National Archives and Records Service is a unit of the General Services Administration.

Code of Ethics: A statement of the archivist's obligations and responsibilities, The Archivist's Code, was first developed in 1955 by Dr. Wayne C. Grover, Third Archivist of the United States (1948-1965), for use in an Inservice Training Program in the National Archives. Later that same year the Code was printed in the American Archivist (volume 18, pages 307-308, October 1955), the quarterly publication of the Society of American Archivists. The Code, in its present form, was issued in 1970 with minor revisions, which were approved by Dr. Grover, drafter of the ethical guide. This code gives general principles of the archivist's obligation to preserve and make available for use valuable documentary records--contemporary as well as those of past times-- which are in his custody.

Professional Insignia: The official emblem of the National Archives and Records Service is its seal--a circular design with an eagle, wings outstretched, facing left; a shield on its breast shows six horizontal stripes at the top and 12 vertical stripes in the lower

portion; the eagle holds an olive branch in its right claw and a sheaf of arrows in its left; the Service motto, "Littera Scripta Manet" ("The Written Letter Remains"), is printed in a scroll over the eagle's head; the organization name, "The National Archives of the United States," is given around the design within a double border banding the emblem; set off by stars, the date, "1934," the year that the National Archives was established, is given at the bottom of the legend. The seal is "in use to legalize documents and copies of Federal service records" in the National Archives and Records Service possession for public use.

Bibliography:
>   National Archives and Records Service. General Services Administration. The Archivist's Code. 1970. 1 page.
>   Professional obligations of the archivist.

"The Archivist's Code"

The Archivist has a moral obligation to society to take every possible measure to ensure the preservation of valuable records, not only those of the past but those of his own times, and with equal zeal.

The Archivist in appraising records for retention or disposal acts as the agent of future generations. The wisdom and impartiality he applies to this task measure his professionalism, for he must be as diligent in disposing of records that have no significant or lasting value as in retaining those that do.

The Archivist must protect the integrity of records in his custody. He must guard them against defacement, alteration, or theft; he must protect them against physical damage by fire or excessive exposure to light, dampness, and dryness; and he must ensure that their evidentiary value is not impaired in the normal course of rehabilitation, arrangement, and use.

The Archivist should endeavor to promote access to records to the fullest extent consistent with the public interest, but he should carefully observe any proper restrictions on the use of records. He should work unremittingly for the increase and diffusion of knowledge, making his documentary holdings freely known to prospective users through published finding aids and personal consultation.

The Archivist should respond courteously and with a spirit of helpfulness to reference requests. He should not place unnecessary obstacles in the way of researchers but should do whatever he can to save their time and ease their work. He should not idly discuss the work and findings of one researcher with another; but where duplication of research effort is apparent, he may properly inform another researcher.

The Archivist should not profit from any commercial exploitation of the records in his custody, nor should he withhold from others any information he has gained as a result of his official duties-- either in order to carry out private professional research or to aid one researcher at the expense of another. He should, however, take every legitimate advantage of his situation to develop his professional interests in historical and archival research.

The Archivist should freely pass on to his professional colleagues the results of his own or his organization's research that add to the body of archival and historical knowledge. He should leave to his successors a true account of the records in his custody and of their organization and arrangement.

SOCIETY OF AMERICAN ARCHIVISTS (SAA)
   160 Rackham Building, University of Michigan
   Ann Arbor, Michigan 48104
   Robert M. Warner, Secretary

Membership: The Society of American Archivists, founded in 1936 and with a present (1973) membership of nearly 2,500, is a professional society for archivists, and admits to membership any person interested in and concerned with "the documentation of human experience." Among professional workers who are members are a variety of individuals with "interests in the preservation of man's recorded heritage"--historians, librarians, educators, archival records managers, and administrators of public or private records collections.

Code of Ethics: The Society has not published a formal guide to professional conduct, but has plans to develop and issue a set of ethical guidelines.

Professional Insignia: The emblem of the Society of American Archivists is its official seal. The design is a round, serrated form, bearing in the center the word, "SEAL," set off by three small diamonds above and below the word; the date of incorporation of the Society, "November 1945," follows the lower half of a dotted circle which encloses the centered area; the organization name, "Society of American Archivists," is given around the bordering band, with the place of incorporation, "Dist of Columbia," at the bottom of the emblem; a corded line forms the outer edge

of this border; the design is enclosed in an outer band with a
serrated edge. The color of the seal is gold, with the lettering
and design embossed [not displayed].

Bibliography:
    Society of American Archivists. The American Archivist.
        Folder.
    Brochure describing SAA journal.

ARTISTS

ARTISTS EQUITY ASSOCIATION (AEA)
    2813 Albemarle St., N.W., Washington, D.C. 20008
    Molly S. Brylawski, Executive Secretary

Membership: Artists Equity Association, founded in 1947 and with
a present (1973) membership of about 1500, is an association of
professional fine artists. Members are grouped in local chapters
across the United States, with five regional areas--East Coast,
South, Midwest, Rocky Mountain, and West Coast. Membership is
open to any person "interested in the promotion of American art."
To be an active member, an applicant must qualify by education,
background, commitment, and present involvement, as a professional artist. No longer is it necessary to have participated in a
juried exhibition or a one-man show to qualify for membership and
membership is likewise not restricted to the traditional painting,
sculpture, and print-making. Those working in the new media,
as well as potters, etc., may
qualify. Eligibility of prospective members is decided by
the local chapters.

Code of Ethics: The professional conduct guide of the AEA
is its Code of Ethics, which
enumerates in 14 points the
rights and obligations of professional artists, including freedom of artistic expression; relationships with clients, employers, dealers, and fellow
artists; ethical conduct principles in entering competitions;
acting as art juror; teaching
and executing commissions.

Professional Insignia: The

emblem of the Artists Equity Association is its logotype--a stylized monogram, "AE." This emblem is shown in black and white on the letterhead.

Bibliography:
    Artists Equity Association. Why Equity--What It Is; How It
        Works; and Code of Ethics. Pamphlet.
    Informational brochure describing AEA--purposes, activities,
    membership requirements, text of Code of Ethics.

"Code of Ethics"
(Artists joining Artists Equity Association
subscribe to the following Code of Ethics.)

In order to establish and build professional and public respect and confidence and to secure to the artist and the society in which he lives the benefits of economic and cultural growth, we establish this code of rights and obligations:

(1) To insure high standards of conduct in the practice of the arts, and to contribute fully to the development of our American cultural heritage the creative artist must constantly strive to act so that his aims and integrity are beyond question.

(2) Freedom of expression is essential for the practice of the fine arts and is the only climate in which health and growth of creative activity is possible. The artist should not, in the practice of his profession, be affected by enmities, political or religious strife, or sectarian aesthetic dissension. He should boycott professional activity involving discrimination as to race, creed or ideology.

(3) The artist shall endeavor to extend public knowledge of, and respect for his profession through dedication to his work and discouragement of all untrue, unfair and distorted ideas of the role of the artist and the practice of his profession.

(4) The artist shall refrain from knowingly injuring or maliciously damaging the professional reputation or work of a fellow artist.

(5) He shall assume full responsibility for work completed under his direction, but freely give credit to his technical advisers and assistants.

(6) When acting as juror the artist shall constantly maintain the objectivity and seriousness required for this important service, taking into account local practices and instructions from those in charge, and giving each entry as careful consideration as he would expect for his own efforts.

(7) When employed as a teacher, the artist shall not make exaggerated claims as to his qualifications, nor permit the school or institution in question to do so in his name.

(8)   The artist shall vigorously oppose vandalism, censorship or destruction of any commissioned work of art, as well as its unauthorized commercial exploitation or defacement.

(9)   The professional artist shall utilize the protection of existing copyright laws.   He should claim all fees to which he is entitled for publication and reproduction rights.

(10)   The artist shall fully assume his responsibility toward his client and shall not misrepresent either the value or permanence of his work.

(11)   Before participating in charity fund-raising sales or auctions, the artist shall assure himself that works will be properly displayed, that established prices will be maintained and that he will receive whatever compensation is agreed upon.

(12)   The artist shall not enter competitions unless the terms are clearly stated, nor when fees are contrary to, or below standards currently established.   Except in the case of open competition, he shall demand compensation for all sketches and models submitted.

(13)   When executing commercial, theatrical or other design commissions, the artist shall familiarize himself with the codes and fair practices of allied trades to avoid misunderstandings in the execution of and remuneration for his work.

(14)   It is unethical for the artist to undertake a commission for which he knows another artist has been employed until he has notified such other artist and has determined that the original employment has been terminated.

JOINT ETHICS COMMITTEE (JEC)
    P. O. Box 179, Grand Central Station
    New York, N. Y. 10017; 2588 Broadway, New York, N. Y.
    Clare Caratti, Executive Director

Membership: The Joint Ethics Committee is composed of three members and one alternate member from each of the following organizations:
        The Art Directors Club,
        The Artists Guild, Inc. of New York,
        Society of Illustrators,
        American Society of Magazine Photographers,
        Society of Photographer and Artist Representatives.

    Established in 1945 by the first three of the above member organizations, the JEC was expanded in 1968 to the present five organizations, in order to include representation of the new communication industries.   The members in the groups subscribing to the Joint Ethics Committee are engaged in various aspects of creating, selling and buying and using graphic arts.   The word "Artist," as defined by the Joint Ethics Committee, is understood "to include creative people in the field of visual communication, such as graphics, photography, film, and television. "

Code of Ethics: Guide to conduct of the JEC is its Code of Fair Practices, adopted in 1945 and revised in 1968. This Code enumerates 22 points to be observed in the relations between artist and buyer, and artist and agent, including such details as form of orders for art work, authorized expense for artists, alterations in art work, date of completion and delivery of art work, art contests, and rebates.

The Joint Ethics Committee acts in interpretation of the Code, and in its enforcement, including the receiving of complaints, and mediating or arbitrating disputes arising under the Code standards. The Committee meets one or more times each month. In over twenty years of practice, it has been instrumental in resolving more than 1000 cases in dispute, following the ethical standards in the Code of Fair Practice, which has been cited as a legal precedent in instances of the Committee's arbitration activity.

Professional Insignia: A design used by the JEC on the back of its printed Code, is an unbordered picture of an easel, on which is a picture of balance scales; the date in Roman numerals, "MCMXLVIII, " is printed below the bars of the balance.

Bibliography:
Joint Ethics Committee. Alternatives to Litigation. Single sheet. Describes activities of the Committee in mediation and arbitration of disputes involving members of component organizations in the field of visual communications.
_____. Code of Fair Practice. Revised edition. 1968. Pamphlet. Explains the workings of the Joint Ethics Committee; gives text of the revised Code.

"Code of Fair Practice"*
(Formulated in 1948   Revised in 1968)

(1)   Dealings between an artist† or his agent and a client
should be conducted only through an authorized buyer.

(2)   Orders to an artist or agent should be in writing and
should include the price, delivery date, and a summarized description of the work.   In the case of publications, the acceptance
of a manuscript by the artist constitutes an order.

(3)   All changes or additions not due to the fault of the
artist or agent should be billed to the purchaser as an additional
and separate charge.

(4)   There should be no charges other than authorized expenses for revisions or retakes made necessary by errors on the
part of the artist or his agent.

(5)   Alterations should not be made without consulting the
artist.   Where alterations or retakes are necessary and time
permits and where the artist has maintained his usual standard
of quality, he should be given the opportunity of making such
changes.

(6)   The artist should notify the buyer of an anticipated delay in delivery.   Should the artist fail to keep his contract through
unreasonable delay in delivery, or non-conformance with agreed
specifications, it should be considered a breach of contract by the
artist and should release the buyer from responsibility.

(7)   Work stopped by a buyer after it has been started
should be delivered immediately and billed on the basis of the time
and effort expended and expenses incurred.

(8)   An artist should not be asked to work on speculation.
However, work originating with the artist may be marketed on its
merit.   Such work remains the property of the artist unless purchased and paid for.

(9)   Art contests except for educational or philanthropic purposes are not approved because of their speculative character.

(10)   There should be no secret rebates, discounts, gifts,
or bonuses requested by or given to buyers by the artist or his
agent.

(11)   If the purchase price of artwork is based specifically
upon limited use and later this material is used more extensively
than originally planned, the artist is to receive adequate additional

---

*Copyright 1954 by The Joint Ethics Committee (Sponsored by the
Society of Illustrators, Inc.; the Art Directors Club, Inc.; the
Artists Guild Inc. of New York; American Society of Magazine
Photographers, Inc.; and the Society of Photographer and Artist
Representatives, Inc.)

†The word artist should be understood to include creative people
in the field of visual communication such as graphics, photography,
film, and television.

remuneration.

(12) If comprehensives, preliminary work or additional photographs from an assignment are subsequently published as finished art the price should be increased to the satisfaction of artist and buyer.

(13) If preliminary drawings, comprehensives, or photographs are bought from an artist with the intention or possibility that another artist will be assigned to do the finished work, this should be made clear at the time of placing the order.

(14) The right of an artist to place his signature upon artwork is subject to agreement between artist and buyer.

(15) There should be no plagiarism of any creative artwork.

(16) If an artist is specifically requested to produce any artwork during unreasonable working hours, fair additional remuneration should be allowed.

(17) An artist entering into an agreement with an agent or studio for exclusive representation should not accept an order from, nor permit his work to be shown by any other agent or studio. Any agreement which is not intended to be exclusive should set for in writing the exact restrictions agreed upon between the two parties.

(18) All artwork or photography submitted as samples to a buyer by artists' agents or studio representatives should bear the name of the artist or artists responsible for the creation.

(19) No agent, studio, or production company should continue to show the work of an artist as samples after the termination of the association.

(20) After termination of an association between artist and agent, the agent should be entitled to a commission on accounts which he has secured, for a period of time not exceeding six months (unless otherwise specified by contract).

(21) Examples of an artist's work furnished to an agent or submitted to a prospective purchaser shall remain the property of the artist, should not be duplicated without his consent, and should be returned to him promptly in good condition.

(22) Interpretation of this code shall be in the hands of the Joint Ethics Committee and is subject to changes and additions at the discretion of the parent organizations.

ASSESSORS

INTERNATIONAL ASSOCIATION OF ASSESSING OFFICERS (IAAO)
1313 E. 60th St., Chicago, Ill. 60637
Paul V. Corusy, Executive Director)

Membership: The International Association of Assessing Officers, founded in 1934 and with a present (1973) membership of over 8000, is "an association of public officials engaged in the assessment of property for taxation, organized to improve standards and to develop better techniques in assessment administration." "Regular Members" of the Association are "employees of a governmental taxing authority or jurisdiction where their duties are related to property tax assessment and administration." The Association issues several professional designations to indicate the competency of its members:

> "Certified Assessment Evaluator"--"CAE";
> "Accredited Assessment Evaluator"--"AAE";
> "Certified Personalty Evaluator"--"CPE."

Code of Ethics: The IAAC guide to professional conduct for its members is the Association Code of Ethics--nine general principles of assessment work, dealing with the public and colleagues, confidentiality of assessment information are covered. The Ethics Committee of the Association receives written complaints of violations of the Code, and--upon investigation and hearing, as required--makes recommendations to the Executive Board of the IAAO for disciplinary action in those cases when complaints are substantiated.

Other Guides to Professional Conduct: The IAAO Standards of Professional Conduct includes the principles of conduct in the Code and groups these guides under five headings:

> Relations with Assessing Officers,
> Relations with Public Officials,
> Relations with Public and Taxpayers,
> Appraisal Standards to be Complied With,
> Relations with the International Association of Assessing
>   Officers.

Professional Insignia: The IAAO emblem is a circular design--a globe with latitude and longitude demarcations--symbolizing land as the basis of assessment--the organization initials, "IAAO," are printed in a horizontal, centered band. The color of this insignia varies--dark blue on white (letterhead); black on buff, or orange on buff (publications).

Other Designations of Professional Status: The professional designations authorized by the Association--as listed above under "Membership," include:

"Certified Assessment
Evaluator"--"CAE";
"Accredited Assessment
Evaluator"--"AAE";
"Certified Personalty
Evaluator"--"CPE."
In addition to the title and
initials, those members (holding the CAE and AAE designations) may display and wear
a visual emblem--a rectangular seal with a triangle in
solid color on a vertically
striped ground, with the letters of the designation ("CAE"
or "AAE," as the case may

be) in the triangle, and the name of the Association around the design in a bordering band.   As the "CPE" designation has just been
established an emblem has not yet been designed.

Bibliography:
        International Association of Assessing Officers.   Code of Ethics.
             11"x14" sheet.
        Conduct guide for IAAO members.
        _____.   International Association of Assessing Officers.
             Pamphlet.
        Brief description of IAAO functions, membership categories,
        and professional designation activity.
        _____.   Professional Designation Program.   Pamphlet.
        Procedures for awarding IAAO professional designations; in-
        cludes Code of Ethics.
        _____.   Professional Designation Program: CAE, CPE, AAE
             Requirements.   December 21, 1972.   Pamphlet.   8 pages.
        Detailed statement of requirements for professional designation.
        _____.   Standards of Professional Conduct.   11" x 14" sheet.
        Principles of assessor's conduct and work performance.

                             "Code of Ethics"

        The functions of the assessing officer and other members of
IAAO are professional in character.   This Code of Ethics is a set
of dynamic principles guiding the members' conduct.   Each member
of IAAO agrees that he will:

        1.   Cooperate fully with other members in all matters af-
fecting his official duties.
        2.   Conduct his activities in a manner that will reflect credit
upon himself, other members and the IAAO.
        3.   Cooperate with the IAAO and its officers in all matters,
including, but not limited to the investigation, censure, discipline
or expulsion of members who by their conduct prejudice their professional status or the reputation of the IAAO.

4.   Protect the professional reputation of other members of IAAO who subscribe to and abide by this Code of Ethics.

5.   Treat as confidential all information concerning persons or their property obtained in his official capacity, except for lawfully authorized uses.   It is proper for members employed by different jurisdictions to exchange factual information concerning persons or their property to aid either or both in the assessment of property legally subject to taxation.

6.   Perform his assessment duties in a manner consistent with statutory requirements without advocacy for accommodation or any particular interests, being factual, objective, unbiased and honest in his conclusion.

7.   Maintain, at all times, a courteous and respectful attitude in his relations with taxpayers, public officials and the public generally, and to compel a similar attitude on the part of his subordinates.

8.   Give full faith and allegiance to his oath of office, apply the law of his jurisdiction to all taxpayers alike, and obey all applicable laws and regulations.

9.   Conform in all respects to this Code of Ethics, The Standards of Professional Conduct and the Constitution of the IAAO as the same may be amended from time to time.

"Standards of Professional Conduct"

In Relations with Assessing Officers
An IAAO Member Will:

Cooperate within the legal and ethical boundaries of his office or profession with other members who request his cooperation in performing the functions of their offices or profession.

Treat information obtained in his professional capacity as confidential unless use of that information is authorized by law.   It is proper for members employed by different jurisdictions to exchange factual information concerning property to aid either or both in the assessment of property legally subject to taxation.

Protect the professional reputation of other members who subscribe to and abide by these Standards of Professional Conduct.

Give full credit to the originator of any material he uses in his writings or speeches.

Conduct his activities in a manner that will reflect credit upon himself, other members and the IAAO.

Cooperate with the officers of the IAAO in all matters, including but not limited to the investigation, censure, discipline or expulsion of members whose conduct cast a shadow on their professional status or the reputation of the IAAO.

In Relations with Public Officials
An IAAO Member:

Has a duty to cooperate with public officials to improve the efficiency and economy of public administration.

Will always maintain an attitude of respect and cooperation toward public officials and governmental agencies to whom the law has assigned official duties relating to the work of the IAAO member.

In Relations with the Public and Taxpayers
An IAAO Member Will:

Maintain at all times a courteous and respectful attitude in his relations with taxpayers, taxing officials and the public generally, and will compel a similar attitude on the part of his subordinates.

Give full faith and allegiance to his oath of office.

Apply the law of his jurisdiction equitable.

Perform his duties in a manner consistent with statutory requirements without advocacy for accommodation of any particular interests; he will be factual, objective, unbiased and honest in his conclusion.

Appraisal Standards To Be Complied With
By IAAO Members:

Any appraisal by an IAAO member shall conform to the highest professional assessment/appraisal standards.

Any value estimate made for assessment purposes by an IAAO member shall be an estimate of true market value as defined by the courts having jurisdiction, regardless of the assessment percentage to be used, except when the law of his jurisdiction requires or the assessment practice in his jurisdiction permits special valuation techniques.

Any value estimate made by an IAAO member shall be a true opinion of value in accordance with generally accepted appraisal practices, except when the law of his jurisdiction requires or the assessment practice in his jurisdiction permits special valuation techniques.

Any fee appraisal assignment accepted by an IAAO member shall be one in which he has no unrevealed personal interest or bias, and one which he is competent to complete without placing his personal integrity or the assessing/appraisal profession in jeopardy.

An IAAO member who accepts fee appraisal assignments which are in addition to his primary employment shall not accept fee appraisal assignments that will conflict with his primary employment, and he shall not become an advocate of any opinion other than his unbiased and objective value conclusion.

In Relations with the International Association
of Assessing Officers, an IAAO Member:

Has a duty to conduct himself in such manner so as not

to prejudice his professional status or the reputation of IAAO.

Shall not use the CAE designation unless duly authorized by IAAO and shall not claim qualifications in reports, testimony or elsewhere which are not factual or which may be subject to erroneous interpretation.

An IAAO member shall strive for individual and collective recognition of the assessing/appraisal field as a profession. It is likewise desirable that members of IAAO continually avail themselves of sources of current information and educational opportunity.

If widely divergent testimony, unethical practices or other acts by members are such as to discredit IAAO or to lower the prestige of membership therein, it is the duty of each member to report such facts and circumstances to the Professional Ethics Committee or the President of IAAO, according to procedures established by the Professional Ethics Committee.

ASSOCIATION EXECUTIVES

AMERICAN SOCIETY OF ASSOCIATION EXECUTIVES (ASAE)
    1101 16th St., N.W., Washington, D.C. 20036
    James P. Low, Executive Vice President

Membership: The American Society of Association Executives, founded in 1920 and with a present (1973) membership of over 4000, is a "professional society of paid executives of national, state, and local trade, professional, technical and business associations." When it was first organized the group was titled "National Trade Organization Secretaries"; this name was changed to "American Trade Association Executives," which--in turn--was replaced by the present name in 1956.

> Regular voting membership in the Society is:
> "limited to full-time staff personnel engaged in the management of trade, technical, educational, philanthropic, business associations, or of individual membership societies with a common professional or business interest, or to individuals who devote 50% or more of their working time to over-all association management duties."

Since 1960 the Society has awarded a professional designation
> "giving special recognition to those association executives who, by passing suitable examinations and fulfilling prescribed standards of performance and conduct have demonstrated a high level of competence and ethical fitness for association management."

The present program awards the professional title and letters:
> "Certified Association Executive"--"CAE."

This designation replaced the previous designation of "Chartered Association Executive" in 1972.

The voluntary certification program is administered by a seven-member Certification Board. Experience and education requirements to take the qualifying certification examinations are:
> "At least five years association management experience in a full-time executive capacity." A bachelor's degree may be substituted for two years of the required experience.

Written examinations are held at stated times and may cover subjects including: law of associations, association financing, publications, staff organization, education, research, statistics, codes of ethics, communications, labor relations, public interest. A bibliography of study materials is made available to help applicants prepare for the tests.

To remain certified "an association executive must accumulate ten professional credits each three years." Such credits are earned through participation in ASAE education programs, completion of college courses related to association management, attendance at ASAE conventions, and participation in education programs of ASAE allied organizations or other selective management programs, such as the institutes for Organization Management.

Code of Ethics: The guide to professional conduct for Association Executives, first issued in 1922, is in its current form, Standards of Conduct, which sets forth twelve general principles to be accepted and observed in the management of organizations. The conduct guide is enforced by the Standards Committee, which receives complaints of a member's violation of the standards of conduct, hears complaints and the response of the member complained against. Decisions of the Committee may be appealed by a member found in breach of the conduct standards to the Society's Board of Directors.

Professional Insignia: The emblem representing the ASAE is the organization's logotype--a bordered square seal, with the Society square seal, with the Society monogram, "ASAE," centered. The color of this insignia is black on white; or it may appear in other colors--buff on brown, yellow-green on white with blue outer border (publications).

Other Designations of Professional Status: As indicated above under "Membership," members are awarded the professional designation:
"Certified Association Executive"--"CAE,"
to indicate high standards of service and professional responsibility. Certified members may use the designation on their Association letterheads and business cards, and may wear the emblem, to show

certification. The design is oval
with "CAE" centered; with "Certi-
fied" above the initials, and "Association Executive" below the monogram; the Society name, "American
Society of Association Executives"
is printed within the bordering
band. The color of the emblem
(shown on the certification information brochure) is black printing
on a central green oval with gold
printing on a black banding border.

Bibliography:
      American Society of Association Executives. ASAE. Pamphlet.
      Informational brochure includes membership requirements
      and definition of "CAE" professional designation.
      _____. ASAE Voluntary Certification Program. 1972.
         Folder.
      Eligibility requirements, qualifying examinations, use of
      professional designation "Certified Association Executive."
      _____. Standards of Conduct. 11"x14" sheet.
      Rules of association service and personal conduct for asso-
      ciation executives.

"Standards of Conduct"

As a member of the American Society of Association Executives, I
pledge myself to:

   Maintain complete loyalty to the association that employs me
and aggressively pursue its objectives.
   Hold inviolate the confidential relationship between the individual members of my association and myself, and the confidential
information entrusted to me through the association office.
   Serve all members of my association impartially, and to
provide no special privilege to any individual member, nor to accept
special personal compensation from an individual member, except
with the knowledge and consent of my association.
   Neither engage in, nor countenance, any exploitation of my
association, industry or profession.
   Recognize and discharge my responsibility and that of my
association to uphold all laws and regulations relating to my association's activities.
   Exercise and insist on sound business principles in the conduct of the affairs of my association.
   Use only legal and ethical means if I should seek to influence
legislation or regulation.
   Issue no false or misleading statements to the public.

Refrain from the dissemination of any malicious information concerning other associations and or other Association Executives.

Accept my responsibility for cooperating in every reasonable and proper way with other Association Executives.

Utilize every opportunity to improve public understanding of the principle of voluntary associations.

Maintain high standards of personal conduct.

ASTRONOMERS

AMERICAN ASTRONOMICAL SOCIETY (AAS)
211 FitzRandolph Rd., Princeton, N.J. 08540
H. M. Gurin, Executive Officer

Membership: The American Astronomical Society, founded in 1899 and with a present (1973) membership of approximately 2300, is an association of professional astronomers. Any person who is seriously interested in the advancement of astronomy, or related fields, is eligible to join the Society. In the categories of membership, professional astronomers are "Members," "deemed capable of preparing an acceptable paper upon subject of astronomy or related branch of science," as determined by the Council of the Society, and who are "sponsored and nominated by two Full Members of the Society," for "Member."

Code of Ethics: The Society does not have a formal printed code of ethics. Any serious matter of professional conduct would be brought before the Council directly for its consideration.

Professional Insignia: The American Astronomical Society and its members are not identified by any pictorial emblem. The initials of the Society name, "A.A.S.," are sometimes used to designate the group.

AUCTIONEERS

NATIONAL AUCTIONEERS ASSOCIATION (NAA)
135 Lakewood Dr., Lincoln, Neb. 68510
Bernard Hart, Secretary

Membership: The National Auctioneers Association, founded in 1946 and with a present (1973) membership of over 3400, is an

organization of auctioneers, whose membership includes:
"Any auctioneer who is honest, upright, worthy of confidence,
of good moral character, and recommended by a member, or
by affiliates through a state organization" (By-Laws, Article
II, Section 1).

Code of Ethics: The guide to professional conduct for auctioneers,
is the Association's Code of Ethics, developed by a Committee of
the NAA, and adopted in 1949. This Code is revised as needed by
the organization Board of Directors. The Code enumerates 14
articles guiding the auctioneer in his Professional Relationships,
Relation to Clients, and Relations to the Public.
    The Code is enforced by the Board of Directors, which investi-
gates and holds hearings on complaints of breaches of the guide to
professional conduct--which have been sent in writing to the Secretary of the Association. When charges of misconduct have been
substantiated, a member may be suspended or his membership revoked (By-Laws, Article II, Section 9).

Professional Insignia: The official emblem of the NAA is a shield
on which the Association
initials, "NAA," are cen-
tered; an oval bisected by
a parallel bar is overprinted
on this monogram, bearing
the group's name, "National
[around the top of the oval]
Auctioneers [across the
horizontal bar] Association
[around the bottom of the
oval]"; a gavel surmounting
the shield symbolizes the
work of the auctioneer.

    Color of the insignia
decal is gold shield and
gavel, red oval and bar,
black printing and outline.
The emblem may appear in
other colors on publications
--as gray on maroon; or
stationery--red on white.
This insignia was adopted in
1949, and its use is limited
to official Association stationery and publications, or to display by
members.

Bibliography:
    National Auctioneers Association. Code of Ethics, Articles of
        Incorporation, By-Laws. 1949. 12 pages. Pamphlet.
    Includes Code of Ethics, with basic organizational documents
    providing for enforcement of the Code.

"Code of Ethics"

PREAMBLE

The public auction subjects all possessions to equitable public appraisal and competitive offer and thereby determines fair and current value of all personal goods and estates.

The Auctioneer is the master of procedure and conduct of the public auction. He is a confident of the public, an instrumentality of community progress and development. Such functions impose grave responsibilities and duty beyond ordinary business policy to which he must dedicate himself and strive to maintain the highest standards of his profession and share with his fellow Auctioneers a common responsibility for its Integrity and Honor.

Accepting the Golden Rule as his standard the Auctioneer pledges himself to observe the Law of God and of the Land in all his dealings and to conduct his business in accordance with the following Code of Ethics adopted by The National Auctioneers Association.

PART I

Professional Relationships

Article 1.   In the best interest of the public, of his fellow Auctioneers and of his own business, the Auctioneer should be loyal to the National Auctioneers Association.

Article 2.   The Auctioneer should so conduct his business as to avoid disputes with his fellow Auctioneers, but in the event of a controversy between two Auctioneers who are members of the National Auctioneers Association, he should not resort to a law suit, but submit his difference to arbitration by the National Auctioneers Association, and the decision of such arbitration should be accepted as final and binding.   If the dispute should be with a non-member, he should offer the services of this Board to arbitrate.

Article 3.   Where a member is charged with unethical practice, he should promptly and voluntarily place all the pertinent facts before the proper committee for investigation and report.

Article 4.   A member should never publicly criticize a competitor, and where an opinion is specially requested, it should be rendered in conformity with strict professional courtesy and dignity.

Article 5.   A member should not solicit the services of an employee of a fellow Auctioneer without his knowledge and consent.

Article 6.   In the best interest of society, of his associates, and of his own business, the Auctioneer should at all times be loyal to the National Auctioneers Association and active in its work; and he should willingly share with his fellow-members the lessons of his experience.

PART II

Relation to Clients

Article 7. In justice of those who place their interests in his hands, the Auctioneer should endeavor to keep abreast of business conditions, to keep informed in matters of law and proposed legislation affecting such interests, so as to give intelligent business advice and effective service.

Article 8. In accepting the sale of real or personal property, the member pledges himself to be fair to both seller and buyer, and to protect the owner's interest as he would his own.

Article 9. When consulted for an appraisal of value or liquidation problem, a member should give a well considered opinion, reflecting expert knowledge and sound judgment, taking requisite time for study, inquiry and deliberation. His counsel represents a professional service which he should render in writing and for which he should make a reasonable charge. A member should not undertake to give an appraisal or offer an opinion on any proposition on which he has a direct or even indirect interests, without a full disclosure of such interest.

Article 10. Before accepting a sale it is the duty of the Auctioneer to advise the owner intelligently and honestly regarding the market value of the business or proposition and the reasonable chance of selling at value or above.

PART III

Relations to the Public

Article 11. It is the duty of every member to protect the public against fraud, misrepresentation or unethical practices in connection with the sale, disposal or liquidation of any real or personal property the Auctioneer is called upon to dispose of at public auction.

Article 12. It is the duty of a member to ascertain all pertinent facts concerning every sale for which he is engaged, so that in offering he may avoid error, exaggeration and misrepresentation.

Article 13. An Auctioneer is a confidential trustee of the information given by the seller or gained by him through relationship, and the Auctioneer must never disclose the gross receipts of a sale or any other information that would tend to be a violation of the profession.

Article 14. No special conditions, real or assumed, or inducements or directions from anyone relieve the member from his responsibility strictly to observe the Code of Ethics in letter and spirit.

AUDITORS

THE INSTITUTE OF INTERNAL AUDITORS, INC. (IIA)
5500 Diplomat Circle, Orlando, Fla. 32810
John E. Harmon, Executive Vice President

Membership: Founded in 1941, The Institute of Internal Auditors, Inc. is a non-profit professional organization with 102 chapters and 8000 members in the United States, Canada and overseas, representing the internal auditing profession in business, government and industry. "Members" of IIA--the fully professional category of membership of The Institute--are internal auditors "in private and government employment who perform administrative and supervisory internal auditing functions, or are full time employees on internal auditing staffs" (Rules of Eligibility for Membership).

"Internal Auditing," as set forth in the Statement of Responsibilities of The Internal Auditor (first issued by the Institute in 1947 and revised in 1957 and 1971) is:
> "an independent appraisal activity within an organization for the review of operations as a service to management. It is a managerial control which functions by measuring and evaluating the effectiveness of other controls."

In carrying out this function, internal auditors are concerned with evaluation of effectiveness of operating controls, extent of compliance with established policies, measures for protection of entity assets, reliability of management data, quality of performance and making recommendations for operating improvements.

Code of Ethics: The IIA guide to professional conduct is its Code of Ethics, adopted in December 1968. The eight principles given in this Code set standards of professional behavior for members, including proper conduct relating to conflict of personal and professional interest, acceptance of gifts, treatment of confidential information. The Board of Directors may discipline members for proved violations of this ethical code by censure, suspension or expulsion after investigation of complaints of unprofessional conduct, and hearings of complaints (Bylaws, Article I, Section 9).

Other Guides to Professional Conduct: The principle guide to the activities of the internal auditor is the Statement of Responsibilities of the Internal Auditor. Here the definition of the internal auditor's professional role and relationships includes the nature of his professional work, objective and scope, responsibility and authority and independence of his activities as a management control in the measure and evaluation of the effectiveness of the other controls of business enterprise and public organizations.

Professional Insignia: The emblem of the IIA is the official seal (provided for, but not specified, in Bylaws, Article XIII). A circular design, it includes a centered open book before which are a lamp and a scroll pen, with The Institute's motto, "Progress Through Sharing," inscribed on the upper part of the book; below the book is the date and place of incorporation, "New York 1941"; a bordering band gives the name, "The Institute of Internal Auditors, Inc.," with the description, "Corporate Seal," at the bottom of the border.   The color of this insignia is shown variously--black on white (letterhead; publications); brown on buff (publications).

Bibliography:
    The Institute of Internal Auditors, Inc. Bylaws; Rules of
        Eligibility. 1969. Pamphlet. 10 pages.
    Includes membership requirements; disciplinary procedure.
            . Code of Ethics. Folder.
    Eight conduct standards governing internal auditing practice.
            . Statement of Responsibilities of the Internal Auditor.
        Revised edition, 1971. Folder.
    Defines professional responsibility and authority of the internal auditor in his relation to management.

"Code of Ethics"

Introduction:

    Recognizing that ethics are an important consideration in the practice of internal auditing and that the moral principles followed by members of The Institute of Internal Auditors, Inc., should be formalized, the Board of Directors at its regular meeting in New Orleans on December 13, 1968, received and adopted the following resolution:

    Whereas, the members of The Institute of Internal Auditors, Inc. represent the profession of internal auditing; and
    Whereas, managements rely on the profession of internal auditing to assist in the fulfillment of their management stewardship; and
    Whereas, said members must maintain high standards of conduct, honor and character in order to carry on proper and meaningful internal auditing practice;

Therefore Be It Resolved that a Code of Ethics be now set forth outlining the standards of professional behavior for the guidance of each member of The Institute of Internal Auditors, Inc.

In accordance with this resolution, the Board of Directors further approved of the principles set forth.

Interpretation of Principles:

The provisions of this Code of Ethics cover basic principles in the various disciplines of internal auditing practice. A member shall realize that individual judgment is required in the application of these principles. He has a responsibility to conduct himself so that his good faith and integrity should not be open to question. While having due regard for the limit of his technical skills, he will promote the highest possible internal auditing standards to the end of advancing the interest of his company or organization.

Articles:

I. A member shall have an obligation to exercise honesty, objectivity and diligence in the performance of his duties and responsibilities.

II. A member, in holding the trust of his employer, shall exhibit loyalty in all matters pertaining to the affairs of the employer or to whomever he may be rendering a service. However, a member shall not knowingly be a party to any illegal or improper activity.

III. A member shall refrain from entering into any activity which may be in conflict with the interest of his employer or which would prejudice his ability to carry out objectively his duties and responsibilities.

IV. A member shall not accept a fee or a gift from an employee, a client, a customer or a business associate of his employer without the knowledge and consent of his senior management.

V. A member shall be prudent in the use of information acquired in the course of his duties. He shall not use confidential information for any personal gain or in a manner which would be detrimental to the welfare of his employer.

VI. A member, in expressing an opinion, shall use all reasonable care to obtain sufficient factual evidence to warrant such expression. In his reporting, a member shall reveal such material facts known to him which, if not revealed, could either distort the report of the results of operations under review or conceal unlawful practice.

VII. A member shall continually strive for improvement in the proficiency and effectiveness of his service.

VIII. A member shall abide by the Bylaws and uphold the objectives of The Institute of Internal Auditors, Inc. In the practice of his profession, he shall be ever mindful of his obligation to maintain the high standard of competence, morality and

dignity which The Institute of Internal Auditors, Inc. and
its members have established.

AUTOMOTIVE SERVICE TECHNICIANS

INDEPENDENT GARAGE OWNERS OF AMERICA (IGOA)
    4001 Warren Blvd., Hillsdale, Ill. 60162
    Donn W. Sanford, Executive Director

Membership: The Independent Garage Owners of America, founded
in 1955 and with a present (1973) membership of about 5000, in
affiliated state and local associations, is a trade association of
garage owners engaged in automotive service and repair work.   The
activities of the IGOA include such "customer satisfaction" programs
as "IGO National Warranty Program," an arrangement by which
customers on vacation or driving outside the area of original repair
may have their car re-repaired by a member of IGOA, who carries
out the original repairer's guarantee of work, without charge to the
customer, by billing the original shop member for the repair work.
The organization also sponsors, with other trade groups, the program of Certification of Automotive Technicians, through the National Automotive Technicians Certification Board.

Code of Ethics: The conduct guide for association members is its
Code of Ethics, a brief statement, in nine points, for fair, dependable and courteous automotive service.   This guide, prepared by
the founders of the group in 1956, covers fair pricing of repair service, presentation of bills itemized to show parts and mechanical
adjustments, retaining replaced parts for customer inspection.
    The Code, which is reviewed periodically by the association's
governing body (House of Delegates), is enforced by state and local
associations in the IGOA federation, who receive complaints of a
member-garage owner's unethical conduct.   Enforcement provisions
for the Code of Ethics are given in the IGOA Bylaws (Article V,
Section 14a), so that a member who violates the conduct guide may
be suspended or terminated as a member.

Professional Insignia: Members of the IGOA are nationally identified by the organization's insignia--a shield with "Personalized Service" across the top; "Member" in a horizontal bar; above "IGO,"
spaced with each letter in a vertical stripe.
    The color of this insignia is red, white and blue--light blue
background, with darker blue "Personalized Service" and shield
border; red background for "Member" and "G" of monogram; white
for the printing of "Member" and the "I" and "O" of monogram,
and the central vertical stripe.   This colored emblem is displayed

by members, and is shown on
the organization stationery
and publications. This emblem may also appear in
other colors on publications--
black on white, or other
paper colors.

Bibliography:
Independent Garage Own-
        ers of America.
        Code of Ethics.
        Member's conduct guide;
        with emblem in red,
        white and blue.
_____ ₒ Don't Turn
        Your Back on Profits.
        Pamphlet.
        Membership brochure,
        with Code of Ethics,
and brief description of IGOA-sponsored voluntary certification program for automotive service technicians.
_____. Pledge To You.... Folder.
        IGO activities; Code of Ethics; emblem in red, white and
blue.

"Code of Ethics"

1. To promote good will between the motorist and members
of this association.

2. To have a sense of personal obligation to each individual
customer.

3. To perform high quality repair service at a fair and
just price.

4. To employ the best skilled mechanics obtainable.

5. To use only proven merchandise of high quality distributed by reputable firms.

6. To itemize all parts and mechanical adjustments in the
price charged for service rendered.

7. To retain all parts replaced for customer inspection.

8. To uphold the high standards of our profession and always seek to correct any and all abuses within the automotive industry.

9. To uphold the integrity of all members of IGOA.

NATIONAL AUTOMOTIVE TECHNICIANS CERTIFICATION BOARD
(NATCB)
     4001 Warren Blvd., Hillside, Ill. 60162
     Mrs. Janet Sanford, Administrator

Membership: The National Automotive Technician Certification
Board, a joint activity of the Independent Garage Owners of America
(IGOA), the Automotive Service Industry Association (ASIA), and
the National Congress of Petroleum Retailers (NCPR), is the voluntary certification program that carries out certifying the competence
of automotive technicians.   The Board--sponsored by the three major
automotive service associations--conducts nationwide certification
designed to safeguard motorists against fraud and incompetence in
auto repair by testing the technician's proficiency through certification examination.   Examining Boards of the NATCB appointed in
each State administer the certifying examinations--all in multiple-
choice form--and award certificates in the following specialties:

1. Engine Overhaul   10. Automatic Air Conditioning
2. Electrical Systems   (Refrigeration, Heating and
3. Carburetion   Cooling)
4. Cooling Systems   11. Body and Fender Repair
5. Braking Systems   12. Automotive Refinishing
6. Automatic Transmission   13. Glass Installation
7. Power Train and Standard   14. Truck Repair (General)
   Transmission   15. Frame Repair
8. Suspensions and Alignment
9. Standard and Power Steering

The number of questions in the tests vary with the subject, from
20 to 60 questions, and are given in sessions that total generally
three hours.

     Qualifications for taking the certifying examinations are by
having "spent at least two years in the trade actively working in
the classification for which he wishes to be certified"--except that
for the specialty Body and Fender Repair three years of experience
is required, and for Truck Repair, four years of experience is
required.
     A "Master Technician Certificate" is awarded when an applicant
has four years of experience in automobile mechanical repair, and
successfully completes eight out of 11 examinations.   These 11
examinations (as listed above) are 1, 2, 3, 4, 5, 6, 7, 8, 9, 10, 14.   In
addition, NATCB offers certification as a "Master Auto Body Repairman."   To qualify for this certification, an applicant must be
employed in that specialty for four years, and must complete Test
#11, 12, plus 13 or 15.

     At the discretion of the local Examining Board, applicants may
receive employment time credit for applicable military automotive
service experience, and for Institutional Vocational-Technical Automotive Training Program completion--up to a maximum of 50% of
the time required for the specific Certification Classification.   Each

applicant passing the examinations receives a certificate "suitable
for framing," and a shoulder patch.   These evidences of technical
competence are issued for a three year period, and at the end of
that time, the repairman must apply for recertification, which involves retaking of examinations.

Code of Ethics: None reported;

Professional Insignia: The Board's emblem is an oval enclosing
the initials of the group, "NATCB," with the central initial, "T,"
framed in a larger outline "T."   The color of this insignia is blue
on white, with the central "T" in red.   The emblem issued as a

shoulder patch to certified automotive service technicians shows the
insignia centered in a half circle, with the specialty designation
above the insignia (as, "Electrical Systems"), and the designation,
"Certified Technician," below the central emblem.   The color of the
sleeve patch is blue on white, with red "T" and outline "T."   For
"Master Technician," the emblem is modified by the word "Master"
printed above the central emblem in gold and the background of the
central oval shown in gold.

BROADCASTERS

NATIONAL ASSOCIATION OF BROADCASTERS (NAB)
    1717 N St., N.W., Washington, D.C. 20036
    Vincent Wasilewski, President

Membership: The National Association of Broadcasters, organized
in 1922, is a broadcasting industry trade association, among whose
active members are approximately 4000 broadcasters in about 4000
radio and television stations throughout the 50 states, the District
of Columbia, Puerto Rico, and seven national radio and television
networks.

Code of Ethics: The NAB adopted its first Code of Ethics in 1929,

and ten years later (1939) a new version of a code of conduct
adopted, resembled the present Radio Code. Today two separate
guides are provided radio and television broadcasters to aid them
in determining acceptable programming and advertising practices--
the Radio Code, first adopted in 1937, and the Television Code,
initially developed in 1952. Both of these Codes are revised frequently to reflect new problems and social changes. The most
recent Code editions were issued in April 1972 (Radio Code), and
April 1973 (Television Code).

The Television Code was "written by 12 practicing and experienced broadcasters" to provide self-regulation of broadcasting practices as an alternative to government regulation in the Federal
Communications Code, the Rules and Regulations of the Federal
Communications Commission, and censorship from "outside interests."

The Codes are added to or amended by recommendations to the
appropriate Code Review Board; changes must be ratified by the
Board of Directors before they become effective. Code subscribers
and advertisers are informed of interpretations of, and policy concerning, a Code through a monthly newsletter, Code News. A
Code Authority Director is provided for each Code, as is a Code
Review Board, a continuing committee which acts in amending and
reviewing its Code, and in enforcement of the Code through investigations, hearings, and recommendations of discipline for "continuous,
willful or gross violation of any of the provisions" of a Code.

The Code Review Board receives complaints of code violation
from the public or other agency, and radio and television programs
are monitored for compliance to Code provisions, in two general
types of review:
    (1)   Qualitative Monitoring--concerned with issues of taste,
             violence, sex, race relations, and similar questions;
    (2)   Quantitative Monitoring--concerned with conformance to
             time standards set in the Code.
For violation or breach of a Code, a member may be suspended or
expelled from membership (Bylaws, Article IV, Section 5), unless
programs or advertising found objectionable are revised or withdrawn.

Other Guides to Professional Conduct: In the Radio Code, the Radio
Broadcaster's Creed introduces the Code and provides a general
conduct guide for radio broadcasters. When day-to-day interpretations of the Television Code provisions develop into Code policy,
they are formalized into "Guidelines." Among Advertising Guidelines issued by the Television Code Authority are those dealing
with such areas as:
      Acne Products;
      Alcoholic Beverages;
      Arthritis and Rheumatism Remedies;
      Bronchitis Products;
      Children's Premiums and Offers;
      Disparagement;

Hallucinogens;
Hypnosis;
Men-in-White;
Non-Prescription Medications;
Personal Products;
Testimonials;
Time Standards;
Toys;
Weight Reducing Products.

The most recently developed NAB standards are the Children's
TV Advertising Statement of Principles, adopted by the Television
Code Review Board at its June 6-7, 1973 meeting, to go into effect
no later than January 1, 1974. The ten principles--based in part
on the content analysis of television commercials directed to children
--conducted by sociologist Dr. Charles Winick, City University of
New York--including provisions to bar commercials that frighten or
exploit children, or that depict violence.

Professional Insignia: The emblem of the National Association of
Broadcasters is a circular seal,
with the initials of the organization, "NAB," shown on a
darker ground, and the name
of the group, "National Association of Broadcasters,"
printed around the seal as an
unbanded border. This insignia is shown on Association
stationery and publications in
various colors--grey on white;
brown on buff; black on white.

In addition to this association emblem, the Radio Code
Authority and the Television
Code Authority each have a
"Seal of Good Practice," which
may be exhibited by a station subscribing to the Code provisions of
programming and advertising.

    Radio Seal of Good Practice: A shield with a horizontal bar
       near the top and a space at the bottom printed in blue;
       the legend, "Radio Code," is centered on the shield;
       "NAB" is shown on the upper blue bar; and crossed radio
       wave and an antenna appear in the lower blue space;
    Television Seal of Good Practice: A design shaped like a
       television screen is framed at the sides with a foliage
       spray; the legend, "Television Code," is centered on the
       emblem, with "National Association of Broadcasters,"
       above, and "Seal of Good Practice," below. The color
       of this emblem is shown variously--black on white; with
       light blue "Television Code" on darker blue ground, and

other legends in white and foliage in green; or black on white, with printing above and below "Television Code" in red. In the 1972 seal, "1972," is printed below "Seal of Good Practice," and the color of the seal is yellow with "Television Code," the date and outside border with foliage in dark green, inner border and other printing in white.

Bibliography:
    Linton, Bruce A. Self-Regulation in Broadcasting. National
        Association of Broadcasters. 1967. 97 pages.
    College-level study guide in the form of a syllabus in outline
    form, in three sections; "Historical Perspective," "Self-
    Regulation in Action," and "Some Problems in Self-Regula-
    tion."
National Association of Broadcasters. Broadcast Self-Regula-
        tion. Looseleaf, in three-ring binder. $20., $10. to
        University Library, to maximum of two copies.
    The Code Authority's working manual, containing NAB Radio
    Code and Television Code, advertising guidelines, interpreta-
    tions of Codes, programming and advertising standards, per-
    tinent government regulations.
        _____. Bylaws. March 13, 1965. 8 pages.
    Includes membership qualifications, and disciplinary action
    that may be taken for Code violation (Article IV, Section 5).
        _____. Children's TV Advertising Statement of Principles.
        (In Code News 6/Number 5-6:1 May-June 1973).
    Ten Principles adopted by the Television Code Review Board
    June 6-7, 1973, to go into effect not later than January 1,
    1974.

_____. History of the NAB, Association of Broadcasters.
1970.
Purpose, functions, and development of the NAB, with official
emblem.
_____. Political Broadcast Catechism and the Fairness Doc-
trine. 6th ed., April 1968, with Addendum of September
8, 1970. 32 pages, and 10 pages.
Interprets Federal Communications Act of 1934 (Section 315
and Section 317), and the Federal Communications Commission Rules and Regulations implementing these sections.
_____. Radio and Television Bibliography. December 1970.
18 pages.
Annotated list of books and pamphlets providing a guide to
reference material on radio and television broadcasting, prepared by the librarian of NAB.
_____. The Radio Code. 17th edition, April 1972. 27 pages.
Includes Radio Broadcaster's Creed, Program Standards,
Advertising Standards, and Regulations and Procedures.
Table of Contents and Subject Index. Official emblem (Seal
of Good Practice) shown in color on cover.
_____. The Television Code. 17th edition, April 1973.
31 pages.
The code of standards subscribed to by television broad-
casters includes Program Standards, Advertising Standards,
Interpretation, Regulations and Procedures. Official emblem
(Seal of Good Practice) shown on cover.
_____. NAB Code Authority. Functions and Procedures of
TV Code Offices. Memorandum 2/18/71. 5 pages.
Discusses establishment of the Code Authority, code sub-
scription, code program and advertising standards, code in-
terpretation, enforcement, and monitoring.

"The Radio Code"

PREAMBLE

The radio broadcasters of the United States first adopted
industry-wide standards of practice in 1937. The purpose of such
standards, in this as in other professions, is to establish guide-
posts and to set forth minimum tenets for performance.
Standards for broadcasting can never be final or complete.
Broadcasting is a creative art and it must always seek new ways
to achieve greater advances. Therefore, any standards must be
subject to change. In 1945, after two years devoted to reviewing
and revising the 1937 document, new standards were promulgated.
Further revisions were made in subsequent years when deemed
necessary.
Through this process of self-examination broadcasters

acknowledge their obligation to the American family.

The growth of broadcasting as a medium of entertainment, education and information has been made possible by its force as an instrument of commerce.

This philosophy of commercial broadcasting as it is known in the United States has enabled the industry to develop as a free medium in the tradition of American enterprise.

The extent of this freedom is implicit in the fact that no one censors broadcasting in the United States.

Those who own the nation's radio broadcasting stations operate them--pursuant to this self-adopted Radio Code--in recognition of the interest of the American people.

The Radio Broadcaster's Creed

We Believe:

That Radio Broadcasting in the United States of America is a living symbol of democracy; a significant and necessary instrument for maintaining freedom of expression, as established by the First Amendment to the Constitution of the United States;

That its influence in the arts, in science, in education, in commerce, and upon the public welfare is of such magnitude that the only proper measure of its responsibility is the common good of the whole people;

That it is our obligation to serve the people in such manner as to reflect credit upon our profession and to encourage aspiration toward a better estate for all mankind; by making available to every person in America such programs as will perpetuate the traditional leadership of the United States in all phases of the broadcasting art;

That we should make full and ingenious use of man's store of knowledge, his talents, and his skills and exercise critical and discerning judgment concerning all broadcasting operations to the end that we may, intelligently and sympathetically:

Observe the proprieties and customs of civilized society;

Respect the rights and sensitivities of all people;

Honor the sanctity of marriage and the home;

Protect and uphold the dignity and brotherhood of all mankind;

Enrich the daily life of the people through the factual reporting and analysis of news, and through programs of education, entertainment, and information;

Provide for the fair discussion of matters of general public concern; engage in works directed toward the common good; and volunteer our aid and comfort in times of stress and emergency;

Contribute to the economic welfare of all by expanding the channels of trade, by encouraging the development and conservation of natural resources, and by bringing together the buyer and seller through the broadcasting of information pertaining to goods and services.

Toward the achievement of these purposes we agree to observe the following:

I. PROGRAM STANDARDS

A. News

Radio is unique in its capacity to reach the largest number of people first with reports on current events. This competitive advantage bespeaks caution--being first is not as important as being right. The following Standards are predicated upon that viewpoint.

1. News Sources. Those responsible for news on radio should exercise constant professional care in the selection of sources--for the integrity of the news and the consequent good reputation of radio as a dominant news medium depend largely upon the reliability of such sources.

2. News Reporting. News reporting shall be factual and objective. Good taste shall prevail in the selection and handling of news. Morbid, sensational, or alarming details not essential to factual reporting should be avoided. News should be broadcast in such a manner as to avoid creation of panic and unnecessary alarm. Broadcasters shall be diligent in their supervision of content, format, and presentation of news broadcasts. Equal diligence should be exercised in selection of editors and reporters who direct news gathering and dissemination, since the station's performance in this vital informational field depends largely upon them.

3. Commentaries and Analyses. Special obligations devolve upon those who analyze and/or comment upon news developments, and management should be satisfied completely that the task is to be performed in the best interest of the listening public. Programs of news analysis and commentary shall be clearly identified as such, distinguishing them from straight news reporting.

4. Editorializing. Broadcasts in which stations express their own opinions about issues of general public interest should be clearly identified as editorials and should be clearly distinguished from news and other program material.

5. Coverage of News and Public Events. In the coverage of news and public events the broadcaster has the right to exercise his judgment consonant with the accepted standards of ethical journalism and especially the requirements for decency and decorum in the broadcast of public and court proceedings.

6. Placement of Advertising. A broadcaster should exercise particular discrimination in the acceptance, placement and presentation of advertising in news programs so that such advertising should be clearly distinguishable from the news content.

B. Controversial Public Issues

1. Radio provides a valuable forum for the expression of responsible views on public issues of a controversial nature. The

broadcaster should develop programs relating to controversial public issues of importance to his fellow citizens; and give fair representation to opposing sides of issues which materially affect the life or welfare of a substantial segment of the public.

  2.   Requests by individuals, groups or organizations for time to discuss their views on controversial public issues should be considered on the basis of their individual merits, and in the light of the contributions which the use requested would make to the public interest.

  3.   Programs devoted to the discussion of controversial public issues should be identified as such. They should not be presented in a manner which would create the impression that the program is other than one dealing with a public issue.

C.   Community Responsibility

  1.   A broadcaster and his staff occupy a position of responsibility in the community and should conscientiously endeavor to be acquainted with its needs and characteristics in order to serve the welfare of its citizens.

  2.   Requests for time for the placement of public service announcements or programs should be carefully reviewed with respect to the character and reputation of the group, campaign or organization involved, the public interest content of the message, and the manner of its presentation.

D.   Political Broadcasts

  1.   Political broadcasts, or the dramatization of political issues designed to influence an election, shall be properly identified as such.

  2.   They should be presented in a manner which would properly identify the nature and character of the broadcast.

  3.   Because of the unique character of political broadcasts and the necessity to retain broad freedoms of policy void of restrictive interference, it is incumbent upon all political candidates and all political parties to observe the canons of good taste and political ethics, keeping in mind the intimacy of broadcasting in the American home.

E.   Advancement of Education and Culture

  1.   Because radio is an integral part of American life, there is inherent in radio broadcasting a continuing opportunity to enrich the experience of living through the advancement of education and culture.

  2.   The radio broadcaster, in augmenting the educational and cultural influences of the home, the church, schools, institutions of higher learning, and other entities devoted to education and culture:

  (a)   Should be thoroughly conversant with the educational and cultural needs and aspirations of the community served;

(b)   Should cooperate with the responsible and accountable educational and cultural entities of the community to provide enlightenment of listeners;

(c)   Should engage in experimental efforts designed to advance the community's cultural and educational interests.

F.   Religion and Religious Programs

1.   Religious programs shall be presented by responsible individuals, groups or organizations.

2.   Radio broadcasting, which reaches men of all creeds simultaneously, shall avoid attacks upon religious faiths.

3.   Religious programs shall be presented respectfully and without prejudice or ridicule.

4.   Religious programs shall place emphasis on religious doctrines of faith and worship.

G.   Dramatic Programs

1.   In determining the acceptability of any dramatic program containing any element of crime, mystery, or horror, proper consideration should be given to the possible effect on all members of the family.

2.   Radio should reflect realistically the experience of living, in both its pleasant and tragic aspects, if it is to serve the listener honestly.   Nevertheless, it holds a concurrent obligation to provide programs which will encourage better adjustments to life.

3.   This obligation is apparent in the area of dramatic programs particularly.   Without sacrificing integrity of presentation, dramatic programs on radio shall avoid:

(a)   Techniques and methods of crime presented in such manner as to encourage imitation, or to make the commission of crime attractive, or to suggest that criminals can escape punishment;

(b)   Detailed presentation of brutal killings, torture, or physical agony, horror, the use of supernatural or climatic incidents likely to terrify or excite unduly;

(c)   Sound effects calculated to mislead, shock, or unduly alarm the listener;

(d)   Disrespectful portrayal of law enforcement;

(e)   The portrayal of suicide as a satisfactory solution to any problem.

H.   Responsibility Toward Children

The education of children involves giving them a sense of the world at large.   It is not enough that programs broadcast for children shall be suitable for the young and immature.   In addition, programs

which might reasonably be expected to hold the attention of children
and which are broadcast during times when children may be normally expected to constitute a substantial part of the audience should
be presented with due regard for their effect on children.

1. Programs specifically designed for listening by children
shall be based upon sound social concepts and shall reflect respect
for parents, law and order, clean living, high morals, fair play,
and honorable behavior.

2. They shall convey the commonly accepted moral, social
and ethical ideals characteristic of American life.

3. They should contribute to the healthy development of
personality and character.

4. They should afford opportunities for cultural growth as
well as for wholesome entertainment.

5. They should be consistent with integrity of realistic production, but they should avoid material of extreme nature which
might create undesirable emotional reaction in children.

6. They shall avoid appeals urging children to purchase the
product specifically for the purpose of keeping the program on the
air or which, for any reason, encourage children to enter inappropriate places.

7. They should present such subjects as violence and sex
without undue emphasis and only as required by plot development
or character delineation. Crime should not be presented as attractive or as a solution to human problems, and the inevitable
retribution should be made clear.

8. They should avoid reference to kidnapping or threats of
kidnapping of children.

I.   General

1. The intimacy and confidence placed in Radio demand of
the broadcaster, the networks and other program sources that they
be vigilant in protecting the audience from deceptive program practices.

2. Sound effects and expressions characteristically assoc-
ciated with news broadcasts (such as "bulletin," "flash," "we interrupt this program to bring you," etc.) shall be reserved for announcement of news, and the use of any deceptive techniques in connection with fictional events and non-news programs shall not be
employed.

3. The acceptance of cash payments or other considerations
for, including identification of commercial products or services,
trade names or advertising slogans, including the identification of
prizes, etc., must be disclosed in accordance with provisions of
the Communications Act.

4. When plot development requires the use of material which
depends upon physical or mental handicaps, care should be taken to
spare the sensibilities of sufferers from similar defects.

5. Stations should avoid broadcasting program material
which would tend to encourage illegal gambling or other violations

of federal, state and local laws, ordinances, and regulations.

6.   Simulation of court atmosphere or use of the term "court" in a program title should be done only in such manner as to eliminate the possibility of creating the false impression that the proceedings broadcast are vested with judicial or official authority.

7.   Quiz and similar programs, that are presented as contests of knowledge, information, skill or luck must in fact, be genuine contests and the results must not be controlled by collusion with or between contestants, or any other action which will favor one contestant against any other.

8.   No program shall be presented in a manner which through artifice or simulation would mislead the audience as to any material fact.   Each broadcaster must exercise reasonable judgment to determine whether a particular method of presentation would constitute a material deception, or would be accepted by the audience as normal theatrical illusion.

9.   Legal, medical and other professional advice will be permitted only in conformity with law and recognized ethical and professional standards.

10.   Narcotic addiction shall not be presented except as a vicious habit.   The misuse of hallucinogenic drugs shall not be presented or encouraged as desirable or socially acceptable.

11.   Program material pertaining to fortune-telling, occultism, astrology, phrenology, palm-reading, numerology, mind-reading, character-reading, or subjects of a like nature, is unacceptable when presented for the purpose of fostering belief in these subjects.

12.   The use of cigarettes shall not be presented in a manner to impress the youth of our country that it is a desirable habit worthy of imitation in that it contributes to health, individual achievement or social acceptance.

13.   Profanity, obscenity, smut and vulgarity are forbidden. From time to time, words which have been acceptable, acquire undesirable meanings, and broadcasters should be alert to eliminate such words.

14.   Words (especially slang) derisive of any race, color, creed, nationality or national derivation, except wherein such usage would be for the specific purpose of effective dramatization, such as combating prejudice, are forbidden.

15.   Respect is maintained for the sanctity of marriage and the value of the home.   Divorce is not treated casually as a solution for marital problems.

16.   Broadcasts of actual sporting events at which on-the-scene betting is permitted should concentrate on the subject as a public sporting event and not on the aspects of gambling.

II.   ADVERTISING STANDARDS

Advertising is the principal source of revenue of the free, competitive American system of radio broadcasting.   It makes possible the presentation to all American people of the finest programs of entertainment, education, and information.
        Since the great strength of American radio broadcasting derives from the public respect for and the public approval of its programs, it must be the purpose of each broadcaster to establish and maintain high standards of performance, not only in the selection and production of all programs, but also in the presentation of advertising.
        This Code establishes basic standards for all radio broadcasting.   The principles of acceptability and good taste within the Program Standards section govern the presentation of advertising where applicable.   In addition, the Code establishes in this section special standards which apply to radio advertising.

A.   General Advertising Standards

        1.   A commercial radio broadcaster makes his facilities available for the advertising of products and services and accepts commercial presentations for such advertising.   However, he shall, in recognition of his responsibility to the public, refuse the facilities of his station to an advertiser where he has good reason to doubt the integrity of the advertiser, the truth of the advertising representations, or the compliance of the advertiser with the spirit and purpose of all applicable legal requirements.
        2.   In consideration of the customs and attitudes of the communities served, each radio broadcaster should refuse his facilities to the advertisement of products and services, or the use of advertising scripts, which the station has good reason to believe would be objectionable to a substantial and responsible segment of the community.   These standards should be applied with judgment and flexibility, taking into consideration the characteristics of the medium, its home and family audience, and the form and content of the particular presentation.

B.   Presentation of Advertising

        1.   The advancing techniques of the broadcast art have shown that the quality and proper integration of advertising copy are just as important as measurement in time.   The measure of a station's service to its audience is determined by its overall performance.
        2.   The final measurement of any commercial broadcast service is quality.   To this, every broadcaster shall dedicate his best effort.
        3.   Great care shall be exercised by the broadcaster to prevent the presentation of false, misleading or deceptive advertising. While it is entirely appropriate to present a product in a favorable

light and atmosphere, the presentation must not, by copy or demonstration, involve a material deception as to the characteristics or performance of a product.

4. The broadcaster and the advertiser should exercise special caution with the content and presentation of commercials placed in or near programs designed for children. Exploitation of children should be avoided. Commercials directed to children should in no way mislead as to the product's performance and usefulness. Appeals involving matters of health which should be determined by physicians should be avoided.

5. Reference to the results of research, surveys or tests relating to the product to be advertised shall not be presented in a manner so as to create an impression of fact beyond that established by the study. Surveys, tests or other research results upon which claims are based must be conducted under recognized research techniques and standards.

C. Acceptability of Advertisers and Products

In general, because radio broadcasting is designed for the home and the entire family, the following principles shall govern the business classifications:

1. The advertising of hard liquor shall not be accepted.

2. The advertising of beer and wines is acceptable when presented in the best of good taste and discretion.

3. The advertising of fortune-telling, occultism, astrology, phrenology, palm-reading, numerology, mind-reading, character-reading, or subjects of a like nature, is not acceptable.

4. Because the advertising of all products and services of a personal nature raises special problems, such advertising, when accepted, should be treated with emphasis on ethics and the canons of good taste, and presented in a restrained and inoffensive manner.

5. The advertising of lotteries is unacceptable. The advertising of tip sheets and other publications seeking to advertise for the purpose of giving odds or promoting betting is unacceptable.

The advertising of organizations, private or governmental, which conduct legalized betting on sporting contests is acceptable, provided it is limited to institutional type of advertising which does not exhort the public to bet.

6. An advertiser who markets more than one product shall not be permitted to use advertising copy devoted to an acceptable product for purposes of publicizing the brand name or other identification of a product which is not acceptable.

7. Care should be taken to avoid presentation of "bait-switch" advertising whereby goods or services which the advertiser has no intention of selling are offered merely to lure the customer into purchasing higher-priced substitutes.

8. Advertising should offer a product or service on its

positive merits and refrain from discrediting, disparaging or unfairly attacking competitors, competing products, other industries,
professions or institutions.

Any identification or comparison of a competitive product or
service, by name, or other means, should be confined to specific
facts rather than generalized statements or conclusions, unless
such statements or conclusions are not derogatory in nature.

9.   Advertising testimonials should be genuine, and reflect
an honest appraisal of personal experience.

10.   Advertising by institutions or enterprises offering instruction with exaggerated claims for opportunities awaiting those
who enroll, is unacceptable.

11.   The advertising of firearms/ammunition is acceptable
provided it promotes the product only as sporting equipment and
conforms to recognized standards of safety as well as all applicable
laws and regulations.   Advertisements of firearms ammunition by
mail order are unacceptable.

D.   Advertising of Medical Products

Because advertising for over-the-counter products involving health
considerations are of intimate and far-reaching importance to the
consumer, the following principles should apply to such advertising:

1.   When dramatized advertising material involves statements
by doctors, dentists, nurses or other professional people, the material should be presented by members of such profession reciting
actual experience, or it should be made apparent from the presentation itself that the portrayal is dramatized.

2.   Because of the personal nature of the advertising of
medical products, the indiscriminate use of such words as "Safe,"
"Without Risk," "Harmless," or other terms of similar meaning,
either direct or implied, should not be expressed in the advertising
of medical products.

3.   Advertising material which offensively describes or
dramatizes distress or morbid situations involving ailments is not
acceptable.

E.   Time Standards for Advertising Copy

1.   The amount of time to be used for advertising should
not exceed 18 minutes within any clock hour.   The Code Authority,
however, for good cause may approve advertising exceeding the
above standard for special circumstances.

2.   Any reference to another's products or services under
any trade name, or language sufficiently descriptive to identify it,
shall, except for normal guest identification, be considered as advertising copy.

3.   For the purpose of determining advertising limitations,
such program types as "classified," "swap shop," "shopping guides,"
and "farm auction" programs, etc., shall be regarded as containing

one and one-half minutes of advertising for each five-minute segment.

F. Contests

1.   Contests shall be conducted with fairness to all entrants,
and shall comply with all pertinent laws and regulations.
2.   All contest details, including rules, eligibility requirements, opening and termination dates, should be clearly and completely announced or easily accessible to the listening public; and
the winners' names should be released as soon as possible after
the close of the contest.
3.   When advertising is accepted which requests contestants
to submit items of product identification or other evidence of purchase of products, reasonable facsimiles thereof should be made
acceptable.   However, when the award is based upon skill and not
upon chance, evidence of purchase may be required.
4.   All copy pertaining to any contest (except that which is
required by law) associated with the exploitation or sale of the
sponsor's product or service, and all references to prizes or gifts
offered in such connection should be considered a part of and included in the total time limitations heretofore provided.   (See Time
Standards for Advertising Copy.)

G. Premiums and Offers

1.   The broadcaster should require that full details of proposed offers be submitted for investigation and approval before the
first announcement of the offer is made to the public.
2.   A final date for the termination of an offer should be
announced as far in advance as possible.
3.   If a consideration is required, the advertiser should
agree to honor complaints indicating dissatisfaction with the premium by returning the consideration.
4.   There should be no misleading descriptions or comparisons of any premiums or gifts which will distort or enlarge their
value in the minds of the listeners.

"The Television Code"

PROGRAM STANDARDS

I. Principles Governing Program Content

It is in the interest of television as a vital medium to encourage programs that are innovative, reflect a high degree of
creative skill, deal with significant moral and social issues and
present challenging concepts and other subject matter that relate
to the world in which the viewer lives.
Television programs should not only reflect the influence of

the established institutions that shape our values and culture, but
also expose the dynamics of social change which bear upon our
lives.

To achieve these goals, television broadcasters should be
conversant with the general and specific needs, interests and aspirations of all the segments of the communities they serve. They
should affirmatively seek out responsible representatives of all
parts of their communities so that they may structure a broad range
of programs that will inform, enlighten the total audience.

Broadcasters should also develop programs directed toward
advancing the cultural and educational aspects of their communities.

To assure that broadcasters have the freedom to program
fully and responsibly, none of the provisions of this Code should be
construed as preventing or impeding broadcast of the broad range
of material necessary to help broadcasters fulfill their obligations
to operate in the public interest.

The challenge to the broadcaster is to determine how suitably
to present the complexities of human behavior. For television,
this requires exceptional awareness of considerations peculiar to
the medium.

Accordingly, in selecting program subjects and themes, great
care must be exercised to be sure that treatment and presentation
are made in good faith and not for the purpose of sensationalism or
to shock or exploit the audience or appeal to prurient interests or
morbid curiosity.

II.   Responsibility Toward Children

Broadcasters have a special responsibility to children. Programs designed primarily for children should take into account the
range of interests and needs of children, and should contribute to
the sound, balanced development of children.

In the course of a child's development, numerous social factors and forces, including television, affect the ability of the child
to make the transition to adult society.

The child's training and experience during the formative
years should include positive sets of values which will allow the
child to become a responsible adult, capable of coping with the
challenges of maturity.

Children should also be exposed, at the appropriate times,
to a reasonable range of the realities which exist in the world sufficient to help them make the transition to adulthood.

Because children are allowed to watch programs designed
primarily for adults, broadcasters should take this practice into
account in the presentation of material in such programs when
children may constitute a substantial segment of the audience.

All the standards set forth in this section apply to both program and commercial material designed and intended for viewing
by children.

III. Community Responsibility

1. Television broadcasters and their staffs occupy positions of unique responsibility in their communities and should conscientiously endeavor to be acquainted fully with the community's needs and characteristics in order better to serve the welfare of its citizens.

2. Requests for time for the placement of public service announcements or programs should be carefully reviewed with respect to the character and reputation of the group, campaign or organization involved, the public interest content of the message, and the manner of its presentation.

IV. Special Program Standards

1. Violence, physical or psychological, may only be projected in responsibly handled contexts, not used exploitatively. Programs involving violence should present the consequences of it to its victims and perpetrators.

Presentation of the details of violence should avoid the excessive, the gratuitous and the instructional.

The use of violence for its own sake and the detailed dwelling upon brutality or physical agony, by sight or by sound, are not permissible.

2. The treatment of criminal activities should always convey their social and human effects.

The presentation of techniques of crime in such detail as to be instructional or invite imitation shall be avoided.

3. Narcotic addiction shall not be presented except as a destructive habit. The use of illegal drugs or the abuse of legal drugs shall not be encouraged or shown as socially acceptable.

4. The use of gambling devices or scenes necessary to the development of plot or as appropriate background is acceptable only when presented with discretion and in moderation, and in a manner which would not excite interest in, or foster, betting nor be instructional in nature.

5. Telecasts of actual sports programs at which on-the-scene betting is permitted by law shall be presented in a manner in keeping with Federal, state and local laws, and should concentrate on the subject as a public sporting event.

6. Special precautions must be taken to avoid demeaning or ridiculing members of the audience who suffer from physical or mental afflictions or deformities.

7. Special sensitivity is necessary in the use of material relating to sex, race, color, creed, religious functionaries or rites, or national or ethnic derivation.

8. Obscene, indecent or profane matter, as proscribed by law, is unacceptable.

9. The presentation of marriage, the family and similarly important human relationships, and material with sexual connotations,

shall not be treated exploitatively or irresponsibly, but with sensitivity. Costuming and movements of all performers shall be handled in a similar fashion.

10. The use of liquor and the depiction of smoking in program content shall be de-emphasized. When shown, they should be consistent with plot and character development.

11. The creation of a state of hypnosis by act or detailed demonstration on camera is prohibited and hypnosis as a form of "parlor game" antics to create humorous situations within a comedy setting is forbidden.

12. Program material pertaining to fortune-telling, occultism, astrology, phrenology, palm-reading, numerology, mind-reading, character-reading, and the like is unacceptable if it encourages people to regard such fields as providing commonly accepted appraisals of life.

13. Professional advice, diagnosis and treatment will be presented in conformity with law and recognized professional standards.

14. Any technique whereby an attempt is made to convey information to the viewer by transmitting messages below the threshold of normal awareness is not permitted.

15. The use of animals, consistent with plot and character delineation, shall be in conformity with accepted standards of humane treatment.

16. Quiz and similar programs that are presented as contests of knowledge, information, skill or luck must, in fact, be genuine contests and the results must not be controlled by collusion with or between contestants, or by any other action which will favor one contestant against any other.

17. The broadcaster shall be constantly alert to prevent inclusion of elements within a program dictated by factors other than the requirements of the program itself. The acceptance of cash payments or other considerations in return for including scenic properties, the choice and identification of prizes, the selection of music and other creative program elements and inclusion of any identification of commercial products or services, their trade names or advertising slogan within the program are prohibited except in accordance with Sections 317 and 508 of the Communications Act.

18. Contests may not constitute a lottery.

19. No program shall be presented in a manner which through artifice or simulation would mislead the audience as to any material fact. Each broadcaster must exercise reasonable judgment to determine whether a particular method of presentation would constitute a material deception, or would be accepted by the audience as normal theatrical illusion.

20. A television broadcaster should not present fictional events or other non-news material as authentic news telecasts or announcements, nor should he permit dramatizations in any program which would give the false impression that the dramatized material constitutes news.

21. The standards of this Code covering program content are also understood to include, wherever applicable, the standards contained in the advertising section of the Code.

V. Treatment of News and Public Events

General

Television Code standards relating to the treatment of news and public events are, because of constitutional considerations, intended to be exhortatory. The standards set forth hereunder encourage high standards of professionalism in broadcast journalism. They are not to be interpreted as turning over to others the broadcaster's responsibility as to judgments necessary in news and public events programming.

News

1. A television station's news schedule should be adequate and well-balanced.

2. News reporting should be factual, fair and without bias.

3. A television broadcaster should exercise particular discrimination in the acceptance, placement and presentation of advertising in news programs so that such advertising should be clearly distinguishable from the news content.

4. At all times, pictorial and verbal material for both news and comment should conform to other sections of these standards, wherever such sections are reasonably applicable.

5. Good taste should prevail in the selection and handling of news:

Morbid, sensational or alarming details not essential to the factual report, especially in connection with stories of crime or sex, should be avoided. News should be telecast in such a manner as to avoid panic and unnecessary alarm.

6. Commentary and analysis should be clearly identified as such.

7. Pictorial material should be chosen with care and not presented in a misleading manner.

8. All news interview programs should be governed by accepted standards of ethical journalism, under which the interviewer selects the questions to be asked. Where there is advance agreement materially restricting an important or newsworthy area of questioning, the interviewer will state on the program that such limitation has been agreed upon. Such disclosure should be made if the person being interviewed requires that questions be submitted in advance or if he participates in editing a recording of the interview prior to its use on the air.

9. A television broadcaster should exercise due care in his supervision of content, format, and presentation of newscasts originated by his station, and in his selection of newscasters,

commentators, and analysts.

Public Events
     1. A television broadcaster has an affirmative responsibility
at all times to be informed of public events, and to provide coverage consonant with the ends of an informed and enlightened citizenry.
     2. The treatment of such events by a television broadcaster
should provide adequate and informed coverage.

VI. Controversial Public Issues

     1. Television provides a valuable forum for the expression
of responsible views on public issues of a controversial nature.   The
television broadcaster should seek out and develop with accountable
individuals, groups and organizations, programs relating to controversial public issues of import to his fellow citizens; and to give
fair representation to opposing sides of issues which materially affect the life or welfare of a substantial segment of the
public.
     2. Requests by individuals, groups or organizations for time
to discuss their views on controversial public issues, should be considered on the basis of their individual merits, and in the light of
the contribution which the use requested would make to the public
interest, and to a well-balanced program structure.
     3. Programs devoted to the discussion of controversial
public issues should be identified as such.   They should not be presented in a manner which would mislead listeners or viewers to believe that the program is purely of an entertainment, news, or
other character.
     4. Broadcasts in which stations express their own opinions
about issues of general public interest should be clearly identified
as editorials.   They should be unmistakably identified as statements
of station opinion and should be appropriately distinguished from
news and other program material.

VII.   Political Telecasts

     1. Political Telecasts should be clearly identified as such.
They should not be presented by a television broadcaster in a manner which would mislead listeners or viewers to believe that the
program is of any other character.
(Ref.: Communications Act of 1934, as amended, Secs. 315 and
317, and FCC Rules and Regulations, Secs. 3.654, 3.657, 3.663,
as discussed in NAB's "Political Broadcast Catechism & The Fairness Doctrine.")

VIII.   Religious Programs

     1. It is the responsibility of a television broadcaster to
make available to the community appropriate opportunity for religious presentations.
     2. Programs reach audiences of all creeds simultaneously.

Therefore, both the advocates of broad or ecumenical religious precepts, and the exponents of specific doctrines, are urged to present their positions in a manner conducive to viewer enlightenment on the role of religion in society.

3.   In the allocation of time for telecasts of religious programs the television station should use its best efforts to apportion such time fairly among responsible individuals, groups and organizations.

IX.   General Advertising Standards

1.   This Code establishes basic standards for all television broadcasting.   The principles of acceptability and good taste within the Program Standards section govern the presentation of advertising where applicable.   In addition, the Code establishes in this section special standards which apply to television advertising.

2.   A commercial television broadcaster makes his facilities available for the advertising of products and services and accepts commercial presentations for such advertising.   However, a television broadcaster should, in recognition of his responsibility to the public, refuse the facilities of his station to an advertiser where he has good reason to doubt the integrity of the advertiser, the truth of the advertising representations, or the compliance of the advertiser with the spirit and purpose of all applicable legal requirements.

3.   Identification of sponsorship must be made in all sponsored programs in accordance with the requirements of the Communications Act of 1934, as amended, and the Rules and Regulations of the Federal Communications Commission.

4.   Representations which disregard normal safety precautions shall be avoided.

Children shall not be represented, except under proper adult supervision, as being in contact with, or demonstrating a product recognized as potentially dangerous to them.

5.   In consideration of the customs and attitudes of the communities served, each television broadcaster should refuse his facilities to the advertisement of products and services, or the use of advertising scripts, which the station has good reason to believe would be objectionable to a substantial and responsible segment of the community.   These standards should be applied with judgment and flexibility, taking into consideration the characteristics of the medium, its home and family audience, and the form and content of the particular presentation.

6.   The advertising of hard liquor (distilled spirits) is not acceptable.

7.   The advertising of beer and wines is acceptable only when presented in the best of good taste and discretion, and is acceptable only subject to Federal and local laws (See Television Code Interpretation No. 4)

8.   Advertising by institutions or enterprises which in their

offers of instruction imply promises of employment or make exaggerated claims for the opportunities awaiting those who enroll for courses is generally unacceptable.

9.   The advertising of firearms/ammunition is acceptable provided it promotes the product only as sporting equipment and conforms to recognized standards of safety as well as all applicable laws and regulations.   Advertisements of firearms/ammunition by mail order are unacceptable.   The advertising of fireworks is acceptable subject to all applicable laws.

10.   The advertising of fortune-telling, occultism, astrology, phrenology, palm-reading, numerology, mind-reading, character-reading or subjects of a like nature is not permitted.

11.   Because all products of a personal nature create special problems, acceptability of such products should be determined with especial emphasis on ethics and the canons of good taste.   Such advertising of personal products as is accepted must be presented in a restrained and obviously inoffensive manner.

12.   The advertising of tip sheets, race track publications, or organizations seeking to advertise for the purpose of giving odds or promoting betting or lotteries is unacceptable.

13.   An advertiser who markets more than one product should not be permitted to use advertising copy devoted to an acceptable product for purposes of publicizing the brand name or other identification of a product which is not acceptable.

14.   "Bait-switch" advertising, whereby goods or services which the advertiser has no intention of selling are offered merely to lure the customer into purchasing higher-priced substitutes, is not acceptable.

15.   Personal endorsements (testimonials) shall be genuine and reflect personal experience.   They shall contain no statement that cannot be supported if presented in the advertiser's own words.

X.   Presentation of Advertising

1.   Advertising messages should be presented with courtesy and good taste; disturbing or annoying material should be avoided; every effort should be made to keep the advertising message in harmony with the content and general tone of the program in which it appears.

2.   The role and capability of television to market sponsors' products are well recognized.   In turn, this fact dictates that great care be exercised by the broadcaster to prevent the presentation of false, misleading or deceptive advertising.   While it is entirely appropriate to present a product in a favorable light and atmosphere, the presentation must not, by copy or demonstration, involve a material deception as to the characteristics, performance or appearance of the product.

Broadcast advertisers are responsible for making available, at the request of the Code Authority, documentation adequate to support the validity and truthfulness of claims, demonstrations and testimonials contained in their commercial messages.

3. The broadcaster and the advertiser should exercise special caution with the content and presentation of television commercials placed in or near programs designed for children. Exploitation of children should be avoided. Commercials directed to children should in no way mislead as to the product's performance and usefulness.

Appeals involving matters of health which should be determined by physicians should not be directed primarily to children.

4. Children's program hosts or primary cartoon characters shall not be utilized to deliver commercial messages within or adjacent to the programs which feature such hosts or cartoon characters. This provision shall also apply to lead-ins to commercials when such lead-ins contain sell copy or imply endorsement of the product by program host or primary cartoon character.

5. Appeals to help fictitious characters in television programs by purchasing the advertiser's product or service or sending for a premium should not be permitted, and such fictitious characters should not be introduced into the advertising message for such purposes.

6. Commercials for services or over-the-counter products involving health considerations are of intimate and far-reaching importance to the consumer. The following principles should apply to such advertising:

a. Physicians, dentists or nurses shall not be employed directly or by implication. These restrictions also apply to persons professionally engaged in medical services (e. g. , physical therapists, pharmacists, dental assistants, nurses' aides).

b. Visual representations of laboratory settings may be employed, provided they bear a direct relationship to bona fide research which has been conducted for the product or service. (See Television Code, X, 11) In such cases, laboratory technicians shall be identified as such and shall not be employed as spokesmen or in any other way speak on behalf of the product.

c. Institutional announcements not intended to sell a specific product or service to the consumer and public service announcements by non-profit organizations may be presented by accredited physicians, dentists or nurses, subject to approval by the broadcaster. An accredited professional is one who has met required qualifications and has been licensed in his resident state.

7. Advertising should offer a product or service on its positive merits and refrain from discrediting, disparaging or unfairly attacking competitors, competing products, other industries, professions or institutions.

8. A sponsor's advertising messages should be confined within the framework of the sponsor's program structure. A television broadcaster should avoid the use of commercial announcements which are divorced from the program either by preceding the introduction of the program (as in the case of so-called "cow-catcher"

announcements) or by following the apparent sign-off of the program (as in the case of so-called trailer or "hitch-hike" announcements). To this end, the program itself should be announced and clearly identified, both audio and video, before the sponsor's advertising material is first used, and should be signed off, both audio and video, after the sponsor's advertising material is last used.

9. Since advertising by television is a dynamic technique, a television broadcaster should keep under surveillance new advertising devices so that the spirit and purpose of these standards are fulfilled.

10. A charge for television time to churches and religious bodies is not recommended.

11. Reference to the results of bona fide research, surveys or tests relating to the product to be advertised shall not be presented in a manner so as to create an impression of fact beyond that established by the work that has been conducted.

ADVERTISING STANDARDS

XI. Advertising of Medical Products

1. The advertising of medical products presents considerations of intimate and far-reaching importance to the consumer because of the direct bearing on his health.

2. Because of the personal nature of the advertising of medical products, claims that a product will effect a cure and the indiscriminate use of such words as "safe," "without risk," "harmless," or terms of similar meaning should not be accepted in the advertising of medical products on television stations.

3. A television broadcaster should not accept advertising material which in his opinion offensively describes or dramatizes distress or morbid situations involving ailments, by spoken word, sound or visual effects.

XII. Contests

1. Contests shall be conducted with fairness to all entrants, and shall comply with all pertinent laws and regulations. Care should be taken to avoid the concurrent use of the three elements which together constitute a lottery--prize, chance and consideration.

2. All contest details, including rules, eligibility requirements, opening and termination dates should be clearly and completely announced and/or shown, or easily accessible to the viewing public, and the winners' names should be released and prizes awarded as soon as possible after the close of the contest.

3. When advertising is accepted which requests contestants to submit items of product identification or other evidence of purchase of products, reasonable facsimiles thereof should be made acceptable unless the award is based upon skill and not upon chance.

    4. All copy pertaining to any contest (except that which is required by law) associated with the exploitation or sale of the sponsor's product or service, and all references to prizes or gifts offered in such connection should be considered a part of and included in the total time allowances as herein provided. (See Television Code, XIV)

XIII. Premiums and Offers

    1. Full details of proposed offers should be required by the television broadcaster for investigation and approved before the first announcement of the offer is made to the public.

    2. A final date for the termination of an offer should be announced as far in advance as possible.

    3. Before accepting for telecast offers involving a monetary consideration, a television broadcaster should satisfy himself as to the integrity of the advertiser and the advertiser's willingness to honor complaints indicating dissatisfaction with the premium by returning the monetary consideration.

    4. There should be no misleading descriptions or visual representations of any premiums or gifts which would distort or enlarge their value in the minds of the viewers.

    5. Assurances should be obtained from the advertiser that premiums offered are not harmful to person or property.

    6. Premiums should not be approved which appeal to superstitition on the basis of "luck-bearing" powers or otherwise.

XIV. Time Standards for Non-Program Material

In order that the time for non-program material and its placement shall best serve the viewer, the following standards are set forth in accordance with sound television practice:

    1. Non-Program Material Definition: non-program material, in both prime time and all other time, includes billboards, commercials, promotional announcements and all credits in excess of 30 seconds per program, except in feature films. In no event should credits exceed 40 seconds per program. The 40-second limitation on credits shall not apply, however, in any situation governed by a contract entered into before October 1, 1971. Public service announcements and promotional announcements for the same program are excluded from this definition.

    2. Allowable Time for Non-Program Material.

        a. In prime time on network affiliated stations, non-program material shall not exceed nine minutes 30 seconds in any 60-minute period. In prime time on independent stations, non-program material shall not exceed 12 minutes in any 60-minute period.

    In the event that news programming is included within the three and one-half hour prime time period, not more than one 30-minute segment of news programming may be governed by time

standards applicable to all other time. Prime time is a continuous
period of not less than three and one-half consecutive hours per
broadcast day as designated by the station between the hours of
6:00 PM and Midnight.
     b. In all other time, non-program material shall not
exceed 16 minutes in any 60-minute period.
     c. Children's Weekend Programming Time--Defined as
that contiguous period of time between the hours of 7:00 AM
and 2:00 PM on Saturday and Sunday. In programming designed primarily for children within this time period, non-program material shall not exceed 12 minutes in any 60-minute
period.
     3. Program Interruptions.
     a. Definition: A program interruption is any occurrence
of non-program material within the main body of the program.
     b. In prime time, the number of program interruptions
shall not exceed two within any 30-minute program, or four within any 60-minute program. Programs longer than 60 minutes
shall be pro-rated at two interruptions per half-hour. The number of interruptions in 60-minute variety shows shall not exceed
five.
     c. In all other time, the number of interruptions shall
not exceed four within any 30-minute program period.
     d. In children's weekend time, as above defined in 2c, the
number of program interruptions shall not exceed two within any 30-
minute program or four within any 60-minute program.
     e. In both prime time and all other time, the following
interruption standard shall apply within programs of 15 minutes or
less in length:
          5-minute program -- 1 interruption;
          10-minute program -- 2 interruptions;
          15-minute program -- 2 interruptions.
     f. News, weather, sports and special events programs
are exempt from the interruption standard because of the nature of
such programs.
     4. No more than four non-program material announcements
shall be scheduled consecutively within programs, and no more than
three non-program material announcements shall be scheduled
consecutively during station breaks. The consecutive non-program material limitation shall not apply to a single sponsor
who wishes to further reduce the number of interruptions in
the program.
     5. A multiple product announcement is one in which two
or more products or services are presented within the framework of
a single announcement. A multiple product announcement shall not
be scheduled in a unit of time less than 60 seconds, except where
integrated so as to appear to the viewer as a single message. A
multiple product announcement shall be considered integrated and
counted as a single announcement if:
     a. the products or services are related and interwoven
within the framework of the announcement (related products or services shall be defined as those having a common character, purpose
and use); and

b. the voice(s), setting, background and continuity are used consistently throughout so as to appear to the viewer as a single message.

Multiple product announcements of 60 seconds in length or longer not meeting this definition of integration shall be counted as two or more announcements under this section of the Code. This provision shall not apply to retail or service establishments. (Effective September 1, 1973)

6. The use of billboards, in prime time and all other time, shall be confined to programs sponsored by a single or alternate week advertiser and shall be limited to the products advertised in the program.

7. Reasonable and limited identification of prizes and donors names where the presentation of contest awards or prizes is a necessary part of program content shall not be included as non-program material as defined above.

8. Programs presenting women's service features, shopping guides, fashion shows, demonstrations and similar material provide a special service to the public in which certain material normally classified as non-program is an informative and necessary part of the program content. Because of this, the time standards may be waived by the Code Authority to a reasonable extent on a case-by-case basis.

9. Gratuitous references in a program to a non-sponsor's product or service should be avoided except for normal guest identification.

10. Stationary backdrops or properties in television presentations showing the sponsor's name or product, the name of his product, his trade-mark or slogan should be used only incidentally and should not obtrude on program interest or entertainment.

INTERPRETATIONS

Interpretation No. 1

June 7, 1956, Revised June 9, 1958
"Pitch" Programs

The "pitchman" technique of advertising on television is inconsistent with good broadcast practice and generally damages the reputation of the industry and the advertising profession.

Sponsored program-length segments consisting substantially of continuous demonstrations or sales presentation, violate not only the time standards established in the Code but the broad philosophy of improvement implicit in the voluntary Code operation and are not acceptable.

Interpretation No. 2

June 7, 1956
Hollywood Film Promotion

The presentation of commentary or film excerpts from

current theatrical releases in some instances may constitute commercial material under the Time Standards for Non-Program Material. Specifically, for example, when such presentation, directly
or by inference, urges viewers to attend, it shall be counted against
the commercial allowance for the program of which it is a part.

Interpretation No. 3

January 23, 1959
Prize Identification
        Aural and/or visual prize identification of up to ten seconds
duration may be deemed "reasonable and limited" under the language
of Paragraph 7 of the Time Standards for Non-Program Material.
Where such identification is longer than ten seconds, the entire
announcement or visual presentation will be charged against the
total commercial time for the program period.

Interpretation No. 4

March 4, 1965
Drinking on Camera
        Paragraph 7, Section IX, General Advertising Standards,
states that the "advertising of beer and wine is acceptable only
when presented in the best of good taste and discretion." This requires that commercials involving beer and wine avoid any representation of on-camera drinking.

"Children's TV Advertising Statement of Principles"

Because of special considerations for children, the following principles shall apply to all advertising designed primarily for children:
        1.   Broadcasters believe that advertising of products or ser-
vices normally used by children can serve to inform children not
only of the attributes of the product/service but also of many aspects of the society and world in which they live.
        2.   Everyone involved in the creation, production and pre-
sentation of advertisements to children has a responsibility to assure that such material serves a positive function and avoids being
exploitative of or inappropriate to a child's still developing cognitive
abilities and sense of values.
        3.   Creative concepts, audio or video techniques and language
addressed to children, shall be non-exploitative in manner, style
and tone.
        4.   Documentation adequate to support the truthfulness and
accuracy of all claims and representations contained in the audio
or video of the advertisement must be made available to broadcasters and/or Code Authority.
        5.   The disclosure of information on the characteristics and
functional aspects of a product/service is strongly encouraged.
This includes, where applicable, relevant ingredient and nutritional

information. In order to reduce the possibility of misimpressions being created, all such information shall be presented in a straightforward manner devoid of language or production techniques which may exaggerate or distort the characteristics or functions of the product.

6. Given the importance of sound health and nutritional practices, advertisements for edibles shall be in accord with the commonly accepted principles of good eating and seek to establish the proper role of the advertised product within the framework of a balanced regimen. Any representation of the relationship between an edible and energy must be documented and accurately depicted.

7. Any representation of a child's concept of himself/herself or of his/her relationship to others must be constructively handled. When self-concept claims are employed, the role of the product/service in affecting such promised benefits as strength, growth, physical prowess and growing up must accurately reflect documented evidence.

8. Appeals shall not be used which directly or by implication contend that if children have a product, they are better than their peers or lacking it will not be accepted by their peers.

9. Advertisements shall portray attitudes and practices consistent with generally recognized social values and customs.

10. Material shall not be used which can reasonably be expected to frighten children or provoke anxiety, nor shall material be used which contains a portrayal of or appeal to violent, dangerous or otherwise antisocial behavior.

11. Advertisements shall be consistent with generally recognized standards of safety.

In addition to the preceding Principles, all advertising designed primarily for children is subject to review under the standards contained in the Television Code. The Principles also cover established Television Code guidelines, interpretations and policies which relate to various aspects of children's advertising.

BUILDING CONSTRUCTION REGULATORS

BUILDING OFFICIALS AND CODE ADMINISTRATORS INTERNATION-
AL, INC. (BOCA International)
    1313 E. 60th St., Chicago, Ill. 60637
    Richard L. Sanderson, Executive Director

Membership: Building Officials and Code Administrators International, founded in 1915, is a professional association--"a non-profit municipal service organization ... in the field of building code administration and enforcement in particular, and in community development in general. " Active membership in BOCA International "is restricted to governmental units, departments or bureaus that administer, formulate, or enforce laws, ordinances, rules or regulations relating to buildings, housing, city planning or zoning. " Such "active members" are entitled to representation in the BOCA based on the population of the jurisdiction:

      to 50, 000 population--2 representatives;
      to 150, 000 population--4 representatives;
      over 150, 000 population--6 representatives.

"Individual active members" are eligible for membership if they are employees "of a federal or state governmental unit" qualified for jurisdictional active membership, but are not active members of BOCA. Among the organization's 3000 members are administrators and specialists in code administration, such as mayors, planners, managers, architects, educators, engineers, lawyers.

Code of Ethics: The conduct guide for BOCA International members is the Code of Ethics, developed by the Ethics Committee of the group and adopted in 1969. The principles of professional conduct are given in the form of a pledge emphasizing public safety and interest, relationships with the public and colleagues, prohibition of use of professional position for private advantage, including acceptance of obligating gifts, favors, or services. The Code is enforced by the Ethics Committee, which investigates alleged violations of the conduct guide and recommends to the BOCA Executive Committee discipline for substantial breaches of the ethical principles, including expulsion from the organization.

Professional Insignia: The BOCA International official emblem is a round seal showing the continent of North America centered, with the name, "Building Officials Code Administrators, " in a circular bordering band; initials of the association, "BOCA, " in a banding arc at the top of the design, and the final portion of the group name, "International, " in a comparable arc at the bottom of the emblem. Colors of the insignia vary--letterhead: brown on buff; publications: blue on white; or white on blue. The colors of the logotype are black on white, with circular banding border in red, and lettering at the top and bottom of the design in gray.

Bibliography:
> Building Officials and Code Administrators International. <u>Facts</u>
> <u>About BOCA International.</u> Folder.
> Describes BOCA programs and services, including its stand-
> ard Codes of Building, Fire Prevention, Mechanics and Plumb-
> ing; and such Code interpretation. Gives membership re-
> quirements.

"Code of Ethics"

I shall place public safety above all other interests.

I shall place public interest above individual, group or special interests and shall consider my profession as an opportunity
to serve society.

I shall maintain the highest standards of integrity.

I shall treat all persons courteously, equally, and fairly.

I shall conduct myself at all times in such a manner as to create
respect for myself, the jurisdiction I represent and Building
Officials and Code Administrators International.

I shall refrain from the use of my position to secure advantage or
favor for myself, my family or my friends.

I shall refrain from representing any private interests in any business or technical affairs of the organization.

I shall refrain from using unfair means to secure an advantage in
the organization or to knowingly injure any individual, company or association to gain such advantage.

I shall not accept, nor offer, any gift, favor or service that might
tend to influence me in the discharge of my duties.

I shall carry on my contacts with other members of the organization
in a spirit of fairness with loyalty and fidelity to the aims
and purposes of Building Officials and Code Administrators
International.

BUSINESSMEN

UNITED STATES DEPARTMENT OF COMMERCE
14th Between E St. and Constitution Ave., N. W.
Washington, D. C. 20230

Code of Ethics: Pursuing the program--"to help the American business community to develop techniques and programs to help itself"
--in 1961 Secretary of Commerce Luther H. Hodges appointed a

Business Ethics Advisory Council to explore "approaches to the development of ethical guidelines that might be useful to the business
community." This action to develop conduct guidelines for businessmen was taken "following the decision of Federal Judge Ganey in
the electrical industry anti-trust case," which had undermined public
confidence in business.

The Council, composed of 26 leading businessmen, educators,
clergymen, and publishers, issued as a first report in January
1962 several documents designed as "starting points from which
businessmen" would "be moved to initiate programs of ethical inquiry in their own companies":
> Statement on Business Ethics and A Call for Action;
> Questions for Businessmen.

Bibliography:
> Hodges, Luther H. The Business Conscience. N. Y., Prentice
> > Hall, 1963. 250 pages.
> > Secretary of Commerce Hodges writing on business ethics
> > discusses value of ethical codes, ethics in education and the
> > organization.
> Thau, Theodore L. "The Business Ethics Advisory Council:
> > An Organization for the Improvement of Ethical Per-
> > formance." Annals of the American Academy of Political
> > and Social Science 343:128-141 September 1962.
> > In an Annals issue devoted to "The Ethics of Business Enter-
> > prise," the Executive Secretary of the Business Ethics Ad-
> > visory Council of the U. S. Department of Commerce writes
> > the history of the Council. An appendix gives the text of
> > the "Statement of Business Ethics..." and the "Questions for
> > Businessmen."
> United States. Business Ethics Advisory Council. Department
> > of Commerce. A Statement on Business Ethics and a
> > Call for Action, with Some Questions for Businessmen.
> > 10 pages. Pamphlet. Washington, D. C., Government
> > Printing Office, 1962. $. 10.
> > Inspirational statements regarding business ethics, and
> > questions "designed to facilitate the examination by American
> > businessmen of their ethical standards and performance."

"Statement of Business Ethics
and a Call for Action"

The ethical standards of American businessmen, like those
of the American people, are founded upon our religious heritage
and our traditions of social, political, and economic freedom. They
impose upon each man high obligations in his dealings with his fel-
lowmen, and make all men stewards of the common good. Immu-
table, well-understood guides to performance generally are effective,
but new ethical problems are created constantly by the ever-increasing
complexity of society. In business, as in every other activity,

therefore, men must continually seek to identify new and appropriate standards.

Over the years, American businessmen in the main have continually endeavored to demonstrate their responsiveness to their ethical obligations in our free society. They have themselves initiated and welcomed from others calls for the improvement of their ethical performance, regarding each as a challenge to establish and meet ever higher ethical goals. In consequence, the ethical standards that should guide business enterprise in this country have steadily risen over the years, and this has had a profound influence on the performance of the business community.

As the ethical standards and conduct of American private enterprise have improved, so also has there developed a public demand for proper performance and a keen sensitivity to lapses from those standards. The full realization by the business community of its future opportunities and, indeed, the maintenance of public confidence requires a continuing pursuit of the highest standards of ethical conduct.

Attainment of this objective is not without difficulty. Business enterprises, large and small, have relationships in many directions--with stockholders and other owners, employees, customers, suppliers, government, and the public in general. The traditional emphasis on freedom, competition, and progress in our economic system often brings the varying interests of these groups into conflict, so that many difficult and complex ethical problems can arise in any enterprise. While all relationships of an enterprise to these groups are regulated in some degree by law, compliance with law can only provide a minimum standard of conduct. Beyond legal obligations, the policies and actions of businessmen must be based upon a regard for the proper claims of all affected groups.

Moreover, in many business situations the decision that must be made is not the simple choice between absolute right and absolute wrong. The decisions of business frequently must be made in highly complex and ever-changing circumstances, and at times involve either adhering to earlier standards or developing new ones. Such decisions affect profoundly not only the business enterprise, but our society as a whole. Indeed, the responsible position of American business--both large and small--obligates each participant to lead rather than follow.

A weighty responsibility therefore rests upon all those who manage business enterprises, as well as upon all others who influence the environment in which business operates. In the final analysis, however, the primary moral duty to establish high ethical standards and adequate procedures for their enforcement in each enterprise must rest with its policymaking body--its board of directors and its top management.

We, therefore, now propose that current efforts be expanded and intensified and that new efforts now be undertaken by the American business community to hasten its attainment of those high ethical standards that derive from our heritage and traditions. We urge all enterprises, business groups, and associations to accept respon-

sibility--each for itself and in its own most appropriate way--to
develop methods and programs for encouraging and sustaining these
efforts on a continuous basis.   We believe in this goal, we accept
it, and we encourage all to pursue its attainment.

"Some Questions for Businessmen"

The following questions are designed to facilitate the examination by American businessmen of their ethical standards and performance.   They are intended to illustrate the kinds of questions
that must be identified and considered by each business enterprise
if it is to achieve compliance with those high ethical standards that
derive from our heritage and traditions.   Every reader will
think of others.   No single list can possibly encompass all of
the demands for ethical judgments that must be met by men
in business.

1.   General Understanding:

Do we have in our organization current, well-considered
statements of the ethical principles that should guide our officers
and employees in specific situations that arise in our business
activities, both domestic and foreign?   Do we revise these statements periodically to cover new situations and changing laws and
social patterns?
Have those statements been the fruit of discussion in which
all members of policy-determining management have had an opportunity to participate?
Have we given to our officers and employees at all levels
sufficient motivation to search out ethical factors in business problems and apply high ethical standards in their solution?   What have
we done to eliminate opposing pressures?
Have we provided officers and employees with an easily
accessible means of obtaining counsel on and resolution of ethical
problems that may arise in their activities?   Do they use it?
Do we know whether our officers and employees apply in
their daily activities the ethical standards we have promulgated?
Do we reward those who do so and penalize those who do not?

2.   Compliance with law:

Having in mind the complexities and everchanging patterns
of modern law and government regulation:
What are we doing to make sure that our officers and employees are informed about and comply with laws and regulations
affecting their activities?
Have we made clear that it is our policy to obey even those
laws which we may think unwise and seek to have changed?
Do we have adequate internal checks on our compliance with
law?

Have we established a simple and readily available procedure
to seek legal guidance in their activities?   Do they use it?

3.   Conflicts of interest:

Do we have a current, well-considered statement of policy
regarding potential conflict of interest problems of our directors,
officers and employees? If so, does it cover conflicts which may
arise in connection with such activities as: transactions with or
involving our company; acquiring interests in or performing services
for our customers, distributors, suppliers and competitors; buying
and selling our company's securities; or the personal undertaking of
what might be called company opportunities?

What mechanism do we have for enabling our directors,
officers and employees to make ethical judgments when conflicts
of interest do arise?

Do we require regular reports, or do we leave it to our
directors, officers and employees to disclose such activities voluntarily?

4.   Entertainment, gifts, and expenses:

Have we defined our company policy on accepting and making
expenditures for gifts and entertainment?   Are the criteria as to
occasion and amount clearly stated or are they left merely to the
judgment of the officer or employee?

Do we disseminate information about our company policy to
the organizations with which we deal?

Do we require adequate reports of both the giving and receiving of gifts and entertainment; are they supported in sufficient
detail; are they subject to review by appropriate authority; and
could the payment or receipt be justified to our stockholders, the
government, and the public?

5.   Customers and suppliers:

Have we taken appropriate steps to keep our advertising and
sales representations truthful and fair?   Are these steps effective?

How often do we review our advertising, literature, labels,
and packaging?   Do they give our customers a fair understanding
of the true quality, quantity, price and function of our products?
Does our service as well as our product measure up to our basic
obligations and our representations?

Do we fairly make good on flaws and defects?   Is this a
matter of stated policy?   Do we know that our employees, distributors, dealers and agents follow it?

Do we avoid favoritism and discrimination and otherwise
treat our customers and suppliers fairly and equitably in all of our
dealings with them?

6.   Social responsibilities:

Every business enterprise has manifold responsibilities to

the society of which it is a part. The prime legal and social obligation of the managers of a business is to operate it for the long-
term profit of its owners. Concurrent social responsibilities pertain to a company's treatment of its past, present and prospective
employees and to its various relationships with customers, suppliers,
government, the community and the public at large. These responsibilities may often be, or appear to be, in conflict, and at times
a management's recognition of its broad responsibilities may affect
the amount of an enterprise's immediate profits and the means of
attaining them.

The problems that businessmen must solve in this area
are often exceedingly perplexing. One may begin his reflections
on this subject by asking--

Have we reviewed our company policies in the light of our
responsibilities to society? Are our employees aware of the interaction between our business policies and our social responsibilities?

Do we have a clearly understood concept of our obligation
to assess our responsibilities to stockholders, employees, customers,
suppliers, our community and the public?

Do we recognize and impress upon all our officers and employees the fact that our free enterprise system and our individual
business enterprises can thrive and grow only to the extent that
they contribute to the welfare of our country and its people?

CHEMISTS

AMERICAN CHEMICAL SOCIETY (ACS)
    1155 Sixteenth St., N. W., Washington, D. C. 20036
    Dr. Robert W. Cairns, Executive Director

Membership: The American Chemical Society, founded in 1876
and with a present (1973) membership of 110, 000, is a scientific
and educational association of professional chemists and chemical
engineers. There are two categories of membership: "member"
and "associate member." In general, a member must have at least
a bachelor's degree in chemistry or chemical engineering and from
two to five years of work experience. Associate members, in general, have completed 3/4th of a curriculum leading to a bachelor's
degree, with at least 24 semester hours in chemistry or chemical
engineering.

There also are student affiliates, local section and division
affiliates, and corporation associates, none of whom are members.
There are no fellows or honorary categories, though persons who
do not meet the normal requirements but have "exceptional achievement" in the field may become members in certain circumstances.

Emeritus members have had at least 35 years of paid membership
and are either retired or over 70 years of age.

Code of Ethics: The ACS guide to professional conduct is the
Chemist's Creed, approved by the Council of the Society on September 14, 1965. This Creed, in the form of brief statements, defines the chemist's responsibility to the public, to science, to his
profession, to his employer, to himself, to his employees, students,
associates, and clients. There are no specific provisions for interpretation or enforcement of these professional guidelines, but
members may be dropped for "charges of conduct."

Professional Insignia: In 1908 at its meeting in Baltimore, the
American Chemical Society appointed a committee of three to consider the question of a permanent badge for the Society. The
following year this committee
presented a design--submitted
by Tiffany & Company, one
of a number of proposed emblems submitted by various
firms--which, with some
modifications from its original form, was recommended
for adoption as the official
pin of ACS. The design was
adopted as the official badge,
and at its 1910 meeting the
Society voted that the official
colors of the organization be
"cobalt blue and gold" (Constitution, Article I, Section
3).

        The official insignia is
described in the American
Chemical Society Constitution (Article I, Section 4):
        "The Society's insignia shall consist of the device of a
        square with one of the points forming the top and another
        the bottom of the emblem; the upper half of the square so
        placed, triangular in shape, shall contain the figure of a
        phoenix rising from the flame, typical of chemical activity
        and of the birth of new substance through the energy of
        chemical change; the lower half of the square shall contain
        the letters ACS and a small Liebig bulb; the whole, when
        used in the form of a pin, shall be finished with cobalt
        blue enamel and gold."

Bibliography:
        American Chemical Society. Charter, Constitution, and Bylaws.
                As revised through January 1, 1972. 17 pages.
                Includes membership requirements; description of insignia.
                        . The Chemist's Creed. 1954. 1 page.
                Professional responsibilities of the chemist.

_____. History of the ACS Emblem. 2 pages. Typed manu-
script.
Development and description of the official insignia of the ACS,
and the Society colors--cobalt blue and gold.

"The Chemist's Creed"

As a chemist, I have a responsibility:

To the public
to propagate a true understanding of chemical science, avoiding
premature, false, or exaggerated statements, to discourage enterprises or practices inimical to the public interest or welfare, and
to share with other citizens a responsibility for the right and beneficent use of scientific discoveries.

To my science
to search for its truths by use of the scientific method, and to enrich it by my own contributions for the good of humanity.

To my profession
to uphold its dignity as a foremost branch of learning and practice,
to exchange ideas and information through its societies and publications, to give generous recognition to the work of others, and to
refrain from undue advertising.

To my employer
to serve him undividedly and zealously in mutual interest, guarding
his concerns and dealing with them as I would my own.

To myself
to maintain my professional integrity as an individual, to strive to
keep abreast of my profession, to hold the highest ideals of personal honor, and to live an active, well-rounded, and useful life.

To my employees
to treat them as associates, being ever mindful of their physical
and mental well-being, giving them encouragement in their work,
as much freedom for personal development as is consistent with
the proper conduct of work, and compensating them fairly, both
financially and by acknowledgment of their scientific contributions.

To my students and associates
to be a fellow learner with them, to strive for clarity and direct-
ness of approach, to exhibit patience and encouragement, and to
lose no opportunity for stimulating them to carry on the great
tradition.

To my clients
to be a faithful and incorruptible agent, respecting confidence, advising honesty, and charging fairly.

CHIROPRACTORS

AMERICAN CHIROPRACTIC ASSOCIATION (ACA)
2200 Grand Ave., Des Moines, Iowa 50312
Louis O. Gearhart, D. C., Executive Director

Membership: The American Chiropractic Association, founded in
1963 and with a present (1973) membership of 8000, is a professional association of chiropractors. "Members" of ACA qualify
for membership
>   "must be graduates of a four-year resident course of a
>   chiropractic college and must be licensed in the state" of
>   practice, "unless that state has no chiropractic licensing
>   laws" (Bylaws, Article III, Section A).

Code of Ethics: To carry out its objective concerning ethics--
"To establish and maintain the standards of ... ethics" (Bylaws,
Article II, Section E)--the ACA adopted a Code of Ethics in June
1966. This Code, in its most recent edition of July 1, 1971, sets
forth general principles concerning a chiropractor's duties and obligations to patients, colleagues, and the public. The Code is enforced by the executive board of governors, which receives complaints of unethical conduct in writing, investigates complaints, and
hold hearings. Disciplinary action for ethical code violation includes reprimand, suspension, or expulsion from ACA membership
(Bylaws, Article III, Section C).

Professional Insignia: The official emblem of the American Chiropractic Association, developed
from designs submitted by members in an emblem contest in
1964, is a round design divided
into quarters by a centered
cross, the vertical arms of
which contain a winged figure
with outstretched arms, surmounted by a torch; the base
of the torch bears the organization initials, "ACA," and a
band entwining the figure the
legend, "Health," and "Chiropractic"; the letters "D" and
"C" (signifying "Doctor of
Chiropractic") are given in
the lower left and right quadrants of the design; the name
of the organization, "American Chiropractic Association,"

appears in one of the bordering bands, at the top of the emblem, "Member" at the bottom of the design, flanked by foliage sprays. The color of the emblem is shown variously--gold on white (letterhead), black on gold (publication), black on gold, with quadrants in red (display emblem).

Bibliography:
American Chiropractic Association. Charter Provisions and Bylaws. Amended edition, 1971. 29 pages.
Contains membership qualifications, disciplinary provisions for enforcement of Code of Ethics, and provides for--but does not specify--official emblem.
_____. Code of Ethics. Amended edition, 1971. 15 pages. Professional conduct guide.

"Code of Ethics"

The scope of a Code of Chiropractic Ethics comprises duties and obligations of chiropractors and patients, the duties and obligations of chiropractors to each other, and the reciprocal obligations of chiropractors and the public.

Fundamental Principles

The transcendent principles upon which chiropractic ethics are based are these:
1.   The ultimate end and object of the chiropractor's effort should be: "The greatest good for the patient."
2.   The rules of conduct of chiropractor and patient, and of chiropractors toward each other, should be but facets of the Golden Rule: "Therefore all things whatsoever ye would that men should do to you, do ye even so to them."
It naturally follows that the various articles of this Code are but special applications of these great principles.

Part 1

RECIPROCAL DUTIES AND OBLIGATIONS OF CHIROPRACTORS AND THEIR PATIENTS

Article 1.   Duties of the Chiropractor to the Patient.

Section 1.   The chiropractic profession has for its objective the greatest service it can render humanity.   Therefore, financial gain becomes a secondary consideration.
Section 2.   The chiropractor should hold himself in constant readiness to respond to calls of the sick. He should bear in mind the great responsibility his vocation involves and should so conduct himself as to acquire the confidence and respect of his patients. The chiropractor is bound to keep secret whatever he may hear or observe respecting the private affairs of his patient and the family,

while in the discharge of his professional duties.   Should it be
evident, however, that such secrecy would result in harm to others,
it becomes his duty to protect the innocent party or parties.   Occasions may arise, however, when he may be compelled by law
to reveal some such confidences in the interests of the commonwealth.

Section 3.   The chiropractor should attend his patient as
often as is necessary to insure continued favorable progress, but
should avoid unnecessary visits lest he expose himself to being accused of mercenary motives.

Section 4.   A chiropractor should not express gloomy fore-
bodings regarding a patient's condition nor magnify the gravity of
the case.   He should endeavor to be cheerful and hopeful in mind
and manner, thus inspiring confidence and courage in the patient.
However, it is the chiropractor's duty to acquaint some judicious
friend or relative of the patient with the true facts, should the
case prove to be of a serious nature.

Section 5.   While the chiropractor has the right to select
his cases, once having accepted one he should not abandon it because it seems incurable or for any other reason, unless he gives
the patient or the patient's friends or relatives sufficient notice of
withdrawal to permit them to secure other attendance.

Section 6.   Since a patient has the right to dismiss a chiropractor for reasons satisfactory to himself, so likewise the chiropractor may decline to attend patients when self respect or dignity
seem to him to require this step; as, for example, when a patient
persistently refuses to follow directions.

Section 7.   In difficult or protracted cases consultations are
advisable, and the chiropractor should be ready to act upon any
desire the patient may express for a consultation, even though he
may not himself feel the need for it.   Nothing is so likely to retain
the patient's confidence as sincerity in this respect.

Section 8.   The intimate relation into which the chiropractor
is brought with his patient gives him the opportunity to exercise a
powerful moral influence, which should always be used in the best
possible manner.   The chiropractor may sometimes be asked to
assist in practices of questionable propriety.   Among these may be
mentioned the pretense of disease in order to avoid jury or military
duty; the concealment of organic disease in order to secure favorable life insurance; or the procurement of abortion when not necessary to save the life of the mother.   To all such propositions the
chiropractor should present an inflexible opposition.

Article II.   Duties of Patients to Their Chiropractors.

Section 1.   Since chiropractors are required by the nature of
their profession to sacrifice comfort, ease, and even their health
for the welfare of their patients, it forthwith becomes the duty of
patients to understand this and to realize that they have certain
obligations toward their chiropractors.

Section 2.   The patient should select a chiropractor in whose
knowledge, skill, and integrity he can place confidence.   A chiro-

practor once having been selected should not be dismissed for light
reasons, because the chiropractor who is acquainted with the conditions, tendencies, and temperaments of a family, can more successfully handle their cases.
     Section 3.   The patient should consult his chiropractor as
early as possible after signs of illness.   He should unreservedly
state any factors he may have in mind that might contribute to his
condition, with the realization that all such statements are of a
confidential nature.
     Section 4.   The patient should obey his chiropractor's direc-
tions as regards frequency of adjustments, diet, sanitation, and
other hygienic measures that may be indicated in his case.   Nor
should he permit himself to deviate from the outlined course
through any advice from outsiders without first consulting his
chiropractor.
     Section 5.   If the patient desires a consultation, he should
make a frank statement to that effect.   On the other hand, if he
wishes to dismiss his chiropractor he should, in justice and
common courtesy, state his reasons in a friendly manner.   Such
a course need not of necessity change the social relations of
the parties.

                                   Part 2

                   DUTIES OF CHIROPRACTORS TO THE
                   PROFESSION AND TO EACH OTHER

Article I.   Duties to the Profession.

     Section 1.   Inasmuch as the chiropractor has of his own free
will and accord chosen chiropractic as his vocation, he must be
willing to assume certain obligations.   Since he is about to profit
from the scientific labor of his predecessors and associates, it becomes his duty to enrich the scientific lore; to elevate the position
of the profession; and always to conduct himself as a gentleman of
pure character and high moral standards.
     Section 2.   The honor and dignity of the chiropractic pro-
fession may best be upheld, its sphere of influence expanded, and
its science advanced through the association of all chiropractors in
state and national organizations.   Hence it is the duty of each chiropractor to associate himself with such bodies.
     Section 3.   The individual chiropractic physician, or doctor
of chiropractic, or chiropractor, shall refrain from personal advertising in order to extend the sphere of respect, recognition and
integrity of the profession.
     Personal advertising is defined as that which in substance
deals with the particular abilities, features, or accomplishments of
the individual.   At no time will a doctor of chiropractic make known
his superiority over that of another, verbal or written--this act
shall be considered as a violation of this Code.   An ACA member
shall never employ a professional agent.

Direct mail public relations to the patient shall contain material of education about chiropractic. At no time will mailed material be flamboyant or showy, make promise of cure, free examination or consultation, special technics or methods, or imply superiority in any manner. Further, the material must not castigate other health sciences or make claims that cannot be substantiated by laboratory and diagnostic procedures. The material should never contain statements of any kind that might be construed as false or misleading.

Group or institutional sponsorship of advertising or public relations news releases is held in the highest regard by the ACA and when utilized must be identified with the group, association or society sponsors and not that of any individual. Radio and TV talks or programs shall propound factual educational material beneficial to the profession and shall not reflect the personal philosophy of any one doctor of chiropractic.

An ACA member shall not employ a solicitor or other agent for the purposes of soliciting patients.

Professional announcements concerning--opening office, closing office, addition of personnel, removal of office--shall be limited to four insertions in all communications media.

Signs used to designate chiropractic offices and clinics shall be of the size and fashion utilized by the other professions in the area or community.

Telephone directory listing is restricted to name, address, hours, phone number and location. An 'if no answer' designation may be used in conjunction with the listing. No display ads are permitted. Type style shall be light face, bold face type is not permitted.

Nothing in this section shall be in conflict with state statutes which regulate professional advertising.

'By their works ye shall know them' is a statement of truth. The best possible public relations is the 'word-of-mouth' commendations of a satisfied public, and this can be procured only through conscientious endeavor and well merited results.

Section 4. It is equally derogatory to professional character for a chiropractor to hold a patent for any special technic, method, device, or appliance that might be applicable to the practice of chiropractic, or to keep secret the nature of any such things. Such concealment or restriction is inconsistent with the beneficence and liberality which should characterize the chiropractic profession, because it is the duty of the chiropractor to avail himself of every opportunity to observe the action and study the merits of all new types of technic or methods of procedure in the application of chiropractic principles to the alleviation of human ailments, and to subject them to the analysis of scientific investigation. For the chiropractor should always bear in mind that the great object of his profession is to cure the sick, and it is his solemn duty to investigate thoroughly and without prejudice whatever offers any probability of adding to his knowledge of the art and science of chiropractic.

Section 5. Chiropractors should safeguard their profession

by exposing those who might attempt to practice without proper credentials, and by reporting acts of dishonesty to the proper authorities.

Section 6.   Procedure for Filing and Handling Complaints in Matters of Ethics.

1.   The Committee on Ethics for the ACA may, upon its own initiative or upon receipt of complaint, meeting the requirements hereinafter set forth, consider and make disposition of matters concerning the conduct of any ACA member.

2.   Any doctor who is a member of the ACA may file a complaint of any alleged violation of the Code of Ethics of the ACA.

3.   With respect to such complaints:

   a.   They shall be submitted in writing with supporting evidence.

   b.   All copies shall be signed by the party or parties making the complaint.

   c.   The district ethics committee member shall, thereupon, furnish the member involved with the contents of the complaint, notifying him of the place and time, not less than ten or more than thirty days after receipt of the complaint, at which the committee member, together with the state delegate from the state in which the problem arises, will hear the matter set forth in said complaint.

4.   The district ethics committee, together with the state delegate from the state where the complaint arises, shall make a thorough investigation and shall hear and consider all proper evidence in support of or contrary to said complaint.

5.   The district ethics member, together with the state delegate from the state where the complaint arises, shall make a determination whether the complaint is true in whole or in part, and on the basis of such findings shall make such disposition of the matter as is consistent with rules governing these procedures.   If such disposition involves affirmative action to be taken against accused member, the district ethics committee member shall make a full report and summary of the case and forward same to the ACA Ethics Chairman along with all evidence heard and received at hearing.

6.   The ACA Ethics Committee shall review the report, findings, and recommendations of the district committee member, make such further investigation, or conduct such hearings as it may deem necessary, whereupon the matter either shall be disposed of or referred to the Board of Censors together with a full report and summary of the case along with all evidence heard and received at the hearing, and include recommendation of the ACA Ethics Committee, if applicable.

Article II.   Professional Services of Chiropractors to Each Other.

Section 1.   All chiropractors and their immediate dependents

are entitled to the gratuitous services of any one or more of the
profession. The chiropractor is unable to care for himself when
ill. Oftentimes the anxiety and solicitude he feels when some one
of his immediate family is ill, renders him incompetent to care for
that one. In these circumstances chiropractors are especially
dependent on each other and professional aid should always be
cheerfully and gratuitously afforded.

Section 2. Should a chiropractor in affluent circumstances
require the services of a distant professional brother for himself
or his immediate dependents, he should pay the travel expenses and
such other honorarium as may at least partially compensate the
visiting chiropractor for his loss of time.

Section 3. When, because of personal illness, a chiropractor
refers his patients to a brother practitioner, the recipient of such
references should consider it a courtesy and permit all fees incident to such services to be paid the sick colleague. If, however, a
chiropractor is absent on holiday pleasures, the fees resulting from
such referred practice may rightfully be retained by the colleague
to whom the patients have been referred.

Article III. Duties of Chiropractors in Regard to Consultations.

Section 1. Whether a consultation is arranged as the result
of a patient's desire or upon the request of the chiropractor
for another opinion, certain procedures should always be followed.

Section 2. The utmost punctuality should be observed by
chiropractors when they are to hold consultations. Unavoidable professional duties may sometimes interfere and delay one or the
other, in which case the first to arrive should wait a reasonable
time for his colleague. If there is no appearance he may consider
the consultation postponed and wait for another appointment. If,
however, the first to arrive is the one who was called in consultation and he has traveled a considerable distance, he may proceed
with his examination and make a private written report of his findings to the attending chiropractor. He should always exercise the
utmost caution in what he says to the patient in the absence of the
attending chiropractor.

Section 3. In consultations the attending chiropractor should
put the necessary questions to the patient. Then the consulting
chiropractor should make such additional inquiries and examinations as may be needed to satisfy him of the nature of the
case but should avoid making a parade of any superior knowledge. Both chiropractors should then retire to a private room
for deliberations.

Section 4. In consultation deliberations the attending chiropractor should voice his opinion first, and other consultants in the
order called. Should there be several consultants and their opinions
equally divided, the attending chiropractor must make the decision.
Should there be a wide diversity of opinion when only two are consulting, they should request a third opinion.

Section 5. The attending chiropractor should communicate

to the patient or his friends such results of the consultation as
have been considered proper to express. But no discussion should
take place before the patient or his friends, except in the presence
of all the consulting chiropractors.

Section 6. The consulting chiropractor should not at any
time take charge of a case on which he has been called as a consultant, without the consent of the attending chiropractor.

Section 7. When a patient is referred by a chiropractor to
another chiropractor for x-rays or other specialty service, the
doctor performing such services must meticulously respect the referring doctor's priority to the patient. He may not offer, suggest,
or perform any other service for the patient except that for which
the patient was referred.

It is recognized that the doctor performing specialty services may have particular instructions and suggestions, but these
must be given to the referring doctor, not to the patient, even
though the patient may request them. The doctor performing
specialized services is obliged to uphold and strengthen the professional image of the referring doctor, and may not detract therefrom
by word or act. If he cannot in good conscience do so, he should
not accept the referral.

Article IV.   Duties of Chiropractors in Cases of Interference.

Section 1. A chiropractor should never permit himself to
feel envious or jealous of a brother practitioner. The distinction
which one successful chiropractor wins is shared by the whole profession.

Section 2. The chiropractor in conversation with a patient
who is under the care of another practitioner should observe the
strictest caution and reserve. No course of conduct should be pur-
sued that might, directly or indirectly, tend to diminish the trust
imposed in the chiropractor employed.

Section 3. A chiropractor should not take charge of a case
which is, or recently has been, under the care of another practitioner in the same illness except in an emergency, or in consultation with the chiropractor in previous attendance, or when the latter
has relinquished the case or has been regularly notified that his services are no longer required.

Section 4. In cases of accident or sudden emergencies,
more than one chiropractor may be sent for by alarmed friends.
Courtesy should assign the patient to the first that arrives, and
he should select from others such additional assistance as he may
require. But he should also request that the family chiropractor
be sent for (if there be one), and on his arrival resign the case
into his hands.

Section 5. In a sparse population, a chiropractor when
visiting a sick person may be requested to see some neighboring
patient who is regularly under the care of another. In such an
event he should do what seems necessary at the time; interfere as
little as possible with previous treatment; and assume no further
direction of the case unless expressly desired, in which case he

should request an immediate consultation with the practitioner
previously employed.

Section 6. A wealthy chiropractor should not give advice
gratuitously to the affluent. In so doing, he injures his professional
brethren. The office of a chiropractor can never be supported as
a beneficent one. Hence it is defrauding the common fund when
fees are dispensed with which might rightfully be claimed.

Section 7. In localities where chiropractors are licensed to
practice obstetrics, if one is absent in a case he has been engaged
to deliver and another chiropractor accomplishes the delivery, the
latter is entitled to the fee but should resign the patient to the
chiropractor originally employed.

Article V. Differences Between Chiropractors and Pecuniary Acknowledgments.

Section 1. Diversity of opinion and of interests may in the
chiropractic profession, as in other professions, sometimes cause
controversy and even contention. When such cases occur and cannot
be readily terminated, they should be referred to the Board of Censors for arbitration.

Section 2. Some general rules should be adopted by chiropractors in every town or district relative to fees from patients.
These should be adhered to by chiropractors as uniformly as circumstances will permit.

Section 3. It shall be considered unprofessional to split
fees or to give or receive a commission in the reference of patients
for chiropractic service, except in cases where laboratory services
are required and then the patient should be informed that there is
an extra charge for such service.

Section 4. Unfortunately every community has within its
population a certain percentage of people who evade every financial
obligation possible. Such persons prey upon the chiropractor as
well as on members of other professions. Therefore, it is perfectly proper for the chiropractors of a community to make a list
of the names of such individuals and to demand, before attending
them, some adequate security that the fees will be paid.

Part 3

RECIPROCAL DUTIES AND OBLIGATIONS OF CHIROPRACTORS AND THE PUBLIC

Article 1. Duties of Chiropractors to the Public.

Section 1. It is the duty of the chiropractor as a good citizen to be vigilant for the welfare of the community and to do his
part in sustaining its burdens. He should be ready to give counsel
to the public on matters pertaining to his profession such as postural
hygiene, general hygiene, and sanitary measures in the control and
prevention of epidemics. He should comply with all local regulations

concerning reportable diseases.

Section 2.   Chiropractors should always be willing to testify in courts of justice on matters pertaining to the profession.

Section 3.   There is no profession by the members of which gratuitous services are more freely dispensed than they are by chiropractors, but justice demands that some limit should be placed on the extent of such services.   Poverty, professional brotherhood, the poorly remunerated occupation of some individual patient, and certain of the public duties referred to in Section 1 of this Article should be recognized as presenting valid claims for gratuitous ser- vices.   However, services rendered endowed institutions, mutual benefit societies, for life insurance or other health certification examinations, as well as services under Section 2 of this Article, should not justly be rendered without an appropriate fee.

Article II.   Obligations of the Public to Chiropractors.

Section 1.   The benefits accruing to the public from the active and constant labors of the chiropractic profession are so numerous that chiropractors are justly entitled to the utmost con- sideration from the community.   The public should be willing to assist in the endowment of nonprofit chiropractic institutions, such as accredited colleges, sanitaria, hospitals, and clinics.   Further- more, the public should demand, through proper legislative chan- nels, that chiropractic services become available to the inmates of all state institutions.

CONCLUSION

Obviously it is impossible to cover all of the innumerable ramifications of professional ethics in a treatise of this length. The foregoing merely points to certain general rules of conduct that should be followed in the interest of public welfare and for the ultimate good of the chiropractic profession.   Application of the same principles should govern the practitioner in his behavior toward any incident that may not herein be specifically mentioned.

CITY MANAGERS

INTERNATIONAL CITY MANAGEMENT ASSOCIATION (ICMA)
    1140 Connecticut Ave., N.W., Washington, D.C. 20036
    Mark E. Keane, Executive Director

Membership: The International City Management Association, founded in 1914 and with a present (1973) membership of 5000, is a professional association of city managers and other urban ad- ministrators.   Experience requirements for the two categories of individual professional membership are:

Member--"City, town and county managers and administrators, chief administrative officers in cities, counties and
towns, and directors of councils of government.   They
must have served in a municipality or a council of
governments which is recognized by the Association as
providing for a position of overall professional management for at least three years."

Assistant Member--An administrator (as described above for
"member") with less than three years experience; and
administrative assistants, assistant city managers, assistant administrators, assistant directors of councils of
government with two years experience.

Code of Ethics: The professional conduct guide of ICMA (Constitution, Article XII) is its City Management Code of Ethics, developed
by a committee of the association, and originally adopted in 1924.
In its most recent edition (1972), the Code enumerates 12 principles
as guides to professional conduct of city managers.   Guidelines, issued in 1972, augment the Code by interpretation and application of
its principles to specific cases.

The Code is revised by membership vote.   It is enforced by
the ICMA Executive Board.   Complaints of breaches of the code of
ethics are received and investigated by the Committee on Professional Conduct (Constitution, Article VIII), which may recommend
disciplinary action to the Executive Board, including reprimand,
censure, suspension, or expulsion from membership.

Other Guides to Professional Conduct: A Suggested Code of Ethics
for Municipal Officials and Employees has been issued by the ICMA
as a conduct guide for municipal officials and employees to be used
in the development of codes of ethics.   This concise review of
ethical questions includes definition of "Ethics," policy questions and
development of ethical guidelines, suggested code of ethics with optional provisions for such a code, and suggested creeds for council-
men, administrative officials and employees of cities.

Professional Insignia: The ICMA emblem is its logotype, consisting
of the name of the organization, "International City Management

International
City
Management
Association

Association," stacked four lines high, either flush right or flush left
of the visual symbol of the square in the circle.   This emblem--
developed by a graphic arts company in Washington, D.C. in early

1969--provides an abstract design identifiable with the ICMA. The
design appears in various colors--gray on white (letterhead), black
on green or green on white, or blue on white (publications).

Bibliography:
        International City Management Association. City Management
             Code of Ethics. 1972 edition. 1 page.
        Enumerates 12 general principles governing professional
        actions of urban administrators.
             _____. City Management Code of Ethics. (Career Develop-
             ment Series) 1972. 19 pages. Pamphlet.
        In addition to text of the City Management Code of Ethics,
        gives background of development of Code, Guidelines for
        Professional Conduct--interpretations of the Code; and Gen-
        eral Policy and Rules of Procedure for the Committee on
        Professional Conduct, in enforcement of the Code.
             _____. International City Management Association. 1972.
        General information brochure giving ICMA goals, membership
        requirements, publications.
             _____. A Suggested Code of Ethics for Municipal Officials
             and Employees. 1962. 40 pages. $2.50.
        Comprehensive statement of ethical ideals and expectations
        of local government service, with suggested code of ethics
        and creeds of service.

"Code of Ethics"

The purpose of the International City Management Association is to
increase the proficiency of city managers, county managers, and
other municipal administrators and to strengthen the quality of urban government through professional management. To further these
objectives, certain ethical principles shall govern the conduct of
every member of the International City Management Association,
who shall:

        1 Be dedicated to the concepts of effective and democratic
local government by responsible elected officials and believe that
professional general management is essential to the achievement
of this objective.
        2 Affirm the dignity and worth of the services rendered by
government and maintain a constructive, creative, and practical attitude toward urban affairs and a deep sense of his social responsibility as a trusted public servant.
        3 Dedicate himself to the highest ideals of honor and in-
tegrity in all public and personal relationships in order that he may
merit the respect and confidence of the elected officials, of other
officials and employees, and of the public which he serves.
        4 Recognize that the chief function of local government at
all times is to serve the best interests of all of the people.
        5 Submit policy proposals to elected officials, provide

them with facts and advice on matters of policy as a basis for making decisions and setting community goals, and uphold and implement municipal policies adopted by elected officials.

6 Recognize that elected representatives of the people are entitled to the credit for the establishment of municipal policies; responsibility for policy execution rests with the member.

7 Refrain from participation in the election of the members of his employing legislative body, and from all partisan political activities which would impair his performance as a professional administrator.

8 Make it his duty continually to improve his ability and to develop the competence of his associates in the use of management techniques.

9 Keep the community informed on municipal affairs; encourage communication between the citizens and all municipal officers; emphasize friendly and courteous service to the public; and seek to improve the quality and image of the public service.

10 Resist any encroachment on his responsibilities, believing he should be free to carry out official policies without interference, and handle each problem without discrimination on the basis of principle and justice.

11 Handle all matters of personnel on the basis of merit so that fairness and impartiality govern his decisions, pertaining to appointments, pay adjustments, promotions, and discipline.

12 Seek no favor; believe that personal aggrandizement or profit secured by confidential information or by misuse of public time is dishonest.

COACHES

NATIONAL COUNCIL OF STATE HIGH SCHOOL COACHES ASSOCIA-
    TIONS (NCSHSCA)
    1201 Sixteenth St., N. W., Washington, D. C. 20036

Membership: The National Council of State High School Coaches Associations, founded in 1965 by the American Association of Health, Physical Education and Recreation, is a professional society of state or regional high school coaches associations. Membership in the Council "is open to any state high school coaches association. In those states where there are no statewide coaches associations, regional associations are eligible for membership."

Code of Ethics: The professional conduct guide for high school coaches was developed by the Ethics Committee of the Council as "a direct result of the National Conference of the Council held in

April 1965." It sets forth the goals and ideals of coaches in the form of a pledge--National Code of Ethics for High School Coaches.

Professional Insignia: The emblem of the Council is its seal--a

circular design set in a black square, with the centered figures of three athletes clearing a hurdle; the motto, "The Joy of Effort," is given in a scroll below the figures; an oak wreath bands the insignia; and the name of the group, "National Council of State High School Coaches Associations," is printed in an unbordered rectangle below the background square. The color of the insignia is black and white. The seal is used by the Council, and its member associations, on letterheads, publications, and other printed materials.

NATIONAL COUNCIL OF STATE HIGH SCHOOL COACHES ASSOCIATIONS

Bibliography:
National Council of State High School Coaches Associations. National Council of State High School Coaches Associations. Folder.

This informational brochure gives the Council purposes, organization, programs, and membership requirements.

"National Code of Ethics
for High School Coaches"

AS A PROFESSIONAL EDUCATOR, I WILL:
Exemplify the highest moral character, behavior, and leadership.
Respect the integrity and personality of the individual athlete.
Abide by the rules of the game in letter and in spirit.
Respect the integrity and judgment of sports officials.
Demonstrate a mastery of and continuing interest in coaching principles and techniques through professional improvement.
Encourage a respect for all athletics and their values.
Display modesty in victory and graciousness in defeat.
Promote ethical relationships among coaches.
Fulfill responsibilities to provide health services and an environment free of safety hazards.

Encourage the highest standards of conduct and scholastic achievement among all athletes.

Seek to inculcate good health habits including the establishment of sound training rules.

Strive to develop in each athlete the qualities of leadership, initiative, and good judgment.

COACHES--FOOTBALL

AMERICAN FOOTBALL COACHES ASSOCIATION (AFCA)
    Box 8705, Durham, N. C. 27707
    William D. Murray, Executive Director

Membership: The American Football Coaches Association, founded in Hanover, New Hampshire in 1921, has a present (1973) membership of approximately 3300. The Association's "Active Members" are "Coaches from the colleges that grant a Bachelor's Degree and who are actively engaged in (or directly associated with) the profession of football coaching, and who are otherwise acceptable to the organization" (By-Laws, Article V). Football coaches from junior colleges, normal schools, high schools, and preparatory schools are eligible for "Allied Membership."

Code of Ethics: Carrying out one of the purposes of the Association ("to maintain the highest possible standards in football and the football coaching profession"), a Code of Ethics was developed in 1952 by the AFCA Committee on Ethics, and adopted by the membership in 1953. The Code groups its guides to professional conduct for football coaches into eight Articles:
    I.   General Principles.
    II.   The Coaches Responsibility to the Institution.
    III.   The Coaches Responsibility to the Player.
    IV.   Rules of the Game.
    V.   Officials.
    VI.   Public Relations.
    VII.   Scouting.
    VIII. Student Recruitment.

Enforcement of the code of ethics is provided in a section on "Enforcement," added to the Code by amendment adopted January 1957. Alleged violations of the Code are investigated by the Committee on Ethics, and a Board of Review considers Committee findings, and carries out appropriate action, including discipline.

Bibliography:
    American Football Coaches Association. Directory. Annual. Includes historical digest of the Association, By-Laws, with membership qualifications and the Code of Ethics.

"Code of Ethics"

PREAMBLE

The distinguishing characteristic of a profession is that its members are dedicated to rendering service to humanity. Financial gain or personal reward must be of secondary consideration. In selecting the football coaching profession, an individual assumes an obligation to conduct himself in accord with its ideals. These are set forth in the Code of Ethics. A coach who is unwilling or unable to comply with the principles emphasized in this Code should have no place in the football coaching profession.

In selecting this profession coaches must be mindful of the history and evolution of the game of football, if they are to serve effectively in the educational development of the young men who play the game. Essentially the game belongs to the players. Justification for including it in the school program rests upon the dual premise that it provides both physical and character values for those who play it. The burden of proof for seeing that these values become a reality rests largely with the coaching profession.

It has become increasingly clear during recent years that because of the vast growth in the popularity of the game in spectator interest, and in the tremendous increase in number of players, teams and coaches, that there is need for an operating code of principles and ethics. In recognition of this need the membership of the American Football Coaches Association, at the Twenty-ninth Annual meeting (January 10, 1952) unanimously approved the formulation, adoption and enforcement of a working Code of Ethics.

In presenting this Code, the Committee on Ethics recognizes that without a genuine and whole-hearted acceptance and practical application of the tenets which it represents, it cannot become an effective instrument in the solution of the problems which have brought occasional criticism and discredit upon the game of football.

The reputation of the football coaching profession, and the fine influence which the game of football can exert upon the people of America, is dependent in large measure upon the manner in which the coaches of the nation live up to both the letter and the spirit which this code represents. As a profession we should be ever mindful of the high trust and confidence which has been placed in us, and which is typified by the comment of one of the nation's outstanding college presidents, when he said:

"The coach is an important person in every hamlet, village and city throughout the land, often times a better known and more influential teacher of the young than his colleagues in other branches of teaching."

Every football coach should study and apply the principles enumerated in this Code to the end that the game of football, and members of the coaching profession may become a more powerful and effective influence in the American educational system.

OBJECTIVES

Among the stated objectives of the American Football Coaches Association are the following: "... to help maintain the highest possible standards in football and the football coaching profession ... to work together for the improvement of conditions in American Football ... and to promote the coaching profession." (Article 1-- By-Laws)

PURPOSE OF CODE OF ETHICS

The Code of Ethics of the American Football Coaches Association has been developed to protect and promote the best interests of the game of football, and the coaching profession. Its primary purpose is to clarify and distinguish ethical and approved professional practices from those which are detrimental and harmful. Its secondary purpose is to emphasize the purpose and values of football in American educational institutions, and to stress the proper functions of coaches in relation to schools and players. Ethics has been defined as the basic principles of right action. Applied to the football coaching profession Ethics imply a standard of character in which the American public has trust and confidence. The ultimate success of the principals and standards emphasized in this Code rests primarily in the hands of those for whom they have been prepared--the football coaches of America.

AUTHORIZATION

The Board of Trustees of the American Football Coaches Association approved the preparation, adoption and enforcement of a Code of Ethics at their Annual Meeting held in Cincinnati, Ohio, on January 8, 1952. On January 10th the Membership of the Association unanimously approved this action and authorized the Committee on Ethics to prepare the Code.

ENFORCEMENT

By a unanimous vote of the membership on January 10, 1952, and amendments ratified January 1957, the following method of enforcement was adopted:

(1) The Committee on Ethics is empowered to investigate any and all alleged violations of the Code which are brought to its attention. It shall be its duty to collect all of the facts surrounding an alleged violation and consider all sides of any controversial issue. When a preliminary investigation by the Ethics Committee shows evidence of a violation, the member involved and his institution's president shall be notified. The member involved shall be requested to answer in writing and invited to appear before the Ethics Committee and state his case. He shall, if the Ethics Committee finds him to be in violation of the Code and recommends disciplinary action, be given an opportunity to appear before the Board of Review to appeal the findings and recommendations of the

Ethics Committee, which shall have been forwarded to the Board of Review for final action.

There is to be no acceptance of prima-facie evidence of a violation in any case. The member coach shall not be presumed in violation of the Code of Ethics because an institution has been found in violation of Article III of the National Collegiate Athletic Association or the Conference Rules and Regulations to which that institution is a member. If there is sufficient evidence in the investigation of the institution to indicate that a member coach might be in violation of the Code of Ethics, normal procedure will then be followed.

Beginning in 1962, the Committee on Ethics shall consist of a chairman and seven members representing eight districts. Two members shall be appointed for four years, two for three years, two for two years, and two for one year. New appointments thereafter shall be for four years. It shall meet each year on a date just prior to the Annual Meeting or at such other time as the chairman deems advisable.

(2) The Board of Review shall review all reports and recommendations of the Committee on Ethics and take such disciplinary action as may seem appropriate. It has been granted power by the membership to suspend or to expel members whose conduct has clearly violated the Code of Ethics. Such violations shall be reported in detail to the administrative head of the institution in which the member is employed, together with a statement covering the disciplinary action which has been taken. The Executive Secretary-Treasurer shall notify the member and the administrative head of his institution of the final findings of the Board of Review.

The Board of Review shall consist of five members: Two past presidents, two trustees, and one Active member who is not in either category. Beginning in 1957, one is to be appointed for five years, one for four years, one for three years, one for two years, and one for one year. New appointments thereafter shall be for five years.

(3) The entire proceedings are to be confidential. Exception: The findings of the Ethics Committee and the Board of Review on violations of the Code, may be announced to the membership at the Annual Meeting of the Association.

ARTICLE I

In becoming a member of the football coaching profession, a man assumes certain obligations and responsibilities to the game of football, and to players and his fellow coaches. It is essential that every member of the profession be constantly aware of these obligations and responsibilities, to the end that football coaching remain always an honorable calling, and that each member conduct himself in such a manner as to maintain the dignity and decency of his profession.

An active coach is involved in three areas of relationships which entail certain obligations, for which some definite standards of conduct may be described.   These are: (1) players, (2) institutions, and (3) with other coaches, teams, officials, sportswriters and others.

In his relationships with players under his care, the coach should always be aware of the tremendous influence he wields, for good or bad.   Parents entrust their dearest possession to the coach's charge, and the coach, through his own example must always be sure that the boys who have played under him are finer and more decent men for having done so.   The coach should never place the value of a win above that of instilling the highest desirable ideals and character traits in his players.   The safety and welfare of his players should always be uppermost in his mind, and they must never be sacrificed for any personal prestige or selfish glory.

In teaching the game of football, the coach must realize that there are certain rules designed to protect the player and provide common standards for determining a winner and loser.   Any attempts to beat these rules, to take unfair advantage of an opponent, or to teach deliberate unsportsmanlike conduct, have no place in the game of football, nor has any coach guilty of such teaching any right to call himself a coach.   The coach should set the example for winning without boasting and losing without bitterness. A coach who conducts himself according to these principles need have no fear of failure, for in the final analysis, the success of a coach can be measured in terms of the respect he has earned from his own players and from his opponents.

In his relationships with the institution for which he works, the coach should remember that he is on public display as a representative of that institution.   It is important, therefore that he conduct himself so as to maintain the principles, the integrity and the dignity of his institution.   Institutional policy regarding football should be adhered to, both in letter and in spirit.   The coach should remember that other members of the faculty also have an interest in the institution and in the students, and his conduct must be such that there arise no criticism of his efforts to develop the common interest and purposes of the institution, along with other faculty members.

In his relationship with other coaches, it should be assumed that all members of the coaching profession intend to follow the precepts set forth in this Code of Ethics.   Incontrovertible evidence of unethical conduct should be brought openly to the Ethics Committee, through the prescribed channels.   Sportswriters and sportscasters should not be used as a means of relieving ill-feelings toward other coaches, players, officials, or other institution.   They also have an interest in the game of football and should be treated with the same respect and honesty which is expected of them.   Offi-

cials are an essential part of the game, and it should be recognized
that they too attempt to maintain high standards of integrity and
honesty.   Just as coaches can make mistakes, so can officials.
It is important that their efforts to secure perfection in performance
be highly respected by coaches.

The essential elements in this Code of Ethics of the American
Coaches Association are honesty and integrity.   Coaches whose conduct reflects these two characteristics will bring credit to the
coaching profession, to the game of football and to themselves.
It is only through such conduct that the profession can earn and
maintain its rightful place in our educational program and make its
full contribution to the American way of life.

ARTICLE II

The Coach's Responsibility
to the Institution

Section 1:   The Coach as an Educator.   The function of the
coach is to educate students through participation in the game of
football.   This primary and basic function must never be disre-
garded.
Section 2:   The Coach and the Administration.   Because of
the unique niche which the football coach holds in the educational
organization, it is highly important that he support the administration in all policies, rules and regulations which may from time to
time be activated.   Where differences of opinion develop, these
should be discussed behind closed doors, and not aired through
public press and radio.
Section 3:   The Coach and the Athletic Council.   By whatever
name the governing body of the school athletic program may be
known, the coach should lend his training and experience to this
body in the solution of football problems.   He should constantly
be alert to see that the game for which he is responsible is being
properly conducted and promoted.   Where differences of opinion
arise, and the Council overrides a coach's judgment, discretion
should be exercised in airing or discussing such differences outside
of Council meetings.
Section 4:   The Coach and the Athletic Director.   Where the
coach is not the Athletic Director, it is important that a harmonious
relationship exist between the two.   The coach should feel free to
suggest and initiate any action which has to do with the conduct or
improvement of the football program.   Controversial matters should
be discussed on a friendly basis, but once final decisions have been
reached they should be accepted and given complete support by the
coach.
Section 5:   The Coach and the Admissions Office.   Every
coach should have the right and privilege of recommending qualified
students for admission.   Official student records and transcripts
should never pass through the coaches office, nor should a coach
ever attempt to bring pressure to bear upon an admissions officer

to admit an applicant merely because he possesses exceptional
athletic ability.

Section 6: The Coach and Eligibility Requirements. Participation in inter-school athletics is generally predicated upon the individual students fulfillment of established rules and regulations.
Every coach should be thoroughly acquainted with these rules and
regulations. He should assume responsibility for their observance
and enforcement in cooperation with the school official who has been
delegated this responsibility. Any attempt by a coach to circum-
vent eligibility rules, or to use ineligible players shall be considered
unethical conduct. Nor shall a coach be a party to exerting pressure of any sort on members of the faculty for the purpose of influencing player grades in academic work.

Section 7: The Coach and Scholarship. One of the coach's
fundamental responsibilities must be to inspire his players to
achieve academic success, not only to make good grades but secure
professional training and graduate with honors.

ARTICLE III

The Coach's Responsibility
to the Player

Section 1: Injured Players. The diagnosis of and prescription of treatment for injuries is strictly a medical problem and
should, under no circumstances, be considered a province of the
coach. A coach's responsibility is to see that injured players are
given prompt and competent medical attention and that the most
minute details of a doctor's orders are carried out.

Section 2: Leadership. Every coach must remember that
he is a living example for all of the young men in the community
in which he coaches. It is vitally important to him, and to the
profession which he represents, that his actions and behavior at
all times bring credit to the game of football. To set down in any
great detail a list of ethical practices which a coach should observe
would go far beyond the confines of this Code. Those which are
listed below are merely illustrative of some of the more important
aspects of his responsibilities.

Section 3: Autographs and Testimonials. In considering
offers of money or goods in return for endorsements of commercial
articles or commodities, a coach must recognize that part of the
consideration which is being offered is tendered him as a successful
representative of the coaching profession. He cannot entirely divorce the payment to him as an individual from that which should
be credited to the game and the profession which he represents.
Accepting money or goods for an endorsement of any product or
commodity which is not in keeping with the traditions of the coaching profession shall be considered unethical. In all endorsements
where a coach's name, and the game of football are involved, it
is the coach's responsibility to be sure that the wording and sense

of the testimonial do not bring discredit upon the game of football, or the coaching profession. Endorsement, directly or indirectly, by Active members of the Association, of alcoholic beverages and/ or tobacco products shall be considered unethical.

Section 4: Publications. Solution of professional problems should be settled within the confines of the profession, and not in the public press. Newspaper columns and magazine articles over the signature or by-line of a member of the coaching profession are exclusively his responsibility. Direct or implied attacks upon those officially associated with the game of football shall be considered unethical.

Section 5: Conduct of Coaches during a Game. (A) Before and after a game rival coaches should meet and exchange friendly greetings. (B) During a game coaches should be as inconspicuous as possible. (C) Coaches are encouraged to demonstrate a friendly and kindly attitude towards their players on the bench. (D) The attitude of coaches towards officials during the progress of a game should be controlled and undemonstrative. (E) After games visitors should not be permitted in team dressing rooms until coaches have had sufficient time to complete all of their post-game responsibilities, including a careful check of player injuries.

ARTICLE IV

Rules of the Game

Section 1: The Football Code which appears in the annual Football Rule Book shall be considered an integral part of this Code of Ethics, and should be carefully read and observed.

Section 2: Knowledge of Rules. Every coach should be thoroughly acquainted with the rules of the game. The official rule book should be studied and frequently reviewed. The coach is primarily responsible for teaching and interpreting the rules to his players.

Section 3: Application of Rules. Both the letter and the spirit of the rules must be respected and adhered to by the coach. Rules are made for the protection of players and in the best interests of the game of football. It is the coach's responsibility to see that they are observed.

Section 4: Beating the Rules. To gain an advantage or win a game by circumvention or disregard of the rules brands a coach or player as a person unfit to be associated with the game of football. It is especially important that coaches stress those rules which involve bodily contact. Where rules permit the use of hands and arms it is the coach's responsibility to see that they are used legally. It is not the purpose of football to hurt or injure an opponent by legal or illegal methods.

Section 5: Good Sportsmanship. Habit formation is developed on the practice field. Where coaches permit, encourage or condone performance which is dangerous to an opponent, they are derelict in their responsibility to teach fair play and good sportsmanship. This aspect of coaching must be attacked just as vigorously as the teaching of offense and defense, and to the players it is far more important than all the technical aspects of the game combined. Any coach who fails to stress this point, or who permits, encourages or defends the use of unsportsmanlike tactics shall be considered guilty of the most serious breach of football coaching ethics.

ARTICLE V

Officials

Section 1: Importance of Officials. No competitive contest can be satisfactorily played without an acceptable code of rules and impartial officials. In large measure the reputation and status of officials depends upon the support which they are accorded by coaches. Officials must have the respect and support of coaches and players if they are to do their jobs efficiently. On and off-the-record criticisms of officials to players or the public shall be considered unethical.

Section 2: Officials Associations. There should be a cooperative relationship between coaches and officials associations, with frequent interchange of ideas and suggestions. Coaches should, whenever possible, accept invitations to attend officials' rules meetings. Similarly coaches should extend officials invitations to discuss rules interpretations with their squads, and on occasion to officiate at scrimmages, for mutual benefits. Wherever possible coaches may find it desirable to join Officials Associations, and serve as officials. It is undesirable for coaches to serve as officials in the league or conference of which their institution is a member, particularly in the sport which they are coaching. It is dangerous and unethical for coaches of rival teams to accept assignment as officials on an exchange basis.

Section 3: Treatment of Officials. On the day of a game officials should be treated in a courteous manner. They should be provided with a private room in which to meet and dress for the game. Conferences between coaches and officials shall always be conducted according to procedures established by the governing Conference or Officials Association. In every respect the official Rule Book shall be followed in coach-official relationships, on the field and during and following a game. Any criticisms which the coach may have to make concerning officiating should be made in writing to the office which assigned the official to the game. For a coach to address, or permit anyone on his bench to address, uncomplimentary remarks to any official during the progress of a game, or to indulge in conduct which might incite players or spectators against the officials, is a violation of the rules of the game and must likewise be considered conduct unworthy a member of the coaching profession.

Section 4: <u>Post-game Comments.</u> Derogatory comments
should be avoided. It should be remembered that criticisms once
made can never be retracted. Coaches must assume full responsibility for whatever comments they may make.

Section 5: <u>Use of Movies in Checking Officials.</u> It should
be recognized that slow motion study of controversial decisions by
officials is far different from on-the-spot decisions which must be
made during the course of a game. To show critical plays to
sportswriters, sportscasters, alumni and the public, which may incite them to label officials as incompetents, must be considered
unethical conduct.

ARTICLE VI

Public Relations

Section 1: <u>Sportswriters and Sportscasters.</u> The responsibility of coaches to accredited writers and radio and television commentators is to provide them news about their team and players.
They should be treated with courtesy, honesty and respect. Derogatory and misleading statements should be avoided. Direct questions
should be answered honestly, or not at all. If good judgment indicates that an honest answer to a question would be prejudicial to the
best interest of the game, ethical procedure demands that it not be
answered. In such cases, "No comment" is entirely justifiable.
Coaches should assume responsibility for and stress the importance
of ethical procedures in teaching their players how to conduct themselves in player-interviews, in the best interests of the game of
football.

The Association recommends that the press be admitted to
the dressing room as soon as practicable after each game so that
they may meet their deadline and capture the dramatic aftermath
of the contest.

Section 2: <u>Good Judgment.</u> It shall be questionable practice
for coaches to stress player injuries, disciplinary measures, academic difficulties, eligibility problems and similar personal items
with the press, radio and television. Disciplinary problems should
be a "family affair," to be solved between the coach and players
involved. Scholastic eligibility is a province of the Deans or
Registrars Office. Injuries are essentially a province of the team
physician and trainer. No good purpose can be served by emphasizing such matters.

Section 3: <u>Football Polls and Picking Game Winners.</u> It
shall be unethical for coaches to pick weekly game winners, or to
participate in pre-season team ratings systems.

Section 4: <u>Alumni, Booster and Quarterback Organizations.</u>
Such organizations can be of value to the game of football if they
have proper objectives. It shall be unethical for coaches to use
such groups to attempt to defeat or obstruct administrative or institutional athletic controls, or to encourage violation of established

rules and regulations in order to strengthen existing football programs. It shall likewise be unethical for coaches to make demands, financial or otherwise, upon such groups which are not in keeping with the letter and spirit of existing controls or in any other manner of misuse such strength and power in violation of accepted rules and regulations.

ARTICLE VII

Scouting

It shall be considered unethical under any circumstances to scout any team, by any means whatsoever, except in regularly scheduled games. Any attempt to scout practice sessions shall be considered unethical. The head football coach of each institution shall be held responsible for all scouting. This shall include the use of moving pictures.

ARTICLE VIII

Student Recruitment

Section 1. General. Any attempt to set down generally acceptable or standardized principles at this time (1952) is impossible because of conditions which have been created by the attempts of so many organizations to assume responsibility for and dictate desirable controls. However there are a number of ethical principles which should be considered in this area. Where Conference or League Rules and Regulations have been adopted, and are in force, they must be strictly observed. In Institutions where no Conference or League Rules exist the following principles shall be observed until such time as national, sectional or Conference Rules may be adopted:

(A) Coaches are entitled to the same rights and privileges as other faculty members, and must assume the same responsibilities as are imposed upon them, in all student recruitment.

(B) Institutional rules and regulations shall be strictly observed in all student recruitment.

(C) Recruitment of students with athletic ability must follow the generally accepted pattern for all students. The first essential qualification is acceptable academic ability; the second, other desirable special abilities including in this case, skill in football.

(D) In discussing the advantages of his institution to a prospect the coach must confine his statements to an honest and forthright presentation of facts and shall refrain from making derogatory statements concerning other institutions and their officials.

(E) In discussing opportunities, part-time work and other institutional advantages it shall be strictly unethical for any coach to make statements to any prospective student which cannot be fulfilled.

(F)   All offers of assistance to prospects must conform to
and be in keeping with the rules and regulations of:
1.   The institution.
2.   The Conference or League to which the institution belongs.
3.   The state or national governing body in control of
athletics.
4.   Any other organization or association to which the institution is responsible in the conduct of its athletic program.

COLLEGE PLACEMENT OFFICERS

COLLEGE PLACEMENT COUNCIL (CPC)
65 E. Elizabeth Ave., Bethlehem, Pa. 18001
Robert F. Herrick, Executive Director

Membership: The College Placement Council, organized in 1956,
is a federation of eight regional college placement associations,
which function as independent and autonomous units:
Eastern College Personnel Officers,
Middle Atlantic Placement Association,
Midwest College Placement Association,
Rocky Mountain College Placement Association,
Southern College Placement Association,
Southwest Placement Association,
University and College Placement Association,
Western College Placement Association.
Individual memberships, which are held in these regional asso-
ciations and not in the Council, total at present (1973) about
5000.

Code of Ethics: The conduct guide for professional college placement officers is the Council's Principles and Practices of College
Placement and Recruitment, developed in 1957, and most recently
revised in 1970.   This code sets forth the ethical principles,
practices and procedures, and compliance provisions to be observed by the three parties to college placement--the employer,
the college, and the student candidate for placement and recruitment.
Enforcement of this conduct guide is the responsibility of the
eight regional associations, who receive complaints of violations
of the code, investigate alleged breaches, and apply "sanctions for
violations" of the obligations and responsibilities, including warning,
suspension, forfeiture or denial of membership to employer and
college members, and sanctions prescribed by a candidate's college
or university.

The Ethics Committee of a regional association may refer a complaint to the College Placement Council's Principles and Practices Compliance Committee for further interpretation or for information on precedents, before making a decision concerning an alleged infraction of the Principles.

Professional Insignia: The emblem of the College Placement Council is an oval logotype, with the initials of the organization, "CPC," spaced within the design. The color of this insignia is shown variously-- black on white (letterhead); white on turquoise, white on blue, maroon on white, white on black (publications).

Bibliography:
> College Placement Council. Principles and Practices of College Placement and Recruitment. 1969 edition, with 1970 amendment. Pamphlet.
> Ethical principles, practices and procedures, and compliance provisions for colleges, employers, and candidates.

"Principles and Practices
of College Placement and Recruitment"

A statement of basic agreements developed for those engaged in college placement and recruitment as a guide to ethical practice.
This document pertains particularly to the relationships of college placement officers and students with employers.

GENERAL PRINCIPLES

It is in the best interests of students, colleges and employers alike that the consideration of careers and selection of employment opportunities be based on an understanding of all the relevant facts and that these considerations be made in an atmosphere conducive to objective thought.
The recruiting of college students should be carried out by employers, candidates, and college authorities, with due regard for established legislation, to serve best the following objectives:

1. The open and free selection of an employment opportunity that will provide the candidate with the optimum long-term utilization of his talents, consistent with his personal objectives.
2. The promotion of intelligent and responsible choice of a career by the candidate for his own greatest satisfaction and the most fruitful long-range investment of his talents for himself, for

his employer, and for society.

3. The development of the placement function as an integral part of the educational system so that it, as well as the total recruiting process, may be oriented toward the establishment of high standards of integrity and conduct among all parties。

4. The fostering of communication and exchange of information between employers and students, faculty members, and administrators。 An employer should not, however, be required to present and defend a corporate position before college and university groups as a condition for recruiting on campus.

PRINCIPLES

<u>The Employer</u>

1. Prior to, or at the time of the offer of employment, the employer should clearly explain to the candidate all conditions of employment.

2. The employer should give the candidate reasonable time to consider his offer, and in no case should the candidate be subjected to undue pressure to make a decision concerning employment。

3. The employer should not offer a candidate special payments, gifts, bonuses, or other inducements, nor should he compensate or favor a third party to prevail upon the candidate to accept an employment offer.

4. The employer should not raise salary offers already made, except when such action can be clearly justified as sound industrial relations practice; such as, when an increase in hiring rate is required on an over-all basis to reflect salary adjustments in the employing organization.

5。 The employer should not ask the placement office to divulge salary offers made by other organizations or for confidential information of any nature.

6. The employer should avoid any arrangements that would provide preferential recruitment or extra assistance from any college by virtue of financial or other special considerations.

7. A. In recognition of the fact that the college placement function plays an integral role in the development of the student, on-campus recruitment activities should be conducted by the individual employer. Where unusual circumstances may require that the employer be represented by other than those directly responsible to management, such representation shall be in the name of the employer and the employer shall assume full responsibility for any negotiations.

B. The employer participating in recruiting activities related to graduating college students, but conducted off-campus, should take every reasonable precaution to assure that the sponsoring organization conducts its program in keeping with the spirit and intent of these Principles and Practices。

C. The employer utilizing external recruiting media or pro-

grams directed toward those college students or graduates antici-
pating their first employment should assume reasonable responsibility for the reliability of representations made by such media or
programs.

8.   When a candidate has declined an offer, the employer
should accept that decision as final.   If for any reason the employer
wishes to re-establish contact with the candidate before graduation,
he should do so only with a copy of his letter sent to the placement
office.

9.   The employer should engage each candidate who has
accepted his offer except when this becomes impossible because of
(a) contingencies explained during the interview or (b) unavoidable
economic factors not foreseen when the offer was made.

Compliance

A complaint against an employer involving violation of these
principles should be made in one of the following ways:

1.   Direct dialog between the placement officer and the employer concerned, or his superior; or

2.   A confidential report to the chairman of the ethics committee of the appropriate Regional Association for adjudication or
hearing.

The Regional committee may refer the complaint to the College Placement Council's Principles and Practices Compliance Committee for further interpretation or for information on past precedents, as required.   Final adjudication, however, is the responsibility of the Regional Association involved.

Sanctions for Violations

In cases referred to the Regional committee any necessary
reprimand may take the form of:

1.   A warning.

2.   Suspension of privileges to attend an annual Regional
meeting during a period of suspension determined by the Regional
Association.

3.   Forfeiture or denial of membership in the Regional
Association.

The College

1.   In counseling candidates, the placement officer and faculty
members should not exert undue influence in the selection of positions.

2.   The placement office constantly should be aware of its
responsibility not to disclose any information given to it in confidence by employers or candidates as distinguished from information provided for general dissemination.   Consequently, no employee
of the placement office should divulge any salary information on a
specific candidate to any employer.

3. The placement office may advise alumni that placement services are available if they are seeking a position. However, the placement officer should not contact an employed alumnus about a specific employment opportunity unless the alumnus has indicated that he is seeking a new position.

4. A college placement officer should avoid any arrangements that would provide preferential placement or extra assistance to organizations by virtue of financial or other special considerations.

5. In recognition of the fact that the college placement function plays an integral role in the development of the candidate, college placement officers and staff members should exercise restraint in the endorsement, or inferential endorsement, of proposed or existing placement and recruitment media. Such restraint shall be exercised especially until such time as the value of such media shall have been established by their contribution to student personnel services on the campus concerned.

Compliance

A complaint against a placement office involving violation of these principles may be made in one of the following ways:

1. Direct dialog between the employer and the placement officer concerned, or his superior; or

2. A confidential report to the chairman of the ethics committee of the appropriate Regional Association for adjudication or hearing.

The Regional committee may refer the complaint to the College Placement Council's Principles and Practices Compliance Committee for further interpretation or for information on past precedents, as required. Final adjudication is the responsibility of the Regional Association involved.

Sanctions for Violations

In cases referred to the Regional committee any necessary reprimand may take the form of:

1. A warning.

2. Suspension of privileges to attend an annual Regional meeting during a period of suspension determined by the Regional Association.

3. Forfeiture or denial of membership in the Regional Association.

PRACTICES AND PROCEDURES

The following are recommended operational procedures which are felt to serve the best interests of the employer, the college, and the candidate--as differentiated from the principles set forth in the preceding section.

The Employer

1. The employer should inform the placement office well in advance regarding desired interview dates, broad categories of employment expected to be available, college degrees, and other pertinent requirements. He should promptly advise the placement office of any change in his original request or subsequent arrangements.

2. The employer should provide suitable material to give students a true and factual picture of the employing organization. This material should be supplied in sufficient quantities and well in advance of the interviewing date.

3. When both the parent organization and subsidiary or affiliated organization conduct interviews in the same college, an explanation of their missions and exact affiliation should be made, both to the placement office and to the candidates.

4. The employer should be punctual. He should advise the placement office about his anticipated arrival and departure times. Every effort should be made to avoid last-minute cancellations.

5. The employer should follow the interview time schedule agreed upon with the placement office.

6. As soon as possible following an interview, the employer should communicate with the candidate and the placement office concerning the outcome of the interview.

7. If the employer invites a candidate to visit his premises for further discussion of employment, the trip should be arranged to interfere as little as possible with class schedules. The employer should explain what expenses will be paid, how, and when. Invitations for this purpose should be made only on an individual basis and the employer should avoid elaborate entertaining or overselling.

8. No more than two and preferably only one interviewer should conduct an interview. The total number of interviewers brought on campus by an employer should not exceed the number necessary to handle adequately the number of candidates scheduled for interviews.

9. Arrangements for interview space requirements should be made in advance with the placement office.

10. Representatives of an employer, including alumni of the college, should notify the placement office of the college, in advance, of any plans for campus visits to acquaint faculty members or candidates with employment activities or opportunities. Such representatives should exercise scrupulous care to avoid undue demands on the time of faculty members or candidates.

11. An employer who desires to meet with a particular candidate at the time of his interview visit should communicate with the candidate well in advance with a notice to the placement office.

12.   The employer should keep the placement office informed concerning his interest in particular candidates and his negotiations with them.

13.   The employer should make certain that its representatives using placement office facilities are acquainted with this statement of "Principles and Practices of College Placement and Recruitment."

The College

1.   The college should provide competent counseling service and such other assistance that will aid the candidate in reaching a career decision based on a full appreciation of his potential.

2.   As soon as the information is available, the placement office should inform employers about graduation dates and the number of candidates who are candidates for degrees in the various curricula of the college.

3.   The placement office should make employment material available to candidates and faculty.

4.   The placement office should not restrict the number of interviews per candidate, except as necessary to discourage indiscriminate "shopping."

5.   The college should provide adequate space and facilities for quiet and private interviews.

6.   Candidate resumes and/or related material should not be released to organizations other than to bona fide employers, and then only with the written permission of the candidate.

7.   The placement office should arrange for employers to meet faculty members who know candidates personally and can provide information about their work and qualifications.

8.   Alumni may establish files with the placement office at an institution other than their own, provided this arrangement is in keeping with the receiving institution's policy.   They will be asked to furnish, for the cooperating institution's files, a statement from the placement officer of the college where they completed their studies.

9.   The placement office should make certain that candidates using its facilities are acquainted with this statement.

10.   As early as practicable, the placement office should announce the names of employers and the dates on which they will be recruiting on campus.   Announcements should be made later to incorporate subsequent changes.

11.   The placement office should inform candidates of the types of positions for which the employer will be interviewing on the proposed campus visit.   To the extent of the time allotted for the campus visit, the placement office should schedule appointments for interested candidates who appear to be qualified.

12.   The placement office should inform employers planning to visit the campus about the response of the candidates.   This will give the employer an opportunity to adjust the number of interviewers in accordance with the appointments scheduled.

The Candidate

1. In preparation for interviews with prospective employers, the candidate should analyze his interests and abilities, consider his career objectives, seek information about the fields of his interest through published materials and counseling, and organize his thoughts so that he may ask and answer questions intelligently.

2. The candidate should notify the placement office as early as possible of the interviews he wishes to have. He should also notify the placement office immediately if he subsequently finds that there is reason for him to cancel any appointments.

3. Before taking an interview, the candidate should read the company material and fill out such forms as may be required. He should arrive on time for his appointment and conduct himself in a businesslike manner.

4. The candidate who is invited to visit an employer's premises should promptly acknowledge the invitation and should accept only if he is sincerely interested in a position with that employer. If the candidate is to set the date of his visit, he should write the employer sufficiently in advance to permit the employer to confirm the date.

5. A candidate making a visit at an employer's expense should seek reimbursement only for those expenditures which pertain to the trip. If he visits other employers on the same trip, he should prorate the total cost among them.

6. When he receives an offer of employment, the candidate should notify the employer as soon as possible, but no later than the deadline specified by the employer, whether he will or will not accept.

7. If a candidate has a legitimate reason for the extended consideration of more than one offer, he should not only notify employers whose offers he is refusing, but also communicate with employers under consideration to attempt to establish a mutually satisfactory decision date. He should make his final choice at the earliest possible date.

8. A candidate should realize that an employment offer is to be accepted in good faith and with sincere intentions of honoring the commitment. He should not thereafter present himself for interviews with other employers.

9. Throughout his negotiations for employment, the candidate should keep the placement office advised of his decisions.

Compliance

A complaint against a candidate involving a breach of ethical conduct in these matters should be made directly to the placement officer concerned. Sanctions, if required, should be as prescribed by that candidate's college or university. The placement officer should advise the employer registering the complaint of the disposition of the case.

COMICS MAGAZINE PUBLISHERS

COMICS MAGAZINE ASSOCIATION OF AMERICA (CMAA)
300 Park Ave. South, New York, N. Y. 10010
Leonard Darvin, Executive Secretary and Code Administrator

Membership: The Comics Magazine Association of America, founded in 1954 and with a present (1973) membership of 14 firms, is a trade association of the comics publications industry that includes "90% of all publishers, distributors, printers and engravers engaged in the industry" of regularly issued comics magazines.

Code of Ethics: The CMAA includes among its objectives "raising the levels through the medium of an industry self-regulation program," and its Code--established and put into effect in 1954 and revised as of February 1 and October 27, 1971--is directed to "maintaining high standards of decency and good taste" in comics publications. The Code's standards for editorial and advertising matter prohibit nudity, details of criminal methods, scenes of horror, ridicule of religious or racial groups, illicit sex, perversion, profanity, and other subject matter offensive to public taste and morals.
    The Comics Code Authority, the agency of CMAA established to enforce the Code, requires that publisher-members of CMAA "submit their original manuscripts and art-work ... well in advance of publication dates" for review to determine compliance with the Code. "Each panel of art and each line of copy" is checked by the Comics Code Authority prior to publication, and changes or deletions are required when the proposed work "violates any tenet or the over-all principles of the Code." "Each individual page of copy must receive the Stamp of Approval of the Code Authority before it may be sent to the engraver. The entire contents of the issue must be so approved before authorization is granted for the Code Authority's Seal of Approval to appear on the upper right-hand corner of the magazine's cover."
    CMAA cites commendations from "public and private agencies concerned with communications media, particularly in their relation to young people," for the Code Authority's prior-to-publication review and its award of the Seal of Approval, as a guarantee that comics content meets "high standards."
    Compliance with the Code is voluntary, applying only to members of the CMAA. If deletions and changes in editorial or advertising contents required by the Code Authority are refused by a member-publisher, the publisher--after investigation and hearing-- may be suspended from membership in the Association.

Professional Insignia: The official insignia of the Comics Magazine Association is its Seal of Approval, placed upon reviewed comics magazines and books. This Seal is rectangular in shape, and bears the legend, "Approved by the Comics Code Authority," with a monogram of the organization, shown between the words "Code" and "Authority." The borders of the rectangle are perforated, and the color of the seal is black on white.

Bibliography:
Comics Magazine Association of America.
Code. Revised, October 1971. Pamphlet.
Code consisting of 18 General Standards, and additional standards grouped under five headings: Dialogue, Religion, Costume, Marriage and Sex, Advertising Matter. Seal of Approval on cover.
_____. Information Brochure. 4 pages.
Facts about the Comics Code and the Comics Code Authority. Shows Seal of Approval.

"Code of the Comics Magazine Association of America"

PREAMBLE

The comics magazine, or as it is more popularly known, the comic book medium, having come of age on the American cultural scene, must measure up to its responsibilities.

Constantly improving techniques and higher standards go hand in hand with these responsibilities.

To make a positive contribution to contemporary life, the industry must seek new areas for developing sound, wholesome entertainment. The people responsible for writing, drawing, printing, publishing and selling comic books have done a commendable job in the past, and have been striving toward this goal.

Their record of progress and continuing improvement compares favorably with other media. An outstanding example is the development of comic books as a unique and effective tool for instruction and education. Comic books have also made their contribution in the field of social commentary and criticism of contemporary life.

Members of the industry must see to it that gains made in this medium are not lost and that violations of standards of good taste, which might tend toward corruption of the comic book as an instructive and wholesome form of entertainment, will not be permitted.

Therefore, the Comics Magazine Association of America, Inc. has adopted this Code, and placed its enforcement in the hands of an independent Code Authority.

Further, members of the Association have endorsed the purpose and spirit of this Code as a vital instrument to the growth of the industry.

To this end, they have pledged themselves to conscientiously adhere to its principles and to abide by all decisions based on the Code made by the Administrator.

CODE FOR EDITORIAL MATTER

General Standards--Part A

1.   Crimes shall never be presented in such a way as to promote distrust of the forces of law and justice, or to inspire others with a desire to imitate criminals.

2.   No comics shall explicitly present the unique details and methods of a crime, with the exception of those crimes that are so far-fetched or pseudo-scientific that no would-be lawbreaker could reasonably duplicate.

3.   Policemen, judges, government officials and respected institutions shall not be presented in such a way as to create disrespect for established authority. If any of these is depicted committing an illegal act, it must be declared as an exceptional case and that the culprit pay the legal price.

4.   If crime is depicted it shall be as a sordid and unpleasant activity.

5.   Criminals shall not be presented in glamorous circumstances, unless an unhappy end results from their ill-gotten gains, and creates no desire for emulation.

6.   In every instance good shall triumph over evil and the criminal punished for his misdeeds.

7.   Scenes of excessive violence shall be prohibited. Scenes of brutal torture, excessive and unnecessary knife and gun play, physical agony, gory and gruesome crime shall be eliminated.

8.   No unique or unusual methods of concealing weapons shall be shown, except where such concealment could not reasonably be duplicated.

9.   Instances of law enforcement officers dying as a result of a criminal's activities should be discouraged, except when the guilty, because of their crime, live a sordid existence and are brought to justice because of the particular crime.

10. The crime of kidnapping shall never be portrayed in any detail, nor shall any profit accrue to the abductor or kidnapper. The criminal or the kidnapper must be punished in every case.

11. The letters of the word "crime" on a comics magazine cover shall never be appreciably greater in dimension than the other words contained in the title. The word "crime" shall never appear alone on a cover.

12. Restraint in the use of the word "crime" in titles or subtitles shall be exercised.

General Standards--Part B

1. No comic magazine shall use the word horror or terror in its title. These words may be used judiciously in the body of the magazine.

2. All scenes of horror, excessive bloodshed, gory or gruesome crimes, depravity, lust, sadism, masochism shall not be permitted.

3. All lurid, unsavory, gruesome illustrations shall be eliminated.

4. Inclusion of stories dealing with evil shall be used or shall be published only where the intent is to illustrate a moral issue and in no case shall evil be presented alluringly nor so as to injure the sensibilities of the reader.

5. Scenes dealing with, or instruments associated with walking dead, or torture shall not be used. Vampires, ghouls and werewolves shall be permitted to be used when handled in the classic tradition such as Frankenstein, Dracula and other high calibre literary works written by Edgar Allan Poe, Saki (H. H. Munro), Conan Doyle and other respected authors whose works are read in schools throughout the world.

6. Narcotics or Drug addiction shall not be presented except as a vicious habit.

Narcotics or Drug addiction or the illicit traffic in addiction-producing narcotics or drugs shall not be shown or described if the presentation:

(a) Tends in any manner to encourage, stimulate or justify the use of such narcotics or drugs; or

(b) Stresses, visually, by text or dialogue, their temporarily attractive effects; or

(c) Suggests that the narcotics or drug habit may be quickly or easily broken; or

(d) Shows or describes details of narcotics or drug procurement, or the implements or devices used in taking narcotics or drugs, or of the taking of narcotics or drugs in any manner; or

(e) Emphasizes the profits of the narcotics or drug traffic; or

(f) Involves children who are shown knowingly to use or traffic in narcotics or drugs; or

(g) Shows or implies a casual attitude towards the taking of narcotics or drugs; or

(h)   Emphasizes the taking of narcotics or drugs throughout, or in a major part, of the story, and leaves the denoue-
ment to the final panels.

General Standards--Part C

All elements or techniques not specifically mentioned herein, but
which are contrary to the spirit and intent of the Code, and are
considered violations of good taste or decency, shall be prohibited.

Dialogue

1.   Profanity, obscenity, smut, vulgarity, or words or symbols which have acquired undesirable meanings--judged and interpreted in terms of contemporary standards--are forbidden.
2.   Special precautions to avoid disparaging references to
physical afflictions or deformities shall be taken.
3.   Although slang and colloquialisms are acceptable, excessive use should be discouraged and wherever possible good
grammar shall be employed.

Religion

1.   Ridicule or attack on any religious or racial group is
never permissible.

Costume

1.   Nudity in any form is prohibited.   Suggestive and salacious illustration is unacceptable.
2.   Females shall be drawn realistically without undue emphasis on any physical quality.

Marriage and Sex

1.   Divorce shall not be treated humorously nor represented
as desirable.
2.   Illicit sex relations are not to be portrayed and sexual
abnormalities are unacceptable.
3.   All situations dealing with the family unit should have as
their ultimate goal the protection of the children and family life.
In no way shall the breaking of the moral code be depicted as rewarding.
4.   Rape shall never be shown or suggested.   Seduction may
not be shown.
5.   Sex perversion or any inference to same is strictly forbidden.

CODE FOR ADVERTISING MATTER

These regulations are applicable to all magazines published

by members of the Comics Magazine Association of America, Inc.
Good taste shall be the guiding principle in the acceptance of advertising.
1. Liquor and tobacco advertising is not acceptable.
2. Advertisement of sex or sex instruction books are unacceptable.
3. The sale of picture postcards, "pin-ups," "art studies,"
or any other reproduction of nude or semi-nude figures is prohibited.
4. Advertising for the sale of knives, concealable weapons,
or realistic gun facsimiles is prohibited.
5. Advertising for the sale of fireworks is prohibited.
6. Advertising dealing with the sale of gambling equipment or printed matter dealing with gambling shall not be accepted.
7. Nudity with meretricious purpose and salacious postures
shall not be permitted in the advertising of any product; clothed
figures shall never be presented in such a way as to be offensive
or contrary to good taste or morals.
8. To the best of his ability, each publisher shall ascertain that all statements made in advertisements conform to fact
and avoid misrepresentation.
9. Advertisement of medical, health, or toiletry products
of questionable nature are to be rejected. Advertisements for
medical, health or toiletry products endorsed by the American
Medical Association, or the American Dental Association, shall be
deemed acceptable if they conform with all other conditions of the
Advertising Code.

CONTRACTORS

ASSOCIATED GENERAL CONTRACTORS OF AMERICA (AGC)
   1957 E St., N.W., Washington, D.C. 20006
   William E. Dunn, Executive Vice President

Membership: The Associated General Contractors of America,
founded in 1918 and with a present (1973) membership of about
9000 firms, is a trade association of general contractors. "Active
Members" are "general contractors who have been engaged in the
business of general contracting for two or more years prior to
application for membership, and have established a reputation for
Skill, Integrity and Responsibility" (Bylaws, Article IV, Section 2).
Members may work in such diverse contracting activities as:
Building--excluding specialty contracting in plumbing, mechanical,
electrical and heating; Industrial, Highway; Heavy and Utilities Construction.

Code of Ethics: Among the special purposes of ACG, as set forth
in the Bylaws (Article I), are the encouragement of High Standards
in the Construction Business, Honorable Dealings, and Fair Practices.   These goals are reflected in the Code of Ethical Conduct
(AGC Governing Provisions, Appendix C), originally adopted in
January 1925, and reissued in 1947 and 1972 with only minor revisions.   The Code contains two main sections:
>   A--Preface: sets forth function of ethics and general prin-
>   ciples; and
>   B--Rules of Ethical Practice: gives the working principles
>   guiding contractors in their relations with client owners
>   and the public, with other agencies of construction and
>   with members of their own profession.

The Ethics and Trade Practices Committee, an AGC standing
committee, receives complaints made concerning ethics and trade
practices of contractor members, and may recommend discipline,
or expulsion to the Executive Committee of the Association, when
complaints of unethical practice are substantiated by investigation.
However, the Code of Ethical Conduct uses the word "should,"
rather than "shall," in setting forth the contractor's obligations
and responsibilities, so that the Code provisions are not mandatory
upon members, but are "rather a recommended guide to business
conduct."

Professional Insignia: The official emblem of the Associated Gen-

eral Contractors is a circular
seal with the name of the
organization, "The Associated
General Contractors of America,"
printed around the design in a
bordering band--black on white;
the central area within the black-
framed white border is red,
with the group's monogram cen-
tered--"AGC" in black, one
letter at the sides and in the center of a larger white"A."   The
motto of the AGC, "Skill, Integrity, Responsibility," appears in a
scroll--shown either over or under the emblem.   The insignia is
used on Association stationery and publications, and members may
display the emblem on stationery, building, job signs, equipment,
and elsewhere (Governing Provisions, IV-D, Section 7), or wear it
as a lapel button.

Bibliography:
    Associated General Contractors of America.   Code of Ethical
         Conduct.   1972.   Pamphlet.
    Guiding principles for contractors' conduct.
    _____.   Governing Provisions and Code of Ethical Conduct.
         Revised edition, 1972.   Pamphlet.
    The Preamble, Bylaws, Appendices (with Code of Ethical
    Conduct in Appendix C), and other basic AGC documents--

Articles of Incorporation.   Detailed Table of Contents, and
Index.

"Code of Ethical Conduct"

A--PREFACE

Preamble. During its comparatively short life, The Associated General Contractors of America has achieved among the
older professional and industrial organizations, a position of confidence and respect, which it earnestly desires to maintain. This
position has been attained principally by persevering effort to promote scientific construction methods, to rid the industry of improper
practices and to eliminate waste in its operations. Scrupulous
avoidance of any action which might not prove compatible with the
public interest or with the rightful interest of other industries together with the practice of opening all Conventions and Directors
Meetings to the public have helped to demonstrate that its purposes
are sound and worthy.

As an Association, we recognize and seek those benefits
which accrue from compliance with high ethical standards.

Function of Ethics. The function of ethical standards for
a society such as this, is essentially twofold; first, to establish
principles of business conduct to be observed by the members in
their relations with each other, and second, to establish principles
to be observed in their transactions with those who utilize their
services. In either sense they represent the minimum requirements for fair competition and honorable dealing.

The philosophy of ethical conduct is not new, nor is it un-
familiar to those men who have grasped the purpose of this Association. It is not necessary therefore, to dwell upon our obligation
to declare and follow what years of commercial experience have
indicated as sound ethical practice. There are, however, certain
practical considerations involved in this matter, which every contractor, and in fact every business man, should recognize.

Practical Considerations. The business structure of America
founded upon private initiative, has grown so complex that successful government of business conduct by legislation is not only undesirable but practically impossible. Industries and individuals, in
order to retain the benefits arising from this free initiative, and
to avoid the hampering burdens of regulatory legislation, must themselves accept responsibility for fair and intelligent self-government.
Such government does not require a profound knowledge of law and
legal procedure, but merely the courage to abide by self-imposed
restraints and principles which the intelligent fair-minded majority
of any industry clearly understand. Especially in construction,
which affects so fundamentally the entire country, is this courage
needed.

The Associated General Contractors of America realizes that the vital bearing of the construction industry upon the well-being, comfort and safety of the entire public, injects into the contractor's function an element of professional responsibility founded upon honor and trust. This responsibility requires, among other things, that we seek to improve construction methods, management and service, to eliminate uneconomical and improper practices, and to build responsibility throughout our industry. It surely cannot mean less than the establishment of construction service which will give to the investing public an assurance of skill and faithful performance.

Acceptable Principles. There are a number of principles to which the members of this Association can subscribe, but which have not yet been clearly formulated. We can accept without reservation the principle recognized by fair-minded men in every industry that contracts whether written or oral should be carried out according to their bona fide intent, and that disagreement concerning their intent should be settled if possible, by impartial arbitration.

The attitude of contractors toward their workmen is an element of ethics or fair dealing, and we recognize the vital relation of the welfare and success of contractors to that of their workmen. They should, in their dealings with labor, be guided by principles of justice and fairness, recognizing in this relation high standards of conduct and craftsmanship.

The Associated General Contractors of America limits its membership to contractors who qualify as to Skill, Integrity, and Responsibility, and whose dealings are honorable and ethical; and it is perhaps superfluous to suggest that no individual possessing these qualifications would attempt to injure the professional reputation, prospects or business of a competitor.

Need of Interpretation. Thus in a measure may be outlined some of the fundamental conceptions of construction ethics which we realize must be clearly expressed and generally accepted if this industry is to maintain its rightful place in the industrial world. Mere acceptance of the principles, however, no matter how sincerely accepted does not assure practical application in the daily transactions of business. Individual minds make individual interpretations and, unless there is some elucidation of principle the many minds do not meet and the principle fails in application. Otherwise we should need only the Golden Rule to govern all human activities.

In developing ethical standards, choice lies somewhere between the shortest possible statement and a complete, explicit set of rules attempting to cover all eventualities of the industry. Each of these conceptions has found favor within the membership of the Association. Approval has already been given to the Golden Rule, and certainly all sound ethical codes must rest upon that inspired foundation, but to go no further would leave this very practical industry at the mercy of individual interpretation and consequently without any standard rules of conduct.

Yet it seems undesirable and well nigh impossible to elaborate upon specific points and to develop a comprehensive structure
which would completely provide for all questions and phases of the
contracting business. This must develop slowly out of experience,
if at all. Consequently the Committee on Ethics rather briefly
suggests the broad principles upon which we stand, and presents
herewith some essential rules upon which we may all approximately
agree.
      No code will be final except in its fundamental principles.
Our rules of practice will inevitably be modified or added to as
experience develops. As ideas on conduct crystallize, various
rules which now are merely suggestive may become mandatory, or
may be abandoned. Therefore, while these rules of ethical practice
are the result of careful thought and study, they are not considered
as either complete or perfect, but are offered as a starting point
or framework which appears fairly adequate today and upon which
a safe ethical structure may in time be developed.

B--RULES OF ETHICAL PRACTICE

      The working principles by which members of The Associated
General Contractors are to be governed in their relations with client
owners and the public, with other agencies of construction, and
with members of their own profession are as follows:

1.   Owners and the Public

      Fair and bona fide competition is a fundamental service of
our industry to which clients and owners are entitled. Any act or
method in restriction thereof is a breach of faith toward this Association and a betrayal of its principles.
      But the competition cannot serve its legitimate purpose unless
it operates under conditions alike fair to owner and to contractor.
      Observance of ethical conduct toward the contractor by those
who utilize his competitive bidding will be encouraged in proportion
as he himself abides by the ethics of fair competition. Only when
he respects the code of this Association can he reasonably ask
others to respect it.
      Ethical conduct with respect to competitive bidding is defined
in the following paragraphs:

      1.   Competitive bids preferably should be submitted only
when a definite time and place for the opening of all proposals has
been fixed, at which all bidders or their representatives are pre-
mitted to be present.
      2.   The contractor's professional knowledge is the result
of his training and experience and if he is called upon for per-
liminary estimates or appraisals it is proper that he should be
paid in the same manner that engineers and architects are paid for
similar service.
      3.   Bidders should neither seek nor accept information con-
cerning a competitor's bid prior to the opening, nor by any method

suppress free competition.   It is equally improper for the
owners to use bids in an effort to induce any contractor to
lower his figures.
    4.   Contractors should cooperate in advising architects, en-
gineers and owners with respect to the relative costs of various
alternates while plans are being prepared and thus seek to reduce
the number of alternates to a nominal maximum.
    5.   When bids are solicited and received by an owner on a
lump sum basis, no competitor other than the low bidder should
solicit the work on a percentage basis, or any other form of cost-
plus contract, provided however, that any competitor shall have
the right to accept the work at his bid price or on a percentage
basis if tendered him without guaranteed maximum cost or at a
guaranteed maximum cost not less than his original bid.

2.   Engineering and Architectural Professions

    Local and national cooperation in matters of mutual concern
should be the basic policy of members of this Association in their
relations with the engineering and architectural professions; the
purpose of this cooperation being to establish a clear conception
of respective functions and responsibilities, to guard against uneconomical or improper practices, and to carry out constructive
measures within the industry.
    Ethical conduct toward architects and engineers demands the
following:

    1.   Support should be given to all efforts of these professions
to maintain and extend high standards of conduct.
    2.   Contractors should give full credit to the value of the
services rendered by the architect and engineer and neither undermine nor disparage their functions or usefulness.

3.   Subcontractors and Those Who Supply Materials

    The operations of the contractor are made possible through
the functioning of those agencies which furnish him with service or
products, and in contracting with them he is rightfully obligated by
the same principles of honor and fair dealing that he desires should
govern the actions toward himself of architects, engineers and
client owners.
    Ethical conduct with respect to subcontractors and those who
supply materials requires that:

    1.   Proposals should not be invited from anyone who is
known to be unqualified to perform the proposed work or to render
the proper service.
    2.   The figures of one competitor shall not be made known
to another before the award of the subcontract, nor should they
be used by the contractor to secure a lower proposal from another
bidder.
    3.   The contract should preferably be awarded to the lowest

bidder if he is qualified to perform the contract, but if the award
is made to another bidder, it should be at the amount of the latter's
bid.

4. In no case should the low bidder be led to believe that
a lower bid than his has been received.

5. When the contractor has been paid by a client owner
for work or material, he should make payment promptly, and in
just proportion, to subcontractors and others.

4. Operating Within the Jurisdiction of a Chapter or Branch

The conduct of any member who traditionally contracts with
the building trades unions when operating within the jurisdiction of
any Chapter or Branch whose members play a principal role in the
local bargaining unit should comply with the following:

1. Prior to estimating work within that area, he should
first contact the appropriate local Chapter or Branch headquarters
which should furnish him with complete information as to local
conditions, prevailing scale of wages and working conditions which
prevail on the proposed work.

2. If awarded work in that area he should become a member
of that appropriate local Chapter or Branch to the end that he may
perform his work under the conditions and scale of wages established
under the jurisdiction of that local Chapter or Branch.

3. Any action which tends to undermine the integrity of
the local bargaining unit such as the use of the interim short-form
agreement and that section of a national agreement which requires
the contractor to continue operations during strikes against, or
lockouts by local contractors, should not be used.

CORPORATE SECRETARIES

AMERICAN SOCIETY OF CORPORATE SECRETARIES, INC. (ASCS)
8 Rockefeller Plaza, New York, N. Y. 10020
John S. Black, Jr., Executive Director

Membership: The American Society of Corporate Secretaries,
founded in 1946 and with a present (1973) membership of over
2000 is a professional service organization, whose members are
officers of their corporations, such as Secretary, Secretary-
Treasurer, Secretary and General Counsel, Vice President and
Secretary. The Society's purpose--as stated in their Year Book--
is "the improvement and simplification of techniques and the maintenance of the highest standards of corporate procedure for the
business corporations of America."

Code of Ethics: No formal code of ethics has been developed.

Professional Insignia: The emblem of the American Society of
Corporate Secretaries is a
quill pen in an inkwell.   This
design appears on the letter-
head--light blue on white
ground, unbordered, and is
shown on the cover of all
Society publications.

COUNSELORS

AMERICAN PERSONNEL AND GUIDANCE ASSOCIATION (APGA)
    1607 New Hampshire Ave., N.W., Washington, D.C. 20009
    Charles Lewis, Executive Director

Membership: The American Personnel and Guidance Association,
organized in 1952 and with a present (1973) membership of over
28,000, is a professional association of counselors.   Its members,
organized in state branches and eight autonomous groups, span
"personnel and guidance work at all educational levels from kinder-
garten through higher education, and in community agencies, government, business and industry."   The eight Divisions--autonomous
groups--within the APGA federation are:
    American College Personnel Association,
    Association for Counselor Education and Supervision,
    National Vocational Guidance Association,
    Student Personnel Association for Teacher Education,
    American School Counselor Association,
    American Rehabilitation Counseling Association,
    Association for Measurement and Evaluation in Guidance,

National Employment Counselors Association.

Entrance requirements for these groups and for professional counseling vary depending upon place of employment and educational institution where trained. The APGA recommends a minimum of two years' graduate preparation for full-time employment as counselor, and most states, training institutions, and employers specify at least a master's degree as prerequisite to professional employment as a counselor.

Code of Ethics: The formulated guide to professional conduct issued by the APGA is the Association's Ethical Standards, which sets forth principles of conduct common to all types of counseling, and groups these responsibilities and obligations into six major areas of professional counseling practice:

> Counseling,
> Testing,
> Research and Publication,
> Consulting and Private Practice,
> Personnel Administration,
> Preparation for Personnel Work.

These Ethical Standards--and the Ethical Standards Casebook, which consists of case studies interpreting the Standards --are revised from time to time. The latest edition of these ethical guides, updated to reflect current standards, are those issued in the fall of 1972. No enforcement procedures for the Ethical Standards are reported.

Professional Insignia: The emblem of the American Personnel and Guidance Association is its logotype-- the organization monogram, "APGA," arranged in a square design. The color of the insignia varies--brown on white (letterhead); black on white, brown on white, tan on white (publications).

Bibliography:
> American Personnel and Guidance Association. Counseling: A Helping Relationship. 1970. Folder.
> Brochure describing the counseling profession--what the counselor does; entrance requirements for professional counseling field.

_____. "Ethical Practice: Preserving Human Dignity."
American Personnel and Guidance Journal.   December
1971. $2.
Special issue of the APGA professional journal assembled
"to increase counselors' awareness and understanding of
the legal, ethical and philosophical issues related to the
counseling process."
_____.   Ethical Standards.   Washington, D. C., Author,
1972.
General principles of counseling and guidance in major
areas of professional counseling.
_____.   Ethical Standards Casebook.   Washington, D. C.,
Author, 1965.   55 pages. $1.
Collection of 56 case studies relating to the statements in
the APGA Ethical Standards, relating the principles to
practice.   Specific situations in counseling illustrate the
application--or failure in application--of the conduct stand-
ards and ethical obligations of counselors.
Huckins, W.   Ethical and Legal Considerations in Guidance.
Boston, Houghton-Mifflin, 1968.

"Ethical Standards"

Preamble

The American Personnel and Guidance Association is an educational, scientific, and professional organization dedicated to service to society.   This service is committed to profound faith in
the worth, dignity, and great potentiality of the individual human
being.
The marks of a profession, and therefore of a professional
organization, can be stated as follows:

1.   Possession of a body of specialized knowledge, skills,
and attitudes known and practiced by its members.
2.   This body of specialized knowledge, skills, and attitudes is derived through scientific inquiry and scholarly learning.
3.   This body of specialized knowledge, skills, and attitudes
is acquired through professional preparation, preferably on the
graduate level, in a college or university as well as through continuous in-service training and personal growth after completion of
formal education.
4.   This body of specialized knowledge, skills, and attitudes,
is constantly tested and extended through research and scholarly inquiry.
5.   A profession has a literature of its own, even though
it may, and indeed must, draw portions of its content from other
areas of knowledge.
6.   A profession exalts service to the individual and society

above personal gain.   It possesses a philosophy and a code of ethics.

7.   A profession through the voluntary association of its members constantly examines and improves the quality of its professional preparation and services to the individual and society.

8.   Membership in the professional organization and the practice of the profession must be limited to persons meeting stated standards of preparation and competencies.

9.   The profession affords a life career and permanent membership as long as services meet professional standards.

10.   The public recognizes, has confidence in, and is willing to compensate the members of the profession for their services.

The Association recognizes that the vocational roles and settings of its members are identified with a wide variety of academic disciplines and levels of academic preparation.   This diversity reflects the pervasiveness of the Association's interest and influence.   It also poses challenging complexities in efforts to conceptualize:

   a.   the characteristics of members;
   b.   desired or requisite preparation or practice; and
   c.   supporting social, legal and/or ethical controls.

The specification of ethical standards enables the Association to clarify to members, future members, and to those served by members the nature of ethical responsibilities held in common by its members.

The introduction of such standards will inevitably stimulate greater concern by members for practice and preparation for practice.   It will also stimulate a general growth and identification with and appreciation for both the common and diverse characteristics of the definable roles within the world of work of Association members.

There are six major areas of professional activity which encompass the work of members of APGA.   For each of these areas certain general principles are listed below to serve as guide lines for ethical practice.   These are preceded by a general section which includes certain principles germane to the six areas and common to the entire work of the Association members.

Section A

GENERAL

1.   The member exerts what influence he can to foster the development and improvement of the profession and continues his professional growth throughout his career.

2.   The member has a responsibility to the institution within which he serves.   His acceptance of employment by the institution implies that he is in substantial agreement with the general policies and principles of the institution.   Therefore, his professional activities are also in accord with the objectives of the institution.   Within the member's own work setting, if, despite his

efforts, he cannot reach agreement as to acceptable ethical standards of conduct with his superiors, he should end his affiliation with them.

3. The member must expect ethical behavior among his professional associates in APGA at all times. He is obligated, in situations where he possesses information raising serious doubt as to the ethical behavior of other members, to attempt to rectify such conditions.

4. The member is obligated to concern himself with the degree to which the personnel functions of non-members with whose work he is acquainted represent competent and ethical performance. Where his information raises serious doubt as to the ethical behavior of such persons, it is his responsibility to attempt to rectify such conditions.

5. The member must not seek self-enhancement through expressing evaluations or comparisons damaging to other ethical professional workers.

6. The member should not claim or imply professional qualifications exceeding those possessed and is responsible for correcting any misrepresentations of his qualifications by others.

7. The member providing services for personal remuneration shall, in establishing fees for such services, take careful account of the charges made for comparable services by other professional persons.

8. The member who provides information to the public or to his subordinates, peers, or superiors has a clear responsibility to see that both the content and the manner of presentation are accurate and appropriate to the situation.

9. The member has an obligation to ensure that evaluative information about such persons as clients, students, and applicants shall be shared only with those persons who will use such information for professional purposes.

10. The member shall offer professional services only, through the context of a professional relationship. Thus testing, counseling, and other services are not to be provided through the mail by means of newspaper or magazine articles, radio or television programs, or public performance.

Section B

COUNSELING

This section refers to practices involving a counseling relationship with a counselee or client and is not intended to be applicable to practices involving administrative relationships with the persons being helped. A counseling relationship denotes that the person seeking help retain full freedom of choice and decision and that the helping person has no authority or responsibility to approve or disapprove of the choices or decisions of the counselee or client. "Counselee" or "client" is used here to indicate the person (or

persons) for whom the member has assumed a professional
responsibility. Typically the counselee or client is the individual
with whom the member has direct and primary contact. However,
at times, "client" may include another person(s) when the other
person(s) exercise significant control and direction over the individual being helped in connection with the decisions and plans
being considered in counseling.

    1.   The member's primary obligation is to respect the in-
tegrity and promote the welfare of the counselee or client with
whom he is working.

    2.   The counseling relationship and information resulting
therefrom must be kept confidential consistent with the obligations
of the member as a professional person.

    3.   Records of the counseling relationship including inter-
view notes, test data, correspondence, tape recordings, and other
documents are to be considered professional information for use
in counseling, research, and teaching of counselors but always with
full protection of the identity of the client and with precaution so
that no harm will come to him.

    4.   The counselee or client should be informed of the con-
ditions under which he may receive counseling assistance at or before the time he enters the counseling relationship. This is particularly true in the event that there exist conditions of which the
counselee or client would not likely be aware.

    5.   The member reserves the right to consult with any
other professionally competent person about his counselee client.
In choosing his professional consultant the member must avoid
placing the consultant in a conflict of interest situation, i. e.,
the consultant must be free of any other obligatory relation to
the member's client that would preclude the consultant being a
proper party to the member's efforts to help the counselee or
client.

    6.   The member shall decline to initiate or shall terminate
a counseling relationship when he cannot be of professional assistance to the counselee or client either because of lack of competence
or personal limitation. In such instances the member shall refer
his counselee or client to an appropriate specialist. In the event
the counselee or client declines the suggested referral, the member
is not obligated to continue the counseling relationship.

    7.   When the member learns from counseling relationships
of conditions which are likely to harm others over whom his institution or agency has responsibility, he is expected to report
the condition to the appropriate responsible authority, but in
such a manner as not to reveal the identity of his counselee
or clients.

    8.   In the event that the counselee or client's condition is
such as to require others to assume responsibility for him, or
when there is clear and imminent danger to the counselee or client
or to others, the member is expected to report this fact to an appropriate responsible authority, and/or take such other emergency
measures as the situation demands.

9.   Should the member be engaged in a work setting which calls for any variation from the above statements, the member is obligated to ascertain that such variations are justifiable under the conditions and that such variations are clearly specified and made known to all concerned with such counseling services.

Section C

TESTING

1.   The primary purpose of psychological testing is to provide objective and comparative measures for use in self-evaluation or evaluation by others of general or specific attributes.
2.   Generally, test results constitute only one of a variety of pertinent data for personnel and guidance decisions.   It is the member's responsibility to provide adequate orientation or information to the examinee(s) so that the results of testing may be placed in proper perspective with other relevant factors.
3.   When making any statements to the public about tests and testing care must be taken to give accurate information and to avoid any false claims or misconceptions.
4.   Different tests demand different levels of competence for administration, scoring, and interpretation.   It is therefore the responsibility of the member to recognize the limits of his competence and to perform only those functions which fall within his preparation and competence。
5.   In selecting tests for use in a given situation or with a particular client the member must consider not only general but also specific validity, reliability, and appropriateness of the test(s).
6.   Tests should be administered under the same conditions which were established in their standardization.   Except for research purposes explicitly stated, any departures from these conditions, as well as unusual behavior or irregularities during the testing session which may affect the interpretation of the test results, must be fully noted and reported.   In this connection, unsupervised test-taking or the use of tests through the mails are of questionable value.
7.   The value of psychological tests depends in part on the novelty to persons taking them.   Any prior information, coaching, or reproduction of test materials tends to invalidate test results. Therefore, test security is one of the professional obligations of the member。
8.   The member has the responsibility to inform the examinee(s) as to the purpose of testing.   The criteria of examinee's welfare and/or explicit prior understanding with him should determine who the recipients of the test results may be。
9.   The member should guard against the appropriation, reproduction, or modifications of published tests or parts thereof without express permission and adequate recognition of the original author or publisher.
    Regarding the preparation, publication, and distribution of

tests reference should be made to:
>"Tests and Diagnostic Techniques"--Report of the Joint Committee of the American Psychological Association. American Educational Research Association, and National Council of Measurements used in Education. Supplement to Psychological Bulletin, 1954, 2, 1-38.

Section D

RESEARCH AND PUBLICATION

1. In the performance of any research on human subjects, the member must avoid causing any injurious effects or after-effects of the experiment upon his subjects.

2. The member may withhold information or provide mis-information to subjects only when it is essential to the investigation and where he assumes responsibility for corrective action following the investigation.

3. In reporting research results, explicit mention must be made of all variables and conditions known to the investigator which might affect interpretation of the data.

4. The member is responsible for conducting and reporting his investigations so as to minimize the possibility that his findings will be misleading.

5. The member has an obligation to make available original research data to qualified others who may wish to replicate or verify the study.

6. In reporting research results or in making original data available, due care must be taken to disguise the identity of the subjects, in the absence of specific permission from such subjects to do otherwise.

7. In conducting and reporting research, the member should be familiar with, and give recognition to, previous work on the topic.

8. The member has the obligation to give due credit to those who have contributed significantly to his research, in accordance with their contributions.

9. The member has the obligation to honor commitments made to subjects of research in return for their cooperation.

10. The member is expected to communicate to other members the results of any research he judges to be of professional or scientific value.

Section E

CONSULTING AND PRIVATE PRACTICE

Consulting refers to a voluntary relationship between a professional helper and help-needing social unit (industry, business, school, college, etc.) in which the consultant is attempting to give help to the client in the solving of some current or potential problem. *

1. The member acting as a consultant must have a high degree of self-awareness of his own values and needs in entering a helping relationship which involves change in a social unit.

2. There should be understanding and agreement between consultant and client as to directions or goals of the attempted change.

3. The consultant must be reasonably certain that he or his organization have the necessary skills and resources for giving the kind of help which is needed now or that may develop later.

4. The consulting relationship must be one in which client adaptability and growth toward self-direction are encouraged and cultivated. The consultant must consistently maintain his role as a consultant and not become a decision maker for the client.

5. The consultant in announcing his availability for service as a consultant follows professional rather than commercial standards in describing his services with accuracy, dignity, and caution.

6. For private practice in testing, counseling, or consulting the ethical principles stated in all previous sections of this document are pertinent. In addition, any individual, agency, or institution offering educational and vocational counseling to the public should meet the standards of the American Board on Professional Standards in Vocational Counseling, Inc.

Section F

PERSONNEL ADMINISTRATION

1. The member is responsible for establishing working agreements with supervisors and with subordinates especially regarding counseling or clinical relationships, confidentiality, distinction between public and private material, and a mutual respect for the positions of parties involved in such issues.

2. Such working agreements may vary from one institutional setting to another. What should be the case in each instance, however, is that agreements have been specified, made known to those concerned, and whenever possible the agreements reflect institutional policy rather than personal judgment.

3. The member's responsibility to his superiors requires that he keep them aware of conditions affecting the institution, particularly those which may be potentially disrupting or damaging to the institution.

4. The member has a responsibility to select competent

---

*This definition is adapted from "Dimensions of the Consultant's Job" by Ronald Lippitt, The Journal of Social Issues, Vol. XV. No. 2, 1959.

persons for assigned responsibilities and to see that his personnel are used maximally for the skills and experience they possess.

5.   The member has responsibility for constantly stimulating his staff for their and his own continued growth and improvement. He must see that staff members are adequately supervised as to the quality of their functioning and for purposes of professional development.

6.   The member is responsible for seeing that his staff is informed of policies, goals, and programs toward which the department's operations are oriented.

Section G

PREPARATION FOR PERSONNEL WORK

1.   The member in charge of training sets up a strong program of academic study and supervised practice in order to prepare the trainees for their future responsibilities.

2.   The training program should aim to develop in the trainee not only skills and knowledge, but also self-understanding.

3.   The member should be aware of any manifestations of personal limitations in a student trainee which may influence the latter's provision of competent services and has an obligation to offer assistance to the trainee in securing professional remedial help.

4.   The training program should include preparation in research and stimulation for the future personnel worker to do research and add to the knowledge in his field.

5.   The training program should make the trainee aware of the ethical responsibilities and standards of the profession he is entering.

6.   The program of preparation should aim at inculcating among the trainees, who will later become the practitioners of our profession, the ideal of service to individual and society above personal gain.

CREDIT MANAGERS

NATIONAL ASSOCIATION OF CREDIT MANAGEMENT (NACM)
   475 Park Ave. South, New York, N.Y. 10016
   Robert D. Goodwin, Executive Vice President

Membership: The National Association of Credit Management, founded in 1896 and with a present (1973) membership of more than 36,000 is an affiliation of 100 local credit associations in the United States, Mexico, and Europe. The members--whose membership in the NACM is automatic when they are members of a local association--are credit and financial executives professionally employed by "manufacturers, wholesalers, financial institutions and varied service organizations. "

Courses and training in credit offered by and for the Association include:

Graduate School of Credit and Financial Management

Advanced courses for credit and financial executives offered at Dartmouth College, Harvard University, and Stanford University, each summer for a two-week period covering a three-year course.

National Institute of Credit Courses

Extension courses in cooperation with colleges and universities; and correspondence courses in such subjects as "Credit and Collection Principles"; "Advanced Credit Analysis"; and "Credit Management Cases. "

Code of Ethics: Carrying out one of the purposes of founding NACM --"to establish a code of ethics"--a professional conduct guide, Canons of Commercial Ethics, was prepared by a committee of the Association in the mid-1950's. The Canons enumerate ten general principles governing ethical conduct in credit and financial management. This ethical code is enforced through the local affiliate associations of NACM, who receive complaints of violations of the Canons, interpret the code, investigate complaints and hold hearings as required, and carry out disciplinary action for proved violations of the ethical guide by censure or expulsion from the Association.

Professional Insignia: The NACM emblem is the organization's

official seal, re-designed in 1958 when the organization's name was changed from "National Association of Credit Men" to the present name. This insignia is a round design bearing a centered horizontal bar with the term, "Vigilantia, " to indicate "the importance of vigilance in extending credit"; the group's founding date is recorded in "Organized, " above the centered bar, and "1896, " below the bar; the name of the group, "National Association of Credit Management, " bands the emblem, and is bordered by uniform fluting, representing an impressed wax seal.

The seal is used by members on letterheads, membership plaque or lapel button, as well as on Association stationery and publications. The color of the emblem is shown variously--black on white; black on green (letterhead).

<u>Other Designations of Professional Status:</u> The current NACM motto
(adopted in 1964 to replace the previous maxim, "Guarding the Nation's Profits") is:
     "Creating Profit Through Credit."

<u>Bibliography:</u>
     National Association of Credit Management. <u>Canons of Com-</u>
          <u>mercial Ethics.</u> Single 8"x11" sheet. $.25.
     Enumerates ten general principles of ethical credit manage-
     ment.
          _____. <u>Credit and Financial Management.</u> Monthly. $5. a
          year; $.50 a copy.
     The monthly journal of the NACM includes descriptive and
     historic facts about the Association--a concise description
     of the purposes and services of the Association (July 1971,
     inside front cover); Diamond Jubilee Anniversary Issue
     (May 1971) gives history of the NACM, goals, and of-
     ficers.

                   "Canons of Commercial Ethics"

                                I
          Justice, equity, and confidence constitute the foundation of
     the credit structure.
                                II
          Agreements and contracts are sacred and should not be
     breached by either party.
                                III
          The interchange of credit information must be based upon
     confidence, cooperation, and reciprocity.
                                IV
          It shall be deemed unethical to be a party to unwarranted
     assignments or transfers of a distressed debtor's assets, nor should
     creditors participate in secret arrangements.
                                V
          Creditors should cooperate for the benefit of all in adjust-
     ment or liquidation of insolvent estates.
                                VI
          Creditors should render all possible assistance to honest
     debtors in distress.
                                VII
          Dishonest debtors should be exposed and punished.
                                VIII
          Cooperation, fairness and honesty must dominate in all dis-
     tressed debtor proceedings.
                                IX
          Expensive administrative procedures in the rehabilitation
     or liquidation of a distressed debtor shall be avoided at all
     times.
                                X
          Members pledge themselves to uphold the integrity, dignity,
     and honor of the credit profession in all their dealings.

DATA PROCESSORS

DATA PROCESSING MANAGEMENT ASSOCIATION (DPMA)
    505 Busse Highway, Park Ridge, Ill. 60060
    R. Calvin Elliott, Executive Director

Membership: The Data Processing Management Association, founded
in 1951 and with a present (1973) membership of about 30,000, is a
professional organization of directors, managers, and supervisors
of information processing and computer installations. Members,
grouped in over 280 local chapters in the United States, Canada,
and other countries, are eligible for "Regular Membership" if they
are "persons engaged as:
    a. Managerial or supervisory personnel in EDP (Electronic
        Data Processing) installations;
    b. Systems and methods analysts, research specialists, and
        computer programmers employed in executive, adminis-
        trative or consulting capacities; and
    c. Staff, managers, educators, and executive personnel with
        a direct interest in data processing. "

    To identify individuals who have reached acceptable levels of
professional knowledge, the Association conducts, through its
"Certification Council," two voluntary examination programs:
    Certificate in Data Processing (CDP)--Since 1962 this pro-
        gram has awarded the "Certificate in Data Processing,"
        and authorized the use of the designation "CDP" after the
        name of individuals who have qualified for such certifica-
        tion with "at least 60 months of direct experience in
        computer-based information systems," and passed a day-
        long written examination, consisting of 300 questions in
        five general information areas: Data Processing Equip-
        ment, Computer Programming and Software, Principles
        of Management, Quantitative Methods, Systems Analysis
        and Design.
    Registered Business Programmer (RBP)--Since 1968 this
        registration procedure has authorized the use of the
        designation "Registered Programmer" to "identify in-
        dividuals who have a common body of technical knowledge
        which should enable them to be efficient, effective busi-
        ness programmers. "
            The 4 1/2 hour written examination qualifying for
        registered programmer is open to applicants "with suffi-
        cient training and experience to reach the level of Senior
        Programmer," and consists of 180 questions "distributed
        between work problems and detailed knowledge in subject
        areas: Principles of Programming, Meta Programming
        Systems, Problem Oriented Language, Data Processing

Systems Design, and Computational Topics, including
Representation of Numbers, Significant Digits, Rounding,
Iteration. "

These examinations, given annually at universities and
colleges throughout the United States and Canada, are developed by experienced data processing managers working
with psychologists and educators skilled in test development and evaluation.

In awarding designations of acceptable levels of knowledge, the
Certification Council acts in "establishing the requirements for
candidates, determining the scope of both Examinations, and in
approving the contents and cut-off scores of the Examinations. "

Code of Ethics: The conduct guide for members is the DPMA Code
of Ethics, which gives, in the form of a pledge, the principles subscribed to by members. No enforcement procedures for this code
were reported.

Other Guides to Professional Conduct: Holders of the "Certificate
in Data Processing" subscribe to a pledge, Code of Ethics, adopted
by the Certification Council in December 1967. This code lists the
general obligations of the data processor. Individuals authorized to
use the designation "Registered Business Programmer" subscribe
to a comparable statement of obligations, Registered Programmer Code of Ethics, approved by the Certification Council in
April 1970.

Professional Insignia: The
official emblem of the DPMA
is its logotype--a rectangular
design, with a centered magnetic tape reel surrounded by
electron rings; to the left of
which is printed inside a punch
card the organization initials,
"DPMA. " This logotype appears in the circular seal of
the Association, and on Association publications. The
colors of the insignia are
shown variously--blue on white
(letterhead, publications); black on white (publications).

Other Identification of Professional Status: As described above under
"Membership, " two professional designations are authorized to indi-
cate acceptable levels of knowledge:
"Certificate in Data Processing" ("CDP");
"Registered Business Programmer" ("RBP").

Bibliography:
Data Processing Management Association. Certificate in Data
Processing. 1972. 30 pages. Pamphlet.

Announcement and study guide for the CDP program, with requirements for examination, detailed outline of subjects covered in examination, references for suggested reading for examinees, and Code of Ethics for Holders of Certificate in Data Processing.

_____. Registered Business Programmer. 1972. 12 pages. Pamphlet.

Announcement and study guide for RBP, with requirements for examination, detailed outline of examination subjects, references for suggested reading for examinees, and Registered Programmer Code of Ethics.

_____. Services and Activities. Pamphlet. Informational brochure.

"Code of Ethics"

I acknowledge:

That I have an obligation to management, therefore, I shall promote the understanding of automatic data processing methods and procedures to management using every resource at my command.

That I have an obligation to my fellow members, therefore, I shall uphold the high ideals of the DPMA as outlined in its International Bylaws. Further, I shall cooperate with my fellow members in the dissemination of knowledge pertaining to the general development of data processing. Further, I shall not use knowledge of a confidential nature pertaining to the business of a fellow member's employer to further my personal interest.

That I have an obligation to my employer whose trust I hold, therefore, I shall endeavor to discharge this obligation to the best of my ability, to guard his interests, and to advise him wisely and honestly.

That as an associate member, I have a further obligation, therefore, I shall not engage in direct selling efforts during a regularly scheduled DPMA meeting unless specifically and officially invited to do so; further, I shall not be indiscreet in any of my dealings wherein the association or a fellow member is involved.

That I have an obligation to my country, therefore, in my personal, business and social contacts I shall uphold this great nation and shall honor the chosen way of life of my fellow citizens.

I accept these obligations as a personal responsibility and, as a member of this association, I shall actively discharge these obligations and I dedicate myself to that end.

"Code of Ethics for Holders
of the Certificate in Data Processing"

The holder of the Certificate in Data Processing, consistent with his obligation to the public at large, should promote the understanding of data processing methods and procedures using every resource at his command.

The holder of the Certificate in Data Processing has an obligation to his profession to uphold the high ideals and the level of personal competence certified by the Certificate.   He should also encourage the dissemination of knowledge pertaining to the development of data processing.

The holder of the Certificate in Data Processing has an obligation to serve the interests of his employer and clients loyally, diligently, and honestly.

The holder of the Certificate in Data Processing must not engage in any conduct or commit any act which is discreditable to the reputation or integrity of the data processing profession.

The holder of the Certificate in Data Processing must not imply that the Certificate in Data Processing which he holds is his sole claim to professional competence.

"Registered Programmer Code of Ethics"

I acknowledge:

That I have an obligation to my employer, whose trust I hold.   Therefore, I shall endeavor to discharge this obligation to the best of my ability, to guard his interests and to serve him efficiently and honestly.

That I have an obligation to my profession.   Therefore, I shall uphold the status of the profession by maintaining a level of competency in the art of programming and by aiding in the dissemination of knowledge pertaining to the general development of data processing programming.

That I have an obligation to the community in which I live. Therefore, I shall endeavor to represent the programming profession in the education and understanding by the public of data processing principles.

That I have an obligation to the agency under whose authority my qualification as a programmer has been examined and registered. Therefore, I shall uphold the reputation of the issuing agency by discharging my duties and responsibilities as a programmer in a competent and professional manner.

I accept these obligations as a personal responsibility and, as a Registered Programmer, I shall actively discharge these obligations and I dedicate myself to that end.

I further acknowledge the power of issuing agency to revoke this registration upon breech of these ethics.

DENTAL ASSISTANTS

AMERICAN DENTAL ASSISTANTS ASSOCIATION (ADAA)
    211 E. Chicago Ave., Chicago, Ill. 60611
    Thomas R. Schedler, Executive Director

Membership: The American Dental Assistants Association, founded
in 1924 and with a present (1973) membership of about 17,000, is
a professional association of dental assistants, organized in 51
state groups and about 450 local groups. "Active Members" are
dental assistants employed by a member of the American Dental
Association or by a dentist whose practice is in accord with the
Principles of Ethics of the American Dental Association, or employed in a dental division of clinics, hospitals, or institutions,
or as an instructor of dental assisting programs in non-proprietary
schools, or as executive officer for a professional dental group,
with active ADAA membership prior to such employment.

    Through its certification program, initiated in 1948, the Asso-
ciation authorizes the use of the professional designation:
    "Certified Dental Assistant"--"C.D.A."
The basic requirement for certification--open to dental assistants
whether or not they are members of ADAA--is graduation from a
training program for dental assistants, which is accredited by the
American Dental Association.
    The certifying program is administered by the ADAA Certify-
ing Board. The certification examination consists of four separate
tests--three written and one clinical:
        Written--Part I.   Sciences and Dental Materials;
                 Part II.   Procedures;
                 Part III. Expanded Duties (Intra-oral);
        Clinical--Part IV. Actual Performance Test involving three
                            aspects of a maxillary stone cast.
Part IV is required only of those candidates who have previously
failed the clinical test. The written examinations consist of multiple-choice and matching questions, and the Handbook for Applicants
for certification includes a subject outline from which information
used in the tests is drawn, and sample questions. Certificates
must be renewed annually, with evidence of continuing education required.

Code of Ethics: The professional conduct guide for dental assistants
is the ADAA Principles of Ethics, which sets forth in five paragraphs the general professional obligations of the dental assistant.
No procedures for enforcement of these principles are reported.

Other Guides to Professional Conduct: The Dental Assistants Pledge
(written by Dr. C. N. Johnson), subscribed to be each member

upon joining the Association, gives the high ideals of loyalty and
devotion for the dental assistant.

Professional Insignia: The
official emblem of the American Dental Assistants Association is a circular design
showing a centered lamp of
learning placed on two horizontal books--signifying study
and education--over the initials of the organization,
"ADAA"; the motto of the
Association, "Education,
Efficiency, Loyalty, Ser-
vice," is printed around the
design in a bordering band,
enclosed in a six-scalloped
band. The color of the
insignia is blue on white
(publication). The emblem
appears on official ADAA publications, and is worn by members as
a pin, in the official colors of the Association--blue and gold.

Bibliography:
    American Dental Assistants Association. Certification Handbook
        for Applicants. Annual.
    Includes qualifications to take the certifying examination, Rules
    and Regulations for Examination and Certification, examination
    outline and sample questions, examination locations and
    schedule.
        . Membership Information Pamphlet. Folder.
    Gives membership requirements, Principles of Ethics, Dental
    Assistants Pledge, and shows official emblem.

"Principles of Ethics"

    Conduct of Members. The conduct of every member shall
be governed by the Principles of Ethics of the American Dental
Assistants Association and the constituent and component societies
within whose jurisdiction she is located. The member shall maintain honesty in all things, obedience to the dental practice act of
the state in which she is employed, and adherence to the professional ethics required of her by her employer.
    Obligations. Every member of this Association has the obli-
gation:
    To hold in confidence the details of professional service ren-
dered by her employer, the salary she receives, and the confidence
of any patients who come under her care.
    To increase her abilities and skills by seeking additional
education in her field through services provided by the Association

and its constituent and component societies.

To participate actively in the efforts of this Association and its constituent and component societies to improve the educational status of the dental assistant.

To support these Principles of Ethics.

To refrain from performing any service for any patient which requires the professional competence of a dentist, or is prohibited by the dental practice act of the state in which she is employed.

"The Dental Assistants Pledge"

"I solemnly pledge that, in the practice of my profession, I will always be loyal to the welfare of the patients who come under my care, and to the interest of the practitioner whom I serve.

I will be just and generous to the members of my profession, aiding them and lending them encouragement to be loyal, to be just, to be studious.

I hereby pledge to devote my best energies to the service of humanity in that relationship of life to which I consecrated myself when I elected to become a Dental Assistant."

--Dr. C. N. Johnson

DENTAL HYGIENISTS

AMERICAN DENTAL HYGIENISTS' ASSOCIATION (ADHA)
211 E. Chicago Ave., Chicago, Ill. 60611
Carl H. Hauber, Executive Director

Membership: The American Dental Hygienists' Association, founded in 1923 and with a present (1973) membership of over 18,000, is a professional society of dental hygienists. A member of ADHA must belong to one of the constituent (state) societies of the Association, have completed training in a school of dental hygiene accredited by the Council on Dental Education of the American Dental Association, and be licensed in state of practice (Bylaws, Chapter I, Section 2).

Code of Ethics: In accordance with one of the objectives of the American Dental Hygienists' Association--"contributing to the improvement of the health of the public; in a manner consistent with the Principles of Ethics of the profession" (Constitution, Article II) --professional obligations of the dental hygienist are set forth in the ADHA Principles of Ethics, which groups broad conduct guides

under the headings:
  Self;
  Professional Organization; and
  The Community.

  These Principles are enforced (Bylaws, Chapter XVIII), by the
constituent and component societies of the Association, who may
hold hearings and set discipline for violation of the ethical code.
Disciplinary measures include censure, probation, or suspension
or expulsion from ADHA membership. A member judged guilty of
violating the ethical code, in a decision of the local society of
which he is a member, may appeal that decision to the ADHA Committee on Judicial Affairs.

Other Guides to Professional Conduct: In the Oath of the American
Dental Association, the dental hygienist pledges obligations to the
public and to his profession.

Professional Insignia: The emblem of the American Dental Hygienists' Association, adopted in
the present form in 1972, is
a circular design with a
stylized winged staff of
Aesculapius, symbolizing
the healing arts; beneath
this symbol are the Asso-
ciation initials, "ADHA,"
in lower case type; a bordering band carries the name
of the organization, "American Dental Hygienists' Association," with the date of
founding, "1923," within the
bordering band. The insignia
incorporates a lavender background for the central circular
area--as lavender is the academic color for dental hygiene.

Bibliography:
  American Dental Hygienists' Association. Constitution, Bylaws,
    Principles of Ethics, Platform, and Oath. 1970. 30
    pages.
  Basic organizational documents of ADHA, including code of
  ethics and oath; official seal on cover.
  Motley, Wilma. Ethics, Jurisprudence, and History for the
    Dental Hygienist. Philadelphia, Lea & Febiger, 1972.
    $7.50.
  The editor of the ADHA Journal brings together information
  about ethics, history of dental hygiene.
  Steele, Pauline. Dimensions of Dental Hygiene. Philadelphia,
    Lea & Febiger, 1968. 520 pages.
  Includes a history of the ADHA to the middle 1960's.

"Principles of Ethics"

The philosophical, practical science of ethics, established by reason and intelligent observation, principles to direct our human conduct. Professional conduct incorporates the knowledge of these principles into practice.

The following principles constitute a guide to the responsibilities of the dental hygienist to:

Self

The dental hygienist, supporting the laws governing dental hygiene, is individually obligated to assume responsibilities for professional actions and judgments when rendering services to the public.

The dental hygienist has an obligation to improve professional competency through continued education and research.

The dental hygienist functions harmoniously with and sustains confidence in all members of the dental health team.

The dental hygienist is obligated to report unethical practice to the appropriate authority.

Professional Organization

The dental hygienist has the responsibility to support and participate in the professional organization.

The dental hygienist participates in the study of and acts on matters of legislation affecting the dental hygienist and dental hygiene services to the public.

The dental hygienist through the professional organization participates responsibly in establishing social and economic status for the practice of dental hygiene.

The Community

The dental hygienist as a member of a community understands and upholds the laws of that community and has a particular responsibility to work with all allied health professions in promoting efforts to meet the general and oral health needs of the public.

"Oath"

Whereas, ages ago in their quest for supernatural aid, the Greeks swore by Aesculapius, son of Apollo, god of health, and by Hygeia, goddess of health; and whereas, the Romans in the Christian era placed themselves under the protection of Apollonia, whose help as Dentistry's patron saint, they besought, so now, do I--humbly acknowledge my human limitations--in accepting this parchment of my Alma Mater, solemnly swear to render health service to those who seek my ministrations, hereby enjoining upon myself the sacred duty of teaching to public, particularly children

and young people, by precept, lecture, and every other available
mode of instruction, the value of dental health as a priceless possession; and further, bind myself, by future study to broaden my
knowledge that I may share with others such information in my
special field as will tend toward the idea of dental health sought by
Dr. Alfred C. Fones, the founder of the profession of Dental Hygiene.

 With this pledge inviolate, may it be granted me to enrich
my life in the practice of my art, thus to worship God in the service of mankind.

DENTISTS

AMERICAN DENTAL ASSOCIATION (ADA)
  211 E. Chicago Ave., Chicago, Ill. 60611
  C. Gordon Watson, D.D.S., Executive Director

Membership: The American Dental Association, founded in 1859
and with a present (1973) membership of over 115,000, is the professional organization of dentists. Members, qualified to practice
dentistry by graduate college training and licensed in the state in
which they practice, are grouped in component local and state
dental societies throughout the United States.

Code of Ethics: Ethical rules governing the professional practice
of dentistry are the ADA Principles of Ethics, first adopted in
1866, and periodically revised, the most recent revision being that
of January 1, 1972. These Principles set forth in 21 sections the
dentist's obligations regarding such questions as "Emergency Service," "Consultation," "Patents and Copyrights," "Contract Practice,"
"Announcement of Limitation of Practice," and promotion of practice
in Advertising, Cards, Letterheads and Announcements; Office Door
Lettering and Signs; Directories.
 The Principles of Ethics are interpreted by the American Dental
Association Judicial Council, and the interpretations are published
periodically in the Journal of the American Dental Association, and
as a separate brochure. Questions of infractions of the code of
ethics are resolved on the local level, in city, regional, or state
professional organizations (Principles of Ethics, Section 21), but in
event that "a satisfactory decision cannot be reached" at the local
level, a question of ethics may be referred, on appeal, to the
Judicial Council of the American Dental Association for consideration (Bylaws, Chapter XI).

Professional Insignia: The official emblem of dentistry, first
adopted in 1940, was approved--after a study of the professional
insignia--by the American Dental Association House of Delegates in

1965. The design "uses as its central figure a serpent entwined about an ancient Arabic cautery in the manner of the single serpent of Aesculapius, the Greek god of medicine, coiled about the rod. The Greek letter, "$\triangle$," (delta), for dentistry and the Greek letter, "O," (omicron), for odont (tooth), form the periphery of the design. The word "Dentistry" appears in the lowest arc of the letter "O." In the background are 32 leaves and 20 berries, representative of the two dentitions of permanent and temporary teeth."

The color of the emblem is specifically described:
"the background in a shade of lilac, the official academic color of dentistry (Descriptive Color Names Dictionary of the Container Corporation of America, 1950, color chip 12 gc); the letter O in gold; the letter D outlined in black; the cautery in gold outlined in black; and the leaves and berries merely outlined in black on the lilac background."
The insignia may be used by all dental organizations, but "its use in advertising or promotion material is not looked on with favor."

Bibliography:
    American Dental Association. "Dental Insigne." American
        Dental Association. Transactions. 1965:228.
    _____. Principles of Ethics with Official Advisory Opinions.
        As revised November 1972. American Dental Association.
        Journal, 86:60-64 January 1973.
    Rules of professional conduct for dentists.

"Principles of Ethics"
with official advisory opinions, as revised November 1972

The Association's Principles of Ethics, although presented in the form of general guides, clearly suggests the conduct which a dentist is expected to follow in carrying out his professional activities whether they be related to his patients or to fellow practitioners.

It should be kept in mind that the Principles are aimed primarily at upholding and strengthening dentistry as a full-fledged member of the learned professions.

The dentist constantly should remind himself that the ethics of dental practice, the basic system for self-regulation of the dental profession, grow out of the obligations inherent in the practice of a profession. The dentist should reflect constantly upon the professional characteristics of his occupation. They are:

1. The provision of a service (usually personal) which is
essential to the health and well-being of society.

2. The necessity of intensive education and training to qualify as competent to provide the essential service.

3. The need for continuing education and training to maintain and improve professional knowledge and skills.

4. The need for joining with professional colleagues in
organized efforts to share new knowledge and new developments of
professional practice.

5. Dedication to service rather than to gain or profit from
service.

Section 1--Education Beyond the Usual Level. The right of
a dentist to professional status rests in the knowledge, skill, and
experience with which he serves his patients and society. Every
dentist has the obligation of keeping his knowledge and skill fresh-
ened by continuing education through all of his professional life.

Advisory Opinions

1. The awarding of certificates to dentists who complete
postgraduate courses does not bring the component society or the
recipient dentists in conflict with the Principles of Ethics. Dentists
should be encouraged to continue their professional education.

2. It is unethical for a dentist to display certificates of
membership and certificates of completion of short courses if the
total display would tend to imply announcement of a specialty practice. The excessive display of such certificates should be discouraged.

Section 2--Service to the Public. The dentist's primary duty
of serving the public is discharged by giving the highest type of
service of which he is capable and by avoiding any conduct which
leads to a lowering of esteem of the profession of which he is a
member.

In serving the public, a dentist may exercise reasonable
discretion in selecting patients for his practice. However, a dentist
may not refuse to accept a patient into his practice or deny dental
service to a patient solely because of the patient's race, creed, col-
or, or national origin.

Advisory Opinions

1. The use of professional letterheads in connection with a
dentist's efforts to promote a commercial endeavor is undignified
and might tend to lower public esteem for the profession.

2. It is not unethical for a local society to announce or publish the availability of a budget payment dental care plan provided
that the announcement is dignified and identifies only the society.

3. It is unethical for a dentist to inform the public that he
will render certain services free of charge.

4. It is unethical for a dentist to sell to his patients, at a

profit, articles such as toothbrushes.

     5. The Principles do not prohibit a dentist from engaging in the normal business practice of instituting service charges for unpaid balances.

     6. Dentists who use patients for teaching or research purposes without their fully informed consent are in violation of Section 2 of the Principles of Ethics.

     Section 3--Government of a Profession. Every profession receives from society the right to regulate itself, to determine and judge its own members. Such regulation is achieved largely through the influence of the professional societies, and every dentist has the dual obligation of making himself a part of a professional society and of observing its rules of ethics.

Advisory Opinions: None.

     Section 4--Leadership. The dentist has the obligation of providing freely of his skills, knowledge, and experience to society in those fields in which his qualifications entitle him to speak with professional competence. The dentist should be a leader in his community, including all efforts leading to the improvement of the dental health of the public.

Advisory Opinions: None.

     Section 5--Emergency Service. The dentist has an obligation when consulted in an emergency by the patient of another dentist to attend to the conditions leading to the emergency and to refer the patient to his regular dentist who should be informed of the conditions found and treated.

Advisory Opinions: None.

     Section 6--Use of Auxiliary Personnel. The dentist has an obligation to protect the health of his patient by not delegating to a person less qualified any service or operation which requires the professional competence of a dentist. The dentist has a further obligation of prescribing and supervising the work of all auxiliary personnel in the interests of rendering the best service to the patient.

Advisory Opinions

     It is unethical for a dentist to refer a patient to a commercial dental laboratory.

     Section 7--Consultation. The dentist has the obligation of seeking consultation whenever the welfare of the patient will be safeguarded or advanced by having recourse to those who have special skills, knowledge, and experience. A consultant will hold the details of a consultation in confidence and will not undertake treatment without the consent of the attending practitioner.

Advisory Opinions: None.

Section 8--Unjust Criticism and Expert Testimony. The
dentist has the obligation of not referring disparagingly, orally or
in writing, to the services of another dentist to a member of the
public.   A lack of knowledge of conditions under which the services
were afforded may lead to unjust criticism and to a lessening of
the public's confidence in the dental profession.   If there is indis-
putable evidence of faulty treatment, the welfare of the patient demands that corrective treatment be instituted at once and in such
a way as to avoid reflection on the previous dentist or on the
dental profession.   The dentist also has the obligation of cooperating
with appropriate public officials on request by providing expert
testimony.

Advisory Opinions

1.   In a malpractice suit both parties have a right to present
expert testimony through witnesses.   A dentist acting as a witness
may not be disciplined merely for presenting his professional opinion.
2.   Section 8 has no application to dental societies or committees thereof acting on grievances, review, or similar matters.
3.   The dentist has the obligation to report instances of
continuous faulty treatment by another dentist to the appropriate
agency of the dental society.

Section 9--Rebates and Split Fees.   The dentist may not accept or tender "rebates" or "split fees."

Advisory Opinions

1.   A fee arrangement between dentists and other practitioners of the healing arts which is not disclosed to the patient constitutes fee splitting and is unethical.
2.   The failure to disclose to the patient an approved government or prepaid dental care plan fee arrangement between a general
practitioner and a specialist does not constitute fee splitting.
3.   A dentist who purchases a retiring or deceased dentist's
practice may ethically agree to pay to the retiring dentist or to the
estate a percentage of the fees collected from patients of record of
the retired or deceased dentist for a limited period of time [note:
this arrangement may violate some state dental practice acts].
4.   A dentist may ethically agree to pay to another dentist a
percentage of his fees as part of an agreement covering the sharing
of office facilities [note: this arrangement may violate some state
dental practice acts].
5.   Dentists in partnership may use any reasonable formula
for determining how partnership profits may be divided among partners.
6.   The practice of dentists billing patients for services provided by pathologists does not constitute fee splitting.
7.   Compensating dental hygienists on a percentage basis

does not constitute fee splitting or violation of the Principles.

8. Whether a dentist may properly enter into a lease agreement in which his office rental will be based on a percentage of the gross income derived from his practice is not governed by the Principles of Ethics.

Section 10--Secret Agents and Exclusive Methods. The dentist has an obligation not to prescribe, dispense, or promote the use of drugs or other agents whose complete formulas are not available to the dental profession. He also has the obligation not to prescribe or dispense, except for limited investigative purposes, any therapeutic agent, the value of which is not supported by scientific evidence. The dentist has the further obligation of not holding out as exclusive, any agent, method, or technique.

Advisory Opinions: None.

Section 11--Patents and Copyrights. The dentist has the obligation of making the fruits of his discoveries and labors available to all when they are useful in safeguarding or promoting the health of the public. Patents and copyrights may be secured by a dentist provided that they and the remuneration derived from them are not used to restrict research, practice, or the benefits of the patented or copyrighted material.

Advisory Opinions: None.

Section 12--Advertising. Advertising reflects adversely on the dentist who employs it and lowers the public esteem of the dental profession. The dentist has the obligation of advancing his reputation for fidelity, judgment, and skill solely through his professional services to his patients and to society. The use of advertising in any form to solicit patients is inconsistent with this obligation.

Advisory Opinions

1. A dentist who arranges for an advertisement of his "Dental Clinic" is engaged in unethical conduct.

2. A dentist in a specialist practice who includes on his referral slips a map or diagram of his office location is merely providing helpful information to the patients of referring dentists and is not engaged in unethical conduct.

3. It is unethical for a dentist to induce any publication that tends to be professionally self-laudatory, or that tends to differentiate him professionally from other dentists.

Therefore, it is unethical for a dentist to induce publication of articles in nonprofessional media that, for example, praise his research, connect him with technological advances in dentistry, or announce his participation in a postgraduate course. It is also unethical for a dentist to sell or distribute health education material containing his name and professional identification.

4.   It is not unethical for a dentist to publish or to have published professional matters of general community interest, such as activities involving National Children's Dental Health Week, school dental programs, or advancements in dental technology, but they should be originated by or cleared in advance by the local society. It is unethical for a dentist to induce publication of professional matters of community interest on his own behalf.

5.   It is not unethical for a local dental society to purchase institutional advertising to counteract the advertising of unethical dentists.   Such a practice, however, may not be in good taste.

6.   A dignified announcement or publication of the availability of a budget payment dental care plan is not unethical if the plan and the announcement are approved by the local dental society.   It is unethical for the announcement to list the names of dentists participating in the plan.

7.   A dentist who permits his name to be used in a dental health education pamphlet to be distributed to the public at large by a commercial firm is engaged in unethical conduct.

8.   A dentist who indicates on a prominent sign outside an unfinished building that he intends to relocate his practice there is engaged in unethical conduct.

9.   A dentist is not prohibited by ethics from engaging in an activity such as that of a radio "sportscaster, " but he should not give undue emphasis to his identity as a practicing dentist.   It is advisable, also, for a dentist to consult with his local society before undertaking such an activity.

10.   A dentist who distributes his professional cards to all persons eligible for dental care under a group health care plan, including many persons not his patients of record, is engaged in unethical conduct even though he is the only dentist who has agreed to render services to the group.

11.   It is unethical for a specialist to distribute reprints of his published articles to a large segment of general practitioners. This practice appears to be an obvious effort to solicit referrals by indicating superiority in the special field.

12.   It is unethical for specialists to furnish so-called patient education pamphlets to general practitioners for distribution to patients where pamphlets, in effect, stress unduly the superiority of the procedures used by specialists.   Publication of such so-called patient education material has the effect of solicitng patients.

13.   It is unethical for a dentist to give lectures or demonstrations before lay groups on a particular technique (such as hypnosis) that he employs in his practice.

14.   The publication of a list of dentists who have agreed to participate in a group dental care plan which is found to be in violation of the American Dental Association's policy on group dental care plans and not approved by the state dental society is unethical.

15.   It is unethical for a dentist to include on his cards, letterheads, bills, signs, and so forth, that he uses anesthesia, X-rays, or does oral diagnosis.

16.   It is unethical for a dentist to allow use of his office or his person as a part of a television advertisement.

Section 13--Cards, Letterheads, and Announcements. A
dentist may properly utilize professional cards, announcement cards,
recall notices to patients of record, and letterheads when the style
and text are consistent with the dignity of the profession and with
the custom of other dentists in the community.

Announcement cards may be sent when there is a change in
location or an alteration in the character of practice, but only to
other dentists, to members of other health professions, and to
patients of record.

Advisory Opinions

1. A dentist who invites his patients of record, other dentists,
and other practitioners of the healing arts to an "open house" in connection with the establishment of a new office is not engaged in unethical conduct.

2. It is not unethical for a dentist who has returned from
military service to send announcements to his former patients.

3. A dentist who purchases or takes over the practice of
another dentist who is retiring may send announcements or recall
cards to the retiring dentist's patients of record. But it would be
unethical for the new dentist to send recall cards at a later date to
those who did not definitely indicate that they wished to be accepted
into the new dentist's practice.

4. The use of pictures and symbols on professional stationery should be discouraged.

5. A dentist may insert a paid announcement of his dental
practice in a local newspaper on a restricted basis only where approved by the local dental society.

6. On establishing a dental practice a dentist may send
announcements to other dentists, members of other health professions, and to relatives.

7. The Principles permit announcement, on a limited basis,
if there is a change in the character of practice, such as from a
general to a specialty practice. Sections 13 and 18, however, do not
permit publication or announcement of matters not representing a
change in the character of a practice such as use of new techniques,
qualification to perform oral rehabilitation, or competency to use
certain anesthetics.

8. A dentist who announces the employment of a dental
hygienist to all dentists and physicians of the community is engaged
in unethical conduct.

9. It is unethical for a dentist to include on his cards or
letterheads the name of a dental hygienist.

Section 14--Office Door Lettering and Signs. A dentist may
properly utilize office door lettering and signs provided that their
style and the text are consistent with the dignity of the profession
and with the custom of other dentists in the community.

Advisory Opinions

1. A building may be identified as the "... Dental Building," except that the full name of the building cannot include the name of a participating dentist.

2. A component society may determine community custom to prohibit dentists from using floodlights to draw attention to their nameplates on the outside of their private practice facilities. Component societies should be aware, furthermore, that the state dental practice acts ordinarily establish regulations on the use of office door lettering and signs.

3. It is unethical for a dentist to include on his door the name of a dental hygienist.

Section 15--Use of Professional Titles and Degrees. A dentist may use the titles or degrees Doctor, Dentist, D. D. S., or D. M. D., in connection with his name on cards, letterheads, office door signs, and announcements. A dentist who also possesses a medical degree may use this degree in addition to his dental degree in connection with his name on cards, letterheads, office door signs, and announcements. A dentist who has been certified by a national certifying board for one of the specialties approved by the American Dental Association may use the title "Diplomate" in connection with his specialty on his cards, letterheads, and announcements if such usage is consistent with the custom of dentists of the community. A dentist may not use his title or degree in connection with the promotion of any commercial endeavor.

The use of eponyms in connection with drugs, agents, instruments, or appliances is generally to be discouraged.

Advisory Opinions

1. The Principles of Ethics permit dentists to use the titles "Doctor" or "Dentist" or the degrees "D. D. S. " or "D. M. D. " in connection with their names on cards, letterheads, office door lettering, or signs. The use of other titles, such as "Dental Surgeon" or "Surgeon Dentist, " is unethical.

2. A dentist may permit his name to be used to identify a dental instrument so long as his degree or title is not added to that identification.

3. It is unethical for a dentist to permit his name with title or degree to be used in advertising circulars and other material promoting a product, such as a denture cleanser, to either the public or professional at large.

4. A practicing dentist who identifies himself by title or degree in material promoting the products of a dental supply house owned or managed by that dentist is engaged in unethical conduct.

5. A dentist who merely demonstrates a new piece of dental equipment within a commercial exhibit at a professional meeting is not engaged in unethical conduct.

6. The use of the title "Diplomate of ... " on office door lettering or signs is not permitted.

7. The limitations on the use of titles and degrees in connection with a dentist's name on cards, letterheads, announcements,

and signs should be strictly observed.

8. A dentist who participates in a dental motion picture film sponsored by a commercial film company in which he has a financial interest is engaged in unethical conduct if he is identified by name and title or degree.

9. Although the House of Delegates has recommended that postgraduate courses for dentists should be conducted under the auspices of recognized educational institutions, hospitals, and dental societies (Trans, 1951:190), that policy has not been incorporated in the Principles of Ethics. It is not unethical for a dentist to participate in a scientific or professional presentation under the sponsorship of a commercial concern, unless that dentist's participation does, in effect, promote the product or products of the sponsoring commercial concern.

10. It is unethical for a dentist employed by a dental supply or other commercial firm to sign his name with title or degree to letters or circulars promoting the products of his employer.

11. A dentist may ethically combine the practice of dentistry with the practice of other branches of the healing arts.

12. A dentist may not use degrees other than D. D. S., D. M. D., or M. D., if earned, in connection with his name on cards, letterheads, and announcements.

13. The mere identification of a dentist as an officer or member of the board of directors of a corporation is not unethical.

Section 16--Health Education of the Public. A dentist may properly participate in a program of health education of the public involving such media as the press, radio, television, and lecture, provided that such programs are in keeping with the dignity of the profession and the custom of the dental profession of the community.

Advisory Opinions

1. It is not unethical for a dentist to mail health education pamphlets to his patients of record.

2. Before a dentist initiates the publication of a dental health column in a newspaper, he should seek the approval of his local and state dental societies.

3. A dentist has the right to speak out against the policies espoused by organized dentistry, including the right to make public pronouncement against flouridation. It is unethical, however, for a dentist to represent his views as those of the dental society or as those of the majority of dentists of the community where in fact his views are opposed to the society's or to the majority of dentists in the community.

4. A dentist who prepared a health education column for a newspaper syndicate is not required to obtain the approval of every component society in whose jurisdiction the column is published.

5. A school dental health education program is a recognized and valued adjunct to a complete program of dental health education. Dental societies are encouraged to select representatives to participate in properly conducted school dental health education programs.

In conformance with sound educational principles recognized
by the Association's Bureau of Dental Health Education, a properly
conducted school dental health education program should utilize only
acceptable and accurate dental health education materials, whether
sponsored by commercial or other agencies, and further should contain safeguards to insure that the dentist will not be placed in the
position of promoting a commercial product in violation of the Principles of Ethics.

Section 17--Contract Practice.   A dentist may enter into an
agreement with individuals and organizations to provide dental health
care provided that the agreement does not permit or compel practices which are in violation of these Principles of Ethics.

Advisory Opinions

1.   The practice of dentistry under contract with, or as an
employee, of a health plan is not of itself unethical.   The health
plan's efforts to promote its dental benefits to the public, however,
may involve participating dentists in unethical conduct.
2.   The inclusion of a clause in a contract between partners
in a dental practice that forbids any partner who withdraws from
the dental partnership from locating a new practice near the partnership's location is not of itself unethical.
3.   Unless the practices and procedures of a dental care
plan require a dentist participating in that plan to violate the Principles of Ethics, participation in such a plan should not be prohibited by a component society as a violation of professional ethics.
4.   A dentist is not in violation of the Principles when he
participates in a bona fide prepaid dental care plan that solicits
patronage from the public as long as the plan is open to participation by all ethical dentists in the community.
5.   The requirement imposed by component or constituent
societies to file a contract between any members and a corporation
is not a matter of ethics and is unenforceable as being outside the
purview of the Principles of Ethics of a professional association.
6.   It is not unethical for a dentist to charge a reasonable
fee for completing a third-party reimbursement form.
7.   The practice of increasing fees when it becomes known
that there is a third-party reimbursing agent is unethical.
8.   A dentist who commits a deliberate "irregularity" in
billing in a third-party reimbursement plan is engaged in unethical
conduct.

Section 18--Announcement of Limitation of Practice.   Only
a dentist who limits his practice exclusively to one of the special
areas approved by the American Dental Association for limited practice may include a statement of his limitation in announcements,
cards, letterheads, and directory listings (consistent with the customs
of dentists of the community), provided at the time of the announcement,
he has met the existing educational requirements and standards* [see
p. 234] set forth by the American Dental Association for members

wishing to announce limitation of practice.

In accord with established ethical ruling that dentists should not claim or imply superiority, use of the phrases "Specialist in ..." or "Specialist on ..." in announcements, cards, letterheads, or directory listings, should be discouraged.   The use of the phrase "Practice limited to ..." is preferable.

A dentist, who uses his eligibility to announce himself as a specialist to make the public believe that specialty services rendered in his dental office are being rendered by ethically qualified specialists when such is not the case, is engaged in unethical conduct. The burden is on the specialist to avoid any inference that general practitioners who are associated with him are ethically qualified to announce themselves as specialists.

[*The following are included within the standards of the American Dental Association for determining the educational experience and other appropriate requirements for announcing a limited practice:

1.   The indicated area of dentistry must be one for which there is a certifying board approved by the American Dental Association.

2.   The dentist's practice must be limited exclusively to the indicated area of dentistry.

3.   The dentist must have completed successfully an educational program accredited by the Council on Dental Education, two or more years in length, as specified by the Council or be a diplomate of a national certifying board.]

Advisory Opinions

1.   A dentist who indicates on his cards, stationery, or in his directory listings, that he specializes in any field not recognized as a specialty by the American Dental Association is engaged in unethical conduct.

2.   A dentist may not properly announce that he limits his practice to two special fields of dentistry.   Only one special field may be announced.

3.   The use of the term "Diplomate" on cards, letterheads, and announcements implies an announcement of a limited practice.

Section 19--Directories.   A dentist may permit the listing of his name in a directory provided that all dentists in similar circumstances have access to a similar listing and provided that such listing is consistent in style and text with the custom of the dentists in the community.

Advisory Opinions

1.   Listings in telephone directories should be in good taste and conform to community custom; directory listings must also conform to those sections of the Principles of Ethics concerned with announcements and prohibitions against advertising.

2.   An unusual method of listing a dental practice in a

telephone directory is not permitted by the Principles of Ethics.

3. Community custom will determine whether dentists may be listed in directories published by fraternal organizations or similar groups.

4. If community custom permits, practitioners ethically qualified to announce limitations of their practice in one of the approved areas may be listed under separate headings in the classified section of telephone directories as long as they are not also listed under the "general dentistry" heading.

5. Unless community custom permits, dentists should not list their names in the classified telephone directories for localities outside their residence or practice locations.

6. If community custom permits, a dentist may indicate in his telephone directory listing that he is a member of the American Dental Association.

7. It is not unethical for a dentist to use the description "children's dentistry" rather than "pedodontia" in a telephone directory listing as long as community custom permits that usage.

8. In a group practice names of the individual dentists may be listed alphabetically, and there may also be one listing for the group name.

9. Group practices may be identified by the name of one or more dentists practicing within the group. The use of "Dr. Smith and Associates" is consistent with this opinion.

Section 20--Name of Practice. A dentist may practice in a partnership, or as a solo practitioner, professional corporation, or professional association. The use of practice names other than the names of participating dentists is unethical, except that corporate designations may be used if required by state law. Designations such as "Professional Corporation," "Inc.," "Group," "Clinic," or similar designations may not be used as a part of the name of a practice on cards, letterheads, signs, directories, and announcements, unless required by state law.

[Note: Resolved, that dentists using assumed names for their dental practices prior to June 1, 1970, be allowed to continue to use ethically such assumed names until not later than January 1, 1972. (Adopted by 1970 House of Delegates.)]

Advisory Opinions

1. Section 20 is intended to apply to solo practitioners and partnerships as well as to corporations.

2. The use of assumed names in answering the telephone in a dental office is unethical. It is permissible to answer "dental office."

3. The use of the term "clinic" should be limited to designate public or quasi-public institutions.

4. It is not unethical for a dentist to practice in a predominantly medical facility that uses an assumed name.

Section 21--Judicial Procedure.   Problems involving questions of ethics should be solved at the local level within the broad boundaries established in these Principles of Ethics and within the interpretation of the code of ethics of the component society.   If a satisfactory decision cannot be reached, the question should be referred, on appeal, to the constituent society and the Judicial Council of the American Dental Association, as provided in Chapter XI of the By-laws of the American Dental Association.

Advisory Opinions

1.   Grievance procedures are not within the jurisdiction of the Judicial Council.
2.   The establishment of a system for collecting overdue accounts by a local dental society is not within the concern of the Judicial Council.
3.   When a Judicial Council opinion on a question raised by an individual dentist will affect the whole dental community, a copy of that opinion will be sent to the secretary of the constituent or component society.

DIETITIANS

THE AMERICAN DIETETIC ASSOCIATION (ADA)
620 North Michigan Ave., Chicago, Ill. 60611
Robert M. Crum, J. D., Executive Director

Membership: The American Dietetic Association, founded in 1917 and with a present (1973) membership of over 23,000, is an organization whose members are professionally trained in the science of nutrition in its various aspects--Community Nutrition, Clinical Dietetics, Food Service Administration, and Education. "Associate Membership" requirements include a bachelor's degree in foods, food service management, nutrition, public health nutrition, or related fields, from an accredited college or university.   In addition to this basic education qualification, the majority of members of the Association complete supervised experience or graduate education requirements by:

> Completion of a dietetic internship approved by the Association--length varies from six to twelve months;
> At least two years of pre-planned supervised experience in dietetics;
> A master's or doctoral degree in foods, nutrition, food service management, education or related fields, providing evidence of qualifying experience.

A program of voluntary registration of dietitians has been

maintained by the ADA since June 1969. ADA members who meet
requirements of continuing education and pass a written test of
"basic knowledge related to the practice of dietetics"--administered
by The Psychological Corporation--are authorized to use the professional designation, "Registered Dietitian," and the initials, "R.D.,"
following their names. This registration is renewed annually, and
requires continuing education within five years of renewal.

Code of Ethics: The guide to professional practice of The American
Dietetic Association is its Code of Professional Practice, which was
adopted in its most recent form October 5, 1970. This Code sets
forth broad principles of the professional dietitian in meeting "Responsibility to Society" and "Responsibility to the Profession." Guidelines to Professional Conduct, adopted October 5, 1971, provides additional ethical standards.

Other Guides to Professional Conduct: The Dietitian's Oath is the
individual member's pledge of professional service, principles, and
standards.

Professional Insignia: The emblem of The American Dietetic Association is its official seal,
adopted in 1940.   The circular
design bears a centered shield
--bordered by stylized acanthus
leaves (representing "life and
growth"), divided vertically
by a staff (symbolic of Aesculapius, the Roman god of
medicine), indicating "the
relationship between the Association and the medical fraternity"; the shield bears on
its left half a balance ("representing accuracy and the necessity for careful evaluation")
supported by the caduceus, or
the Wand of Mercury, with its
two entwined serpents (symbolic of healing); the right
half of the shield bears a cook-

ing vessel ("representing the art of food preparation"). The crest
of the emblem is a cornucopia on a wreath, symbolizing "abundance
of food."

   The motto of the Association is born on a scroll below the
shield: "Quam Purimis Predesse" ("To benefit as many as possible"); the sprays of wheat terminating the scroll signify bread,
the staff of life. The seal, within a uniformly fluted border, is
banded with the name of the organization, "The American Dietetic
Association," and the date of its founding, "MCMXVII."

The color of the seal is green on gold--the official colors of
the American Dietetic Association. The seal appears on stationery
and publications of the ADA and affiliated state and district associations, and is available for wear by members as a sleeve emblem.

Other Designations of Professional Status: As described above under
"Membership, " the professional designation awarded by the ADA is:
"Registered Dietitian" ("R. D. ").

Bibliography:
   The American Dietetic Association.   About The American
      Dietetic Association. 1971.   8 pages.
   Brochure giving membership requirements, qualifications
   for "Registered Dietitian" designation.
   _____.   Code of Professional Practice.   October 5, 1970.
      1 page.
   Ethical code for professional dietitians.
   _____.   Constitution.   1959, with amendments through Febru-
      ary 9, 1971.   16 pages.
   Includes membership requirements, disciplinary forfeiture of
   membership, program for Registered Dietitian.
   _____.   The Dietitian's Oath.   1 page.
   Pledge of professional service subscribed to upon admission
   to membership in ADA.
   _____.   Guidelines for Professional Conduct.   October 5,
      1971.   1 page.
   Conduct standards for the professional dietitian.

"Code of Professional Practice"

The profession of dietetics is dedicated to improvement of
the nutrition of human beings, advancement of the science of dietetics
and nutrition and promotion of education in these and allied areas.
The dietitians' responsibility for nutritional care is unique among
professions because the dietitian is the only professional person who
concentrates on the application of concepts of nutrition in everyday
health care of individuals and groups.

Responsibility to Society

The dietitian, with commitment to excellence in the nutritional
care of individuals and groups shares responsibility with associated
professionals in meeting the health needs of the public.
The dietitian, with specialized knowledge of food and its implications for health, participates in the protection of the public against
fraud, misinformation and unethical practices.

Responsibility to the Profession

The dietitian identifies and accepts those responsibilities requiring professional competence and delegates other functions to

those qualified to perform them.

The dietitian participates in establishing and maintaining conditions of employment conducive to high quality nutritional care.

The dietitian recognizes that continuing education is an essential element in the development of personal competence and reliable professional performance.

The dietitian avoids conduct which may lower esteem for the profession.

"Guidelines for Professional Conduct"

Society gives a profession the right to regulate itself and to evaluate and judge its members. The American Dietetic Association, as the professional society for dietitians, assumes this responsibility. Each member has the obligation to follow these guidelines for professional conduct.

The terms, "Registered Dietitian" and "ADA Member," are used only by dietitians entitled to these designations.

The dietitian uses the name of the national, state, or district association and speaks in the name of the association only when such authority is specifically designated.

The dietitian observes only those business practices which avoid personal obligation and is not influenced by special compensation or gifts.

The dietitian in fulfilling the requirements for continuing education reports accurately the time expended in the learning experience.

The dietitian has a professional responsibility to effect improvement in nutritional care; to make certain no facility uses his name unless required services are being provided.

The dietitian is objective in the evaluation of the work of another dietitian.

The dietitian follows the testimonial advertising policy as stated in "General Information for Members of The American Dietetic Association."

"The Dietitian's Oath"

I do solemnly affirm
That as a member of The American Dietetic Association
I shall, to the best of my ability, so conduct myself
As to reflect credit upon the profession of which I am a member.
To this end
I shall adhere to the principles of honor, integrity,
Spirit of service, and devotion to duty
On which The American Dietetic Association was founded
And shall uphold the common good which is symbolized in its Seal.
I shall do all in my power
To maintain high standards of competence and deportment.
I pledge myself as a dietitian

To support the healing arts and the physician and nurse
And strive toward the improvement of human nutrition
In whatever capacity I may serve.

ECOLOGISTS

INSTITUTE OF ENVIRONMENTAL SCIENCES (IES)
      940 E. Northwest Highway, Mt. Prospect, Ill. 60056
      Mrs. Betty Peterson, Executive Director

Membership: The Institute of Environmental Sciences, founded in
1959 and with a current (1973) membership of over 2200 "is a
professional society of engineers, scientists and educators dedicated
to the researching, simulating, testing and teaching of the environments of earth and space, for the betterment of mankind and the
advancement of industry, science and education." The Institute grew
from the Environmental Equipment Institute, a trade association for
equipment manufacturers (formed in 1954) when the Institute of Environmental Engineers--scientists grouped in the aeroplane and related industry--merged with a separate Society of Environmental
Engineers, and later combined with the Environmental Equipment
Institute to form the present IES.

      Education and experience requirements for the categories of In-
stitute membership are:
      Senior Member--Twelve years' experience as an engineer or
            scientist working in environmental engineering or allied
            sciences; instructing in engineering or science in an ac-
            credited college; an executive directing technical work in
            environmental engineering. Graduation from an accredited
            college with a degree in science or engineering may sub-
            stitute for four years of the required experience.
      Member--Seven years of the type of experience described
            above, with the same education substitution.
Additional categories of membership are "Associate Member," an
individual employed in the field of environmental engineering or related areas who cannot meet the requirements for "Member"; and
"Student Member," a full-time student enrolled in an institution of
higher learning.

      The Society awards the designation of "Fellow"--an honor, not
to be applied for--to a Member or a Senior Member with 15 years
of professional experience, who has made "substantial or vital contribution to the advancement of the environmental sciences." In
addition to the substitution of college graduation in science or engineering for four years of the required experience, as much as
three years' full-time postgraduate study which had led to an

advanced degree may be substituted for three additional years of
the required professional experience.

Code of Ethics: None reported. Disciplinary action concerning
members' professional conduct is provided for in that "the Council
of National Directors may suspend a member for a definite or an
indefinite period, or expel a member for cause," after investigation
and hearing (Bylaws, Section 7E).

Professional Insignia: The official emblem of the IES is an oval

design, with an outlined arm and hand upholding a globe showing
the western hemisphere; the name of the organization, "Institute
of Environmental Sciences," borders the lower portion of the oval
in a band. An alternate form of the emblem shows the oval central
design without the oval border, but framed in a rectangle of solid
color, with the organization initials, "IES," above the oval. The
color of the emblem is shown variously--depending on paper color
of publications and design of color: black on green; black on yellow; red on white; blue on white.

Bibliography:
        Institute of Environmental Sciences. Constitution; Bylaws.
            November 30, 1970 revision. 6, and 17 pages.
            Gives categories and qualifications for membership; disci-
            plinary suspension of member for cause.
                    . Institute of Environmental Sciences. Brochure.
            Information folder giving brief history of the IES, member-
            ship qualifications; emblem on cover.

ECONOMISTS

AMERICAN ECONOMIC ASSOCIATION (AEA)
    1313 21st Ave. South, Nashville, Tenn. 37212
    Mrs. Mary Bobo, Administrative Director

Membership: The American Economic Association, founded in 1885
and with a present (1973) membership of over 18,000, is composed
of professional workers--economics teachers in universities and colleges, business executives, government officials, journalists, and
lawyers--"interested in the study of economics or the economic
aspects of political and social questions." "Anyone interested in
becoming a member" of the Association is eligible for membership.

Code of Ethics: The Association has issued no formal code of
ethics.

Professional Insignia: The emblem of the ASA is a circular seal--

a centered bearded seated
figure (signifying "Economics")
holds a torch in his raised left
hand, and a branch of olive
leaves in his right hand;
"Economica" (Economics) is
printed vertically by the up-
raised left arm; two basic aspects of economic science are
shown at either side of the
central figure--to the left is
a path of wheat, below the
legend "Terra" (Earth)--sig-
nifying "Land"; to the right of
the figure is a spoked wheel,
below the legend "Labor"--
representing another element
of economic wealth; beneath the seated figure is the name of the
organization, "American Economic Association," and the date of
the group's organization, "Founded 1885." The insignia is shown
in black on white (letterhead; publication).

Bibliography:
        American Economic Association. Information Booklet of Pur-
            poses and Activities. 1971. 10 pages.
        Brief statement of AEA history, objectives, publications,
        awards, application for membership.

ENGINEERING TECHNICIANS

AMERICAN SOCIETY OF CERTIFIED ENGINEERING TECHNICIANS
(ASCET)
  2029 K St., N. W., Washington, D. C. 20006
  C. J. Knezek, C. E. T., President

Membership: The American Society of Certified Engineering Technicians, founded in 1964 and with a present (1973) membership of
over 4,000, is an association, each of whose "Members" has been
certified as a competent engineering technician, by the Institute for
the Certification of Engineering Technicians (ICET):
  2029 K Street, N. W.
  Washington, D. C. 20006
    Joseph M. Srarponis, Executive Secretary
  The Institute, sponsored by the National Society of Professional
Engineers (NSPE), is "an examining body ... evaluating the qualifications of those who voluntarily apply for certification." It has
issued certificates of competence to engineering technicians since
1961. According to the official Institute definition, an engineering
technician is:
> "one who, in support of and under the direction of profession-
> al engineers or scientists, can carry out in a responsible
> manner either proven techniques, which are common knowl-
> edge among those who are technically expert in a particular
> technology, or those techniques especially prescribed by pro-
> fessional engineers."
  Three grades of Engineering Technician Certificates are issued
by the Institute, each of which requires specified technical, academic
education, or experience:
  Certified Senior Engineering Technician,
  Certified Engineering Technician,
  Certified Associate Engineering Technician.
The ICET's certified engineering technician examination "is based
on knowledges and skills normally expected of Associate degree
graduates of engineering technology programs." The examination--
an objective multiple choice, open book test--is given in two three-
hour parts:
  Part A--"same for all fields and contains three sections of
      125 questions each: communications skills, mathematics,
      and physical science."
  Part B--"directed towards the specialized fields of engineering
      technology." At present (1973) there are five fields:
        Architectural and Building Construction,
        Civil Engineering Technology,
        Electrical-Electronics Engineering Technology,
        Industrial Engineering Technology,
        Mechanical Engineering Technology.
These fields will be increased to "more than twenty" by

May 1975. In 1973 two fields to be added are: Metallurgy, and Fluid Power.

Code of Ethics: The ASCET--carrying out one of its objectives (the "Promotion of the educational, social, economic, and ethical responsibility of the engineering technicians")--has issued a guide to conduct: the Code of Ethics. This Code enumerates five general obligations of the engineering technician to the public and to the profession. A standing committee of the Society is the "Ethics Committee," but no procedures for enforcement of the Code of Ethics are reported.

Professional Insignia: The emblem of the Society is a design consisting of a horizontal lozenge, with the organization initials, "ASCET," printed within a banded border. The color of the design is shown variously --blue on white (letterhead, publication); three-color (vinyl decal). The design is also available to members as a lapel pin:

"Members" (gold);
"Associate Members" (bronze);
"Student Members" (silver).

Other Identification of Professional Status: As described above under "Membership," members of the Society identify themselves with the title and letter designations of competence awarded by the Institute for Certifying Engineering Technicians: "Certified Engineering Technician" ("C. E. T. ").

Bibliography:
    American Society of Certified Engineering Technicians. Member's Manual. Pamphlet.
    ASCET Constitution, By-Laws, organization structure and Engineering Technician's Code of Ethics.
    _____. The Voice of Engineering Technicians. Folder. Includes brief ASCET history, membership requirements and Code of Ethics.
    Institute for the Certification of Engineering Technicians. The Certification of Engineering Technicians. June 1973. Folder.
    Defines an "Engineering Technician," and gives requirements for the three grades of certified engineering technicians.
    _____. Examination Information. Folder. Describes the form and content of ICET's certification examinations for engineering technicians in 5 fields: Architectural and Building Construction, Civil Engineering Technology, Electrical-Electronics Engineering Technology, Industrial Engineering Technology, Mechanical Engineering Technology.

_____ . Guide for Preparing Technical Essays. Folder.
Outline, format, and content of the 5,000 word technical essay
required for initial certification as Senior Engineering Technician after January 1, 1973, and for upgrading to Senior
after January 1, 1976.

"Code of Ethics"

Honesty, justice, and courtesy form a moral philosophy which,
associated with mutual interest among men, constitutes the foundation of ethics. The technician should recognize such a standard, not
in passive observance, but as a set of dynamic principles guiding
his conduct and way of life. It is his duty to practice his profession
according to these rules of ethics.

Because the keystone of professional conduct is integrity, the
technician:
1. Will discharge his duties with fidelity, fairness, and impartiality to all.
2. Will use his knowledge and skill for the advancement of
human welfare.
3. Will strive to increase competence and prestige of the
profession of the engineering technician.
4. Will uphold the honor and dignity of his profession and
avoid association with any enterprise of questionable character.
5. Will, in his dealings with fellow engineering technicians,
be fair and tolerant.

ENGINEERS

ENGINEERS' COUNCIL FOR PROFESSIONAL DEVELOPMENT (ECPD)
345 E. 47th St., New York, N. Y. 10017
David R. Reyes-Guerra, Executive Director

Membership: The Engineers' Council for Professional Development,
founded in 1932, is a large federation of the leading engineering
societies in the United States. The twelve member societies and
two affiliate groups of the ECPD are:
American Institute of Aeronautics and Astronautics,
American Institute of Chemical Engineers,
American Institute of Industrial Engineers,
American Institute of Mining, Metallurgical and Petroleum
Engineers,
American Nuclear Society,
American Society of Agricultural Engineers,
American Society of Civil Engineers,

American Society of Mechanical Engineers,
Institute of Electrical and Electronics Engineers,
Society of Automotive Engineers,
National Council of Engineering Examiners,
American Society for Engineering Education.

Affiliates
National Institute of Ceramics Engineers,
National Society of Professional Engineers.

The Council has published its definition of engineering:
"Engineering is the profession in which a knowledge of the
mathematical and natural sciences gained by study, experience, and practice is applied with judgment to develop ways
to utilize, economically, the materials and forces of nature
for the benefit of mankind. "

Code of Ethics: The Engineers' Council for Professional Development is active in the field of ethics on behalf of its member and
affiliated societies。 In 1963 the Ethics Committee developed an
EPCD Canons of Ethics, setting forth fundamental principles as a
guide for professional engineers in their "Relations with the Public, "
"Relations with Employers and Clients, " and "Relations with Engineers. "
These Canons--or their fundamental principles--have been
adopted or endorsed by six of the EPCD member and affiliate societies (Chemical Engineers, Industrial Engineers, Agricultural En-
gineers, Civil Engineers, Mechanical Engineers, and Ceramics En-
gineers)。 In addition, the Canons have been adopted by the American Association of Cost Engineers; American Society of Heating,
Refrigerating and Air-Conditioning Engineers; Society of Packaging
and Handling Engineers; Society for Quality Control; and the American
Society of Safety Engineers.

While the American Association of Cost Engineers has not
formally adopted the Canons, their Bylaws (Article I, Section 8)
provide for discipline of any of their members who violate the
Canons。 The American Institute of Plant Engineers encourages
their members to follow the Canons in their professional work.
Enforcement procedures for these guides to professional engineering
conduct are established and carried out in the component societies
of the EPCD.

Other Guides to Professional Conduct: The EPCD Ethics Committee
has also developed a creed for professional engineers--Faith of the
Engineer--setting forth the engineer's obligation to society and to
his profession in the form of a pledge.

Professional Insignia: The emblem of the Engineers' Council for
Professional Development is its logotype--a circular design with the
linked letters of the organization name, "EPCD, " centered, and
the name of the group, "Engineers' Council for Professional

Development" imprinted on
a dark bordering band. The
colors of EPCD are wine
and gray.

Bibliography:
  Alger, Philip L., N.A.
          Christensen, and
          Sterling P. Olmsted.
          Ethical Problems in
          Engineering.   N.Y.,
          Wiley, 1965.   299
          pages.

          Presents 127 day-to-
          day problems of pro-
          fessional engineering
          ethics, drawn from
actual engineering practice.   The problems are based upon
a survey sponsored by the Ethics Committee of the American
Society for Engineering Education, and the co-sponsorship of
the Engineers' Council for Professional Development and the
National Society for Professional Engineers.   The case-
studies are applications of professional engineering ethics--
"rules of conduct designed to control engineers' relations
(a) among themselves, (b) between themselves and their
employers and clients, and (c) between themselves and the
public."   Appendixes include three codes of ethics: Engineers' Council for Professional Development Canons of
Ethics of Engineers, National Society of Professional Engineers Code of Ethics, American Society of Civil Engineers
Code of Ethics.   "Selected Bibliography," p. 293-295.
  Engineers' Council for Professional Development.   Annual Re-
          port.
          Gives address, corresponding officer and emblem of the
          member and affiliate societies, and the two EPCD ethical
          guides for professional engineers: Canons of Ethics of
          Engineers, and Faith of the Engineer.

                    "Canons of Ethics of Engineers"
          Fundamental Principles of Professional Engineering Ethics

          The Engineer, to uphold and advance the honor and dignity
of the engineering profession and in keeping with high standards of
ethical conduct:
          I.   Will be honest and impartial, and will serve with devotion
                    his employer, his clients, and the public;
          II.   Will strive to increase the competence and prestige of
                    the engineering profession;
          III.   Will use his knowledge and skill for the advancement of
                    human welfare.

Relations with the Public

1.1   The Engineer will have proper regard for the safety, health and welfare of the public in the performance of his professional duties.

1.2   He will endeavor to extend public knowledge and appreciation of engineering and its achievements, and will oppose any untrue, unsupported, or exaggerated statements regarding engineering.

1.3   He will be dignified and modest in explaining his work and merit, will ever uphold the honor and dignity of his profession, and will refrain from self-laudatory advertising.

1.4   He will express an opinion on an engineering subject only when it is founded on adequate knowledge and honest conviction.

1.5   He will preface any ex parte statements, criticisms, or arguments that he may issue by clearly indicating on whose behalf they are made.

Relations with Employers and Clients

2.1   The Engineer will act in professional matters as a faithful agent or trustee for each employer or client.

2.2   He will act fairly and justly toward vendors and contractors, and will not accept from vendors or contractors, any commissions or allowances, directly or indirectly.

2.3   He will inform his employer or client if he is financially interested in any vendor or contractor, or in any invention, machine or apparatus, which is involved in a project or work of his employer or client.   He will not allow such interest to affect his decisions regarding engineering services which he may be called upon to perform.

2.4   He will indicate to his employer or client the adverse consequences to be expected if his engineering judgment is overruled.

2.5   He will undertake only those engineering assignments for which he is qualified.   He will engage or advise his employer or client to engage specialists and will cooperate with them whenever his employer's or client's interests are served best by such an arrangement.

2.6   He will not disclose information concerning the business affairs or technical processes of any present or former employer or client without his consent.

2.7   He will not accept compensation--financial or otherwise-- from more than one party for the same service, or for other services pertaining to the same work, without the consent of all interested parties.

2.8   The employed engineer will engage in supplementary employment or consulting practice only with the consent of his employer.

Relations with Engineers

3.1   The Engineer will take care that credit for engineering work is given to those to whom credit is properly due.

3.2   He will provide a prospective engineering employee with complete information on working conditions and his proposed status of employment, and after employment will keep him informed of any changes in them.

3.3   He will uphold the principle of appropriate and adequate compensation for those engaged in engineering work, including those in subordinate capacities.

3.4   He will endeavor to provide opportunity for the professional development and advancement of engineers in his employ or under his supervision.

3.5   He will not injure maliciously the professional reputation, prospects, or practice of another engineer. However, if he has proof that another engineer has been unethical, illegal, or unfair in his practice, he should so advise the proper authority.

3.6   He will not compete unfairly with another engineer.

3.7   He will not invite or submit price proposals for professional services which require creative intellectual effort, on a basis that constitutes competition on price alone. Due regard should be given to all professional aspects of the engagement.

3.8   He will cooperate in advancing the engineering profession by interchanging information and experience with other engineers and students, and by contributing to public communication media, to the efforts of engineering and scientific societies and schools.

"Faith of the Engineer"

I am an engineer. In my profession I take deep pride, but without vain-glory; to it I owe solemn obligations that I am eager to fulfill.

As an Engineer, I will participate in none but honest enterprise. To him that has engaged my services, as employer or client, I will give the utmost of performance and fidelity.

When needed, my skill and knowledge shall be given without reservation for the public good. From special capacity springs the obligation to use it well in the service of humanity; and I accept the challenge that this implies.

Jealous of the high repute of my calling, I will strive to protect the interests and the good name of any engineer that I know to be deserving; but I will not shrink, should duty dictate, from disclosing the truth regarding anyone that, by unscrupulous act, has shown himself unworthy of the profession.

Since the Age of Stone, human progress has been conditioned by the genius of my professional forbears. By them have been rendered usable to mankind Nature's vast resources of material and energy. By them have been vitalized and turned to practical account the principles of science and the revelations of technology. Except for this heritage of accumulated experience, my efforts would be feeble. I dedicate myself to the dissemination of engineering knowledge, and, especially to the instruction of younger members of my profession in all its arts and traditions.

To my fellows I pledge, in the same full measure I ask of them, integrity and fair dealing, tolerance and respect, and devotion to the standards and the dignity of our profession; with the consciousness, always, that our special expertness carries with it the obligation to serve humanity with complete sincerity.

NATIONAL SOCIETY OF PROFESSIONAL ENGINEERS (NSPE)
    2029 K Street, N.W., Washington, D.C. 20006
    Paul H. Robbins, P.E., Executive Director

Membership: The National Society of Professional Engineers, founded in 1934 and with a present (1973) membership of approximately 68,000, is a federation of 54 state societies and over 500 local chapters in the United States and Canada. Members are engineers, qualified by education or state registration, in all types of engineering, including private practice, government, education, and industry, and most NSPE members are also members of the technical society in their engineering field.

In addition to "Student Members" (undergraduate or graduate engineering students), there are four categories of membership with specific education and experience requirements:
    Member: Registered to practice engineering, by a state
        board of engineering examiners.
    Senior Associate Member: Graduation from an engineering
        curriculum accredited by the Engineers' Council for Professional Development; minimum of 12 years acceptable
        engineering experience, and member of an engineering
        society in an approved grade.
    Associate Member: Certified Engineer-in-Training; or a
        graduate engineer working as an engineer or in postgraduate engineering study.
    Surveyor Member: Land Surveyor licensed in state of
        practice.

Code of Ethics: Since the Society was founded in 1934, a "strict Code of Ethics" has been maintained "to uphold the honor and dignity of the engineering profession and in keeping with high standards of ethical conduct." This Code of Ethics--continuously reviewed and revised in the light of experience and changing times, and issued most recently in a revision of January 1971--provides in its 15 sections standards for professional service performed by an engineer.

Enforcement of the Code is the responsibility of local chapters and affiliated state societies of NSPE. The Society's Board of Ethical Review renders opinions pertaining to the interpretation of the Code. The Board's opinions are based on actual facts and circumstances (hypothetical and real cases), as submitted by state societies or by individual members. These interpretations, published

as Opinions of the Board of Ethical Review, have been issued in
three volumes (1958-1971).

Other Guides to Professional Conduct: The Engineers' Creed,
adopted by the NSPE in June 1954, is a pledge of high standards
of professional engineering conduct, that is "used in a number of
ceremonies by the engineering profession, " such as "registration
certificate presentations" and "officer installation ceremonies at
all levels of the Society. "

Professional Insignia: The emblem of the National Society of Professional Engineers is a shield, bearing in a circle the name of the

organization, "National Society of Professional Engineers, " and the
date of founding, "Founded 1934. "   The color of this insignia is gold
on black.

Other Identification of Professional Status: The Society provides a
"Professional Engineer" emblem, in the form of a six-spoked wheel,
with the initials, "PE, " one letter on each side of a mathematical
integral sign--signifying the integration of all engineers into one
profession; the designation, "Professional Engineer, " is shown at the
top of the banding border.   This emblem is shown in black and white.
      Registered Engineers are authorized to use the professional
designation, "Professional Engineer, " and the initials, "PE, " with
their names, as an indication of competence.   Both the NSPE shield
and the PE emblem are available to members in miscellaneous
jewelry.

Bibliography:
      National Society of Professional Engineers.   Code of Ethics.
            1934, latest revision January 1971.   1 sheet.
      Guide for the engineer's professional conduct and practice.

_____₀ Engineers' Creed. June 1954. 1 page.
Pledge used in registration certificate presentations, installation of Society officers, and other ceremonies.
_____. Ethics for Engineers. May 1970. 13 pages.
Gives the Engineers' Creed, Code of Ethics, with subject reference to Code and index to opinions of the NSPE Board of Ethical Review.
_____. A Shoulder to the Wheel for the Concerned Engineer. 1970. 13 pages. Pamphlet.
Information brochure includes definition of member grades of NSPE, and list of state societies of NSPE.
_____₀ Board of Ethical Review. Opinions. 3 volumes. 1958-1971. $1.50 each volume.
Applications and interpretations of the Code of Ethics, with detailed index.

"Code of Ethics"

Preamble

The Engineer, to uphold and advance the honor and dignity of the engineering profession and in keeping with high standards of ethical conduct:
Will be honest and impartial, and will serve with devotion his employer, his clients, and the public;
Will strive to increase the competence and prestige of the engineering profession;
Will use his knowledge and skill for the advancement of human welfare.

Section 1--The Engineer will be guided in all his professional relations by the highest standards of integrity, and will act in professional matters for each client or employer as a faithful agent or trustee.
a. He will be realistic and honest in all estimates, reports, statements, and testimony.
b. He will admit and accept his own errors when proven obviously wrong and refrain from distorting or altering the facts in an attempt to justify his decision.
c. He will advise his client or employer when he believes a project will not be successful.
d. He will not accept outside employment to the detriment of his regular work or interest, or without the consent of his employer.
e. He will not attempt to attract an engineer from another employer by unfair methods.
f. He will not actively participate in strikes, picket lines, or other collective coercive action.
g. He will not use his professional affiliations or public office to secure personal advantage and will avoid any act tending to promote his own interest at the expense of the dignity and integrity of the profession.

Section 2--The Engineer will have proper regard for the safety, health, and welfare of the public in the performance of his professional duties. If his engineering judgment is overruled by non-technical authority, he will clearly point out the consequences. He will notify the proper authority of any observed conditions which endanger public safety and health.

    a. He will regard his duty to the public welfare as paramount.

    b. He shall seek opportunities to be of constructive service in civic affairs and work for the advancement of the safety, health and well-being of his community.

    c. He will not complete, sign, or seal plans and/or specifications that are not of a design safe to the public health and welfare and in conformity with accepted engineering standards. If the client or employer insists on such unprofessional conduct, he shall notify the proper authorities and withdraw from further service on the project.

Section 3--The Engineer will avoid all conduct or practice likely to discredit or unfavorably reflect upon the dignity or honor of the profession.

    a. The Engineer shall not advertise his professional services but may utilize the following means of identification:

    (1) Professional cards and listings in recognized and dignified publications, provided they are consistent in size and are in a section of the publication regularly devoted to such professional cards and listings. The information displayed must be restricted to firm name, address, telephone number, appropriate symbol, name of principal participants and the fields of practice in which the firm is qualified.

    (2) Signs on equipment, offices and at the site of projects for which he renders services, limited to firm name, address, telephone number and type of services, as appropriate.

    (3) Brochures, business cards, letterheads and other factual representations of experience, facilities, personnel and capacity to render service, providing the same are not misleading relative to the extent of participation in the projects cited, and provided the same are not indiscriminately distributed.

    (4) Listings in the classified section of telephone directories, limited to name, address, telephone number and specialties in which the firm is qualified.

    b. The Engineer may advertise for recruitment of personnel in appropriate publications or by special distribution. The information presented must be displayed in a dignified manner, restricted to firm name, address, telephone number, appropriate symbol, name of principal participants, the fields of practice in which the firm is qualified and factual descriptions of positions available, qualifications required and benefits available.

    c. The Engineer may prepare articles for the lay or technical press which are factual, dignified and free from ostentations or laudatory implications. Such articles shall not imply other than his direct participation in the work described unless credit is given to others for their share of the work.

d. The Engineer may extend permission for his name to be used in commercial advertisements, such as may be published by manufacturers, contractors, material suppliers, etc., only by means of a modest dignified notation acknowledging his participation and the scope thereof in the project or product described. Such permission shall not include public endorsement of proprietary products.

e. The Engineer will not allow himself to be listed for employment using exaggerated statements of his qualifications.

Section 4--The Engineer will endeavor to extend public knowledge and appreciation of engineering and its achievements and to protect the engineering profession from misrepresentation and misunderstanding.

a. He shall not issue statements, criticisms, or arguments on matters connected with public policy which are inspired or paid for by private interests, unless he indicates on whose behalf he is making the statement.

Section 5--The Engineer will express an opinion of an engineering subject only when founded on adequate knowledge and honest conviction.

a. The Engineer will insist on the use of facts in reference to an engineering project in a group discussion, public forum or publication of articles.

Section 6--The Engineer will undertake engineering assignments for which he will be responsible only when qualified by training or experience; and he will engage, or advise engaging, experts and specialists whenever the client's or employer's interests are best served by such service.

Section 7--The Engineer will not disclose confidential information concerning the business affairs or technical processes of any present or former client or employer without his consent.

a. While in the employ of others, he will not enter promotional efforts or negotiations for work or make arrangements for other employment as a principal or to practice in connection with a specific project for which he has gained particular and specialized knowledge without the consent of all interested parties.

Section 8--The Engineer will endeavor to avoid a conflict of interest with his employer or client, but when unavoidable, the Engineer shall fully disclose the circumstances to his employer or client.

a. The Engineer will inform his client or employer of any business connections, interests, or circumstances which may be deemed as influencing his judgment or the quality of his services to his client or employer.

b. When in public service as a member, advisor, or employee of a governmental body or department, an Engineer shall not participate in considerations or actions with respect to services provided by him or his organization in private engineering practice.

c.   An Engineer shall not solicit or accept an engineering contract from a governmental body on which a principal or officer of his organization serves as a member.

Section 9--The Engineer will uphold the principle of appropriate and adequate compensation for those engaged in engineering work.

a.   He will not undertake or agree to perform any engineering service on a free basis, except for civic, charitable, religious, or eleemosynary nonprofit organizations when the professional services are advisory in nature.

b.   He will not undertake work at a fee or salary below the accepted standards of the profession in the area.

c.   He will not accept remuneration from either an employee or employment agency for giving employment.

d.   When hiring other engineers, he shall offer a salary according to the engineer's qualifications and the recognized standards in the particular geographical area.

e.   If, in sales employ, he will not offer, or give engineering consultation, or designs, or advice other than specifically applying to the equipment being sold.

Section 10--The Engineer will not accept compensation, financial or otherwise, from more than one interested party for the same service, or for services pertaining to the same work, unless there is full disclosure to and consent of all interested parties.

a.   He will not accept financial or other considerations, including free engineering designs, from material or equipment suppliers for specifying their product.

b.   He will not accept commissions or allowances, directly or indirectly, from contractors or other parties dealing with his clients or employer in connection with work for which he is responsible.

Section 11--The Engineer will not compete unfairly with another engineer by attempting to obtain employment or advancement or professional engagements by competitive bidding, by taking advantage of a salaried position, by criticizing other engineers, or by other improper or questionable methods.

a.   The Engineer will not attempt to supplant another engineer in a particular employment after becoming aware that definite steps have been taken toward the other's employment.

b.   He will not offer to pay, either directly or indirectly, any commission, political contribution, or a gift, or other consideration in order to secure work, exclusive of securing salaried positions through employment agencies.

c.   He shall not solicit or submit engineering proposals on the basis of competitive bidding. Competitive bidding for professional engineering services is defined as the formal or informal submission, or receipt, of verbal or written estimates of cost or proposals in terms of dollars, man days of work required, percentage

of construction cost, or any other measure of compensation whereby
the prospective client may compare engineering services on a price
basis prior to the time that one engineer, or one engineering organization, has been selected for negotiations. The disclosure of
recommended fee schedules prepared by various engineering societies
is not considered to constitute competitive bidding. An Engineer
requested to submit a fee proposal or bid prior to the selection of
an engineer or firm subject to the negotiation of a satisfactory contract, shall attempt to have the procedure changed to conform to
ethical practices, but if not successful he shall withdraw from consideration for the proposed work. These principles shall be applied
by the Engineer in obtaining the services of other professionals.

     d. An Engineer shall not request, propose, or accept a pro-
fessional commission on a contingent basis under circumstances in
which his professional judgment may be compromised, or when a
contingency provision is used as a device for promoting or securing
a professional commission.

     e. While in a salaried position, he will accept part-time
engineering work only at a salary or fee not less than that recognized as standard in the area.

     f. An Engineer will not use equipment, supplies, laboratory,
or office facilities of his employer to carry on outside private
practice without consent.

     Section 12--The Engineer will not attempt to injure, mali-
ciously or falsely, directly or indirectly, the professional reputation, prospects, practice or employment of another engineer, nor
will he indiscriminately criticize another engineer's work in public.
If he believes that another engineer is guilty of unethical or illegal
practice, he shall present such information to the proper authority
for action.

     a. An Engineer in private practice will not review the work
of another engineer for the same client, except with the knowledge
of such engineer, or unless the connection of such engineer with the
work has been terminated.

     b. An Engineer in governmental, industrial or educational
employ is entitled to review and evaluate the work of other engineers when so required by his employment duties.

     c. An Engineer in sales or industrial employ is entitled to
make engineering comparisons of his products with products by
other suppliers.

     Section 13--The Engineer will not associate with or allow the
use of his name by an enterprise of questionable character, nor will
he become professionally associated with engineers who do not conform to ethical practices, or with persons not legally qualified to
render the professional services for which the association is intended.

     a. He will conform with registration laws in his practice of
engineering.

     b. He will not use association with a nonengineer, a cor-
poration, or partnership, as a "cloak" for unethical acts, but must
accept personal responsibility for his professional acts.

Section 14--The Engineer will give credit for engineering work to those to whom credit is due, and will recognize the proprietary interests of others.

a. Whenever possible, he will name the person or persons who may be individually responsible for designs, inventions, writings, or other accomplishments.

b. When an Engineer uses designs supplied to him by a client, the designs remain the property of the client and should not be duplicated by the Engineer for others without express permission.

c. Before undertaking work for others in connection with which he may make improvements, plans, designs, inventions, or other records which may justify copyrights or patents, the Engineer should enter into a positive agreement regarding the ownership.

d. Designs, data, records, and notes made by an engineer and referring exclusively to his employer's work are his employer's property.

Section 15--The Engineer will cooperate in extending the effectiveness of the profession by interchanging information and experience with other engineers and students, and will endeavor to provide opportunity for the professional development and advancement of engineers under his supervision.

a. He will encourage his engineering employees' efforts to improve their education.

b. He will encourage engineering employees to attend and present papers at professional and technical society meetings.

c. He will urge his engineering employees to become registered at the earliest possible date.

d. He will assign a professional engineer duties of a nature to utilize his full training and experience, insofar as possible, and delegate lesser functions to subprofessionals or to technicians.

e. He will provide a prospective engineering employee with complete information on working conditions and his proposed status of employment, and after employment will keep him informed of any changes in them.

[Note: In regard to the question of application of the Code to corporations vis-a-vis real persons, business form or type should not negate nor influence conformance of individuals to the Code. The Code deals with professional services, which services must be performed by real persons. Real persons in turn establish and implement policies within business structures. The Code is clearly written to apply to the Engineer and it is incumbent on a member of NSPE to endeavor to live up to its provisions. This applies to all pertinent sections of the Code.]

"Engineers' Creed"

As a Professional Engineer, I dedicate my professional knowledge and skill to the advancement and betterment of human welfare.

I pledge:
To give the utmost of performance;
To participate in none but honest enterprise;
To live and work according to the laws of man and the highest standards of professional conduct;
To place service before profit, the honor and standing of the profession before personal advantage, and the public welfare above all other considerations.
In humility and with need for Divine Guidance, I make this pledge.

ENGINEERS--AGRICULTURAL

AMERICAN SOCIETY OF AGRICULTURAL ENGINEERS (ASAE)
    2950 Niles Rd., St. Joseph, Mich. 49085
    J. L. Butt, Executive Secretary

Membership: The American Society of Agricultural Engineers, founded in 1907 and with a present (1973) membership of about 7000, is the professional association of engineers engaged in various phases of work associated with the production of food and fibre, and the conservation and use of the country's soil and water resources.   Education and experience requirements for the several grades of membership include:
> Fellows--An honorary status to which members may be elected, but for which they may not apply.
> Members--Engineering degree from an ECPD accredited curriculum and six years of experience; or twelve years of experience; three years of experience must have been in responsible charge of engineering work.
> Associate Members--Engineering degree from an EPCD accredited curriculum; or six years of engineering experience.
> Affiliate Members--Interest in agricultural engineering-- engineering degree not required.

Code of Ethics: The ASAE guide to professional conduct is the Canons of Ethics for Engineers, adapted from a statement developed by the Engineers' Council for Professional Development. These Canons, an article of the Constitution and Bylaws of the ASAE (Article B15, "Professional Practice"), are enforced by the Board of Directors when a charge of violation of the conduct guide is formally presented to them. Disciplinary action for infractions of the Canons may include dismissal from the Society.

Professional Insignia: The emblem of the American Society of Agricultural Engineers, worn by members as a lapel button or pin,

is octagonal in shape, and is shown
with the following colors and legends
for professional member grades including:

> Fellows: Initials of the Asso-
> ciation, "ASAE," in gold on
> blue octagon, bordered in
> gold, with a horizontal white
> bar imprinted in gold with
> the professional designation,
> "Fellow."
>
> Members and Associate Mem-
> bers: Initials of the Society,

"ASAE," in gold on a blue octagon, bordered in gold.

> Affiliate Members: Same as for Members (above),   except
> on a red octagon.

Bibliography:

> American Society of Agricultural Engineers.   Agricultural En-
> gineers Yearbook.   1972.   610 pages. $10.
> Contains all current ASAE standards, recommendations, data.
> _____. Know and Display your ASAE Membership Certificate
> and Emblem.   Folder.
> Pictures ASAE emblem in color for the different categories
> of membership; shows Membership Certificate.
> _____. You're On the Right Track with ASAE.   10 pages.
> Pamphlet.
> ASAE goals, services, membership requirements.   Emblem
> on cover.

"Canons of Ethics for Engineers"

see pages 247-249.

ENGINEERS--AUTOMOTIVE

SOCIETY OF AUTOMOTIVE ENGINEERS (SAE)
>   Two Pennsylvania Plaza, New York, N.Y. 10001
>   Joseph Gilbert, General Manager

Membership: The Society of Automotive Engineers, founded in 1905
and with a present membership of over 26,000, is the technical
society of engineers engaged in the design, construction and utilization of self-propelled mechanisms, prime movers, their components,
and related equipment.   Requirements for the various grades of
membership are:

>   Member: (a) a baccalaureate degree in engineering, plus

a minimum of five years of professional experience; or
    (b) a related science or engineering technology degree,
plus a minimum of seven years of professional experience.
Associate: (a) a baccalaureate degree in engineering; or
          (b) equivalent education and experience.   The grade
of Associate is the normal entry grade into the Society.
Affiliate: qualified to cooperate technically with engineers
    in an automotive or related engineering field by virtue of
    competence gained through experience, education, or re-
    sponsibility.

Code of Ethics: While fully subscribing to ethical guides, SAE has
no formally enunciated code of ethics.   The members have generally
felt that they know what ethical behavior is and have lived up to it
as well as any other engineering group; they refuse to adopt a code
merely to be numbered among Societies having such a Code.

Professional Insignia: The emblem of the Society of Automotive
Engineers is a slightly rounded equilateral triangle set on its base,
bearing the Society's initials, "SAE"; the shield is dark blue, the
initials white.   The emblem may be incorporated into a logotype

which is a rectangle having rounded
corners, bearing the shield in its
left-hand two-thirds, and the legend,
"land sea air space," set vertically
on four lines, in its right-hand third,
the two sections being separated by
a thin ruled vertical line.

Bibliography:
        Society of Automotive Engineers.
    SAE in Profile.   17 pages.   Pamphlet.
Summary of the Society's operations.   Includes membership
qualifications.

ENGINEERS--CERAMIC

NATIONAL INSTITUTE OF CERAMIC ENGINEERS (NICE)
    4055 N. High St., Columbus, Ohio 43214
    Tom Stone, Executive Director

Membership: The National Institute of Ceramic Engineers, founded
in 1938 and with a current (1973) membership of over 1,700, is
the professional organization of Ceramic Engineering, which involves
all phases of research, teaching, and application of technical knowledge in the manufacture and use of ceramics and glass.   Both types
of Institute membership--Associate Membership and Full Membership

--require "a degree in Ceramic Engineering from an educational institution having a curriculum in Ceramic Engineering accredited by
the Engineers' Council for Professional Development. "

The Full Member, in addition to this education qualification,
must have "a minimum of nine years active practice in ceramic
engineering, with at least five years of responsibility for technical
charge of important engineering work. " Education with a degree in
a branch of engineering other than ceramics, or in a physical
science, is acceptable when experience of a specified length in
ceramic engineering can be substituted for specialized study in
ceramic engineering.

Code of Ethics: The Canons of Ethics for Engineers, prepared by
the Engineers' Council for Professional Development, is the official
NICE ethical guide, endorsed by the Executive Committee of the
National Institute of Ceramic Engineers on December 10, 1955.
Any revisions or modifications in the ethical code would be considered by an Ethics Education Committee of the Institute.   Complaints of professional conduct violating the ethics code are received
and processed by the Executive Committee of the NICE.

Professional Insignia: The emblem of the National Institute of
Ceramic Engineers, adopted as the official insignia on March 26,
1958, is a circular design--a twelve-cogged wheel with a central
figure of a robed woman
seated on a horizontally
striped bench, in front of a
periodic kiln of the "beehive"
or "bottle" type, holding in
her left hand a chemical retort, and in her right scales,
symbolizing the "blending of
technology and science to produce ceramic products. "
Such ceramic products are
shown in the design by traditional utensils around the feet
of the seated figure.   The
background of the central area
is dotted, and this dotting is
also shown in twelve cogs on
a second border.   The first
border banding the central area

bears the name of the society, "American Ceramic Society, " and a
third border, the association name, "The National Institute of Ceramic Engineers. "   The inner portion of the emblem is a replica of
the American Ceramic Society insigne, except for the background,
which has been dotted to distinguish it from the Society's seal, with
its solid white or black background.   The emblem appears in various colors--brown on white (letterhead); black on orange (publication).

Bibliography:
    National Institute of Ceramic Engineers. National Institute of
        Ceramic Engineers. Folder.
    Information brochure giving brief history and objectives of
    the Institute, with membership qualifications, Canons endorse-
    ment, Engineering Registration Boards.

            "Canons of Ethics for Engineers"

              see pages 247-249.

ENGINEERS--CHEMICAL

AMERICAN INSTITUTE OF CHEMICAL ENGINEERS (AIChE)
    345 E. 47th St., New York, N.Y. 10017
    F. J. Van Antworpen, Executive Secretary

Membership: The American Institute of Chemical Engineers, founded
in 1908 and with a present (1973) membership of 38,000, is the professional association of chemical engineers, whose work is defined as:
    "engaged in the application of the principles of the sciences,
    together with the principles of economics and human relations,
    to fields that pertain to processes and process equipment in
    which matter is treated to effect a change in state, energy,
    content, or composition."
The grades of AIChE membership are Fellow, Members, Associate
Members, Affiliate Members, and Student Members. To qualify as
a Member, a chemical engineer must have a Bachelor's degree in
chemical engineering from a school in which that specialty is recognized by the Engineers' Council for Professional Development, and
six years chemical engineering experience, of which three years
must have been in "responsible charge." Member applicants with
the M.S. or Ph.D. degree may substitute such an advanced academic
degree for one, or two years, respectively, of the general experience required for membership.
    An Associate Member is required to have an academic degree in
chemical engineering, but need have no work experience. Applicants
with degrees in other fields of engineering, with degrees from a
school not of recognized standing, or in fields other than engineering
or science, or "no degree," may qualify for Institute membership
if they have a sufficient amount and type of prescribed engineering
experience.
    After ten years as a Member, an engineer may be nominated
a Fellow of the Institute if he has had a minimum of 25 years of
experience in chemical engineering practice; has achieved professional
attainment based on "contribution to the professional advancement of

chemical engineers and the engineering profession"; has given valuable service to AIChE and other professional societies; and has significant accomplishments in engineering "based on process or product
developments." The number of Fellows is limited to "10 percent of
the total number of Members who meet the criterion of ten years in
the Member grade" (Constitution, Article III, Section 2c).

Code of Ethics: The guide to professional conduct of the AIChE (according to Bylaws, Section XIII) is the Canons of Ethics for Engineers, prepared by the Engineers' Council for Professional Development. The Institute Committee of Ethics investigates all complaints "of abuse or misuse of the privileges of the Institute or of
conduct unbecoming a member," submitted to it by the Council of
the Institute (Bylaws, Section VI, 5), and reports its findings and
recommendations to the Council for disposition of the complaint.

Professional Insignia: The professional emblem of the AIChE
is a maroon shield, with the
initials of the association,
"AIChE," and a narrow border
in gold.

Other Identification of Professional Status: Each Institute member is authorized
to represent himself in the
appropriate grade of member-
ship--as Fellow, Member,
Associate Member--by using
the appropriate title designation, as "Fellow, American
Institute of Chemical En-
gineers," and letters, as "FAIChE," with his name. The emblem
for each grade of membership is the basic official emblem of the
Institute, worn by members as an Institute pin. The Fellow pin is
gold, and only this pin shows the grade. The pin and other jewelry
for other membership grades are maroon and gold.

Bibliography:
        American Institute of Chemical Engineers. Constitution and
            Bylaws. Amended to February 27, 1970.
        Includes membership requirements and Code of Ethics.
        _____. Professionalism and the Individual. 2 volumes,
            Volume 1, 1966, 100 pages, $4.; Volume 2, 1970, 124
            pages, $5.

            "Canons of Ethics for Engineers"

see pages 247-249.

ENGINEERS--CIVIL

AMERICAN SOCIETY OF CIVIL ENGINEERS (ASCE)
345 E. 47th St., New York, N. Y. 10017
Eugene Zwoyer, Executive Director

Membership: Developing from professional organizations first established in 1852, the American Society of Civil Engineers has a current (1973) membership of over 67,000. "Civil Engineering" was defined by the Society Board of Directors in October, 1961, as:
> "the profession in which a knowledge of the mathematical
> and physical sciences gained by study, experience, and
> practice is applied with judgment to develop ways to utilize
> economically the materials and forces of nature for the
> progressive well-being of mankind in creating, improving
> and protecting environment, in providing facilities for com-
> munity living, industry and transportation, and in providing
> structures for the use of mankind."

Of the several grades of Society membership (Fellow, Member,
Associate Member, Affiliate, Honorary Member), an applicant
qualifies for "Member" by graduation in engineering from a school
accredited by the Engineers' Council for Professional Development
(ECPD), and five years of responsible professional practice.   An
"Associate Member" is required to have an ECPD-accredited degree,
or have graduated from an approved four year program and have a
license to practice in engineering (Constitution, Article II).   To
qualify for "Fellow" of the ASCE, an engineer must be licensed as
a professional engineer in the state of practice, have a minimum of
four years of experience in the grade of "Member," in "responsible
charge" of important engineering work, and be qualified to direct,
conceive, plan or design engineering works, or to be in charge of
"important industrial, business, construction, educational, editorial,
research or engineering society activity."
Society members are authorized to use the appropriate member
grade of professional designation, abbreviation, and emblem (Rules
of Policy and Procedure, Article II).

Code of Ethics: The first ASCE Code of Ethics was developed in
1914 by a committee of the Board of Direction. This guide to professional conduct--consisting of nine principles--has been amended
several times, most recently on October 19, 1971. The Guide to
Professional Practice under the Code of Ethics, issued at that time,
applies and interprets each of the nine principles of the Code.
Amendments to the Code are proposed by the Professional Activities
Committee for approval by the Board of Direction (Bylaws, Article
VII, Section 1).

The ASCE Professional Activities Committee is also responsible
for enforcing the Code of Ethics (Bylaws, Article VII, Section 5A).
It investigates all charges of unprofessional conduct against a Society
member, presenting sustained or proven charges to the Board of
Direction for disciplinary action, which may include reprimand,
suspension, or expulsion from membership (Bylaws, Article III,
Section 1). Statistical summaries of professional conduct cases are
reported in Civil Engineering, the official monthly magazine of the
Society. An annual award of the Society (the Daniel W. Mead Prizes)
is offered to Associate and Student Members for the best papers on
professional ethics (Official Register, 1971, p. 180-181).

Other Guides to Professional Conduct: In 1964 the ASCE endorsed
the Fundamental Principles of Engineering Ethics--the broad preliminary statements from the Canons of Ethics of Engineers, prepared by the Engineers' Council for Professional Development. The
ASCE Committee on Professional Conduct recently prepared a statement on professional conduct, which was published in the December
1969 issue of the Society's monthly magazine, Civil Engineering.

Professional Insignia: The official emblem of the ASCE is a blue
shield imprinted with the or-
ganization name, "American
Society of Civil Engineers, "
and the founding date of the
organization, "Founded 1852. "
This insignia--adopted in 1894
from the design prepared by a
committee composed of Des-
mond Fitzgerald, William Craig-
hill, and John Thompson--was
derived from an older badge
with a wider shield, developed
in 1852.   The form of the emblem, generally termed in
heraldry a "shield, " is described by the ASCE (Civil
Engineering, February 1934,
page 99):

"for a very short dis-
tance the upper parts of
the sides of the badge
are straight; the lower
parts of the sides are
cycloidal curves gen-
erated by a point on a 4-in. circle that rolls downward
along a vertical axis. "

The color of the emblem is shown variously--blue shield, with
white printing and border, banded in black; dark blue on white (letterhead), white on black (publication).   Use of the emblem is restricted to official Society stationery, official badges, charms and

pins, official banners and placards, and Society publications (<u>Rules</u> <u>of Policy and Procedure,</u> Article I. Emblem). Student chapters of <u>the ASCE</u> may use the emblem, but the shield must be red, not blue.

<u>Other Identification of Professional Status:</u> While the ASCE official emblem may not be used on private or business stationery of members, a member is authorized to identify himself on his stationery through the use of professional designation of member grade, followed by the society initials, "ASCE," and to wear the appropriate emblem:

Member Grade	Professional Abbreviation	Emblem
Honorary Member	Hon. M. ASCE	Gold enamel on Blue
Fellow	F. ASCE	same
Member	M. ASCE	same
Affiliate	Aff. ASCE	same
Associate	A. M. ASCE	Blue shield, white border
Student		Maroon shield, white border

A gold lapel clasp with the official Society emblem is available to Fellows, Members, and Affiliate Members. Gold lapel buttons and tie tacks are available to Associates (blue and white), and Student Members (maroon and white). <u>Flag:</u> a 5x7 foot banner, bearing the seal of the Society on a maroon bunting background, is available for purchase and display by student chapters (price $40., postpaid). <u>Tie:</u> A tie for ASCE members shows the official emblem in black and white on a blue, or maroon tie.

Bibliography:
        American Society of Civil Engineers. <u>Annual Report.</u> 1972.
        General information and activities of the ASCE.
                  . <u>Code of Ethics.</u> 1972.
        Includes the professional conduct guides of the Society--Code
        of Ethics, Guide to Professional Practice under the Code of
        Ethics, and Canons of Ethics of Engineers as Fundamental
        Principles of Engineering Ethics.
                  . <u>Consulting Engineering--A Guide for the Engagement</u>
        <u>of Engineering Services.</u> Report No. 45. July 1972. $1.
                  . <u>Official Register.</u> 1973. November 1972.
        Includes Society Constitution, Bylaws, Guide to Practice and
        Code of Ethics.
                  . Committee on Professional Conduct. "Statement on
        Professional Conduct." <u>Civil Engineering,</u> July 1969.
        Wisely, William H. "Maintaining Ethical Standards." <u>Civil</u>
        <u>Engineering,</u> April 1964, page 31.
        Statistical summary of professional conduct cases, 1952-
        1964, with highlights of the ten years of enforcement of the
        Code of Ethics.

_____ . "Administration of Ethical Standards." Civil Engineering, August 1967, page 37.
Statistical summary of professional conduct cases, 1952-1967, with brief statement of policies of enforcement.

"Code of Ethics"

It shall be considered unprofessional and inconsistent with honorable and dignified conduct and contrary to the public interest for any member of the American Society of Civil Engineers:

1. To act for his client or for his employer otherwise than as a faithful agent or trustee.

2. To accept remuneration for services rendered other than from his client or his employer.

3. To attempt to supplant another engineer in a particular engagement after definite steps have been taken toward his employment.

4. To attempt to injure, falsely or maliciously, the professional reputation, business, or employment position of another engineer.

5. To review the work of another engineer for the same client, except with the knowledge of such engineer, unless such engineer's engagement on the work which is subject to review has been terminated.

6. To advertise engineering services in self-laudatory language, or in any other manner derogatory to the dignity of the profession.

7. To use the advantages of a salaried position to compete unfairly with other engineers.

8. To exert undue influence or to offer, solicit or accept compensation for the purpose of affecting negotiations for an engineering engagement.

9. To act in any manner derogatory to the honor, integrity or dignity of the engineering profession.

[Under the Code of Ethics of the American Society of Civil Engineers, the submission of fee quotations for engineering services is not an unethical practice. ASCE is constrained from prohibiting or limiting this practice and such prohibition or limitation has been removed from the Code of Ethics. However, the procurement of engineering services involves consideration of factors in addition to fee, and these factors should be evaluated carefully in securing professional services. (Added July 1972)

[The Society has also endorsed the Fundamental Principles of Professional Engineering Ethics of the Canons of Ethics as adopted by Engineers' Council for Professional Development on September 30, 1963, by Board action on May 11-12, 1964.

[On foreign engineering work, for which only United States engineering firms are to be considered, a member shall order his practice in accordance with the ASCE Code of Ethics. On other engineering works in a foreign country he may adapt his conduct

according to the professional standards and customs of that country,
but shall adhere as closely as practicable to the principles of this
Code.   (Adopted by ASCE Board of Direction October 7-8, 1963.)]

ENGINEERS--CONSULTING

AMERICAN INSTITUTE OF CONSULTING ENGINEERS (AICE)
     345 E. 47th St., New York, N.Y. 10017
     C. Einersen, Administrator

Membership: The American Institute of Consulting Engineers,
founded in 1910 and with a present (1953) membership of about
500, is a professional organization of engineers who practice as
consultants in recognized branches or specialized fields of engineering.
An applicant for membership may qualify for AICE "Member" by
being a consultic engineer who practices as proprieter or partner in
an engineering firm, or performs comparable independent work in
engineering, is at least 35 years of age, and is a "Member," or
higher grade of membership, of an engineering society, including
American Society of Civil Engineers; American Institute of Mining,
Metallurgical and Petroleum Engineers; American Society of Mechanical Engineers; Institute of Electrical and Electronic Engineers;
American Institute of Chemical Engineers.

Code of Ethics: One of the objectives of the AICE (as set forth in
the Institute Constitution) is "to promote ethical principles and practice."   The AICE guide to professional conduct is set forth in its
Code of Ethics, which enumerates 10 principles concerning relations
to clients, colleagues, commission and advertising activities; and in
the Standards of Professional Conduct, which expand and interpret--
through applications--the principles of the Code.   Both of these professional conduct guides were approved by the Institute Council on
June 17, 1958, amended later that year, and adopted by the Institute
membership on January 19, 1959.   Written complaints of unprofessional conduct of a member are addressed to the Council of the
Institute, which investigates the charges, may hold a hearing, and
may discipline an offending member by suspension or expulsion
(Bylaws, Article 1, Section 8).

Professional Insignia: The emblem of the AICE is its seal--penta-
gon in form, with the symbols of the five engineering specialties in
which members may practice in the center:
        Theodolite--Civil Engineering;
        Lightning Bolt--Electrical and Electronic Engineering;
        Retort--Chemical Engineering;
        Hammer and Pick, crossed--Mining, Metallurgical and Petro-
            leum Engineering;

Wheel, eight-cogged--Mechanical Engineering.
A circular band enclosing these
central symbols bears the name
of the association, "American
Institute of Consulting Engineers, "
and shows at the bottom of the
band, the date of the organization founding, "1910. " In the
border there is an equilateral
triangle, surface shaded, at each
point of the pentagon, and two
shaded triangles at the crest of
the design. The color of the
emblem--as shown on publications
--is blue and white.

Bibliography:
American Institute of Consulting Engineers. Code of Ethics,
and Standards of Professional Conduct. 1959. Folder.
_____. Objectives of the Institute and Requirements for
Admission to Membership. 3 pages.
Pertinent sections for the AICE Constitution and Bylaws,
giving qualifications for membership; procedures for enforcing
Code of Ethics and Standards of Professional Practice.

"Code of Ethics"

It shall be considered unprofessional and inconsistent with
honorable and dignified conduct for any member of the American
Institute of Consulting Engineers:
1. To act for his clients in engineering matters otherwise
than as a faithful agent or trustee;
2. To accept any remuneration other than his agreed
charges for services rendered his clients;
3. To pay commissions or make donations to other than
regular employees in negotiating for engineering work;
4. To compete with a fellow engineer for employment on
the basis of fee, or to invite another engineer to do so;
5. To attempt to supplant another engineer knowing that
definite steps have been taken towards his engagement;
6. To engage to review the work of another engineer for
the same client, if such engineer is still employed, except with
his consent;
7. To attempt to injure the reputation, prospects, or business, of another engineer;
8. To be associated in the conduct of engineering work with
others who do not conform to the basic principles of this code;
9. To advertise or make public statements, in a self-laudatory manner;
10. To engage in any practice which will tend to bring discredit on the honor or dignity of the engineering profession.

"Standards of Professional Conduct"

1. A member shall abide by the Code of Ethics of the American Institute of Consulting Engineers.

2. A member who has proof that another member has violated the Code of Ethics will bring the matter to the attention of the Council of the Institute.

3. A member shall inform his clients of business connections, interests or circumstances which might influence his judgment or the quality of his services.

4. A member shall promptly disclose to his client any interest in a business which may compete with or affect the business of his client. He will not allow such interest to affect his decisions.

5. A member shall not disclose information concerning the business affairs or technical processes of clients without their consent.

6. A member shall not divulge any findings of studies or actions of an engineering commission of which he is a member, without the official permission of the commission.

7. A member shall not make use of information or discoveries, or the results therefrom, obtained while in the service of a client, in any manner adverse to the interests of the client.

8. A member shall engage or advise his client to engage, and he shall cooperate with, experts and specialists whenever the client's interests would be best served by such services.

9. A member who serves on a public or quasi-public board which is required to pass upon plans, specifications, and designs of engineering works shall debar himself from accepting any engagement involving matters that may come before him in his public capacity.

10. A member shall not accept compensation, financial or otherwise, from more than one interested party for the same service, or for services pertaining to the same work, without the consent of all interested parties.

11. A member shall not accept for himself, commissions or allowances from contractors or other parties dealing with his client in connection with work for which he is responsible.

12. A member shall not accept for himself any trade commissions, discounts, or allowances in connection with a professional engagement.

13. A member shall not accept for himself, unless authorized by the client, any royalty, gratuity or commission on any patented or protected article or process used on work upon which he is retained.

14. A member shall not compete with another engineer by reducing his usual charges or attempting to underbid, after being informed of the charges named by his competitor.

15. A member will not use the advantage of a salaried position to compete unfairly with other engineers.

16. A member will not knowingly submit a proposal for rendering engineering services on a competitive price basis.

17. A member will not invite proposals for the performance

of engineering services on a competitive price basis.

18.   A member will not attempt to supplant another engineer before that engineer's services have been terminated.

19.   A member will, as soon as possible, sever his relations with an engineering organization whose representatives, whether or not under his direct control, refuse to conduct themselves and the business of the organization in accord with the Code of Ethics of the American Institute of Consulting Engineers.

20.   A member will not advertise or make public statements or releases on his professional practice, qualifications, or achievements, in misleading, self-laudatory, or undignified language or manner.

21.   A member will decline to give a bond for the faithful performance of engineering services, unless required by foreign practice.

22.   A member will not enter competitions for designs for a specific project, unless provision is made for reasonable compensation for all designs submitted.

23.   A member will warn his client of the consequences to be expected from any deviations from his engineering recommendations proposed by others.

24.   A member will not issue comments, criticisms, or arguments on matters connected with public policy that are inspired or paid for by private interests, unless he indicates on whose behalf he is acting.

ASSOCIATION OF CONSULTING MANAGEMENT ENGINEERS (ACME)
    347 Madison Ave., New York, N.Y. 10017
    Philip W. Shay, Executive Director

Membership: The Association of Consulting Management Engineers, founded in 1929 and with a present (1973) membership of about 50, is a professional organization of engineers engaged in managerial services to commercial, governmental, industrial, and other organizations.

Code of Ethics: The guide to professional conduct for Association members is the ACME Standards of Professional Conduct and Practice, adopted in its current form on February 1, 1972.   The Standards consist of two sections:
    I.   Code of Professional Responsibility--Enumerates responsibilities of the consulting engineer, including Basic Client Responsibilities; Client Arrangements; Client Fees.
    II.   Professional Practices--Enumerates 11 standards of good practice in management consulting.
The Executive Secretary receives requests regarding interpretation of the Standards and complaints of violations of these guides to pro-

fessional conduct. Complaints of unprofessional conduct are investigated, and disciplinary action taken against any member found
"guilty of code violation."

Professional Insignia: The
emblem of the Association of
Consulting Management En-
gineers is its seal--a round
design with the initials of the
organization in a central circle,
"ASME," with the name of
the group, "Association of
Consulting Management En-
gineers," in the bordering
band. The color of this em-
blem--as shown on publica-
tions--is black and white, or
blue and white.

Bibliography:
       Association of Consulting
Management Engineers. Standards of Professional Con-
duct and Practice. February 1, 1972. 8 pages.
Includes ACME Code of Professional Responsibility, and
Professional Practices.

"Standards of Professional Conduct and Practice"

PREAMBLE

Purposes of Standards of Professional Conduct

        These Standards of Professional Conduct and Practice signify
voluntary assumption by members of the obligation of self-discipline
above and beyond the requirements of the law. Their purpose is
to let the public know that members intend to maintain a high level
of ethics and public service, and to declare that--in return for the
faith that the public places in them--the members accept the obligation to conduct their practice in a way that will be beneficial to the
public.   They give clients a basis for confidence that members will
serve them in accordance with professional standards of competence,
objectivity, and integrity.

        They express in general terms the standards of professional
conduct expected of management consulting firms in their relationships with prospective clients, clients, colleagues, members of
allied professions, and the public. The Code of Professional Responsibility, unlike the Professional Practices, is mandatory in
character.   It serves as a basis for disciplinary action when the
conduct of a member firm falls below the required standards as
stated in the Code of Professional Responsibility. The Professional

Practices are largely aspirational in character and represent objectives and standards of good practice to which members of the Association subscribe.

The Association enforces the Code of Professional Responsibility by receiving and investigating all complaints of violations and by taking disciplinary action against any member who is found to be guilty of code violation.

The Professional Attitude

The reliance of managers of private and public institutions on the advice of management consultants imposes on the profession an obligation to maintain high standards of integrity and competence. To this end, members of the Association have basic responsibilities to place the interests of clients and prospective clients ahead of their own, maintain independence of thought and action, hold the affairs of their clients in strict confidence, strive continually to improve their professional skills, observe and advance professional standards of management consulting, uphold the honor and dignity of the profession, and maintain high standards of personal conduct. These Standards have evolved out of the experience of members since the Association was incorporated in 1933. In recognition of the public interest and their obligation to the profession, members and the consultants on their staffs have agreed to comply with the following articles of professional responsibility.

1--CODE OF PROFESSIONAL RESPONSIBILITY

1. Basic Client Responsibilities

1. 1   We will at all times place the interests of clients ahead of our own and serve them with integrity, competence, and independence.
We will assume an independent position with the client, making certain that our advice to clients is based on impartial consideration of all pertinent facts and responsible opinions.

1. 2   We will guard as confidential all information concerning the affairs of clients that we gather during the course of professional engagements; and we will not take personal, financial, or other advantage of material or inside information coming to our attention as a result of our professional relationship with clients; nor will we provide the basis on which others might take such advantage.   Observance of the ethical obligation of the management consulting firm to hold inviolate the confidence of its clients not only facilitates the full development of facts essential to effective solution of the problem but also encourages clients to seek needed help on sensitive problems.

1. 3   We will serve two or more competing clients on sensitive problems only with their knowledge.

1. 4   We will inform clients of any relationships, circumstances, or interests that might influence our judgment or the objectivity of our services.

2.   Client Arrangements

2. 1   We will present our qualifications for serving a client solely in terms of our competence, experience, and standing, and we will not guarantee any specific result, such as amount of cost reduction or profit increase.

2. 2   We will accept only those engagements we are qualified to undertake and which we believe will provide real benefits to clients.   We will assign personnel qualified by knowledge, experience, and character to give effective service in analyzing and solving the particular problem or problems involved.   We will carry out each engagement under the direction of a principal of the firm who is responsible for its successful completion.

2. 3   We will not accept an engagement of such limited scope that we cannot serve the client effectively.

2. 4   We will, before accepting an engagement, confer with the client or prospective client in sufficient detail and gather sufficient facts to gain an adequate understanding of the problem, the scope of study needed to solve it, and the possible benefits that may accrue to the client.   The preliminary exploration will be conducted confidentially on terms and conditions agreed upon by the member and the prospective client.   Extended preliminary or problem-defining surveys for prospective clients will be made only on a fully compensated fee basis.

2. 5   We will, except for those cases where special client relationships make it unnecessary, make certain that the client receives a written proposal that outlines the objectives, scope, and, where possible, the estimated fee or fee basis for the proposed service or engagement.   We will discuss with the client any important changes in the nature, scope, timing, or other aspects of the engagement and obtain the client's agreement to such changes before taking action on them--and unless the circumstances make it unnecessary, we will confirm these changes in writing.

2. 6   We will perform each engagement on an individualized basis and develop recommendations designed specifically to meet the particular requirements of the client situation.   Our objective in each client engagement is to develop solutions that are realistic and practical and that can be implemented promptly and economically. Our professional staffs are prepared to assist, to whatever extent desired, with the implementation of approved recommendations.

2. 7   We will not serve a client under terms or conditions that might impair our objectivity, independence, or integrity; and

we will reserve the right to withdraw if conditions beyond our control develop to interfere with the successful conduct of the engagement.

2. 8   We will acquaint client personnel with the principles, methods, and techniques applied, so that the improvements suggested or installed may be properly managed and continued after completion of the engagement.

2. 9   We will maintain continuity of understanding and knowledge of clients' problems and the work that has been done to solve them by maintaining appropriate files of reports submitted to clients. These are protected against unauthorized access and supported by files of working papers, consultants' log-books, and similar recorded data.

2. 10   We will not accept an engagement for a client while another management consulting firm is serving that client unless we are assured, and can satisfy ourselves, that there will be no conflict between the two engagements.   We will not endeavor to displace another management consulting firm or individual consultant once we have knowledge that the client has made a commitment to the other consultant.

2. 11   We will review the work of another management consulting firm or individual consultant for the same client, only with the knowledge of such consultant, unless such consultant's work which is subject to review has been finished or terminated.   However, even though the other consultant's work has been finished or terminated, it is a matter of common courtesy to let the consulting firm or individual know that his work is being reviewed.

3.   Client Fees

3. 1   We will charge reasonable fees which are commensurate with the nature of services performed and the responsibility assumed.   An excessive charge abuses the professional relationship and discourages the public from utilizing the services of management consultants.   On the other hand, adequate compensation is necessary in order to enable the management consulting firm to serve clients effectively and to preserve the integrity and independence of the profession.   Determination of the reasonableness of a fee requires consideration of many factors, including the nature of the services performed; the time required; the consulting firm's experience, ability, and reputation; the degree of responsibility assumed; and the benefits that accrue to the client.   Wherever feasible, we will agree with the client in advance on the fee or fee basis.

3. 2   We will not render or offer professional services for which the fees are contingent on reduction in costs, increases in profits, or any other specific result.

3.3 We will neither accept nor pay fees or commissions to others for client referrals, or enter into any arrangement for franchising our practice to others. Nor will we accept fees, commissions, or other valuable considerations from individuals or organizations whose equipment, supplies, or services we might recommend in the course of our service to clients.

II--PROFESSIONAL PRACTICES

In order to promote highest quality of performance in the practice of management consulting, ACME has developed the following standards of good practice for the guidance of the profession. Member firms subscribe to these practices because they make for equitable and satisfactory client relationships and contribute to success in management consulting.

1. We will strive continually to advance and protect the standards of the management consulting profession. We will strive continually to improve our knowledge, skills, and techniques, and will make available to our clients the benefits of our professional attainments.

2. We recognize our responsibilities to the public interest and to our profession to contribute to the development and understanding of better ways to manage the various formal institutions in our society. By reason of education, experience, and broad contact with management problems in a variety of institutions, management consultants are especially qualified to recognize opportunities for improving managerial and operating processes; and they have an obligation to share their knowledge with managers and their colleagues in the profession.

3. We recognize our responsibility to the profession to share with our colleagues the methods and techniques we utilize in serving clients. But we will not knowingly, without their permission, use proprietary data, procedures, materials, or techniques that other management consultants have developed but not released for public use.

4. We will not make offers of employment to consultants on the staffs of other consulting firms without first informing them. We will not engage in wholesale or mass recruiting of consultants from other consulting firms. If we are approached by consultants of other consulting firms regarding employment in our firm or in that of a client, we will handle each situation in way that will be fair to the consultant and his firm.

5. We will not make offers of employment to employees of clients. If we are approached by employees of clients regarding employment in our firm or in that of another client, we will make certain that we have our clients' consent before entering into any negotiations with employees.

6.   We will continually evaluate the quality of the work done by our staff to insure, insofar as is possible, that all of our engagements are conducted in a competent manner.

7.   We will endeavor to provide opportunity for the professional development of those men who enter the profession, by assisting them to acquire a full understanding of the functions, duties, and responsibilities of management consultants, and to keep up with significant advances in their areas of practice.

8.   We will administer the internal and external affairs of our firm in the best interests of the profession at all times.

9.   We will not advertise our services in self-laudatory language or in any other manner derogatory to the dignity of the profession.

10.   We will respect the professional reputation and practice of other management consultants. This does not remove the moral obligation to expose unethical conduct of fellow members of the profession to the proper authorities.

11.   We will strive to broaden public understanding and enhance public regard and confidence in the management consulting profession, so that management consultants can perform their proper function in society effectively. We will conduct ourselves so as to reflect credit on the profession and to inspire the confidence, respect, and trust of clients and the public. In the course of our practice, we will strive to maintain a wholly professional attitude toward those we serve, toward those who assist us in our practice, toward our fellow consultants, toward the members of other professions, and the practitioners of allied arts and sciences.

Adopted February 1, 1972

ENGINEERS--COST

AMERICAN ASSOCIATION OF COST ENGINEERS (AACE)
308 Monongahela Bldg., Morgantown, W. Va. 26505
Kenneth K. Humphreys, Executive Director

Membership: The American Association of Cost Engineers, founded in 1956 and with a present (1973) membership of over 2300, is a professional organization of engineers engaged in "Cost Engineering," defined by the group as
    "that area of engineering practice where engineering judgment and experience are utilized in the application of scientific principles and techniques to problems of cost estimation

cost control, business planning and management science"
(Constitution, Article I, Section 2).
To qualify as a professional member of the Association, an engineer
engaged in cost engineering must meet one of the following requirements:
> "1.   Graduate of recognized engineering curricula with at
>   least five years of experience in responsible positions;
> 2.   Hold a license to practice Professional Engineering; or
> 3.   Have at least ten years of experience in an engineering
>   profession and at least seven years of these in a respon-
>   sible engineering position."

Code of Ethics: Although the AACE has issued no formal code of
ethics, its members are required to subscribe to the Constitution .
and Bylaws.   These AACE Bylaws provide (Article I, Section 8) for
the discipline of members who have violated the Canons of Ethics
for Engineers of the Engineers' Council for Professional Development.   Complaints about an AACE member's professional misconduct
are submitted in writing to the association Secretary, and--after investigation and hearing of the complaint--the AACE Board of Directors may expel a member.

Professional Insignia: The emblem of the American Association of

Cost Engineers is a horizontal
oval, with a center design of
a slide rule, bearing a "$" on
its cursor; the name of the
organization, "American Association of Cost Engineers," is
arranged around the oval to
form an unenclosed border.
The official colors of the emblem are "white or silver and
a greenish gray."   The official
seal of the Association is of
the same shape and design as the emblem, but carries the legend
of the date of establishment, "Founded 1956."

Bibliography:
>   American Association of Cost Engineers.   American Association
>   of Cost Engineers.   Folder.
>   Informational brochure with definition of "Cost Engineering,"
>   and objects, membership requirements of AACE.
>   .   Constitution, Bylaws.   Adopted June 2, 1956; amended
>   March 1970.   Folder.
>   Sets forth membership requirements, disciplinary procedure
>   for unprofessional conduct, and describes and pictures official
>   emblem.

"Canons of Ethics for Engineers"

see pages 247-249.

ENGINEERS--ELECTRICAL AND ELECTRONIC

INSTITUTE OF ELECTRICAL AND ELECTRONICS ENGINEERS
(IEEE)
345 E. 47th St., New York, N.Y. 10017
Donald G. Fink, General Manager

Membership: The Institute of Electrical and Electronics Engineers, founded in 1884, is the "world's largest engineering society," with a current (1973) membership of over 165,000. Its professional engineer members are grouped in more than 210 local IEEE Sections, administered in ten Regions, which cover the world--with six Regions in the United States. In addition to the geographic division into Regions and Sections, the Institute is organized technically into 31 groups or Societies reflecting the diversity of interest of its members (Bylaws, Section 405, Division 8):

Groups

Aerospace and Electronic Systems
Antennas and Propagation
Audio and Electroacoustics
Broadcast and Television Receivers
Broadcasting
Education
Electrical Insulation
Electromagnetic Compatibility
Electron Devices
Engineering Management
Engineering in Medicine and Biology
Geoscience Electronics
Industrial Electronics and Control Instrumentation
Information Theory
Instrumentation and Measurement
Manufacturing Technology
Microwave Theory and Technique
Part, Materials and Packaging
Professional Communication
Reliability
Sonics and Ultrasonics
Vehicular Technology

Societies

Circuits and Systems
Communications
Computer
Control Systems
Industry Applications
Magnetics
Nuclear and Plasma Sciences
Power Engineering
Systems, Management and Cybernetics

Requirements for membership in those member grades applied for (in addition to Student) are:
Associate--Graduation "from a course of study of at least two

academic years' duration or its equivalent in the fields of
electrical, electronics, or radio technology or an allied
branch of engineering or related arts and sciences in a
'school of recognized standing'," or proved interest and
capability in electrical or electronics engineering, radio
or allied branches of engineering or related arts and
sciences.

Member--Graduation from a course of study of at least four
academic years' duration in a school of "recognized standing," or three years of professional experience; or specified equivalents.

Senior Member--Minimum of ten years' active professional
practice, five of which must have shown distinction attained through publication of important original engineering or scientific papers, books or inventions; technical
direction with evidence of accomplishment of important
scientific or engineering work; creative contributions to
the welfare of the scientific or engineering profession; or
establishment or furtherance of important scientific or
engineering courses in a "school of recognized standing";
or equivalent contributions in technical editing, patent prosecution or patent law.

Honorary Member; Fellow--Honorary grades of membership
conferred by the Board of Directors as marks of unusual
professional distinction.   An IEEE member who has been
a member of the Institute for seven years and who meets
the education and experience requirements for Senior
Member, may be considered for Fellow.

Code of Ethics: Although the IEEE has not adopted ethical guides
in the form of a Code of Ethics or Ethical Standards, members may
be disciplined by suspension or expulsion from the organization (Bylaws, Section 112) when complaints of unprofessional conduct are
submitted in writing to the Board of Directors, and the alleged infraction of professional conduct
is substantiated by investigation
and hearing.

Professional Insignia: The emblem of the IEEE is diamond
shaped, and bears a centered
symbol of a vertical arrow encircled at the center by an
orthogonal arrow. These arrows symbolize the flow of
electric current through a wire
with the resultant encircling
magnetic field. The use of
this emblem is restricted to
"official business" of the Institute, and it appears on
IEEE stationery and publications.

The color of the design varies--light blue on black (Bylaws), white on royal blue (membership folder), white on gray-blue (letterhead).

Other Identification of Professional Status: While the official emblem of IEEE may not be used on members' personal or business stationery, it may be worn by them as professional jewelry (tie tac, lapel pin, tie bar). Members may also identify themselves by use of the following professional designation in connection with their names (Bylaws, Section 104, Division 12):

Designation	Emblem Color
Hon. Mem. IEEE	Gold
Fel. IEEE	Gold
Mem. IEEE	Dark Blue
Assoc. IEEE	Light Blue
Student Member	Green

Bibliography:
    Institute of Electrical and Electronics Engineers. Bylaws.
        Effective January 1, 1972. 23 pages.
        Gives purposes, classes of membership, membership require-
        ments, approved initials of professional designation of mem-
        bers, restrictions on emblem use, component groups and
        societies.
    _____. Membership Benefits. Folder.
    Brief statement of membership requirements, educational
    activities, groups and societies.

ENGINEERS--ENVIRONMENTAL

AMERICAN ACADEMY OF ENVIRONMENTAL ENGINEERS (AAEE)
    P. O. Box 9728, Washington, D. C.   20016
    Frank Butrice, Executive Director

Membership: The American Academy of Environmental Engineers, founded in 1955 and with a present (1973) membership of approximately 2500, represents--through its parent organization the Environmental Engineering Intersociety Board (EEIB), and its Specialty Committee certification program--the first licensure "for specialty engineering certification beyond state registration requirements." Every engineer who holds a certificate of special knowledge in environmental engineering granted by the Environmental Engineering Intersociety Board is designated a "Diplomate" and is automatically a member of the Academy.

    "Environmental Engineering," according to the official definition of the Academy, means:
        "the application of engineering principles and practice to one

or more elements of the environment for the purpose of protecting or improving man's health and well-being. It includes
the control of the air, land and water resources, man's personal and working environment in relation to his health,
social and economic well-being, and the design and maintenance of systems to support life in alien and hostile environments."
To be eligible for examination for EEIB certification an engineer
must be licensed in a state (U.S.A.) or province (Canada) of
practice, have graduated from a recognized university or college
with an engineering degree, plus eight years' experience in an environmental engineering specialty, four years of which must be "in
responsible charge of work." This certifying examination consists
of two parts:

Written--Tests knowledge and ability in specialty field;
Oral--Measures personal qualifications, including knowledge
of professional ethics.

Applicants take an examination and are issued certificates in
one of the following four specialties of environmental engineering:
Air Pollution Control--AP;
Industrial Hygiene--IH;
Sanitary--(Including Water Supply, Water and Land Pollution
Control, and Public Health Engineering)--SE;
Radiation and Hazard Control--RH.
Each diplomate is listed with specialty designation in the annual
Roster of the Academy, and is entitled to use the specialty designa-
tion with his name as an indication of competence certified to by
his professional peers. Also the engineer certified by the Academy
may use the professional designation following his name, "Diplomate
AAEE."

Code of Ethics: No special conduct guide has been issued by the
American Academy of Environmental Engineers, many of whose mem-
bers are members of sponsoring engineering associations with pro-
fessional codes of ethics, such as Air Pollution Control Association,
American Institute of Chemical Engineers, American Society of Civil
Engineers.

Professional Insignia: The emblem of the AAEE is a circular design, with a centered five-pointed star in a circle; radial divisions
from each point of the star divide the surrounding circle into fifths,
showing clockwise starting at the top right--rural scene; chemical
tools, such as retort, balance, Bunsen burner, microscope; engineering measurement tools, such as T-square, right angle; atom
nucleus; urban scene; a five-part beaded border, each part joined
by a link, encloses this central design, with the name of the organization, "The Environmental Engineering Intersociety Board,
Inc.," outside the border, and the date of founding, "1955," at the
bottom of the emblem. Color of the emblem is shown variously--
black on white (letterhead); black on various color paper (publications).

Other Identification of Professional Status: As described above under "Membership," professional competence of certified engineers is indicated by the professional designation, following the member's name, "Diplomate AAEE," or as Diplomate in one or more of the four specialty fields of environmental engineering.

Bibliography:
American Academy of Environmental Engineers. Roster. Annual, as of December 31. Environmental Engineering Intersociety Board. Includes Academy and Board Bylaws, with requirements for membership, examination, and certification as Diplomate.

ENGINEERS--FIRE PROTECTION

SOCIETY OF FIRE PROTECTION ENGINEERS (SFPE)
60 Batterymarch St., Boston, Mass. 02110
Peter Lund, Executive Director

Membership: The Society of Fire Protection Engineers, founded in 1950 and with a present (1973) membership of approximately 1500, is a professional organization of engineers--also scientists, technologists, and administrators--concerned with fire science and technology in its various aspects of prevention, detection, and control.

Code of Ethics: The guide to professional conduct for SFPE members is the Canons of Ethics for Engineers, adopted by the Society on May 23, 1962. The Canons give principles of conduct in 28 sections which are grouped under four headings:
Professional Life,
Relations with the Public,
Relations with Clients and Employers,
Relations with Engineers.
No enforcement procedures for these Canons are reported.

Professional Insignia: The insignia of the Society is triangular in shape, representing the "triangle of fire" (prevention, detection, control): "The lines at the corners symbolize the separability of

the three components of fire."
In a centered triangle, flames
of a fire are shown; this centered triangle is divided horizontally into a smaller upper
triangle and a base--about one-
third up the triangle sides.
The name of the organization,
"Society of Fire Protection Engineers," is spaced around
the triangle within a bordering
band. In color the emblem
is gold on white, with the central triangle blue on top, red
on base. This emblem of the Society may be worn by members as
a lapel button, which is gold for Members, and silver for Junior
Members.

Bibliography:
    Society of Fire Protection Engineers.   Canons of Ethics for
        Engineers.   3 pages.

"Canons of Ethics for Engineers"

Foreword

Honesty, justice, and courtesy form a moral philosophy which,
associated with mutual interest among men, constitutes the foundation of ethics. The engineer should recognize such a standard, not
in passive observance, but as a set of dynamic principles guiding
his conduct and way of life. It is his duty to practice his profession
according to these Canons of Ethics.

As the keystone of professional conduct is integrity, the engineer will discharge his duties with fidelity to the public, his employers, and clients, and with fairness and impartiality to all. It
is his duty to interest himself in public welfare, and to be ready
to apply his special knowledge for the benefit of mankind. He should
uphold the honor and dignity of his profession and also avoid association with any enterprise of questionable character. In his dealings with fellow engineers he should be fair and tolerant.

Professional Life

Section 1: The engineer will cooperate in extending the effectiveness of the engineering profession by interchanging information and experience with other engineers and students and by contributing to the work of engineering societies, schools, and the
scientific and engineering press.
    Section 2: He will not advertise his work or merit in a
self-laudatory manner, and he will avoid all conduct or practice

likely to discredit or do injury to the dignity and honor of his profession.

Relations with the Public

   Section 3:   The engineer will endeavor to extend public knowledge of engineering and will discourage the spreading of untrue, unfair, and exaggerated statements regarding engineering.

   Section 4:   He will have due regard for the safety of life and health of the public and employees who may be affected by the work for which he is responsible.

   Section 5:   He will express an opinion only when it is found on adequate knowledge and honest conviction while he is serving as a witness before a court, commission, or other tribunal.

   Section 6:   He will not issue ex parte statements, criticisms, or arguments on matters connected with public policy which are inspired or paid for by private interests, unless he indicates on whose behalf he is making the statement.

   Section 7:   He will refrain from expressing publicly an opinion on an engineering subject unless he is informed as to the facts relating thereto.

Relations with Clients and Employers

   Section 8:   The engineer will act in professional matters for each client or employer as a faithful agent or trustee.

   Section 9:   He will act with fairness and justice between his client or employer and the contractor when dealing with contracts.

   Section 10:   He will make his status clear to his client or employer before undertaking an engagement if he may be called upon to decide on the use of inventions, apparatus, or any other thing in which he may have a financial interest.

   Section 11:   He will guard against conditions that are dangerous or threatening to life, limb, or property on work for which he is responsible or, if he is not responsible, will call promptly such conditions to the attention of those who are responsible.

   Section 12:   He will present clearly the consequences to be expected from deviations proposed if his engineering judgment is overruled by nontechnical authority in cases where he is responsible for the technical adequacy of engineering work.

   Section 13:   He will engage, or advise his client or employer to engage, and he will cooperate with, other experts and specialists whenever the client's or employer's interests are best served by such services.

   Section 14:   He will disclose no information concerning the business affairs or technical processes of clients or employers without their consent.

   Section 15:   He will not accept compensation, financial or otherwise, from more than one interested party for the same service, or for services pertaining to the same work, without the consent of all interested parties.

   Section 16:   He will not accept commissions or allowances,

directly or indirectly, from contractors or other parties dealing
with his client or employer in connection with work for which he is
responsible.

Section 17: He will not be financially interested in the bids
as or of a contractor on competitive work for which he is employed
as an engineer unless he has the consent of his client or employer.

Section 18: He will disclose promptly to his client or employer any interest in a business which may compete with or affect
the business of his client or employer. He will not allow an interest
in any business to affect his decision regarding engineering work for
which he is employed, or which he may be called upon to perform.

Relations with Engineers

Section 19: The engineer will endeavor to protect the engineering profession collectively and individually from misrepresentation and misunderstanding.

Section 20: He will take care that credit for engineering work
is given to those to whom credit is properly due.

Section 21: He will uphold the principle of appropriate and
adequate compensation for those engaged in engineering work, including those in subordinate capacities, as being in the public interest and maintaining the standards of the profession.

Section 22: He will endeavor to provide opportunity for the
professional development and advancement of engineers in his employ.

Section 23: He will not injure directly or indirectly the professional reputation, prospects, or practice of another engineer.
However, if he considers that an engineer is guilty of unethical,
illegal, or unfair practice, he will present the information to the
proper authority for action.

Section 24: He will exercise due restraint in criticizing another engineer's work in public, recognizing the fact that the engineering societies and the engineering press provide the proper
forum for technical discussions and criticism.

Section 25: He will not try to supplant another engineer in
a particular employment after becoming aware that definite steps
have been taken toward the other's employment.

Section 26: He will not compete with another engineer on
the basis of charges for work by underbidding, through reducing
his normal fees, after having been informed of the charges named
by the other.

Section 27: He will not use the advantages of a salaried
position to compete unfairly with another engineer.

Section 28: He will not become associated in responsibility
for work with engineers who do not conform to ethical practices.

ENGINEERS--HEATING, REFRIGERATING, AND AIR-CONDITIONING

AMERICAN SOCIETY OF HEATING, REFRIGERATING AND AIR-
   CONDITIONING ENGINEERS (ASHRAE)
      345 E. 47th St., New York, N.Y. 10017
      Andrew T. Boggs III, Executive Director

Membership: The American Society of Heating, Refrigerating and
Air-Conditioning Engineers, founded in 1894 and with a present
(1973) membership of approximately 28,000, is a society of persons
employed in the fields relating to air-conditioning, heating, refrigerating and ventilation. Categories of membership and requirements set by the ASHRAE (other than for Student Member) are:
> Member--Equivalent of 12 Society-accredited years of experi-
> ence composed of any combination of approved completed
> education beyond high school, work experience, and en-
> gineering registration.
> Associate Member--Graduate of an engineering curriculum
> accredited by ECPD or the American Society of Heating,
> Refrigerating and Air-Conditioning Engineers' Board of
> Directors, or shall have the equivalent of 8 Society-ac-
> credited years of experience composed of an approved com-
> bination of completed education, work experience, and
> engineering registration.
> Affiliate--Shall have had experience in technical matters,
> design, operation, or maintenance in heating, refrigerating,
> air-conditioning, or ventilating fields, or shall possess
> sufficient qualifications to cooperate with heating, refrig-
> erating, air-conditioning or ventilating engineers in the ad-
> vancement of knowledge relating to these fields.

Code of Ethics: The professional conduct guide for members of
the Society is based upon Canons of Ethics for Engineers, 1947
edition, prepared by the Engineers' Council for Professional Development. Enforcement of the Canons is carried out by the Society
Board he is guilty of professional misconduct, or of abuse or
misuse of the privileges of Society membership, or of action
Board he or she is guilty of professional misconduct, or of abuse
or misuse of the privileges of Society membership, or of action
prejudicial to the best interest of the Society or profession.

Professional Insignia: The ASHRAE
emblem is hexagonal in shape, with
a centered hexagon bearing a con-
ventionalized sun symbol--12 rays,
alternately long and short; the initials of the organization,
"ASHRAE," are spaced in a wide
bordering band, beginning in the
lower left face, one letter on
each face of the hexagon. The
color of the emblem shows the
central hexagon and the initials in
dark blue on a gold ground. The

color of the emblem on the letterhead is dark blue on white. While use of the emblem is restricted to Society stationery and other official items, members are authorized to wear the insignia on jewelry --lapel button-tie tac, or key (gold with blue enamel insets); tie bar (rolled gold with golden emblem).

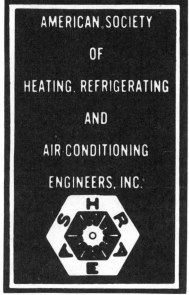

Other Designations of Professional Status: According to Society rules,

"No member shall describe himself in connection with the Society in any advertisement, letterhead, printed matter, or any other manner other than as an Honorary Member, Presidential Member, Fellow, Life Member, Member, Associate Member, Affiliate, or Student Member, as the case may be, except in official business of the Society.

Banner: The Society banner--a vertical rectangle, hung from the top--contains the society name, printed in six lines from the top of the banner, and the emblem at the bottom. Colors are gold (name, emblem, and line border) on blue.

Bibliography:
  American Society of Heating, Refrigerating and Air-Conditioning Engineers. An Invitation. Folder.
  Includes membership requirements.
  _____. What ASHRAE Membership Can Mean To You.
  Informational brochure, pictures emblem and banner.

"Canons of Ethics for Engineers"

see pages 247-249.

ENGINEERS--INDUSTRIAL

AMERICAN INSTITUTE OF INDUSTRIAL ENGINEERS (AIIE)
  25 Technology Park/Atlanta, Norcross, Georgia 30071
  Jack F. Jericho, P.E., Executive Director

Membership: The American Institute of Industrial Engineers, founded in 1948 and with a present (1973) membership of approximately 20,000, is the professional association for industrial engineers, whose work (as defined by the Institute):
> "is concerned with the design, improvement, and installation of integrated systems of men, materials and equipment. It draws upon specialized knowledge and skill in mathematical, physical and social sciences together with the principles and methods of engineering analysis and design to specify, predict and evaluate the results to be obtained from such systems."

According to the AIIE, industrial engineering differs from other branches of professional engineering in the breadth of its application --all types of industry, commercial and governmental activity--and in its concern with people, both as individuals and as social groups, Professionals in this engineering specialty may work in management, plant design and engineering, electronic data processing, systems engineering, production and quality control, performance standards and measurements, operations research, organization planning, and methods and process design.

Members, distributed in about 200 chapters in the United States, Canada, and Mexico, have broadened their skills to make the AIIE "the most diverse professional engineering society in the world." This variety of work is reflected in the divisions of the Society:

Industry Divisions--Aerospace, Government, Graphic Arts, Hospital and Health Services, Sewn Products, Transportation and Distribution.

Management Division.

Systems and Engineering Divisions--Computer and Information Systems, Engineering Economy, Operations Research, Production Planning and Control, Quality Control, Reliability Engineering, and Manufacturing Systems.

Technical Divisions--Ergonomics, Facilities Planning and Design, Industrial and Labor Relations, Value Engineering, Work Measurement and Methods Engineering.

Professional members of the AIIE are in two categories of "Corporate Grade" of membership:

Senior Member--Registered Professional Industrial Engineer, who has worked in a "responsible position" in Industrial Engineering for at least one year; or a registered professional engineer, other than industrial, with two years such experience.

Associate Member--Graduate from a curriculum accredited by the Engineers' Council for Professional Development, with specialization in Industrial Engineering; or five years experience.

For both these grades of membership, when the education is not at an institution approved by the Engineers' Council for Professional Development, or is not in the specialty of Industrial Engineering, other combinations of education and experience may be accepted as qualifying.

Affiliate and Professional Affiliate are non-Corporate grades of membership, with educational qualifications below those required for Associate Member. Two categories of membership are considered awards in recognition of outstanding contribution to the field, and are not applied for:

> Fellow--A Senior Member, at least forty years of age, registered in state of practice, and with at least 10 years important engineering work, qualified to direct, conceive, plan or design engineering work.
>
> Honorary Member--May be awarded to engineers who have practiced for ten years with distinction as Senior Members, Fellows, or Emeritus Members, and "have made outstanding contributions to the field of Industrial Engineering which have significantly increased the effectiveness of Human endeavor."

Code of Ethics: The AIIE subscribes to the Canons of Ethics of Engineers, prepared by the Engineers' Council for Professional Development. The Ethics Committee and the AIIE Board of Trustees act in enforcement of these ethical conduct guides (Constitution III, Bylaws III).

Other Guides to Professional Conduct: The society Code of Work Measurement Principles provides a professional guide for engineers dealing with work measurement, goal setting, and wage payment, through its 20 numbered rules for judging the soundness and propriety of such work.

Professional Insignia: The AIIE emblem is its seal--a circular

design, with a central shield bearing the group's initials, "AIIE," on a slanted bar; an hour glass is shown in the upper left of the shield, signifying the importance of time in the work of the Industrial Engineer; and the lamp of knowledge is shown in the lower right portion of the shield; the shield is set in a darker circle, and the bordering band bears the name of the organization, "American Institute of Industrial Engineers," with the legend at the bottom of the band, "Founded 1948."

The color of the emblem is blue, with hour glass, bar, and lamp in white, and lettering and border outlines in gold. The emblem is shown on the letterhead in blue on white. The emblem may be used only upon official items issued by the Institute and its chapters. Membership pins, given to each member, show the central part of the seal; with member grades identified by different colors.

Bibliography:
       American Institute of Industrial Engineers.   Code of Work

Measurement Principles. 1963. Brochure.
Standards to be followed by the industrial engineer in work
measurement, goal setting, and wage payment; includes
Canons of Ethics for Engineers.
_____. Constitution; Bylaws. July 1971 edition. 38 pages.
Includes membership qualifications; ethics enforcement; em-
blem.
_____. Membership Qualifications Manual. Revised edition,
October 1967. 13 pages.
Definitions and clarifications of education and experience re-
quirements for various categories of AIIE membership.

"Canons of Ethics for Engineers"

see pages 247-249.

ENGINEERS--MECHANICAL

AMERICAN SOCIETY OF MECHANICAL ENGINEERS (ASME)
345 E. 47th St., New York, N.Y. 10017
Rogers B. Finch, Executive Director and Secretary

Membership: The American Society of Mechanical Engineers,
founded in 1880 and with a present (1973) membership of over
60,000, is a professional association of engineers in the special
field of mechanical engineering. Applicants for the following
grades of ASME membership qualify with education and experience
specified:
Member--Equivalent of 12 years active practice in the profession of engineering or teaching, 5 years of which must
have been in responsible charge of engineering work. A
bachelor's degree from an approved engineering or engineering technology curriculum may be substituted for 8
years of the required active practice. Other education
may substitute in part for the required experience.
Associate Member--Eight years of experience as described
above; or a bachelor's degree in an approved engineering
or engineering technology curriculum. Other education
may substitute in part for the required experience.
Executive Affiliate--No formal education in engineering or
practice in engineering required, but must have attained
"a position of policy-making authority and recognized
leadership in some pursuit related to engineering," and
personal qualifications of aptitude and interest.
Affiliate--"Capable of and interested in rendering service in
the field of engineering."

Code of Ethics: The ASME adopted in 1947 the Canons of Ethics
of Engineers, prepared by the Engineers' Council for Professional
Development. The latest edition of the Canons was ratified by the
Society Council on November 17, 1953. No enforcement procedures
for the Canons are reported.

Professional Insignia: The emblem of the Society is a quatrefoil,

with one initial of the organization,
"ASME, " on each of the four
petals of the design, beginning
with the top petal. The color of
the design is shown variously--
blue on white (letterhead), gold
on blue (publication), white on
black (publication). The insignia
is available to members as an
official badge on jewelry (lapel
button, watch charm), the enameled
color of the background denoting
membership grade:

Fellow--Gold,
Member--Blue,
Executive Affiliate--Green,
Associate Member--Maroon,
Affiliate--Grey.

Bibliography:
     American Society of Mechanical Engineers. Canons of Ethics
          of Engineers. 1963. Single sheet.
     Professional conduct guide, developed by Engineers' Council
     for Professional Development, with ASME emblem.
     King, W. J. The Unwritten Laws of Engineering. N. Y., Ameri-
          can Society of Mechanical Engineers, 1947. Pamphlet
          49 pages. (Reprint from Mechanical Engineering of May,
          June, July 1944).
     Principles of professional engineering relationship.

"Canons of Ethics of Engineers"

see pages 247-249.

ENGINEERS--MILITARY

SOCIETY OF AMERICAN MILITARY ENGINEERS (SAME)
     800 17th St. , N. W. , 500 Fleming Bldg. , Washington, D. C. 20006
     Brig. Gen. W. C. Hall, Executive Secretary

<u>Membership</u>: The Society of Military Engineers, founded in 1920 following World War I and with a current (1973) membership of over 23,000, is dedicated to national defense. The Society's members, in about 125 posts (local sections) throughout the United States and abroad, include over 19,000 civilian engineers--most of whom have had military service and hold National Guard or reserve commissions. Among the members are engineers in all fields of industry, in education, or in government service, and some 2000 officers from all branches of the United States armed forces. Qualifications for the several types of Society membership include:

> <u>Military Engineer Members</u>--Commissioned officers in the engineer services of the military forces of the United States, or engineers who have held such commission, and have been honorably separated from service.

> <u>Military Members</u>--Service in the military forces of the United States, or honorably separated from such service, and who have completed at least two years in the Reserve Officers Training Corps.

> <u>Engineering Members</u>--Graduates from an engineering school of recognized standing; or eight years practice in professional engineering; or license as professional engineer in state of practice; or a voting member of a professional engineering society.

> <u>Affiliate Members</u>--Attendance at an engineering school of recognized standing for at least two years; or two years experience as engineering technician; or demonstrated interest in military engineering and in preparedness for national defense.

<u>Code of Ethics</u>: The Society has issued no formal code of conduct. Its members conform to the code of conduct of the United States Armed Forces.

<u>Professional Insignia</u>: The emblem of the Society of American Military Engineers is a shield, the upper part horizontally striped, the lower part with vertical stripes made up of five lines; a three-towered castle--symbolic of military engineering and constructive national defense--is centered on the shield. Foliated, fruited olive branches border the shield, and there is an eagle crest (conventional symbol of the United States) with outspread wings, looking left, and holding an olive branch in left talons, and arrows in right talons; the scroll below

the shield bears the legend of the Society name, "American Military
Engineers. "

     The colors of the emblem are--red, white and blue shield;
brown eagle and castle; green leaves; and black ribbon with white
lettering for scroll; background of emblem is red. Members are
authorized to wear the Society insignia as jewelry, patch, decal
and printed wall emblem, bar ribbon and medal for uniform. The
emblem is the same for all member grades. Colors: The official
colors of the Society are red, white, and black.

Bibliography:
     Society of American Military Engineers. Aims and Activities.
          1972-1973. Folder.
     Informational brochure giving brief Society history, member-
     ship qualifications, local and student posts, officers; emblem
     on cover.
          . Fact Book. 1972-1973.
     This publication, sent to all new members, "contains the con-
     stitution and bylaws, history, awards, officers, and other
     pertinent information concerning the Society. "

ENGINEERS--NUCLEAR

AMERICAN NUCLEAR SOCIETY (ANS)
     244 E. Ogden Ave. , Hinsdale, Ill. 60521
     Octave J. Du Temple, Executive Secretary

Membership: The American Nuclear Society, founded in 1954 and
with a current (1973) membership of approximately 9000, is a professional organization of scientists and engineers active in work relating to the atomic nucleus. Diversity of member activities, in
"fundamental and applied research, teaching consultation, administration and engineering, " is indicated by the subject range of the 12
Divisions and three technical Groups into which the Society is organized:

Divisions
Aerospace   Reactor Operations
Civil Explosion Application   Reactor Physics
Isotope and Radiation Edu-   Remote Systems Technology
   cation   Shielding and Dosimetry
Materials Science and
   Technology
Mathematics and Computation
Nuclear Criticality Safety
Nuclear Fuel Cycle
Power

Technical Groups
Controlled Nuclear Fusion   Nuclear Reactor Safety
Environmental Sciences

Qualifications for Society membership are:
  Members--Three years' professional experience, and pres-
    ently engaged in "professional activity in or closely related
    to one or more of the fields of nuclear science and en-
    gineering or allied fields" and who:
    1. Holds a Bachelor or advanced degree from a recog-
       nized institution in the field of physics, chemistry,
       mathematics, life sciences, engineering, or metal-
       lurgy, or
    2. Have had eight years' or more responsible scientific
       or engineering experience (MS degree in appropriate
       field equivalent to one year of this required experience,
       Ph. D. equivalent to three years of required experience),
       or
    3. Have recognized record of attainment or leadership in
       some science, profession or branch of industry rele-
       vant to nuclear science technology.
  Associate Members--Academic degrees as specified for Mem-
    bers, or three years of professional level experience in
    the fields of nuclear technology or of allied fields.

Code of Ethics: The American Nuclear Society has formulated no
published guide to professional conduct of members.

Professional Insignia: The emblem of the American Nuclear Society
--designed by N. W. Rubel & Company--was adopted in 1956, and
modified in 1958 and 1965.
The design--circular in form
--shows at its center electrons
orbiting the nucleus of an
atom (symbolic of nuclear
technology); bounded by the
bordering lettering, "American Nuclear Society, Hinsdale,
Illinois, U. S. A." The Society
initials, "ANS," are imprinted
across the central electron-
nucleus design. The color of
the emblem is black and white.
Use of the insignia is restricted to official Society
stationery and publications,
but members are authorized
to wear it on a lapel pin.

Bibliography:
  American Nuclear Society. Information. 30 pages. Folder.
    Includes ANS Divisions and Technical Groups, membership
    qualifications; shows emblem on cover.

ENGINEERS--PACKAGING AND HANDLING

SOCIETY OF PACKAGING AND HANDLING ENGINEERS (SPHE)
14 E. Jackson Blvd., Chicago, Ill. 60604
Charles R. Goerth, Executive Director

Membership: The Society of Packaging and Handling Engineers,
founded in 1945 and with a present (1973) membership of approximately 1700, is an organization composed of engineers and other
professional workers in the field of packaging and material handling.
The qualifications for professional members of the Society are:
  (1)   age 26;
  (2)   currently working in the fields of packaging or materials
        handling;
  (3)   Bachelor's degree and 3 years experience in the field,
        or seven years experience in the field.

Code of Ethics: The Society subscribes to the Engineers' Creed and
the Canons of Ethics for Engineers, prepared by the Engineers'
Council for Professional Development. Procedures for enforcement
of the Canons are provided (By-Law 11) and discipline for infraction of the Canons includes expulsion from the Society.

Professional Insignia: The SPHE emblem is circular in design, with
a centered circle, a box in the
upper segment--to signify pack-
aging--and a hand in the lower
segment--to signify "handling"
--the engineering specialty
title; the centered circle is
divided by a horizontal band
showing the organization initials,
"SPHE"; the group's name,
"Society of Packaging and
Handling Engineers," is printed
around the design as an unbounded border. Official colors
for the design are orange (background of upper and lower
panel of centered circle) and
black. The emblem is also
shown in white on black, or
black on white (letterhead).

Bibliography:
      Society of Packaging and Handling Engineers. What's Your
          Question About SPHE? 4 pages. Folder.
      Informational brochure, with emblem on cover.

"Canons of Ethics for Engineers"

see pages 247-249.

"Engineers' Creed"

see pages 249-250.

ENGINEERS--PLANT

AMERICAN INSTITUTE OF PLANT ENGINEERS (AIPE)
1021 Delta Ave., Cincinnati, Ohio 45208
Walter Schaw, Executive Director

Membership: The American Institute of Plant Engineers, founded in
1915 and with a current (1973) membership of approximately 6000,
is a professional organization of manufacturing plant engineers,
whose work includes responsibility for all installation engineering
except that associated with service product or production. Among
the Plant Engineers responsibilities are:
    Plant Engineering Administration,
    Plant Layout and Design,
    Construction and Installation,
    Maintenance Repairs and Replacements,
    Operation of Utilities,
    Plant Protection.

    Among the grades of membership in the Institute for which edu-
cation and experience qualifications have been set are:
    Member--Degree of Bachelor of Science in any field of en-
        gineering or equivalent degree from a university, college
        or technical school of recognized standing, and at least
        six years of experience in engineering, with two years of
        this experience in responsible charge of engineering work.
            A license to practice professional engineering work may
        by substituted for the required education. Other combina-
        tions of experience and types and levels of education are
        also qualifying.
    Associate Member--Degree of Bachelor of Science in any
        branch of engineering or physical science, or license to
        practice professional engineering, and two years of ex-
        perience in plant engineering. Other combinations of
        experience and education are also qualifying.

Code of Ethics: The Institute encourages the Plant Engineer members to follow the Code of Ethics for Engineers of the National
Society of Professional Engineers, as this Code is pertinent to their

activities (Code of Plant Engineers, Section V). No procedure for
enforcement of the Code of Ethics are reported.

<u>Professional Insignia</u>:   The American Institute of Plant Engineers'

emblem shows a banded globe
with the centered American
continents; the profile of an
urban scene with skyscrapers
appears across the lower portion of the globe; the organization name is shown in a banding
border, "American Institute of,"
around the top of the globe, and
in a bar, "Plant Engineers,"
across the bottom of the circular design.   The color of the
emblem may be shown variously
--purple on white (publication).

<u>Bibliography</u>:
                American Institute of Plant
                Engineers.   <u>Code of</u>
<u>the Plant Engineer</u>.   1961.   17 pages.
Contains a definition of the Plant Engineer's responsibility,
with detailed description of functions and operations, and
aspects of cooperation with other plant departments.   States
following the Code of Ethics for Engineers of the National
Society of Professional Engineers is encouraged (Section V).

<u>"Code of Ethics for Engineers"</u>

see pages 252-257.

ENGINEERS--PLASTICS

SOCIETY OF PLASTICS ENGINEERS (SPE)
        656 W. Putnam Ave., Greenwich, Conn. 06830
        Robert D. Forger, Executive Secretary

<u>Membership</u>: The Society of Plastics Engineers, founded in 1942
and with a present (1973) membership of approximately 17,000, is
the professional organization of engineers and scientists engaged in
the development, manufacture and use of plastics.   The two classes
of professional membership require experience to qualify for acceptance by the Society:
        <u>Senior Member</u>--12 years of responsible experience in plas-
                tics engineering; and continuous membership for a mini-

mum of two years; one degree in science and engineering
may be substituted for experience according to the following scale:
     Doctorate--6 years,
     Master's--5 years,
     Bachelor's--4 years,
     Associate in Plastice--2 years.
Member--six years of experience, as described above; same
    degree substitution.

Code of Ethics: The Society of Plastics Engineers has issued no
formal code of ethics.

Professional Insignia: The emblem of the Society of Plastics Engineers is in the form of a truncated shield, with rounded corners
and straight vertical boundaries.
In one-color reproductions of
the emblem (black on white),
the initial outline, "SPE," born
in the center of the insignia,
and other outlines and borders
are shown in black. In two-
color reproduction of the em-
blem--black and red on white--
the central background of the
design is bright red, in a
shade of red specified as:
    "Maerz and Paul, Dic-
       tionary of Color.
       Plate 3 L6
    Lewis Roberts. Royal
      Red 3525

    Sinclair & Valentine Zephyr Offset Cherry Red No. 384 (on
      coated stock)
    Pall Mall cigarette wrapper."
The Society emblem as well as the Society name and abbreviation,
may "not be used or referred to by any member in an advertisement
or commercial exploitation of himself, his employer or its products"
(Bylaws, Section 5). Jewelry bearing the emblem is available to
members to indicate Society membership.

Bibliography:
    Society of Plastics Engineers. Constitution and Bylaws. Amend-
        ed to April 9, 1970. (Reprint from SPE Journal 26:237-
        246 August 1970).
    Gives membership qualifications; allowable emblem use.

ENGINEERS--SAFETY

AMERICAN SOCIETY OF SAFETY ENGINEERS (ASSE)
   850 Busse Hwy., Park Ridge, Ill. 60068
   Wayne C. Christensen, Managing Director

Membership: The American Society of Safety Engineers, founded
in 1911 and with a current (1973) membership of over 11,000, is
the organization of engineers and other workers in the Safety Profession.   There are three categories of membership (in addition to
honorary memberships, such as "Fellow" and "Honorary Member"--
granted by award, not upon application), that require experience
or education:
   Professional Members--30 years of age, or more; employed
      full time in the safety profession for at least five years;
      and presently engaged in the broad practice of safety or
      one of its relevant specialties; and
      (a)   hold a degree from an accredited college or univer-
            sity in the field of employment; or
      (b)   have been registered or licensed by a State agency
            as a professional appropriate to his field of employ-
            ment:
      (c)   have been certified as competent within the practice
            of safety or one of its specialties by an organiza-
            tion recognized as qualified by the Admissions
            Committee.
   Member--21 years of age, or more; one full year employ-
      ment in safety practice or one of its specialties;
   Affiliate Member--21 years of age, or more; two years' con-
      secutive employment in pursuits and functions qualifying
      him to cooperate with members of the Society and to
      render service to the Society.

Code of Ethics: A new code of ethics is now (1973) being prepared
                   for adoption by the Ameri-
                   can Society of Safety En-
                   gineers.

Professional Insignia: The
ASSE emblem is "a gold
cross on a green enamel
background shaped like a
Norman shield, with the letters ASSE (in gold), superimposed within the four
angles formed by the cross"
(By-Laws, Articles XIX).
This symbol may be used on
official stationery and publications of the Society, and
also may be worn by mem-
bers to signify membership
in the ASSE.   The authorized
color of the emblem in

reproduced copies is specified:
> "Reproduced in green, gold, black and white only or any combination of these colors" (By-Laws, Article XIX, Section 4).

Bibliography:
> American Society of Safety Engineers. By-Laws. 1969.
> Gives membership grades and qualifications; code of conduct enforcement; official symbol and its prescribed use.

FASHION DESIGNERS

COUNCIL OF FASHION DESIGNERS OF AMERICA (CFDA)
32 E. 57th St., New York, N.Y. 10022
David Evins, Secretary-Treasurer

Membership: The Council of Fashion Designers of America is "a national honorary society of creative leaders in various fields of fashion." Among the eighty members of the Council are leading designers in the apparel, footwear, textile, jewelry, and accessory fields. CFDA, founded in 1963, "limits its membership strictly to individuals known for their creative force within a fashion firm. Membership is personal and does not extend to the firm or association" in which a designer member is employed. Membership is invitational, or may be applied for.

Code of Ethics: Although one of the purposes of the Council, according to its charter, is "to establish and maintain a code of ethics and practice in professional, public and trade relations," no formal code of ethics has been issued by the Council.

Professional Insignia: The Council of Fashion Designers of America does not have an official insignia, but does use a logotype on its letterhead that may be identified with the organization—a rectangular flag-shaped design with 15 stripes--eight impressed between seven raised stripes, with the initials of the organization, "CFDA," in a rectangle at the left of the top three impressed stripes, which are shortened to provide space for the initials. The color of the design (as shown on Council stationery) is red letters on a grey ground [not displayed].

FINANCIAL ANALYSTS

THE FINANCIAL ANALYSTS FEDERATION (FAF)
   Tower Suite, 219 E. 42nd St. , New York, N. Y. 10017
   Theodore R. Lilley, Executive Director

THE INSTITUTE OF CHARTERED FINANCIAL ANALYSTS (I. C. F. A.)
   Monroe Hall, University of Virginia
   Charlottesville, Va. 22903
   Dr. W. Scott Baumen, C. F. A. , Executive Director

Membership: The Financial Analysts Federation, founded in 1947
and with a present (1973) membership of over 13, 000 in 43 Financial Analysts Societies located in major cities of the United States
and Canada, is an organization of financial analysts, who work for
brokerage houses, investment banking concerns, insurance companies, bank trust departments, and endowment and pension or
profit-sharing funds.   "The modern profession of financial analysis
involves the primary functions of investigation, evaluation, selection
and management of all types of investments, particularly in bonds
and preferred and common stock. "

   "Regular Members" of Financial Analysts Societies are required
to qualify for membership with "a minimum of three years experience in financial analysis as related to securities investment, " and
be engaged in such pertinent work as financial analysis--in private
business or public agency; college teaching or research in investments; or act as economist concerned with financial analysis related
to securities investment (By-Laws, Article XIV, Section 1).   A
recent survey of FAF membership showed that the educational
preparation of members was: bachelor's degree 92%, master's
degree 48%, doctorate 3%.

   To establish standards of professional competence in the field
of financial analysis, The Financial Analysts Federation--in cooperation with the University of Virginia Graduate School of Business
Administration--formed The Institute of Chartered Financial Analysts
in 1959.   This Institute, affiliated with the Financial Analysts Federation, conducts tests of competence, and authorizes use of the
professional designation, "Chartered Financial Analyst" ("C. F. A. "),
to qualified applicants who pass a series of examinations.

Code of Ethics: Carrying out one of the stated objectives of the
Federation--"to develop, promulgate and enforce a Code of Ethics
and Standards for persons practicing the profession of financial
analysis" (Articles of Incorporation, Article II)--a Code of Ethics
was established by the FAF By-Laws in 1962, and adopted in its
present form on October 19, 1969.   The Code of Ethics and Standards of Professional Conduct sets forth several general principles of
professional practice, and enumerates nine guides to professional
conduct for financial analysts.   A Professional Ethics Committee
reviews the Code and Standards on a continuing basis (By-Laws,
Article VI, Section 1K), and enforcement of these professional
guides is the responsibility of the local member societies, whose

disciplinary action--following investigation and hearing of charges of unprofessional conduct--may include suspension from membership (By-Laws, Article XII, Section 2).

Professional Insignia: The emblem of the FAF is its corporate seal, which (following specifi- cations in the Articles of In- corporation, Article I, Section 3) is circular in form, with the initials of the organization, "FAF," shown in a centered shaded or colored circle, the incorporation and founding dates are shown at the bottom and top of a bordering band, "In- corporated 1965," "Founded 1947"; the association name, "The Financial Analysts Fed- eration," is printed in an outer border, which is set off with eight uniform scallops. The centered association ini- tials may be printed in block

style (letterhead), or in script (publications).   The color of the seal is shown variously--black and white (letterhead), blue-grey or purple (publications).

Other Identification of Professional Status: As mentioned above under "Membership," The Institute of Chartered Financial Analysts authorizes use of a professional designation, "Chartered Financial Analyst" ("C.F.A."), to applicants demonstrating their professional competence by passing a series of examinations.   Five basic sub- ject matter areas extend through a series of three examinations in: (1) investment principles; (2) applied security analysis; and (3) in- vestment management decision making.   These five subject matter areas are: accounting, economics, financial analysis, portfolio management, and ethical standards.   Annual Study Guides and Read- ing Lists for each examination are available for purchase from the Institute.

The Institute Code of Ethics and Standards of Pro- fessional Conduct are identical with those of the FAF, with the exception of the inclusion of a paragraph concerning pro- fessional use of the designation, "Chartered Financial Analyst." The emblem of the Institute is its seal, showing a circular design with the letters, "C.F.A.,"

centered; the name of the group and date of incorporation in a bordering band, "The Institute of Chartered Financial Analysts, Inc
1962"; set off by several bordering bands and a serrated border.
The color of the emblem is shown variously--white on blue, black
on blue (publications).

Bibliography:
   The Financial Analysts Federation.   Articles of Incorporation;
      By-Laws; Code of Ethics and Standards of Professional
      Conduct.   Amended October 4, 1970.   Folder.   31 pages.
   Basic documents of the Federation, giving membership quali-
   fications, text of professional guides, and ethics enforcement
   procedures.
   _____. The Financial Analysts Federation.   Folder.   8
      pages.
   Informational brochure including FAF objectives, organization,
   activities.
   The Institute of Chartered Financial Analysts.   Basic Documents.
      Revised 1971.   Folder.   20 pages.
   Includes Articles of Incorporation, By-Laws, Code of Ethics
   and Standards of Professional Conduct, with rules of procedure for their enforcement.
   _____. The C. F. A. Program, 1972-1973.   Folder.   36
      pages.
   Gives eligibility requirements for examinations, describes
   examination form and content, and professional designation.
   _____. The Profession of Financial Analysts and the Char-
      tered Financial Analyst, 1971.   Pamphlet.   28 pages.
   Defines occupation, history and objectives of professional
   designation program, topical outline of C. F. A. Program
   examinations.

"Code of Ethics"

     Whereas, the profession of financial analysis has evolved
because of the increasing public need for competent, objective and
trustworthy advice with regard to investments and financial management; and

     Whereas, The Institute of Chartered Financial Analysts was
organized to establish educational standards in the field of financial
analysis, to conduct examinations of financial analysts and to award
the professional designation of Chartered Financial Analyst, among
other objectives; and

     Whereas, despite a wide diversity of interest among analysts
employed by banks, brokers and security dealers, investment advisory organizations, financial relations counselors, insurance companies, investment companies, investment trusts, pension trusts and
other institutional investors and corporate bodies, there are nevertheless certain fundamental standards of conduct which should be

common to all engaged in the profession of financial analysis and accepted and maintained by them; and

Whereas, The Institute of Chartered Financial Analysts adopted a Code of Ethics on March 14, 1964; and

Whereas, it is now deemed appropriate to make certain amendments to this Code;

Now, therefore, The Institute of Chartered Analysts hereby adopts the following Code of Ethics and Standards of Professional Conduct:

A Chartered Financial Analyst should conduct himself with integrity and dignity and encourage such conduct by others in the profession.

A Chartered Financial Analyst should act with competence and strive to maintain and improve his competence and that of others in the profession.

A Chartered Financial Analyst should use proper care and exercise independent professional judgment.

Standards of Professional Conduct

1. The Chartered Financial Analyst shall conduct himself and encourage the practice of financial analysis in a manner that shall reflect credit on himself and on the profession. The financial analyst shall have and maintain knowledge of and shall comply strictly with all federal, state and provincial laws as well as all rules and regulations of any governmental agency governing his activities. The financial analyst shall also comply strictly with the rules and regulations of the stock exchanges and of the National Association of Securities Dealers if he, or his employer, is a member of these organizations.

2. The Chartered Financial Analyst shall ascertain that his employer is aware of the existence and content of the Code of Ethics and of these Standards of Professional Conduct.

3. The Chartered Financial Analyst shall conduct himself in such manner that transactions for his customers, clients or employer have priority over personal transactions, that personal transactions do not operate adversely to their interests and that he act with impartiality. Thus, if an analyst has decided to make a recommendation as to the purchase or sale of a security, he shall give his customers, clients and employer adequate opportunity to act on such recommendation before acting on his own behalf.

4. The Chartered Financial Analyst shall, in addition to the requirements of disclosure required by law and rules and regulations of organizations governing his activities, when making recommendations, disclose to his customers, clients or employer any

material conflict of interest relating to him and any material beneficial ownership of the securities involved which could reasonably be
expected to impair his ability to render unbiased and objective advice.

5.   The Chartered Financial Analyst shall be objective in
his opinions in advising his customers, clients and employer and
when making a recommendation must have a basis which can be substantiated as reasonable.   He must be accurate and complete when
reporting facts.

6.   The Chartered Financial Analyst shall inform his customers, clients and employer of compensation arrangements in connection with his services to them which are in addition to compensation from his employer or from the customer or client for
such services.

7.   The Chartered Financial Analyst shall not pay any consideration to others for recommending his services unless such arrangement has been appropriately disclosed.

8.   The Chartered Financial Analyst shall not undertake independent practice for compensation in competition with his employer
unless he has received written consent from both his employer and
the person for whom he undertakes independent employment.

9.   The Chartered Financial Analyst shall not, in the preparation of material for distribution to customers, clients, or the general public, copy or use in substantially the same form material
prepared by other persons without acknowledging its use and identifying the name of the author or publisher of such material.

10.   The Chartered Financial Analyst may use the professional designation Chartered Financial Analyst, or the abbreviation
C. F. A. , but only in a dignified and judicious manner.   The only
proper use of the professional designation in advertising media shall
be the designation itself.   In printed advertising media, the professional designation shall be used only after the name of the holder of
such designation appearing in such media and in type no larger
than the type used in his name.   The professional designation shall
not be used in the text in such advertising.   The term advertising
media used herein shall not apply to promotional booklets, annual
reports and similar publications that may be published from time to
time by various financial institutions for limited distribution.

FIRE PREVENTION AND CONTROL

INTERNATIONAL ASSOCIATION OF FIRE CHIEFS (IAFC)
    1725 K St., N.W., Suite, 1108, Washington, D.C. 20006
    Donald M. O'Brien, General Manager

Membership: The International Association of Fire Chiefs is one
of the oldest professional associations in the United States, as it
was founded in 1873--two years after the great Chicago fire of
October 8-10, 1871--as the "National Association of Fire Engineers."
The organization's present name was adopted in 1926. Active members of the IAFC are fire chiefs--and the chief officers in municipal
fire departments, industries, military installations, state and provincial fire marshals, fire commissioners or fire directors, who
devote full-time to their duties in fire prevention, fire protection,
or fire fighting--all aspects of protection of life and property from
fire. Members of the International Association are also members
of one of the Association's component groups, eight regional associations, including one in Canada.

Code of Ethics: Since the Fire Service "is dedicated solely to the
protection of life and property against fire," no public code of
ethics has been published.

Professional Insignia: The emblem of the IAFC is its seal--a circular design with a centered globe, bearing in the lower portion
five crossed speaking trumpets, symbolizing the command insignia
of the fire chief, and a crest
with the legend, "Org. 1872."
The name of the association
is shown in a border, "Association of Fire Chiefs," with
the word, "International," on
a band circling the centered
globe.   A rope, symbolic of
fire fighting, as one of the
common tools of fire control,
bands the border of the design.

    The color of the emblem--
as shown on the letterhead--is
shaded black (grey) on white
for the globe and the rope
banding the design; gold for
the crest and base; red for
the border; blue for the band
circling the globe.   The founding date in the emblem is
printed in black, and the association name in white.   These colors
are also shown on the decal emblem (except the association name
here is shown in gold), and on various jewelry (lapel buttons, tie
tacks, cuff links, circle or bow pin and earrings for women, blazer
buttons, and jacket crest) worn or used by members.

Bibliography:
    International Association of Fire Chiefs. <u>A Brief History of the</u>
       <u>International Association of Fire Chiefs.</u> 4 pages. Pro-
       cessed.
       Origin, development, former influential officers, and present
       officers.
    <u>   </u>. <u>International Association of Fire Chiefs.</u> Pamphlet.
       IAFC history, operation, functions, and membership require-
       ments.

FOREIGN TRADE WORKERS

AMERICAN SOCIETY OF INTERNATIONAL EXECUTIVES (ASIE)
    734 Land Title Bldg., Broad and Chestnut Sts.,
    Philadelphia, Pa. 19110
    Melvin R. Kerr, EIE-TM, President

Membership: The American Association of International Executives, founded in 1963 and with a present (1973) membership of about 400, is a "professional Society for career personnel engaged in international trade." The Society gives a semi-annual Career International Trade Professional Examination and awards recognition of competence to members with skills important to international commerce. The ASIE does not offer or require specific courses for examination, but does encourage course offerings in colleges and universities. In addition to corporate memberships, the Society offers individual memberships in various fields of international business, in two general classes--those requiring examinations and those not requiring examinations.

    Examinations (three-hour, essay-type) are administered and professional designations awarded in the following trade areas, given here with their education and experience requirements.
    Certified Documentary Specialist (CDS)
       one year experience in export documentary work; typing ability.
    Certified International Executive (CIE-)
       Four categories: Export Management (EM)
                  Traffic Management (TM)
                  Freight Forwarding (FF)
                  Air Forwarding (AF)
       Minimum of two years' experience in specialty as assistant manager.
    Qualified International Executive (QIE-)
       Four categories--same as above.
    Minimum of five years' experience in charge of specialty.
Examination subjects for the CDS and CIE designations include:

Foreign Trade Terminology, Payment Terms, Business Terms
in one foreign language, Drafts and Letters of Credit, U. S.
and foreign trade controls, export shipping documents; traffic
procedures; marine insurance, CIF quotation.
The designations CIE and QIE require additional examinations, and
QIE a research paper.

An additional designation is awarded, for which no examination
is required:
Experienced International Executive
11 categories:
Export Management (EIE-EM)
Traffic Management (EIE-TM)
Freight Forwarding (EIE--FF)
Air Forwarding (EIE-AF)
Marketing (EIE-M)
Credit (EIE-C)
Banking (EIE-B)
Finance (EIE-F)
Shipping (EIE-S)
Operations (EIE-O)
Insurance (EIE-I)
These all require 15 years' experience, including 10 years in charge
of international business operations, or an important area of opera-
tion. ASIE devises and grades the examinations required for com-
petency designation. Study Outline, in each of the nine trade areas
in which examinations are given, may be purchased from the Society
($5. for each examination area).

Code of Ethics: No formal code of ethics has been published.

Professional Insignia: The emblem of the American Society of
International Executives is its
official seal--an unbanded oval,
bearing a flattened globe with
the organization initials, "ASIE, "
printed over the center; laurel
sprays frame the lower half of
the globe; seven stars mark the
upper half of the globe as a
border.   The color of the design is blue on white.

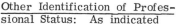

Other Identification of Professional Status: As indicated
above under "Membership, " title and letter designations are awarded
on the basis of qualifying examinations, or experience requirements.

Bibliography:
American Society of International Executives.   American Society
of International Executives.   1970.   15 pages.   Pamphlet.
Informational brochure giving membership requirements,

professional title and letter designations awarded on basis of
qualifying examinations or experience; subject matter listing
for examinations.
_____. Study Outline. Nine subject Areas. $5. each.
For each of the nine subject areas in which examinations are
given by ASIE, a study outline, with bibliography, is available.

FORESTERS

SOCIETY OF AMERICAN FORESTERS (SAF)
1010 16th St., N. W., Washington, D. C. 20036
H. R. Glasscock, Jr., Executive Vice President

Membership: The Society of American Foresters, founded in 1900
by Gifford Pinchot and six other pioneer foresters, and with a
present (1973) membership of approximately 18, 000, is the organization for all segments of the forestry profession, "including public
and private practitioners, researchers, administrators, educators
and forestry students."   The Society defines "Forestry" (The Forest
Policies, Preamble) as:
     "the science and art and the practice of managing and using
     for human benefit the natural resources that occur on and in
     association with forest lands.   These resources include trees,
     and other plants, animals of all description, the climate,
     the soil, and related air and water."

SAF "Members" are
     "(1)   graduates of curricula approved by the Council in insti-
            tutions either accredited or affiliated by the Council   or
      (2)   scientists or practitioners in fields closely allied to
            forestry who hold a bachelor or higher degree in their
            special field and who are rendering or have rendered
            substantial service to forestry."
Another category of Society membership--Technician--requires edu-
cation that is of shorter duration, or experience in forestry.   The
"Fellow" member category is awarded by the organization for out-
standing service to forestry and to the Society (Constitution, Article
III).

Code of Ethics: In accordance with provisions of the SAF Constitution
Article VII), a guide to professional conduct for foresters was developed by a committee of the Society, and adopted on November 12,
1948; and amended most recently by Referendum on December 4,
1971.   This Foresters' Code of Ethics--which must be published at
least annually in the official monthly publication of the Society,
Journal of Forestry--consists of 25 canons of conduct as a profes-

sional guide to relations with colleagues, employers, and the public. Enforcement of the Code is provided for in detail (Constitution, Article VIII; By-Laws, VIII). Written charges of unprofessional conduct against a member signed by five "voting members" are submitted to the Society Council; the Committee on Ethics, or other specially appointed committee, investigates the charges, which--when substantiated--may result in disciplinary action, including reprimand, censure, or expulsion from membership.

Professional Insignia: The official emblem of the Society of American Foresters is "a shield with 'Society of American Foresters 1900' in gold letters on a green background surrounded by a gold border" (By-Laws, I-B). This insignia (shown on letterhead and publications in green and white) may be worn or displayed only by members, in the form of a decal; wall plaque; bumper strip; and jewelry (cuff links, lapel button, tie tack, or tie bar).

Bibliography:
 Society of American Foresters. Constitution and Bylaws, Amended December 5, 1970, and December 4, 1971. (Journal of Forestry 10:295-302 May 1972).
 Includes membership qualifications; authorization for and enforcement of Foresters' Code of Ethics; description of official emblem.
 _____. Foresters' Code of Ethics. Adopted November 12, 1948, amended December 4, 1971. 1 page.
 Guide to professional conduct of Foresters in relations with colleagues, the public, and employers.
 _____. Sound American Forestry. 1972. 9 pages. Folder.
 Informational brochure briefly describes SAF membership categories, defines "Forestry." Emblem on cover.

"Foresters' Code of Ethics"

The purpose of these canons is to formulate guiding principles of professional conduct for foresters in their relations with each other, with their employers, and with the public. The observance of these canons secures decent and honorable professional and human relationships, establishes enduring mutual confidence and respect, and enables the profession to give its maximum service.

In order to apply these canons to the diverse circumstances arising in practice, guidelines are issued from time to time by the Council of the Society. They are incorporated by reference and made a part hereof.

Professional Life

1. The professional forester will utilize his knowledge and skill for the benefit of society. He will cooperate in extending the effectiveness of the forestry profession by interchanging information and experience with other foresters, and by contributing to the work of forestry societies, associations, schools, and publications.

2. He will advertise only in a dignified manner, setting forth in truthful and factual statements the services he is prepared to render for his prospective clients and for the public.

Relations with the Public

3. He will strive for correct and increasing knowledge of forestry and the dissemination of this knowledge, and will discourage and condemn the spreading of untrue, unfair, and exaggerated statements concerning forestry.

4. He will not issue statements, criticism, or arguments on matters connected with public forestry policies, without indicating, at the same time, on whose behalf he is acting.

5. When serving as an expert witness on forestry matters, in a public or private fact finding proceeding, he will base his testimony on adequate knowledge of the subject matter, and render his opinion on his own honest convictions.

6. He will refrain from expressing publicly an opinion on a technical subject unless he is informed as to the facts relating thereto, and will not distort or withhold data of a substantial or other nature for the purpose of substantiating a point of view.

Relations with Clients, Principals, and Employers

7. He will be loyal to his client or to the organization in which he is employed and will faithfully perform his work and assignments.

8. He will present clearly the consequences to be expected from deviations proposed if his professional forestry judgment is overruled by nontechnical authority in cases where he is responsible for the technical adequacy of forestry or related work.

9. He will not voluntarily disclose information concerning the business affairs of his employers, principals or clients, which they desire to keep confidential, unless express permission is first obtained.

10. He will not, without the full knowledge and consent of his client or employer, have an interest in any business which may influence his judgment in regard to the work for which he is engaged.

11. He will not, for the same service, accept compensation of any kind, other than from his client, principal, or employer, without full disclosure, knowledge, and consent of all parties concerned.

12. He will engage, or advise his client or employer to engage, other experts and specialists in forestry and related fields whenever the client's or employer's interests would be best served by such actions, and will cooperate freely with them in their work.

Relations with Professional Foresters

13. He will at all times strive to protect the forestry profession collectively and individually from misrepresentation and misunderstanding.

14. He will aid in safeguarding the profession against the admission to its ranks of persons unqualified because of lack of good moral character or of adequate training.

15. In writing or in speech he will be scrupulous to give full credit to others, in so far as his knowledge goes, for procedures and methods devised or discovered and ideas advanced or aid given.

16. He will not intentionally and without just cause, directly or indirectly, injure the reputation or business of another forester.

17. If he has substantial and convincing evidence of unprofessional conduct of a forester, he will present the information to the proper authority for action.

18. He will not bid competitively to supply professional forestry services, but shall expect the prospective client to make the selection by comparison and negotiation.

Guidelines: The objectives of the Society of American Foresters are "to advance the science, technology, education, and practice of professional forestry in America and to use the knowledge and skills of the profession to benefit society."

The term "bid competitively" as used in Canon 18 refers to the practice of competitive bidding, where price is the only basis on which a client selects a supplier of professional forestry services. It is an employment procedure which could result in lower standards of professional forestry services. Low standards of services do not "benefit society" nor do they "advance the practice of professional forestry in America." Therefore, the Society of American Foresters considers it unethical for its members to bid competitively on the basis of price alone to supply professional forestry services.

"Professional forestry services" are those services which are based on forestry theories, principles and practices and involve primarily the preparation and submission of recommendations and/ or a plan. Supervision of a plan is also considered to be a "professional forestry service." Such services are subject to Canon 18 of the SAF Code of Ethics and guidelines issued by the Council of the SAF pursuant thereto.

Proposals presented by SAF members to prospective clients for professional forestry services should include a program of work, estimated time required to complete the work and fee. The member's professional qualifications, his experience and the personnel and equipment available to him should also be presented to the prospective client. The prospective client is expected to base his selection on comparison of all information received. Proposals presented by SAF members should remain firm unless the prospective client changes the specifications of the work to be done. If the client changes the work specifications, proposals presented by SAF members should be resubmitted accordingly.

19. He will not use the advantages of a salaried position to compete unfairly with another forester.

20. He will not attempt to supplant another forester in a particular employment, after becoming aware that the latter has been definitely engaged.

21. He will not review the work of another forester, for the latter's employer, without the other's knowledge, unless the latter's connection with the work has been terminated.

22. He will base all letters of reference or oral recommendation on a fair and unbiased evaluation of the party concerned.

23. To the best of his ability he will support, work for, and adhere to the principles of the merit system of employment.

24. He will not participate in soliciting or collecting financial contributions from subordinates or employees for political purposes.

25. He will uphold the principle of appropriate and adequate compensation for those engaged in forestry work, including those in subordinate positions, as being in the public interest and maintaining the standards of the profession.

FUNERAL DIRECTORS

NATIONAL FUNERAL DIRECTORS ASSOCIATION (NFDA)
  135 W. Wells St., Milwaukee, Wisc. 53203
  Howard C. Raether, Executive Director

Membership: The National Funeral Directors Association, founded in 1882 and with a present (1973) membership of over 14,000, is a professional society of funeral directors. NFDA is a federation of state funeral directors associations, whose individual and/or firm members qualify by licensure in the state of practice.

Code of Ethics: The Association Code of Ethics--professional guide for the funeral service profession in dealings with the public and colleagues--sets forth broad principles of practice in the form of a pledge. No national enforcement procedures for the Code are reported.

Other Guides to Professional Conduct: In addition to its Code of
Ethics, the National Funeral Directors Association has issued a
Code of Professional Practices for Funeral Directors, adopted in
1965 and revised in part in 1969, and again in 1972. Conduct guides
to be followed by the funeral director are given in some detail in
this code of practice, including relationships with the family of the
deceased, the clergy, and colleagues.

Professional Insignia: The official emblem of the Association is its
seal--a circular design with a
centered cross whose arms are
in the form of a triangle with
curved sides; one letter of the
organization's initials, "NFDA,"
is printed on each of the four
arms of the cross (upper, left,
right, bottom); and the legend,
"U.S.," in the center. The
color of the emblem is shown
variously--black and white (logotype), blue and white (publication).

Bibliography:
        National Funeral Directors
              Association. Code of
              Ethics. Single page.
        Principles of conduct in the form of a pledge.
_____. Code of Professional Practices for Funeral Direc-
        tors. Revised edition, October 1972. 4 pages.
        Practices to be followed by the funeral director in relation-
ships with those he serves, the clergy, and colleagues.
_____. National Funeral Directors Association. Folder.
        Includes NFDA membership requirements, structure, func-
tions, program and services.

"Code of Ethics"

I

        As funeral directors, we herewith fully acknowledge our in-
dividual and collective obligations to the public, especially to those
we serve, and our mutual responsibilities for the proper welfare of
the funeral service profession.

II

        To the public we pledge: vigilant support of public health
laws; proper legal regulations for the members of our profession;
devotion to high moral and service standards; conduct befitting good
citizens; honesty in all offerings of service and merchandise, and
in all business transactions.

III

To those we serve we pledge: confidential business and professional relationships; cooperation with the customs of all religions and creeds; observance of all respect due the deceased; high standards of competence and dignity in the conduct of all services, truthful representation of all services and merchandise.

IV

To our profession we pledge: support of high educational standards and proper licensing laws: encouragement of scientific research; adherence to sound business practices; adoption of improved techniques; observance of all rules of fair competition; maintenance of favorable personnel relations.

As an affiliate of our state and national association, we subscribe to the ʰrinciples set forth in the Code of Ethics and pledge our best efforts to make them effective.

(Signed)_____
                          Funeral Director

"Code of Professional Practices for Funeral Directors"

When a death occurs a survivor in the immediate family or the person or persons who will be responsible for the funeral of the deceased should be advised to contact their family funeral director or should direct that said funeral director be notified.   This should be done regardless of where or when death takes place.   The funeral director then becomes the representative of the family for the purpose of the funeral arrangements.

When once a funeral director is called by the family or their representative and as a result of such call removes the body, he shall provide the necessary services and merchandise in keeping with the wishes and finances of the family or their representative.

Before any funeral arrangements are made the funeral director should determine, if he does not know, who is the minister, priest or rabbi of the deceased and/or of the family.   The funeral director should ascertain if such clergyman has been notified of the death.   If this has not been done the funeral director should suggest it be done and should offer to do so for the family.

Before the specifics as to any and all aspects of the religious part of the funeral are decided, they should be discussed and cleared with the clergyman.   This can be done either by the family or the funeral director as their representative or by both.

Before the family selects the funeral service, the funeral director should explain the various aspects of the funeral and the costs thereof as to the services and the merchandise he provides and as to that obtained from others such as cemeteries, florists and so forth. This should be done before the family goes into the casket selection room. In such explanation the funeral director should make clear the range of prices of funerals he has available. Also the funeral director should welcome any questions or discussions as to that which is or is not required by laws and/or regulations to such laws.

The funeral director should review for the family the various death benefits and/or burial allowances that may be available to them such as those involving Social Security, the Veterans Administration, labor unions, fraternal and other organizations. He will assist in the preparation and filing of the necessary forms to secure these benefits and allowances for the family. Where further professional assistance is required he should suggest that the families seek the advice of other professionals.

Because the price of the funeral as to the funeral director is related to the casket selection, there should be a card or brochure in each casket in the selection room. Such card or brochure should outline the services offered by the funeral home. Services and merchandise not included where a unit price method is used should be listed on the card or brochure as separate items.

Representations of the funeral director with respect to caskets should be as to material, construction, design, hardware, mattressing and interior. The use of an outside receptacle in which the casketed body is placed should be fully explained. Facts should be given regarding the requirements of cemeteries as to such receptacles where they exist. The various kinds of receptacles and their materials, construction and design should be reviewed.

When a family decides on the kind of service desired the funeral director should provide a memorandum or agreement for the family to approve or sign showing (1) the price of the service that the family has selected and what is included therein; (2) the price of each of the supplemental items of service and/or merchandise requested; (3) the amount involved for each of the items for which the funeral director will advance monies as an accommodation to the family; and (4) the method of payment agreed upon by the family and the funeral director.

When death occurs in a place other than where the funeral and/or burial are to take place, most times the services of two funeral directors are necessary. Under such circumstances the family should not pay for a complete service both where death occurred and also where the burial or cremation is held.

The forwarding funeral director should make an allowance or adjustment for those of his services not required and should notify the receiving funeral director thereof. Likewise the receiving funeral director should not charge the family for the services already provided by the forwarding funeral director unless there is a duplication thereof desired by the family.

The family should pay for only one complete service plus any additional charges incurred because the place of death and the place of final disposition require the services of two funeral firms.

As soon as the details and schedule in the transporting of remains are known to the forwarding funeral director, he shall immediately notify the receiving funeral director thereof.

It is suggested that when a body is transported a report made out by the person who did the embalming should accompany the remains. Such a report could be of assistance to the receiving funeral director in the event additional professional work is required on the body.

Where burial is at a point distant from where the funeral service is to be conducted and a concrete or metal burial vault is to be used, the funeral director called for the service should suggest the funeral director who will be responsible for the interment provide said vault for a number of reasons including the saving to the family of the added cost of handling and transporting the vault to the place of burial.

When a funeral service is conducted in a place other than the church of the clergyman, his wishes and desires should be considered to whatever extent possible.

In the matter of the honorarium or the stipend the personal wishes of the clergyman should be respected. If the family is a member of the clergyman's church or parish it is a personal matter between the family and the clergyman. When the funeral director assumes the responsibility for the honorarium at the direction of the family, it is desirable to use a check for the transaction for record keeping purposes. If the clergyman does not accept honoraria, the family should be so informed in order that they may express their appreciation in other ways. When the family has no choice of a clergyman and the funeral director makes arrangements for one, the matter of the honorarium becomes the responsibility of the funeral director and a cash advance for the family.

When conducting a funeral in a church the polity, rules and regulations of that church must serve as the guide to the conduct of the service. Any exceptions to such procedures requested by the family should be cleared with the clergyman or proper authority well in advance of the time of their actual performance.

The funeral director should remain alert to the needs of the families he serves and when the need for religious or pastoral counseling is indicated he should make proper referrals whenever possible.

Funeral directors should be available to discuss with anyone all matters relative to the conduct of a funeral. Whenever possible the funeral director should assume active leadership in seminars or discussions which will bring a deeper understanding to all concerned about death, the funeral and bereavement.

GENEALOGISTS

AMERICAN SOCIETY OF GENEALOGISTS (ASGA)

Membership: The American Society of Genealogists, founded in
1940, is "a learned society devoted to genealogy and heraldry."
Members are limited to fifty, and "Membership is an honor,
granted in recognition of the quality and quantity of published works"
in genealogy and related fields. An individual does not apply for
membership, but is nominated for membership by a Member of the
society, and sponsored by at least two other members.   A nominee,
after his qualifications have been evaluated by a committee of the
society, is elected to membership by vote of the members.

Members are designated, "Fellows," and are authorized to
affix to their names the designation: "F. A. S. G." (Fellow American
Society of Genealogists). Since the American Society of Genealogists
is purely an honorary society, it refers inquiries concerning Genealogy or Genealogists to the National Genealogical Society or the
Board for Certification of Genealogists, both organizations located
at 1307 New Hampshire Avenue, N. W. , Washington, D. C. 20036.

Code of Ethics: The Society has issued no formal code of ethics,
although one of its purposes is "to improve the scholarship and
ethics of the profession, " and a Fellow may be dropped from the
Roll of the Society "for conduct deemed prejudicial to the Society"
(Constitution and Bylaws, Article IX).

Professional Insignia: The official emblem of the ASG is its seal--
a circular design, with a centered Crusader's shield upon which is

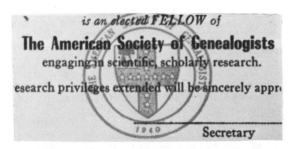

a cross bearing six stars in the vertical bar, and seven stars on
the horizontal; the Liberty Bell is shown in the upper left-hand
angle; the name of the organization, "The American Society of Genealogists, " is printed around the upper half of the design in a bordering band; and the founding date, "1940, " within the bordering

band at the bottom of the design.   The color of the emblem (membership card) is grey on blue.

Other Identification of Professional Status: As described above under
"Membership," members of the Society are designated "Fellows,"
and are "authorized to affix the initials 'F. A. S. G.' (Fellow, American Society of Genealogists) to their names."

Bibliography:
    American Society of Genealogists.   Constitution and Bylaws.
       January 1969.   3 pages.
       Includes membership requirements, designation "F. A. S. G.,"
       and disciplinary procedure.

BOARD FOR CERTIFICATION OF GENEALOGISTS (BCG)
    1307 New Hampshire Ave., N. W., Washington, D. C. 20036
    Richard E. Spurr, Executive Secretary

Membership: The Board for Certification of Genealogists, organized
in 1964, certifies workers in American genealogical research, formu-
lates standards of genealogical research, and maintains a register
of competent genealogists and record searchers.   The Board, composed of leading genealogists and historians, receives applications
for certification, and--based on inspection of training and experience
qualifications and work samples of certification candidates--issues
three certificates signifying competence to engage in professional
research in American genealogy:
    Certified Genealogist (C. G.)--"conducts research among
       primary sources and studies secondary works, but also
       constructs genealogies of families based upon investigation
       of the sources and careful analysis of the evidence."
    Certified American Lineage Specialist (C. A. L. S.)--"prepares
       a lineage (single line of descent) and is competent to de-
       termine the authenticity of evidence and acceptability of
       original source material and compiled and printed material."
    Certified Genealogical Record Searcher (G. R. S.)--"searches
       original records (census enumerations, wills, deeds,
       Orphans Court records, pensions, military and naval
       records, etc.), but makes no attempt to reconstruct a
       pedigree or to prepare a family history."

    Judges selected by the Board consider the training and experi-
ence and professional reports submitted by candidates for certification, for which no specific amount or kind of education or experience
is required.   Candidates certified as competent are authorized by
the Board to use the appropriate professional initials with their
name (as shown above), and the appropriate insignia on letterheads.
These letterheads must be ordered through the Executive Secretary

of the Board from the Board's printer. Certificates are issued for
five years, and may be renewed for additional periods of five years
when expired.

Code of Ethics: Each candidate certified as competent in professional genealogical research is required to subscribe to The Genealogist's Code, which sets forth the researcher's professional
obligations to the public, client, and profession. No procedures
for enforcing this Code are reported.

Professional Insignia: The Board for Certification of Genealogists
has no official emblem.

Other Designations of Professional Status: As described above under
"Membership," researchers are certified as competent by the Board
and authorized to use appropriate professional designations and initials with their names. The professional seals authorized for use of
Certified researchers are:

> Certified Genealogical Record Searcher (G. R. S.)--A round
>   design, a centered scroll bearing the name of the specialty,
>   "Genealogical Record Searcher"; a bordering band carries
>   the name of the certifying agency and the date of its found-
>   ing, "Board for Certification of Genealogists 1964." Shown
>   in black on white.
> Certified American Lineage Specialist (C. A. L. S.)--Identical
>   design, except the centered symbol is two sheets of records,
>   with the designation printed around the design below the
>   bordering band, "Certified American Lineage Specialist."
> Certified Genealogist (C. G.)--Identical design, except the cen-
>   tered symbol is a shield bearing a three-generation an-
>   cestral chart, as "the visual record of progenitors," with
>   the designation "Certified" above the shield, and "Genealo-
>   gist" below the shield.

Bibliography:
    Board for Certification of Genealogists. The Board's Position
        on Genealogists' Fees. 2 pages.
    Guideline for fees charges by genealogists.
    _____. The Genealogist's Code. Single sheet.
    Statement of professional ethics accepted by certified genea-
    logical researchers.
    _____. Heraldry for United States Citizens. 2 pages.

Professional genealogists' statement about the registration and use of coats of arms in the United States.
_____. Information Sheet. 1973. 3 pages.
Certification qualifications and procedures. Pictures seals indicating certification.
_____. (Work Description and Requirements for Professional Genealogical Researchers): Genealogist; American Lineage Specialist; Genealogical Record Searcher. 3 separate sheets.
What the professional genealogical searcher does, and the knowledges, skills, and abilities required for such work.

"The Genealogist's Code"

The profession of genealogy calls for accurate research, personal and scholarly integrity, and creative analysis. A genealogist must realize that he has moral obligations to society as well as to his client, beyond the requirements of law and business practice. His honesty of purpose must be above suspicion, his findings from the best available evidence, and his analysis sound.

Realizing my moral obligations as a genealogist, I make the following commitments:

I have obligations to the public. Whether engaged in independent research or acting as consultant, adviser, or assistant on a mutually acceptable basis of fee, I will strictly maintain my professional integrity. I will not indulge in exaggerated, misleading, or false advertisement or publicity. I will not publish or publicize as fact anything I know to be false or unproven; nor will I be a party, either directly or indirectly, to such action by others.

I have obligations to my client. To avoid unnecessary duplication of effort I will, before undertaking research, request from the client such information as he has assembled, with its documentation; and on the basis of that information I will give a candid opinion of the possible or probable results of the projected research. I will make my communications to the client definite and clear. If unable to resolve his problem, I will explain why, and, if possible, suggest other avenues of research.
I will inform my client that my conclusions must be based on the preponderance of evidence, and that absolute proof of ancestral relations is usually impossible.
I will not knowingly misquote any document nor cite as authoritative any questionable source. I will not assert as a fact that which I have not substantiated by adequate documentation, nor conceal or withhold data which would break down the chain of evidence necessary for the client's purpose.
I will consider work done for a client as confidential, and will not divulge any information concerning the client or his interests without prior consent. Nor will I publish under my own name and

in his lifetime, without authorization, the results of research for which the client has paid.

I will have no personal or financial interests which might tend to compromise my obligations to the client.

I have obligations to the profession.
I will not act in a manner detrimental to the best interests of the profession.

I will not knowingly injure or attempt to injure, without demonstrable justification, the professional reputation, prospects, or practice of another genealogist. I will, however, participate in exposing genealogical charlatans.

I will not attempt to supplant another genealogist already employed by a client; nor will I substitute for another unless and until a written form of substitution has been signed by all concerned.

I will not present as my own, the work of another.

Signed at
this   day of   19   _____

NATIONAL GENEALOGICAL SOCIETY (NGS)
    1921 Sunderland Place, N. W. , Washington, D. C. 20036
    Dr. Kenn Stryker-Rodda, President

Membership: The National Genealogical Society, founded in 1903 and with a present (1973) membership of about 3000, "was created to collect, preserve and publish genealogical information, to inculcate and promote interest in research, and to foster careful documentation, and to champion ethical standards." Any person "interested in genealogy and related fields of biography, local history and heraldry" may become a member of the Society.

Code of Ethics: The National Genealogical Society endorses the Code of Ethics, developed by the Board for Certification of Genealogists.

Professional Insignia: The official insignia of the Society is "a shield of blue, white and red enamel, surrounded by a ribbon of gold bearing the name, 'National Genealogical Society,' in blue letters. In heraldic terms the blazon of the shield is 'Argent, three acorns gules, with a border azure'" (Bylaws, Article XIII). The seal of the Society is used on publications (Application for Membership). It is
    "one and thirteen sixteenths of an inch in diameter, consisting of the bearings of the society displayed on the breast of a conventional eagle, below which is a ribbon or scroll containing the motto, 'Non Nobis Solum' ('Not For Ourselves Alone'), and above a similar ribbon with the words, 'The

National Genealogical Society,'
all contained within two or
more concentric circles.   The
date of the founding of the
society, '1903,' in figures,
appears between the eagle's
claws" (Bylaws, Article III).

Bibliography:
National Genealogical
   Society.   Application
   for Membership.
   Folder.
Brief description of
NGS purposes and ac-
tivities; pictures seal.
_____. Bylaws. Re-
   vised edition, 1969.
Includes specifications for insignia and seal.

"Code of Ethics"

see pages 322-323.

GEOGRAPHERS

AMERICAN GEOGRAPHICAL SOCIETY (AGS)
      Broadway at 156th St., New York, N.Y. 10032
      Burton K. Adkinson, Director

Membership: The American Geographical Society, founded in 1852
and with a present (1973) membership of over 3000, includes among
its members professional geographers and any person who qualifies
for membership with "an interest in exploration and travel, and in
the accumulation, analysis, and spread of geographical knowledge."
Members include "statesmen, scientists, educators, and leaders in
business and the professions." "Geography" is defined by the
Society as that
         "science that aims at bringing all the earth's resources--
         land, air, water, and living things--into human focus, and
         at giving shape and meaning to the places of man's abode."

Code of Ethics: As the American Geographical Society is open to
all interested in geography, the organization has not formulated a
professional code of ethics for geographers.

Professional Insignia: The official emblem of the Society is the

seal--adopted in 1859, and re-
designed in 1873 and 1881.
The design, circular in form,
bears a tilted globe, resting
on four books--two larger
books lying flat to the right
and two leaning, smaller books,
to the left. These symbols
of the scope of geography and
its accumulated records and
research show, in front and
on the books to the right,
three common instruments of
the explorer--astrolabe, tele-
scope, and compass. The
motto of the Society, "Ubique"
(Latin term that may be trans-

lated "Everywhere") appears around the equator of the globe, symbolizing the earth-wide scope of geography. The original name of
the group, "American Geographical Society of New York," and the
year of the AGS organization, "1852," appear in a bordering band.
The color of the emblem is shown variously--blue on white (letterhead, publications), and gold on white (publications).

Bibliography:
        The American Geographical Society. The American Geographical
            Society. Folder.
        Informational brochure with brief history of the Society,
            description of services and activities.
        Wright, John Kirkland. Geography in the Making: The Ameri-
            can Geographical Society, 1851-1951. N.Y., American
            Geographical Society, 1952. 490 pages.
        Includes a brief history of the Society emblem (pages 19-
        20).

GEOLOGISTS

THE GEOLOGICAL SOCIETY OF AMERICA (GSA)
        3300 Penrose Place, Boulder, Colo. 80301
        Edwin B. Eckel, Executive Secretary

Membership: The Geological Society of America, founded in 1888
and with a present (1973) membership of about 10,000, is a professional association of geologists. Within the Society are six regional
sections, and the range of interest of members is indicated by the
five topical divisions of the Society: Coal Geology, Engineering
Geology, Quaternary Geology and Geomorphology, Hydrogeology,

and Geophysics. Membership qualifications for the various categories
of membership--other than "Student Associate"--are:
> Members--Persons engaged in either geologic work, the
> teaching of geology, or in graduate study of geology.
> Bachelor's Degree with a major in Geology or a related
> science, or equivalent training through practical experi-
> ence required.
> Fellows--Persons engaged in either geologic work or the
> teaching of geology, who have contributed to the advance-
> ment of the science, and have been a member of the GSA
> for at least one year before nomination for Fellow.
> Honorary Fellow--Persons distinguished for their attainments
> in geologic science in countries outside the North Ameri-
> can Continent.

Code of Ethics: The Geological Society of America has published no
formal code of ethics.

Professional Insignia: The emblem of The Geological Society of
America is the GSA logo--which consists of the GSA seal and the
organization name. The Seal is circular in form with the continent
of North America shown on a horizontally striped ground; a leather
belt, as indicated by the buckle at the bottom right, borders this
central shaded area, and bears the name of the group, "The Geological Society of America, " and at the bottom of the design--the

THE
GEOLOGICAL SOCIETY
OF AMERICA

date of organization's founding, "1888, " and a geologist's pick,
common tool of the field geologist. The Society and its units show
the GSA signature "on all printed matter including: publications,
announcements, stationery, reports, programs. "

Bibliography:
> Geological Society of America. Facts About the Society. 2
> pages.
> Information sheet giving purpose, organization, membership
> qualifications, publications, and awards of the GSA.
> _____. The GSA Signature and Its Applications. 1966. 4
> pages.
> Describes the GSA Signature--Seal and Name--giving purpose,
> application and use on stationery and publications. Pictures
> signature in dimensions of from 1" to 2"; and signature used
> for geographic regions and topical divisions.

GERIATRICIANS

AMERICAN GERIATRICS SOCIETY (AGS)
   10 Columbus Circle, New York, N.Y. 10019
   Edward Henderson, M.D., Executive Director

Membership: The American Geriatrics Society, founded in 1942, is a clinical medical society whose members--currently (1973) over 8000--are licensed M.D.'s in the state of their practice, who have an interest in the medical specialty of geriatrics--the treatment of older patients.

Code of Ethics: As an organization of physicians, the American Geriatrics Society subscribes to the canons of ethics of the American Medical Association.

Professional Insignia: The emblem of the American Geriatrics Society is its seal--a circular device with three symbols: at upper left a rayed sun, shining on a centered time marker of a sundial and a sheaf of wheat--representing the benefits of a full life that may be enjoyed by individual matured through time; the organization initials, "AGS," and the date of the group's founding (in Roman numerals), "MCMXLII," are also shown in the central area of the design; the name of the association, "American Geriatrics Society," appears in the border banding the emblem. The color of the insignia is grey on white (letterhead).

"Code of Ethics"

see page 564

GOVERNMENT EMPLOYEES--CIVILIAN

Ethical conduct standards for employees of the United States government are included in federal laws, executive orders, and executive department regulations (see also JUDGES), and such standards, adopted in the past decade, are found in the federal statutes, presidential executive orders, U. S. Civil Service Commission regulations, and publications of executive department.

Civilian Employees of the United States Government--One basic conduct guide for federal civilian officers, employees, or advisors of any executive department, independent agency, or any government corporation in the executive branch of the federal government is the Presidential Order (Executive Order 11222), signed by President Lyndon B. Johnson on May 8, 1965. This order prescribes standards of ethical conduct for government officers and employees pertaining to conflict of interest between government employees' private and official interests and actions, including the "using of public office for private gain," and provides for the reporting of financial interest, which "may indicate a conflict between the financial interests of the officer or employee concerned and the performance of his services for the Government" (Part IV, Section 404 of Executive Order 11222).

To carry out provisions in this executive order, the United States Civil Service Commission issued rules and regulations (5 Code of Federal Regulations 735, November 9, 1965, Revised July 1969) directed to "the maintenance of unusually high standards of honesty, integrity, impartiality, and conduct by Government employees" (735.101). Specifically proscribed (735.201a) is any action which "might result in, or create the appearance of:

    (a)   Using public office for private gain;
    (b)   Giving preferential treatment to any person;
    (c)   Impeding government efficiency or economy;
    (d)   Losing complete independence or impartiality;
    (e)   Making a government decision outside official channels;
    (f)   Affecting adversely the confidence of the public in the integrity of the government."

Other aspects of ethical conduct and responsibilities of government employees considered in these Civil Service Commission rules include regulations concerning:
    Gifts, entertainment and favors;
    Outside employment and other activities;
    Financial interests;
    Use of government property;
    Misuse of official information;
    Statements of employment and financial interests.
These rules also list miscellaneous statutory provisions in the United States Code relating to ethical, and other, conduct of employees (735.210), including the Code of Ethics for Government Service, adopted by the United States Congress on July 14, 1958 (House Concurrent Resolution 175, 85th Congress, 2d Session, 72 Stat. B12). This code of ethics enumerates ten principles of conduct to be followed by "any person in Government service." Although (according

to Library of Congress report) no formal procedures for enforcement of these Congressional rules of conduct have been created, disciplinary and other remedial action for violation of the ethical code regarding conflict of interests set forth penalties ranging from reassignment, through divestment of conflicting interest, to disqualification for a particular assignment.   During the past several years, 379 bills pertaining to standards of official conduct have been introduced in Congress--House of Representatives (336 bills) and Senate (47 bills)--from the 85th through the 90th Congress, 1st Session.

United States Congress.   House of Representatives--The Committee on Standards of Official Conduct of the House of Representatives (created April 13, 1967) has conducted hearings from the year of its appointment through each session to the present.   After hearings (August and September 1967), the Committee formulated the Code of Official Conduct, United States House of Representatives (March 14, 1968), and this Code was adopted by the House of Representatives on April 3, 1968 (House Resolution 1099, 90th Congress, 2d Session).

The eight standards enumerated in the Code govern general conduct and receipt and identification of nongovernmental compensation and campaign funds.

Subsequent reports of this House of Representatives Committee on Standards of Official Conduct pertain to Financial Disclosure (1970), proposing requirement of:
> "public disclosure of (1) the sources of honorariums of $300 or more, and (2) the identity of each creditor to whom $10,000 or more was owed for 90 consecutive days or more in the preceding calendar year without the pledge of specific security."

Other aspects of legislators' conduct considered by the Committee are Regulations of Lobbying (1970, and 1971), and Campaign Finances (1970).

United States Congress.   Senate--In the United States Senate rules of official conduct for Senators (adopted March 22, 1968, as S. Res. 266, Report No. 1015, 90th Congress, 2d Session) were introduced by a member of the Senate's Select Committee on Standards and Conduct.   These rules (incorporated in the Standing Rules of the United States Senate, January 3, 1971, as Rule XLI-XLIV) concern:
> Outside business or professional activity or employment by officers and employees;
> Contributions;
> Political fund activity by officers and employees;
> Disclosure of financial interests.

Bibliography:
> Congressional Quarterly.   Guide to the Congress of the United States: Origins, History and Procedure.   Washington, D.C.,

Congressional Quarterly Service. 1971.
"Ethics in Congress" (Chapter 7, p. 627-638) gives "Expulsion, Exclusion and Censure" provisions, "Restrictions on Members." Includes Senate Ethics Rules, House Ethics Rules, and Government's Code of Ethics (p. 636).

U. S. Civil Service Commission. Employee Responsibilities and Conduct. (Code of Federal Regulations, Chapter 735 of Title 5). November 9, 1965, Revised June 1969.
Current ethics regulations governing Federal employees, drafted by the Civil Service Commission under authority of the President's Executive Order No. 11222, referred to as the "ethical conduct code."

U. S. Congress. House of Representatives. Code of Ethics for Government Service. (H. Con. Res 175, 85th Congress, 2d Session, July 14, 1958)

U. S. Congress. House of Representatives. Committee on Standards of Official Conduct. Standards of Official Conduct. Hearings. August and September 1967. 90th Congress, 1st Session. 1967. 310 p.
Testimony from individuals and organizations on proposals for Standards of official legislator conduct, including "Congressional Ethics," by Bob Wilson, p. 196-200.

_____. Report of the Committee on Standards of Official Conduct. March 14, 1968. 90th Congress, 2d Session. 1968. 45 p.
Recommends the 8-point "Code of Official Conduct," adopted by the House of Representatives April 3, 1968. Includes a "Short History of Rules of Conduct Enforcement in the House of Representatives (p. 34-37) prepared by the Legislative Reference Service, Library of Congress.

_____. Code of Official Conduct. United States House of Representatives. April 3, 1968. House Resolution 1099, 90th Congress, 2d Session.
Eight principles of professional conduct for U. S. representatives.

_____. Standards of Official Conduct. Hearings. February 19, 1970. 1970. 52 p.
Testimony and statements on H. Res. 796, proposed amendments to Financial Disclosure Rule (House Rule XLIV).

_____. Amending the Rules of the House of Representatives. Report. March 24, 1970. 91st Congress, 2d Session. 1970. 6 pages.
Favorable report on House Resolution 796--to amend and clarify provisions of House Rule XLIV on financial disclosure.

_____. Regulation of Lobbying. Hearings. October 1970. 91st Congress, 2d Session. 1970. 134 p.
Testimony and statements on House Resolution 1031, 91st Congress, 2d Session on amendment of House Rules regulating lobbying. The present basic statute regulating lobbying (Federal Regulation of Lobbying Act, a disclosure statute which came into existence as Title III of the Legislative Reorganization Act of 1946) is 25 years old.

_____. Campaign Finances. Hearings. December 1, 8, 9, and 15, 1970. 91st Congress, 2d Session. 1970. 209 p.
Hearings and statements concerning regulation of lobbying and management of campaign money.

_____. [Campaign Funds Disclosure.] Report. 91st Congress, 2d Session. December 21, 1970. 1970. 19 pages.
Report on campaign financing defines the problems and establishes priorities in dealing with them, rather than offering specific remedies. The present basic statute on campaign financing (Federal Corrupt Practices Act of 1925, a regulatory statute) is 45 years old.

_____. Lobbying. Hearings. March 1971. 92nd Congress, 1st Session. 1971. 145 p.
Testimony and statements on H.R. 5259, introduced March 1, 1971, cited as the "Legislative Activities Disclosure Act."

United States Congress. Senate. Standing Rules of the United States Senate.... January 3, 1971. 181 p.
Includes the written standards (p. 60-68) of conduct adopted by the Senate (S. Res. 266. Report No. 1015, 90th Congress, 2d Session. March 15, 1968).

United States Postal Service. Laws Relating to Ethical Conduct and Conflict of Interest. (POD Pubn 74). Washington, D.C., Post Office Department, July 1971. 43 p.
Contains Federal Statutes pertaining to ethical conduct of employees of the U.S. government, Executive Order 11222, Civil Service Commission Regulations (5 CFR 735) relating to ethical conduct and conflict of interests.

United States. President. Executive Order 11222. Prescribing Standards of Ethical Conduct for Government Officers and Employees.
Rules to guide ethical conduct.

Wilson, Bob. "Congressional Ethics," in: We Propose: A Modern Congress. N.Y., McGraw-Hill, 1966.

CONCURRENT RESOLUTION

Resolved by the House of Representatives (the Senate concurring), That it is the sense of the Congress that the following Code of Ethics should be adhered to by all Government employees, including officeholders:

"Code of Ethics for Government Service"

Any person in Government service should:

1. Put loyalty to the highest moral principles and to country above loyalty to persons, party, or Government department.

2. Uphold the Constitution, laws, and legal regulations of

the United States and of all governments therein and never be a
party to their evasion.

3. Give a full day's labor for a full day's pay; giving to the
performance of his duties his earnest effort and best thought.

4. Seek to find and employ more efficient and economical
ways of getting tasks accomplished.

5. Never discriminate unfairly by the dispensing of special
favors or privileges to anyone, whether for remuneration or not;
and never accept, for himself or his family, favors or benefits
under circumstances which might be construed by reasonable persons as influencing the performance of his governmental duties.

6. Make no private promises of any kind binding upon the
duties of office, since a Government employee has no private word
which can be binding on public duty.

7. Engage in no business with the government, either directly
or indirectly, which is inconsistent with the conscientious performance
of his governmental duties.

8. Never use any information coming to him confidentially in
the performance of governmental duties as a means for making private profit.

9. Expose corruption wherever discovered.

10. Uphold these principles, ever conscious that public
office is a public trust.

"Code of Official Conduct,
United States House of Representatives"

I.   A Member, officer, or employee of the House of Representatives shall conduct himself at all times in a manner which shall
reflect creditably on the House of Representatives.

II.   A Member, officer, or employee of the House of Representatives shall adhere to the spirit and the letter of Rules of the
House and to the rules of duly constituted committees thereof.

III.   A Member, officer, or employee of the House of Representatives shall receive no compensation nor shall he permit any
compensation to accrue to his beneficial interest from any source,
the receipt of which would occur by virtue of influence improperly
exerted from his position in the Congress.

IV.   A Member, officer, or employee of the House of Representatives shall accept no gift of substantial value, directly or indirectly, from any person, organization, or corporation having a
direct interest in legislation before the Congress.

V.   A Member, officer, or employee of the House of Representatives shall accept no honorarium for a speech, writing for publication, or other similar activity, from any person, organization,
or corporation in excess of the usual and customary value for such
services.

VI.   A Member of the House of Representatives shall keep his campaign funds separate from his personal funds.   He shall convert no campaign funds to personal use in excess of reimbursement for legitimate and verifiable prior campaign expenditures. He shall expend no funds from his campaign account not attributable to bona fide campaign purposes.

VII.   A Member of the House of Representatives shall treat as campaign contributions all proceeds from testimonial dinners or other fund-raising events if the sponsors of such affairs do not give clear notice in advance to the donors or participants that the proceeds are intended for other purposes.

VIII.   A Member of the House of Representatives shall retain no one from his clerk hire allowance who does not perform duties commensurate with the compensation he receives.

"Code of Official Conduct, United States Senate"
[Standing Rules of the Senate--XLI-XLIV]
[*S. Jour. 247, 90-2, Mar. 22, 1968]

[41]   RULE XLI*
Outside Business or Professional Activity or Employment by Officers or Employees
[41.1] 1.   No officer or employee whose salary is paid by the Senate may engage in any business or professional activity or employment for compensation unless--
(a)   the activity or employment is not inconsistent nor in conflict with the conscientious performance of his official duties; and
(b)   he has reported in writing when this rule takes effect or when his office or employment starts and on the 15th day of May in each year thereafter the nature of any personal service activity or employment to his supervisor.   The supervisor shall then, in the discharge of his duties, take such action as he considers necessary for the avoidance of conflict of interest or interference with duties to the Senate.

[41.2] 2.   For the purpose of this rule--
(a)   a Senator or the Vice President is the supervisor of his administrative, clerical, or other assistants;
(b)   a Senator who is the chairman of a committee is the supervisor of the professional, clerical, or other assistants to the committee except that minority staff members shall be under the supervision of the ranking minority Senator on the committee;
(c)   a Senator who is a chairman of a subcommittee which has its own staff and financial authorization is the supervisor of the professional, clerical, or other assistants to the subcommittee except that minority staff members shall be under the supervision of the ranking minority Senator on the subcommittee;
(d)   the President pro tempore is the supervisor of the Secretary of the Senate, Sergeant at Arms and Doorkeeper, the Chaplain, and

the employees of the Office of the Legislative Counsel;

(e)   the Secretary of the Senate is the supervisor of the employees of his office;

(f)   the Sergeant at Arms and Doorkeeper is the supervisor of the employees of his office;

(g)   the Majority and Minority Leaders and the Majority and Minority Whips are the supervisors of the research, clerical, or other assistants assigned to their respective offices;

(h)   the Majority Leader is the supervisor of the Secretary for the Majority.   The Secretary for the Majority is the supervisor of the employees of his office; and

(i)   the Minority Leader is the supervisor of the Secretary for the Minority.   The Secretary for the Minority is the supervisor of the employees of his office.

[41.3] 3.   This rule shall take effect ninety days after adoption.

[42]   RULE XLII*

Contributions

[42.1] 1.   A Senator or person who has declared or otherwise made known his intention to seek nomination or election, or who has filed papers or petitions for nomination or election, or on whose behalf a declaration or nominating paper or petition has been made or filed, or who has otherwise, directly or indirectly, manifested his intention to seek nomination or election, pursuant to State law, to the office of United States Senator, may accept a contribution from--

       (a)   a fundraising event organized and held primarily in his behalf, provided--
       (1)   he has expressly given his approval of the fundraising event to the sponsors before any funds were raised; and
       (2)   he receives a complete and accurate accounting of the source, amounts, and disposition of the funds raised; or
       (b)   an individual or an organization, provided the Senator makes a complete and accurate accounting of the source, amount, and disposition of the funds received; or
       (c)   his political party when such contributions were from a fundraising event sponsored by his party, without giving his express approval for such fundraising event when such fundraising event is for the purpose of providing contributions for candidates of his party and such contributions are reported by the Senator or candidate for Senator as provided in paragraph (b).

[42.2] 2.   The Senator may use the contribution only to influence his nomination for election, or his election, and shall not use, directly or indirectly, any part of any contribution for any other purpose, exxept as otherwise provided herein.

[42.3] 3.   Nothing in this rule shall preclude the use of contributions to defray expenses for travel to and from each Senator's home

State; for printing and other expenses in connection with the mailing of speeches, newsletters, and reports to a Senator's constituents; for expenses of radio, television, and news media methods of reporting to a Senator's constituents; for telephone, telegraph, postage, and stationery expenses in excess of allowance; and for newspaper subscriptions from his home State.

[42.4] 4. All gifts in the aggregate amount or value of $50 or more received by a Senator from any single source during a year, except a gift from his spouse, child, or parent, and except a contribution under sections 1 and 2, shall be reported under rule XLIV.

[42.5] 5. This rule shall take effect ninety days after adoption.

[43]   RULE XLIII*

              Political Fund Activity by Officers and Employees

[43.1] 1. No officer or employee whose salary is paid by the Senate may. receive, solicit, be the custodian of, or distribute any funds in connection with any campaign for the nomination for election, or the election of any individual to be a Member of the Senate or to any other Federal office. This prohibition does not apply to any assistant to a Senator who has been designated by that Senator to perform any of the functions described in the first sentence of this paragraph and who is compensated at a rate in excess of $10,000 per annum if such designation has been made in writing and filed with the Secretary of the Senate. The Secretary of the Senate shall make the designation available for public inspection.

[43.2] 2. This rule shall take effect sixty days after adoption.

[44]   RULE XLIV*

                  Disclosure of Financial Interests

[44.1] 1. Each Senator or person who has declared or otherwise made known his intention to seek nomination or election, or who has filed papers or petitions for nomination or election, or on whose behalf a declaration or nominating paper or petition has been made or filed, or who has otherwise, directly or indirectly, manifested his intention to seek nomination or election, pursuant to State law, to the office of United States Senator, and each officer or employee of the Senate who is compensated at a rate in excess of $15,000 a year, shall file with the Comptroller General of the United States, in a sealed envelope marked "Confidential Personal Financial Disclosure of _ _ _ _ _ _ _ _ _ _ _ _ _ _ (Name) _," before the 15th day of May in each year, the following reports of his personal financial interests:

(a)   a copy of the returns of taxes, declarations, statements, or other documents which he, or he and his spouse jointly, made for the preceding year in compliance with the income tax provisions of the Internal Revenue Code;

(b)   the amount or value and source of each fee or compensation of $1,000 or more received by him during the preceding year from a client;

(c)   the name and address of each business or professional corporation, firm, or enterprise in which he was an officer, director, partner, proprietor, or employee who received compensation during the preceding year and the amount of such compensation;

(d)   the identity of each interest in real or personal property having a value of $10,000 or more which he owned at any time during the preceding year;

(e)   the identity of each trust or other fiduciary relation in which he held a beneficial interest having a value of $10,000 or more, and the identity if known of each interest of the trust or other fiduciary relation in real or personal property in which the Senator, officer, or employee held a beneficial interest having a value of $10,000 or more, at any time during the preceding year. If he cannot obtain the identity of the fiduciary interests, the Senator, officer, or employee shall request the fiduciary to report that information to the Comptroller General in the same manner that reports are filed under this rule;

(f)   the identity of each liability of $5,000 or more owed by him, or by him and his spouse jointly, at any time during the preceding year; and

(g)   the source and value of all gifts in the aggregate amount or value of $50 or more from any single source received by him during the preceding year.

[44.2] 2.   Except as otherwise provided by this section, all papers filed under section 1 of this rule shall be kept by the Comptroller General for not less than seven years, and while so kept shall remain sealed.   Upon receipt of a resolution of the Select Committee on Standards and Conduct, adopted by a recorded majority vote of the full committee, requesting the transmission to the committee of any of the reports filed by any individual under section 1 of this rule, the Comptroller General shall transmit to the committee the envelopes containing such reports.   Within a reasonable time after such recorded vote has been taken, the individual concerned shall be informed of the vote to examine and audit, and shall be advised of the nature and scope of such examination.   When any sealed envelope containing any such report is received by the committee, such envelope may be opened and the contents thereof may be examined only by members of the committee in executive session.   If, upon such examination, the committee determines that further consideration by the committee is warranted and is within the jurisdiction of the committee, it may make the contents of any such envelope available for any use by any member of the committee, or any member of the staff of the committee, which is required for the discharge of his official duties.   The committee may receive the papers as evidence, after giving to the individual concerned due notice and opportunity for hearing in a closed session. The Comptroller General shall report to the Select Committee on Standards and Conduct not later than the 1st day of June in each year the names of Senators, officers, and employees who have filed a report. Any paper which has been filed with the Comptroller General for longer than seven years, in accordance with the provisions of this section, shall be returned to the individual concerned or his legal representative. In the event of the death or termination of service of a Member of the Senate, an officer or employee, such papers shall be returned unopened to such individual, or to the surviving spouse or legal representative of such individual within one year of such death or termination of service.

[44.3] 3. Each Senator or person who has declared or otherwise made known his intention to seek nomination or election, or who has filed papers or petitions for nomination or election, or on whose behalf a declaration or nominating paper or petition has been made or filed, or who has otherwise, directly or indirectly, manifested his intention to seek nomination or election, pursuant to State law, to the office of United States Senator, and each officer or employee of the Senate who is compensated at a rate in excess of $15,000 a year, shall file with the Secretary of the Senate, before the 15th day of May in each year, the following reports of his personal financial interests:

    (a) the accounting required by rule XLII for all contributions received by him during the preceding year except that contributions in the aggregate amount of value of less than $50 received from any single source during the reporting period may be totaled without further itemization; and
    (b) the amount or value and source of each honorarium of $300 or more received by him during the preceding year.

[44.4] 4. All papers filed under section 3 of this rule shall be kept by the Secretary of the Senate for not less than three years and shall be made available promptly for public inspection and copying.

[44.5] 5. This rule shall take effect on July 1, 1968. No report shall be filed for any period before office or employment was held with the Senate, or during a period of office or employment with the Senate, of less than ninety days in a year except that the Senator, or officer or employee of the Senate, may file a copy of the return of taxes for the year 1968, or a report of substantially equivalent information for only the effective part of the year 1968.

GOVERNMENT EMPLOYEES--MILITARY

All members of the United States armed services are governed by the Code of Conduct for Members of the Armed Forces of the United States (also referred to as the U. S. Fighting Man's Code), a standard of conduct issued as an official publication by the United States Department of Defense for the use of personnel in all of the Military Services.

The Code, in its present written form, grew out of the Korean war, and was drawn up by a special advisory committee appointed by President Eisenhower to develop "guidelines for the professional conduct of the United States fighting man." This guide in its present written form was distributed as the official ethical code for members of the United States Armed Services by President Eisenhower's Executive Order 10631 (August 17, 1955). While this Code put conduct standards for the fighting man in specific form, the declarations of the conduct rules are old in the customs and traditions of American military service, as they have been followed for some two hundred years, dating back to the American Revolution, and have been "honored in all the wars this country has fought."

The Code of Conduct is a brief document, written in the form of a creed, with six Articles setting standards for conduct on the battlefield and in the prisoner of war compound (U. S. Department of Defense, DoD Directive No. 1300. 7, July 8, 1964).

> "Articles I and VI of the Code of Conduct are general statements affirming dedication to American security and devotion to American principles. Resistance is the keynote of Article II, which prescribes the behavior required on the battlefield. Articles III, IV, and V tell what is expected of the American fighting man who has the misfortune to be captured by the enemy."

There are more detailed conduct guides for military personnel in other government documents, including Uniform Code of Military Justice, military regulations, and rules of military courtesy, and in the "well established traditions and customs of each of the Services."

In addition to the conduct guides which apply to officers and enlisted men alike, there are principles of the officer's code--expressed in the Oath of Office, subscribed to by every individual upon accepting an officer's commission in any branch of the armed services. Where armed services officers are trained (at each of the United States military academies, and colleges and universities), the ethical code associated with the profession of arms forms part of instruction. Supporting and elaborating the standards for conduct of military personnel found in tradition, in law, and in the Oath of Office, each academy may give training in an informal and strict code of ethics:

> United States Military Academy, West Point--The Academy's motto, "Duty, Honor, Country," describes its "unwritten code." Details of ethical code and conduct are discussed in the text prepared by the Academy: Samuel H. Hays, Taking Command.

United States Naval Academy, Annapolis--Midshipmen at
Annapolis, as are officer trainees in the schools of other
branches of the armed services, are required to take an
oath upon entrance to the Academy and to execute a loyalty certificate (Annapolis, The United States Naval
Academy. Catalog). The Honor Concept of the Academy
gives general guidelines for conduct, and has served as
the model for the Honor Concept, a similar publication
of the Regiment of Midshipmen of the United States
Merchant Marine Academy, Kings Point, New York.
United States Air Force Academy, Colorado--The Code of
Ethics--other than conduct guides in the public law, ser-
vice regulations, and Oath of Office--is given in several
Academy publications, including: AFA Decorum Manual;
Ethics Manual, Air Force Cadet Wing Manual; and Honor
Reference Handbook, Air Force Cadet Wing.

The United States Coast Guard administers the Oath of Office
taken by a military officer upon receiving a commission, and also
an oath which is attested to by each individual upon receiving a
Coast Guard license as Merchant Marine Officer, a civilian license
in categories ranging from Chief (First) Mate to Third Assistant
Engineer. Violation of the oath by a Merchant Marine Officer may
(according to established procedure--United States Code, Revised
Statute 4450) result in the suspension or revocation of license.

Bibliography:
    Hays, Samuel H. Taking Command. Harrisburg, Pa., Stack-
        pole, 1967. 317 pages.
    Includes a description of the ethics of the armed services--
    Chapter III. Morality Aspects of Leadership; and the "U.S.
    Fighting Man's Code," p. 250-251.
    United States Air Force Academy. Decorum. Commandant of
        Cadets. USAFA. June 1971.
    Military customs and courtesies, and social etiquette.
    _____. The Ethics Manual. (Air Force Cadet Wing Manual,
        NR. 30-2). USAFA, March 1, 1965.
    Manual prescribing policy and procedures for the Cadet Pro-
    fessional Ethics Committee.
    United States Department of the Army. I Am an American
        Fighting Man. (Troop Topics, DA Pam 360-225). Sep-
        tember 1966. Washington, D.C., Department of the Army.
    History and application of the Code of Conduct.
    _____. Standards of Conduct, A Part of the Officer's Code
        (Officer's Call February 15, 1965, DA Pam 360-301).
    Washington, D.C. Department of the Army.
    Standards of behavior that apply with respect to the acceptance
    of gratuities.
    _____. Standards of Conduct for Department of the Army
        Personnel. (Army Regulations AR 600-50), with Changes).
    June 1966, and subsequent changes. Washington, D.C.,
    Department of the Army.

Regulations prescribing standards of conduct, relating to possible conflict between private interests and official duties, required of all Department of Defense personnel.

United States Department of Defense. Code of the U.S. Fighting Man. (DoD Gen-11; DA Pam 360-512; NAVPERS 92483A; AFP 34-10-10).

Includes Code text, with explanation of principles, and a statement of armed forces personnel standards of conduct.

———————. The U.S. Fighting Man's Code. (DoD Gen 28; DA Pam 360-522; NAVPERS 92538A; AFP 34-10-1; NAVMC 2512 (Rev-67). Washington, D.C. Government Printing Office, 1968. 92 pages.

The current explanation and application of the United States Armed Service Code.

"U.S. Fighting Man's Code"
"Code of Conduct for Members
of the Armed Forces of the United States"

I

I am an American fighting man. I serve in the forces which guard my country and our way of life. I am prepared to give my life in their defense.

II

I will never surrender of my own free will. If in command I will never surrender my men while they still have the means to resist.

III

If I am captured I will continue to resist by all means available. I will make every effort to escape and aid others to escape. I will accept neither parole nor special favors from the enemy.

IV

If I become a prisoner of war, I will keep faith with my fellow prisoners. I will give no information or take part in any action which might be harmful to my comrades. If I am senior, I will take command. If not, I will obey the lawful orders of those appointed over me and will back them up in every way.

V

When questioned, should I become a prisoner of war, I am bound to give only name, rank, service number, and date of birth. I will evade answering further questions to the utmost of my ability. I will make no oral or written statements disloyal to my country and its allies or harmful to their cause.

VI

I will never forget that I am an American fighting man, responsible for my actions, and dedicated to the principles which made my country free. I will trust in my God and in the United States of America.

[Department of Defense]
"Officer's Oath of Office"

"I, _____, do solemnly swear (or affirm) that I will
support and defend the Constitution of the United States against all
enemies, foreign and domestic; that I will bear true faith and allegiance to the same; that I take this obligation freely, without any
mental reservation or purpose of evasion; and that I will well and
faithfully discharge the duties of the office on which I am about to
enter. So help me God."

[U. S. Coast Guard]
"Merchant Marine Officer's Oath"

"I, _____, do solemnly (swear or affirm) that I am a
citizen of the United States and that I will faithfully and honestly,
according to my best skill and judgment, and without concealment
or reservation, perform all the duties required of me by the laws
of the United States as _____."

HEALTH PHYSICISTS

AMERICAN BOARD OF HEALTH PHYSICS (ABHP)
   Health Physics Department Bldg. 72
   Lawrence Berkeley Laboratory, Berkeley, Calif. 94720
   H. Wade Patterson, Chairman

Members: The American Board of Health Physics, formally founded
on October 29, 1959 as a certification board for health physicists,
includes in its purposes the establishment and encouragement of
"the highest standards of professional ethics and integrity in the
practice of health physics." The Board grants certificates to voluntary applicants to indicate completion of specified requirements of
study and professional experience in health physics, and the passing
of an examination designed to test competence in the field.

The seven members of the ABHP--five sponsored by the Health
Physics Society, one by the American Association of Physicists in
Medicine, and one by the American Public Health Association--con-
sider an applicant's total professional record when issuing a certificate in Health Physics, which qualifies the applicant as a health
physicist, and authorizes the use with his name of the professional
designation, "Certified Health Physicist" ("CHP").

Basic education and experience requirements for the Board
examination are:

Bachelor's Degree in a physical science or in a biological
science, with a minor in a physical science;
Six years of responsible professional experience in health
physics, at least three years of which must have been in
applied radiation protection work.
Substitution of experience may be allowed for the required academic
training, and graduate study and degree (MS, PhD, and ScD) may
be substituted, in part, for the required experience.

The examination--prepared, administered, and graded by an
Examination Panel of 16 Certified Health Physicists--is a written
test in two parts:
Part I.   Fundamental Aspects of health physics;
Part II.   Practical health physics topics.
In addition to this written examination, a candidate for certifica-
tion may be required to demonstrate his professional competence
through submission of written reports on radiation protection evalu-
ations, made or supervised by him, on installations or operations
involving possible radiation hazards, such as:
Radiographic installation--industrial or medical;
Fluoroscopic installation;
Therapy installation;
Radionuclide laboratory;
Air and water sampling and environmental survey;
Nuclear fuel processing plant;
Nuclear reactor;
Major decontamination operation;
Particle accelerator.

Code of Ethics: The professional conduct guide for Certified Health
Physicists is the ABHP statement of Professional Responsibilities of
Certified Health Physics, containing general principles of technical competence and professional integrity. Certificates may be
revoked for actions found by the Board in violation of these Professional Responsibilities.

Professional Insignia: The emblem of the Health Physics Society is

its seal--a triangle with curving sides
and blunted angles; with a centered
globe and several symbols representing
interests of the group, including an
atom nucleus; the name of the organization, "Health Physics Society," is
printed in a banding border, each word
on one side of the design, beginning
with the left side. The color of the
emblem is black on white, and it may
be shown in various other colors, as
red on yellow (publication).

Other Identification of Professional Status: As described above under
"Membership," the professional designation indicating competence

that is authorized for use with a Certified Health Physicist's name
is, "Certified Health Physicist" ("CHP").

Bibliography:
    American Board of Health Physics. American Board of Health
        Physics. Pamphlet. 7 pages.
    General requirements for certification, statement of Respon-
    sibilities of Certified Health Physicists, and history, pur-
    poses, and examinations administered through the Board.

"Professional Responsibilities of Certified Health Physicists"

    In achieving certification, the Certified Health Physicist
recognizes and assumes responsibilities due the profession of health
physics.
    In order to maintain his technical competence, the Certified
Health Physicist has a commitment to remain active in the field of
health physics and acquainted with the scientific, technical and regulatory developments in his field.
    In order to uphold the professional integrity of health physics
implied in this certification, his relations with others, including
clients, colleagues, governmental agencies, and the general public
shall always be based upon and reflect the highest standards of
professional ethics and integrity.
    The Certified Health Physicist shall represent himself as an
authority only in those areas in which he has extensive experience
and in which he is considered expert by his peers.

HEARING AID DEALERS

NATIONAL HEARING AID SOCIETY (NHAS)
    24261 Grand River Ave., Detroit, Mich. 48219
    Anthony Di Rocco, Executive Secretary

Membership: The National Hearing Aid Society, founded in 1951 and
with a present (1973) membership of approximately 3000, is a trade
association in the hearing aid field. Members, who are retail
"hearing aid dealer/consultants," may also be members of one of
the 46 state and provincial chapters in the United States and Canada
affiliated with the national organization. They are "engaged in the
testing of human hearing, and in the selection, adaptation, fitting,
and servicing of hearing aids." Since 1951, the NHAS has certified
the competence of members, engaged in the retail selling and fitting
of hearing aids, by issuing a Certificate as Hearing Aid Audiologist,
and granting use of the designation, "Certified Hearing Aid Audiologist," a title, which is not abbreviated.

Members qualify for certification if they have demonstrated their ability by:

(1) Education--Completion of the NHAS Basic Course in Hearing Aid Audiology, or equivalent approved course. This two-year basic course is available from NHAS for $48, and includes instructions in "acoustics, the human ear and hearing process, type of hearing disorders, audiometry, hearing analysis, and selection and fitting of hearing aids." Texts recommended for study in the Basic Course include: Newby, Hayes A., Audiology, N.Y., Appleton-Century, Crofts, 1972; Davis, Hallowell, Hearing and Deafness, N.Y., Holt, 1970; and Efram, Alexander, Sound, N.Y., John F. Rider, 1957.

(2) Experience--Two years' supervised experience in fitting hearing aids.

(3) Examination--Passing the NHAS Certification Examination, or equivalent examination.

The examination consists of a written test--true-false, multiple choice and essay questions--and may include a practicum.

Code of Ethics: The guide to acceptable conduct in the hearing aid retail business, sponsored by the National Hearing Aid Society, is the Code of Ethics of the Hearing Aid Industry, first adopted January 1, 1960, and most recently revised January 1, 1963. This Code, prepared by the NHAS National Committee on Ethics, in consultation with manufacturers of hearing aids and components and with hearing aid dealers in the United States and Canada, "details rules regulating guarantees and warranties, advertising, conduct of business, scientific claims, testimonials, disparagement, misrepresentation in general, and other business practices," of industry members of NHAS, and Certified Members.

The National Committee on Ethics interprets and recommends changes in the Code of Ethics (By-Laws, Article XII), and a National Grievance Committee enforces the provisions of the Code. Grievances--complaints of violations of the code of ethics--may be handled in local chapters, but may be considered by the National Grievance Committee, whose disciplinary action includes recording of its opinion on a substantiated complaint, reprimand, fine of up to $200, suspension or expulsion from membership (By-Laws, Article XIII).

Professional Insignia: The official emblem of the NHAS is its seal--circular in design with a centered symbol signifying "Hearing" (sound waves activating the three bones of the middle ear--malleus, incus, stapes, also referred to as the "hammer, anvil, and stirrup bones"--which in turn send vibrations through the fluid of the internal ear); the legend "Seal of Excellence" appears above ("Seal of") and below ("Excellence") the centered design; and the organization name, "National Hearing Aid Society," forms the upper unbanded border of the seal, which is completed at the bottom by

three stars. The color of
this insignia is shown variously on publications: black
on white; black on blue;
brown on white; green on
yellow.

Other Identification of Professional Status: A member
of the NHAS is authorized to
use the designation, "Member,
National Hearing Aid Society."
A Certified Member of NHAS,
as described above under
"Membership," is granted use
of the designation, "Certified
Hearing Aid Audiologist." Use of these designations is governed by
the rules in the Code of Ethics, and in the detailed instructions in
Proper Use of Society's Name and Title by Members (NHAS Policy
Statement No. 2, 1963).

Bibliography:
> Berger, Kenneth W. The Hearing Aid: Its Operation and De-
> velopment. Washington, D. C., National Hearing Aid
> Society. 1970. 212 pages. $11.85; paper $9.60.
> Textbook with "complete description of hearing aids, both
> past and present; list of manufacturers; hearing aid legisla-
> tion and codes; hearing aid battery numbers and signs."
>
> National Hearing Aid Society. Basic Course. $48.
> Techniques and methods used in fitting hea: ng aids.
>
> _____. By-Laws. Revised edition, October 30, 1970. 14
> pages.
> Membership requirements, certification, functions of National
> Committee on Ethics, procedures of National Grievance Com-
> mittee in enforcement of Code of Ethics.
>
> _____. Certification by the National Hearing Aid Society.
> 1971. Brochure.
> Purpose and requirements for certification.
>
> _____. Code of Ethics of the Hearing Aid Industry. Revised
> edition, 1963. 11 pages.
> Standards of conduct for industry and other members of NHAS.
>
> _____. How to Choose the Right Hearing Aid for You.
> Pamphlet. Revised 1971. 16 pages.
>
> _____. Proper Use of the Society's Name and Title by Mem-
> bers. (Policy Statement No. 2). Revised edition, April
> 5, 1963. Folder.
> Examples of acceptable use of membership and certification
> designation.
>
> _____. What Is the National Hearing Aid Society. Pamphlet.
> 1971.
> Describes NHAS membership, certification, code of ethics.

"Code of Ethics of the Hearing Aid Industry"

Preamble

So that we can best serve the hard of hearing, provide correction for their impairment, and contribute toward their participation in the world of sound and speech, we, in the hearing aid industry, including manufacturers, distributors, dealers and salesmen (hereafter referred to as "industry members"), pledge ourselves to observe this code of ethics:

(a)   All advertising and public announcements covering hearing aids and other industry products relating to performance, appearance, benefits, elements, and use will state only the true facts and will not, in any way, attempt to misrepresent our products or mislead the persons we seek to serve.

(b)   Industry members engaged in dispensing hearing aids are to provide thorough and ethical consulting services, including appropriate testing and proper fitting of a hearing aid that would be most suitable for the particular type of loss.

(c)   We shall, at all times, provide the best possible service to the hard of hearing, offering counsel, understanding, and technical assistance contributing toward their deriving the maximum benefit from their hearing aids.

(d)   We shall constantly engage in independent and combined research, cooperating whenever possible with medical and other professional individuals and societies to employ the maximum accumulation of scientific knowledge and technical skills in the manufacturing and fitting of hearing aids.

Specifically, we agree as follows:

I   Misrepresentation in General:

It is unethical for any industry member to use, or cause or promote the use of, any trade promotional literature, advertising matter, testimonial, guarantee, warranty, mark, insignia, depiction, brand, label, designation, or representation, however disseminated or published, which has the effect of misleading or deceiving purchasers or prospective purchasers:

(a)   with respect to the characteristics and terms of sales of its products;

(b)   with respect to any services offered or promised by such member in connection with its products;

(c)   with respect to limitations concerning the use or efficient application of its products.

II   Guarantees and Warranties:

It is unethical to use, or cause to be used, any guarantee or warranty which is false, misleading, deceptive, or unfair to the purchasing or consuming public, whether in respect to the quality, construction, serviceability, performance, or method of manufacture of any industry product, or the terms and conditions of refund of purchase price thereof, or in any other respect.

The foregoing inhibitions of this rule are to be considered as applicable with respect to any guarantee or warranty in which the terms and conditions relating to the obligation of the guarantor or warrantor are deceptively minimized or stated, or in which the obligations of the guarantor or warrantor are impractical of fulfillment; and is also applicable to the use of any guarantee or warranty in respect to which the guarantor or warrantor fails or refuses to observe scrupulously his obligations hereunder.

Any guarantee or warranty made by the dealer or vendor which is not backed up by the manufacturer must clearly state that the guarantee is offered by the dealer or vendor only.

III 'Bait' Advertising:

(a) It is unethical for any industry member to advertise a particular model or kind of hearing aid for sale when purchasers or prospective purchasers responding to such advertisements cannot have it demonstrated to them or cannot purchase the advertised model or kind from the industry member and the purpose of the advertisement is to obtain prospects for the sale of a different model or kind of hearing aid than that advertised;

(b) It is unethical to advertise or represent an installment sales contract as a lease or rental plan;

(c) It is unethical for an industry member to advertise or offer as an aid to hearing a device which has less than 18 decibels of amplification as averaged at 500, 1,000 and 2,000 cycles per second (as determined by HAIC standards);

(d) It is unethical when an industry member:
(1) uses in his advertising the name or trademark of a manufacturer in such a way as to imply a relationship which does not exist;
(2) uses in his advertising the name or trademark or model name of a manufacturer or displays on his premises the name or trademark of a manufacturer in such a way as to imply a relationship which does not exist, or whose products he neither has in stock nor has arranged to stock;
(3) advertises services and/or accessories in such a manner as to imply a relationship with a manufacturer that does not exist;
(4) in any other manner tries to benefit from the use of a trade name of an industry member when he is not authorized or legally entitled to do so.

(e) It is unethical when an industry member advertises a hearing aid utilizing bone conduction as having no cord, no tube, no ear mold, no buttons, or receivers without disclosing the instrument utilizes bone conduction;

(f)   It is unethical for an industry member to advertise that no buttons, wires, or cords are attached to an instrument unless there is disclosed in the same advertisement and in reasonable proximity to such statement the fact that a tube runs from the instrument to the ear, if such is the fact;

(g)   It shall be considered unethical for an industry member to use or cause, or promote any advertising material which shall show only a single part, accessory, or component of the hearing aid such as a battery on the finger, or a transistor held in the hand, where such has the effect of misleading or deceiving purchasers or prospective purchasers into believing that said parts are all that need be worn or carried, when such is not the fact.

IV   Earnings of Industry Members:

It is unethical for any industry member to make or publish, or cause to be made or published, any advertisement, offer, statement, or other form of representation which directly or by implication is false, misleading, or deceptive:

(a)   concerning the salary, commission, income, earnings, or other remuneration which industry members receive or may receive; or

(b)   concerning any conditions or contingencies affecting such remuneration or the opportunities therefor.

V   Character of Business:

It is unethical for any member of the industry to represent, directly or indirectly, through the use of any word of term in his corporate or trade name, in his advertising or otherwise, that he is a manufacturer of hearing aids, or of batteries or other parts or accessories therefor, or that he is the owner or operator of a factory or producing company manufacturing them, or that he owns or maintains an acoustical research laboratory devoted to hearing aid research or development, when such is not the fact, or in any other manner to misrepresent the character, extent, or type of his business.

VI   Medical, Professional and Scientific Claims:

(a)   It is unethical, in connection with the sale and offering for sale of industry products, for any industry members to represent or imply that the services or advice of a doctor have been used in the designing or manufacturing of an industry product, or will be used or made available in the selecting, testing, or adjusting of industry products to the individual needs of consumer-purchasers, when such is not the fact;

(b) The inhibitions of the above rule are applicable to the use of such terms as doctor, physician, otologist, specialist, audiologist, or certified hearing aid audiologist, and to any abbreviation of such terms, and are also applicable to the use of any symbol or depiction which connotes the medical profession;

(c) It is considered unethical to use terms in hearing aid advertising that have medical connotations, such as clinic, and so forth;

(d) Industry members must not use such terms as "Hearing Center," "Hearing Institute," "Hearing Bureau," "Hearing Clinic," and the like, that can cause confusion between a commercial hearing aid establishment and a governmental or non-profit medical, educational or research institution. "Hearing Center" is not acceptable although "Hearing Aid Center" is acceptable. Any public hearing aid center or medical clinic or practitioner which might undertake to sell hearing aids should identify its commercial interest plainly by the words "Hearing Aid Dealer."

(e) Industry members recognize the professional and non-commercial status of the physician, optometrist, clinical audiologist and other professional and scientific practitioners. There shall be no fee-splitting or kickbacks on referrals from the aforementioned groups.

(f) It is unethical for an industry member to advertise or offer as an aid to hearing, medicines, ear oils, drugs, vitamins, or remedies of any kind, or treatment, rehabilitation by machine, vibrations, sound "treatment," or surgery. Medicine and surgery are the province of the physician and may in no way be offered or advertised by industry members.

VII Visibility or Construction:

It is unethical to represent that any hearing aid or part thereof is concealed or unrecognizable as a hearing aid when worn by any user if, for practical purposes, such is not the fact.

VIII Novelty of Products:

It is unethical, in the sale, offering for sale, or distribution of industry products, to use any advertisement or other representation which misleads or deceives purchasers or prospective purchasers into the belief that any such product, or part or accessory thereof, is a new invention or involves a new mechanical or scientific principle, when such is not the fact.

IX Used or Rebuilt Products:

It is unethical for any industry member to represent, directly or indirectly, that any industry product or part thereof is new, unused, or rebuilt, when such is not the fact.

In the marketing of industry products which are second-hand or rebuilt, or which contain second-hand or rebuilt parts, is is unethical to fail to make full and nondeceptive disclosure in writing to the purchaser and by a conspicuous tag or label firmly attached to the product, and in all advertising and promotional literature relating thereto, of the fact--

(a)   that such products are second-hand, rebuilt, or contain second-hand or rebuilt parts, as the case may be, or

(b)   that the rebuilding of rebuilt products was done by other than the original manufacturer, when such is the case.

X   Tests, Acceptance, or Approval:

It is unethical, in the sale, distribution, or promotion of hearing aids, for any industry member--

(a)   to represent, or to use any seals, emblems, shields, or other insignia which represent or imply in any manner, that a hearing aid or other industry product has been tested, accepted, or approved by any individual, concern, organization, group, or association, unless such hearing aid has in fact been tested in such manner as reasonably to insure the quality and performance of the instrument in relation to the intended usage thereof and the fulfillment of any material claims made, implied, or intended to be supported by such representation or insignia; or

(b)   to represent that a hearing aid or other industry product tested, accepted, or approved by any individual, concern, organization, group, or association has been subjected to tests based on more severe standards of performance, workmanship, quality than is in fact true; or

(c)   to make any false, misleading or deceptive representation respecting the testing, acceptance, or approval of a hearing aid by any individual, concern, organization, group or association.

XI   Endorsement and Testimonials:

It is unethical for any industry member to advertise that a certain individual, organization, or institution:

(a)   endorses, uses or recommends his hearing aids or other industry products when such is not the case; or

(b)   personally wears his hearing aid when such is not the case.

XII   Disparagement:

(a)   It is unethical to defame industry members by falsely imputing to them dishonorable conduct, inability to perform contracts, questionable credit standing, or by other false representations, or the false disparagement of the products of competitors in any respect, or their business methods, selling prices, values, credit terms, policies, or services.

   (b)   It shall be considered unethical for an industry member to:

   (1)   display the products of his competitor in his window, shop or advertising in such manner as to convey a false comparison of the products, thereby resulting in a false disparagement of the competitor's product.   This shall not prevent him from displaying or advertising in such manner as to convey a true and accurate comparison of competitive products, and shall not prevent him from making specific or generalized truthful comparisons to point out the features and superiorities of his product;

   (2)   represent, without substantial and specific grounds for such representation, that competitors are unreliable whereas he himself is not;

   (3)   quote prices of competitive devices when such are not the true current prices, or to show, demonstrate or discuss competitive models as current models when such are not current models.

   (c)   It shall be considered unethical for an industry member to attempt to foster an unfavorable impression of a competitor with the medical profession, hearing societies, clinics, or public groups by falsely disparaging his motives, his methods, his products, and his prices with such groups.

HERALDS

THE HERALDRY SOCIETY
   25 Museum St. , London WC 1, England
   Mrs. Linda Biermann, Secretary

Membership: The Heraldry Society, first organized in 1947 under the title, The Society of Heraldic Antiquaries, has operated since 1950 under the present name.   Any person over 21 years of age, who is interested in heraldry, armory, chivalry, genealogy, and related subjects may apply for membership in the Society.   The category "Associate Member" is for applicants under 21 years of age.   The Society is international in scope, as it includes members in the United States, Canada, and other countries, as well as in England.

   To further the aims and objects of the organization--"the encouragement and extension of interest in and knowledge of heraldry" --an excellent heraldic library is maintained, courses and instruc-

tion are given in heraldry, and a number of publications are issued.
Also, certificates are awarded by the Society to candidates passing
examinations that are held annually.   The two types of certificates
granted are:
        Elementary Heraldry;
        Intermediate Heraldry.
These examinations are written and--as in the Elementary Heraldry
Test of 1971--consist of two sessions of two hours each, with
questions designed to test an applicant's knowledge of the terms of
heraldry, basic coats of arms, and blazoning and painting arms.
The examination requires ability to describe and illustrate elements
and terms of arms, and to complete coats of arms.

Code of Ethics: No code of ethics reported.

Professional Insignia: The Society's description of their arms
reads "The arms were designed by a special committee set up by
the Council of The Heraldry Society and may be blazoned thus:

The Heraldry Society.

Quarterly azure and gules a Lion's face crowned with an Ancient crown or within a tressure flory on the outer edge of the same, and for the Crest on a wreath or azure and gules a demi figure of a Knight in armour habited in a Tabard of the Arms his hands gauntleted proper the dexter holding the Hilt and the sinister resting on the Quillons of a sword point downward also proper hilt and pommel or on his head a Chapeau gules turned up ermine encircled by an Ancient crown gold, mantled azure and gules doubled or. Supporters. On either side an Unicorn sable armed unguled crined and tufted or wreathed about the neck with a torse argent and gules. Motto. 'Entalente A Parler d'Armes, ' may be translated, 'Able to speak of Arms. ' Badge. A lion's face crowned with an Ancient crown or within an annulet flory on the outer edge of the same.

"The Arms are intended to represent the essence of heraldry. They have about them the suggestion of the ancient Royal Arms, they contain the face of that most heraldic charge the lion, crowned with an ancient crown and the graceful single tressure flory, which has about it a suggestion of Scotland and contains perhaps the most beautiful charge in heraldry--the fleur-de-lys. Its continuous line is, of course, symbolic of the eternal unity of the Society. The knight with sword reversed and no helmet on his head symbolises chivalry and nobility of purpose. His tabard and armour are those worn in about 1484, the year in which the College of Arms was first incorporated. The supporters are taken from the crest of Mr. J. P. Brooke-Little, the founder of the Society, their red and gold collars being here replaced with a torse of the Duke of Norfolk's livery colours, his Grace being the first President of the Society: The motto is taken from a mediaeval poem 'Le Tournoi de Chauvency. ' The Badge is a reflection of the motif of the Arms. (Extract from The Coat of Arms, Vol. IV, No. 31, July 1957, the quarterly magazine of The Heraldry Society.)"

Bibliography:
    The Heraldry Society. The Heraldry Society. 4 pages.
    Informational brochure includes officers, aims, history,
    membership requirements; arms on cover.

HOME ECONOMISTS

AMERICAN HOME ECONOMICS ASSOCIATION (AHEA)
    2010 Massachusetts Ave. , N. W. , Washington, D. C. 20036
    Doris E. Hanson, Executive Director

Membership: The American Home Economics Association, founded in 1909 and with a present (1973) membership of approximately 50, 000--including 35, 000 members with bachelor's or advanced

Professional Ethics and Insignia

degrees in home economics, or one of its specialities, and 15,000
undergraduate students of home economics--is among the largest
professional associations in the United States.   Members of AHEA
are also members of the affiliated state home economics associations in the state where they practice.   The diverse activities of
members are shown in the variety of the eight professional sections
of the Association:

Colleges and Universities,   Business,
Research   Health and Welfare,
Elementary, Secondary and   Homemaking,
  Adult Education,   Students.
Extension,

The field of "Home Economics" is defined by the AHEA as:
"the field of knowledge and service primarily concerned
with strengthening the family life through educating the individual for family living, improving the goods and services
used by families, conducting research to discover changing
needs of individuals and families and means of satisfying
these needs, furthering community, national, and world conditions favorable to family living."

Code of Ethics: No formal code of ethics has been developed by
the American Home Economics Association.

Professional Insignia: The emblem of the AHEA is the Betty
Lamp--a light source of great antiquity, identified in this country

with pioneer settlers before
and after the American Revolution.   This insignia was designed by Mildred Chamberlain,
a member of the Association,
and adopted in 1926.   The design symbolizes "the application
of science to the improvement
of the home."   The emblem is
shown in the official academic
color of home economics--
maroon--and in the AHEA
colors--maroon and gold--and
also appears in other colors.
The emblem is on the
official seal of the organization,
and is available for display and
wear by members as jewelry (including pin, charm bracelet, neck-
lace, and plaque), and as a logotype--where it is bordered in
rounded-corner square, with the legend of the group's name,
"American Home Economics Association," and founding date, "Est.
1909," forming the border.

Bibliography:
American Home Economics Association.   AHEA Policy Handbook.   1970. $2.

Procedural guidelines, including description of official emblem and seal, and restrictions of use.
_____. Fact Sheet. Fall 1971. 1 sheet.
Brief statement of AHEA membership requirements, purposes, programs.

HOSPITAL ADMINISTRATORS

AMERICAN COLLEGE OF HOSPITAL ADMINISTRATORS (ACHA)
   840 N. Lake Shore Dr., Chicago, Ill. 60611
   Richard J. Stull, FACHA, Executive Vice President

Membership: The American College of Hospital Administrators,
founded in 1933 and with a present (1973) membership of approximately 9000, is a professional society in the field of "hospital and
health care service and administration." In addition to the special
memberships ("Student Associate," and "Honorary Fellowship"),
there are three categories of ACHA membership:
   Affiliates--admitted formally as "Nominees," who advance to
      "Membership" by successfully completing prescribed writ-
      ten and oral examinations;
   Members--who advance, in turn, to Fellowship by successfully
      completing certain project requirements "indicative of a
      basic standard of excellence in hospital administration."

Education and experience requirements for these three types of
membership in the College are:
   Nomineeship: Bachelor's degree and three years' responsible
      hospital administrative experience, OR Master's degree in
      health-care administration;
   Membership: Three years as Nominee, while maintaining "a
      responsible administrative position in hospital or related
      health activity," and passing prescribed oral and written
      examinations administered by ACHA;
   Fellowship: Six years as Member, while participating in
      programs of continuing education, and completion of a
      special project, such as a thesis, or four case reports--
      evidencing "service to the hospital field beyond the ordinary
      demands" of hospital administrator.
As an indication of highest professional competence, "Fellows may
use the designation 'FACHA' following their names upon official
stationery, articles for publication, and upon other appropriate occasions."

Code of Ethics: The Code of Ethics for Hospital Administrators,
prepared by a special committee of 12 representatives of the
American Hospital Association and the American College of Hospital

Administrators, as a guide for "both personal and professional conduct," outlines "hospital ethics, principles of conduct for hospital administrators, and administrative principles of the hospital administrator in his professional relations." First adopted in 1941, the Code has been revised several times (1956, 1965), with the latest revision adopted in 1971. The Code of Ethics applies, as a guideline for self-discipline, to those "members of the administrative staff who have responsibility and authority in maintaining and administering health care programs, including chief executive officer, assistant administrators, administrative assistants, and other administrative personnel."

The Code is enforced and interpreted by the Committee on Ethics, which investigates charges of unprofessional conduct brought to the attention of the Director of Membership, holds hearings as required, and determines disciplinary action, which may include expulsion from College membership.

Other Guides to Professional Conduct: Upon admission to each of the three types of ACHA membership described above, the candidate repeats a pledge in which he "solemnly dedicates" himself to basic professional principles appropriate to the category of membership:

     Pledge of Nomineeship;
     Pledge of Membership;
     Pledge of Fellowship.

Professional Insignia: The official emblems of the ACHA are the College Key--which may be worn by Fellows and Members--and the

College Seal. The emblem on both these insignia--designed by J. Dewey Lutes, former Director General of the College--was adopted in 1933. The design is circular, with a centered inner circle bearing a rising sun in the background with a lamp of knowledge resting upon two books in the foreground, symbolizing "education, learning, and enlightenment"; a chevron shown in back of books and lamp, and extending from the center of the inner design to the bottom, depicts "service"; a caduceus above the lamp, divides the central circle vertically, and indicates "healing or medicine"; and a cross at the bottom of the bordering band, signifies "nursing." The name of the organization, "American College of Hospital Administrators," is spaced around the design within the bordering band.

Other Designations of Professional Competence: Fellows, as indicated above under "Membership," may use the professional designation, "F. A. C. H. A."

Bibliography:
    American College of Hospital Administrators.   ACHA ... A
        Brief Description. Brochure.
    ACHA history, types of membership, objectives and
    activities.
        _____ . Code of Ethics for Hospital Administrators.   1971
        edition.   6 pages. $. 20.
    Hospital administrative personnel professional conduct guide,
    with general principles, and obligations and functions in re-
    lationships with patients, fellow workers, vendors.

"Principles of Conduct for Hospital Administrators"

The life of the hospital administrator is dedicated to the
achievement of the highest possible level of performance in the
competent and humane delivery of health services, and in education
and research conducted in the interests of health care.   In pursuing
this objective the administrator shall be guided by the following
principles:

1.   Conduct himself at all times in a dignified exemplary
manner.

2.   Be objective, understanding, and fair in his professional
performance and relationships.

3.   Avoid use of his position or influence for selfish personal advantage or gain.

4.   Not seek to displace another administrator.

5.   Not denigrate the work of his colleagues.

6.   Encourage, assist, and teach others in the principles and
practice of health care administration.

7.   Foster and support sound programs of recruitment and
education to assure manpower for existing and emerging health service programs.

8.   Contribute his interest, support, and leadership toward
the general improvement of the community, with special emphasis
on delivery of health care, health education, and related objectives.

9.   Support endeavors which are constructive and in the interests of quality and efficiency in professional practice by all participants in the field of health services.

10.   Continually strive to improve his professional skills
and knowledge.

11.   Respect and protect the rights, privileges, and beliefs
of others under his position of public trust.

In the health services field, acceptance and continuity of the
system for providing care depends upon the public's confidence in
the system's capacity and in the integrity and impartiality of its
administration.

This demands performance in compliance with an established
code of professional conduct governing administrative efforts for
public benefit and relationships with the multiple vested interest

groups involved in the overall provision of health services.

To guide the administrator in his endeavors to maintain the public's trust and to assist him in his working contacts with others, the following guidelines for administrative conduct, with interpretations, have been developed as indices of the performance criteria set forth in the Code of Ethics.

A. Obligations and Functions.

The administrator, as the chief executive officer, is responsible for the effective management of the organization. Because of this, his personal and public conduct cannot be divorced from the reputation of the organization he directs. Further, he shall be concerned with and participate in programs for his own professional growth and development. For that reason he shall:

Administer the organization so that it promotes the full confidence and active support of the community it serves; generates the loyalty and trust of allied professions; allies itself with scientific advancement and education; and fulfills its rightful place among the health forces of the community.

Conduct himself at all times in a manner befitting the dignity and responsibility of his office.

Improve and increase continually his knowledge of health care administration and executive skills to enhance his effectiveness and broaden his potential for leadership in the health field.

B. The Administrator and Patients

The welfare of patients is the primary concern of the health care system. Toward implementing this responsibility, the administrator shall:

Provide the best possible patient care within the resources available, and accommodate reasonable requests of patients, including the opportunity for their observance of religious practices.

Safeguard confidential information about patients and impress upon others respect for the patient's essential right of privacy.

Encourage and support research and education insofar as they are compatible with the provision of quality patient care.

C. The Administrator and the Public

As a vital resource person having special skills and knowledge in planning and managing for health services, an understanding of health needs and a sense of appreciation of the need to mesh his organization with other community health services, the administrator can impart professional leadership to community endeavors, both within and without the health services field. To make his talents available for this purpose he shall:

Participate in and provide leadership for activities contributing

to community betterment, especially those directed toward meeting
health needs.

Cultivate reasonable opportunities for favorable public relations throughout the community served by his organization.

Interpret the work of the organization in a dignified, ethical,
non-competitive manner and avoid personal aggrandizement in public
speaking, in submitting information to the press, or in broadcasting
over radio and television.

D.   The Administrator and the Governing Body

Effectiveness in administrative performance depends on mutual respect and harmonious relationships between the administrator
and the governing authority.   Such accord can be maintained best
when the functions and prerogatives of each are carefully defined,
understood, and followed.   As the chief executive officer, the administrator, in the fulfillment of his obligations, shall:

Exercise the necessary authority assigned in his responsibility for the administration of the overall organization in all of its
various activities and operating units, in accordance with policies
adopted by the governing authority.

Manifest his personal integrity and high professional standards
with capable leadership which will command confidence and respect.

Consider the interests of the organization and its community
relations in all matters affecting the conditions of his employment.

E.   The Administrator and the Medical Staff

In organizations having a medical staff, the administrator
shall foster effective channels of communication among the governing board, the medical staff, and administration.   To effect this,
he shall:

Provide coordinative effort, support and understanding in
assisting the medical staff to fulfill its role in the organization.

Enforce, through appropriate channels, the policies established for the welfare of patients and the continued effectiveness of
the organization.

Be considerate and helpful to members of the medical profession in the community who are not members of the medical
staff; and encourage them to participate in hospital activities for
continuing education within guidelines determined by the medical
staff.

F.   The Administrator and Personnel

To ensure the most effective utilization of the talents and
services of professional and supportive personnel, and a high degree
of self-fulfillment for each individual, the administrator shall be
responsible for enlightened personnel practices.   To accomplish
this, the administrator shall:

Be interested in developing skills at all levels so that these persons may achieve their highest potential of leadership, initiative, and contribution to the total program of the organization.

G.   The Administrator and Vendors

The administrator shall maintain impartiality in his relationships with representatives of commercial organizations. To achieve this, he shall:

Avoid being obligated to a commercial firm or its representative by accepting gifts, social favors, or through any other practice that might be suspect.

Not accept personal commissions, rebates, or gifts which might imply an obligation.

Not solicit contributions to his organization on the promise of granting special business favors or on the threat of withholding future purchases.

H.   The Administrator and Other Administrators

The administrator shall maintain a spirit of cooperation with representatives of other health care organizations, since there is a sharing of a common objective: the delivery of health services. Therefore, he shall:

Assist other administrators and their organizations through participation in activities and services which will improve the quality of health care services and programs, and enhance the effectiveness and economy of the health care system.

I.   The Administrator and Conflict of Interest

The administrator shall so conduct his personal and professional relationships as to assure himself, his organization, and the community that he may make decisions for the best interest of the organization without impairment. To maintain his integrity and avoid criticism or suspicion, he shall:

Engage in no outside employment or activities that might impair his effectiveness as the executive of his organization.

Permit no commercial exploitation of his position.

Shun inconsistent duties or activities and avoid becoming involved in any investment which might in any way interfere with the expeditious and proper administration of his organization.

Make readily available to his governing authority, if requested, a statement of his holdings, interests, or investments which might possibly be interpreted as a conflict of interest in the administration of his health services organization.

"Pledge of Nomineeship"

In accepting Nomineeship in the American College of Hospital Administrators, I solemnly dedicate myself:

> To contribute to the advancement of the profession by conscientious endeavor in the performance of my administrative duties;
>
> To participate in the opportunities afforded for education in hospital administration; and
>
> To support the objectives of the American College of Hospital Administrators.

"Pledge of Membership"

In accepting Membership in the American College of Hospital Administrators, I solemnly dedicate myself:

> To serve my community by efficient and cooperative administration of my hospital;
>
> To assist in the educational program for hospital administrators; and
>
> To uphold and further the objectives of the American College of Hospital Administrators.

"Pledge of Fellowship"

In accepting Fellowship in the American College of Hospital Administrators, I solemnly dedicate myself:

> To administer my hospital in the best interest of the patient, the physician, and the community;
>
> To contribute to the advancement of honest and competent hospital administration;
>
> To promote diligently the education of hospital administrators; and
>
> To further faithfully the objectives of the American College of Hospital Administrators.

HYPNOTISTS

SOCIETY FOR CLINICAL AND EXPERIMENTAL HYPNOSIS, INC. (SCEH)
> 140 West End Ave., New York, N.Y. 10023
> Marion Kenn, Administrative Secretary

Membership: The Society for Clinical and Experimental Hypnosis, founded in 1949 and with a present (1973) membership of 650, is

an organization of professionals in medicine, psychiatry, psychology
and dentistry who have had special training and experience in hypnosis. The requirements for SCEH membership are:

> Associate Member--Doctor's degree in medicine (including
> psychiatry), dentistry, or psychology, and completion of
> an acceptable initial course in hypnotic techniques and
> active utilization of hypnosis in clinical practice or re-
> search.
>
> Full Member--In addition to the education and experience
> qualifications for Associate Member, two more years of
> acceptable experience in research or clinical uses of hyp-
> nosis, and publication of a scientific paper in the field.
>
> Fellow--Elevation to Fellowship in SCEH is made by the
> designation and recommendation of the Executive Council.
>
> Student Affiliate--Students in pursuit of their doctorates
> (Ph. D. or Ed. D. in Psychology), or who are serving
> either internship or residency.

As a result of the publication requirements for Full Membership,
"at least three-fourths of all English-language publications in the
field of scientific hypnosis appearing in the past decade have been
written by members of SCEH. "

To provide recognition of professional competence of physicians,
dentists, and psychologists whose background and training enable
them to provide expert skills in using hypnosis, the American
Board of Clinical Hypnosis was created in 1958. This Board
established three sub-boards for accreditation in each modality;

> American Board of Medical Hypnosis
> 67 Chestnut Street
> Lewistown, Pa. 17044
> Milton Cohen, M. C. , Secretary
>
> American Board of Hypnosis in Dentistry
> 200 Central Park South
> New York, N. Y.   10019
> George D. Roston, D. D. S. , Secretary
>
> American Board of Psychological Hypnosis
> (formerly American Board of Examiners in Psychological
> Hypnosis)
> Peter B. Field, Ph. D. , Secretary

These three Boards, operating autonomously and independently
from the SCEH, award certificates or diplomas to qualified candi-
dates--already certified by their own professions as competent
clinicians or scientists--who have "demonstrated ability to use hyp-
notic techniques with a high level of proficiency, " as "an adjunctive
skill in the practice of the professions of medicine, dentistry, or
psychology. "

> The American Board of Medical Hypnosis awards certificates
> when physicians either have a diploma from a medical
> specialty board or are an active member of the American
> Academy of Family Practice; have had a minimum of
> seven years "substantial experience in the clinical use of

hypnosis"; and satisfactorily complete written and oral
examinations.

The American Board of Hypnosis in Dentistry awards certificates to dentists who have had a minimum of seven
years of substantial experience in the clinical use of hypnosis as it pertains to dentistry; and satisfactorily complete an oral examination, and submit several typical case
histories, explaining techniques used, in problems that
were treated with hypnosis.

The American Board of Psychological Hypnosis issues diplomas in clinical Hypnosis and in Experimental Hypnosis.
By agreement with the American Psychological Association,
requirements for these diplomas are:

Clinical Hypnosis: Psychologists who hold ABPP
(American Board of Professional Psychology) diplomas, have five years of "creditable experience in
the clinical uses of hypnosis," and pass prescribed
oral examinations.

Experimental Hypnosis: Psychologists who have had five
years of creditable experience in experimental uses
of hypnosis, plus research publication, and pass a
prescribed oral examination.

Since 1961, Diplomates of the ABPH have been indicated
as qualified in hypnosis in the Directory of the American
Psychological Association.

Code of Ethics: The SCEH guide to professional conduct is its
Code of Ethics, developed by a Committee of the Society. This
Code is directed to establishing and maintaining high standards for
responsible professionals who use hypnosis as one of the techniques
in practicing their profession. Four ethical principles directed to
the use of hypnosis as a professional tool and not as an entertainment are set forth in Section A of the code of ethics, while Section
B outlines procedures to be followed in the event of Violations of
Ethical Principles. These procedures expand the enforcement process and disciplinary action in the Society Bylaws (Article XIV).
Charges of unprofessional conduct are submitted in writing to the
Executive Council of the SCEH. This Council may discipline a member, based on investigation and hearing conducted by the Committee
on Ethics, by censure, suspension, or expulsion from membership.

Professional Insignia: The SCEH has adopted no official emblem.

Other Identification of Professional Status: The professional designations awarded by the specialty certifying Boards--described above
under "Membership"--indicate professional competence in the technique of hyponsis:

Physicians: Diplomate--ABMH,
Dentists: Diplomate--ABHD,
Psychologists: Diplomate--ABPH.

Bibliography:
      Society for Clinical and Experimental Hypnosis.   Bylaws; Con-
         stitution.   As amended March 1971.
      Enforcement of the Code of Ethics is provided for in Article
      XIV: Problems of Ethics.
      _____.   Code of Ethics.   September 1964.   7 pages.
      Includes broad ethical guides, and details of procedure in
      enforcement of the code.
      _____.   Society for Clinical and Experimental Hypnosis.   6
         pages.
      Informational brochure giving SCEH history, purposes, and
      structure.

"Code of Ethics"

The Society for Clinical and Experimental Hypnosis is dedicated to the clinic and scientific utilization of hypnosis at the highest professional level.   The history of hypnosis and its use call
for some basic principles to maintain high standards for responsible
professional workers.   In addition, the multi-disciplinary character
of the professional membership of SCEH requires an explicit statement of the ethical guidelines to which a member of the Society is
required to subscribe and for whose observance he is responsible.

Section A: Ethical Principles
Principle I

A member of SCEH shall be a member in good standing of
the recognized professional organization in his field (e.g. AMA,
ADA, APA, et al.).
      I-1.   If a member is not affiliated with his professional
organization, he may be requested to obtain such membership or
to show cause as to why he should not meet this requirement.
      I-2.   Item I-1 requires acceptance of the ethical and scien-
tific standards of a responsible professional organization.   It does
not imply endorsement by SCEH of particular policies or practices
of any particular organization.

Principle II

Each member of SCEH shall limit his clinical and scientific
use of hypnosis to the area of his competence as defined by the
professional standards of his field.
      II-1.   Professional training, qualifications, and competence,
as defined by the member's professional organization and his own
achievements in his professional field shall guide the member's
practices within his area.
      II-2.   A member who encounters a problem in the use of
hypnosis shall seek the help of qualified specialists, competent to
deal with the problem.
      II-2-a.   This help may be obtained either by consultation with

the specialist, or by referral of his patient to the specialist.

II-3.   A member may seek to broaden the usefulness of hypnosis in his professional field in the interest of his individual patients as well as in the interests of extending the professional and scientific knowledge of hypnosis.

II-3-a.   Such extension of the use of hypnosis must be carried out with all appropriate safeguards as specified in IV.

Principle III

The clinical and scientific utilization of hypnosis is an important contribution to mankind's health.   It should not be used as a source of entertainment.

III-1.   No member of SCEH shall offer his services for the purpose of public entertainment or collaborate with any person or agency engaged in public entertainment.   He shall not cooperate with or participate in lectures, demonstrations or publications of lay or stage hypnotists.   He shall not give courses in hypnosis to lay people.

III-1-a.   A lay person is defined as one who is not a member in good standing of a recognized therapeutic or scientific profession: a person whose sole qualification is in the use of hypnosis for entertainment, treatment or research is a lay person within the meaning of the Code.

III-1-b.   Paragraph III-1 shall not apply to the advising and consultative function which a member, acting as a representative of SCEH, shall perform towards the mass media in order to minimize distortions, misrepresentations, etc., and in order to assure the accurate presentation of clinical and scientific material and knowledge.

III-2.   Each member when dealing with the subject of hypnosis in any form shall observe the professional standards of his own professional society with respect to advertising, promotion and display of his service, in addition to the standards as set forth under this Code.

III-2-a.   No member of SCEH shall offer his professional use of hypnosis via newspapers, radio, television or similar media.

III-2-b.   In the announcement of his services to the profession, statements of membership in SCEH, the American Boards of Hypnosis, and similar accredited affiliations, are appropriate when presented with accuracy and dignity along with his other professional credentials.

III-2-c.   Each member makes a statement or writes an article for publication in the lay press or appears on radio, T.V. or similar media, he shall behave in conformity with the requirements of his own professional society and with the provisions of the Code of Ethics of SCEH.   If in doubt, he shall consult beforehand with the Committee on Ethics of SCEH.

III-2-d.   Each member shall be responsible, within the limit of his possibilities for statements made by other agencies such as book publishers, drug manufacturing firms, etc., which deal with his creative products (e.g. book, film, publications), and shall use his influence and prestige to avoid exaggerations or false statements about hypnosis.

Principle IV

A member of SCEH shall make clinical and scientific use of hypnosis if it contributes to the welfare of the patient and/or to the advancement of professional knowledge in his field.

IV-1. The standards of professional relationships which guide the physician, dentist, or psychologist within his professional field shall prevail in his use of all special therapeutic techniques.

IV-2. Research investigations utilizing hypnosis shall maintain the strongest safeguards for the well-being of the subject.

IV-2-a. Proper safeguards shall be maintained whenever a human subject is exposed to stress. The problem should be of sufficient importance to justify such a procedure; and adequate facilities during and after the procedure should be available to assure the well-being of the subject. When there is doubt as to the appropriateness of the stress exposure, the member shall consult with one or more colleagues or specialists or with the Committee on Ethics before undertaking the procedure.

Section B: Violations of Ethical Principles

Procedure to be followed:

1. Any person, whether a member or not of SCEH, may initiate a charge of ethical violation.

a. A non-professional individual may also initiate a charge through the offices of a professionally qualified person.

2. The charge must be submitted, in writing, to the Executive Council of SCEH. It must be specific as to time, place, person and event; it must be signed by the complainant, with the address and professional identification.

3. The Executive Council may refer the complaint to the Committee on Ethics for investigation, and ask the Committee to report back at a specific time.

a. The Ethics Committee's preliminary investigation may lead to a report either that the complaint does not merit further attention, or that it merits further exploration.

b. The Executive Council may accordingly dismiss the complaint and order that all reference to it be deleted from the records or direct that a notation about it be made in the minutes of the Executive Council. If it does not dismiss the complaint, it must direct the Ethics Committee to make a full review of the charges.

4. When directed by the Executive Council to make a full review of the charges, the Ethics Committee shall:

a. In writing, inform the member who has been charged with an ethical violation, of the complaint and the specific charges upon which the complaint is made; and solicit the member's response to the charges in question.

b. Appoint a sub-committee to hold a hearing. Neither

the charged member nor the complainant may act as members
of the sub-committee concerned with the particular complaint.

    c.   Set a time for a hearing and advise the member and
the complainant by written notice, sent by certified mail at
least ten (10) days in advance, of the hearing. The hearing
must be held within sixty (60) days after the Executive Council
has directed the Committee on Ethics to proceed with the hearing, except in cases of extreme hardship. In such a case sufficient and convincing proof must be submitted with the request
for postponement.

    5.   The Ethics Committee Hearing shall be conducted in a
spirit of professional inquiry, directed toward obtaining as accurate
a statement of the facts as possible.

    a.   The member shall have the privilege of appearing in
person to defend himself, or of being represented by someone
of his choice, or he may present a written defense. If the
choice is a written defense, then this document must be available to the sub-committee of the Committee on Ethics at least
one day before the date set for the hearing.

    b.   The charged member shall have the right, at said
hearing, to cross examine the person or persons who have
initiated the complaint and any witnesses who may appear
against him. He shall also have the right to present witnesses.

    c.   The complainant shall not have the right of direct
examination. He shall be able to direct his questions only
through the sub-committee members.

    d.   A full record shall be made by a stenographer or
recording device and a transcript made of the proceedings.
The charged member shall be provided with a copy of the
transcript at cost, or without charge. The question as to
whether the transcript shall be provided at cost or without
charge shall be decided by the Executive Council.

    e.   The Committee on Ethics shall submit its report and
recommendations to the Executive Council, no later than sixty
(60) days following the hearing. Their recommendations may
be, (1) dismissal of charges because of insufficient evidence or
unsubstantiated evidence; (2) censure or warning; (3) suspension
of member for a period of up to one (1) year; (4) and order
that the member submit his resignation and in the event that he
fails or refuses to do so, that he be expelled from SCEH; (5) expulsion of member.

    6.   The Executive Council shall review the findings and
recommendations of the Committee on Ethics and reach a decision.

    a.   If the decision is for censure or warning, this may
be a matter for Executive Council record alone or the Executive
Council may decide to inform the membership of SCEH as in 6b.

    b.   If the decision is for suspension, resignation or expul-
sion, then each member of SCEH shall be individually informed
of the action of the Executive Council in the next regular mailing
which is distributed to all members of SCEH, as a privileged

communication, available only to them as members.

    c. A member found guilty of the charges brought against him or any part thereof, shall have the right to appeal to the Executive Council, which shall review such appeal as soon as is feasible following its receipt. Such notice of appeal must be submitted in writing within sixty (60) days after the decision has been communicated and if not submitted by the member within such a period of time, the right of appeal shall be lost.

    d. A member found guilty of violation of any of the ethical principles adopted and subscribed to by all members of the SCEH shall be advised in writing of his right to appeal.

INDUSTRIAL TRAFFIC MANAGERS

AMERICAN SOCIETY OF TRAFFIC AND TRANSPORTATION (ASTT)
547 W. Jackson Blvd., Chicago, Ill. 60606
Charles C. Glasgow, CM, Executive Director

<u>Membership</u>: The American Society of Traffic and Transportation, founded in 1946 and with a current (1973) membership of about 3500, is a professional association of workers in traffic and transportation management. Three categories of membership--in addition to Founder, Sustaining, and Member Emeritus--with their required education and experience are:

    <u>Certified Member</u>--Completion of two years' education in an accredited college, or five years' "increasingly responsible traffic and transportation experience," and passing four written examinations and write an original research paper in traffic and transportation management.

    <u>Educator Member</u>--A terminal degree (such as Ph.D., D.B.A.), and actively engaged in teaching in traffic and transportation, or a related area or discipline.

    <u>Associate Member</u>--Candidates for "Certified Member," who have met one or more of the requirements of passing four examinations and the writing of an original research paper.

The required research paper must be on a special aspect of traffic transportation or distribution management, must be original, documented, and from 3000 to 5000 words in length.

The four written examinations that a candidate for "Certified Member" must pass are four hours each in length, and in the subjects of:
1. Economics of Transporation,
2. Traffic Transportation and Physical Distribution Management,
3. Management Tools and Concepts,
4. Transportation Law and Regulation.

Waivers of the four required tests may be granted for--
  Tests 1, 2, and 3--Completion of two or more years' course
    work at an accredited college or recognized vocational
    school in specific courses:
  Test 1--One year sophomore economics; one course in
    Economics of Transportation; two or more courses in
    Applied Economics and Business (i.e., managerial labor
    economics, foreign trade, international business, or closely
    related areas).
  Test 2--One course in fundamentals of traffic management and
    two or more courses in physical distribution, logistics,
    channels of distribution, or closely related areas.
  Test 3--One course in at least seven of the following eight
    fields: Accounting, Business Law, Corporate Finance,
    Money and Banking, Principles of Management, Principles
    of Marketing, Basic Statistics, and Government.

Code of Ethics: The ASTT guide to professional conduct is its Code
of Ethics which gives six principles of conduct to be observed by
members, including use of the designation "Certified Member," and
other membership designations authorized by the ASTT, use of the
title "Traffic Manager," and relations with colleagues, employers,
and the public. No enforcement procedures for the Code are reported.

Professional Insignia: The emblem of the American Society of
Traffic and Transportation is
its logotype--two crossed lines
terminating in arrows (symbolizing the four directions of
the compass in traffic and
transportation, and physical
distribution management movement of the goods of com-
merce); with one of the initials of the Society monogram,
"ASTT," in each angle of the

crossed-direction lines, reading clockwise from the upper left-hand
corner. The motto of the Society is "Toward Excellence in Traffic,
Transportation and Physical Distribution Management."

Other Identification of Professional Status: The ASTT authorizes use
of the designation, "Certified Member" ("CM"), as indicated above
under "Membership," as well as other designations denoting membership category (as, "Founder," "Sustaining"). The authorized designation may be used with a member's name, or worn on official
insignia jewelry--octagonal seal of the Society, with the appropriate
member initial, as "CM," at the center--including lapel emblem,
cuff links, tie bar, tie tac. Jewelry is gold with the imprint in
black enamel.

Bibliography:
   American Society of Traffic and Transportation.   Code of Ethics.
      1 leaf.
   The six principles of ASTT ethics, with the Society Motto.
                  .   Professional Examinations for Certified Membership.
         1972-1974.   79 pages.
   Describes the examination program, with eligibility requirements, waivers, enrollment and examination procedure,
   preparation for the examinations, including local study groups,
   lists of suggested textbooks and study materials, with "Guidelines for Study" for each of the four examinations, and "Selected Examination Questions and Answers. "

"Code of Ethics"

One.   A person holding membership in the Society, by virtue of having successfully met all of its examination requirements,
may describe himself as a "Certified Member--American Society of
Traffic and Transportation. " A person holding membership in the
Society, by virtue of having qualified under the Founder's requirement, may describe himself as a "Founder Member--American
Society of Traffic and Transportation. "   A person holding membership in the Society, by virtue of having qualified under the Sustaining requirements, may describe himself as a "Sustaining Member--
American Society of Traffic and Transportation. "   A person holding
membership in the Society, by virtue of having qualified under the
Educator requirements, may describe himself as an "Educator
Member"--American Society of Traffic and Transportation. "   A
person holding membership in the Society, by virtue of having qualified under the Associate requirements, may describe himself as
an "Associate Member--American Society of Traffic and Transportation. "   A person who has qualified in any of the above categories
and who has retired from active pursuit of his profession shall be
entitled to describe himself as a "Member Emeritus--American
Society of Traffic and Transportation. "

Two.   A person holding membership in the Society shall
strictly observe any law or laws regarding the use and application
of the title "Traffic Manager, " or other similar designations, which
may be in effect in the particular state or states in which such
member resides, is employed, or engaged in practice.

Three.   The conduct of those holding membership in this
Society with each other and before the public generally should be
characterized by candor and fairness, and should be such as to
uphold at all times the honor of their calling and to maintain the
dignity of their profession.

Four.   A person holding membership in the Society shall
consider and hold confidential all information imparted to him in
the course of his employment, and shall not disclose same except

upon authority of the client or clients to which such information properly belongs, or when required to do so by a mandate of law.

Five. No one holding membership in the Society shall undertake to render professional services under any circumstances or upon any terms that would jeopardize the good name of the profession or impair the standing of any other person.

Six. Those holding membership in the Society are hereby deemed responsible for the professional conduct of persons in their employ. Consequently, they should, through exemplary conduct on their own part, strive at all times to secure observance by their employees of this code of ethics.

INSURANCE AGENTS AND BROKERS

NATIONAL ASSOCIATION OF INSURANCE AGENTS, INC. (NAIA)
    85 John St., New York, N.Y. 10038
    Arthur Blum, Executive Vice President

Membership: The National Association of Insurance Agents, founded in 1896 and with a current (1973) membership of over 31,000 insurance agencies--representing approximately 150,000 individual insurance agents--is one of the ten largest trade associations in the United States. The NAIA is a federation of state associations of insurance agents.

Code of Ethics: The Association Code of Ethics, providing a conduct guide for members, was adopted in 1929. This Code contains in credo or pledge form the rules for relationships with the public, insurance companies, and colleagues. No enforcement procedures for the Code are reported.

Professional Insignia: The emblem of the National Association of Insurance Agents, which appears on its stationery and publications, is a horizontal oval design, with the legend, "Your Independent Insurance Agent Serves You First"; an eagle, facing right with outstretched wings, is perched on the "I" of the word "Independent"--symbolizing the independent resourcefulness of the competent independent insurance agent; a line border encloses the design. The color of

the emblem is black on white, with five words of the legend ("Your
... Agent Serves You First") and the bordering line in red.

Bibliography:
    National Association of Insurance Agents.   Code of Ethics.
        1929.   1 page.
    Guide to conduct for insurance agents in relations with the
    public, employers, and colleagues.
    _____.   This is the N. A. I. A.   July 1970.   Folder.
    Informational brochure includes NAIA history, structure,
    program, and services.

"Code of Ethics"

I believe in the insurance business and its future, and that
the American agent is the instrumentality through which it reaches
its highest point and attains its widest distribution.

I will do my part to uphold and upbuild the American Agency
System which has developed insurance to its present fundamental
place in the economic fabric of our nation, and to my fellow-members of the National Association of Insurance Agents I pledge myself always to support right principles and oppose bad practices in
the business.

I believe that these three have their distinct rights in our
business; first, the Public; second, the Insurance Companies; and
third, the Insurance Agents; and that the rights of the Public are
paramount.

To the Public

I regard the insurance business as an honorable profession
and realize that it affords me a distinct opportunity to serve society.

I will strive to render the full measure of service that should
be expected from an intelligent, well-informed insurance man.   Anything short of this would be a violation of the trust imposed in me.

I will thoroughly analyze the insurance needs of my clients
and recommend the forms of indemnity best suited to these needs,
faithfully advising as to the best insurance protection available.

I will do my part to help bring the public to a better understanding of insurance, always so conducting my business that the
fullest light of publicity can be turned upon it.

I will consider it a duty to cooperate with the national, state
and local authorities in the prevention of fire waste and accidents.

I will take an active part in recognized civic, charitable and
philanthropic movements which contribute to the public good of my
community.

To the Companies

I will respect the authority vested in me to act in their behalf in serving the public, striving at all times to live up to the

agreements made with my companies.

I will use care in the selection of risks, and do my utmost to merit the confidence of my companies by rendering them the fullest information attainable to enable them to underwrite their insurance intelligently; nor will I withhold any facts, that may come to my knowledge, detrimental to their interests.

I will expect my companies to give me the same fair treatment that I give to them, and will favor those companies that subscribe to the principles of the National Association of Insurance Agents and in the conduct of their business carry out these principles.

To Fellow Members

I pledge myself to maintain friendly relations with other agencies in my community. I will compete with them on an honorable and fair basis, make no false statements, nor any misrepresentation by omission of facts, inference or subterfuge.

I will consider unethical, the obtaining of business by commercial bribery, coercion or unfair influence.

I will adhere to a strict observance of all insurance laws relative to the conduct of my business and will studiously avoid any practices which might cause the business adverse notoriety or disrepute.

I will cooperate in every reasonable way with my competitors for the betterment of the insurance business and its advancement to a still higher level of service.

Realizing that only by unselfish service can the insurance business have the public confidence it merits, I will at all times seek to elevate the standards of the insurance profession by governing all my business and community relations in accordance with the provisions of this Code and by inspiring others to do likewise.

INSURANCE UNDERWRITERS--LIFE

AMERICAN SOCIETY OF CHARTERED LIFE UNDERWRITERS (ASCLU)
270 Bryn Mawr Ave., Bryn Mawr, Pa. 19010
Paul S. Mills, C. L. U., Executive Vice President

Membership: The American Society of Chartered Life Underwriters, founded in 1928 (present name taken in 1940) and with a current (1973) membership of approximately 17,000 in about 200 chapters, is an organization of life and health insurance underwriters who have been granted the professional designation, "C. L. U." ("Chartered Life Underwriter"). A "C. L. U." qualifies for this designation of professional competence by passing ten written examinations,

which usually take five years to complete. To be eligible for the
examinations--prepared and graded by the American College of
Life Underwriters--a candidate must be a high school graduate
(although half of enrollees in the CLU study are college graduates),
and have had at least "three years of experience in activities related to the insuring of human life values." The subject areas of
the two-hour written examinations are:
> Indidivual Life and Health Insurance,
> Life Insurance Law and Company Operations,
> Group Insurance and Social Insurance,
> Pension Planning,
> Income, Estate and Gift Taxation,
> Investments and Family Financial Planning,
> Accounting and Finance,
> Economics,
> Business Insurance,
> Estate Planning.

Code of Ethics: The professional conduct guide subscribed to by all
members of the Society is the ASCLU Code of Ethics, adopted in
1961.   There are two sections in this guide for insurance underwriters' "professional conduct in their relationships with the public,
clients, fellow underwriters and companies":
> I.   Guides to Professional Conduct--The Professional Pledge
>   of the Chartered Life Underwriter is the first of eight
>   enumerated obligations of the CLU;
> II. Rules of Professional Conduct--Sets forth six rules.

No enforcement procedures for this Code are reported.

Professional Insignia: The emblem of the ASCLU is an unbordered
design--the Society monogram, "CLU," in a nested square of letters,
with "American" above, and
"Society" below these initials.

AMERICAN

The colors of this emblem are
shown variously--black and
white (logotype); blue and
white (publication, letterhead).

Other Identification of Professional Competence: Individuals
who have been awarded the professional designation, "C. L. U."
by the American College of Life
Underwriters, as described

SOCIETY

above, are entitled to wear a key--comparable in form to a Phi Beta
Kappa key, with the letters, "CLU," in a centered circle superimposed on a formée (a cross with arms narrow at the center and expanding toward the sides, the ends of the arms being straight).
The key may also be shown on business cards. The color of the
key is gold, with the "CLU" in black enamel. Use of the professional designation "CLU" is authorized with designees' names, and
other identification of their professional services.

Bibliography:
    American Society of Chartered Life Underwriters.   <u>Commitment.</u>
       Pamphlet.
    ACLU history, activities, and Code of Ethics. Shows em-
    blem.
    _____. <u>The Meaning of CLU.</u> Folder.
    Gives requirements for obtaining the professional designa-
    tion "CLU." Includes Guides to Professional Conduct and
    Rules of Professional Conduct. Key shown in color on cover.
    _____. <u>What is CLU?</u> Folder.
    Significance and qualifications of the designation "CLU," with
    Professional Pledge of the Chartered Life Underwriter (which
    is 1, of the Guides to Professional Conduct).

"Professional Attitude"

The true professional man places the public's welfare above his own. Such concern for the patient or client is characteristic of a professional calling. The objective of the C. L. U. program is not only to help a life underwriter gain the subject knowledge that is needed to serve his clients well, but to instill in him the attitude of placing their interests above his own. Both within the life and health insurance industry and with the general public, C. L. U. has come to be recognized as the symbol of professional competence.

"The Code of Ethics"
subscribed to by all members of the
American Society of Chartered Life Underwriters

It is the desire of the members of the American Society of Chartered Life Underwriters to serve the insuring public in accordance with the purposes set forth in the Society's Bylaws.

And because Society members recognize and accept collective and individual responsibility for professional conduct in their relationships with the public, clients, fellow underwriters and companies, they pledge themselves to the Code of Ethics, consisting of Guides to Professional Conduct and Rules of Professional Conduct, as set forth below:

I.   Guides to Professional Conduct

    1.   I shall, in the light of all the circumstances surrounding my client, which I shall make every conscientious effort to ascertain and to understand, give him that service which, had I been in the same circumstances I would have applied to myself. *

    2.   I shall place the welfare and interests of my clients above my own interests.

    3.   I shall render continuing service and counsel to my clients.

---

*The professional pledge of Chartered Life Underwriters.

4. I shall continue to study and to improve my technical competency.

5. I shall keep abreast of changing conditions and legislation which may affect the financial plans of the insuring public and keep my clients informed of such changes as relate to them.

6. I shall accord the same courtesy and consideration to others engaged in related professions as I would wish to receive from them.

7. I shall refrain from engaging in any activity which, if practiced by a substantial number of members, would bring discredit to the institution of life insurance in general and to the American Society of Chartered Life Underwriters in particular.

8. I shall encourage others with the proper qualifications to earn the C. L. U. designation in the belief that this is in the best interests of the insuring public.

II.   Rules of Professional Conduct

1. A member shall obey all applicable laws governing life and health insurance.

2. A member shall conduct his personal and business affairs in such a manner as to avoid discrediting his reputation and impairing the public regard for life underwriting as a profession.

3. A member shall respect the confidential nature of the relationship existing between himself and his client.

4. A member shall respect the agent/principal relationship existing between himself and the company he represents.

5. A member shall avoid impairing the reputation or practice of another life underwriter.

6. Advertising the C. L. U. designation or its significance shall be done only in a manner approved by the American Society of Chartered Life Underwriters and the American College of Life Underwriters.

NATIONAL ASSOCIATION OF LIFE UNDERWRITERS (NALU)
    1922 F St., N. W., Washington, D. C. 20006
    Horace Flickinger, Director

Membership: The National Association of Life Underwriters, founded in 1890 and with a present (1973) membership of approximately 115,000 in local associations, is a trade association federation. Any life insurance underwriter or general insurance agent may join an NALU local association, as an individual, provided he works "full time" in life insurance selling (e. g., 50 percent or more of his income comes from life insurance sales).

Code of Ethics: The guide to professional conduct for an Association member is the NALU Code of Ethics, directed to improvement of the quality of insurance agent management through a recognized ethical guide.   Principles set forth in the Code refer to the responsibility of the life underwriter to his clients and the general rendering of service to his insurance business.   No procedures for enforcement of the Code are reported.

Professional Insignia: The emblem of the NALU is its seal--circular in form, the design shows the liberty bell at the top of a centered scroll bearing the legend: "Life Insurance: A Declaration of Financial Independence"; the organization name, "The National Association of Life Underwriters," is spaced around the design as an unbanded border, with the date of organization of the group, "Founded 1890," at the bottom of the insignia. The color of the emblem is black on white (letterhead, publications).   The NALU insignia is available for wear and display by members in the form of decals, membership stickers, and as auto emblem, paper weight, office plaque, and on jewelry and lighters.

Bibliography:
    Kobel, Marvin A.   The NALU Ethic.   15 pages.   Processed.
        Speech by the Director of Public Relations of the National Association of Life Underwriters.
    National Association of Life Underwriters.   Code of Ethics.
        1 page.
    Principles to govern conduct of NALU members.

"Code of Ethics"

Preamble: The position of the Life Underwriter is unique in that he is the liaison between his client and his company.   As a life insurance advisor he owes a high professional duty toward his client, while, at the same time, he also occupies a position of trust and loyalty to his company.   Only by observing the highest ethical balance can he avoid any conflict between these two obligations.   Therefore:

I Believe it to be my Responsibility ... TO hold my business in high esteem and strive to maintain its prestige.   TO keep the needs of my clients always uppermost.   TO respect my clients' confidence and hold in trust personal information.   TO render continuous service to my clients and their beneficiaries.   TO employ

every proper and legitimate means to persuade my clients to protect insurable obligations; but to rigidly adhere to the observance
of the highest standards of business and professional conduct. TO
present accurately, honestly, and completely every fact essential
to my clients' decisions. TO perfect my skill and to add to my
knowledge through continuous thought and study. TO conduct my
business on such a high plane that others emulating my example
may help the standards of our vocation. TO keep myself informed
with respect to insurance laws and regulations and to observe them
in both letter and spirit. TO respect the prerogatives and cooperate with all others whose services are constructively related to ours
in meeting the needs of our clients.

INSURANCE UNDERWRITERS--PROPERTY AND CASUALTY

SOCIETY OF CHARTERED PROPERTY AND CASUALTY UNDER-
   WRITERS (SCPCU)
      Penn State Bldg., Media, Pa. 19063
      Dr. Ronald T. Anderson, CPCU, C.L.U., Managing Director

Membership: The Society of Chartered Property and Casualty Underwriters, founded in 1944 and with a current (1973) membership of
approximately 6700 in over 100 chapters, is a professional association of insurance men and women specializing in property and
casualty insurance, who have been granted the professional designation, "CPCU" ("Chartered Property and Casualty Underwriter").
Members authorized to use this professional designation have been
qualified as competent through meeting the education and experience
requirements for examinations and passing the required examinations
in their insurance specialty. These examinations, given in June of
each year, are administered by the
      American Institute for Property and Liability Underwriters
         (AIPLU)
      Insurance Institute of America
      Providence and Sugartown Road
      Malvern, Pennsylvania 19355
      Edwin S. Overman, Ph.D., CPCU, President
Information regarding study materials, procedures for taking the
CPCU examinations, fees, and locations of examination centers--as
well as qualifications for examination--is obtainable from the American Institute.

Code of Ethics: The guide to professional conduct subscribed to be
members of the SCPCU is the Canons of Ethics, approved by the
Directors of the Society. These Canons set forth the obligations of
members in relationships with business associates, clients, and in

professional practice.   No enforcement procedures for the Canons
are reported.

Other Guides to Professional Conduct: At the time of receiving
the professional designation, "CPCU" ("Chartered Property and
Casualty Underwriter"), each
candidate takes an oath--The
CPCU Charge--concerning the
Chartered Property and Casualty Underwriter's concern
with the client's interest and
high standards of business
honor and integrity.

Professional Insignia: The
emblem of the SCPCU is its
gold key, bearing the professional designation: CPCU.
Members are authorized to
wear the key (in yellow or
white gold, with letters in
enamel).   In addition to the
full size key or pin, the emblem is available to members
as a miniature key or pin,
shortie tie bar with key, tie
tac or tie chain with key.

Bibliography:
    Insurance Institute of
          America, The Amer-
          ican Institute for
          Property and Lia-
          bility Underwriters.
          Catalogue, 1973-1974.
          94 pages.
    Annual publication giving
    details of requirements
    for CPCU designation,
    preparation for CPCU
    Examinations, including
    procedure, fees, study
    text references.
          .   Personal Growth Through Continuing Education--IIA
          and CPCU.   Folder.
    Gives information about the CPCU professional designation--
    requirements, study materials, local classes, national ex-
    amination registration.
    Overman, Edwin S.   The Professional Concept and Business
          Ethics.   75 pages.   Paper. $1.
    Reviews the "nature and significance of professionalism, "
    including applications for the clergy, medicine, law, ac-

counting business management, insurance. "
Society of Chartered Property and Casualty Underwriters.
What is CPCU?   Folder.
Information about CPCU designation and examination quali-
fications, preparation, and content.   Shows CPCU Charge,
and key.

"Canon of Ethics"

1.   No Society member shall be relieved of his obligations
for ethical standards because of a business association with a non-
designee, who has no such obligation.   No member shall carry out,
through others, acts which he is prohibited from directly performing
as a result of the Society Code of Professional Ethics.

2.   Each member has an obligation to advise himself of
each and every law and regulation pertaining to his business operations and may not plead lack of such knowledge as a defense for
improper conduct, unless he can demonstrate that he has made a
reasonable effort, in good faith, and through no fault of his own
such knowledge was not available to him.

3.   Every Society member shall have an obligation to assist
in contributing to the raising of professional standards in the insurance business, and should contribute his time and efforts to those
organizations and activities designed to produce this result.   Such
a C. P. C. U. also has as his obligation to bring to the attention of
the proper authority any such actions of himself or others that
should bring or would bring discredit upon the designation.   To have
knowledge of such conditions or such situations and to not bring
them to the attention of the proper authorities constitutes an unethical act on the part of the individual who possesses such knowledge.

"The CPCU Charge"

In all of my business dealings and activities I agree to abide
by the following rules of professional conduct:
I shall strive at all times to ascertain and understand the
needs of those whom I serve and act as if their interests were my
own; and
I shall do all in my power to maintain and uphold a standard
of honor and integrity that will reflect credit on the business in
which I am engaged.

INTERIOR DESIGNERS AND DECORATORS

AMERICAN INSTITUTE OF INTERIOR DESIGNERS (AID)
750 Fifth Ave., New York, N.Y. 10019
W.D. Hamilton, Executive Director

Membership: The American Institute of Interior Designers, founded
in 1931 and with a present (1973) membership of over 5000, is a
professional association of interior designers. The Institute has
defined "interior designer" as:
    "a person qualified by training and experience to plan and
    supervise the design and execution of interiors and their
    furnishings, and to organize the various arts and crafts
    essential to their completion."
The AID membership is grouped in over 40 chartered Chapters,
located throughout the United States and in the countries of Latin
America, Europe, the Orient, and Near East.
    Candidates for professional categories of membership--Corporate
Membership and Affiliate Membership--must be qualified by education
and current employment in a recognized establishment of interior
design. Affiliate Members may qualify for membership on the basis
of education in interior design; Corporate Members are required--
in addition to such education--to have specified amounts of practical
experience in "a recognized establishment of interior design and
decoration."

    The qualifying combinations of training and experience are:

Education Requirement for Affiliate and Corporate Members (Academic and Technical Training in Interior Design--after High School Graduation)	Experience Requirement for Corporate Members
I. 5-year course in Interior Design	1 year
II. 4-year course in Interior Design	2 years
III. 2 years college, plus 2/3 years technical school	2 years
IV. 3 years technical school	3 years
V. 2 years technical school	4 years
Qualifying for Corporate Membership Only	
VI. Secondary School	6 years
VII. After having fulfilled the foregoing requirements to the satisfaction of the Committee of Admissions, the applicant then will be required to take and pass the Accreditation Examination.	

Code of Ethics: Carrying out one of the stated organization pur-
poses--"to uphold in practice a code of ethics of mutual benefit in
professional and trade relations"--the AID has issued a Code of
Ethics and Professional Practices. This Code provides a basis for
professional conduct of members by setting forth principles in four
sections:
    Obligations,
    Client Relations,

Professional Relations,
Institute Relations.
Enforcement provisions of the Code (contained in its "Conclusion
paragraph) directs that charges of violations of the professional conduct guide be made by the National Board of Governors of AID, the
Board of Governors of a Chapter, or by three Members of AID.
The National Board of Governors is the sole judge of alleged unprofessional conduct, and--after investigation and hearing--may take
disciplinary action, which could result in expulsion from membership in the Institute.

Professional Insignia: The emblem of AID is a square design consisting of a black centered square with a line border; on the square
is a lozenge with bordered segments; the upper left and lower right

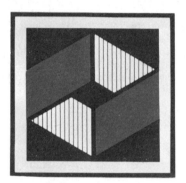

are solid dark orange in color,
and the other two segments are
striped by black vertical lines on
a white background.   This insignia
appears on Institute stationery and
publications.   It is also shown in
blind embossed form (letterhead).
The emblem was designed by Eck-
stein and Stone, N.Y., N.Y., and
adopted by the Institute in 1966.

Bibliography:
American Institute of Interior
Designers. Information
Bulletin. 1970. 8 pages.
AID purposes, membership requirements, Code of Ethics and
Professional Practices. Insignia shown in color on front and
back covers.

"Code of Ethics and Professional Practices"

The following Code shall be considered the basis for the professional conduct of members.   This Code may be amended in the
same manner as prescribed in Article XII of the Bylaws of the Institute.

Any deviation by a member from any of the standards of this
Code, or from any of the rules of the Board of Governors supplemental thereto, or any action of his that is detrimental to the best
interests of the profession and the Institute shall be deemed to be
unprofessional conduct on his part, and ipso facto he shall be subject
to discipline by the Institute.

Preface

The profession of interior design demands that its members
have high standards, training, integrity, imagination and creative
ability.   The services of the interior designer should include any

service that shall further the ultimate goal of creating an environment of orderliness and beauty.   The interior designer shall maintain his professional integrity: his motives, abilities and conduct shall always be such as to command respect and confidence.

Obligations

A-1.   The interior designer shall conform to the Code of Ethics and Standards governing the practice of interior design in any state in which he practices, as well as to this Code of Ethics.

A-2.   The interior designer shall perform his professional services with competence and shall properly serve the interests of his client.   He may offer his services on the generally accepted basis of retail price, commission, fee, salary, as consultant or adviser, provided he strictly maintains his professional integrity.

A-3.   The interior designer shall exercise great care in the use of his name in any advertising or other publicity concerning the product, merchandise or services of any manufacturer or distributor.   Officers of the Institute, or its Chapters, may not permit the use of their titles in any such advertising, merchandising or promotion.

A-4.   Since adherence to these high principles is the obligation of every member of the Institute, any deviation is subject to discipline in proportion to the gravity of the charge, as outlined in the Conclusion of this Code.

Client Relations

A-1.   Before undertaking any commission the interior designer shall determine with his client the scope of the project, the nature and extent of the services he will perform, and his compensation for same, and shall provide complete confirmation thereof in writing.   In performing his services he shall constantly maintain an understanding with his client regarding the project, its potential solutions and its estimated probable costs.   He shall pledge that his work measures up to highest standards of his profession.

A-2.   The interior designer shall guard the interests of his client and the rights of those whose contracts he administers.   If compensation is derived by the designer from any supplementary source or contractor, the client should be apprized of such compensation.

A-3.   The interior designer shall preserve any confidential information derived from his client.   He shall not release information concerning his projects without the consent of his client.

Professional Relations

A-1.   A member shall seek every opportunity to advance the

dignity of the profession, the prestige of the Institute and the well-being of the community.

A-2. A member of this Institute shall maintain a satisfactory credit standing, as an obligation to his profession and as part of his position of respect in the community and industry.

A-3. A member shall maintain the good will of his resources to uphold his professional standing and the reputation of the Institute.

A-4. A member shall not make any statement which unjustifiably injures the reputation, prospects or business of another designer. When a designer has made a contract with, or been employed by a client, no other designer shall knowingly interfere with the performance of the contract or the rendering of any services by the designer employed, or by his subcontractors.

A-5. A member shall not practice in any manner inconsistent with this Code of Ethics and Professional Practices, nor shall a member be, or continue to be associated with a firm that in any way violates this Code.

A-6. A member shall offer encouragement to qualified young people wishing to study interior design, students in design schools and colleges, and will assist, to the best of his abilities, those who are entering the field. He shall encourage a continuing education in the design profession, in its functions, duties and responsibilities, as well as the technical advancement of the art and science of environmental design.

A-7. A member shall contribute to the interchange of technical information and experience between the interior designer and other allied professions, and respect the interest and contributions of associated professionals.

Institute Relations

A-1. A member upon election, shall assume the responsibility of participating in the affairs of the Institute on a Chapter and National level.

A-2. A member is required, when asked, to serve on Chapter or National Committees or in some alternate manner contribute to the furtherance of the aims and principles as outlined in this Code of Ethics and in the Bylaws of the Institute.

A-3. A member is obligated to keep informed of workshops, seminars, lectures, demonstrations and other educational projects sponsored by the Institute in Chapter or National meetings, and to attend at least one such program or series of programs each year.

A-4. Failure to conform to the requirements set forth in paragraphs 1, 2, and 3 may cause any membership to be reviewed by the Chapter and the National Board of Governors to determine whether the continuation of that membership is in the best interests of the Institute. Lack of interest or participation may be considered grounds for termination of membership.

Conclusion

Since adherence to the principles outlined here is the obligation of every member of the Institute, any deviation therefrom shall be subject to discipline by the National Board of Governors. Charges against any member may be made by the National Board of Governors, or the Board of Governors of a Chapter, or by three (3) Members in good standing. A hearing upon such charges shall be held under such conditions and procedures as may be prescribed from time to time by the National Board of Governors. The accused shall be given ten (10) days notice in writing of such hearing: he shall then have the right to appear before the National Board of Governors in person. The National Board of Governors shall be the sole judge of such discipline, and its action shall be final, subject only to the right of the Board to grant a re-hearing. With the termination of membership all rights and privileges of the member in the Institute shall cease.

NATIONAL SOCIETY OF INTERIOR DESIGNERS (NSID)
     315 E. 62nd St., New York, N.Y. 10021
     John Hammon, Executive Director

Membership: The National Society of Interior Designers, founded in 1951 and with a current (1973) membership of approximately 5000, is a professional organization of interior designers. The Society defines "interior designer" as:

> a professional who plans, counsels and guides the "design, decoration, or arrangement of the interior areas of any private or public building or structure"; with services including "evaluation, planning and layout, esthetic and structural design and decoration of such interior areas and the responsible supervision of the composition and specifications of the furniture, fabrics, wall and floor covering, accessories, ornaments, or other items to be used in connection with such interior areas."

In addition to Industry, Trade, Research, Press, Communications Memberships--available to ancillary activities for the interior furnishings field--and Student Membership, Professional Affiliate Memberships in NSID are granted to individuals practicing as architects, artists, educators in appropriate areas, graphic designers, landscape architects, lighting designers, museum executives, photo-

graphers, screen, stage and television designers, product designers.
Qualifications for NSID Professional Membership and Associate
Membership are:

> Professional Membership--Five-year college level degree and
> one year full-time practical interior design experience;
> or completion of four-year college level degree course and
> two years' experience; or a three-year certificate or di-
> ploma course in chartered school of design or equivalent
> technical school and three years' experience and passing
> the Society's Qualification Examination; or eight years'
> combined education and experience in Interior Design and
> passing Society's Qualification Examination.

> Associate Membership--Be regularly engaged in the practice
> of Interior Design, and completion of a four- or five-year
> college level degree course; or a three-year certificate
> or diploma course in a chartered school of design or equiva-
> lent technical school; or six consecutive years of combined
> education and practical experience in Interior Design.

Code of Ethics: The NSID guide to professional conduct is its Code
of Ethics, developed by a committee of the organization appointed
to formulate standards of professional practice.   This Code enumerates 17 principles to be followed in dealing with clients, colleagues, and the public.   Enforcement of this ethical code is the
responsibility of the National Board of Directors (Bylaws, Chapter
II, Article 10).   The Board investigates complaints of unprofessional
conduct, holds hearings, and takes appropriate disciplinary action--
which may include reprimand, suspension, or removal from Society
membership.

Professional Insignia: The
emblem of the Society is its
logotype--a stylized monogram
of the Society name, "NSID, "
in lower case letters, arranged
to form a square design.   This
emblem is shown in white--
with embossed monogram (letterhead; Code of Ethics), and
in black and white (publication).
The emblem is reserved for
official use of the NSID, and
is not authorized for use by
individual members.

Other Identification of Professional Status: The Professional
Membership of the Society is
authorized to designate their Society affiliation by use of "NSID, "
with their names, or as:

> "Professional Member, National Society of Interior Designers";
> "Member, National Society of Interior Designers";

"Member, NSID."
Authorized use of membership by Society initials or name for firms
and other classes of membership is given in the brochure, NSID
Appellation Procedure Guide.

Bibliography:
    National Society of Interior Designers. Appellation Procedure
        Guide. Pamphlet. 4 pages.
    Specific forms to be followed when using NSID appellation
    and name with advertising stationery, cards, correspondence,
    and other professional listings.
          . Code of Ethics. Pamphlet. 4 pages.
    Seventeen standards for NSID members in their professional
    practice.
          . Membership Qualification Examination for the Na-
        tional Society of Interior Designers: Handbook for Candi-
        dates. Annual. 5 pages.
    Contains necessary information about the NSID Membership
    Qualification Examination, including examination schedule for
    application and testing, application qualifications and pro-
    cedure for examinations; sample examination questions.
          . NSID Qualification Examination Study Guide. 9
        pages.
    Outlines subject content of examination; gives study bibli-
    ography.
          . National Organization of Professional Interior De-
        signers. Folder.
    Gives NSID purpose and activities, qualifications for various
    membership categories.

"Code of Ethics"
Standards of Professional Practice

       Members of the National Society of Interior Designers are
required to conduct their professional practice in a manner that will
command the respect and confidence of clients, suppliers, fellow interior designers and the general public. The professional conduct of
every regular member of the Society shall be governed by the following code:

       1. He shall conform to any existing laws and regulations
governing the practice of interior design in any state or community
in which he practices, as well as to this code.

       2. He may offer his design services to a client as a con-
sultant, specifier or supplier on the basis of a fee, salary, commission, or the retail price of merchandise, provided that the professional service shall be performed with competence in a manner
that is in the best interest of the client without sacrificing the professional integrity of the designer.

       3. He will, before entering into a contract with a client,

clearly determine and define with the client the scope and nature of
the project involved, the services to be performed and the method
of compensation for those services. He will perform such services
as defined in accordance with the highest standards of the profession.

4.   He will at all times keep his client informed regarding
the progress of the project, its estimated cost, and any circumstances that might delay its eventual completion. He will not make
any substitutions of materials without the client's knowledge and approval.

5.   He shall guard the interest of his client in any sub-con-
tract necessary to complete a project and shall not accept any supplemental compensation resulting from such sub-contracts without
the full knowledge and consent of the client.

6.   He shall not divulge any confidential information derived
from his client nor will he release any information on a project
without the consent of the client.

7.   He shall consider the maintenance of a satisfactory credit
standing an obligation to his profession.

8.   He shall maintain the good will of his trade sources, subcontractors, business associates and the community.

9.   He shall consider it a part of his professional responsibility to take an active interest in community projects designed to
improve the quality of man's environment, conducting such activities
in a manner that will enhance the dignity of the profession and the
Society.

10.   He shall at no time injure the reputation or business
relations of another interior designer.

11.   He shall not knowingly approach a client who has a
contract with another interior designer nor will he in any way interfere with the performance of such a contract by another designer,
his trade sources, or his subcontractors, nor will he enter into an
agreement with such a client until that client represents that he has
severed his relationship with the original designer.

12.   He shall not permit any representative of his business
organization to present himself to the general public as an interior
designer unless such representative is qualified by education and/
or experience.

13.   He shall not permit his name nor the name of his firm
to be used by any individual for the purpose of making direct purchases from wholesale sources unless such purchases are a part of
a design project for which proper compensation is received.

14.   He shall not, while serving as a Chapter or Society

officer use his title to promote through advertising or any other
means the product, merchandise or services of any manufacturer
or distributor.

15.   He shall not imply, through advertising or other means
that his staff or the employees of his firm are members of the
Society unless such be the fact, since the right to use the Society's
appellation is granted to the individual only.

16.   He shall encourage and contribute to the sharing of
ideas and information between the interior designer and other allied
professions, and in any association with these professions be
governed by the same high standards of professional practice which
apply to his relations with his fellow interior designers.

17.   He shall consider it his professional responsibility to
encourage young students interested in the study of interior design
and to offer assistance whenever possible to those who enter the
profession.

Any deviation from this code, or from subsequent revisions
by the Board of Directors of the National Society of Interior Designers, or any action detrimental to the Society and the profession
as a whole shall be deemed unprofessional conduct subject to discipline by the Society's Board of Directors under Chapter II, Section
10, of the Bylaws of the Society.

JOURNALISTS

THE NEWSPAPER GUILD (TNG)
    1126 16th St., N.W., Washington, D.C. 20036
    Robert M. Crocker, Secretary-Treasurer

Membership: The Newspaper Guild (name changed in 1971 from
"American Newspaper Guild"), founded in 1933 and with a present
(1973) membership of approximately 33,000, is a labor union affiliated with the American Federation of Labor-Congress of Industrial Organizations (AFL-CIO) and the Canadian Labour Congress
(CLC).   Guild "membership is open to anyone engaged in the editorial, advertising, circulation, maintenance, promotion and related
departments of
        1.   News and News-Feature publications;
        2.   Enterprises supplying such material or services to pub-
             lications or distributors who pay for the service;
        3.   Newsreel companies, radio and television broadcasting
             companies;
        4.   Informational and publication activities of governmental

agencies, bureaus or department in the United States,
its territories and possessions, and Canada."

Code of Ethics: The conduct guide for members of The Newspaper
Guild is its Code of Ethics, adopted at the Guild's first annual
convention in 1934.   Revision of this ethical code is under study
(1973).   The Code--listing seven practices to be followed--"is intended to be a guideline for voluntary adherence by working news-
men and newswomen; there is no enforcement process, discipline,
or hearings."

Professional Insignia: The emblem of the Guild is its seal--a circular design bearing a centered shield with the organization's initials,

"TNG"; this shield is placed
on symbols of news gathering
and distribution: an eye,
above the shield, for observation of news events; crossed
pen and pencil, behind the
shield, the working tools of
recording observations; and
electronic waves surrounding
the shield, signifying means
of transmitting and broadcasting news by telephone, tele-
type, telegraph, radio and television.   The Guild's name,
"The Newspaper Guild," is
printed around the design, inside a bordering band, which
is a cable.   The color of the
insignia is shown variously--black on gold (letterhead); black on
white (logotype).

Bibliography:
     The Newspaper Guild.   Code of Ethics.   1 page.
     Conduct guide for TNG members.

"Code of Ethics"

     (1)   That the newspaper man's first duty is to give the public
accurate and unbiased news reports, and that he be guided, in his
contacts with the public, by a decent respect for the rights of individuals and groups.
     (2)   That the equality of all men before the law should be
observed by the men of the press; that they should not be swayed
in news reporting by political, economic, social, racial or religious
prejudices, but should be guided only by fact and fairness.
     (3)   That newspaper men should presume persons accused of
crime of being innocent until they are convicted, as is the case under
the law, and that news accounts dealing with accused persons should

be in such form as not to mislead or prejudice the reading public.

(4)   That the Guild should work through efforts of its members, or by agreement with editors and publishers, to curb the suppression of legitimate news concerning 'privileged' persons or groups, including advertisers, commercial powers and friends of newspaper men.

(5)   That newspaper men shall refuse to reveal confidences or disclose sources of confidential information in court or before other judicial or investigating bodies; and that the newspaper man's duty to keep confidences shall include those he shared with one employer even after he has changed his employment.

(6)   That the news be edited exclusively in the editorial rooms instead of in the business office of the daily newspaper.

(7)   That newspaper men shall behave in a manner indicating independence and decent self-respect in the city room as well as outside, and shall avoid any demeanor that might be interpreted as a desire to curry favor with any person.

JUDGES

AMERICAN BAR ASSOCIATION (ABA)
    1155 E. 60th St., Chicago, Ill. 60637
    Bert W. Early, Executive Director

<u>Membership</u>:   The American Bar Association, founded in 1878 and with a present (1973) membership of over 165, 000, is a professional organization of attorneys and judges in the United States.   Attorneys admitted to the bar in any state of the United States are eligible for membership.   Judges, court administrators, and federal court executives who are not members of the legal profession may be admitted to the American Bar Association as Judicial Associate members.   State Bar Associations are affiliated with the American Bar Association.

<u>Code of Ethics</u>:   The Bar Association has a long leadership in setting standards of professional conduct--for judges, as well as lawyers, and its regular committees concerned with professional ethics include those for Ethics and Professional Responsibility; and Special Committee on the Evaluation of Ethical Standards and Evaluation of Disciplinary Enforcement.   "Almost fifty years ago the American Bar Association formulated the original <u>Canons of Judicial Ethics</u>," which were kept current by amendment, and were adopted in most states.   In August 1969 a Special Committee on Standards of Judicial Conduct was appointed to consider changes in the Canons, "required by current needs and problems."   "With the aid of suggestions from Bench, Bar, legal educators and interested laymen," the Committee prepared and issued a tentative draft of revised Canons of Judicial Ethics in May 1971.   Based on the revisions,

a new Code of Judicial Conduct was adopted by the ABA House of Delegates on August 16, 1972.

The rules of judicial conduct--applicable to all levels of judges from local courts through the United States Supreme Court--are grouped in seven Canons:

1. A Judge should uphold the integrity and independence of the judiciary.
2. A Judge should avoid impropriety and the appearance of impropriety in all his activities.
3. A Judge should perform the duties of his office impartially and diligently.
4. A Judge may engage in activities to improve the law, the legal system, and the administration of justice.
5. A Judge should regulate his extra-judicial activities to minimize the risk of conflict with his judicial duties.
6. A Judge should regularly file reports of compensation received for quasi-judicial and extra-judicial activities;
7. A Judge should refrain from political activity inappropriate to his judicial office.

In the Code, each Canon--statement of norms--is accompanied by "text setting forth specific rules, and the commentary, states the standards that judges should observe. The Canons and text establish mandatory standards unless otherwise indicated." The ABA Standing Committee on Ethics and Professional Responsibility interprets the Code of Judicial Conduct in Formal and Informal Opinions. Formal Opinions are published in full in the American Bar Association Journal and subsequently in bound volumes of Opinions. Informal Opinions are summarized in the Journal. State Bar Associations are encouraged to adopt the Code--it has now been adopted by 48 states--and to "establish effective disciplinary procedure for its enforcement."

Professional Insignia: The American Bar Association reports no official emblem.

Bibliography:
    American Bar Association. Code of Professional Responsibility and Code of Judicial Conduct. 1972. 55 pages.
    Newly revised Code of Judicial Conduct (p. 43-52).

JUDICIAL CONFERENCE OF THE UNITED STATES
    Supreme Court Bldg., Washington, D.C. 20544
    Chief Justice Warren E. Burger, Chairman of the Conference

The Judicial Conference of the United States--a 25-member group of judges that acts as the rule-making body for federal judges--

adopted on April 6, 1973 standards of conduct governing the 650 federal trial and appellate judges--but not the Supreme Court justices.

The Conference--whose membership is made up of the chief judge and a district court judge from each of the 11 judicial circuits of the United States, and representatives of two specialty courts (Court of Claims, and Court of Customs and Patent Appeals) --set standards which would bar most extra-judicial activities of a political or business nature.

Adoption of the code of ethics for United States judges followed four years of controversy and consideration of ethical conduct guides for the federal judiciary, beginning with the resignation of Supreme Court Justice Abe Fortas over legal work for the Wolfson family, and the question of Justice Douglas' acting as president of the Parvin Foundation. By its order, the Conference adopts for federal judges the Code of Judicial Conduct approved by the American Bar Association in August 1972, with specific modifications. The rules require that a federal judge guard against conflict-of-interest between his professional judicial and private activities by publicly making periodic reports of gifts and outside legal work, and by disqualifying himself for even minor financial interest in a party to a case, where he would act as judge. Off-the-bench legal work is restricted, as is any activity that might disregard the "appearance of propriety."

The new rules are stricter than the American Bar Association Code for judges--which applies to all judges--as the resolution of the Conference provides that where the Bar Association Code differs from federal statutes or previous Conference resolutions, the more restrictive provisions will apply to federal judges.

The provisions of the Conference standards of conduct are effective immediately, and must be complied with within one year from the date of resolution adoption. While the Conference has no means of enforcing its code of judicial conduct, the "moral suasion" it exercises has insured, with few exceptions, compliance with Conference directives.

Bibliography:
    Jackson, Robert L. "Judges Meet to Frame First Code of
        Ethics for U.S. Bench." Los Angeles Times. 1:1,
        May 25, 1969.
    McKenzie, John F. "Code of Ethics for U.S. Judges Issued."
        Los Angeles Times. 1:1, April 6, 1973.
    Ostrow, Ronald J. "Ethics Code Issued for Federal Judges."
        Los Angeles Times. 1:1, June 11, 1969.
    U.S. Administrative Office of the United States Courts. Annual
        Report. 1970.
        Includes a Public Report for Extrajudicial Services form.
    U.S. Judicial Conference. Proceedings. Washington, D.C.,
        March 15-16, 1971, and October 28-29, 1971. Washington,

D. C. , Government Printing Office, 1972.
Legislation governing judicial ethics to be formulated after
the American Bar Association Code of Judicial Ethics is completed (p. 76-77).

_____. Resolution. April 6, 1973.
Conference action adopting a conduct guide for federal judges.

"Resolution. April 6, 1973"

The Judicial Conference adopts the Code of Judicial Conduct
approved by the American Bar Association in August, 1972, with
the following modifications:

(1) The adoption of the Code will not restrict any functions
or privileges accorded by statute or resolution of the Conference
to part-time magistrates, part-time referees in bankruptcy or special masters;
(2) The adoption of the Code will not abrogate or modify
any conflicting provisions of statutes or resolutions of the Conference.   Except as provided in number (1) above, to the extent that
any part of the enumerated statutes or Conference action is less
restrictive than the Code, the latter will control.
(3) The provisions of the Code relating to "Effective Date
of Compliance" shall be modified to read as follows:
A person to whom this Code becomes applicable should arrange his affairs as soon as reasonably possible to comply
with it and should do so in any event within the period of
one year.   If, however, the demands on his time and the
possibility of conflicts of interest are not substantial, a person who holds judicial office on the date this Code becomes
effective may continue to act, without compensation, as an
executor, administrator, trustee, or other fiduciary for the
estate or person of one who is not a member of his family,
if terminating such relationship would unnecessarily jeopardize
any substantial interest of the estate or person.
(4) The entire commentary under Canon 5C(2), (including the
blackface, bracketed material) is deleted.
The Joint Committee is directed to give further study to the
provision of Canon 7 as it uniquely relates to federal judges.

LANDSCAPE ARCHITECTS

AMERICAN SOCIETY OF LANDSCAPE ARCHITECTS (ASLA)
    1750 Old Meadow Rd. , McLean, Va. 22101
    Alfred B. La Gasse, Executive Director

Membership: The American Society of Landscape Architects,

founded in 1899 and with a present (1973) membership of approximately 4000, is the professional organization of landscape archi-
tects--those design professionals concerned with the planning of
outdoor areas.   As experts in the "art of developing land and the
objects thereon for optimum human use and enjoyment," landscape
architects define themselves as the only planners who cover "the
physical problem of fitting man's entire environment to appropriate
use."

A professional "Member" of ASLA is required to be a graduate
of an accredited landscape architecture curriculum, and have at
least three years acceptable experience in the practice or teaching
of landscape architecture.   A one year's apprenticeship may be substituted for one year of the qualifying experience.   Other categories
of membership are:

> Associate--Graduates of accredited school of landscape archi-
> tecture, or persons evidencing professional competence
> to a Chapter Examining Board.
> Fellow--An honorary membership designation, that may be
> awarded to ASLA Members of ten years standing who
> have made an outstanding contribution to the profession.

Enrolled students in a course of landscape architecture and certain
other individuals working in related fields, or without a landscape
architecture degree may be admitted to Affiliation of the Society.

Code of Ethics: The guide to professional conduct for ASLA members is the Society's Code of Professional Practice, first adopted
in 1927, and revised in its present edition as of June 15, 1962.
This Code consists of ten rules or precedents, each followed by a
short commentary interpreting or explaining the rule.   Among the
subjects considered are relationships with clients, the public; obtaining commissions; source and type of remuneration; participation
in competitions.   The professional conduct rules are enforced by
the Committee on Code of Professional Practice, which acts in investigating complaints of unprofessional conduct, hearing appeals,
and making recommendations for disposition of alleged infractions
of the Code to the Board of Trustees of the ASLA.   The Board
may censure or remove a member from membership for unprofessional conduct.

Other Guides to Professional
Conduct: The ASLA Code of
Competition specifies the circumstances under which a
Society member may participate in competitions, accept
commissions purportedly
awarded in competition, or
make competition awards
(Code of Professional Practice, 10).

Professional Insignia: The

THE
AMERICAN
SOCIETY OF
LANDSCAPE
ARCHITECTS
FOUNDED
1899

emblem of the Society is its seal--a circular device, with the organization name and founding date printed in the center, "The American
Society of Landscape Architects.   Founded 1899"; the border is an
oak wreath with acorns.   The color of the insignia is shown in the
official colors of the ASLA--greyed green on white.

Bibliography:
    American Society of Landscape Architects.   The ASLA Code of
        Professional Practice vs. Emerging Forms of Practice.
        (ASLA Bulletin, No. 213, November 1972), pages 1-10.
        An ASLA Task Force report on a revision of the Society's
        Code of Professional Practice.
    _____.   Code of Competition.   4 pages.   Folder. $. 25.
        Rules governing landscape architecture competitions, and
        ASLA member participation as competitors or officials.
    _____.   Code of Professional Practice, with Commentary.
        June 15, 1962.   4 pages.   Folder. $. 20.
    _____.   Constitution and Bylaws.   January 1972.   25 pages.
        Includes definition of occupation, ASLA membership require-
        ments.
    _____.   What is ASLA?   Folder.
        Informational brochure, with Society activities and categories
        of membership.

"Code of Professional Practice"

    Ethical, responsible professional behavior results not from
edict but rather from a positive inward force of the individual.
Even by the most careful selection of members a professional
society cannot overcome basic inadequacies in a person's character
resulting from his family, church, or school background.   The most
effective influence toward a high ethical standard is positive, consistent ethical actions in the practice of their profession by the
members of the Society.
    Unfortunately we seem to be living in an era of low ethical
standards.   These are reflected only too frequently in actions taken
by responsible officials in government, in industry and in other professions.   Nor are the landscape architects exempt from criticism
on this score.   That all of this is so, however, is not an excuse.
Good standards are even more important in an era of low ethical
standards.   The simple qualities of honesty, trustworthiness, truthfulness and in fact observance of the "golden rule" itself are also
good business and professional practices as well.
    It is necessary for a professional society to have rules (and
rather specific rules) for the conduct of its members.   All professional societies have codes of professional practice.   The only
enforcement of such a code is either censure of an individual by
the Society or the removal of an individual from membership.   In
the American Society of Landscape Architects enforcement of the
Code of Professional Practice usually results from a complaint
made against an individual.   Such a complaint is investigated by the

Committee on Code of Professional Practice which acts as a Board
of Appeals for implementing the provisions of the code.   Following
such investigation and report, final action is taken by the Board of
Trustees.
        This is a code for all landscape architects, whether or not
they are on public or private payrolls and whether or not they are
teaching, doing research, or working in a private or public office.
        While the Code of Professional Practice has been drafted to
be self-explanatory, a commentary is included for the purposes of
clarity.   The commentary is not a part of the code.   The code consists of 10 rules or precepts; following each of these there is the
short commentary interpreting or explaining the rule:

1   The professional landscape architect acts and practices always
in a manner bringing credit to the honor and dignity of the profession of landscape architecture.

Commentary
        This is a broad recognition of the principle that "one bad
apple spoils the barrel" and the principle that a group of people in
the same boat should pull together.
        Under this rule it would not be professional for a firm or
partnership to use the term "members of the American Society of
Landscape Architects" unless all members or associates of the firm
were either Fellows or Members of the Society.   Legal proceedings
to protect the name of the Society could be taken in such a case as
they certainly would be in the case of a single practitioner who
falsely claimed membership in the Society.
        Also, it would be unprofessional for a landscape architect to
allow his name to be associated with an undertaking in any professional capacity unless he served in that capacity.   A landscape
architect should not, for example, allow his name to be published
as the designer of a subdivision unless he is actually familiar with
the circumstances and responsible for the design and considers it
worthy of the standards of his office.   Similarly, he should not
accept a position as consultant or consent to review the plans of
another practitioner unless the circumstances are such that he can,
in fact, become familiar with the problem and the design.

2   The professional landscape architect promotes the public interest,
placing it above gain to himself or to his client.

Commentary
        The landscape architect is expected to be interested in all
civic and public affairs.   He should make his views known in connection with matters affecting the physical development of communities, including those in which he lives.   He would be expected to
make his views known, for example, on the regulations of land use,
such as zoning and land subdivision ordinances.   However, he
should not assist a client to obtain a special privilege in connection
with a zoning or subdivision matter and appear before a zoning or
planning commission as an advocate of a client endeavoring to obtain
a special privilege contrary to public interest.

3 The professional landscape architect is a faithful agent or trustee for his employer or his client, providing the full benefit of an objective professional opinion unaffected by other personal or financial commitments.

Commentary

Landscape architects, as is true of doctors or lawyers, may undertake other business activities "on the side" such as investments in stocks and bonds, real estate development and the like, to which the knowledge and the ability learned in the practice of their profession may contribute to a personal profit. Such activities are not deemed to be unprofessional so long as (1) they are fully disclosed, (b) they do not impair the objectivity of the landscape architect's advice to his client, and (c) they are a minor or subsidiary activity of the landscape architect.

The intent here is to prevent the landscape architect from either being or appearing to be in such a relation to others that he may not exercise his best judgment for the benefit of his client. For the same reasons it is undesirable for the landscape architect to maintain any other business or professional connection which might influence his judgment on behalf of the client without the full knowledge of the client in the case affected.

The landscape architect may legitimately, where it will best serve the interest of the client and the welfare of the work, organize a working force and purchase materials for his client and supervise operations through his office, rendering bills to the client at stated intervals for the actual amounts paid out. This is not a generally desirable procedure because it emphasizes the executive function rather than the advisory function of the landscape architect and so tends to a confusion of his services with those of the contractor.

The landscape architect shall not, however, undertake in any form the execution of construction work or planting on a lump sum basis. The crucial point here is that the landscape architect's remuneration must not be in the form of a commercial or speculative profit on materials or labor. Moreover, it is not equitable to ask the landscape architect to guarantee an uncertain cost as by a bond or otherwise--i.e., take a speculative risk--when he may not take a speculative profit.

It is legitimate for a landscape architect to give a bond for the faithful performance of his own work in design when this is required by law. It is not desirable, however, because his employment must be based upon trust and his integrity; he can do no more than give his best advice and is legally entitled to remuneration for it in the same manner as a doctor or a lawyer.

4 The professional landscape architect furthers the welfare and advancement of his profession by participating in activities of his professional society, encouraging professional development of those who enter the profession, and never doing any act that would falsely or maliciously injure the professional reputation, prospects, practice or employment position of another landscape architect.

Commentary
     This rule is quite similar to Rule 1. Each individual land-
scape architect will prosper as the entire Society prospers. It is
to the long-range benefit of each landscape architect to see the profession grow in numbers and esteem. This rule is in basic con-
tradiction to any actions that might tend toward restriction of the
number of qualified practitioners.
     A landscape architect should avoid both the act and the ap-
pearance of maliciously injuring the reputation of a rival practitioner.
Any adverse criticism of a fellow practitioner to a third party is
therefore undesirable, except where unavoidable in carrying out a
professional trust. This is especially true of matters of design
and to some extent of technical procedure, about which honest and
reasonable differences of opinion may exist.
     Matters of common honesty are usually regarded as more
capable of categorical definition, and dishonesty should never be
condoned because of considerations of professional solidarity; but
here also, before making any accusations, officially or unofficially,
the landscape architect should be certain:
     1   that the facts are actually and correctly before him;
     2   that a good purpose is served by revealing them; and
     3   that he is not rendering himself liable to the laws of libel.
     This rule is not intended to prohibit intelligent adverse criti-
cism of the advisability or design of public works or reports on
public works by a landscape architect in his capacity as a citizen
as long as the criticism is made in good faith and with no deliberate
attempt maliciously or otherwise to injure the professional reputation of another practitioner.
     Before a member of the Society either as an individual takes
action or in his or her capacity as representative of an organized
group votes to express an adverse opinion regarding a design, he
should give the practitioner whose work is being criticized an opportunity to present his reasons for the design.

5   The professional landscape architect obtains commissions solely
on the basis of his experience and ability, advertising in only a
dignified and responsible manner and not soliciting clients of another
landscape architect.

Commentary
     A known reputation for doing excellent work is the landscape
architect's most effective advertisement. It is entirely legitimate
for a landscape architect to bring himself to public attention so
long as in so doing he does not make himself and his Society appear: (a) to have bad manners or bad taste, (b) to be commercial
rather than professional, (c) to be self-seeking rather than public
spirited, and (d) to be under such obligations as to be incapable of
giving honest and disinterested advice.
     In this connection the landscape architect:
     1   May publish his name and profession and address, tele-
phone number, etc. in such publications as the telephone directory
or in the advertising pages of a periodical. However, display

advertisements or descriptive advertisements which are not distinguishable from ordinary commercial advertising associate a landscape architect in the public mind with nonprofessional sales methods
and are therefore to be avoided;

2   May furnish information, illustrations, etc. for articles
or prepare at his own expense articles about his own work for any
legitimate publication, provided that the material has real general
interest and is not blatantly laudatory or misleading or in any way
suggestive of commercial advertising methods;

3   May give lectures on professional or other subjects with
the same restrictions as above noted.

4   May show photographs, drawings, models, etc., of his
work in public exhibitions;

5   May serve as a public official or on committees, commissions, etc. for the public benefit (but avoid the giving of professional service without pay to communities or agencies which are
capable of paying for such service); and

6   May send out professional announcements on the occasion
of a change of address, change in firm membership, etc.

The Society and its Chapters should make their influence felt
in public affairs. Resolutions on public questions, letters to public
officials, newspaper articles, etc., are entirely legitimate.

The landscape architects is to take reasonable precautions to
determine whether another landscape architect has recently preceded
him in relation to each new piece of work. If such is the case the
second landscape architect should not proceed with the work until he
has communicated the facts to the first landscape architect and
satisfied himself that he may properly accept the employment. The
employment of a landscape architect by a client is considered to
have taken place when the landscape architect has been authorized
to make sketches by the client verbally or in writing. Mere solicitation of the client by a landscape architect is not a step toward
employment.

The landscape architect should not review, criticize or supplement the plans or work of another landscape architect for the
same client without the consent of the other landscape architect
except when the landscape architect first employed has entirely
severed his connection with the work. This statement is not intended to prohibit the otherwise proper soliciting of a former client
of another landscape architect nor the soliciting of a present client
of another landscape architect in regard to an entirely different
piece of work from that on which the other landscape architect is
employed.

6   The professional landscape architect receives his remuneration
solely from his stated charges for services rendered his client and
never in whole or in part from commissions from commercial or
speculative profit emanating from materials or services provided to
a client by others.

Commentary
     It is absolutely unprofessional to accept payment from

gardeners, superintendents, contractors, material men, etc., for
obtaining employment or sales for them and the landscape architect
should not lay himself open to the suspicion of having done this. It
is equally unprofessional to accept from another practitioner a payment for a portion of his fee in consideration of procuring work
for him.

7   The professional landscape architect refuses to invite proposals
or state a price for services in response for such an invitation
when there are reasonable grounds for belief that price will be the
prime consideration in the selection of the landscape architect.

Commentary
        The cost, safety and excellence of undertakings in landscape
architecture result from the experienced judgment and professional
competence and integrity of landscape architects selected for such
work and as the landscape architect's fees are a minor consideration in the over-all cost and because it is the duty of professional
societies to protect the unwary client against incompetence, inadequate experience or unethical practice, the American Society of
Landscape Architects strongly condemns the practice on the part of
some public and private individuals, firms and corporations of
soliciting competitive bids from landscape architects for the rendering of professional landscape architectural service.   Further it is
unprofessional for a landscape architect occupying a public position
to participate in a public action involving "competitive bidding" for
a professional assignment.

8   The professional landscape architect neither pays nor accepts
commissions for securing work.

Commentary
        This provision does not apply to those in regular employ of
a landscape architect as assistants, etc.   Such persons bringing
work into an office may properly be paid a percentage of the profits
or be otherwise remunerated.   To hire a person to secure work
when he has no other connection with the office is not a desirable
practice.   To offer payment directly or indirectly to other practitioners, as for instance to architects, in order to obtain work is
absolutely unprofessional.

9   The professional landscape architect will not reduce his standard
fee to obtain work or use a salaried position to compete unfairly
with other landscape architects.

Commentary
        It is highly undesirable for a landscape architect to offer
professional services on approval and without compensation unless
justified by previous personal or business relations with a particular client.   Where advice or service are knowingly under-valued for
good reasons in any particular case, this should be made perfectly
plain to a client so that the client may not obtain a false conception

of the real value of such services. Charges of different landscape
architects for employment upon the same problem will be different
according to their reputation and efficiency.

The Society recognizes that it is desirable for persons in
teaching positions to also undertake other professional assignments
"on the side" because to do so may be essential to improved quality
of teaching. However, the fees charged and the quality of services
performed should be comparable with those in private practice.
There should be no implication that the services were being provided by the institution to which the landscape architect is attached
or that special favors from said institution will be obtained by
virtue of the landscape architect's employment. Further, the use
of inexperienced student assistants at low rates of pay is not a good
practice. Landscape architects on a public payroll should not perform professional services for private clients when said professional
services are of a nature that will require review by the public agency
the landscape architect works for. While the practice of "Moon-
lighting" or undertaking secondary work on the side in "after office
hours" is primarily a problem for the individuals and the organizations concerned, it is unprofessional for a landscape architect to
engage in a secondary employment of a type that will conflict with
his primary employment: to thereby compete with the private office
he works for in the daytime, for example.

10 The professional landscape architect participates in competitions
only in accordance with the ASLA Code for Competitions.

Commentary
The ASLA Code of Competitions has been developed primarily
for the long-range protection of the landscape architect.

It may be legitimate for a landscape architect to accept a
commission to do a piece of work for which there has been a competition in which he has been concerned not as a winner, when no
award was made and a long time has elapsed and especially if the
requirements of the problem had been radically changed.

However, it is unprofessional for a landscape architect to
take part in any competition which is conducted contrary to the
principles sanctioned by the Society and to accept the commission
to do any work in connection with which he has acted in an advisory
capacity in drawing the program for a competition or in making the
award in such a competition.

LAW ENFORCEMENT OFFICERS

AMERICAN FEDERATION OF POLICE (AFP)
     1100 N. E. 125th St., N. Miami, Fla. 33161
     Gerald S. Arenberg, Executive Director

<u>Membership</u>:   The American Federation of Police, founded in 1966 and with a current (1973) membership of approximately 33,000, is a "national fraternal organization of law enforcement officers of all ranks, all departments." Among the AFP "Active Members"--who qualify for membership by being employed in full or part-time law enforcement, are officers and agents of law enforcement agencies (Federal, State, County, and City), including (in addition to Federal and Military Special Agents, Sheriffs and their deputies, Chiefs of Police, patrolmen, detectives, police technicians, fingerprint technicians, radio operators) military police of the armed forces, prison wardens and guards, parole and probation officers, and individual security officers of industry and business firms, special officers of patrol and guard services.

Through its National Commission of Professional Law Enforcement Standards--appointed from AFP elected national officers--the Federation accredits law enforcement officers as professionals by issuing a Professional Certificate in Law Enforcement Science "to those who qualify through experience, service, ability and character examination." The qualifying interview and written examination (of about 100 questions)--designed to test general knowledge of law enforcement and philosophy in administration of justice--are prerequisites for the Certificate. Eligible to take the interview and examination are full time law enforcement officers with a minimum of five years experience, who have completed advanced training in police science or techniques "sponsored by any governmental police agency, any school, or private institution or through a proved home study course of the government, military, or private institutions."

<u>Code of Ethics</u>: A guide to conduct for law enforcement officers is the AFP <u>Law Enforcement Profession's Code of Ethics</u>, in effect since 1955 as "a standard to which policemen may be guided." This Code enumerates seven obligations and responsibilities of the police officer. No procedures for enforcement of the professional conduct code are reported.

<u>Professional Insignia</u>: The emblem of the AFP is its seal--circular in shape, with an American eagle--"symbolic of the nation's unity and strength" --centered, the eagle bears a vertically striped shield (with a horizontal bar across the top bearing six stars), on its breast; the organization name, "American Federation of Police," is printed around the design, within a banding border.   The color of the emblem is blue on white (letterhead, publication). The emblem is also available

to members for display and wear as a wall plaque, sleeve patch, and jewelry--where the design is modified by superimposition of the seal on a five-pointed star, with the legend, "Member," at the top, and "Lex et Ordo" ("Law and Order") at the bottom; banded by a wreath of laurel leaves.

Bibliography:
    American Federation of Police. American Federation of Police.
        1973. 24 pages. Pamphlet.
        Informational brochure describing AFL membership, professional certificate in police science; pictures emblem.
    _____. Code of Ethics. 1955. 1 page.
        Seven principles providing a conduct guide for law enforcement officers.

                "Law Enforcement Profession's Code of Ethics"

    I As a law enforcement officer, I regard myself as a member of an important and honorable profession.
    II As a law enforcement officer, I will keep myself in the best physical condition, so that I may at all times, perform my police duty with efficiency, and if necessary defend my uniform with honor. It is my duty to know the art of defense and be proficient in the use of my revolver.
    III As a law enforcement officer, it is my duty to know my work thoroughly and to inform myself on all other phases of law enforcement work. It is my further duty to avail myself of every opportunity to learn more about my professional work.
    IV As a law enforcement officer, I should be exemplary in my conduct, edifying in my conversation, honest in my dealings, and obedient to all the laws of my city, state, and nation, and I shall regard these as my sacred honor.
    V As a law enforcement officer, I should not, in the performance of duty, work for personal advantage or profit. I shall, at all times, recognize that I am a public servant obliged to give the most efficient and impartial service of which I am capable and I will be courteous in all my contacts.
    VI As a law enforcement officer, I will regard my brother officer with the same standards as I hold for myself. It is my duty to guard his honor and life as I guard my own.
    VIII As a law enforcement officer, I should be loyal to my superiors, who determine my policies and accept responsibilities for my actions. It is my duty to do only those things which will reflect honor upon them, upon myself, and upon my profession.

_____

INTERNATIONAL ASSOCIATION OF CHIEFS OF POLICE (IACP)
    11 Firstfield Rd., Gaithersburg, Md. 20760
    Quinn Tamm, Executive Director

<u>Membership</u>: The International Association of Chiefs of Police, founded in 1893 and with a present (1973) membership of 9300, is an association of police executives "from every echelon of federal, state, and local law enforcement agencies and sixty-three foreign countries." "Active Members" of the Association must be of executive police rank--that is of command level, such as Chief, or Assistant Chief:

> "The following persons shall be eligible for active membership: commissioners, superintendents, chiefs, and directors having actual supervision of, and receiving salaries from, any legally constituted national, state, provincial, county, municipal, or other police department of any governmental jurisdiction; assistant chiefs of police, deputy chiefs of police, executive heads and division, district, or bureau commanding officers of such departments, when recommended for such membership by the chief of police or other highest commanding officer of such a prospective member's department, if such chief or other commanding officer is an active member in good standing of this Association, and chief executive officers of railroad police systems and railway express company police systems."

"Associate Members" are:

> "Any person not eligible for active membership, but qualified by training and experience in police or other law enforcement activity, or by other professional attainments in police science or administration." Eight "classes of persons" qualifying for this category of membership are enumerated in the IACP Requirements for Membership.

<u>Code of Ethics</u>: The professional conduct guide of the IACP is its <u>Law Enforcement Code of Ethics</u>, which sets forth in the form of a pledge the fundamental duties of the law enforcement officer, and the objectives and ideals of personal and professional conduct. No procedures for enforcement of this Code are reported.

<u>Professional Insignia</u>: The official emblem of the Association is circular in form, with a monogram of the organization name, "IAC," above the word "Police," in a wreath, which rests on a foundation consisting of a horizontal bar, a short vertical support between two "V"-shaped elements. The color of the insignia is shown variously--embossed (letterhead); black on white (Code of Ethics); dark blue on grayed blue (publication).

Bibliography:
  International Association of Chiefs of Police.   International Asso-
      ciation of Chiefs of Police. 14 pages. Pamphlet.
  Informational brochure describing law enforcement services
  provided by the Association; emblem on cover.
  _____. Law Enforcement Code of Ethics. 1 page.
  Professional conduct guide for members of the IACP.

"Law Enforcement Code of Ethics"

As a Law Enforcement Officer, my fundamental duty is to
serve mankind; to safeguard lives and property; to protect the innocent against deception, the weak against oppression or intimidation,
and the peaceful against violence or disorder; and to respect the
Constitutional rights of all men to liberty, equality and justice.

I will keep my private life unsullied as an example to all;
maintain courageous calm in the face of danger, scorn, or ridicule;
develop self-restraint; and be constantly mindful of the welfare of
others. Honest in thought and deed in both my personal and official
life, I will be exemplary in obeying the laws of the land and the
regulations of my department. Whatever I see or hear of a confidential nature or that is confided to me in my official capacity will
be kept ever secret unless revelation is necessary in the performance
of my duty.

I will never act officiously or permit personal feelings, prejudices, animosities or friendships to influence my decisions. With
no compromise for crime and with relentless prosecution of criminals,
I will enforce the law courteously and appropriately without fear or
favor, malice or ill will, never employing unnecessary force or violence and never accepting gratuities.

I recognize the badge of my office as a symbol of public faith,
and I accept it as a public trust to be held so long as I am true to
the ethics of the police service. I will constantly strive to achieve
these objectives and ideals, dedicating myself before God to my
chosen profession ... law enforcement.

NATIONAL SHERIFFS' ASSOCIATION (NSA)
     1250 Connecticut Ave., Suite 320, Washington, D.C. 20036
     Ferris E. Lucas, Executive Director

Membership: The National Sheriffs' Association, founded in 1940
and with a present (1973) membership of over 28,000, is an organization of peace officers "from any level of law enforcement."
Among members are sheriffs, deputy sheriffs, and municipal, state,
and federal law enforcement officers.

Code of Ethics: As part of the NSA purpose is "to professionalize law enforcement," the Association adopted, as a conduct guideline for its members, the Law Enforcement Code of Ethics. This Code --in the general form of a pledge--sets standards for the public service, obligations, and personal conduct of police officers. No procedure for enforcing the Code are reported.

Professional Insignia: The emblem of the National Sheriffs' Association is circular in form, with a superimposed five-pointed star--the points signifying friendship, guidance, honesty, integrity, and merit; a bordered shield centered on the star symbolizes defense, protection, and faith; its color--white--denotes purity; a mace in the center of the shield indicates authority; while the circular border of the emblem symbolizes eternity, and the olive spray in the bordering band at each side represents peace; the organization name, "National Sheriffs' Association," ap-pears spaced at the top and bottom within the bordering band. The insignia is shown in color (on the letterhead)--black on white background, with the star and the Association name in gold, and the border background for the group's name in blue. The emblem is also shown in black on white (publications, logotype).

Bibliography:
    National Sheriffs' Association. Policies and Procedures for Law Enforcement Administrators. 27 pages. Pamphlet.
    Includes Law Enforcement Code of Ethics (pages 2-3), standards of law enforcement procedure, law enforcement terminology.
    Walrod, Truman. The Role of Sheriff--Past--Present--Future. Washington, D.C., National Sheriffs' Association, 1968. Folder. $.25.
    History of the office of "Sheriff," from earliest times to the present, with derivation of the word, "Sheriff."

"Law Enforcement Code of Ethics"

    Whereas, The National Sheriffs' Association is constitutionally pledged to the professionalization of law enforcement; and
    Whereas, The National Sheriffs' Association recognizes that if the peace officer is to achieve the status of a professional, he must have moral integrity that is above reproach;
    Now, therefore be it resolved, That the National Sheriffs'

Association hereby adopts, and urges that all practitioners of law
enforcement adhere to, the Law Enforcement Code of Ethics.

As a Law Enforcement Officer, my fundamental duty is to
serve mankind; to safeguard lives and property; to protect the innocent against deception, the weak against oppression or intimidation,
and the peaceful against violence or disorder; and to respect the '
Constitutional rights of all men to liberty, equality and justice.

I will keep my private life unsullied as an example to all;
maintain courageous calm in the face of danger, scorn, or ridicule;
develop selfrestraint; and be constantly mindful of the welfare of
others.   Honest in thought and deed in both my personal and official life, I will be exemplary in obeying the laws of the land and
the regulations of my department. Whatever I see or hear of a confidential nature or that is confided to me in my official capacity
will be kept ever secret unless revelation is necessary in the performance of my duty.

I will never act officiously or permit personal feelings, prejudices, animosities or friendships to influence my decisions.   With
no compromise for crime and with relentless prosecution of criminals, I will enforce the law courteously and appropriately without
fear or favor, malice or ill will, never employing unnecessary force
or violence and never accepting gratuities.

I recognize the badge of my office as a symbol of public faith,
and I accept it as a public trust to be held so long as I am true to
the ethics of the police service.   I will constantly strive to achieve
these objectives and ideals, dedicating myself before God to my
chosen profession ... law enforcement.

LAWYERS

AMERICAN BAR ASSOCIATION (ABA)
1155 E. 60th St., Chicago, Ill. 60637
Bert W. Early, Executive Director

Membership: The American Bar Association, founded in 1878 and
with a present (1973) membership of over 165, 000, is a professional society of attorneys and judges in the United States.   Members are grouped in affiliated local and state bar associations, and
qualify for membership by being admitted to the bar in any state of
the United States.   Since December 1972, membership has been
expanded to include two categories of Associate Members:
   International Associates--members of the legal profession
      of another country who have not been admitted to the bar
      of any state of the United States; and
   Judicial Associates--judges, court administrators and fed-
      eral court executives who are not members of the legal
      profession.

<u>Code of Ethics</u>: The American Bar Association has been active for
a number of years in the setting of standards of ethical practice for
lawyers.   The original 32 Canons of Professional Ethics, adopted in
1908, were "based principally on the 1887 Code of Ethics of the
Alabama Bar Association, which in turn had borrowed the professional guides largely from the lectures of Judge George Sharswood,
as published in 1854 under the title, <u>Professional Ethics</u>."
    From 1908 until 1964, a limited number of amendments to the
original 32 Canons of Ethics had been adopted on a piecemeal basis.
Special Committees of the American Bar Association were appointed
in 1928, 1933, 1937 and 1954 for the purpose of investigating the
subject of overall revision, but no action was taken until 1964, when
work was begun on the new Code.   The revision was directed to
criticisms of the older canons--important areas of lawyers' conduct
were only partially covered or omitted, many canons needed editorial revision, most canons "did not lend themselves to practical
sanctions for violation," and changed and changing social conditions
required new statements of professional principles.

    The revised canons "incorporating professional responsibilities
and obligations--as well as etiquette and deportment"--were issued
in the current Code of Professional Responsibility, adopted by the
ABA House of Delegates on August 12, 1969, to be effective January 1, 1970, and amended February 24, 1970.   The basic source
for the new code was the book, <u>Legal Ethics</u> (1953), by Henry S.
Drinker, who for nine years was Chairman of the Committee on
Professional Ethics, and the opinions of the ABA Committee on
Professional Ethics, collected in a single published volume (1967),
and more recently issued in loose-leaf form.

    The Code of Professional Responsibility consists of nine Canons:
1. A lawyer should assist in maintaining the integrity and
   competence of the legal profession.
2. A lawyer should assist the legal profession in fulfilling
   its duty to make legal counsel available.
3. A lawyer should assist in preventing the unauthorized
   practice of law.
4. A lawyer should preserve the confidence and secrets of
   a client.
5. A lawyer should exercise independent professional judgment on behalf of a client.
6. A lawyer should represent a client competently.
7. A lawyer should represent a client zealously within the
   bounds of the law.
8. A lawyer should assist in improving the legal system.
9. A lawyer should avoid even the appearance of professional impropriety.

    Each of the nine Canons may include:
    <u>Canon</u>--"Statement of axiomatic norms, expressing in gen-
    eral terms the standards of professional conduct expected
    of lawyers in their relationships with the public, with the

legal system, and with the legal profession";
Ethical Considerations--Aspirational objectives, principles
   providing guidance for many specific situations the lawyer
   may meet;
Disciplinary Rules--Mandatory "minimum level of conduct below which no lawyer can fall without being subject to disciplinary action."
The standing Committee on Ethics and Professional Responsibility interprets and revises the Code of Professional Responsibility.   Interpretations are issued as Formal Opinions and Informal Opinions.
Formal Opinions--on matters of widespread interest--are published
in full in the American Bar Association Journal, and are subsequently
published in volumes of Opinions.   Informal Opinions are summarized
in the Journal.

   The Code of Professional Responsibility is enforced by state and
local Bar Associations, whose grievance agencies receive complaints
and act on them through the state courts.   The ultimate authority
rests with the highest court in the state, usually the Supreme Court,
which is the agency that admits lawyers to practice.   The ABA Committee on Professional Grievances has been disbanded, as the American Bar Association as a private organization "has no power to
discipline or disbar an attorney."   Although the American Bar Association does not participate in the grievance procedures, the Association's new Code of Professional Responsibility has now been adopted
by 48 states.   The Association also engaged in a national program
to tighten disciplinary enforcement and to encourage the states to
improve their disciplinary structures.

Other Guides to Professional Conduct: The Oath of Admission to the
Bar sets forth the "general principles which should ... control the
lawyer in the practice of his profession."   It is formulated upon the
Oath used by the Bar Association in the State of Washington.   The
American Bar Association "recommends the form of oath for adoption by the proper authorities in all the States and Territories" of
the United States.

Professional Insignia: The American Bar Association reports no
official emblem.

Bibliography:
   American Bar Association.   Code of Professional Responsibility
      and Code of Judicial Conduct.   Chicago, American Bar
      Association, 1972.   55 pages.   (Printed by Martindale-
      Hubbell, Inc. as a service to the legal profession.)
   Includes a historical preface, detailed Table of Contents, the
   Code with nine Canons, Ethical Considerations and Disci-
   plinary Rules.   Gives composition, duties and procedural
   rules of pertinent committees, such as standing committee on
   Ethics and Professional Responsibility.   Text of Oath of Ad-
   mission to the Bar (p. 55).   Detailed index (p. 38-42).
   American Bar Association.   Committee on Ethics and Professional

Responsibility. Opinions. 1967, and looseleaf, 1967-
The opinions published in the American Bar Association
Journal (the Formal Opinions) are preserved in this publi-
cation.

Drinker, Henry. Legal Ethics. N.Y., Columbia University
Press, 1953. 448 pages.
A basic source of the current American Bar Association
Code of Professional Responsibility.

Maru, Olavi. Digest of Bar Association Ethical Opinions.
Chicago, Bar Foundation, 1970. 633 pages.

Matthews, Robert Elden. Problems Illustrative of the Responsibilities of Members of the Legal Profession. 2nd rev
ed. N.Y., Council on Legal Education for Professional
Responsibility. 1968. 263 pages.

Wise, Raymond L. Legal Ethics. 2nd ed. N.Y., Matthew
Bender, 1970. 505 pages.
In addition to text of the canons and disciplinary rules of the
current Code of Professional Responsibility of the American
Bar Association, gives explanation and comparisons of the
purpose, meaning, and derivation of each canon, with cita-
tion of relevant ABA decisions and opinions.

"Oath of Admission"

The general principles which should ever control the lawyer
in the practice of his profession are clearly set forth in the following Oath of Admission to the Bar, formulated upon that in use in the
State of Washington, and which conforms in its main outlines to the
"duties" of Lawyers as defined by statutory enactments in that and
many other States of the Union--duties which they are sworn on
admission to obey and for the wilful violation of which disbarment
is provided:

I Do Solemnly Swear:

I will support the Constitution of the United States and the
Constitution of the State of ....

I will maintain the respect due to Courts of Justice and
judicial officers;

I will not counsel or maintain any suit or proceeding which
shall appear to me to be unjust, nor any defense except such as I
believe to be honestly debatable under the law of the land;

I will employ for the purpose of maintaining the causes confided to me such means only as are consistent with truth and honor,
and will never seek to mislead the Judge or jury by any artifice or
false statement of fact or law;

I will maintain the confidence and preserve inviolate the
secrets of my client, and will accept no compensation in connection
with his business except from him or with his knowledge and approval;

I will abstain from all offensive personality, and advance no
fact prejudicial to the honor or reputation of a party or witness,

unless required by the justice of the cause with which I am charged;
    I will never reject, from any consideration personal to my-
self, the cause of the defenseless or oppressed, or delay any man's
cause for lucre or malice.   So help me God.

        The American Bar Association commends this form of oath
for adoption by the proper authorities in all the States and Territories.

INTERNATIONAL BAR ASSOCIATION (IBA)
    14 Waterloo Place, London SW 1 Y 4AR
    Sir Thomas Lund, C. B. E. , Director General
    (G. J. McMahon, Secretary-General
    501 Fifth Ave. , New York, N. Y. 10017)

Membership: The International Bar Association, founded in 1947
and with a present (1973) membership of 65 members and one sustaining member from 49 countries, is a federation of national Bar
Associations and Law Societies.   Also, included as active Patrons
and Subscribers, are 2800 individual lawyers, who are members of
the IBA.   "Any National Bar Association or Law Society may be
elected a member and any State, Provincial, District or Local Bar
Association or Law Society may be elected a 'Sustaining Member', "
of the Association.   Any attorney licensed to practice law in the
State (or other administrative area) of his practice may become a
Patron or Subscriber of the International Bar Association.

Code of Ethics: Among the topics discussed at the bienniel Conferences of the International Bar Association--held since 1948--are
ethical codes for lawyers.   Such a guide for the legal profession is
published by the IBA--the International Code of Ethics for the Legal

Profession.   The Code, which
was adopted in 1956 and most
recently amended by the General Meeting of the IBA at
Mexico City on July 29, 1964,
consists of 20 principles, which
set forth the duties and responsibilities of the lawyer--rang-
ing from personal conduct,
confidentiality of communication,
conflict-of-interest, soliciting
business, to conduct in dealing
with foreign colleagues and
handling cases of international
character.

Professional Insignia: The

emblem of the International Bar Association is a circular design, with a centered line outline of the scales of justice held in a closed right hand; the organization initials, "IBA," are shown below the scales. The colors of this insignia are white on gold (as shown on publication).

Bibliography:
International Bar Association. International Code of Ethics for the Legal Profession. Adopted at Oslo on July 25, 1956, and amended ... July 29, 1964.
Background and significance of legal ethics.
_____. Introducing the International Bar Association. 1973. Folder.
Informational brochure giving IBA purposes, membership and activities; emblem on cover.
Lund, Sir Thomas George. Professional Ethics. London, Sweet & Maxwell, Ltd., 1970. (Distributed by International Bar Association, New York). 51 pages. $3.
This second in a series of books "designed to assist developing Bar Associations and Law Societies and Practitioners," includes history and significance of legal ethics; and text of the International Bar Association International Code of Ethics for the Legal Profession (p. 39-43).

"International Code of Ethics"

1 This Code of International Ethics in no way is intended to supersede existing national or local rules of legal ethics or those which may from time to time be adopted.
A lawyer shall not only discharge the duties imposed upon him by his own national or local rules, but he shall also endeavour when handling a case of an international character to adhere to the rules of this Code subject necessarily to the rules existing in those other countries in which he is active.
2 A lawyer shall at all times maintain the honour and dignity of his profession.
He shall, in his practice as well as in his private life, abstain from any behaviour which may tend to discredit the profession of which he is a member.
3 A lawyer shall preserve independence in the discharge of his professional duty.
A lawyer, practising on his own account or in partnership where permissible, shall not engage in any other business or occupation if by doing so he may cease to be independent.
4 A lawyer shall treat his professional colleagues with the utmost courtesy and fairness.
A lawyer who undertakes to render assistance to a foreign colleague shall always keep in mind that his foreign colleague has to depend on him to a much larger extent than in the case of another lawyer of the same country. Therefore his responsibility is much greater, both when giving advice and when handling a case.

For this reason it is improper for a lawyer to accept a case unless he can handle it promptly and with due competence, without undue interference by the pressure of other work. To the fees in these cases Rule 19 applies.

5   Except where the law or custom of the country concerned otherwise requires, any oral or written communication between lawyers shall in principle be accorded a confidential character as far as the Court is concerned, unless certain promises or acknowledgments are made therein on behalf of a client.

6   A lawyer shall always maintain due respect towards the Court.   A lawyer shall without fear defend the interests of his client and without regard to any unpleasant consequences to himself or to any other person.

A lawyer shall never knowingly give to the Court incorrect information or advice which is to his knowledge contrary to the law.

7   It shall be considered improper for a lawyer to communicate about a particular case directly with any person whom he knows to be represented in that case by another lawyer without the latter's consent.

8   It is contrary to the dignity of a lawyer to resort to advertisement.

9   A lawyer should never solicit business and he should never consent to handle a case unless at the direct request of the party concerned.   However, it is proper for a lawyer to handle a case which is assigned to him by a competent body, or which is forwarded to him by another lawyer or for which he is engaged in any other manner permissible under his local rules or regulations.

10   A lawyer shall at all times give his client a candid opinion on any case.

He shall render his assistance with scrupulous care and diligence.   This applies also if he is assigned as counsel for an indigent person.

A lawyer shall at any time be free to refuse to handle a case, unless it is assigned to him by a competent body.

A lawyer should only withdraw from a case during its course for good cause, and if possible in such a manner that the client's interests are not adversely affected.

The loyal defence of a client's case may never cause an advocate to be other than perfectly candid, subject to any right or privilege to the contrary which his clients choose him to exercise, or knowingly to go against the law.

11   A lawyer shall when in the client's interest endeavour to reach a solution by settlement out of court rather than start legal proceedings.

A lawyer should never stir up litigation.

12   A lawyer should not acquire financial interest in the subject matter of a case which he is conducting.   Neither should he, directly or indirectly, acquire property about which litigation is pending before the Court in which he practices.

13   A lawyer should not represent conflicting interests in litigation and should only do so in other matters where he considers to do so is in the best interests of both clients and they do not

object.   This also applies to all members of a firm or partnership of lawyers.

14   A lawyer should never disclose, unless lawfully ordered to do so by the Court or as required by Statute, what has been communicated to him in his capacity as lawyer, even after he has ceased to be the client's counsel.   This duty extends to his partners, to junior lawyers assisting him and to his employees.

15   In pecuniary matters a lawyer shall be most punctual and diligent.

He should never mingle funds of others with his own and he should at all times be able to refund money he holds for others.

He shall not retain money he received for his client for longer than is absolutely necessary.

16   A lawyer may require that a deposit is made to cover his expenses, but the deposit should be in accordance with the estimated amount of his charges and the probable expenses and labour required.

17   A lawyer shall never forget that he should put first not his right to compensation for his services, but the interest of his client and the exigencies of the administration of justice.

His right to ask for a deposit or to demand payment for his services, failing which he may withdraw from a case or refuse to handle it, should never be exercised at a moment on which the client or prospective client may be unable to find other assistance in time to prevent irreparable damage being done.

The lawyer's fee should, in the absence or non-applicability of official scales, be fixed on a consideration of the amount involved in the controversy and the interest of it to the client, the time and labout involved and all other personal and factual circumstances of the case.

18   A contract for a contingent fee, where sanctioned by the law or by professional rules and practice, should be reasonable in all the circumstances of the case, including the risk and uncertainty of the compensation and subject to supervision of a court as to its reasonableness.

19   A lawyer who engaged a foreign colleague to advise on a case or to cooperate in handling it, is responsible for the payment of the latter's charges except express agreement to the contrary.   When a lawyer directs a client to a foreign colleague he is not responsible for the payment of the latter's charges, but neither is he entitled to a share of the fee of this foreign colleague.

20   No lawyer should permit his professional services or his name to be used in any way which would make it possible for persons to practice law who are not legally authorised to do so.

No lawyer shall delegate to a legally unqualified person not in his employ and control any functions which are by the law or custom of the country in which he practices only to be performed by a qualified lawyer.

LIBRARIANS

AMERICAN LIBRARY ASSOCIATION (ALA)
    50 E. Huron St., Chicago, Ill. 60611
    Robert Wedgeworth, Executive Director

Membership: The American Library Association, organized in 1876
and with a present (1973) membership of approximately 37,000, is
the national professional organization of librarians. ALA has more
than 50 state, regional and territorial chapters, and the diversity
of interest of its members is reflected in 14 divisions and seven
round tables, devoted to special types of libraries and the various
activities of libraries and all types of information centers. Membership is open to any individual or organization with an interest in
any aspect of librarianship. To be eligible as a "Personal Member," an applicant must be:
    "a librarian
    a library trustee
    in library service in any capacity [or]
    an interested individual."

Code of Ethics: The professional conduct guide of the American
Library Association is its Code of Ethics for Librarians, adopted in
1938, and at present being revised by an ALA Committee. The
Code consists of 25 numbered paragraphs, that give principles of
ethical behavior for the professional librarian in relation to:
    Governing Authority of the Library,
    Constituency of the Librarian,
    Library in which the Librarian Works,
    The Library Profession,
    Society in which the Library Operates.
No procedures for enforcement of the Code are reported.

Professional Insignia: The emblem of the American Library
Association is its seal--circu-
lar in shape, the design shows
a centered open book with the
organization initials, "ALA,"
above the book; the bordering
band of the design bears the
group's name, "American Library Association," with the
Association's founding date,
"1876," at the bottom within
the border. The color of the
emblem is shown variously--
blue on white, with the central

circular portion of the design in blue (letterhead); black on greyed blue (publication).

Bibliography:
> American Library Association. The American Library Association and You. 8 pages. Pamphlet.
> Informational brochure includes ALA membership categories, organization, purpose, activities, and publications.
>> Code of Ethics for Librarians. 1938. 3 pages. Processed.
> Conduct guide for professional librarians.

"Code of Ethics for Librarians"

Preamble

1. The library as an institution exists for the benefit of a given constituency, whether it be the citizens of a community, members of an educational institution, or some larger or more specialized group. Those who enter the library profession assume an obligation to maintain ethical standards of behavior in relation to the governing authority under which they work, to the library constituency, to the library as an institution and to fellow workers on the staff, to other members of the library profession, and to society in general.

2. The term librarian in this code applies to any person who is employed by a library to do work that is recognized to be professional in character according to standards established by the American Library Association.

3. This code sets forth principles of ethical behavior for the professional librarian. It is not a declaration of prerogatives nor a statement of recommended practices in specific situations.

I. Relation of the Librarian to the Governing Authority

4. The librarian should perform his duties with realization of the fact that final jurisdiction over the administration of the library rests in the officially constituted governing authority. This authority may be vested in a designated individual, or in a group such as a committee or board.

5. The chief librarian should keep the governing authority informed on professional standards and progressive action. Each librarian should be responsible for carrying out the policies of the governing authority and its appointed executives with a spirit of loyalty to the library.

6. The chief librarian should interpret decisions of the governing authority to the staff, and should act as liaison officer in maintaining friendly relations between staff members and those in authority.

7. Recommendations to the governing authority for the appointment of a staff member should be made by the chief librarian solely upon the basis of the candidate's professional and personal

qualifications for the position. Continuance in service and promotion should depend upon the quality of performance, following a definite and known policy. Whenever the good of the service requires a change in personnel, timely warning should be given. If desirable adjustment cannot be made, unsatisfactory service should be terminated in accordance with the policy of the library and the rules of tenure.

8. Resolutions, petitions, and requests of a staff organization or group should be submitted through a duly appointed representative to the chief librarian. If a mutually satisfactory solution cannot be reached, the chief librarian, on request of the staff, should transmit the matter to the governing authority. The staff may further request that they be allowed to send a representative to the governing authority, in order to present their opinions in person.

II.   Relation of the Librarian to His Constituency

9. The chief librarian, aided by staff members in touch with the constituency, should study the present and future needs of the library, and should acquire materials on the basis of those needs. Provision should be made for as wide a range of publications and as varied a representation of viewpoints as is consistent with the policies of the library and with the funds available.

10. It is the librarian's responsibility to make the resources and services of the library known to its potential users. Impartial service should be rendered to all who are entitled to use the library.

11. It is the librarian's obligation to treat as confidential any private information obtained through contact with library patrons.

12. The librarian should try to protect library property and to inculcate in users a sense of their responsibility for its preservation.

III.   Relations of the Librarian within His Library

13. The chief librarian should delegate authority, encourage a sense of responsibility and initiative on the part of staff members, provide for their professional development, and appreciate good work. Staff members should be informed of the duties of their positions and the policies and problems of the library.

14. Loyalty to fellow workers and a spirit of courteous cooperation, whether between individuals or between departments, are essential to effective library service.

15. Criticism of library policies, service, and personnel should be offered only to the proper authority for the sole purpose of improvement of the library.

16. Acceptance of a position in a library incurs an obligation to remain long enough to repay the library for the expense incident to adjustment. A contract signed or agreement made should be adhered to faithfully until it expires or is dissolved by mutual consent.

17. Resignations should be made long enough before they are to take effect to allow adequate time for the work to be put in shape and a successor appointed.

18. A librarian should never enter into a business dealing on behalf of the library which will result in personal profit.

19. A librarian should never turn the library's resources to personal use, to the detriment of services which the library renders to its patrons.

IV. Relation of the Librarian to His Profession

20. Librarians should recognize librarianship as an educational profession and realize that the growing effectiveness of their service is dependent upon their own development.

21. In view of the importance of ability and personality traits in library work, a librarian should encourage only those persons with suitable aptitudes to enter the library profession and should discourage the continuance in service of the unfit.

22. Recommendations should be confidential and should be fair to the candidate and the prospective employer by presenting an unbiased statement of strong and weak points.

23. Librarians should have a sincere belief and a critical interest in the library profession. They should endeavor to achieve and maintain adequate salaries and proper working conditions.

24. Formal appraisal of the policies or practices of another library should be given only upon the invitation of that library's governing authority or chief librarian.

25. Librarians, in recognizing the essential unity of their profession, should have membership in library organizations and should be ready to attend and participate in library meetings and conferences.

V. Relation of the Librarian to Society

26. Librarians should encourage a general realization of the value of library service and be informed concerning movements, organizations, and institutions whose aims are compatible with those of the library.

27. Librarians should participate in public and community affairs and so represent the library that it will take its place among educational, social, and cultural agencies.

28. A librarian's conduct should be such as to maintain public esteem for the library and for library work.

SPECIAL LIBRARIES ASSOCIATION (SLA)
    235 Park Ave. South, New York, N. Y. 10003
    F. E. McKenna, Executive Director

Membership: The Special Libraries Association, founded in 1909

and with a present (1973) membership of more than 7500, is an
"international organization of professional librarians and information experts"--"individuals and organizations, with educational,
scientific and technical interests in library and information science
and technology--especially as these are applied in the selection,
recording, retrieval and effective utilization of man's knowledge."
A "special library" is defined by the Association as:

"a. A library information center maintained by an individual,
     corporation, association, government agency or any
     other group; or

b.   A specialized or departmental collection within a library,
     for the organization and dissemination of information,
     and primarily offering service to a specialized clientele
     through the use of varied media and methods."

Any person interested in library work may join the SLA; however, the fully professional category of membership is "Member,"
which requires one of the following combinations of education and
experience:

a.   Graduate degree in library or information science;

b.   Bachelor's degree or higher degree and three or more
     years of professional experience in a special library;

c.   At least seven years experience in a special library,
     determined by the Association committee concerned with
     membership to be professional experience. (One year of
     undergraduate college credit equals one year of profes-
     sional experience);

d.   A teaching position in a university or college and is
     engaged in educating students in one or more disciplines
     related to the professional aspects of professional li-
     brarianship or information science;

e.   Bachelor's degree or higher degree and has or has had
     general administrative responsibility for one or more
     special divisions or subject areas in an academic or
     public library.

**SPECIAL LIBRARIES
ASSOCIATION**

Code of Ethics: The Special
Libraries Association has considered adoption of a guide to
professional conduct for its
members, but because of the
diversity of membership has
not issued a formal code of
ethics.

Professional Insignia: The
official emblem of the SLA is
its logotype--a circular design
with the initials of the organization, "SLA," in script with
the unbounded border of the
design formed by the Association

motto, "Putting Knowledge to Work," above the printed name, "Special Libraries Association." The insignia--shown in black and white--was adopted in 1958, although the motto has been in use by the group since about 1909. The emblem, which was designed by the Special Libraries Association Public Relations Committee, is restricted in use to SLA publications, or other items, as officially approved by the Association's Board of Directors.

Bibliography:
 Special Libraries Association. Bylaws. Folder.
   Includes definition of "special library," and SLA membership requirements.
   _____. A Resume. Folder.
   Informational brochure giving SLA purposes, organization, activities and services, membership application.
   _____. What is a Special Librarian? Folder.
   Guidance information about special library work.
   _____. The World of the Special Librarian is a World of Information. Folder.
 Scope of work; places of education and employment for special librarians.

MANAGERIAL OCCUPATIONS

SOCIETY FOR ADVANCEMENT OF MANAGEMENT (SAM)
 Suite 1050, 135 W. 50th St., New York, N.Y. 10020
 William H. Latham, Executive Director

Membership: The Society for Advancement of Management, founded in 1912 and with a present (1973) membership of over 16,000, is a professional organization of management executives and management administrators in business, industry and the public service, including government and education. The present organization grew from two parent societies, The Taylor Society--founded in 1912 to "promote the science of management," and the Society of Industrial Engineers, organized in 1917. Among the pioneers in management science initiating and active in these early groups were Frederick W. Taylor, Frank and Lillian Gilbreth, and Carl Barth. Diverse aspects of management are represented among executive members of SAM, including directors, presidents, comptrollers, research and development directors, plant managers, production and sales managers, industrial engineers, economists and business consultants, and officials in federal, state, and local governments.

 Education and experience requirements for several categories of SAM membership are:
   Member--Minimum of five years' experience in managerial

activity; graduation from accredited college or university
curriculum may substitute for three years of this required
experience;
<u>Associate Member</u>--Minimum of five years' experience in an
area related to the art and science of management; or
graduation from an accredited college or university curriculum, and present employment as a management
trainee.
Other types of membership include student memberships and honorary memberships, such as "Fellow"--which requires "significant
attainments in art and science of management," and 10 years' managerial experience, and membership as an SAM "Member."

<u>Code of Ethics</u>: No formal guide to professional activity in the form
of a code of ethics has been issued by SAM.

<u>Professional Insignia</u>: The emblem of the Society is its logotype--
a stylized monogram of the
organization initials, "sam,"
shown in lower case and with

the middle horizontal line of
the "a" ending in an arrow--
similar to the mathematical
symbol of an arrow meaning
"yields"; this element of the
design is emblematic of the
application of scientific study
and quantification to "organized effort in industrial and economic
life." The color of the insignia is shown variously--blue (letterhead); black (publications).

<u>Bibliography</u>:
Society for Advancement of Management. <u>Constitution and By-</u>
<u>Laws</u>. June 11, 1968. 20 pages. Pamphlet.
Includes membership requirements, and purpose and mission
of SAM.
_____. <u>A Funny Thing Happened to Me on the Way to the</u>
<u>Top</u>. 20 pages. Pamphlet.
Informational brochure gives brief SAM history, membership
requirements, and activities.

MANUFACTURERS

NATIONAL ASSOCIATION OF MANUFACTURERS (NAM)
277 Park Ave., New York, N.Y. 10017
W. P. Gullander, President

Membership: The National Association of Manufacturers is a trade association, founded in 1897 and with a present (1973) membership of 12,000. Its members are "industrial and business firms, large and small, located in every state" of the United States.

Code of Ethics: Guides to conduct have been formulated by NAM as the Association's Code of Business Practices, which enumerates five policies of business practice, to which NAM members are urged to subscribe.

Other Guides to Professional Conduct: The purposes of the National Association of Manufacturers--as a voluntary organization of thousands of member companies in all types and sizes of industries --is expressed in the NAM Credo, which is "dedicated to the economic and social well-being of the nation and the freedom and progress of the American people."

Professional Insignia: The emblem of the NAM is its logotype--stylized monogram of the organization initials, "NAM." The color of this insignia is shown variously--red and white (stationery); black and white (publications).

Bibliography:
> National Association of Manufacturers. Official Policy Positions. Annual, in January.
> This manual--published each year, as provided in the NAM By-Laws--states "the official views of the Association on the significant economic, political, and social issues of the day." Includes the Code of Business Practices and the NAM Credo.

"Code of Business Practices"

While there can be no question as to the right of American citizens to engage in private business under our Constitution and form of government, this right like all rights has accompanying responsibilities. Business organizations must serve the public interest, as separate entities and in the over-all sense, if this right is to be respected and maintained.

NAM and its member companies are committed to policies and practices which will strengthen faith in our free economy and inspire public confidence in our business enterprises and those who manage them.

All members of the Association are urged to subscribe to the official CODE OF BUSINESS PRACTICES adopted by the Board of Directors, which is as follows:

1. We will strive at all times to conduct the affairs of this company to merit public confidence in American business and

industry and faith in our free private competitive enterprise system.

2. We will see that our employees are given every opportunity to progress with the company and are appropriately compensated
for their work.

3. We will deal fairly with customers and suppliers and extend to them the same treatment we wish to receive ourselves.

4. We will compete vigorously to serve our customers and
expand our business, but we will avoid unfair or unethical practices.

5. We will seek through sound management practices to
produce the profit necessary to the continued progress of the business and so fulfill our responsibilities to our stockholders, employees, customers, community and nation.

"NAM Credo"

The National Association of Manufacturers is a voluntary
organization of many thousands of member companies, located in
every state, representative of industry of all sizes from the smallest
to the largest, and dedicated to the economic and social well-being
of the nation and the freedom and progress of the American people.

The purposes of the National Association of Manufacturers
are defined as follows:

To formulate policies and objectives based on the enduring
economic, social and governmental principles embodied in the Constitution of the United States, and without regard to partisan political
considerations or the fortunes of any political party or candidate.

To provide leadership in bringing about a steady improvement:
(a) in the economic strength of the nation; (b) in the contribution
of industry to the public welfare; (c) in the operation of the American system of free capital and free labor so as to afford opportunity
and incentive for the individual to progress and provide for the well-
being and security of himself and his family.

To assist manufacturers in appraising the significance of
social, legislative, and economic trends as they affect industry,
people, the community and the nation.

To contribute to a continuing improvement in the relations
and cooperation between employer and employee, between government and industry, and between the public and industry.

To join with others in bringing to the public and to government the viewpoint of manufacturers as to how national and international issues affect industry and the future of every citizen.

To help create understanding of how the American free competitive enterprise system works for the benefit of every individual.

To formulate its policies and conduct its operations so as to
merit the respect and support of the American people.

MARKETING RESEARCH WORKERS

AMERICAN MARKETING ASSOCIATION (AMA)
    230 N. Michigan Ave., Chicago, Ill. 60601
    Wayne A. Lemburg, Executive Director

Membership: The American Marketing Association, founded in 1915
and with a present (1973) membership of 18,000, is a professional
association "dedicated to the advancement of science in marketing."
Diverse interests of the membership are shown in the seven major
professional divisions in:

Marketing Education,	Industrial Marketing,
Marketing Management,	International Marketing,
Marketing Research,	Public Policy and Issues.
Consumer Marketing,	

The wide range of members' interest is also reflected in the
subject sections and committees of the Association, which cover
marketing of products and services, such as Grocery Products,
Pharmaceuticals, Travel and Passenger Transportation, Construction, Financial Services, Agricultural Marketing. The Association
defines "marketing" (Constitution, Article I) as:
    "the performance of business activities that direct the flow
    of goods and services from producer to consumer or user,"
    and admits to membership individuals "actively engaged or
    interested in teaching, developing, or applying effective and
    efficient marketing methods."

Code of Ethics: Following one of the purposes of the Association--
"To encourage and uphold sound, honest practices, and to keep
marketing work on a high ethical plane"--a Committee of the AMA
developed the Marketing Research Code in 1920. This Code
enumerates obligations and responsibilities of members, under four
headings:
    Research Users, Practitioners and Interviewers;
    Research Practitioners;
    Users of Marketing Research;
    Field Interviewers.
The Association follows specified procedures in enforcement of the
Codes of conduct it has developed. The Executive Director of the
AMA reviews written complaints of codes violation and an AMA
Ethics Review Board reviews and takes "appropriate action on complaints relating to alleged violations of the Association's Code of
Ethics and the Marketing Research Code. When those refused mem-
bership or expelled from membership contest the AMA decision,
the question is referred to arbitration for decision binding upon all
parties.

Other Guides to Professional Conduct: Another statement of professional obligation and responsibility for market research workers
is the pledge by which a member recognizes the significance of his
professional conduct and his responsibilities to society and other
members of his profession, as stated in the six principles--Our
Code of Ethics. This pledge is signed by all members as a part

of their application, and each member states he has read this code and agrees to abide by it.

Professional Insignia: The insignia, used by the AMA or its chapters on official stationery and publications, is a rectangular unbordered design, formed by the stylized monogram of the group, "AMA," printed above the organization name, "American Marketing Association." The color of the logotype is black on white.

Bibliography:

    American Marketing Association. "AMA Board Backs New Ethics Procedure." The Marketing News. 6:1 August 15, 1972. Describes the procedure for enforcement of the AMA code of ethics and the Marketing Research Code.

    ——————. Fact Book: This is the American Marketing Association. Annual. Includes Association history, membership qualifications, Constitution and Bylaws, Marketing Research Code, and Our Code of Ethics.

"Our Code of Ethics"

As a member of the American Marketing Association, I recognize the significance of my professional conduct and my responsibilities to society and to the other members of my profession:

1.   By acknowledging my accountability to society as a whole as well as to the organization for which I work.
2.   By pledging my efforts to assure that all presentations of goods, services and concepts be made honestly and clearly.
3.   By striving to improve marketing knowledge and practice in order to better serve society.
4.   By supporting free consumer choice in circumstances that are legal and are consistent with generally accepted community standards.
5.   By pledging to use the highest professional standards in my work and in competitive activity.
6.   By acknowledging the right of the American Marketing Association, through established procedure, to withdraw my

membership if I am found to be in violation of ethical standards of professional conduct.

"Marketing Research Code of Ethics"

The American Marketing Association, in furtherance of its central objective of the advancement of science in marketing and in recognition of its obligation to the public, has established these principles of ethical practice of marketing research for the guidance of its members. In an increasingly complex society, marketing management is more and more dependent upon marketing information intelligently and systematically obtained. The consumer is the source of much of this information. Seeking the cooperation of the consumer in the development of information, marketing management must acknowledge its obligation to protect the public from misrepresentation and exploitation under the guise of research.

Similarly the research practitioner has an obligation to the discipline he practices and to those who provide support for his practice--an obligation to adhere to basic and commonly accepted standards of scientific investigation as they apply to the domain of marketing research.

It is the intent of this code to define ethical standards required of marketing research in satisfying these obligations.

Adherence to this code will assure the users of marketing research that the research was done in accordance with acceptable ethical practices. Those engaged in research will find in this code an affirmation of sound and honest basic principles which have developed over the years as the profession has grown. The field interviewers who are the point of contact between the profession and the consumer will also find guidance in fulfilling their vitally important role.

For Research Users, Practitioners and Interviewers

1. No individual or organization will undertake any activity which is directly or indirectly represented to be marketing research, but which has as its real purpose the attempted sale of merchandise or services to some or all of the respondents interviewed in the course of the research.

2. If a respondent has been led to believe, directly or indirectly, that he is participating in a marketing research survey and that his anonymity will be protected, his name shall not be made known to anyone outside the research organization or research department, or used for other than research purposes.

For Research Practitioners

1. There will be no intentional or deliberate misrepresentation of research methods or results. An adequate description of methods employed will be made available upon request to the sponsor of the research. Evidence that field work has been completed according to

specifications will, upon request, be made available to buyers of research.

2. The identity of the survey sponsor and/or the ultimate client for whom a survey is being done will be held in confidence at all times, unless this identity is to be revealed as part of the research design. Research information shall be held in confidence by the research organization or department and not used for personal gain or made available to any outside party unless the client specifically authorizes such release.

3. A research organization shall not undertake marketing studies for competitive clients when such studies would jeopardize the confidential nature of client-agency relationships.

For Users of Marketing Research

1. A user of research shall not knowingly disseminate conclusions from a given research project or service that are inconsistent with or nor warranted by the data.

2. To the extent that there is involved in a research project a unique design involving techniques, approaches or concepts not commonly available to research practitioners, the prospective user of research shall not solicit such a design from one practitioner and deliver it to another for execution without the approval of the design originator.

For Field Interviewers

1. Research assignments and materials received, as well as information obtained from respondents, shall be held in confidence by the interviewer and revealed to no one except the research organization conducting the marketing study.

2. No information gained through a marketing research activity shall be used directly or indirectly, for the personal gain or advantage of the interviewer.

3. Interviews shall be conducted in strict accordance with specifications and instructions received.

4. An interviewer shall not carry out two or more interviewing assignments simultaneously unless authorized by all contractors or employers concerned.

Members of the American Marketing Association will be expected to conduct themselves in accordance with the provisions of this Code in all of their marketing research activities.

MARRIAGE AND FAMILY COUNSELORS

AMERICAN ASSOCIATION OF MARRIAGE AND FAMILY COUNSELORS (AAMFC)

225 Yale Ave., Claremont, Calif. 91711
C. Ray Fowler, Ph.D., Executive Director

Membership: The American Association of Marriage and Family
Counselors, founded in 1942 and with a present (1973) membership
of over 1500, is a professional association of counselors, engaged in
the relatively new field of personal and social service--that of marriage and family counseling. Among members of AAMFC are
psychologists, psychiatrists, social workers, ministers, physicians,
sociologists, attorneys, and educators--who as "highly-trained professional marriage counselors" work to help couples solve their
marriage and family problems.

The academic training and professional experience requirements
qualifying for the three categories of Association membership are:

    Fellow--Minimum of five years as a member of AAMFC, and
       a significant contribution to the field of marriage counsel-
       ing. This category of membership is honorary so is
       awarded rather than being applied for.

    Member--Professional training for and a minimum of five
       years' experience in clinical marriage counseling.

    Associate Member--Professional training for clinical mar-
       riage counseling and a minimum of two years' experience
       in that field.

Code of Ethics: Directed by its stated purpose of promoting and
maintaining "standards at a professional level in a new field of
clinical specialization," the Association has developed a guide to professional conduct, to which each member subscribes: Code of Professional Ethics. This Code was prepared by a specially appointed
AAMFC Committee during 1960-1961, and approved in 1962. It
enumerates principles governing professional practice and relationships with clients, colleagues, and the public. The Code contains
provisions for its enforcement by including procedures for receiving,
investigating, and recommending disposition of alleged Code violations, by the Committee on Ethics
and Professional Practices. Final
disposition of substantiated complaints is determined by the
AAMFC Board of Directors, which
may admonish, reprimand, or dismiss from membership an unethical
member.

Professional Insignia: The emblem of the American Association
of Marriage and Family Counselors is a monogram of the organization, "AAMFC," printed in
rectangular form.

Bibliography:
   American Association of Marriage and Family Counselors.
      American Association of Marriage and Family Counselors
      --What It is ... What It Does. 4 pages. Folder.
      Informational brochure giving brief history, membership re-
      quirements, activities of the Association; emblem on cover.
               . Constitution and By-Laws; Code of Ethics. Pamphlet.
      Includes membership requirements; ethical code, and pro-
      cedures for code enforcement.
               . The First 25 Years: 1942-1967. 16 pages. Pam-
      phlet.
      History of AAMFC, and its founders.

"Code of Professional Ethics"

This Code was drawn up by a specially-appointed Committee
of the A.A.M.C. during 1960-61. It was then studied by the Board
of Directors and sent out to the entire clinical membership for
further suggestions. After these suggestions had been examined by
the Board of Directors the final revision of the Code was approved
at the Annual Business Meeting on May 19th, 1962.

All clinical members of the A.A.M.C.--Fellows, Members,
and Associate Members--are under obligation to abide by the rules
set out in this Code.

Section 1. It shall be the duty of each member to safeguard
high standards of ethical practice, particularly as defined in the following Sections. Should a fellow member appear to violate this
Code he may be cautioned, through friendly remonstance, or formal
complaint against him may be made in accordance with the following procedure:

a. Complaint of unethical practice shall be made in writing
to the Standing Committee on Ethics and Professional Practices. A
copy of the complaint shall be furnished simultaneously to the person
or persons against whom it is directed.

b. The Standing Committee on Ethics and Professional
Practices shall decide whether the complaint warrants investigation.
If investigation is indicated, the Standing Committee on Ethics shall
constitute itself an Investigating Committee and shall include in its
membership at least one member of the Board and at least two
members from the local area involved. This Investigating Committee shall make one or more local visits of investigation of the
complaint. After full investigation the Committee shall report its
findings and recommendations to the Board, upon which the Board
shall take appropriate action.

c. The defendant shall have free access to all charges and
evidence cited against him. He shall have full freedom to defend
himself before the Investigating Committee and before the Board, including the right to legal counsel.

d. Recommendations to be made by the Committee shall

include advice that the charges are unfounded; recommendation of specified admonishment; reprimand; and dismissal from membership.

e. In accepting membership in the Association each member binds himself to accept the judgment of his fellow members as to standards of professional ethics, subject to the safeguards provided in this section. Acceptance of membership involves explicit agreement to abide by the acts of discipline herein set forth. Should a member be finally expelled from the Association he shall at once surrender his membership diploma to the Board of Directors. Failure to do so may be countered by such action as legal counsel may recommend.

Section 2. Should a member of this Association be expelled from another professional group for unethical conduct the Standing Committee on Ethics shall investigate the matter and act in the manner provided in Section 1 respecting charges of unethical conduct.

Section 3. Advertising of professional services is prohibited, except as to simple professional signs and brief telephone listings, devoid of all claims about service, and the indirect advertising involved in professional communications and participation in community projects relating to marriage and family life. In the course of public speaking and writing care should be exercised to avoid emphasis upon one's personal professional competence.

Section 4. Affiliates and Associates-in-Training shall not represent themselves as having membership status in the Association.

Section 5. When expressing professional opinions or points of view no officer or member shall make it appear, directly or indirectly, that he speaks in behalf of the Association or represents its official position, except as authorized by the Board of Directors.

Section 6. The affiliation of members with professional groups, clinics or agencies operating in the marriage and family life field is encouraged and advised. Similarly, interdisciplinary contact and co-operation are encouraged.

Section 7. The counselor should be cautious in his initial prognosis. He should avoid unwarranted optimism, while offering dignified and reasonable support.

Section 8. Financial arrangements should always be discussed at the start and handled in a business-like manner, including the rendering of periodic statments, unless some other procedure is agreed upon. In establishing fees the client's ability to pay should be taken into consideration.

Section 9. Receipt or payment of a commission for referral of a client is prohibited.

Section 10. Referrals generally should be acknowledged.

Significant information in aid of the referral process usually should be sought from the referral source.

Section 11. Records indicative of the problems and the scope of service shall be kept for each client and shall be stored in a space assuring security and confidentiality.

Section 12. Except by written permission, all communications from clients shall be treated in complete confidence and never revealed to anyone. When a client is referred to in a professional case report his identity shall be thoroughly disguised and the report shall so state.

Section 13. The counselor should always bear in mind that he may meet clients with whose problems he is not fully qualified to deal. In such case he should make appropriate referral.

Section 14. While the marriage counselor will feel satisfaction in the strengthening of a marriage he should not feel obligated to urge that the married partners continue to live together at all costs. There are situations in which all resources fail and in which continued living together may be severely damaging to one or several persons. In such event it is the duty of the counselor to assess the facts as he sees them. However, the actual decision concerning separation or divorce is a responsibility that must be assumed by the client and this should be made clear to him. If separation or divorce is decided upon it is the continuing responsibility of the counselor to give further support and counsel during a period or readjustment, if that appears to be wanted and needed, as it often is.

Section 15. The counselor should recognize that the religious convictions of a client may have powerful emotional significance and should be approached with caution and sensitivity. If there are problems in this area, consideration should be given to the desirability of consultation with a clergyman of the client's faith.

Section 16. Disparagement of a colleague to a client should be avoided; to do otherwise is unprofessional.

Section 17. It is desirable for the counselor to seek opportunities for community leadership and public education in matters relating to marriage and the family and to cooperate with others so engaged.

Section 18. The counselor has an obligation to continue postgraduate education and professional growth in all possible ways, including active participation in the meetings and affairs of the Association.

"Addenda to Code of Professional Ethics"
(Approval by the Committee on Ethics and Professional
Practices, and by the Board of Directors)

One-Counselor Agencies

It shall be unethical for a member to represent to the public
that a marriage counseling clinic, agency, or center is being
operated if in fact the member is engaged in independent individual
practice. Legal incorporation shall not in itself be satisfactory
evidence of existence of a de facto clinic. There must be actual
association of three or more qualified professional persons working
together at least half-time as a clinical team at the same location.
The advertising of a clinic shall be subject to the same restrictions
as apply to individual members.

Telephone Listings

For listing in the yellow pages of the telephone directory:
Nothing in the listing should make one individual or firm's listing
stand out from other listings in the directory. Bold face type, or
other than ordinary type size, should be avoided. Space should not
be enclosed in a lined box nor exceed that needed to contain the information; generally no more than five lines should be used. The
listing may consist of the person's name; highest earned degree;
A. A. M. C. clinical membership category; state certification if obtained (e. g., Certified Psychologist); diplomate status if attained
(e. g., Diplomate of the American Board of Examiners in Professional Psychology); address; and telephone number. If a person
wishes, he may list an additional address and telephone number
but his name should be listed only once. Office hours (or the statement "by appointment only") may be listed if permitted by the local
telephone company. Whereas joint practice is not to be discouraged,
a title such as "Family Institute" or "Marriage and Family Relations Clinic" is an acceptable telephone listing only if the joint
venture is truly a clinic of three or more professional people. Titles
utilizing the name of a city, county, or state imply the group to be
a community agency. If such a listing is used, it should be clearly
evident in the listing that the clinic or group is a private group and
not community sponsored. Three or more A. A. M. C. members in
a given community may list themselves together under the A. A. M. C.
heading and may use the A. A. M. C. insignia. In this case only, a
lined box may be used.

For listing in the white pages of the general telephone directory: Listing may include, in addition to name, address, and
telephone number, the words "Marriage Counselor" or "Marriage
and Family Counselor" in small light type, thus:

Jones, John B.   Marriage Counselor
    500 West 38 Street   462-4537
    Res. 111 Park Rd.   462-4828

MATHEMATICIANS

THE MATHEMATICAL ASSOCIATION OF AMERICA (MAA)
    1225 Connecticut Ave., N. W., Washington, D. C. 20036
    Alfred B. Willcox, Executive Director

Membership: The Mathematical Association of America, founded in
1915 and with a present (1973) membership of over 18,000, is a
professional organization of mathematicians, with the purpose "to
assist in promoting the interests of mathematics in America, especially in the collegiate field." Any person interested in the field
of mathematics is eligible for membership, and the members--in-
cluding 800 residing in foreign countries and more than 300 academic
and corporate members--are organized into 28 regional Sections.

Code of Ethics: The Association, as an interest group with no
minimum qualifications of academic training or experience required
for membership, does not have a formulated code of professional
ethics.

Professional Insignia: The emblem of the MAA is its seal--circular

in form, with a centered
icosahedron (20-faced poly-
hedron), the lower faces of
which are variously shaded by
parallel lines or solid color;
the organization name, "The
Mathematical Association of
America," is printed around
the design in a bordering
band.   The color of the emblem is shown variously--black
(letterhead, publication); blue
(publication).

Bibliography:
        The Mathematical Associa-
        tion of America.
        Information Booklet.
        Pamphlet.
Gives brief history and services available to universities and
colleges from the Association; emblem on cover.

MEDICAL LABORATORY WORKERS

AMERICAN MEDICAL TECHNOLOGISTS (AMT)
    710 Higgins Rd., Park Ridge, Ill. 60068
    Chester B. Dziekonski, Executive Secretary

Membership: The American Medical Technologists, founded in 1939
and with a present (1973) membership of approximately 11,500, is a
registry of medical laboratory workers, that issues designations of
professional competence, in the form of four specialty registration
certificates:
        "Medical Technologist"--"M. T. ";
        "Medical Laboratory Technician"--"M. L. T. ";
        "Certified Technician"--"C. T. ";
        "Registered Medical Assistant"--"R. M. A. "
"All applicants for certification ... must take and pass the AMT
registry examinations for specific certifications. " The examinations
are 2-1/2 hour tests, with questions in objective form. Training
and experience requirements for certification are:

Medical Technologist--M. T.

Duties: Conducts clinical laboratory tests, reports results; under general supervision, and functions when laboratory director on duty or on call; may supervise or assist in training of technicians and aides.

Education/Experience: Completion of 90 semester hours of college with appropriate science credits, plus one year's approved laboratory experience; or M. L. T. certificate, plus three years' experience.

Medical Laboratory Technician--M. L. T.

Duties: Performs clinical laboratory tests, working under immediate supervision, particularly performing other than routine tests.

Education/Experience: Accredited vocational school with classroom courses and laboratory experience combined as a two-year program; or completion of the 50-week Armed Forces medical laboratory course, plus 12 months' laboratory experience; or 60 semester hours of college with appropriate science credits, plus six months' experience.

Certified Technician--C. T.

Duties: Conducts clinical laboratory tests of a routine nature (urinalysis, hematology, serology, bacteriology, and some clinical chemistry) under immediate and close supervision.

Education/Experience: Two years' on-the-job training.

Registered Medical Assistant--R. M. A.

Duties: Aids the practicing physician through the application of general knowledge

Education/Experience: Accredited course in medical assisting; or completion of a medical assisting

and skills in office, examination room, and laboratory
procedures.

course prior to 1970, plus two
years' experience; or graduation
from an accredited nursing program, plus one year's experience
as a medical assistant; or five
years' experience completed prior
to 1970.

Code of Ethics: The guide to professional conduct of the AMT is its
Code of Ethics, which includes in the form of a pledge, principles
and standards of medical technology practice, and relationships with
physicians. No enforcement procedures for the Code are reported.

Professional Insignia: The emblem of the AMT is its official seal--

an octagon with centered symbols of medical laboratory work,
including beaker, microscope,
test tubes in rack, and the wand
of Mercury--the caduceus, a
winged staff with two entwined
serpents--signifying healing;
the organization name, "American Medical Technologists, "
is around the upper portion
within a bordering band; with
the printed initials of the group,
"AMT, " at the bottom of the
design within the border.   The
emblem is shown in blue on
white (letterhead, publications).

Bibliography:
     American Medical Tech-
          nologists. Code of
          Ethics. 1 page.
Pledge of standards of professional conduct for AMT certifi-
cated.

"Code of Ethics"

     Recognizing that the American Medical Technologists seeks to
encourage, establish and maintain the highest standards, traditions,
and principles of our profession as a condition of Registration and
maintaining membership in good standing in the American Medical
Technologists, I pledge myself to practice Medical Technology in
strict accord with the principles, standards, traditions and regulations of the American Medical Technologists and in accordance with
the laws of the state in which I practice.
     While engaged in the Arts and Sciences which constitute the
practice of Medical Technology, I shall practice with thorough self-
restraint, always placing the welfare of the patients, entrusted to

my care for tests or examinations, above all else, with full realization of my personal responsibility for the patients' best interests.

Realizing that it is incumbent upon me, as a Medical Technologist to continually keep abreast of the times, I pledge myself to strive constantly to increase my technical knowledge of Medical Technology and to participate in the interchange of knowledge with other competent practitioners of Medical Technology and/or other para medical Arts and Sciences that our joint knowledge shall benefit the profession and my practice.

I pledge accuracy and reliability in the performance of tests and to seek competent professional council when in doubt of my own judgment or competence in a particular test or examination.

As a further consideration for registration, I pledge myself to avoid dishonest, unethical or illegal compensation for such services as I shall render to the patients in my charge and I shall shun unwarranted professional publicity or unjust discrimination among the patients in my charge.

I pledge myself to protect the judgment of the attending physician in all cases in which I am directed to make laboratory tests or examinations, and to report the results of my findings free from all personal opinion to the attending physician only. I shall not make or offer a diagnosis or interpretation unless I be a duly licensed physician, except as the results of the report may of itself so indicate, or unless I am asked to by the attending physician.

I pledge myself to protect the identity and the integrity of all patients placed in my charge and to make only such reports public as shall be required by me by the laws of the state in which I practice or as the patient's physician shall direct.

As a final condition of Registration and Membership in the American Medical Technologists, I pledge my honor and my integrity to cooperate in the advancement and expansion, by every lawful means within my power, of the influence of the American Medical Technologists and to defend its principles.

AMERICAN SOCIETY OF MEDICAL TECHNOLOGY (ASMT)
   Hermann Professional Bldg., Suite 1600, Houston, Texas 77025
   Stephen B. Friedheim, Executive Director

Membership: The American Society of Medical Technology (formerly the American Society of Medical Technologists), founded in 1932 and with a present membership of about 21,000, is a professional society in medical technology. Members, grouped in constituent societies at the state and local level, "cover the entire field of medical technology: medical technologists, technicians, laboratory assistants, researchers, educators, administrators, students and specialists working in hospitals, clinics, private, governmental, research and industrial medical laboratories."

An "Active Member" of ASMT qualifies for membership with a graduate degree in science, education, or administration and activity in the field of medical technology; or by other level or combination of education and experience, as specified by the Society. One of these qualifying requirements is certification--upon passing a written examination--by the Board of Registry of Medical Technologists of the American Society of Clinical Pathologists, which is operated jointly with the representatives of ASMT.

Basic requirement for the examination is graduation from an American Medical Association approved program in medical technology, or a bachelor's degree in science, plus five years of experience in an accredited clinical laboratory. Since 1928, the Board of Registry has examined applicants, issued certificates, and authorized the use of professional designations to indicate competence as:

> Medical Technologists--MT (ASCP), in general technology, or with specialty indicated in blood banking, chemistry, microbiology, or nuclear medicine.
> Cytotechnologist--CT (ASCP)
> Histologic Technician--HT (ASCP)
> Certified Laboratory Assistant--CLA (ASCP)
> Medical Laboratory Technician--MLT (ASCP).

<u>Code of Ethics</u>: The conduct guide of ASMT is its <u>Code of Ethics,</u> a brief pledge of three paragraphs, accepting responsibilities of ethical practice in medical technology. The Society has a Judicial Committee for enforcement of their Code of Ethics.

<u>Professional Insignia</u>: The symbol of the American Society of

Medical Technology is a round design with a centered circle bearing a caduceus--serpent-wreathed, winged staff, "the traditional symbol of the profession of medicine"--and a microscope and retort, "among the first instruments used in the clinical laboratory"; an eight-cogged border carries the organization initials, "ASMT," in alternate cogs from left to right, with jewels in the cogs between initials. Color of the emblem is shown variously in publications-- grey on white, black on brown, brown on black.

<u>Other Identification of Professional Status</u>: As described above under "Membership," five professional designations are awarded upon completion of required examinations.

Bibliography:
American Society of Medical Technology. The ASMT Story.
Brochure.
Includes general description of the Society organization and
structure, emblem, and code of ethics.
_____. An Invitation to Membership in the American Society
of Medical Technology. 4 pages. Pamphlet.
Membership classifications and requirements, with an applica-
tion for membership.
Simkins, Tania. "A Fight for Freedom." Association and
Society Manager. November 1970.
ASMT Executive Director discusses problems of cooperation
with the American Society of Clinical Pathologists in voluntary
certification of medical technologists and technicians, and
other professional problems of the Society.

"Code of Ethics"

Being fully cognizant of my responsibilities in the practice of
Medical Technology, I affirm my willingness to discharge my duties
with accuracy, thoughtfulness, and care.

Realizing that the knowledge obtained concerning patients in
the course of my work must be treated as confidential, I hold inviolate the confidence (trust) placed in me by patient and physicians.

Recognizing that my integrity and that of my profession must
be pledged to the absolute reliability of my work, I will conduct myself at all times in a manner appropriate to the dignity of my profession.

INTERNATIONAL SOCIETY OF CLINICAL LABORATORY TECH-
NOLOGISTS (ISCLT)
805 Ambassador Bldg., 411 N. 7th St., St. Louis, Mo. 63101
David Birenbaum, Administrator

Membership: The International Society of Clinical Laboratory Technologists, founded in 1966 and with a present (1973) membership of
4000, is an organization of medical laboratory workers who have
qualified for examination as:
Registered Laboratory Technician (RLT)--Graduation from a
junior college; or comparable academic training (60 hours
of college credit with a major in laboratory science,
graduation from a medical laboratory school accredited by
the ISCLT, or completion of military laboratory procedure
course); and one year of clinical laboratory experience;
Registered Medical Technologist (RMT)--Graduation from an
accredited college with a major in chemical, physical, or
biological science; and one year of clinical laboratory

experience.   An additional year of experience may be substituted for each year of the four years of college education lacking.
The examinations are written and cover all of the laboratory disciplines.   The multiple-choice questions are developed from lists of
questions submitted by educators from colleges, universities, and
proprietary schools.

Code of Ethics: The conduct guide developed by the Society for its
members is the Creed of a Laboratory Technician, which gives--in
the form of a pledge--the obligations and responsibilities of laboratory technicians.

Professional Insignia: The emblem of the International Society of
Clinical Laboratory Technologists is its seal--circular in form, the

design has a centered caduceus
--winged and with two entwined
serpents--superimposed on a
globe showing the American
continent; the two professional
designations awarded by the
Society--"RMT" (Registered
Medical Technologist) and
"RLT" (Registered Laboratory
Technician)--are printed on
the design--one above, the
other below the caduceus.   The
color of the emblem is shown
variously--black on white (letterhead); blue on white (publication).

Other Identification of Professional Status: The professional designations, as described above under "Membership," are shown

on insignia authorized for use as shoulder patches on uniforms:
"RMT"--Blue with gold caduceus, letters centered in red, on
globe background of white;
"RLT"--Red, with gold caduceus, letters centered in blue,
on globe background of white.
This same emblem is shown on the certificate awarded to indicate
professional competence. Here its colors are grey on gold, with
professional designation in black.

Bibliography:
International Society of Clinical Laboratory Technologists. By-
Laws. Revised edition, June 1970. 15 pages.
Includes membership requirements.
_____. Requirements for Eligibility for Examination for
Registration of Laboratory Technologists and Technicians.
Revised edition, August 1968. 2 pages.

"Creed of a Laboratory Technician"

I shall at all times devote myself to the high purposes of my
calling with honor and dignity.
I shall conscientiously perform my laboratory duties accurately and efficiently, unswayed by partiality or outside influences.
I shall report candidly and honestly on all my laboratory findings to those authorized to receive them.
I shall preserve in strictest confidence all information obtained in my technical investigations and disclose them only to the
proper hospital officials and medical men.
I shall accept responsibility for all duties entrusted to me
and fulfill these to the fullest extent of my capabilities.
I shall confer with medical and hospital authorities on any
finding about which I have the slightest doubt in order to assure accuracy in all my reports.
I shall be loyal to the institution in which I work and the
persons with whom I am associated.
I shall conduct myself with morality, integrity, consideration,
and calmness in keeping with the high principles of the healing arts.
I shall be cooperative and helpful to all hospital and medical
personnel with whom I have contact.
All this I shall ever bear in mind in order that I, as a
Laboratory Technician, may help in succoring the sick, in furthering
the healing arts, and in improving the standards and practice of my
vocation.
To this I pledge myself.

MEDICAL RECORD ADMINISTRATORS

AMERICAN MEDICAL RECORD ASSOCIATION (AMRA)
    875 N. Michigan Ave., Suite 1850, Chicago, Ill. 60611
    Mary Waterstraat, Executive Director

Membership: The American Medical Record Association (formerly
American Association of Medical Record Librarians), founded in
1928 and with a present (1973) membership of over 10,000, is a
professional organization of the employees in hospitals, clinics and
extended care medical facilities who plan, prepare, maintain and
analyze records and reports on patients' illness and treatment. Two
designations of professional competence are awarded by AMRA:
        Medical Record Administrator: "Registered Record Adminis-
            trator," "RRA." Initiated in 1932, basic requirements
            are graduation from AMRA approved program with bach-
            elor's degree in medical record administration;
        Medical Record Technician: "Accredited Record Technician,"
            "ART." Initiated in 1955, basic requirement is graduation
            from AMRA approved program with AA degree in medical
            record technology, or successful completion of 25-lesson
            AMRA independent home study course.
Both certificate programs are administered by the AMRA Committee
on Education and Registration, and both programs require passing
a written examination, which is prepared, given, and graded by the
Psychological Corporation of New York.

Code of Ethics: The guide to professional conduct for AMRA members is its Code of Ethics, approved in 1957. Twelve tenets of
ethical conduct are enumerated in the Code, and the publication--A
Guide to the Interpretation of the Code of Ethics--cites specific
examples of conduct cited by these principles. No procedures for
enforcement of the Code are reported.

Professional Insignia: The emblem of the Association is its seal--

a circular design, with a centered
caduceus--winged wand with two entwined serpents--on which is superimposed an open book; the organization
name, "American Medical Record
Association," is printed at the top of
the insignia, and the founding date of
the group, "1928," at the bottom.
The color of the emblem is shown
variously--white on green (letterhead);
brown on white, black on white (publications).

Other Identification of Professional Status: As described above
under "Membership," qualified members are authorized to use the
professional designations:
        "Registered Medical Record Administrator" ("RRA");
        "Accredited Medical Record Technician" ("ART").
These designations are authorized for use with an individual's name,

and as a sleeve patch.   The uniform emblem is green and gold, its
round design shows the emblem from the insignia--caduceus and book;
with the professional designation printed around the patch as a border.

Bibliography:
American Medical Record Association.   Code of Ethics.   1957.
1 page.
Tenets of professional practice in 12 principles.
_____.   An Educational Opportunity: Correspondence Course
for Medical Record Personnel.   Folder.
Description of 25-lesson AMRA home study course, satis-
factory completion of which qualifies an applicant to take the
examination for ART (Accredited Record Technician).
_____.   Guide to the Interpretation of the Code of Ethics.
1957.   4 pages.
Specific examples of practice governed by the Code of Ethics,
grouped by type of relationship: Patient, Employer, Medical
Staff, Medical Record Profession, Professional Society.

"Code of Ethics for the Practice of
Medical Record Administration"

Medical Record Administration is concerned with the development, use, and maintenance of medical and health records for
medical care and treatment, administrative, reference, professional
education and research purposes.   Medical record practice is a trust
delegated by the medical and health services.   To protect and merit
the trust placed in it, the medical record profession has the responsibility of defining basic principles governing the professional conduct
of its members.   The American Medical Record Association has
therefore adopted this Code of Ethics.
The following code of ethical conduct defines the tenets necessary for carrying out the purposes of the medical record profession,
is binding upon any member of the American Medical Record Association, and upon any person, certified, registered, or accredited by
this Association.   As a member of one of the paramedical professions, he shall:

1.   Place service before material gain, the honor of the profession before personal advantage, the health and welfare of patients
above all personal and financial interests, and conduct himself in
the practice of this profession so as to bring honor to himself, his
associates, and to the medical record profession.
2.   Preserve and protect the medical records in his custody
and hold inviolate the privileged contents of the records and any
other information of a confidential nature obtained in his official
capacity, taking due account of applicable statutes and of regulations
and policies of his employer.
3.   Serve his employer loyally, honorably discharging the
duties and responsibilities entrusted to him, and give due consideration to the nature of these responsibilities in giving his employer

notice of intent to resign his position.

4.   Refuse to participate in or conceal unethical practices or procedures.

5.   Report to the proper authorities but disclose to no one else any evidence of conduct or practice revealed in the medical records in his custody that indicates possible violation of established rules and regulations of the employer or of professional practice.

6.   Preserve the confidential nature of professional determinations made by the staff committees which he serves.

7.   Accept only those fees that are customary and lawful in the area for services rendered in his official capacity.

8.   Avoid encroachment on the professional responsibilities of the medical and other para medical professions, and under no circumstances assume or give the appearance of assuming the right to make determinations in professional areas outside the scope of his assigned responsibilities.

9.   Strive to advance the knowledge and practice of medical record administration, including continued self-improvement, in order to contribute to the best possible medical care.

10.   Participate appropriately in developing and strengthening professional manpower and in representing the profess on to the public.

11.   Discharge honorably the responsibilities of any Association post to which appointed or elected, and preserve the confidentiality of any privileged information made known to him in his official capacity.

12.   State truthfully and accurately his credentials, professional education, and experience in any official transaction with the American Medical Record Association and with any employer or prospective employer.

MICROBIOLOGISTS

AMERICAN ACADEMY OF MICROBIOLOGY (AAM)
1913 I St., N.W., Washington, D.C. 20006
R. W. Sarber, Executive Secretary

Membership: The American Academy of Microbiology, founded in 1955 and with a present (1973) membership of 800, is a professional association of microbiologists. The Academy was incorporated into the American Society for Microbiology (founded in 1899) as the Society's professional arm in 1968. The 800 "Fellows" of the Academy have qualified for fellowship with education and training requirements of a doctor's degree (such as Ph.D., M.D., D.Sc.), and a minimum of 5 to 10 years full time post-doctoral experience in microbiology. The Academy's professional designation of "Fellow" indicates "professional excellence, recognized competence and high ethical standards."

The AAM has established two agencies in the field of microbiology, each of which conducts a voluntary licensing program, with
examinations, and awards professional designations indicating adequate preparation for and competence in medical laboratory work:
American Board of Medical Microbiology--established in 1959,
National Registry of Microbiologists--established in 1961.
The American Board of Medical Microbiology, through its Standards
and Examination Committee, offers certification at the post-doctoral
level, awarding--after examination--the professional designations:
1. Public Health (P. H.) and Medical Laboratory (M. L.) in
   Immunology.
2. Public Health (P. H.) and Medical Laboratory (M. L.) in
   Mycology.
3. Public Health (P. H.) and Medical Laboratory (M. L.) in
   Parasitology.
4. Public Health (P. H.) and Medical Laboratory (M. L.) in
   Virology.
5. Public Health (P. H.) and Medical Laboratory (M. L.) in
   Microbiology.
   (the fifth designation includes the first four specialty
   areas).

Applicants for examination must have:
1. An acceptable doctoral degree (M. D., Ph. D., D. V. M.,
   D. P. H., D. D. S.);
2. A minimum of five years of post-doctoral experience
   pertinent to microbiology; residency or clinical internship, approved by the American Medical Association,
   or one year of teaching or independent research in
   microbiology may be substituted in part for the required experience.
Each examination consists of two parts:
I. Written Examination--three-hour examination of multiple-
   choice questions, covering basic knowledge and its
   application in P. H. and M. L. Bacteriology, Immunology, Mycology, Parasitology, Virology, Microbiology;
II. Advanced Test--written and oral test in designated areas
    of applicant's competence.
The successful examination candidate becomes a "Diplomate" of the
American Board of Medical Microbiology, and receives a certificate
of competence in public health and medical microbiology, or in his
designated specialty areas in microbiology. The examinations conducted by the National Registry of Microbiologists (since 1961),
through its Committee on Standards and Examinations, are directed
to recognizing the "training and scientific understanding in the field
of microbiology" at the college graduate level, but does "not provide for appraisal of laboratory competence. "

The Registry defines a "microbiologist" "as one who, by education and training, is possessed of a knowledge of the nature,
characteristics, cultural and metabolic properties of microorganisms,
has the necessary skills to isolate, cultivate and identify such

organisms, and can evaluate and interpret technically the results obtained." To qualify for Registry examination, an applicant must have graduated from an accredited college with specialization in a biological science, and have specified study in basic sciences-- chemistry and physics, mathematics, and microbiology.

For each candidate, the examination consists of:
    General Examination--"Comprehensive written examination in general microbiology, covering the methods of isolation, cultivation, identification and some knowledge of the nutrition, metabolism, and physiology of microorganisms, with special emphasis on bacteria."
    Specialty Examinations--At least 2 tests in the following specialty fields:
    1. Agricultural and Industrial Microbiology,
    2. Food, Dairy and Sanitation Microbiology,
    3. Pathogenic Bacteriology,
    4. Immunology and Serology,
    5. Virology (including Rickettsia),
    6. Mycology,
    7. Parasitology.
Candidates passing the examinations receive a: "Certificate as Registered Microbiologist."

The Registry also issues a certificate as: "Specialist in Public Health and Medical Laboratory Microbiology" to recognize "capacity to supervise the effective operation of the microbiological procedures in a public health or medical laboratory." To qualify for the examination for this Certificate, an applicant must have: "Master's degree in microbiology, medicine or science from an accredited college, with specified study in basic sciences--chemistry and physics; in mathematics; and in microbiology; and four years of experience in a public health or medical microbiology laboratory." The comprehensive written examination in public health and medical microbiology covers bacteriology, immunology, mycology, parasitology, and virology. Until June 30, 1974, a Specialist may be registered without examination, provided the applicant meets the above-described requirements to the satisfaction of the Registry Committee.

Code of Ethics: The American Academy of Microbiology approved on December 7, 1970 a guide to ethical practices for public health and medical laboratory biology--its Code of Ethics, which is endorsed by the two examining and voluntary licensing committees of the Academy, The National Registry of Microbiologists and the American Board of Medical Microbiology. General principles of professional conduct are grouped in six articles in the Code:
        General Standards, Definitions,
        Publication, Patents and Advertising,
        Obligations as a Microbiologist,
        Duties to the Physician and Patient,
        Revision of the Code,
        Application and Enforcement of the Code.

Enforcement of the Code is carried out by the Ethics Committee of the American Academy of Microbiology, which investigates, holds hearings as necessary, and recommends disciplinary action to the Board of Governors of the Academy. Discipline for violations of the Code may range from reprimand to expulsion from membership and revocation of certificate or registration.

Professional Insignia: The emblem of the AAM is an unbordered design consisting of the van Leeuwenhoek microscope, bearing the association initials, "AAM," at the top, and the organization name, "The American Academy of Microbiology," overprinted across the center.   The design is shown in black on white (letterhead, publication).

The American Academy of Microbiology

Other Identification of Professional Status: As indicated above under "Membership," the professional designations awarded by the AAM include:

American Academy of Microbiology: Fellow
American Board of Medical Microbiology: Diplomate in Microbiology, or one of its specialties.
National Registry of Microbiologists: Registered Microbiologist, Specialist in Public Health and Medical Laboratory Microbiology.

Bibliography:
American Academy of Microbiology.   Code of Ethics.   December 7, 1970.   Folder.
Professional conduct guide, endorsed by the American Board of Medical Microbiology, and the National Registry of Microbiologists.
. Qualifications and Procedures for Nomination for Fellowship in the American Academy of Microbiology; Certification by the American Board of Medical Microbiology; Registration in the National Registry of Microbiologists.   4 pages.   Folder.
American Board of Medical Microbiology.   American Board of Medical Microbiology.   2 pages.
Organization and purpose of the Board; description of its certification program for "Diplomate," including qualifications for examination and description of examination.
. Nature of Part I Examination.   2 pages.
Gives question form, test length, subjects covered, with sample questions in each of the six examination subject areas.
. Rules and Regulations.   April 1970.   9 pages.
Procedural guide for examination and certification of Diplomates.
National Registry of Microbiologists.   National Registry of

Microbiologists. 2 pages.
Procedural guide for examination and registration of Regis-
tered Microbiologist, or as Specialist in Public Health and
Medical Laboratory Microbiology.

"Code of Ethics"

ARTICLE I
General Standards, Definitions

Section 1. Public Health and Medical Laboratory Microbiology and its subdivisions of Bacteriology, Mycology, Virology, Immunology and Parasitology concern the application of microbiological
theory and practice, including the isolation, identification and char-
acterization of microbial agents of disease and the evaluation of
measurable reactions of the patient which indicate infection or resistance.
Section 2. The Public Health and Medical Laboratory Microbiologist is one equipped by education and experience to engage in
the practice of microbiology as defined above.
Section 3. Practitioners of the profession of Public Health
and Medical Laboratory Microbiology hold their contribution to the
welfare of the public as their ultimate concern and responsibility.
The microbiologist shall, to the best of his ability, use his scientific
skills and knowledge for the benefit of man.
Section 4. The microbiologist accepts as professional obligations the acquisition of the best available education and experience
in the science and its advancement through his personal contribution.
He shall strive constantly to enlarge, extend and improve his knowledge of the science to his own advantage and that of his colleagues.
Section 5. The Public Health and Medical Laboratory Microbiologist shall maintain the highest professional standards in his
dealings with the medical and related professions.
Section 6. The microbiologist shall offer no rebates or commissions to any person for the solicitation or referral of patients
for professional services. Microbiologists, with the exception of
those qualified as physicians, shall, in keeping with the welfare of
the patient, refrain from engaging in activities which constitute the
diagnosis of disease as those activities are performed by licensed
medical practitioners.

ARTICLE II
Publications, Patents and Advertising

Section 1. The microbiologist shall freely discuss with his
colleagues and with scientists in related fields, advances in the
science of microbiology. To withhold information for personal gain
shall be considered unethical. This Section shall not apply to information classified by a government agency for reasons of national
security.
Section 2. The microbiologist is encouraged to publish,

after critical evaluation, new knowledge pertaining to the science of microbiology obtained through research or other observations.

Section 3. It shall be considered unethical for any microbiologist to advertise, announce or solicit requests for his services except through bona fide scientific or professional channels normally used by physicians, microbiologists, and other health specialists.

Section 4. Microbiologists shall require manufacturers and suppliers to provide all significant information on reagents, laboratory diagnostic agents, and biological products, proposed for use by him, or in applications under his supervision or direction. He shall not knowingly use, endorse, or promote such products about which significant information has been concealed.

ARTICLE III
Obligations As a Microbiologist

Section 1. The microbiologist shall not use any procedure except for research purposes that has not been adequately evaluated in his laboratory and found appropriate for the intended purpose.

Section 2. The microbiologist shall, in the pursuit of his profession, observe the highest scientific standards at all times and shall conduct himself as a scientist.

Section 3. The microbiologist shall carefully supervise the technicians working in his laboratory. He shall train these workers to the best of his ability, encourage them to attain the highest technical competence and teach them by word and example to adhere to the ethical standards herein outlined.

Section 4. The microbiologist shall contribute to research and to the advancement of his specialty, and shall encourage those working in his laboratory to do likewise. He shall accept as collaborators, whenever possible, the junior members of his staff and shall encourage these members to contribute to the science of microbiology. To the best of his ability he shall cooperate with other scientists and physicians in their efforts to advance microbiology and medical science.

ARTICLE IV
Duties to the Physician and Patient

Section 1. The Microbiologist shall, when appropriate, outline to the physician the significance of microbiological findings and he shall suggest further determinations that would aid the physician in treatment of the patient or would contribute to the prevention of disease.

Section 2. The microbiologist shall under no circumstances transmit to the patient the results or the interpretation of results of tests conducted by him.

ARTICLE V
Revision of the Code

Section 1. The outline here presented can serve only as a

general guide and shall be periodically reviewed and revised by the
Ethics Committee of the American Academy of Microbiology.

ARTICLE VI
Application and Enforcement of the Code

Section 1. The Ethics of the Public Health and Medical
Laboratory Microbiologist shall at all times be at least comparable
to the standards to which medical, engineering, scientific and other
comparable professions subscribe.

Section 2. It shall be the obligation of the microbiologist
to report to the Ethics Committee of the American Academy of
Microbiology any infractions of these principles of professional conduct and behavior by individuals subject to this Code which may
come to his attention.

Section 3. The Ethics Committee of the American Academy
of Microbiology shall consider all reported infractions. When a
person has been charged with a violation, he shall be so informed in
writing. The notice of the charge shall state the charged offense
with particularity sufficient to enable the accused to prepare a defense. The accused shall have the opportunity to appear and present
his defense with the assistance of counsel or to submit written
statements of his defense, if he so elects. A written record of the
proceedings, but not of the deliberations of the Committee, shall
be prepared and made available to the accused. On the basis of
all evidence presented and recorded, the Ethics Committee shall
determine whether or not the charges have been substantiated.

Section 4. Should the Ethics Committee determine that a
microbiologist subject to this Code of Ethics has violated its
principles or any of its specific provisions, it shall recommend to
the Board of Governors of the American Academy of Microbiology
such disciplinary or corrective action as is deemed appropriate
under the circumstances. The permissible range of disciplinary
action shall vary from a simple reprimand to expulsion from membership in the American Academy of Microbiology, removal of certification by the American Board of Medical Microbiology or registration by the National Registry of Microbiologists. Expulsion
from membership or removal of certification or registration shall
be limited to instances where an individual subject to this Code of
Ethics is found to have willfully, repeatedly, or flagrantly violated
its provisions.

MIDWIVES

AMERICAN COLLEGE OF NURSE-MIDWIVES (ACNM)
    50 E. 92nd St., New York, N.Y. 10028
    Norma Pilegard, Executive Secretary

Membership: The American College of Nurse-Midwives, founded in
1955 and with a present (1973) membership of 400, is a professional organization for nurse-midwives in the United States, dedicated to "the improvement of services for mothers and babies in
cooperation with other allied groups." Members are registered
professional nurses who have "successfully completed a recognized
program of study and clinical experience leading to a certificate in
nurse-midwifery." The Nurse-Midwife (always functioning "within
the framework of a medically directed health service") provides
prenatal, intra partum and post partum care, and teaches about
and interprets pregnancy, birth, infant care and family health, including methods of birth control and family planning.

         The ACNM gives a national examination for voluntary certifica-
tion as: "Certified Nurse-Midwife" ("C. N. M. "). Registered nurses
licensed to practice, who complete the post-RN and master's degree
level nurse-midwife curriculum offered by the ACNM are eligible
to take the certification examination. This curriculum is offered in
three programs:
            Basic Curriculum,
            Internship Program,
            Refresher Program.

Code of Ethics: The College has prepared no formal written code
of ethics. Members who violate the by-laws or standing rules of
the College are subject to discipline by the Executive Board (By-
Laws, Article XII), and may be suspended or expelled from membership.

Professional Insignia: The emblem of the ACNM is its official seal
(By-Laws, Article II, Section 4)--a circular design with a centered
shield bearing a lamp (designating
"learning"), three interlocked rings
with the lower ring shaded by cross-
hatching (symbolizing the family),
and a small shield with stars in the
upper portion and vertical stripes in
the lower (indicating the United States).
The College motto--"Vivant" ("Let
Them Live")--appear on a wavy
horizontal band crossing the centered
shield about one-third of the distance
from its point. Above the centered shield are the words, "Corporate Seal"; a bordering band around

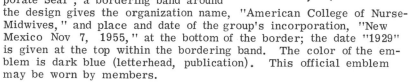

the design gives the organization name, "American College of Nurse-
Midwives, " and place and date of the group's incorporation, "New
Mexico Nov 7, 1955, " at the bottom of the border; the date "1929"
is given at the top within the bordering band. The color of the emblem is dark blue (letterhead, publication). This official emblem
may be worn by members.

Other Identification of Professional Status: Members may use the initials showing College membership after their names: "ACNM, " and, as described above under "Membership, " the professional designation: "Certified Nurse-Midwife" ("C. N. M. ").

Bibliography:
    American College of Nurse-Midwives. Articles of Incorporation
        and By-Laws. 1955, amendments through April 1969.
        Gives membership qualifications, describes emblem, mentions
        disciplinary procedures.
    _____ . What is a Nurse-Midwife? Folder.
    Defines occupation, describes certification procedure, lists
    approved schools offering programs for Nurse-Midwife.

MOTION PICTURE DISTRIBUTORS

MOTION PICTURE ASSOCIATION OF AMERICA, INC. (MPAA)
    522 Fifth Ave., New York, N. Y. 10036
    Jack J. Valenti, President

Membership: The Motion Picture Association of America, Inc., founded in 1922 and with a present (1973) membership of 22 companies and individuals, is a trade association whose members are the principal producers and distributors of motion pictures in the United States.

Code of Ethics: The Motion Picture Code and Rating Program is the formal name for the current voluntary system of self-regulation carried on by MPAA, in cooperation with the International Film Importers & Distributors of America, Inc. (IFIDA) and the National Association of Theatre Owners, Inc. (NATO). This Code became effective on November 1, 1968, and contains "Standards for Production, " "Standards for Advertising, " and "Standards for Titles, " which are distinct from the ratings assigned. This Code supplanted previous MPAA codes--the Motion Picture Production Code, 1930-1966, and the Code

FILM RATING GUIDE
For Parents and Their Children

G — GENERAL AUDIENCES
All Ages Admitted

PG — PARENTAL GUIDANCE SUGGESTED
Some Material May Not Be
Suitable For Pre-Teenagers

R — RESTRICTED
Under 17 requires accompanying
Parent or Adult Guardian

X — NO ONE UNDER 17 ADMITTED
(Age limit may vary in certain areas)

— MOTION PICTURE ASSOCIATION OF AMERICA.

of Self-Regulation, 1966-1968. The purpose of the ratings is to "inform parents about the suitability of films so that they can decide whether their children should see a motion picture or not." The MPAA, through its Code and Rating Administration, determines the ratings for motion pictures distributed by its member companies and for any other motion pictures voluntarily submitted by producers and distributors who are not members of MPAA. The current rating symbols for motion pictures are given in the box on page 452.

Film ratings and/or descriptive reviews for specific motion pictures are found in newspapers and in magazines of general circulation, such as:

Parents' Magazine,	Newsweek,
Time,	Good Housekeeping,
Ladies' Home Journal,	Family Circle,
Woman's Day,	McCall's,
PTA Magazine,	

and in periodicals covering film ratings and reviews, including: Film Information and Catholic Film Newsletter. A motion picture producer or distributor may appeal the rating assigned to a film by the Code and Rating Administration. These appeals are considered by a separate and distinct body known as the Code and Rating Appeals Board, which comprises representatives of MPAA, IFIDA and NATO.

Aside from MPAA's member companies, who are pledged to submit all of their films for rating, compliance with the Code by producers and distributors who are not members of MPAA and by theatre owners is done on an entirely voluntary basis. There is no Code provision for imposition of sanctions against producers and distributors who do not submit their films for rating, or against theatre owners who do not enforce the ratings. However, MPAA may revoke a rating certificate for violation of any of the conditions attached to its issuance, such as requirement that all advertising material be submitted for approval by the Director of the Code for Advertising, and only such advertising material as is approved by him be used in connection with a film.

Professional Insignia: The emblem of the MPAA--oval in shape, with a motion picture reel centered in an inner oval, both ovals bisected by a horizontal line. This insignia appears with ratings of G, PG and R, but not with X.
The X is the only rating which a producer or distributor may apply to a film without first submitting it for review and rating by the MPAA's Code and Rating Administration.

Bibliography:
    Motion Picture Association of America, Inc. The Motion Picture Code and Rating Program. 16 pages. Pamphlet.

Includes Standards for Production, Advertising, and Titles;
regulations governing these standards and the motion picture
ratings; and industry appeals procedure. (This pamphlet has
not yet been reprinted to reflect the current rating symbols
and some changes in the appeals procedure.)
_____. Film Rating Guide for Parents and Their Children. 8
pages. Folder.
A simplified description of the rating system, answering questions frequently asked about it.

"Standards for Production"

In furtherance of the objectives of the Code to accord with
the mores, the culture, and the moral sense of our society, the
principles stated above and the following standards shall govern
the Administrator in his consideration of motion pictures submitted
for Code approval:

The basic dignity and value of human life shall be respected
and upheld. Restraint shall be exercised in portraying the taking
of life.
Evil, sin, crime and wrong-doing shall not be justified.
Special restraint shall be exercised in portraying criminal
or anti-social activities in which minors participate or are involved.
Detailed and protracted acts of brutality, cruelty, physical
violence, torture and abuse shall not be presented.
Indecent or undue exposure of the human body shall not be
presented.
Illicit sex relationships shall not be justified. Intimate sex
scenes violating common standards of decency shall not be portrayed.
Restraint and care shall be exercised in presentations dealing
with sex aberrations.
Obscene speech, gestures or movements shall not be pre-
sented. Undue profanity shall not be permitted.
Religion shall not be demeaned.
Words or symbols contemptuous of racial, religious or na-
tional groups, shall not be used so as to incite bigotry or hatred.
Excessive cruelty to animals shall not be portrayed and
animals shall not be treated inhumanely.

"Standards for Advertising"

The principles of the Code cover advertising and publicity
as well as production. There are times when their specific application to advertising may be different. A motion picture is viewed as
a whole and may be judged that way. It is the nature of advertising,
however, that it must select and emphasize only isolated portions
and aspects of a film. It thus follows that what may be appropriate
in a motion picture may not be equally appropriate in advertising.
Furthermore, in application to advertising, the principles and standards of the Code are supplemented by the following standards for
advertising:

Illustrations and text shall not misrepresent the character of a motion picture.

Illustrations shall not depict any indecent or undue exposure of the human body.

Advertising demeaning religion, race, or national origin shall not be used.

Cumulative overemphasis on sex, crime, violence, and brutality shall not be permitted.

Salacious postures and embraces shall not be shown.

Censorship disputes shall not be exploited or capitalized upon.

"Standards for Titles"

A salacious, obscene, or profane title shall not be used on motion pictures.

MUSEUM WORKERS

AMERICAN ASSOCIATION OF MUSEUMS (AAM)
    2233 Wisconsin Ave., N.W., Washington, D.C. 20007
    Kyran M. McGrath, Director

Membership: The American Association of Museums, founded in 1906 and with a present (1973) membership of 6000, includes as members all types of museum institutions--art, history, science-- as well as individuals interested in museum work--professionals in the museum field, museum trustees, and educators.

Code of Ethics: The AAM published a Code of Ethics for Museum Workers in 1925. More recently (1969), the Association published a Code of Ethics for Museum Personnel in its official magazine, Museum News. This Code (devised by the Museums Section of the Ontario Historical Society; R. Alan Douglas, Curator of the Hiram Walker Historical Museum, Windsor, Ontario, Canada--Chairman of the Section) provides a guide for individual museum workers in their obligations to:
    Governing Authority of museum,
    The Museum and its staff,
    Museum Materials in the museum worker's care,
    Other members of the museum Profession,
    The Public.
A second document, Recommended Policy for Museums, applies to questions of policy for each Museum as an institution.

Professional Insignia: For some years the emblem of the American Association of Museums was an unbordered symbol composed of

acanthus leaves--a theme widely used in design from earliest times
to the present. This emblem has recently been replaced by a logo-

type--the Association monogram, showing the organization initials,
"aam, " in lower case script. The color of the emblem is shown
variously--blue (publication); embossed (letterhead).

Bibliography:
    American Association of Museums. AAM Membership: Become
        a Professional. Folder.
    Purposes, services, membership information; emblem on
    cover.
         . Code of Ethics for Museum Workers. 1925.
    The original professional guide for museum workers; now out
    of print.
        . Invitation to Membership. Folder.
    Descriptive brochure of AAM activities and membership.
    Douglas, R. Alan. "Museum Ethics, Practice and Policy."
        Museum News. September 1969.
    Code of Ethics for Museum Personnel, and Recommended
    Policy for Museums, developed by the Museums Section,
    Ontario Historical Society, Canada.

"Code of Ethics for Museum Personnel"*

    Preamble: For the purpose of this Code, "Member" means
an individual member of the Museum Section of the Ontario Historical Society;
    "Museum" means a museum as defined by the Canadian
Museums Association at its 1964 meeting at Hamilton, Ontario:
the word "Museum" shall be deemed to mean a non-profit, permanent establishment, not existing primarily for the purpose of conducting temporary exhibitions, exempt from Federal and Provincial
income taxes, open to the public and administered in the public interest, for the purpose of conserving and preserving, studying, interpreting, assembling and exhibiting to the public for its instruction
and enjoyment, objects and specimens of educational and cultural
value, including artistic, scientific (whether animate or inanimate),
historical and technological material. Museums thus defined shall
include Botanical Gardens, Zoological Parks, Aquaria, Planetaria,

Historical Societies and Historic Houses and Sites which meet the
requirements set forth in the preceding sentence; and

"Museology" means the science or profession of museum
organization, equipment, and management (definition from Webster's
Third New International Dictionary, 1965).

A member shall at all times have in mind that he is under
great obligation to all who have made museology a dignified and
learned profession, and he shall endeavor to give recognition to that
obligation in every appropriate way.

Upon accepting a position in a museum a member assumes
an obligation to maintain ethical standards of conduct in relationship to:

A. The Governing Authority under which he practices
B. The Museum and its staff
C. The museum Materials in his care
D. Other members of the Profession
E. The Public

A. Relationship to the Governing Authority:

1. A member shall perform his duties with realization of
the fact that final jurisdiction over the administration of the museum
rests in the officially constituted governing authority; members
should, however, expect freedom from interference from their
governing bodies in matters of professional practice.

B. Relationship to the Museum and its staff:

1. Museum personnel should, while respecting each other's
special functions and responsibilities, work together in a spirit of
cooperation, each freely advising and assisting the other when called
upon to do so.
2. No member shall enter into a business dealing on behalf
of the museum which will result in a personal profit.
3. A member shall never use a museum's resources for
his personal advantage, to the detriment of the museum.
4. No member shall engage in anything outside his profession that would conflict with his duties and responsibilities; he should,
however, participate in community activities related to his profession.

C. Relationship to museum Materials:

1. A member shall treat and display the materials in his
custody with the dignity that is their due; restoration shall be based
on adequate research; and while seeing to it that an object is clean,
sanitary, and structurally sound, he shall refrain from removing
legitimate marks of normal use, wear, and age. All substantial
replacements shall be made to resemble, but not duplicate, the
original. Accidental or non-original accretions shall be removed
whenever possible.

D. Relationship to the Profession:

1. A member shall have membership in as many applicable museum organizations as possible, and shall be ready to attend and participate in professional meetings and conferences; he shall be willing to do a reasonable share of the work of the Museums Section of the Ontario Historical Society.

2. A member shall extend his knowledge of museum practice through reading professional journals and taking training courses.

3. Every member shall assist any other member who seeks information or advice from him in a matter of professional service.

4. Formal evaluation of the policies and practices of another museum shall be given only upon the invitation of that museum's governing authority, and then only with the approval of the member's own governing authority.

5. A member shall confine his public criticism to evaluation of exhibitions, avoiding all questions as to the personality or competence of another member of the profession; private criticism must be guided by the discretion of the individual.

E. Relationship to the Public:

1. It is a member's responsibility to make all the resources and services of the museum known to its potential users: impartial service shall be rendered to all who are entitled to use such resources and services.

2. A member shall work to extend the public knowledge of museum practices, and to discourage unfair, untrue, or exaggerated statements with respect to the profession.

3. A member shall treat as confidential any private information obtained through contact with museum patrons or through museum materials.

4. In cases where the twofold responsibilities of preserving and disseminating information come into conflict, priority shall be given to preservation since many materials are irreplaceable.

5. No member shall divulge information which would enable private individuals to compete with museums in developing collections.

"Recommended Policy for Museums"*

Preamble: For the purpose of this Recommended Policy, "Museum" means a museum as defined by the Canadian Museums Association at its 1964 meeting at Hamilton, Ontario: The word "Museum" shall be deemed to mean a non-profit, permanent establishment, not existing primarily for the purpose of conducting temporary exhibitions, exempt from Federal and Provincial income taxes, open to the public and administered in the public interest, for the purpose of conserving and preserving, studying, interpreting, assembling and exhibiting to the public for its instruction and enjoyment, objects and specimens of educational and cultural value, including artistic, scientific (whether animate or inanimate), historical and technological material. Museums thus defined shall include Botanical Gardens, Zoological Parks, Aquaria, Planetaria, Historical Societies and Historic Houses and Sites which meet the requirements set forth in the preceding sentence; and

"Indemnity" means replacement with goods of like kind and quality.

Upon its inception a museum assumes an obligation to maintain ethical standards of conduct in relationship to:

A. Museum Materials
B. Other Museums
C. The Public

A. Relationship to Museum Materials:

1. A museum should adequately catalogue and index its holdings.

2. Adequate safeguards should be established regarding the acquisition and disposal of museum materials; every effort should be made to identify and document such materials through the consultation of reliable authorities; and in particular, problematical objects should not be rejected without being identified.

3. Museum materials should be displayed for the purpose of public instruction and enjoyment; they should not be used to present undignified aspects of an individual's life story unless such aspects are specifically related to his historical significance.

B. Relationship with Other Museums:

1. Museums should strive to cooperate with each other, not compete, in the answering of reference questions; various aspects of a complex question might be shared among those museums that are best qualified to answer them.

2. No museum should employ any guile, deception, scheme, or trick to entice material from the collection of another museum.

3. No museum should knowingly retain material which would be more appropriately placed in another museum, without consultation with that museum; provided always, however, that such material may be taken into temporary custody for the purpose of transferring it to the other museum.

4. In cases of the transfer of material from one museum to another, each such transfer should be considered as a completely independent transaction; it is contrary to the public interest for a museum to withhold such material until the other museum can exchange it in order to obtain it.

C. Relationship with the Public:

1. Donors of museum material should be made aware that their donations, whether single objects or series or collections, become the exclusive and absolute property of the recipient museum, to be dealt with in all respects as the museum alone sees fit; a

statement to this effect should appear on the gift form.

2. Materials should be borrowed only for specific purposes of display or research; upon the death of a lender the museum should negotiate a new loan with the heirs.

3. Museums should attempt to confine their collecting:
(a) if representative and anonymous material, to one of a kind;
(b) if material associated with a personality, to those things which are specifically related to his historical significance. It is not the museum's function to accept materials whose significance is purely personal and not of public concern.

4. Museums should not allow undesirable visitors to endanger their holdings, or to interfere with other visitors; the tolerating of such interference is a breach of public trust.

5. No museum should knowingly allow an inaccuracy to remain in a caption beyond such reasonable time as might be required to correct it.

6. No museum should appraise materials brought to its attention. In dealing with the public the sole concern of the museum should be identification, and/or authentication. Discussions of monetary values are speculative, and unrelated to the museum's interpretive function.

7. Museums should resist commercialized offers of materials in which price is speculative, and cannot be justified in terms of (a) an appropriate return for the vendor's own efforts, or (b) the indemnity of the owner for the actual loss of use of his material.

8. No museum charging an admission fee should arrange its displays in such a way that they cannot be understood without the purchase or rental of explanatory aids.

Much of the foregoing was written with historical museums in mind, for the simple reason that almost all Ontario's museums are historical. Adaption to serve broader purposes would therefore be necessary.

In retrospect, certain points perhaps deserve a little explanation. In the Code, point E3 arose when a museum was consulted by both sides of a legal case. Point E4 was included primarily with such things as archaeological sites in mind. A responsible museologist should display and interpret archaeological materials to the public, but he should stop short of divulging the precise location of an uncompleted dig since such information would lead to amateur looting.

In the Policy, point A3 is in part an outgrowth of a discussion at an earlier workshop of the hypothetical question "Should Great Uncle Willie's chamber pot be accepted by a museum for its association with Great Uncle Willie (who of course was a pillar of the community and a sainted ancestor of the donor), or because it represents mid-Nineteenth Century ceramics; or should it be rejected because it's a chamber pot and therefore censorable?" It might be added parenthetically that the daily press appears to

regard chamber pots as censorable. When this discussion was reported in the papers, it was said to have centered on Great Uncle
Willie's snuffbox!

In point C3 of the Policy, the phrase "one of a kind" should
be interpreted broadly. A museum could easily develop a collection
of 150 molding planes without a duplication. A set of dishes would
still be one of a kind, even though it might include twelve settings.

Policy point C6 was included because so many museums head
straight for trouble through not being able to cite something in print
on the subject of "value." The use of the word in a monetary sense
is nonsense for museums anyway. The popular impression seems
to be that every last bit of matter has an absolute cash value, just
because it exists. Actually, monetary value is entirely a phenome-
non of the human intellect, and very largely subjective.

A private collector once pulled a glass target ball out of his
pocket and presented it to a museum, before an audience of museum
people. He had long since forgotten where the piece was collected,
but he doubted if it was in the area served by the museum (see
Policy, B3). A member of the audience, a private collector on
the side, leaped to his feet and said "That's worth twenty dollars,
and I'll give you twice that!" (Code, B4; Policy, B2).

More recently a box containing seventy-two target balls has
come to light. Now, was the original "worth" twenty dollars, or
forty dollars? And are the additional seventy-two "worth" $1440,
or $2880? Or are they "worth" even more because they were
found together, or less because of supply and demand? Or are they
"worth" nothing at all, because their only value is educational and/
or cultural and/or aesthetic? And by what process did the first
one come to be "worth" even twenty dollars? Target balls were
made to be broken, and therefore must have been decidedly inex-
pensive to begin with. Who gets the profit, and how does he justify
it?

Refusal to quote prices can have its distinct advantages.
One museum declined to answer a reporter's question about the
value of a pistol that had been stolen, which resulted in the gun's
being described as "priceless" in the story that followed, and perhaps more column inches than would otherwise have been devoted
to the subject. The thief was alarmed to read that he had a "priceless" gun which was described down to the last scratch thanks to
thorough cataloguing (Policy, A1), and must have concluded that he
could never run the risk of showing it to anyone. His only alternative was to abandon it and tip the police, which he did. The gun
was recovered, and back on display, while the paper containing the
story of the theft was still being sold.

It might be noticed that both Code and Policy are devoid of
penalty clauses. The committee felt, and I think wisely so, that

museology and the other academic and service professions are
among the last outposts of nobility and selflessness in contemporary
life, and hence the provision of a policing arrangement for violators
would demean them and in a sense defeat the whole purpose. In
short it is taken for granted that museum people are respectable,
and all that is necessary to keep them that way in the fact of an
imperfect world is to give them a set of standards to fall back on.

Museums have traditionally been the champions of Truth and
Beauty. Let us restore Goodness to the triad of platonic values
(that word again!)--and let us remember which comes first.

*"Code" and "Recommended Policy" reprinted by permission of the
Museums Section, Ontario Historical Society, Ontario, Canada.

MUSIC TEACHERS

MUSIC EDUCATORS NATIONAL CONFERENCE (MENC)
     1201 16th St., N.W., Washington, D.C. 20036
     Charles L. Gary, Executive Secretary

Membership: Music Educators National Conference, an affiliate of
the National Education Association, was organized in 1907 as a
national organization of music supervisors in the public schools and
has a present (1973) membership of 62,000. Among members are
music teachers or professionals engaged in other music education
work "at all institutional levels, from pre-school through college
and university. " Component music organizations in each state are
federated with MENC in six geographic regions. MENC active
membership is "open to all persons engaged in music teaching or
other music education work. "

Code of Ethics: While MENC has issued no formal code of professional ethics, it did adopt in 1947 a statement of policy dealing with
ethical standards involved in the question of student performing
groups as distinct from professional musicians. This Music Code
of Ethics--adopted in conjunction with the American Federation of
Musicians and the American Association of School Administrators--

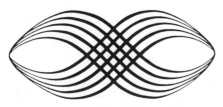

defines the jurisdictions of
student groups (I. Music Education) and of professional
musicians (II. Entertainment).

Professional Insignia: The
symbol identifying MENC was
adopted in 1969, and registered

as a trademark in 1971. It combines the five-line musical staff with the symbol for infinity--designated the "Infinite Staff"--"symbolic of music education's linking of the old and new, " and acting as a "bridge between classical and modern, past, present, and future. " The emblem, which may be reproduced in any color, may be shown with the legend "MENC, " or "Music Educators National Conference, " in any combination with the symbol. The "Infinite Staff" appears on national and state MENC stationery, membership cards, publications, and is also available for members' wear as jewelry (pin, tie-tack, tie bar, charm).

Bibliography:
    Music Educators National Conference. MENC. August 1971. Folder.
    Descriptive brochure including MENC purpose, organization, history, functions; emblem on cover.
    _____. MENC Symbol--Guidelines for Use. 1 page. Pictures emblem, giving meaning, adoption history, authorized form and use.
    _____. The Music Code of Ethics. 4 pages. Folder. Agreement defining the jurisdictions of professional musicians and school musicians--adopted jointly in 1947 by the American Federation of Musicians, the MENC, and the American Association of School Administrators.

"The Music Code of Ethics"

    The competition of school bands and orchestras in the past years has been a matter of grave concern and, at times, even hardship to the professional musicians.
    Music educators and professional musicians alike are committed to the general acceptance of music as a desirable factor in the social and cultural growth of our country. The music educators contribute to this end by fostering the study of music among the children, and by developing an interest in better music among the masses. The professional musicians strive to improve musical taste by providing increasingly artistic performances of worthwhile musical works.
    This unanimity of purpose is further exemplified by the fact that a great many professional musicians are music educators, and a great many music educators are, or have been, actively engaged in the field of professional performance.
    The members of high school symphonic orchestras and bands look to the professional organizations for example and inspiration; they become active patrons of music in later life. They are not content to listen to a twelve-piece ensemble when an orchestra of symphonic proportions is necessary to give adequate performance. These former music students, through their influence on sponsors, employers and program makers in demanding adequate musical performances, have a beneficial effect upon the prestige and economic status of the professional musicians.

Since it is in the interest of the music educator to attract
public attention to his attainments for the purpose of enhancing his
prestige and subsequently his income, and since it is in the interest
of the professional musician to create more opportunities for employment at increased remuneration, it is only natural that upon
certain occasions some incidents might occur in which the interests
of the members of one or the other group might be infringed upon,
either from lack of forethought or lack of ethical standards among
individuals.

In order to establish a clear understanding as to the limita-
tions of the fields of professional music and music education in the
United States, the following statement of policy, adopted by the Music
Educators National Conference and the American Federation of
Musicians, and approved by the American Association of School
Administrators, is recommended to those serving in their respec-
tive fields:

I Music Education

The field of music education, including the teaching of music
and such demonstrations of music education as do not directly conflict with the interests of the professional musician, is the province
of the music educator. It is the primary purpose of all the parties
signatory hereto that the professional musician shall have the fullest
protection in his efforts to earn his living from the playing and rendition of music; to that end it is recognized and accepted that all
music to be performed under the "Code of Ethics" herein set forth
is and shall be performed in connection with non-profit, non-commercial and non-competitive enterprises.   Under the heading of
"Music Education" should be included the following:

(1)   School Functions initiated by the schools as a part of a
school program,   whether in a school building or other building.

(2)   Community Functions organized in the interest of the
schools strictly for educational purposes, such as those that might
be originated by the Parent-Teacher Association.

(3)   School Exhibits prepared as a part of the school district's courtesies for educational organizations or educational conventions being entertained in the district.

(4)   Educational Broadcasts which have the purpose of demonstrating or illustrating pupils' achievements in music study, or
which represent the culmination of a period of study and rehearsal.
Included in this category are local, state, regional and national
school music festivals and competitions held under the auspices of
schools, colleges, and/or educational organizations on a non-profit
basis and broadcast to acquaint the public with the results of music
instruction in the schools.

(5)   Civic Occasions of local, state or national patriotic

interest, of sufficient breadth to enlist the sympathies and cooperation of all persons, such as those held by the G. A. R., American
Legion, and Veterans of Foreign Wars in connection with their
Memorial Day services in the cemeteries. It is understood that
affairs of this kind may be participated in only when such participation does not in the least usurp the right and privileges of local
professional musicians.

(6)   Benefit Performances for local charities, such as the
Welfare Federations, Red Cross, hospitals, etc., when and where
local professional musicians would likewise donate their services.

(7)   Educational or Civic Services that might beforehand be
mutually agreed upon by the school authorities and official representatives of the local professional musicians.

(8)   Audition Recordings for study purposes made in the
classroom or in connection with contest or festival performances by
students, such recordings to be limited to exclusive use by the students and their teachers, and not offered for general sale or other
public distribution. This definition pertains only to the purpose and
utilization of audition recordings and not to matters concerned with
copyright regulations. Compliance with copyright requirements
applying to recordings of compositions not in the public domain is
the responsibility of the school, college or educational organization
under whose auspices the recording is made.

II Entertainment

The field of entertainment is the province of the professional
musician. Under this heading are the following:

(1)   Civic parades, ceremonies, exposition, community concerts, and community-center activities (See I, Paragraph 2 for
further definition); regattas, non-scholastic contests, festivals,
athletic games, activities or celebration, and the like; national,
state and county fairs (See I, Paragraph 5 for further definition).
(2)   Functions for the furtherance, directly or indirectly, of
any public or private enterprise; functions by chambers of commerce,
boards of trade, and commercial clubs or associations.
(3)   Any occasion that is partisan or sectarian in character
or purpose.
(4)   Functions of clubs, societies, civic or fraternal organizations.

Statements that funds are not available for the employment
of professional musicians, or that if the talents of amateur musical
organizations cannot be had, other musicians cannot or will not be
employed, or that the amateur musicians are to play without remuneration of any kind, are all immaterial.

MUSIC TEACHERS NATIONAL ASSOCIATION (MTNA)
    1831 Carew Tower, Cincinnati, Ohio 45202
    Dr. Albert G. Huetteman, Executive Secretary

Membership: The Music Teachers National Association, the oldest
organization of professional music educators in the United States,
was founded in 1876 and has a present (1973) membership of over
14,000. MTNA Active Membership is "open to all persons professionally engaged in the field of musical activity subject to membership regulations of affiliated states or regularly organized national
music organizations." Among the members are many private music
teachers, and faculty members of college and university music
schools.

    In order to evaluate and designate qualified music teachers and
to require teaching accomplishments and professional competence
in music education, MTNA instituted a National Certification Plan
in April 1967. MTNA Certification Plan--directed to promoting
"recognition of private music teaching as a profession"--issues a
professional designation, "Nationally Certified," which is valid for
five years from date of issue. According to Certificate Regulations:
    "1.   The MTNA will recognize for certification in applied
          music any member in good standing who holds an
          earned degree in music from an institution approved
          by the National Certification Board with a major in
          the performing medium he desires to teach, and who
          is recommended by his State Association for certifi-
          cation...."
    "2.   The MTNA will grant certification in applied music to
          any member in good standing who does not hold an
          earned degree, but who has successfully completed
          comprehensive written, oral, and performance exam-
          inations in theory, music history and literature,
          pedagogy, and performance in the area in which the
          applicant wishes to teach. These examinations are
          prepared, administered, and evaluated by the National
          Certification Board...."

Code of Ethics: The professional conduct guide for MTNA members
is the organization's Code of Ethics, which gives standards of professional conduct and personal integrity, under several areas of
music teaching:
        Studio Music Teaching,
        Public School and College Music Teaching,
        Cooperative Activity, including relationships with students,
            parents of students, announcements of professional service.
The Code includes (V) a provision concerning the obligation of
every MTNA member to report to the Association in writing any
violations of the code of ethics.

Professional Insignia: The emblem of the MTNA is its official seal
--a circular device with a centered five-stringed harp--symbolizing

music--in which a ribbon is
entwined; the organization's
founding date, "1876," is
given at the base of the harp;
the name of the group,
"Music Teachers National
Association," appears around
the design in a dark border.
The color of the emblem is
green (publications).

Other Identification of Professional Status: As indicated above under "Membership," members certified by
MTNA as professionally
competent, indicate certification with their name by,
"Nationally Certified."

Bibliography:
    Bryant, Celia Mae. "The second 70's." Folder reprint from
        American Music Teacher Magazine, January 1970; rev.
        1973.
    History and future of MTNA.
    Music Teachers National Association. Code of Ethics. 1 page.
        Principles of ethical practices subscribed to by MTNA mem-
        bers.
           . MTNA National Certification Handbook. 1969. 10
        pages. Pamphlet.
    History and purpose of MTNA certification; requirements for
        certification and certification renewal.
           . Music Teachers National Association. Folder.
    Informational brochure describing MTNA functions, organiza-
    tion, membership categories; emblem on cover.

"Code of Ethics"

      We, the members of Music Teachers National Association,
having dedicated ourselves to the advancement of music and the
growth of young musicians, subscribe to the following principles
of ethical practice as standards of professional conduct:

      I It shall be the obligation of every member to maintain the
highest standards of moral and professional conduct, and personal
integrity.

      II In the Area of Studio Music Teaching

      1. teachers will refrain from exploiting the student primarily
for the teacher's own prestige.

2.   teachers will cooperate in the support of public education and encourage students to participate in school ensembles and activities.

3.   teachers, if affiliated with the public schools in instructional capacity, will conform to the policies of the school and cooperate with the administration.

III   In the Areas of Public School and College Music Teaching

1.   teachers will not show partiality when advising those seeking guidance in selecting a private teacher, but will, if requested, suggest the names of two or more private teachers in the community, the final choice to be made by the parent and student.

2.   teachers will secure advance approval from the properly constituted authorities for the use of a cost-free room in a publicly-owned building for the purpose of teaching privately for personal monetary gain.

3.   teachers will, after a period of basic music instruction through groups or classes, encourage qualified students to study with private teachers so the students' abilities can be more thoroughly developed.

4.   when serving for limited time as an interim instructor of a student from a private studio, teachers will employ the utmost tact in order to avoid undermining the instruction of the student's regular teacher.

5.   teachers will never solicit or accept a student for individual instruction who is already receiving instruction in the same subject from another teacher.

IV   In the Areas of Cooperative Activity

1.   teachers will refrain from discussing with parents or students the work of another teacher in such a way as to injure the professional reputation of that teacher.

2.   teachers will not claim sole credit for the achievement of students under cooperative or individual instruction, if such claims shall imply discredit upon a previous or presently cooperating teacher.

3.   teachers will not claim credit for the achievement of any student until the student has studied with that teacher for a term of not less than six months.

4.   teachers will offer opportunities for a study to gifted but underprivileged students in the form of free lessons or scholarships only upon merit and not as inducements to study with a particular teacher.

5.   teachers will not solicit another teacher's students.

6.   teachers will not accept a student who is or has been studying the same subject with another teacher until relations with the previous teacher have been terminated and his just indebtedness paid in full.

7.   teachers will rely upon their professional qualities to attract students and will avoid using their positions in the community

churches or schools as pressure on students to study with them.

8. teachers will not represent themselves as a "pupil of" or a "student of" any teacher unless they have completed a continuous course of three months study.

9. teachers will not make exaggerated claims or misleading statements in any printed matter; advertising copy will be dignified, strictly truthful, and representative of the art of music and its responsibility to the community.

V It shall be the duty of every member to report to the respective National or State Executive Boards the violation of any article of this Code, supported by written evidence of such unethical conduct.

NATIONAL ASSOCIATION OF SCHOOLS OF MUSIC (NASM)
One Dupont Circle, Suite 650, Washington, D. C. 20036
Robert Glidden, Executive Secretary

Membership: The National Association of Schools of Music, founded in 1924 and with a present (1973) institutional membership of about 400, is an organization of institutions engaged in music education-- schools of music in colleges, universities, independent schools of music, junior colleges, and institutions offering graduate work only in music. The NASM has been designated by the National Commission on Accrediting as the agency responsible for the accreditation of music curricula in higher education. Institutions are admitted to membership, provided they meet qualifications for:

Associate Membership--Initial applicants meeting a substantial portion of the standards of the NASM are granted Associate Membership for minimum period of two years, and are expected to apply within five years for Full Membership;

Full Membership--Institutions holding Associate Membership and meeting Association standards for all music curricula offered; re-examined for Full Membership on a ten-year cycle.

Individual Membership and Honorary Membership may be granted to qualified individuals.

Code of Ethics: The professional conduct guide for members of NASM is the Association's Code of Ethics. This guide lists in eleven Articles principles of practice for schools of music, including the awarding of academic appointments, financial aid to students, advertising and informational materials. Provisions for enforcement of these standards are contained in the Code (Article X)--complaints of violation of professional ethics are considered by the Ethics Committee, which--after investigation and hearing--refers questions for appropriate action to the NASM Board of Directors.

Professional Insignia: None reported.

Bibliography:
    National Association of Schools of Music. Directory of Full
        and Associate Member Institutions, Individual and Honor-
        ary Members. 1973. 96 pages. $1.50.
                . Handbook. Annual. 1972. 40 pages. Pamphlet. $1.
    Includes NASM purpose, organization, membership categories,
    and code of ethics.
                . Music in Higher Education, 1971-1972. 48 pages.
        Pamphlet. $4.
    Statistical information compiled from the annual reports of
    member institutions.

"Code of Ethics"

Article I.   Institutional members of the Association agree
that the granting or conferring of degrees and diplomas shall be in
accordance with the standards of this Association.

Article II.   Inquiries about an individual's interest in and
conversation concerning a new, full-time, academic appointment are
in order at any time of the year, but after May 1, an offer for an
appointment to take effect in the next academic year will not be
made unless the administrative head (usually the Dean or his designated substitute) of the offering college, school, or institute, has
determined that the date at which the appointment is to take effect
is agreeable to the administrative head of the college, school, or
institute which the individual will be leaving if he accepts the new
appointment.

Article III.   Institutional members of the Association recognize the importance of moral, ethical, and professional integrity in
the conduct of their faculty.

Article IV.   Financial aid shall be awarded according to the
criteria established by the member institution granting the award.
The acceptance of financial aid by a candidate shall be a declaration
of intent to attend the institution making the award and he must be
so informed. *

Article V.   A transferring student who has not completed a
degree program can be considered eligible for financial aid during
the first term of enrollment in the new institution only if the Music
Executive of the school from which he is transferring specifically
approves.   Junior College transfers who have completed a two-year
program of study or whatever part of the university parallel curriculum is available at the Junior College attended, are exempt from
this regulation.

Article VI.   Institutional members of this Association shall
refuse to accept as a student, until after full investigation of the
circumstances, one who has been expelled for just cause (disciplinary
action, not academic suspension).

Article VII.   Institutional members shall not make exaggerated
or misleading statements during interviews, auditions, nor in printed

matter. All brochures, catalogs, and yearbooks shall be an accurate statement of the curriculum, objectives, equipment, and accommodations of the institution.

Article VIII. Advertising shall be dignified and truthful.

Article IX. Institutional members of this Association shall be at all times cognizant of the school's responsibility to a student. Exploitation, with or without financial compensation, of a student to the detriment of his normal academic progress shall be considered a violation of this code.

Further, when it has been determined that a student, either graduate or undergraduate, is not acceptable as a candidate for a degree or diploma, the student shall be so informed.

Article X. If the parties involved cannot resolve an alleged violation, an appeal, in the form of a detailed letter, shall be filed with the Chairman of the Ethics Committee and the NASM Executive Secretary. The Ethics Committee shall after due inquiry and consideration, make the appropriate recommendations to the Board of Directors of the National Association of Schools of Music.

Article XI. The Code of Ethics may be amended by a two-thirds vote of the membership present and voting at any annual meeting, provided a written notice of the proposed amendment be sent to all institutional members at least two weeks before the said meeting.

---

*It is recommended that the following format be incorporated in making any offer of financial aid:

"In accepting this offer of financial aid from _____ __(institution)____ I recognize that I may not consider any other offer from an institutional member of the National Association of Schools of Music for the academic year_____-_____ except with the express consent of the music executive of the above-named institution."

(signed)_____
(date) _____

MUSIC THERAPISTS

NATIONAL ASSOCIATION FOR MUSIC THERAPY (NAMT)
P. O. Box 610, Lawrence, Kansas 66044
Mrs. Margaret Sears, Coordinating Secretary

Membership: The National Association for Music Therapy, founded in 1950 and with a present (1973) membership of about 1200, is a professional association of workers engaged in "the use of music in the accomplishment of therapeutic aims: the restoration, maintenance, and improvement of mental and physical health." Qualified

for "Active Membership" in NAMT are "all persons engaged in the
use of music therapy: music therapists, physicians, psychologists,
administrators, and educators."

The Association registers therapists and authorizes the use of
a professional designation, "Registered Music Therapist" ("RMT"),
which is granted without examination. The requirement for registration is the completion of a baccalaureate degree in music therapy
(B. M., A. B., or B. M. E. in Music Therapy, or Bachelor of Music
Therapy) in a university approved by the NAMT to offer such a degree,
or the equivalent. In addition to 128 semester hours of on-campus
education, the degree requires a six-month period of clinical training, following academic study, in an approved program under the
direction of a Registered Music Therapist.

Code of Ethics: The NAMT has developed no written code of ethics.

Professional Insignia: The official emblem of the National Association for Music Therapy is an unbordered design, devised by Sister M.

Xaveria, and adopted by the
Association in 1952. The insignia signifies the interrela-
tionship of music and medicine
in music therapy, by showing
a caduceus--the winged, serpent-
entwined staff of medicine--
superimposed on two musical
notes; the legend "Music" appears at the top of the design,
and "Therapy" toward the bottom of the emblem. The color
of the insignia is shown vari-
ously--black on white, green
on white, turquoise blue on
white. A pin, available for
wear by Registered Music Therapists, is a shield enclosing this
official insignia.

Other Identification of Professional Status: As described
above under "Membership,"
the NAMT awards the professional designation: "Registered Music
Therapist" ("RMT").

Bibliography:
      National Association for Music Therapy.   A Career in Music
            Therapy. 6 pages. Pamphlet.
         Duties, approved curriculum and colleges offering, and brief
         description of qualifications for RMT (Registered Music
         Therapist.)
      _____. The National Association for Music Therapy.

Pamphlet.
Descriptive brochure giving NAMT purposes and activities,
membership requirements, and application for membership.

MUSICIANS

AMERICAN SOCIETY OF COMPOSERS, AUTHORS AND PUBLISHERS (ASCAP)
575 Madison Ave., New York, N. Y. 10022
Stanley Adams, President

Membership: The American Society of Composers, Authors and
Publishers, organized in 1914 and with a present (1973) membership
of about 16, 000 American composers and lyricists and their over
5500 publishers, is a clearing house for performing rights in music.
ASCAP "licenses the right to perform ... in public ... for profit in
the United States the copyrighted musical works of its American
members and the members of affiliated societies in more than
thirty countries. " Any composer, lyricist or musical publisher may
join ASCAP by giving copyright proof that they have had a musical
work "regularly published, " or are "actively engaged in the music
publishing business and assuming the normal financial risks involved
in publishing. "

The Society collects income for licensing the performance rights
of the copyrighted music of its members, from some 35, 000 licensed
users of ASCAP music, including radio and television stations and
networks, nightclubs and hotels, wired music systems such as
MUZAK, symphony orchestras, colleges and universities sponsoring
concerts. This ASCAP income from licensing musical performances
is distributed to its members as quarterly-paid royalty. In 1969
operating costs of ASCAP deducted were less than 16% of income
(based primarily upon a Survey of Performances--a statistical sampling of ASCAP music performances of television, radio, wired
music and similar devices).

Code of Ethics: ASCAP has issued no written code of ethics.

Professional Insignia: The emblem of ASCAP is its official seal--
a circular design bearing the Society initials, "AS of CAP, " in the
center, and the organization name, "American Society of Composers,
Authors, Publishers, " in five bordering band segments. The color
of the emblem as shown on letterhead and publications is black on
white. Members are forbidden by Society rules "from using the
ASCAP seal, or referring to their membership in the Society in
connection with the solicitation of funds from writers for the purpose
of revising, adapting, publishing or exploiting their works. "

Bibliography:
American Society of Com-
posers, Authors and
Publishers. ASCAP
Biographical Diction-
ary. 1966. 845 p.
$5.25.
Biographical sketches of
writer members, and
list of all publisher members.
_____. ASCAP Index.
3 volumes. $15.
List of popular songs
performed in ASCAP
survey.
_____. ASCAP: The
Facts. Folder.

Twenty question-and-answer paragraphs provide information
about ASCAP functions, membership, licensees, fees, publications.
_____. Questions and Answers. 8 pages. Pamphlet.
Includes ASCAP operation, membership, branch offices, managers.

MUSICIANS--ORGANISTS

AMERICAN GUILD OF ORGANISTS (AGO)
     630 Fifth Ave., New York, N.Y. 10020
     Charles D. Walker, President

Membership: The American Guild of Organists, founded in 1896 and
with a present (1973) membership of approximately 16,000 in over
300 chapters and branches, is a non-sectarian organization of professional church musicians--Organists and Choir Masters.   There
are several categories of membership.   "Member" is open to any
person interested in professional church music, and requires no
examination.   Three other types of membership require examination,
an important Guild activity in:
          "raising the standard of efficiency of organists and choir-
          masters, by examinations to evaluate the training and the
          attainments of candidates in Practical Organ Playing, Choir-
          Training, and Theory and General Knowledge of Music, and
          to grant certificates in their respective classes of member-
          ship."

Requirements and examinations for such memberships are:

Choir Master (Ch. M.)--Open to Fellows, Associates, and Members; 30-minute practical test with choir, rehearsing and directing the choir in singing specified compositions, including demonstrating with the choir methods of breathing, tone production, purity of vowels, clear enunciation, three hour paper test in theory and general music, including Ear Tests involving writing from dictation and recognition of wrong notes.

Associate (A. A. G. O.)--Open to Members; 30-minute test at Organ, including playing at sight, harmonizing, transposing, two 3-hour paper tests in theory and general music, including counterpoint; construction, design and maintenance of the organ; standard repertoire of church music; ear tests, including dictation and composition.

Fellow (F. A. G. O.)--Open to Associates who have passed their Associateship examination in a previous year; 40-minute Test at Organ, including more difficult playing, sight reading, transposing, in addition to improvising; two 3-1/2 hour tests including counterpoint; fugue; ear tests, including counterpoint, string quartet; composition for organ; twentieth century music.

The AGO also issues to qualified members of the Guild and to Student Guild Groups, a certificate in "Service Playing."

Code of Ethics: The AGO guide to professional conduct for members is its Code of Ethics, which consists of three rules of practice in securing positions as organist or director of the choir in churches, contract length and termination, duties of regular organist. This Code was developed by the Committee on Code of Ethics, of which George Mead was Chairman. Provisions of the Code are enforced by the Committee on Ethical Practices, which receives and investigates complaints of irregular or unfair practices on the part of organists, choirmasters, and churches. Upon this Committee's recommendation, the AGO Council may discipline a member by censure, suspension, or expulsion (Constitution, Article IV, Section 4).

Other Guides to Professional Conduct: At its inception in 1896, the Guild issued standards to be followed by members in service: A Declaration of the Religious Principles of the American Guild of Organists. This Declaration, which is in the form of a credo, is enforced by the Committee on Ethical Practices.

Professional Insignia: The emblem of the American Guild of Organists is its official seal--an ellipsoid, with angular terminations; an organ case is centered with a superimposed

banner bearing the legend, "Soli Deo Gloria" ("To God Alone Be
Glory"); a bordering band carries the organization name, "American
Guild of Organists," with the date of the group's founding, "1896," at
the bottom of the border.   This border is banded on the inside with
two borders--the inner carrying dotting, the outer, dark half circles
with dotted band; the outer band has alternate light and dark spaces,
stemmed flowers shown from the light spaces.   The color of the
official seal is gold; and the emblem is shown in various colors--
red; black (publications).

Other Identification of Professional Status: As described above under
"Membership," professional designations are awarded by the Guild,
to indicate professional competence: "Choir Master" ("Ch. M. ");
"Service Playing"; and two classes of Guild Academic Membership:
"Associate" ("A. A. G. O. "); "Fellow" ("F. A. G. O. ").

Bibliography:
    American Guild of Organists.   American Guild of Organists.
        Folder.
        Information brochure giving AGO purposes and membership
        qualifications.
        _____.   A Brief Sketch of A. G. O.   Folder.
        Includes "A Declaration of the Religious Principles of the
        American Guild of Organists."
        _____.   Code of Ethics and Recommendations.   1 page.
        Three rules of the Code; recommendations for acceptable
        practice; enforcement procedure.
        _____.   Examination Requirements.   Annual.
        For each certificate issued gives examination requirements,
        and may describe content, form and subjects of examination;
        textbooks recommended for study.

"Code of Ethics and Recommendations"

Rule 1.   No organist or choirmaster shall apply for a position, nor shall any teacher or school of music seek to place anyone
in a position, unless a present or prospective vacancy definitely has
been determined.
     Rule 2.   When requested, churches should give organists
and choirmasters a yearly contract, which may be terminated upon
expiration only, at ninety days notice.
     Rule 3.   None but the regular organist of a church shall play
at weddings or funerals.   Any exception to this rule must be made
with the consent of the organist.

The Committee Recommends:

A.   That a "Committee on Ethical Practices" be appointed
by The Council to receive and act on complaints of irregular and
unfair practices on the part of organists, choirmasters and churches.
These complaints should be submitted in writing to this committee.

This committee, with the ratification of the Council, has the power to act in behalf of the interests of the Guild as stipulated in the Code of Ethics and has the power to take steps to correct any situation presented to them, where this Code is being broken.

B.   That organists and choirmasters be cautioned against breaking this Code of Ethics in spirit or letter and that at all times our "Declaration of Religious Principles" be their standard of service.

C.   That the attention of all Guild members be called to the following article from our Constitution in regard to discipline as the result of neglecting or violating our Code of Ethics:

Article IV, Section 4, Page 18--"Discipline"

"In case of charges deemed inimical to the interests of the Guild being brought against a member, he may be censured, suspended or expelled from membership by a vote of the Council, after opportunity shall have been given him for a hearing in his own defense and after discussion. For this purpose a quorum shall consist of not less than fifteen members and not less than four-fifths shall be in favor of censure, suspension or expulsion before such action can be taken.   A member who has been expelled shall not be eligible to re-election, nor shall he be admitted to the rooms of the Guild as a visitor. "

We hope that the attention of those in authority will be called to this Code of Ethics, and that these unethical and unprofessional practices may cease.

"A Declaration of the Religious Principles of the American Guild of Organists"

"For the greater glory of God, and for the good of His Holy Church in this land, we, being severally members of the American Guild of Organists, do declare our mind and intention in the things following:

We believe that the office of music in Divine Worship is a Sacred Oblation before the Most High.

We believe that they who are set as Choir Masters and as Organists in the House of God ought themselves to be persons of devout conduct, teaching the ways of earnestness to the Choirs committed to their charge.

We believe that the unity of purpose and fellowship of life between Ministers and Choirs should be everywhere established and maintained.

We believe that at all times and in all places it is meet, right, and our bounden duty to work and to pray for the advancement of Divine Worship in the holy gifts of strength and nobleness; to the end that the Church may be purged of her blemishes, that the minds of men may be instructed, that the honor of God's House may be guarded in our time and in the time to come.

Wherefore we do give ourselves with reverence and humility to these endeavors, offering up our works and our persons in the Name of Him, without Whom nothing is strong, nothing is holy. Amen. "

NEWSPAPER EDITORS

AMERICAN SOCIETY OF NEWSPAPER EDITORS (ASNE)
Box 551, 1350 Sullivan Trail, Easton, Pa. 18042
Gene Giancarlo, Executive Secretary

Membership: The American Society of Newspaper Editors, founded in 1922 and with a current (1973) membership of nearly 800, is a professional association of editors of daily newspapers in every section of the United States.   Membership is limited, with few exceptions, to directing editors having immediate charge of editorial or news policies on newspapers with circulation over 20,000. Publishers are eligible only if they are also editors, and spend a major part of their time on editorial affairs.   The Society purpose, according to its Constitution, is "to interchange ideas for the advancement of professional ideals ... and to work collectively for the solution of common problems. "

Code of Ethics: The guide to professional conduct of members of ASNE is the organization's Code of Ethics or Canons of Journalism, which codify "sound practice and just aspirations of American journalism" under six headings:
I.   Responsibility;
II.   Freedom of the Press;
III.   Independence;
IV.   Impartiality;
V.   Fair Play, Decency.
Adherence to the Code is at the voluntary level.

Professional Insignia: No official emblem has been adopted by the Society.

Bibliography:
    American Society of Newspaper Editors. ASNE--Brief History. 1 page.
        Society organization, purpose, and programs, including Freedom of Information, and free press and fair trial.
    _____ . Code of Ethics or Canons of Journalism. 2 pages. Codification of "sound practice and just aspiration" of American journalism. "
    _____ . Problems of Journalism. Annual. 1923- (1972 $6.25; 1973, late summer).
        Proceedings of the Society Annual Convention.

"Code of Ethics; or, Canons of Journalism"

The primary function of newspapers is to communicate to the human race what its members do, feel and think. Journalism, therefore, demands of its practitioners the widest range of intelligence, or knowledge, and of experience, as well as natural and trained powers of observation and reasoning. To its opportunities as a chronicle are indissolubly linked its obligations as teacher and interpreter.

To the end of finding some means of codifying sound practice and just aspirations of American journalism, these canons are set forth:

I

Responsibility--The right of a newspaper to attract and hold readers is restricted by nothing but considerations of public welfare. The use a newspaper makes of the share of public attention it gains serves to determine its sense of responsibility, which it shares with every member of its staff. A journalist who uses his power for any selfish or otherwise unworthy purpose is faithless to a high trust.

II

Freedom of the Press--Freedom of the press is to be guarded as a vital right of mankind. It is the unquestionable right to discuss whatever is not explicitly forbidden by law, including the wisdom of any restrictive statute.

III

Independence--Freedom from all obligations except that of fidelity to the public interest is vital.

1. Promotion of any private interest contrary to the general welfare, for whatever reason, is not compatible with honest journalism. So-called news communications from private sources should not be published without public notice of their source or else substantiation of their claims to value as news, both in form and substance.

2. Partisanship, in editorial comment which knowingly departs from the truth, does violence to the best spirit of American journalism; in the news columns it is subversive of a fundamental principle of the profession.

IV

Sincerity, Truthfulness, Accuracy--Good faith with the reader is the foundation of all journalism worthy of the name.

1. By every consideration of good faith a newspaper is constrained to be truthful. It is not to be excused for lack of thoroughness or accuracy within its control, or failure to obtain command of these essential qualities.

2. Headlines should be fully warranted by the contents of the articles which they surmount.

V

Impartiality--Sound practice makes clear distinction between news reports and expressions of opinion. News reports should be free from opinion or bias of any kind.
1.   This rule does not apply to so-called special articles unmistakably devoted to advocacy or characterized by a signature authorizing the writer's own conclusions and interpretation.

VI

Fair Play--A newspaper should not publish unofficial charges affecting reputation or moral character without opportunity given to the accused to be heard; right practice demands the giving of such opportunity in all cases of serious accusation outside judicial proceedings.
1.   A newspaper should not invade private rights or feeling without sure warrant of public right as distinguished from public curiosity.
2.   It is the privilege, as it is the duty, of a newspaper to make prompt and complete correction of its own serious mistakes of fact or opinion, whatever their origin.

Decency--A newspaper cannot escape conviction of insincerity if while professing high moral purpose it supplies incentives to base conduct, such as are to be found in details of crime and vice, publication of which is not demonstrably for the general good.   Lacking authority to enforce its canons the journalism here represented can but express the hope that deliberate pandering to vicious instincts will encounter effective public disapproval or yield to the influence of a preponderant professional condemnation.

NEWSPAPER PUBLISHERS

AMERICAN NEWSPAPER PUBLISHERS ASSOCIATION (ANPA)
    11600 Sunrise Valley Dr., Reston, Va. 22070
    Stanford Smith, President and General Manager

Membership: The American Newspaper Publishers Association, founded in 1887 and with a current (1973) membership of about 1100 daily newspapers, is a trade association which represents the publishers (owners) of daily newspapers in the United States, Canada, and off-shore islands.   The membership of ANPA represent more than 90 percent of the total daily newspaper and Sunday circulation in the United States, and over 80 percent of daily circulation in Canada.

Code of Ethics: The ANPA has issued no formal code of ethics. Certain standards and goals of newspaper publishing appear among

the purposes of the Association (By-Laws, Article II) in statements,
including:
> the gathering and diffusing of "reliable information relating
> to all phases of the newspaper publishing business";
> "through counsel to be represented in legal proceedings ...
> concerned with the constitutionally guaranteed right of the
> people to have a press free from government control or
> restraint."

A member may be expelled from the Association (By-Laws, Article
X) "whenever such action is believed necessary to protect the welfare of the association and its members." This procedure requires
that a written motion to expel be signed by five members and passed
(after hearing) by a four-fifths vote of the Board of Directors.

Professional Insignia: The ANPA has no official insignia. Several
monograms are used on letter-
head and publications--the
most frequently used and most
recognized is that on the
Association letterhead. This
monogram shows the organ-
ization initials, "ANPA,"
printed on a dark rectangular background (black and
white).

Bibliography:
> American Newspaper Publishers Association. By-Laws. April
> 1972.
> Includes Association purposes; membership requirements.
> _____. What a Member Newspaper May Expect from the
> ANPA. Folder.
> Informational brochure describing ANPA activities and pub-
> lications.

"Purposes"
(Article II of By-Laws)

The purposes of the association shall be to foster the business and business interests of its members; to obtain for its members accurate and reliable information as to the standing and character of persons, firms and corporations with whom the members
are doing business; to foster amicable relationships among its members; to act on behalf of members in legal proceedings against
debtors, in the administration of their estates, and in settlement
with them and to employ counsel to represent the association or its
members in connection therewith; and to do all such other and further
acts and things relating thereto or otherwise, which may be found
necessary or expedient, so far as the same are permitted by the
laws of the Commonwealth of Virginia to corporations organized
under the Virginia Non-Stock Corporation Act; to encourage in the

broadest and most liberal manner the advancement of the daily
newspaper business in all of its branches and departments; to engage in and otherwise to promote research in the newspaper publishing field and to make available to its members the results of
such research; to gather and diffuse among its members accurate
and reliable information relating to all phases of the newspaper publishing business in respect of customs and usages of the business,
and particularly in respect of relations between its members and
their employees, between its members and their customers, and
between its members and the public at large; through counsel to
be represented in legal proceedings, including, but without limitation thereto, proceedings concerned with the constitutionally guaranteed right of the people to have a press free from government
control or restraint; by its meetings, contacts, reports, papers,
discussions, publications and activities, to promote generally the
highest standards of journalism, thereby fostering the dissemination of information vital to the public welfare and adding to the
material prosperity and happiness of the people served by its members, and generally to further the interests of its members.

    To do any and all things deemed necessary and proper in
connection with or incidental to any of the foregoing, subject to
such limitations as are prescribed by law.

NUMISMATISTS

AMERICAN NUMISMATIC SOCIETY (ANS)
    Broadway and 156th St., New York, N.Y. 10032
    Leslie A. Elam, Director

Membership: The American Numismatic Society, founded in 1858
and with a current (1973) membership of approximately 1800, is

the professional and avocation-
al organization of individuals
interested in any aspect of
coins--their history, identification, value and collecting.
The Society, a member of the
American Council of Learned
Societies, admits to membership any person with an interest in coins.

Code of Ethics: No formal
code of ethics has been developed.

Professional Insignia: The

emblem of the American Numismatic Society is its seal--circular
in form, the insignia shows a spray of three oak leaves curving
from lower left to right and upper portions of the design, the base
of the spray bearing two acorns; the Society motto, "Parva Ne
Pereant" ("Let Not the Little Things Perish"), is shown in the upper left, and the organization name, "The American Numismatic
Society," in the lower left of the design.   The emblem was designed by Victor D. Brenner, from an earlier seal cut by George
Lovett (adopted in 1867), from a design by the classical scholar,
Charles Anthon.

Bibliography:
    Adelson, Howard L.   The American Numismatic Society, 1858-
        1958.   New York, The American Numismatic Society,
        1958. $15.
    Includes history of the Society seals (p. 38, 158).

NURSES

AMERICAN NURSES' ASSOCIATION (ANA)
    2420 Pershing Rd., Kansas City, Mo. 64108
    Eileen M. Jacobi, Ed. D., R. N., Executive Director

Membership: The American Nurses' Association, founded in 1896
and with a present (1973) membership of 200,000, is the national
professional association of registered nurses in the United States.
Members, grouped in 50 state associations of professional nurses
and associations in the District of Columbia, Guam and Virgin Islands, qualify for membership by being graduate nurses licensed
as Registered Nurse (R. N.).   Public Health Nurses, once a separate professional association, are now members of the ANA, in
the Community Health Section.

Code of Ethics: The professional conduct guide for Registered
Nurses is the Code for Nurses with Interpretive Statements, adopted
in 1950, and revised in 1960 and 1968.   The ten enumerated principles of practice for nurses are clarified by the interpretive statements.   The Code was originally prepared by the ANA Committee
on Ethical, Legal and Professional Standards, and is now interpreted and enforced through the ANA Congress for Nursing Practice.
Complaints of violations of this professional conduct guide are generally investigated, heard, and disposed of by the State Nurses'
Associations' Committees on Practice.

Professional Insignia: The emblem of the American Nurses' Association is a round design with the lamp of learning in the left
lower quadrant; the association initials, "ANA," are shown in script

in the upper right of the emblem.
The insignia was selected by
popular vote of the membership,
during the 1956 convention, from
three different designs suggested
by members.   The colors of
the emblem are shown variously
--black on white; grey on white
(letterhead).

Other Identification of Professional Status: The professional
designation, "Registered Nurse"
("R. N."), indicates completion
of basic education preparation
for nursing and state licensure
as nurse.

Bibliography:
     American Nurses' Association.   Code for Nurses with Interpre-
          tive Statements.   1970.   Folder.
     The principles of professional conduct for nurses, with
     clarifying statements.
               .   The Nurse in Research: ANA Guidelines on Ethical
          Values.   1968.   Pamphlet.
     Responsibilities of the professional nurse in research, "an
     extension of the principles enunciated in the ANA Code for
     Professional Nurses."

"Code for Nurses with Interpretive Statements"

Introduction

     The development of a code of ethics is an essential charac-
teristic of a profession, and provides one means whereby professional standards may be established, maintained, and improved.
A code indicates a profession's acceptance of the responsibility and
trust with which it has been invested.   Each practitioner, upon
entering a profession, inherits a measure of that responsibility and
trust and the corresponding obligation to adhere to standards of
ethical practice and conduct set by the profession.

     The Code for Nurses, adopted by the American Nurses' Asso-
ciation in 1950 and revised in 1960 and 1968, is intended to serve
the individual practitioner as a guide to the ethical principles that
should govern her nursing practice, conduct, and relationships.
The Code and the accompanying interpretive statements clarify the
essential areas in which definite standards of practice and conduct
are seen as essential to the full and ethical discharge of the nurse's
responsibility to the public, to other groups with whom she may be
associated, and to the profession of which she is a member.   Each

nurse has an obligation to uphold and adhere to the Code in her individual practice and to ensure that her colleagues do likewise.

Guidance and assistance in implementing the Code in local situations may be obtained from committees or councils on nursing practice of State Nurses Associations. Further information about the Code and its interpretation may be obtained from the ANA Nursing Practice Department.

The Code for Nurses

1   The nurse provides services with respect for the dignity of man, unrestricted by considerations of nationality, race, creed, color, or status.

2   The nurse safeguards the individual's right to privacy by judiciously protecting information of a confidential nature, sharing only that information relevant to his care.

3   The nurse maintains individual competence in nursing practice, recognizing and accepting responsibility for individual actions and judgments.

4   The nurse acts to safeguard the patient when his care and safety are affected by incompetent, unethical, or illegal conduct of any person.

5   The nurse uses individual competence as a criterion in accepting delegated responsibilities and assigning nursing activities to others.

6   The nurse participates in research activities when assured that the rights of individual subjects are protected.

7   The nurse participates in the efforts of the profession to define and upgrade standards of nursing practice and education.

8   The nurse, acting through the professional organization, participates in establishing and maintaining conditions of employment conducive to high-quality nursing care.

9   The nurse works with members of health professions and other citizens in promoting efforts to meet health needs of the public.

10   The nurse refuses to give or imply endorsement to advertising, promotion, or sales for commercial products, services, or enterprises.

1   The nurse provides services with respect for the dignity of man, unrestricted by considerations of nationality, race, creed, color, or status.

The need for nursing care is universal, cutting across all national, ethnic, religious, cultural and economic differences, as does nursing's response to this fundamental human need. Whoever the individual and whatever his background and circumstances, his nursing care should be determined solely by his needs as a unique human being. Individual differences in background, customs, attitudes, and beliefs influence nursing practice only insofar as they represent factors that the nurse must understand, consider, and respect in tailoring care to personal needs and in maintaining the individual's self-respect and dignity. In whatever employment setting she may be, the nurse herself should adhere to this principle of nondiscriminatory, nonprejudicial care and endeavor to promote its acceptance by others.

The nurse's respect for the worth and dignity of the individual human being extends throughout the entire life cycle, from birth to death, and is reflected in her care of the defective as well as the normal, the patient with a longterm in contrast to an acute illness, the young and the old, the recovering patient as well as the one who is terminally ill or dying. In the latter instance the nurse should use all the measures at her command to enable the patient to live out his days with as much comfort, dignity, and freedom from anxiety and pain as possible. His nursing care will determine, to a great degree, how he lives this final human experience and the peace and dignity with which he approaches death.

2   The nurse safeguards the individual's right to privacy by judiciously protecting information of a confidential nature, sharing only that information relevant to his care.

The nurse has a clear obligation to safeguard any confidential information about the patient that she may acquire from the patient himself or from any other source. The nurse-patient relationship is built on trust; this relationship could be destroyed and the patient's welfare and reputation jeopardized by the nurse's injudicious disclosure of confidential information.

In some instances, however, knowledge gained in confidence is relevant or essential in planning the patient's care. Under these circumstances, and guided by her professional judgment, the nurse may share the pertinent information with others who are directly concerned with the patient's care. But she discloses only the information relevant to the patient's welfare, and only to those who are responsible for maintaining and promoting it. The rights, well-being, and safety of the individual patient should be the determining factors in the decision to share this information.

Occasionally, the nurse may be obligated to give testimony in court in relation to confidential information about a patient. Under these circumstances, she should obtain legal counsel before testifying in order to be fully informed as to her rights and responsibilities in relation to both her patient and herself.

3   The nurse maintains individual competence in nursing practice, recognizing and accepting responsibility for individual actions and judgments.

The nature of nursing is such that inadequate or incompetent practice could result in the loss of health or even the life of the patient. Therefore, the maintenance of competence in practice is the personal responsibility of each individual practitioner. Over and above the moral obligation this imposes on the individual nurse, she can be held legally responsible--in the event of injury to a patient-- if it is proved that she has failed to carry out the actions or to exercise the judgment that is considered standard nursing practice within the particular area and at the time of the injury. Neither physician's orders nor the employing agency's policies relieve the nurse of responsibility for her own nursing actions or judgments.

Competence is a relative term; and an individual's competence in any field may be diminished or otherwise affected by the passage of time and the emergence of new knowledge. This means that for the patient's optimum well-being and for the nurse's own professional development, her nursing care should reflect and incorporate new techniques and knowledge in health care as these develop, and especially as they relate to her particular field of practice.

Nursing knowledge, like that in the other health disciplines, is rendered rapidly obsolete by mounting technological and scientific advances, changing concepts and patterns in the provision of health services, and increasingly complex nursing responsibilities. The nurse must therefore be aware of the need for continuous updating and expansion of the body of knowledge on which her practice is based, and must keep her knowledge and skills current by whatever means are appropriate and available to her: inservice education, academic study, professional reading, conferences, workshops, and the like. Only by such continuing infusion of new knowledge and skills into her practice can the nurse maintain her individual competence and provide nursing care of high quality to the public.

4   The nurse acts to safeguard the patient when his care and safety are affected by incompetent, unethical, or illegal conduct of any person.

Inasmuch as the nurse's primary commitment is to the patient's care and safety, she must be alert to, and take appropriate action regarding, any instances of incompetent, unethical, or illegal practice by any member of the health care team, or any action on the part of others that is prejudicial to the patient's best interests. "Appropriate action" may take the form of expressing her concern to the person carrying out the questionable practice and calling attention to the possible detrimental effect upon the patient's welfare. If indicated, the practice should be reported to the appropriate authority within the institutional or agency setting. It is highly desirable that there be an established mechanism for the reporting and handling of incompetent, unethical or illegal practice within the employment setting, so that such reporting can go through official channels and be done without fear of reprisal.

When incompetent, unethical, or illegal practice on the part of anyone concerned with the patient's care (nurses, ancillary workers, technical specialists, or members of other professional disciplines, for instance) is not corrected within the employment

setting and continues to jeopardize the patient's care and safety,
additional steps need to be taken. It should be reported to such
other appropriate authorities as the practice committees of the
various professional organizations, or the legally constituted bodies
concerned with licensing of specific categories of health workers or
professional practitioners.   Some situations may warrant the concern and involvement of all these groups.

Reporting should be both factual and objective, and the nurse
should be fully aware of the state laws governing practice in the
health care field and of the employing institution's policies in relation to incompetent, unethical, or illegal practice.   Whenever a
practice threatens the patient's health, welfare, or safety, the nurse
has no choice but to take appropriate action in his behalf.

5 The nurse uses individual competence as a criterion in
accepting delegated responsibilities and assigning nursing
activities to others.

Because of the increased complexity of health care, changing
patterns in the delivery of health services, and continuing shortages
in skilled health manpower, nurses are being requested or expected
to carry out functions that have formerly been performed by physicians.   In turn, nurses are assigning some former registered
nurse functions to variously prepared ancillary personnel.   In this
gradual shift of functions, the nurse is the "middle man." It is
fully as important that she exercise judgment in accepting responsibilities as in assigning responsibilities to others.

Medical and nursing practice acts are usually expressed in
broad and general terms, and offer little guidance, direction, or
protection to the nurse in relation to her acceptance or performance
of specific delegated medical functions.   A recognition by nurses of
the need for a more definitive delineation of medical and nursing
roles and responsibilities has resulted in collaborative efforts on
the part of the official nursing, hospital, and medical organizations
to develop joint policy statements.   These statements specify the
functions that are agreed upon as appropriate and proper for the
nurse to perform.   They include the circumstances under which she
should and should not carry out these functions, and the required
preparation in the skills and judgments necessary to perform the
functions.   Such statements represent a body of expert judgment
that can be used as authority where responsibilities are not defini-
tively outlined by legal statute.   Similar formulations have been
developed and made official policy within many individual health care
agencies and institutions.

The nurse should look to such mutually agreed-upon policy
statements for guidance and direction; but even where such statements exist, the individual nurse should also assess her personal
competence carefully before accepting these responsibilities.   If
she does not consider herself competent or adequately prepared to

carry out a specific function, she should feel free, without fear of censure, to refuse to do so; in so doing, she protects both the patient and herself.

The reverse of the coin is also true. The nurse should not accept delegated responsibilities that do not utilize her nursing skills and competencies or that prevent her from providing needed nursing care to patients.

Inasmuch as the nurse is responsible for the patient's total nursing care, she must also assess individual competence in assigning selected components of that care to other nursing service personnel. The nurse should not delegate to any member of the nursing team a function which that person has not been prepared for or is not qualified to perform.

Concern for the patient's welfare and safety is the nurse's primary consideration in both accepting and assigning these various responsibilities. Decisions in this area call for knowledge of, and adherence to, the joint policy statements and to the laws regulating medical and nursing practice, as well as for the exercise of informed, professional nursing judgment.

6 The nurse participates in research activities when assured that the rights of individual subjects are protected.

Nurses today find themselves increasingly involved in research activities, as members of many disciplines, including nursing, search for improved methods of patient care and treatment. Generally speaking, nurses in the research setting assume one of two roles: that of investigator, including membership on a research team; or that of practitioner, giving care to patients serving as subjects in a research study. The latter role may call for specified nursing performance as part of the research design and/or the gathering or reporting of specific data.

This item in the Code focuses on the role of the nurse as a practitioner in a research setting as guidelines for the nurse investigator have been delineated in the ANA publication The Nurse in Research: ANA Guidelines on Ethical Values.

The nurse practitioner is, first of all, responsible for rendering quality nursing to all patients entrusted to her ca_e. Implicit in this care is the protection of the individual's rights as outlined in the above publication: privacy, self-determination, conservation of personal resources, freedom from arbitrary hurt and intrinsic risk of injury, and the special rights of minors and incompetent persons. While the research investigator assumes primary responsibility for the preservation of these rights, the individual nurse practitioner within the research setting should also be aware of them and of her share in this responsibility.

Research projects may call for specific observations, treatments, or care procedures that represent variations from the usual.
The nurse participates in such research or experimental activity only
with the assurance that the project has the official sanction of the
research committee or other appropriate authority within the institutional or agency setting. For her own and the patient's protection,
she needs sufficient knowledge of the research design to enable her
to participate in the required activities in an informed, effective,
and ethical fashion. With this knowledge, she is conscientious in
carrying out her specific functions and responsibilities as outlined in
the research design.

Investigational drugs, potentially harmful to the patient, may
represent a special problem. The nurse administering such drugs
should have basic information about them: method of administration,
strengths, actions and uses, side effects, symptoms of toxicity, and
so on.

Occasionally, the research may be of such a nature as to
give rise to questions, and perhaps conflicts, for the nurse where it
appears that the well-being and safety of the patient are adversely
affected by procedures prescribed as part of the project. In such
instances the nurse is obligated to voice her concern to appropriate
persons in the agency. She should also bear in mind that participation in research activities does not relieve her of responsibility for
her own acts and judgments.

Participation in research activities carries the implication
that the nurse will want and is entitled to information about the
study findings, and that she will utilize in her own practice appropriate findings from research studies related to nursing education
and practice.

7   The nurse participates in the efforts of the profession to
define and upgrade standards of nursing practice and education.

The professional association, through its membership, is
responsible for determining standards of nursing practice and education. The key phrase "through its membership" means that each
nurse should share in the activities that go into developing, evaluating, disseminating, and implementing these standards. These
standards, furthermore, should be reflected in the individual nurse's
preparation and practice. Standards represent not only professional
goals but also a means of ensuring a high quality of nursing care
for the public. As such, each nurse has a vested interest in developing and maintaining them.

Standards can never be static because of the constantly
changing nature of health care and of educational patterns. As an
active participant in the necessarily continuous process of defining,
maintaining, and upgrading standards of nursing practice and education, the nurse must keep herself informed of present and projected

standards. She should adhere to these standards in her own practice; help to disseminate them and provide for their implementation ιn the institution or agency with which she is associated; and take responsible and remedial action when standards are violated. Through the channels provided by her professional association, she should work to support the standards that have been adopted, or endeavor to revise or upgrade them as indicated.

8 The nurse, acting through the professional organization, participates in establishing and maintaining conditions of employment conducive to high-quality nursing care.

The nurse must be concerned with the conditions of economic and general welfare within her profession because these conditions are important determinants in the recruitment and retention of well-qualified personnel and in the opportunity for each nurse to function to her fullest potential in the working situation. If the needs and demands of society for both quantity and quality of nursing care are to be met, the professional association and the individual nurse must share in the effort to establish conditions that will make it possible to meet these needs.

An appropriate channel through which the nurse can work constructively, ethically, and with professional dignity to promote the employment conditions conducive to high-quality nursing care is the economic security program of her professional association. This program, encompassing commitment to the principle of collective bargaining, promotes the right and responsibility of the individual nurse to participate in determining the terms and conditions of her employment.

This participation, to be most productive, should be in the form of a group approach to economic action, through the channels provided by the professional organization and with that organization providing assistance and representation in nurses' collective negotiations with employers. In this way, the nurse can work most effectively to achieve working conditions that will be commensurate with her preparation, qualifications, functions, and responsibilities today and in so doing, will promote the welfare of the public.

9 The nurse works with members of health professions and other citizens in promoting efforts to meet health needs of the public.

It is increasingly recognized that society's need and mounting demand for comprehensive health services can be met only through a broad and intensive effort on the part of both the community and the health professions. The nurse, with her special knowledge and skills in the health field, her essential role in the provision of health services, and her traditional commitment to ever higher standards of health care, has an obligation to participate actively and responsibly in professional, interprofessional, and community endeavors designed to meet the health needs of the public.

She should involve herself in both the planning and implementation of the health services needed, maintaining open and constructive communication with the citizen and professional groups involved. Especially important in this process is the exploration by
physician and nurse of their interdependent functions as these relate to the delivery of comprehensive health services. Such exploration calls for a continuous exchange of ideas between members of
the two professions on local, state, regional, and national levels,
the goal being closer liaison between the two groups in the interest
of improved patient care.

A similar and continuing communication should also be carried
on with representatives of the other disciplines in the health field--
pharmacy, social service, nutrition, physical, occupational, and
recreational therapy, hospital or agency administration--as well as
with specialized technical groups providing various health services.
Nurses must work together with representatives of these groups in
defining, exploring, and enhancing the relationships created by
their interaction and mutual concern with health care.

The nurse, because of her close and continuing contact with
patients and families, and awareness of both individual and community health needs, has much to contribute to community planning
for health services. By assuming an active and, on occasion, a
leadership role in these activities, nurses can help to shape programs that will provide the public with care that takes full advantage
of the resources of modern science.

10   The nurse refuses to give or imply endorsement to
advertising, promotion, or sales for commercial products,
services, or enterprises.

Over the years the public has learned to trust and respect the
nurse and to have confidence in her judgment and advice. Very
often, the individual nurse represents the entire profession to patients and others. This means that what one nurse says or does
may be interpreted as reflecting the action, opinion, or judgment
of the profession as a whole. Therefore, this favorable professional image should not be used in ways that might be misleading
or harmful to the public and bring discredit upon the nurse and her
profession. The nurse should not permit her name, title, professional status, or symbols--uniform, pin, or the letters "R. N.", for
instance--to be used or associated with the promotion of any commercial product or service.

The right to use the title "Registered Nurse" is granted by
state governments through licensure by examination for the protection of the public. Use of the title carries with it the responsibility
to act in the public interest. This title, and other symbols of the
profession, should not be used for the personal benefit of the nurse
or those who may seek to exploit them for other purposes.

By permitting her professional self or the nursing profession's symbols or representations to be used in association with a particular product or service, the nurse places herself in the position of seeming to endorse, or recommend, or make the judgment that one among several similar and competing products is preferable to the others. She has neither the qualifications nor authority to make this judgment. The public, because of its tendency to identify the individual with the profession, may construe this individual action as reflecting endorsement or approval of a product or service by the profession as a whole. In some instances, such action on the part of an individual nurse could also be interpreted as a violation of the legal statutes forbidding nurses to make medical diagnosis or to prescribe medications or treatments.

Nursing symbols and representations of nurses may be used in advertisements directed to members of the health professions, but only in such advertisements, and never to imply medical diagnosis or prescription, or professional endorsement of commercial products.

The nurse may indicate the availability of her own services by listing herself in directories or professional publications available to the public. Properly used, such advertising may prove of benefit to the public in securing needed care. It is expected, however, that nurses will present the necessary information in a manner consistent with the dignity of the profession and in keeping with the general practices of other professional groups within the community.

Not only should the nurse herself adhere to the above principles; she should also be alert to any instances of their violation by others. She should report promptly, through appropriate channels, any advertisement or commercial which involves a nurse, implies her involvement, or in any way suggests nursing endorsement of a commercial product, service, or enterprise. The nurse who knowingly involves herself in such unethical activities negates her professional responsibility for personal gain, and jeopardizes the public confidence and trust in the nursing profession that have been created by generations of nurses working together in the public interest.

NURSES--PRACTICAL

NATIONAL ASSOCIATION FOR PRACTICAL NURSE EDUCATION
AND SERVICE, INC. (NAPNES)
    122 E. 42nd St., New York, N.Y. 10017
    Rose G. Martin, R.N., Executive Director

Membership: The National Association for Practical Nurse Education

and Service, founded in 1941 and with a present (1973) membership
of approximately 35,000, is a professional association "totally committed to practical nursing and practical nurse education."

Code of Ethics: The professional conduct guide for licensed prac-
tical/vocational nurses--adopted by the Board of Directors and membership of the Association in April 1971, is the Code of Ethics, which
sets forth the obligations and responsibilities for the licensed prac-
tical/vocational nurse.

Professional Insignia: The emblem of NAPNES--as it appears on

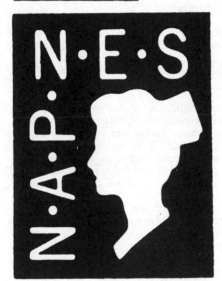

Association stationery and pub-
lications--is a rectangular design, with the profile of a
nurse in cap in the lower right
of the rectangle; the organization initials, "NAPNES," are
printed around the left and
upper sides of the design; a
base rectangle shows the
printed name of the group,
"National Association for Practical Nurse Education and Service." The color of the insignia is white on red for the
upper rectangle; and red on
white for the lower rectangle.

Bibliography:
   National Association for
        Practical Nurse Edu-
        cation and Service.
        Code of Ethics.
        1971. 1 page.
   Ten principles guiding
   conduct of practical/
   vocational nurses.

NATIONAL ASSOCIATION FOR
PRACTICAL NURSE
EDUCATION AND SERVICE

"Code of Ethics
for the Licensed Practical/Vocational Nurse"

The Licensed Practical/Vocational Nurse shall:

1. Consider as a basic obligation the conservation of life and the
    prevention of disease.
2. Promote and protect the physical, mental, emotional, and
    spiritual health of the patient and his family.
3. Fulfill all duties faithfully and efficiently.
4. Function within established legal guidelines.
5. Accept personal responsibility (for his acts) and seek to merit
    the respect and confidence of all members of the health
    team.

6. Hold in confidence all matters coming to his knowledge, in the
   practice of his profession, and in no way and at no time violate this confidence.
7. Give conscientious service and charge just remuneration.
8. Learn and respect the religious and cultural beliefs of his
   patient and of all people.
9. Meet his obligation to the patient by keeping abreast of current trends in health care through reading and continuing
   education.
10. As a citizen of the United States of America, uphold the laws
   of the land and seek to promote legislation which shall meet
   the health needs of its people.

NURSING HOME ADMINISTRATORS

AMERICAN COLLEGE OF NURSING HOME ADMINISTRATORS
(ACNHA)
   8641 Colesville Rd., Suite 409, Silver Springs, Md. 20910
   Lynn W. Norris, Executive Director

Membership: The American College of Nursing Home Administrators, founded in 1962 and with a present (1973) membership of
1800, is a professional organization of administrators of long-term
health care institutions. "Members of the College are predominantly
health care administrators," who have qualified for one of the following categories of membership with required training and experience:
   Nominee--At least three years' experience in long-term
      health care administration; a bachelor's degree in a per-
      tinent field may be substituted for two years of the required
      experience;
   Member--Nominee in good standing for at least one year,
      who has completed at least two years of training beyond
      high school and has a minimum of four years' administra-
      tive practice in long-term health care; a bachelor's de-
      gree may be substituted for two years of the required ex-
      perience; attended at least one ACNHA national, regional,
      or state meeting;
   Fellow--In addition to meeting Member requirements and
      having been a Member for two years, have completed at
      least four years of acceptable training beyond high school;
      and attended at least four meetings of ACNHA during a
      three year period.

Code of Ethics: ACNHA standards of professional practice for
nursing home administrators are set forth in its Code of Ethics,
which--in the form of a pledge administered to all categories of

members upon induction into membership--gives broad principles
of obligations and responsibilities of Nursing Home Administrators.
No procedures for enforcement of the Code are reported.

Professional Insignia: The emblem of the College--adopted in 1966--

is its seal: a circular design
with a centered shield bearing
four professional symbols
(clockwise, beginning with
upper left quadrant):
lamp of knowledge--
academic achievement
and dedication of self-
improvement through
continuing education;
nursing home institu-
tion--physical struc-
ture in which nursing
home administrators'
services are rendered;
caduceus--staff with two
entwined serpents,
symbolic of healing
(administration of health care service);
pine-tree--professional commitment to the health and long
life of the patients entrusted to care.

Below this centered shield in a scroll, is the legend, "Ars
Vertus Caritas," which may be translated:
Skill (in health care administration),
Integrity (ethical conduct), and
Concern (for humanity, human dignity, and human values).
A bordering band carries the organization name, "American College
Nursing Home Administrators." This emblem is shown in black
and white (letterhead, publications). Members may wear the em-
blem jewelry (pin or tie tac)--in silver for Nominees, gold for
Members and Fellows, with Fellows distinguished by a sapphire
stone. Fellows and Members may also wear the official key of
the College.

Other Identification of Professional Status: The only category of
ACNHA member authorized to use a professional designation with
his name is: "F. A. C. N. H. A."--"Fellow."

Bibliography:
American College of Nursing Home Administrators. Code of
Ethics. 1 page.
Pledge of professional obligations and responsibilities of the
nursing home administrators.
_____. Information Statement. 4 pages.
Includes organization objectives, Code of Ethics, member-
ship requirements.

_____. What is the American College of Nursing Home Ad-
ministrators. 1971.
ACNHA purpose, history, activities.

"Code of Ethics"

As a Fellow, a Member or a Nominee of the American College of Nursing Home Administrators:

I will insure that my personal, professional and business conduct at all times, is dedicated to the welfare and interest of the
Patients/Residents entrusted to my care, and in no way discredit
the American College of Nursing Home Administrators.
I will administer the Home or Homes under my jurisdiction
at all times on the highest professional level possible.
I will accept my responsibility to The Nursing Home Profession, and will constantly seek to broaden my professional knowledge,
and will actively engage in research projects designed to improve
Patients/Residents care.
I will accept my responsibility as a part of the community
health team and will participate directly and contribute my whole
hearted support toward improving and meeting the health needs of
the community, disregarding race, creed or color.
I will treat those who are under my care with the respect,
honor and dignity that befits each of us as human beings, making
provisions not only for their medical and physical requirements, but
also for their social and spiritual needs.

OCCUPATIONAL THERAPISTS

AMERICAN OCCUPATIONAL THERAPY ASSOCIATION (AOTA)
    6000 Executive Blvd., Rockville, Md. 20852
    Harriet Tiebel, Executive Director

Membership: The American Occupational Therapy Association,
founded in 1917 and with a present (1973) membership of over
14,000, is the professional association of occupational therapists.
According to the AOTA definition, "occupational therapy" is:
    "The art and science of directing man's response to selected
    activity to promote and maintain health, and to prevent dis-
    ability, to evaluate behavior and to treat or train patients
    with physical or psychological dysfunction."
As part of the community health team, members are engaged in
"purposeful activities planned and controlled to bring about specific
changes in physical and emotional behavior."

Two voluntary licensure programs for members are directed by the AOTA Committee on Registration and Certification. These programs in which professional designations are awarded to qualified applicants with required training, education, and skills are:

Registered Occupational Therapist (OTR)--The professional category of membership. Requires "a baccalaureate or master's degree" from "a basic professional occupational therapy educational program approved by the American Medical Association in collaboration with the American Occupational Therapy Association, who has passed the national registration examination and maintains registration in AOTA." This registration program was initiated in 1931; and the examination in 1945.

Certified Occupational Therapy Assistant (COTA)--The technical category of membership. Requires "an associate degree or certificate of graduation" from "a basic technical occupational therapy program approved by the American Occupational Therapy Association, and [that one] holds current certification from AOTA." This certification program was initiated in 1959.

The "Registered Occupational Therapist" is responsible for the professional and administrative activities of the occupational therapy department, and may evaluate individuals and plan treatment programs, act in guidance and counseling, administration and consultation. The "Certified Occupational Therapy Assistant" works with supervision and consultation in assisting with specific treatment.

Code of Ethics: The professional conduct guide for occupational therapists is the code of ethics ("Ethics," Bylaws, Article XIV), which sets forth in eight Sections the responsibilities and obligations of members. Enforcement of the ethical code is considered in "Disciplinary Action" provisions of the Bylaws (Article XV), where procedures are given for dealing with alleged violations of the conduct guide--from receipt of written complaint by the Executive Board, investigation, hearing, to possible disciplinary action by expulsion from the AOTA.

Other Guides to Professional Conduct: The Pledge and Creed for Occupational Therapists provides an additional goal of professional activity.

Professional Insignia: The emblem of the AOTA--Bylaws, Article I, Section 2 provides for an official "collective membership mark of the Association," which may supplant the currently used insignia --is oval in shape, a caduceus centered; the words "Occupational Therapy" superimposed, following the oval bordering lines. The color of the insignia (letterhead) is blue printing and border, red caduceus, on white background. This insignia is also the OTR emblem, discussed and pictured below.

Other Designations of Professional Status: As indicated above under "Membership," the professional designation (title and initial) indicated competence as:

"Registered Occupational Therapist" (OTR);
"Certified Occupational Therapy Assistant" (COTA).
The OTR emblem, to be worn as an arm band, uniform insignia, or
as a pin, is identical in form and color with the current AOTA in-
signia.   The uniform insignia and pin emblem of the "Certified
Occupational Therapy Assistant" is lozenge shaped--with right and

**THE REGISTERED
OCCUPATIONAL THERAPIST**

**THE CERTIFIED
OCCUPATIONAL THERAPY ASSISTANT**

CERTIFIED
OCCUPATIONAL THERAPY
ASSISTANT

The OTR: The COTA:

left end truncated; the designation, "Certified Occupational Therapy
Assistant, " is spaced within the design.   The color of this insignia
is red on a white ground.

Bibliography:
        American Occupational Therapy Association.   Bylaws.   Revised
             October 1972.   8 pages.
        Gives membership categories and qualifications; authorizes
        official mark (emblem or insignia); includes "Ethics"--
        ethical code (Article XIV), and enforcement procedures for
        ethical code ("Disciplinary Action, " Article XV).
               .   Occupational Therapy Is....   2 pages.
        Informational brochure defines occupation, gives duties and
        requirements, pictures insignia of OTR and COTA.

                                "Ethics"

        Section 1.   Registered members may accept referrals from
qualified physicians and from others seeking occupational therapy
services.   They shall collaborate with qualified professionals in
those instances where collaboration is indicated.
        Section 2.   Advertising by registered members under their
professional title shall be in accordance with propriety and precedent in health professions.
        Section 3.   Members shall maintain competency in occupational
therapy practice through standards established by the Delegate Assembly.
        Section 4.   Members shall provide only those services for
which they are properly qualified by registration or certification.
        Section 5.   The registered member shall assume responsi-
bility for services provided to clients and is obligated to provide
continuing supervision when any portion of the service is delegated
to supportive personnel.   He shall not delegate to an unqualified

person any services which require professional skill and judgment.
    Section 6. Members shall respect the confidentiality of all
privileged information.
    Section 7. Registered members shall charge only for ser-
vices actually rendered by them or under their supervision.
    Section 8. Members shall be responsible for clearly deline-
ated documentation of all professional services provided.

"Pledge and Creed
for Occupational Therapists"

Reverently and earnestly do I pledge my whole-hearted service in aiding those crippled in mind and body.
    To this end that my work for the sick may be successful, I
will ever strive for greater knowledge, skill and understanding in
the discharge of my duties in whatsoever position I may find myself.
    I solemnly declare that I will hold and keep inviolate what-
ever I may learn of the lives of the sick.
    I acknowledge the dignity of the cure of disease and the
safeguarding of health in which no act is menial or inglorious.
    I will walk in upright faithfulness and obedience to those
under whose guidance I am to work and I pray for patience, kind-
liness and strength in the holy ministry to broken minds and bodies.

OPERATING ROOM TECHNICIANS

ASSOCIATION OF OPERATING ROOM TECHNICIANS (AORT)
    1100 W. Littleton Blvd., Suite 101, Littleton, Colo. 80120
    Mack N. Whitaker, Administrative Director

Membership: The Association of Operating Room Technicians,
founded in 1969 and with a present (1973) membership of about
8500, is an organization of paramedical workers who assist with
care to a hospital patient undergoing surgery and perform related
services in the operating room. An "Active Member" of AORT
must have passed the national certifying examination or be preparing to take this examination within two years (Bylaws, Article
II, Section 3A). The professional designation authorized by AORT,
to applicants successful in the examination is "CORT" ("Certified
Operating Room Technician").

    The examination is conducted by the certifying body of the
Association--the AORT Advisory Board--which includes, in addition
to AORT members, representatives from three other professional
organizations: American College of Surgeons (ACS), American
Hospital Association (AHA), and Association of Operating Room
Nurses (AORN). Programs qualifying an applicant to take the

certifying examinations are offered in vocational schools, junior colleges and hospitals, with course length ranging from nine months to two years.

The three written tests comprising the examination (each containing 100 five-part multiple-choice questions) are:

    I. Surgical Procedures in Case or Problem Situations;

    II. Basic Sciences, including anatomy, physiology, and microbiology;

    III. Operating Room Care of the Patient--before, during and after surgery.

Code of Ethics: The conduct guide for AORT--its Code of Ethics-- consists of ten principles ranging from general statements for high standards of conduct and patient care, to specific provisions of practice ("To always follow the principles of asepsis"). Enforcement procedures for the Code of Ethics (Bylaws, Article III, Section 5) provide that a member found in violation of the ethical guide, after hearing, may be censured, suspended, or expelled by a two-thirds vote of the AORT Board of Directors.

Professional Insignia: The official emblem of the Association of Operating Room Technicians is its logotype--an original drawing by Oscar Erikson, CORT. This triangular design depicts in a

centered diagram the Operating Room Team, and the Operating Room Technician's place on the team; the organization name is shown on the three sides of the triangle, "Association of Operating Room Technicians, Inc." AORT pins, as well as other types of jewelry, are available to members. The jewelry carries the official logo of the Association. Certified Operating Room Technicians are entitled to purchase and wear pins with a year guard, showing the year of their certification.

Other Identification of Professional Status: As described above under membership, the Association awards to applicants, qualifying by education and experience and passing the examination, the professional designation, "CORT" ("Certified Operating Room Technician").

Bibliography:
Association of Operating Room Technicians. Bylaws. Revised edition, June 1971. 12 pages. Pamphlet.
Gives membership requirements, procedures for enforcement of ethical standards.
_____. What is an Operating Room Technician? Folder.
Informational brochure defining work of operating room technician, describing certification procedure, including examination. Includes Code of Ethics; pictures emblem.

"Code of Ethics"

1. Maintain the highest standards of professional conduct and patient care.
2. Hold in confidence with respect to patient's beliefs on all personal matters.
3. To respect and protect the patient's legal and moral right to good patient care.
4. Will not knowingly cause injury or any injustice to those entrusted to my care.
5. To work with fellow technicians and other professional health groups to promote harmony and unity for better patient care.
6. To always follow the principles of asepsis.
7. To maintain a high degree of efficiency through continuing education.
8. Maintain and practice my skills willingly, with pride and dignity and with full regard to limitations.
9. Will report any unethical conduct or practice to proper authority.
10. Will adhere to code of ethics at all times in my relationship with all members of the health care team.

OPHTHALMOLOGISTS

AMERICAN ASSOCIATION OF OPHTHALMOLOGY (AAO)
1100 17th St., N. W., Washington, D. C. 20036
Lawrence A. Zupan, Executive Secretary

Membership: The American Association of Ophthalmology, founded in 1956 and with a present (1973) membership of over 3300, is a professional society of medical doctors specializing in ophthalmology

--the functions and treatment of the eye, which involves diagnosis
and treatment of defects and diseases of the eye, performing surgery, prescribing drugs, and other types of treatment, including
corrective lenses. Members are physicians, licensed in state of
practice, with special training and practice in the eye and the
visual system, who may also be members of state groups of ophthalmologists, affiliated with AAO.

Code of Ethics: Members of the American Association of Ophthalmology, as physicians, subscribe to, and are bound by, the Principles of Medical Ethics of the American Medical Association.

Professional Insignia: The seal of the American Association of
Ophthalmology appearing on the organization stationery and publications, is composed of two forms--at the left a circular design
with a centered serpent en-
twined on a staff (symbolic of
medicine), the border marked
off by degrees; the second element of the design, overlying
the right border of the circle,
is shaped like a human eye,
bearing in a round band, comparable to the iris of the eye,
the organization name, "American Association of Ophthalmology."

The color of the insignia, as shown on the letterhead, is dark blue
on white. The Association has adopted no insignia for the identification of its members.

"Code of Ethics"

see page 564

OPTICIANS

AMERICAN BOARD OF OPTICIANRY (ABO)
     10480 Main St., Clarence, N.Y. 14031
     Frank X. Brandstetter, Executive Secretary

Membership: The American Board of Opticianry, founded in 1947,
is a national accrediting agency, whose "primary function is to
examine qualified Dispensing Opticians who desire to become Certified and Master Opticians." "Opticianry," as defined by the Board,
is:
> "the art and science of optics as applied to the compounding,
> filling and adapting of ophthalmic prescriptions, products
> and accessories."

Certification examinations are given the first Sunday in June, and are prepared "by recognized and qualified educators under the supervision of the Board."

Education and experience requirements for the two examinations are:

Certified Optician (CT)--High school graduation, or equivalent; and one of the following:
(1) Five years' experience as an ophthalmic dispenser under the supervision of an experienced optician (who qualifies for Certification);
(2) Graduation from a Board accredited School of Opticianry;
(3) Licensed as optician in a state giving licensure examinations.

Master in Ophthalmic Optics (MOO)--Three years practice as an optician, after having been licensed as a Certified Optician.

The examinations for the two accredited types of opticians are:

Certified Optician--Written examination of multiple-choice questions in basic areas of knowledge:
Ophthalmic Dispensing,
Opthalmic Materials,
Ophthalmic Laboratory Procedures,
Geometric/opthalmic Optics,
Anatomy and Physiology of the Eye,
Contact Lenses.
Applicants must file applications to take the examination by March 31, and upon qualification for examination will receive a set of 100 Review Questions, as a study aid.

Master in Ophthalmic Optics--Must submit with his application for examination "an original paper of not less than 2000 words"; the subject to be selected from a list provided by the Board, or one of the applicant's choice, subject to Board approval. The written examination consists of a set of 50 multiple-choice questions, and essay and problem solving questions.

Code of Ethics: The ABO has issued no formal code of ethics.

Professional Insignia: The emblem of the American Board of Opticianry is its seal--a circular emblem with a centered shield bearing the legend, "For Excellence in Optical Craftsmanship Through Adequate Education and Training"; olive sprays are shown at each of the four sides of the shield; a circular bordering band of the design gives the organization name and date of establishment, "American Board of Opticianry Founded 1947." The color of the insignia is shown variously--blue

on white (publication; certificate); brown on yellow (publication).

Bibliography:
    American Board of Opticianry. Handbook for Applicants for
        Certification. 1973. 9 pages. Pamphlet.
    Qualifications required and examination content for Certified
    Optician, and Master in Ophthalmic Optics. Emblem on
    cover.
        _____. Opticianry. 10 pages. Pamphlet.
    Descriptive brochure defines occupation, pictures insignia
    and certificates.

GUILD OF PRESCRIPTION OPTICIANS OF AMERICA (GPOA)
    1250 Connecticut Ave., N.W., Washington, D.C. 20036
    Jerome A. Miller, Executive Secretary-Treasurer

Membership: The Guild of Prescription Opticians of America,
founded in 1926 and with a present (1973) membership of over 1000,
is a trade association of retail optical dispensing firms in the
United States and Canada. The Guild--operating in the tradition of
the craftsmen's guilds of Europe--seeks "to maintain and keep up
to date standards of quality and service." Any firm engaged in
retail optical dispensing in the United States or Canada is eligible
for membership in the Guild, provided that it is completely independent of any refractionist, is conducting its business in accordance
with the GPOA Code of Ethics, and is a member of the local Guild.

Code of Ethics: The guide to conduct and practice for Guild members is the GPOA Code of Ethics, which gives the obligations and
responsibilities in conduct of business, and the standards for relationships of the optician with the professional refractionist, the
public and colleagues. No procedures for enforcement of the Code
are reported.

Professional Insignia: The Guild insignia is its seal--a round design with "RX," the symbol for "prescription," centered; place and
date of founding of the group, "Organized in Philadelphia 1926," is
printed around the lower portion of the prescription symbol; and the
group name, "Guild of Prescription Opticians of America," around
the circular border of the emblem. The color of the insignia is
shown variously--dark blue on white (publications); brown on turquoise blue on white (publications); gold on black (photoplate sign
for member display). The insignia is used on Guild stationery and
publications and is available to all members for use on stationery,
and for display in place of business--where the design is modified
to show "Guild Optician," in place of the organization name, and
the place and date of the group's founding is deleted from the design.

Bibliography:
Guild of Prescription Opti-
cians of America.
Guild of Prescription
Opticians of America.
Pamphlet.
Informational brochure in-
cluding purposes, activi-
ties, and membership re-
quirements.
_____. Code of Ethics.
Pamphlet.
Obligations and responsi-
bilities of dispensing op-
tical firms, members of
the Guild.

"Code of Ethics"

Section 1.   PREAMBLE

The retail optical dispensing business of America is dedicated to providing, economically and efficiently, to the people of
the United States and Canada a high quality of optical dispensing ser-
vice--independent of control by any person or organization engaged
in examination or refraction of the eyes--a service that is vital and
necessary to eye physicians and other refractionists and to the
public.

Section 2.   CODE OF ETHICS

The Guild of Prescription Opticians of America declares:

1.   That it is in the best interests of the public (that is,
the individual who is a patient of the refractionist and a customer
of the retail optical dispensing firm that
    a.   the function of examination including refraction of the
patient's eyes and
    b.   the function of filling ophthalmic prescriptions through
the preparation of lenses, assistance in the selection of
frames, the fitting of frames to the needs of the customer
and after service, as well as the business of maintaining a
      minimum balanced inventory of ophthalmic merchandise,
should be performed by persons or organizations which are mutually
independent of each other.

2.   That it is the obligation of every member firm and all
its principals and employees to provide its customers with the finest
ophthalmic products that conform to close tolerances to the prescriptions, prepared by professional refractionists licensed to examine eyes and to prescribe lenses that will correct or compensate
for visual defects or deficiencies.

3. That it is in the best interest of the public that the judgment of the professional and licensed refractionist as to whether he should prescribe glasses for his patient and what the prescription should require should be entirely unaffected by a commercial interest in or financial benefit from the sale of ophthalmic products either through rebating in any of its forms or by ownership, either directly or indirectly, or an ophthalmic dispensing business.

4. That it is the obligation of every member firm to price its services and the ophthalmic products it sells both
a. fairly, taking into account both quality and value, and
b. competitively in conformity with our traditional system of free competitive enterprise and in conformity with public law.

5. That it is the obligation of every member firm to dispense ophthalmic products and provide optical dispensing services only after eye examination by a refractionist who is entirely independent of, not employed by, and not under obligation to, the retail ophthalmic dispensing firm.

6. That it is the obligation of every member firm to present and explain fairly the quality, performance characteristics, convenience, use and style values of the products it sells and the services it performs and specifically not to engage in deceptive or bait advertising or unfair and deceptive acts.

7. That it is the obligation of every member firm to guard, jealously, its complete freedom and independence in the marketing and pricing of services and the products it sells and the terms and conditions under which they are sold and to make certain that it does not abdicate its authority, independence and responsibility therein to any competitor and to accept and support the principle that competition and the survival of the free enterprise system presupposes and is dependent upon, free and competitive pricing of services and products.

8. That it is the obligation of every member firm so to conduct its dispensing business, including the training, supervision and leadership of its employees, in both the craft or technical skills and the special retail business skills and other aspects of their respective duties, as to create and maintain the confidence of both professional refractionists and customers of the firm in the quality of performance and business integrity of a firm so that they may take pride in the services they perform, the business with which they are associated and the vital function it performs.

9. That it is the special obligation of each member firm to keep informed on and to master and apply to a high degree the retail business management skills and methods that can contribute to conducting the business in a manner that, while keeping the business on a reasonably profitable basis at fair prices, will eliminate so

far as practicable any unnecessary wasteful costs to the end that
the firm's customers may be served on a technically sound basis
and so that the reputation of retail optical dispensing firms in
performing their dispensing functions may be maintained and even
enhanced, recognizing that, without efficient business management,
the quality of the dispensing function is always in danger of deterioration and finally extinction.

    10.   That it is the obligation of every member firm:
    a.   to promote the education of the public regarding the risks
that accrue from indifference to or disregard of the danger
signals of eye diseases or of other diseases which manifest
themselves in the eyes and that regular eye examinations are
vital to health.
    b.   to promote the education of the public as to the impor-
tance of having the ophthalmic prescription filled accurately--
to close tolerances and of having frames chosen wisely and
correctly along with adequate after-service.

    11.   That every member firm is encouraged to exchange with
other optical dispensing firms ideas and methods which have been or
may be developed which can contribute to a more efficient, more
satisfactory, or less costly dispensing service to the public in the
field of eye care.

    12.   That it is the obligation of the owners and management
of every member firm to accept and to indoctrinate all employees
of the firm in the following philosophy:
    a.   That the standards of conduct of the firm, its manage-
ment and its employees, shall have in them a note of sym-
pathy for all humanity.
    b.   That the business and all vocations in retail optical dis-
pensing afford a distinct opportunity to serve society.
    c.   That the firm and each of its employees should wish no
success that is not founded on the highest plane of justice
and fairness.
    d.   That the firm and each of its employees should perform
their functions and duties in such a manner that it and they
may contribute fully to providing a perfect service.
    e.   That it and all its employees will do everything possible
to promote the conservation of human eye sight.
    f.   That the firm and all its employees should make them-
selves worthy of the confidence placed in the firm by the
Guild of Prescription Opticians of America and do everything
possible to maintain the worthiness of the firm's membership
in the Guild.
    g.   That neither firm nor any employee will take any unfair
and unlawful advantage of a competitor or potential competitor
nor consider any practice ethical or legitimate that takes any
unfair and unlawful advantage of any opportunity not equally
open to and lawful if practiced by a competitor.
    h.   That the firm and every employee should share their

knowledge and experience and contribute their endeavors to
elevate the craft and technical skills and business management skill used in the retail optical dispensing business to
the end that a high quality of optical dispensing service may
be available to the public and to strive to set an example
to other optical dispensing firms and to the employees that
will be wise, conducive to personal happiness and satisfaction and, in the long run, profitable as well as beneficial
to all customers for optical dispensing service.
i.   That the firm and its employees believe in the univer-
sality of the golden rule, "All things whatsoever ye would
that men should do unto you, do ye unto them."
j.   That the firm accepts and all employees should accept
the obligation that in all their dealings it and they should
take into consideration their highest duties as a member of
society and in every position in ophthalmic dispensing and in
every responsibility the chief thought should be to fill that
responsibility and discharge that duty so that when it has been
ended the level of human ideals and achievements will have
been lifted a little higher.

OPTOMETRISTS

AMERICAN OPTOMETRIC ASSOCIATION (AOA)
      7000 Chippewa St., St. Louis, Mo. 63119
      J. Harold Bailey, Executive Director

Membership: The American Optometric Association, founded in
1898 and with a current (1973) membership of 18,000 (making it the
"third largest independent health care profession in the United
States"), is a federation of State Optometric Associations.   According to the approved definition of the profession (adopted at the 66th
Annual Congress of the AOA in 1963):

> "An optometrist, doctor of optometry (O.D.), is a person
> specifically educated, trained and state licensed to examine
> the eyes and related structures to determine the presence
> of vision problems, eye diseases or other abnormalities.
> He prescribes and adapts lenses or other optical aids and
> may use visual training when indicated to preserve or re-
> store maximum efficiency of vision."

Active members of AOA are members of state optometric associations, affiliated with the American Optometric Association.   Military
and special class members pay their AOA dues directly.

Code of Ethics: The national guide to professional conduct for

optometrists is the AOA Code of Ethics, which contains minimum
standards of conduct for members.   The first Code of Ethics of
the Association was drafted by A. J. Cross, John Eberhardt, and
William Huston.   This code, adopted in 1908, served until 1935,
when it was replaced by a revised version, in force until 1944,
when the present Code of Ethics was adopted.   This current Code,
drafted by John O'Shea, E. F. Richardson, and Charles Sheart to
"represent the ideals and practice of modern optometry," is a nine-
point guide that sets forth "certain basic duties of members and reaffirms the fundamental principles of the profession of optometry:
To protect, conserve and improve human vision."

     To "clarify the Code of Ethics and to define specific situations,"
Supplements to the code were adopted in 1946, and were later revised (1968 and 1970).   These ethical guides are grouped under
four headings:
          Basic Responsibilities of an Optometrist;
          Relations Between an Optometrist and His Patient;
          Responsibilities to Other Optometrists and the Public;
          Relations Between the Optometrist and Other Professions.
The state optometric associations have the responsibility in matters
relating to professional ethics.   The Judicial Council of the AOA
occasionally gives advisory opinions on ethical matters referred to
it.

Other Guides to Professional Conduct: An additional standard of
ethical practice for optometrists is the AOA Rules of Practice.
The present four basic rules of practice were adopted in 1968.
They represent a revision (prepared by a Committee consisting of
Robert Phillips, Harvey Arnold, Jack Potter, Jack Keith, and
Richard Dexter) of those rules initially adopted in 1948, and pat-
terned after the rules of practice developed by the New Jersey
Optometric Association.   "Enforcement of the provisions of the
Rules of Practice shall be the duty of the various state associations.
It is recommended that when a member is doubtful of the ethics
or advisability of any action he contemplates, he shall submit a
detailed statement to the proper committee of his state association
for its consideration."

Professional Insignia: In addition to the official seal for the non-
profit corporation, the symbol most widely used by, and associated
with, the AOA is the "Australian Eye" logotype, developed by the
Australian Optometric Association, which is now an international
symbol of "Optometry."   The "Australian Eye" is a design in the
form of a human eye, with heavy borders, a centered circle symbolizing the pupil.   The American Optometric Association logotype
(membership mark) shows the Eye in a rectangle, the association
name, "American Optometric Association," below the rectangle; a
base rectangle carries the monogram, "AOA."   The color of this
symbol is shown variously--black on background color (publications);
black eye on red background, with black association name and base
rectangle; white pupil of eye and monogram (folder explaining the
emblem and its use).

Bibliography:
American Optometric Association.
Code of Ethics and Supplement; Rules of Practice.
7 pages.   Pamphlet. $1.
Nine basic duties of the optometrist set forth in the Code,
are expanded and interpreted
in the Supplements.
_____. Optometry Today:
The Vision Care Profession.
1971.   31 pages.
AOA purpose, functions, history, membership qualifications; official definition of the
profession.
_____. What's In a Name?
1970.   4 pages.   Folder.
Pictures, describes, and indicates uses of AOA logotype,
which includes the "Australian
Eye."
Gregg, James R. American Optometric Association: A
History, 1898-1972.   St.
Louis, American Optometric
Association, 1972.   399
pages. $7.95.
Definitive history of AOA
serves as a social history of
the development of a profession, including licensure, occupational associations, educational preparation, ethical code.
Illustrations picture Association

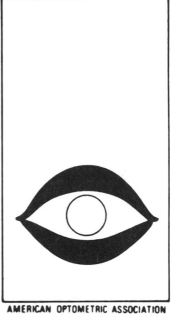

AMERICAN OPTOMETRIC ASSOCIATION

officers and other groups and individuals important in the
group's development.   Indexed by name and subject.

"Code of Ethics"

The Code of Ethics of the American Optometric Association sets
forth certain basic duties of its members, and it reaffirms "the
benevolent and humane fundamental purpose of the profession of
optometry: To protect and conserve and improve human vision"
(from the preamble to the Code of Ethics.)

It Shall Be the Ideal, the Resolve, and the Duty of the Members of
the American Optometric Association:

        To keep the visual welfare of the patient uppermost at all
times;

To promote in every possible way, in collaboration with the Association, better care of the visual needs of mankind;

To enhance continuously their educational and technical proficiency to the end that their patients shall receive the benefits of all acknowledged improvements in visual care;

To see that no person shall lack for visual care, regardless of his financial status;

To advise the patient whenever consultation with an optometric colleague or reference for other professional care seems advisable;

To hold in professional confidence all information concerning a patient and to use such data only for the benefit of the patient;

To conduct themselves as exemplary citizens;

To maintain their offices and their practices in keeping with professional standards;

To promote and maintain cordial and unselfish relationships with members of their own profession and of other professions for the exchange of information to the advantage of mankind.

"AOA Rules of Practice"

A.   Members shall abide by the Constitution and By-Laws, Code of Ethics and its Supplements, and Rules of Practice of their national, state and local optometric organizations.

B.   Members shall practice in such location and manner as is customary with other health care professionals in the area.

C.   Members shall maintain their offices so that the physical appearance is similar to that customary with other health care professionals in the area:

Signs shall be unpretentious, limited to four inch letters at street level, seven inches above. Ophthalmic materials and certificates shall be visible only from within.

D.   Members shall present themselves to the public in a manner similar to that customary with other health care professionals in the area:

Telephone and other directory listings shall be in ordinary type size. Announcements shall be limited in size to two columns by two inches, and limited in context to name, profession, address, telephone number, office hours, and practice limited to....

"Supplements"

I.   BASIC RESPONSIBILITIES OF AN OPTOMETRIST

Section A.   The Welfare of Humanity

A profession has for its prime object the service it can render to humanity; reward or financial gain should be a subordinate consideration. The practice of optometry is a profession. In choosing his profession an individual assumes an obligation to conduct himself in accord with its ideals.

Section B. Self-Improvement

It is the duty of every optometrist to keep himself in touch with every modern development in his profession, to enhance his knowledge and proficiency by the adoption of modern methods and scientific concepts of proven worth, and to contribute his share to the general knowledge and advancement of his profession by all means in his power. All these things he should do with that freedom of action and thought that provides first for the welfare of the public within the scope and limits of his endeavor.

Section C. Scientific Attitude

An optometrist should approach all situations with a scientific attitude, weighing all that is new against the present fund of knowledge and his experience, and accepting only that which is truth as nearly as he can ascertain.

Section D. Personal Deportment

An optometrist should be an upright man. Consequently he must keep himself pure in character, must conform to a high standard of morals, and must be diligent and conscientious in his studies.

Section E. Optometrists as Public Citizens

An optometrist should bear his full part in supporting the laws of the community and sustaining the institutions that advance the interests of humanity.

II. RELATIONS BETWEEN AN OPTOMETRIST AND HIS PATIENTS

Section A. Confidential Aspects of Patient Relations

Patience and delicacy should characterize all the acts of an optometrist. The confidence concerning individual or domestic life entrusted by a patient to an optometrist and the defects of disposition or flaws of character observed in patients during attendance should be held as a trust and should never be revealed except when imperatively required by the laws of the state.

Section B. The Presence of a Pathological Condition Should be Communicated by an Optometrist to His Patient

An optometrist should give to the patient a timely notice of manifestations of disease. He should neither exaggerate nor minimize the gravity of the patient's condition. He should assure himself that the patient or his family has such knowledge of the patient's condition as will serve the best interests of the patient.

Section C. Patients Must Not be Neglected

An optometrist is free to choose whom he will serve. He should respond to any request for his assistance in an emergency. Once having undertaken a case formally, an optometrist shall not abandon or neglect the patient. Frequently the immediate, prior need of the patient for the professional services of another must be

recommended by the optometrist. In any event, he shall not withdraw from a case until a sufficient notice has been given the patient
or his family to make it possible to secure other professional services.

Section D.   Compensations and Fees
           The fee charged the patient is determined by the skill, knowl-
edge, and responsibility of the optometrist.   Additional factors are
the time and overhead costs, and the relative value of the service
given.

Section E.   The Relations of Services and Materials
           Materials utilized by the optometrist are charged to the pa-
tient on the basis of their costs to the optometrist.

Section F.   Gratuitous Service
           The poverty of a patient and the humanitarian, professional
obligations of optometrists should command the gratuitous services
of an optometrist.   Other individuals and endowed institutions and
organizations have no claim on the optometrist for gratuitous services.

Section G.   Contract Practice
           It is unethical for optometrists to enter into contracts which
impose conditions that make it possible to deal fairly with the public
or fellow practitioners in the locality.

Section H.   Interference of Unrelated Practices
           The acts which an optometrist performs and which are outside
the confines of his profession must not mislead the public as to the
scope of his profession, and must not be inimical to the public welfare or to that of his fellow practitioners.

III. RESPONSIBILITIES TO OTHER
OPTOMETRISTS AND TO THE PUBLIC

Section A.   Uphold the Honor of the Profession
           The obligation assumed upon entering the profession requires
the optometrist to comport himself as a gentleman, and demands that
he use every honorable means to uphold the dignity and honor of
his vocation, to exalt its standards and to extend its sphere of usefulness.

Section B.   Optometric Societies
           In order that the dignity and honor of the optometric profes-
sion may be upheld, its standards exalted, its sphere of usefulness
extended, and the advancement of optometric science promoted, an
optometrist should associate himself with optometric societies.   He
should contribute his time, energy, and means to the end that these
societies may represent the ideals of the profession.

Section C. Advertising
        The following are deemed, among others to be unethical and
to constitute unprofessional conduct in accordance with the laws and
regulations of each particular state.

        Soliciting patients directly or indirectly, individually or
collectively through the guise of groups, institutions, or organizations.
        Employing solicitors, publicity agents, entertainers, lec-
turers, or any mechanical or electronic, visual or auditory device
for the solicitation of patronage.
        Advertising professional superiority, or the performance of
professional services in a superior manner.
        Any advertising or conduct of a character tending to deceive
or mislead the public.
        Advertising one or more types of service to imply superiority
or lower fees.
        Holding one's self forth to the public under the name of any
corporation, company, institution, clinic, association, parlor, or
any other name than the name of the optometrist.
        Holding one's self forth as possessed of, or utilizing exclu-
sive methods of practice or peculiar styles of service.
        Displaying certificates, diplomas, or similar documents un-
less the same have been earned by the optometrist.
        Guaranteeing or warranting the results of professional ser-
vices.
        Advertising of any character which includes or contains any
fee whatsoever, or any reference thereto, or any reference to the
cost to the patient, whether related to that examination or the cost
or fee for lenses, glasses, frames, mountings, or any other optometric services, article, or device necessary for the patient.
        Offering free examination or other gratuitous services,
bonuses, premiums, discounts, or any other inducements.
        Permitting the display of his name in any city, commercial,
telephone, or other public directory; or directory in the lobby of
public halls in any office or public building, using any type which is
in any way different from the standard size, shape, or color of the
type regularly used in such medium.
        Permitting his name to be put in any public directory under
a heading other than "Optometrist."
        Printing professional cards, billheads, letterheads and sta-
tionery with illustrations or printed materials other than his name,
title, address, telephone number, office hours, and specialty, if
any.
        Displaying large, glaring or flickering signs, or any sign
or other depiction containing as a part thereof the representation of
an eye, eyeglasses, spectacles, or any portion of the human head.
        Using large lettering or other devices or unusual depictions
upon the office doors or windows.

Section D. Patients
        It is unprofessional for an optometrist to exploit a patent for

lenses, appliances, or instruments used in the practice of optometry
in such a way as to deprive the public of its benefits, either through
refusal to grant licenses to competent manufacturers who can assure adequate production and unimpeachable quality, or through
exorbitant demands in the form of royalty; or for similar forms of
monopolistic control in which the interests of the public are exploited.

Section E.   Rebates
        It is unprofessional and unethical to accept rebates on pre-
scriptions, lenses, or optical appliances used in the practice of
optometry.

Section F.   Safeguarding the Profession
        An optometrist should expose without fear or favor, before
the proper optometric tribunals, corrupt or dishonest conduct of
members of the profession. All questions affecting the professional
reputation or standing of a member or members of the optometric
profession should be considered only before proper optometric tribunals in executive sessions, or by special or duly appointed committees on ethical relations. Every optometrist should aid in safeguarding the profession against the admission to its ranks of those
who are unfit or unqualified because deficient either in moral character or education.

Section G.   Professional Services of Optometrists to Each Other
        An optometrist should always cheerfully and gratuitously re-
spond with his professional services to the call of any optometrist
practicing in his vicinity, or of the immediate family dependents of
optometrists.

Section H.   Consultations of Optometrists Should be Encouraged
        In doubtful or difficult conditions where the services of an-
other may be required, the optometrist should request consultations.

Section I.   Consultant and Attendant
        When an optometrist has been called on a case as a consultant,
it is his responsibility to insure that the patient be returned to the
original optometrists for any subsequent care that the patient requires.

Section J.   Criticism to be Avoided in Consultation
        The optometrists, in his relations with a patient under the
care of another optometrist, should observe the strictest caution
and reserve; should give no derogatory hints relative to the nature
and care of the patient's disorder; nor should the course of conduct
of the optometrist directly or indirectly tend to diminish the trust
reposed in the attending optometrist. In embarrassing situations
or wherever there may seem to be a possibility of misunderstanding
with a colleague, the optometrist should always seek a personal
interview with his fellow.

Section K.   General Practitioner Responsible
     When the general practitioner of optometry refers a patient
to another optometrist, the former remains in charge of the case
and is responsible for the care of the patient until properly dismissed.

Section L.   Services to Patient of Another Optometrist
     An optometrist should never take charge of, or prescribe
for, a patient who is under the care of another optometrist, except
in an emergency, until after the other optometrist has relinquished
the case or has been properly dismissed.

Section M.   Criticism of a Colleague to be Avoided
     When an optometrist succeeds another optometrist in the
charge of a case, he should not make comments on, or insinuations
regarding the practice of the one who preceded him.   Such comments
or insinuations tend to lower the esteem of the patient for the optometric profession and so react against the critic.

Section N.   A Colleague's Patient
     When an optometrist is requested by a colleague to care for
a patient during his temporary absence; or when, because of an
emergency, he is asked to see a patient of a colleague, the optometrist should treat the patient in the same manner and with the
same delicacy as he would have one of his own patients cared for
under similar circumstances.   The patient should be returned to
the care of the attending optometrist as soon as possible.

Section O.   Arbitration of Differences Between Optometrists
     Should there arise between optometrists a difference of
opinion which cannot be properly adjusted, the dispute should be referred for arbitration to an appropriate committee of impartial optometrists.

Section P.   Fee Splitting
     When a patient is referred by one optometrist to another for
consultation or for care, whether the optometrist in charge ac-
companies the patient or not, it is unethical to give or receive a
commission or secret division of fees, by whatever term it may be
called or under any guise or pretext whatsoever.

Section Q.   Official Postion
     A member holding an official position in any optometric or-
ganization shall avoid any semblance of using this position for
self-aggrandizement.

IV.   RELATIONS BETWEEN AN OPTOMETRIST AND OTHER PROFESSIONALS

Section A.   Interprofessional Relations
     Dignity, propriety and a proper regard for their individual
fields of service must characterize the relationship between optometrists and members of other professions.

Section B.   Referring Patients
        Whenever, to complement the services of an optometrist, the
patient's condition requires the professional services of another,
every cooperative effort shall be made to the end that the patient's
welfare be safeguarded.

Section C.   Public Health
        Professional responsibility demands that the optometrist
actively participate in public health measures to the end that every
step be taken to safeguard the welfare of society.

ORGANIZED LABOR

AMERICAN FEDERATION OF LABOR AND CONGRESS OF INDUS-
TRIAL ORGANIZATIONS (AFL-CIO)
        815 16th St., N.W., Washington, D.C. 20006
        George Meany, President

Membership: The American Federation of Labor and Congress of
Industrial Organizations, founded in 1881 and with a present (1973)
membership of over 13,500,000, is a union of unions--"a voluntary
federation of 113 national and international labor unions in the United
States," including workers in such diverse occupations as actors and
entertainers, barbers, mechanics, railroad workers, newspaper reporters, engineers, printers, telephone operators, television camera-
men, school teachers, farm and cannery workers, post office clerks.
The 113 craft and industrial unions, made up of more than 60,000
local unions, were organized into a single trade union, when the
American Federation of Labor and the Congress of Industrial Organizations merged on December 5, 1955 to form the AFL-CIO.

Code of Ethics: While member unions of the AFL-CIO are autonomous and retain control over their own affairs, they are required
to comply with the AFL-CIO Ethical Practices Codes, which "established basic standards of union democracy and financial integrity,"
and forbade union control by Communists, fascists, or other totali-
tarians.   The six Codes of Ethical Practice--prepared by the AFL-
CIO Ethical Practices Committee, adopted by the Executive Council,
and affirmed by the 1957 convention--are:
        Code
        I.   Local Union Charters.
        II.   Health and Welfare Funds.
        III. Racketeers, Crooks, Communists and Fascists.
        IV.   Investments and Business Interests of Union Officials.
        V.   Financial Practices and Proprietary Activities of Unions.
        VI.   Union Democratic Processes.
The AFL-CIO Standing Committee on Ethical Practices enforces the

provisions of the Code.   The Committee is empowered (Constitution, Article XII, Section 1(d)) to conduct investigations and hold hearings concerning violations of the Ethical Practices Codes (Executive Council, Resolution, June 1956) on its own initiative or in answer to complaints of such violation, and to make recommendations to the Executive Council for disposition of the alleged or reported non-compliance with the established basic standards.

Union Insignia: The official emblem of the AFL-CIO, adopted at the time of the merger in 1955, is a circular design--two clasped hands are centered in a circle, on the left arm are the initials, "AFL, " and on the right, the initials, "CIO"; the clasped hands are superimposed upon the continent of North America; a circular bordering band of the design shows at the top, the organization name, "American Federation of Labor, " and at the bottom, "Congress of Industrial Organizations. " The color of the insignia is shown variously--black on white (publication); blue on white (letterhead).

Other Identification of Union Affiliation:
An insignia long identified with organized labor is the "Union Label, " which varies from union to union, and is developed by and is the property of a single union using it.   The Union Label indicates "quality in labor relations (good wages and working conditions under a union contract), " and appears on products produced in union shops.   The union label that is the mark of the Allied Printing Trades and found on union produced printed material, is the "Union Bug"--a horizontal oval, bisected by a horizontal band, both bearing the name of the union of workers producing the labelled material. A particular chapter of the union may be indicated by a number at each end of the horizontal band.

Bibliography:
        American Federation of Labor and Congress of Industrial Organizations.   AFL-CIO Codes of Ethical Practices.   May 1958.   48 pages.   Pamphlet. $.10.
        Official texts of Ethical Practices Codes and AFL-CIO statements against corruption, racketeering, and subversion.
        _____ . This is the AFL-CIO.   Revised edition, November 1969.   24 pages.   Pamphlet. $.10.
        Informational brochure describing the functions, structure and policies of the AFL-CIO.

"Ethical Practices Code"

I.   LOCAL UNION CHARTERS
(Approved by the AFL-CIO Executive Council, August 29, 1956)

        The AFL-CIO, as one of its specific objectives, has a constitutional mandate "to protect the labor movement from any and

all corrupt influences...."
        The Committee on Ethical Practices has been vested by the
AFL-CIO constitution with the "duty and responsibility" to assist the
Executive Council in its determination to keep the AFL-CIO "free
from any taint or corruption...."
        As the Statement on Ethical Practices adopted unanimously
by our First Constitutional Convention pointed out, "The vast majority of labor union officials accept their responsibility and trust....
Yet the reputations of the vast majority are imperiled by the dishonest, corrupt, unethical practices of the few who betray their
trust and who look upon the trade union movement not as a brotherhood to serve the general welfare, but as a means to advance their
own selfish purposes...."
        The statement of our constitutional convention specifically
called upon our affiliated national and international unions "to take
whatever steps are necessary within their own organizations to
effect the policies and ethical standards set forth in the constitution
of the AFL-CIO." The same resolution pledged the "full support,
good offices and staff facilities" of the Ethical Practices Committee
to our affiliated national and international unions in "their efforts
to carry out and put into practice the constitutional mandate" to keep
our organization free of corruption.
        At its June, 1956, meeting the Executive Council directed
the Committee on Ethical Practices "to develop a set of principles
and guides for adoption by the AFL-CIO in order to implement the
constitutional determination that the AFL-CIO shall be and remain
free from all corrupt influences" and directed that such recommended guides and principles be submitted to the Council.
        In accordance with these constitutional responsibilities and
mandates, the Committee on Ethical Practices, in the period since
its formal creation, undertook an analysis of the issuance of local
union charters as it relates to the problem of corruption. The
code recommended in this report is the first in a series which the
Committee plans to develop in accordance with the Executive Council's direction.
        The Committee found that in this area, as in the field of
union welfare funds, the instances of corruption are relatively rare.
The vast majority of local union charters are issued by the affiliated national and international unions of the AFL-CIO for legitimate
trade union purposes and without any taint or possibility of corruption. In a few instances, however, local union charters have fallen
in the hands of corrupt individuals who have used these charters for
their own illicit purposes instead of legitimate trade union objectives.
        The possession of charters covering "paper locals" has en-
abled such racketeers to victimize individual workers, employers
and the general public, while giving a black eye to the labor movement. They have used these charters to enter into conspiracies
with corrupt employers to prevent, for a price, the genuine organization of workers into legitimate unions, thus depriving these workers of the benefit of honest collective bargaining agreements. These
racketeers also use a charter as a basis to falsely invoke the collective strength of the trade union movement for their illegitimate

ends, thus demeaning the trade union's historic respect for the legitimate picket line, and injuring honest businessmen in the conduct of their affairs. A local union charter, improperly issued, can be used to control a local union unit vote, which negates the legitimate unit vote of bona fide local unions and thus subverts the democratic process within the trade union movement at various levels. A racketeer treats a charter as a "hunting license" to invade the jurisidictions of other national or international unions, in the interests only of corruption and dishonest gain, and to cloak with a respectable name a whole range of nefarious and corrupt activities.

Such corrupt practices are not widespread. But even the few instances in which local union charters have been corruptly used are too many. The name of the AFL-CIO, and of the national and international unions affiliated with it, must always be a hallmark of ethical trade union practices.

Scrupulous adherence, the Committee believes, to certain traditional practices and principles of the trade union movement with reference to the issuance of local union charters will serve to prevent and to eliminate the specific evils in this area.

The basic principle with reference to the issuance of a local union charter is that the charter is, in all unions, a solemn instrument establishing a subordinate or affiliated body of the international union, composed of organized workers in a particular subdivision of the union. The Committee has made a study of the practices and constitutions of a greater number of national and international unions with respect to the issuance of local union charters. In the vast majority of cases, the Committee found, there is a constitutional prohibition against the issuance of charters in the absence of application by a minimum number of bona fide employees, eligible for membership in the union, within the jurisdiction covered by the charter.

The specific rules governing the issuance of charters necessarily vary greatly from union to union. And each national and international union, as part of its autonomous right, has complete authority to prescribe the particular procedures governing the issuance of local union charters. But whatever the particular procedures, each autonomous union has the duty to see to it that the purpose of issuing local union charters is to promote the general welfare of workers. The constitution of the AFL-CIO makes it clear that no affiliate has an autonomous right to permit corrupt or unethical practices which endanger the good name of the trade union movement.

The Committee believes that implementation and enforcement of the basic principle that local union charters are to be issued only to give recognition to workers joining together in a subordinate or affiliated body of a national or international union, which is in fact expressed in the vast majority of union constitutions, will provide an effective method of preventing the kind of evils described in this statement.

Therefore, the Ethical Practices Committee, under the authority vested in it by the constitution of the AFL-CIO and pursuant to the mandate of the first constitutional convention of the

AFL-CIO, recommends that the Executive Council of the AFL-CIO
adopt the following policies to safeguard the good name of the AFL-
CIO and its affiliated unions and to prevent any taint or possibility
of corruption in the issuance of local union charters:

1. A local union charter, whether issued by the AFL-CIO
or by any national or international union affiliated with the AFL-CIO,
should be a solemn instrument establishing a subordinate or affiliated
body. To assure this, the AFL-CIO and each national and international union, by constitution or administrative regulation, should
require, for issuance of a local union charter, application by a
group of bona fide employees, eligible for membership in the union,
within the jurisdiction covered by the charter.

2. The purpose of issuing such charters should be to promote the general welfare of workers and to give recognition to their
joining together in a subordinate or affiliated body.

3. A charter should never be issued to any person or persons who seek to use it as a "hunting license" for the improper invasion of the jurisdictions of other affiliated unions.

4. A charter should never be issued or permitted to continue in effect for a "paper local" not existing or functioning as a genuine local union of employees.

5. A charter should never be issued to persons who are
known to traffic in local union charters for illicit or improper purposes.

6. The provision of the AFL-CIO constitution prohibiting
the AFL-CIO and any affiliated national or international union from
recognizing any subordinate organization that has been suspended or
expelled by the AFL-CIO or any national or international union
plainly includes and prohibits the issuance of a local union charter
by the AFL-CIO or any affiliated national or international union to
any group of individuals or any individuals suspended or expelled
from the AFL-CIO or any affiliated national or international union
for corruption or unethical practices.

7. The AFL-CIO and each national and international union
shall take prompt action to eliminate any loop-holes through which
local union charters have been or can be issued or permitted to
continue in effect contrary to these policies.

8. The AFL-CIO and each national and international union
shall take prompt action to insure the forthwith withdrawal of local
union charters which have been issued and are now outstanding in
violation of these policies.

II. HEALTH AND WELFARE FUNDS
(Approved by the AFL-CIO Executive Council, January 31, 1957)

At its June, 1956, meeting the Executive Council directed the
Committee on Ethical Practices "to develop a set of principles and
guides for adoption by the AFL-CIO in order to implement the constitutional determination that the AFL-CIO shall be and remain free
from all corrupt influences" and directed that such recommended
guides and principles be submitted to the Council. In accordance
with this direction, and its constitutional responsibilities, the

Committee on Ethical Practices submitted to the Executive Council
at its August, 1956, meeting the first of a proposed series of recommended codes. This code covering the issuance of local union
charters was unanimously adopted by the Council.

This report, and the recommended code contained in it, is
the second in the series which the Committee, in accordance with
the Council's direction, is developing to implement the constitutional
mandate that the AFL-CIO shall be and remain free from any and
all corrupt influences and the determination of the first Constitutional Convention of the AFL-CIO that the reputations of the vast
majority of labor union officials, who accept their responsibilities
and trust, are "imperiied by the dishonest, corrupt, unethical
practices of the few who betray their trust and who look upon the
trade union movement not as a brotherhood to serve the general welfare, but as a means to advance their own selfish purposes...."

Both the American Federation of Labor and the Congress of
Industrial Organizations prior to the merger of these two organizations into the AFL-CIO gave thorough consideration to the subject of
Health and Welfare Funds. This subject was also considered by and
dealt with by the First Constitutional Convention of the AFL-CIO
and a resolution dealing with this subject matter was adopted by
that convention.

As stated in the resolution adopted by the First Constitutional
Convention of the AFL-CIO, the task of administering and operating
health and welfare programs which have been developed through collective bargaining has placed heavy new responsibilities upon the
shoulders of trade union officials. The funds involved are paid for
through the labor of the workers covered by the plans. They must
be administered, therefore, as a high trust for the benefit only of
those workers.

Most trade union officials have been faithful to the high trust
which has been imposed upon them because of the development of
health and welfare funds. The malfeasances of a few, however,
have served to bring into disrepute not only the officials of the particular unions involved, but also the good name of the entire American labor movement. For this reason, it is imperative that the
AFL-CIO and each of the national and international unions affiliated
with it rigorously adhere to the highest ethical standards in dealing
with the subject of health and welfare funds.

For these reasons, the Ethical Practices Committee, under
the authority vested in it by the Constitution of the AFL-CIO and
pursuant to the mandate of the First Constitutional Convention of the
AFL-CIO, recommends that the Executive Council of the AFL-CIO
adopt the following policies to safeguard the good name of the AFL-
CIO and its affiliated unions:

1. No union official who already receives full-time pay from
his union shall receive fees or salaries of any kind from a fund
established for the provision of a health, welfare or retirement program. Where a salaried union official serves as employee representative or trustee in the administration of such programs, such service
should be regarded as one of the functions expected to be performed

by him in the normal course of his duties and not as an extra function requiring further compensation from the welfare fund.

2. No union official, employee or other person acting as
agent or representative of a union, who exercises responsibilities
or influence in the administration of welfare programs or the placement of insurance contracts, should have any compromising personal
ties, direct or indirect, with outside agencies such as insurance
carriers, brokers, or consultants doing business with the welfare
plan.   Such ties cannot be reconciled with the duty of a union official
to be guided solely by the best interests of the membership in any
transactions with such agencies.   Any union official found to have
such ties to his own personal advantage or to have accepted fees,
inducements, benefits or favors of any kind from any such outside
agency, should be removed.   This principle, of course, does not
prevent the existence of a relationship between a union officer or
employee and an outside agency where

(a) no substantial personal advantage is derived from the
relationship, and

(b) the outside agency is one in the management of which
the union participates, as a union, for the benefit of its members.

3. Complete records of the financial operations of all welfare funds and programs should be maintained in accordance with the
best accounting practice.   Each such fund should be audited regularly
by internal auditors.   In addition, each such fund should be audited
at least once each year, and preferably semi-annually, by certified
public or other independent accountants of unquestioned professional
integrity, who should certify that the audits fully and comprehensively show the financial condition of the fund and the results of the
operation of the fund.

4. All audit reports should be available to the membership of
the union and the affected employees.

5. The trustees or administrators of welfare funds should
make a full disclosure and report to the beneficiaries at least once
each year.   Such reports should set forth, in detail, the receipts
and expenses of the fund; all salaries and fees paid by the fund, with
a statement of the persons to whom paid; the amount paid and the
service or purpose for which paid; a breakdown of insurance premium paid, if a commercial insurance carrier is involved, showing,
insofar as possible, the premiums paid, dividends, commissions,
claims paid, retentions and service charges; a statement of the person to whom any commissions or fees of any kind were paid; a
financial statement on the part of the insuring or service agency, if
an agency other than a commercial insurance carrier is employed;
and a detailed account of the manner in which the reserves held by
the fund are invested.

6. Where health and welfare benefits are provided through
the use of a commercial insurance carrier, the carrier should be
selected through competitive bids solicited from a substantial number
of reliable companies, on the basis of the lowest net cost for the
given benefits submitted by a responsible carrier, taking into consideration such factors as comparative retention rates, financial

responsibility, facilities for and promptness in servicing claims, and the past record of the carrier, including its record in dealing with trade unions representing its employees.

The trustees of the fund should be required to include in reporting to the membership the specific reasons for the selection of the carrier finally chosen. The carrier should be required to warrant that no fee or other remuneration of any kind has been paid directly or indirectly to any representative of the parties in connection with the business of the fund.

7. Where a union or union trustees participate in the administration of the investment of welfare fund reserves, the union or its trustees should make every effort to prohibit the investment of welfare fund reserves in the business of any contributing employer, insurance carrier or agency doing business with the fund, or in any enterprise in which any trustee, officer or employee of the fund has a personal financial interest of such a nature as to be affected by the fund's investment or disinvestment.

(This is not to be construed as preventing investment in an enterprise in which a union official is engaged by virtue of his office, provided (i) no substantial personal advantage is derived from the relationship, and (ii) the concern or enterprise is one in the management of which the union participates for the benefit of its members.)

8. Where any trustee, agent, fiduciary or employee of a health or welfare program is found to have received an unethical payment, the union should insist upon his removal and should take appropriate legal steps against both the party receiving and the party making the payment. Where health and welfare funds are negotiated or administered by local unions or by other organizations subordinate to or affiliated with a national or international union, provision should be made to give the national or international union the authority to audit such funds and to apply remedies where there is evidence of a violation of ethical standards.

9. Every welfare program should provide redress against the arbitrary or unjust denial of claims so as to afford the individual member prompt and effective relief where his claim for benefits has been improperly rejected. Every program should provide for the keeping of complete records of the claims experience so that a constant check can be maintained on the relationship between claims and premiums and dividends, and on the utilization of the various benefits.

10. The duty of policing and enforcing these standards is shared by every union member, as well as by local, national and international officials. The best safeguard against abuses lies in the hands of a vigilant, informed and active membership, jealous of their rights and interests in the operation of health and welfare programs, as well as any other trade union program. As a fundamental part of any approach to the problem of policing health and welfare funds, affiliated unions, through education, publicity and discussion programs, should seek to develop the widest possible degree of active and informed interest in all phases of these programs on the part of the membership at large. International

unions should, wherever possible, have expert advice available for
the negotiation, establishment and administration of health and welfare plans, and should provide training for union representatives in
the techniques and standards of proper administration of welfare plans.
11. Where constitutional amendments or changes in internal
administrative procedure are necessary to comply with the standards
herein set forth, such amendments and changes should be undertaken
at the earliest practicable time.

III. RACKETEERS, CROOKS, COMMUNISTS AND FASCISTS
(Approved by the AFL-CIO Executive Council, January 31, 1957)

This is the third in a series of recommended codes which
the Committee on Ethical Practices has developed in accordance
with the direction of the Executive Council that it should "develop
a set of principles and guides for adoption by the AFL-CIO in order
to implement the constitutional determination that the AFL-CIO shall
be and remain free from all corrupt influences."
Article VIII, Section 7 of the Constitution of the AFL-CIO
establishes that "it is a basic principle of this Federation that it
must be and remain free from any and all corrupt influences and
from the undermining efforts of communist, fascist or other totalitarian agencies who are opposed to the basic principles of our democracy and of free and democratic trade unionism." Under this
constitutional provision there is no room within the Federation or
any of its affiliated unions for any person in a position of leadership or responsibility who is a crook, a racketeer, a communist or
a fascist. And it is the obligation of every union affiliated with the
AFL-CIO to take appropriate steps to ensure that this principle is
complied with.
To be sure, neither the AFL-CIO nor its affiliated unions
are law-enforcing agencies. It is not within the purview or authority
of a trade union to convict its members of a violation of statutory
law. But it is the duty and responsibility of each national and international union affiliated with the federation to see to it that it
is free of all corrupt, communist or fascist influences. Consequently, a trade union need not wait upon a criminal conviction to
bar from office corrupt, communist or fascist influences. The
responsibility of each union to see to it that it is free of such influences is not a responsibility placed upon our unions by law. It
is a responsibility which rests upon our unions by the AFL-CIO
Constitution and by the moral principles that govern the trade union
movement. Eternal vigilance in this area is the price of an honest
democratic trade union movement.
It is not possible, nor is it desirable, to set down rigid rules
to determine whether a particular individual in a position of responsibility or leadership in the trade union movement is a crook, a
racketeer, a communist, or a fascist. Obviously, if a person has
been convicted of a crime involving moral turpitude offensive to trade
union morality, he should be barred from office or responsible
position in the labor movement. Obviously also, a person commonly
known to be a crook or racketeer, should not enjoy immunity to prey

upon the trade union movement because he has somehow managed to escape conviction. In the same manner, the fact that a person has refrained from formally becoming a member of the Communist Party or a fascist organization should not permit him to hold or retain a position of responsibility or leadership in the trade union movement if, regardless of formal membership, he consistantly supports or actively participates in the activities of the Communist Party or any fascist or totalitarian organization.

In this area, as in all others, determinations must be made as a matter of common sense and with due regard to the rights of the labor unions and the individuals involved.

On the basis of these considerations, the Ethical Practices Committee, under the authority vested in it by the Constitution of the AFL-CIO, pursuant to the mandate of the First Constitutional Convention of the AFL-CIO, recommends that the Executive Council of the AFL-CIO adopt the following policies to safeguard the good name of the AFL-CIO and its affiliated unions:

1. The AFL-CIO and each of its affiliated unions should undertake the obligation, through appropriate constitutional or administrative measures and orderly procedures, to insure that no persons who constitute corrupt influences or practices or who represent or support communist, fascist or totalitarian agencies should hold office of any kind in such trade unions or organizations.

2. No person should hold or retain office or appointed position in the AFL-CIO or any of its affiliated national or international unions or subordinate bodies thereof who has been convicted of any crime involving moral turpitude offensive to trade union morality.

3. No person should hold or retain office or appointed position in the AFL-CIO or any of its affiliated national or international unions or subordinate bodies thereof who is commonly known to be a crook or racketeer preying on the labor movement and its good name for corrupt purposes, whether or not previously convicted for such nefarious actvities.

4. No person should hold or retain office or appointed position in the AFL-CIO or any of its affiliated national or international unions or subordinate bodies thereof who is a member, consistent supporter or who actively participates in the activities of the Communist Party or of any fascist or other totalitarian organization which opposes the democratic principles to which our country and the American trade union movement are dedicated.

IV. INVESTMENTS AND BUSINESS INTERESTS OF UNION OFFICIALS
(Approved by the AFL-CIO Executive Council, January 31, 1957)

This is the fourth in a series of recommended codes which the Committee on Ethical Practices has developed in accordance with the direction of the Executive Council that it should "develop a set of principles and guides for adoption by the AFL-CIO in order to implement the constitutional determination that the AFL-CIO shall be and remain free from all corrupt influences." Prior codes have dealt with the issuance of local union charters; welfare funds;

racketeers, crooks and communists. The code herein recommended deals with conflicts of interest in the investment and business interests of union officials.

It is too plain for extended discussion that a basic ethical principle in the conduct of trade union affairs is that no responsible trade union official should have a personal financial interest which conflicts with the full performance of his fiduciary duties as a workers' representative.

Obviously an irreconcilable conflict of interest would be present if a trade union official, clothed with responsibility and discretion in conducting the representation of workers, simultaneously maintains a substantial interest in the profits of the employer of the workers whom he is charged with representing. Even though, in a particular instance, there may be no actual malfeasance in the representation of the employees involved, the opportunity for personal gain at the expense of the welfare of the employees whom the union official represents obviously exists.

Such a simple case, however, does not fully present the problems which exist, or may exist, in this area. There may be cases in which the conflict of interests is not so clear, but nevertheless exists. There are, on the other hand, forms of private investment which seem wholly devoid of any possibility of corruption or dereliction in trade union responsibility. It will be the purpose of this report to discuss some of the varying situations which may arise in this area and, on the basis of such discussion, to present a recommended code of minimum standards to which the Committee believes all trade union officials should adhere in their investment and business interests.

The problems in this area, of course, could all be eliminated by adoption of the simple principle that no trade union official should, under any circumstances, use his own personal funds or property in any form of business enterprise or investment. But the committee feels that it is both unnecessary and unwise to establish such a rigid standard for trade union officials; union officers and agents should not be prohibited from investing their personal funds in their own way in the American free enterprise system so long as they are scrupulously careful to avoid any actual or potential conflict of interest. The American trade union movement does not accept the principle that either its members or its leaders should own no property. Both union leaders and members have the right to set aside their own personal reserves for themselves and their families, and to invest and use those reserves in legitimate ways.

But the trade union leader does have certain special responsibilities which he must assume and respect because he serves as a leader in the trade union movement. And those responsibilities, the Committee believes, necessarily imply certain restraints upon his right to engage in personal investment, even with his own funds and on his own time. In a sense, a trade union official holds a position comparable to that of a public servant. Like a public servant, he has a high fiduciary duty not only to serve the members of his union honestly and faithfully, but also to avoid personal economic interest which may conflict or appear to conflict with the full performance of his responsibility to those whom he serves.

Like public servants, trade union leaders ought to be paid compensation commensurate with their services. But, like public servants, trade union leaders must accept certain limitations upon their private activities which result from the nature of their services. Indeed, the nature of the trade union movement and the responsibilities which necessarily must be accepted by its leaders, make the strictest standards with respect to any possible conflict of interest properly applicable.

It is plain, as already stated, that a responsible trade union official should not be the owner in whole or in part of a business enterprise with which his union bargains collectively on behalf of its employees.   The conflict in such a case is clear.

It is almost equally clear, the Committee believes, that a trade union official should not be the owner of a business enterprise which sells to, buys from, or in other ways deals, to any significant degree, with the enterprise with which he conducts collective bargaining.   Again, the possibility that the trade union official may be given special favors or contracts by the employer in return for less than discharge of his obligations as a trade union leader, exists.

Somewhat different considerations, however, apply to the ownership, through purchase on the open market or other legitimate means, of publicly traded securities. Employee ownership of stock is certainly a fairly common practice in American life.   Often, indeed, there are special stock purchase plans designed to stimulate such employee investments.

On the other hand, ownership, even of publicly traded securities, in sufficient amounts to influence the course of management decision seems to the Committee incompatible with the proper representation of the employees by a trade union official.

The Committee believes, therefore, that the minimum standards of ethical conduct in this area should not forbid all investment by a trade union official in the corporate securities of companies employing the workers he represents.   Such investment by a trade union official, however, should always be subject to the restriction that it is not acquired in an illegitimate or unethical manner, that it is limited to securities which are publicly traded, and that his interest should never be large enough so as to permit him to exercise any individual influence on the course of corporate decision.

There is nothing in the essential ethical principles of the trade union movement which should prevent a trade union official, at any level, from investing personal funds in the publicly traded securities of corporate enterprises unrelated to the industry or area in which the official has a particular trade union responsibility. Such securities offer a wide choice of investment and are, generally speaking, so far removed from individual stockholder control or influence that with the exceptions above noted, there is no reason to bar investment by trade union officials.

The same principles apply with respect to privately owned or closely held businesses which are completely unrelated to the industrial area in which the trade union leader serves.

On the basis of these considerations, the Ethical Practices

Committee, under the authority vested in it by the Constitution of
the AFL-CIO and pursuant to the mandate of the First Constitutional
Convention of the AFL-CIO, recommends that the Executive Council
of the AFL-CIO adopt the following policies to safeguard the good
name of the AFL-CIO and its affiliated unions:

1. No responsible trade union official should have a personal
financial interest which conflicts with the full performance of his fiduciary duties as a workers' representative.

2. No responsible trade union official should own or have a
substantial business interest in any business enterprise with which
his union bargains collectively, or in any business enterprise which
is in competition with any other business enterprise with which his
union bargains collectively.

3. No responsible trade union official should own or have a
substantial business interest in a business enterprise a substantial
part of which consists of buying from, selling to, or otherwise
dealing with the business enterprise with which his union bargains
collectively.

4. The provisions of paragraphs 2 and 3 above do not apply
in the case of an investment in the publicly traded securities of
widely-held corporations which investment does not constitute a
substantial enough holding to affect or influence the course of corporate decision.

5. No responsible trade union official should accept "kickbacks," under-the-table payments, gifts of other than nominal value,
or any personal payment of any kind other than regular pay and
benefits for work performed as an employee from an employer or
business enterprise with which his union bargains collectively.

6. The policies herein set forth apply to: (a) all officers
of the AFL-CIO and all officers of national and international unions
affiliated with the AFL-CIO, (b) all elected or appointed staff representatives and business agents of such organizations, and (c) all
officers of subordinate bodies of such organizations who have any
degree of discretion or responsibility in the negotiation of collective
bargaining agreements or their administration.

7. The principles herein set forth apply not only where investments are made by union officials, but also where third persons
are used as blinds or covers to conceal the financial interests of
union officials.

V.   FINANCIAL PRACTICES AND PROPRIETARY
ACTIVITIES OF UNIONS
(Approved by the AFL-CIO Executive Council, May 22, 1957)

This is the fifth in a series of recommended codes which
the Committee on Ethical Practices has developed in accordance
with the direction of the Executive Council that it should "develop
a set of principles and guides for adoption by the AFL-CIO in
order to implement the constitutional determination that the AFL-
CIO shall be and remain free from all corrupt influences." On
August 29, 1956, the Council approved a code dealing with the
issuance of local union charters; on January 31, 1957, the Executive

Council approved codes dealing with health and welfare funds, racketeering, crooks and communists, and investment and business interests of union officials.

There are principles inherent in the conception of a free, honest, and democratic trade union movement, which, the Committee believes, virtually dictate the outlines of any Code of Ethical Practices dealing with union finances. The first of these principles hardly requires statement. It is simply that a labor union is an organization whose primary function is to improve the wages, hours and working conditions of the employees it represents, through the processes of collective bargaining with employers. It is not a business enterprise or an investment company. Unions, of course, must have funds with which to operate and it is clearly desirable that they should maintain reserves to cover contingencies which may arise in the course of the performance of their functions as workers' representatives. But, equally clearly, the accumulation of funds per se is not the objective for which the union exists. A union is not a profit-making institution but a democratic organization with definite social aims and principles. Union funds are held in trust for the benefit of the membership. But a union, unlike a bank, a trustee, or other fiduciaries, is not primarily a manager of funds vested with the duty of enhancing their value and making distributions. Increasing the value of the union's funds should never become an objective of such magnitude that it in any way interferes with or obscures the basic function of the union, which is to devote its resources to representing its members, honestly and faithfully.

A second basic principle which dictates the terms of a Code of Ethical Practices with respect to the handling of union funds is again simple. It is that unions are democratic organizations. The fact that a union is a democratic organization plainly implies that the members of the union are entitled to assurance that the union's funds, which are their funds, are not dissipated. They are also entitled to be reasonably informed as to how the funds of the organization are being used or invested. Finally, their delegated representatives in the union's governing body and conventions should have the power and responsibility to oversee the expenditure of the union's monies so that the members can be guaranteed that funds are expended solely for the purposes for which the organization exists.

A final fundamental principle, the Committee believes, is involved. That principle is that each national or international union affiliated with the AFL-CIO, in the words of the Resolution on Ethical Practices which was unanimously adopted by the founding Convention of the AFL-CIO in December 1955, "has clearly accepted the responsibility for keeping its own house in order and to protect the movement 'from any and all corrupt influences and from the undermining efforts of communist agencies and all others who are opposed to the basic principles of our democracy and free democratic unionism.' "

From these three basic principles, the Committee believes that certain conclusions necessarily follow. Since a union holds its funds for the benefit of its membership and to further their

interests it should comply with standards generally applicable to
fiduciaries or trustees with respect to the manner in which it keeps
its records and accounts. Regular audits should be made and there
should be appropriate distribution of summaries of such audits so
that the membership and the public are adequately apprised of the
state of the organization's finances.

In this connection, a Committee of Secretary-Treasurers of
AFL-CIO affiliates has drawn up a suggested set of minimum accounting and financial controls for affiliates of the AFL-CIO. This set
of controls represents, the Committee believes, the minimum with
which any affiliated organization should comply in order to fulfill
the constitutional mandate that the labor movement should be kept
free from any taint of corruption. Almost all unions, the Committee believes, today comply with the minimum controls set forth in
the recommendation of the Secretary-Treasurers. Many, indeed,
have much stricter controls. The minimum controls suggested by
the Secretary-Treasurers, therefore, should not be regarded as an
optimum. Unions are to be commended and encouraged to establish
and maintain even more stringent accounting and financial controls.

In addition to accounting and financial procedures necessary
to conform to the controls applicable generally to well-run business
organizations and fiduciaries, the Committee believes that certain
other rules follow from the basic principles set forth above. Because a union is a union, not a business organization or a trust
company, the rules which guide its use and investment of funds are
necessarily different. For example, investments by business organizations in other businesses from which they buy or sell, so
that the investing business may get favored treatment in its sales
or purchases, may be an acceptable business practice; similar investment by a labor union in business enterprises with which it bargains collectively presents serious problems. Such investment is
not good practice for a union.

The fact that the basic objective in the management of trade
union funds is not the maximizing of profit, but to further the objectives of the members' joining together in a union leads to additional conclusions.

A business organization has one function: to make money
for its stockholders. A fiduciary's primary obligation is to preserve and, within limits defined by the necessity for safety, to augment the funds which the trustee is charged with holding for the
benefit of the beneficiaries.

Since these are not a union's primary functions, a union's
investment policy may properly be governed by different considerations. For example, business institutions and corporate trustees
might question today the propriety of investing all of their reserves
in government bonds because of their comparatively low yield. Yet,
for a trade union, one of whose fundamental objects is "to protect
and strengthen our democratic institutions," such an investment
policy is to be commended. Similarly, since another object of a
trade union is to aid and assist other unions and "to promote the
organization of the unorganized into unions of their own choosing"
loans and grants for mutual aid and assistance are part of the proud

tradition of the labor movement even though foreign to the business community and not justified by any considerations of financial gain or even security.

Similarly, the business community may not regard it to be a bad business practice for a business enterprise to buy or sell from firms in which the officers of the business have a financial interest. Nor may the business community regard it as bad practice for a business organization to lend money, on adequate security, to members of the organization. Because the funds of a labor union are both held in trust for the benefit of its members and are held to further legitimate trade union purposes, practices which may be acceptable in business organizations, the Committee believes, should be limited if not completely eliminated among labor organizations.

All of these considerations lead to this ultimate conclusion. With respect to accounting and financial controls and the expenditure of its funds for proprietary (housekeeping) functions the labor movement, it goes almost without saying, should follow the strictest rules applicable to all well-run institutions. With respect to the policies governing its financial and proprietary decisions, a higher obligation rests upon the trade union movement: to conduct its affairs and to expend and invest its funds, not for profit, but for the benefit of its membership and the great purposes for which they have joined together in the fraternity of the labor movement.

On the basis of these considerations the Committee on Ethical Practices, under the authority vested in it by the Constitution of the AFL-CIO and pursuant to the mandate of the First Constitutional Convention of the AFL-CIO and of the Executive Council, recommends that the Executive Council of the AFL-CIO adopt the following policies to safeguard the good name of the AFL-CIO and its affiliated unions:

1. The AFL-CIO and all affiliated national and international unions should comply with the minimum accounting and financial controls suggested by the Committee of Secretary-Treasurers and approved by the Executive Council, which is annexed hereto.

2. The AFL-CIO and all affiliated national and international unions should conduct their proprietary functions, including all contracts for purchase or sale or for the rendition of housekeeping services, in accordance with the practices of well-run institutions, including the securing of competitive bids for all major contracts.

3. Neither the AFL-CIO nor any national or international union affiliated with the AFL-CIO should permit any of its funds to be loaned, invested, or otherwise dealt with in a manner which inures to the personal profit or advantage of any officer, representative or employee of the union.

4. Neither the AFL-CIO nor any national or international union affiliated with the AFL-CIO should enter into any contracts of purchase or sale or for the rendition of services which will inure to or result in the personal profit or advantage, including gifts of more than nominal value, other than his regular salary or compensation, of any officer, representative or employee of the union.

5. Neither the AFL-CIO nor any national or international

union affiliated with the AFL-CIO should invest in or make loans to
any business enterprise with which it bargains collectively.

6.   The provisions of paragraph 5 shall not be construed as
prohibiting investment by unions in the publicly-traded securities of
widely-held corporations which investment does not constitute a substantial enough holding to affect or influence the course of corporate
decision; the provisions of paragraphs 3 and 4 shall not be construed
as applying to the profit that may result from a proper investment
by a union officer, representative or employee.   Nor shall such
provisions be construed as preventing investment in a business or
enterprise in which an official of an affiliate is engaged by virtue
of his office, provided (a) no substantial personal advantage is derived from the relationship, and (b) the business or enterprise is
one in the management of which the affiliate participates for the
benefit of its members.   The provisions of such paragraphs, however, shall apply wherever third persons are used as blinds or
covers to conceal the personal profit or advantage of union officials。

7。   Neither the AFL-CIO nor any national or international
union affiliated with the AFL-CIO should make personal loans to
its officers, representatives, employees, or members, or members
of their families, for the purpose of financing the private business
or investment of such persons.

8.   Each national or international union affiliated with the
AFL-CIO should promptly take whatever internal steps are needed to
ensure that the standards set forth in this Code are made applicable
to itself and each of its locals and other subordinate or affiliated
bodies.   Wherever constitutional amendments or changes in internal
administrative procedures are necessary to fully comply with those
standards, such amendments and changes should be undertaken by
the affiliates at the earliest practicable opportunity.

("Supplemental Code":)

MINIMUM ACCOUNTING & FINANCIAL CONTROLS
(Drafted by Special Committee of Union Secretary-Treasurers;
Approved by Executive Council, May 22, 1957)

A.   Detailed and accurate records of accounts, in conformity
with generally recognized and accepted principles of accounting,
should be currently maintained by all affiliates of the AFL-CIO.
These records should include, as a minimum need, a cash receipt
record, a cash disbursements record, a general ledger, a dues or
per capita tax record, an investment record, and a payroll record.

B.   All receipts should be duly recorded and currently deposited.   No disbursements of any nature should be made from un-
deposited cash receipts.

C.   All expenditures should be approved by proper authority
under constitutional provision and be recorded and supported by
vouchers, providing an adequate description of the nature and purpose
of the expenditure sufficient for a reasonable audit by internal and
independent auditors.   Disbursements should be made only by check,
with the exception of disbursements from petty cash, in which situation, an imprest petty cash fund should be established.

D.   Salaries of elected officials should be established only by constitutional provision.   Compensation to non-salaried elected officials, and to other officials, representatives and employees, if not fixed by constitutional provision, should be established and paid in strict conformity with such authority as is provided by the constitution and in accordance with its applicable provisions.

E.   Reimbursement of expenses, including per diem expenses, should be made only where such expenses have been duly authorized and are supported in a manner that will permit a reasonable audit.

F.   Every precaution should be taken to ensure the soundness and safety of investments and that investments are made only by persons duly authorized to act for and on behalf of the affiliate. Investments in securities should either be restricted to the type of securities which legally qualify for trust fund investments in the domicile state or a person or persons authorized to invest funds of an affiliate should, in making such investment, be required to exercise the judgment and care under the circumstances then prevailing which men of prudence, discretion and intelligence exercise in the management of their own affairs, not in regard to speculation but in regard to the permanent disposition of their funds, considering probable safety of their capital as well as probable income.   No investment should be made by an affiliate in a business or enterprise in which any officer of that affiliate has a direct or indirect personal financial interest of such a nature as to be affected by the affiliate's investment or withdrawal of investment.   (This last stated provision is not to be construed as preventing investment in a business or enterprise in which an official of an affiliate is engaged by virtue of his office, provided (a) no substantial personal advantage is derived from the relationship, and (b) the business or enterprise is one in the management of which the affiliate participates for the benefit of its members.)   Securities owned by the affiliate should be under dual officer control and held by a bank or a trust company as agent or if that is not feasible, such securities should be placed in a safety deposit vault.   All investments and legal title to all assets of an affiliate should be in the name of the affiliate or its duly designated agent or trustee.

G.   Periodic, but not less than semi-annual, detailed financial reports should be prepared in accordance with generally recognized and accepted standards of financial reporting.   These reports should be prepared and submitted by the elected financial officer of the affiliate to the executive body of such affiliate for its study and such action as may be required.

H.   A record of each meeting of the executive body of an affiliate should be made and maintained.   These records should note all official actions taken by that body, in relation to accounting and financial matters.

I.   Adequate fidelity bond coverage should be required by an affiliate for all officers, representatives and employees of that affiliate in positions of trust, including officers and employees of subordinate bodies of such affiliate.

J.   Affiliates and their subordinate bodies should be subject

to a system of internal audits made by auditors or by other competent persons in accordance with generally accepted standards of
auditing so as to maintain current vigilance over all financial transactions.

K.   At least annually, an audit of the accounts of each affiliate,
except directly affiliated local unions of the AFL-CIO, should be made
by independent certified public accountants. A summary of such audit
approved by such independent certified public accountants should be
made available to the membership of the affiliate and the public.

Each such affiliate should require, at least annually, that an
audit be made of the accounts of its subordinate bodies by competent
persons.   A summary of such audit approved by such competent
persons should be made available to the membership of such subordinate body.

An annual audit of the accounts of directly affiliated local
unions should be made by authorized competent representatives of
the AFL-CIO designated by the Secretary-Treasurer of the AFL-
CIO.   A summary of such audit, approved by such representative,
shall be made available to the membership of such directly affiliated
local unions.

L.   All financial and accounting records of affiliates and their
subordinate bodies, and all supporting vouchers and documents, or
microfilm copies thereof, should be preserved for a period of time
not less than that prescribed by applicable statutes of limitations.

M.   Neither the AFL-CIO nor any national or international
union affiliated with the AFL-CIO should make personal loans to its
officers, representatives, employees, or members, or members of
their families, for the purpose of financing the private business or
investment of such persons.

N.   No "kickbacks" or any other improper payments should
be accepted or made, directly or indirectly, by any officer, representative or employee of an affiliate in connection with any financial
transaction of such affiliate.

O.   Affiliates should take every precaution necessary to insure their full compliance with all properly authorized and applicable
requirements of state or federal law pertaining to financial and accounting matters and to reporting.

P.   In order to protect and safeguard the good name and
reputation of the AFL-CIO and its affiliates, the financial and accounting controls set forth herein are made applicable to itself and
each of the affiliates of the AFL-CIO and their subordinate bodies
and to all their funds of whatever nature.

Q.   Where constitutional amendments or changes in internal
administrative procedure are necessary to a full compliance with the
standards set forth herein, such amendments and changes should be
undertaken by affiliates at the earliest practicable opportunity.

VI.   UNION DEMOCRATIC PROCESSES
(Approved by the AFL-CIO Executive Council, May 23, 1957)

This is the sixth in a series of recommended codes developed
by the AFL-CIO Committee on Ethical Practices.   The prior codes
have dealt, primarily, with the questions related to corruption and

conflicts of interest. The present code has been developed by the
Committee pursuant to the mandate contained in Article II, Sections
10 and 11, of the Constitution of the AFL-CIO which sets forth the
basic objectives of the Federation to protect the labor movement not
only from corrupt influences and communist agencies but also from
"all others who are opposed to the basic principles of our democracy
and free and democratic unionism, " and "to safeguard the democratic
character of the labor movement. "

These constitutional provisions of the AFL-CIO give effect to
the democratic tradition upon which the entire labor movement is
based. Freedom and democracy are the essential attributes of our
movement. Labor organizations lacking these attributes, like Hitler's
Labor Front, Franco's syndicates, and Moscow's captive unions,
are unions in name only. Authoritarian control, whether from within the labor movement or imposed from without by government, is
contrary to the spirit, the tradition and the principles which should
always guide and govern our movement.

We are proud of our record. Just as the Constitution of the
AFL-CIO proclaims its dedication to the concepts of freedom and
democracy and contains machinery for their implementation in the
Federation's operations, so also do the constitutions of its affiliates.
Almost without exception, they provide for the basic elements of
union democracy: the right of full and equal participation by each
member in the affairs and processes of union self-government, in
accordance with the principles of representative democracy, and the
necessity for protecting the rights of individual members.

The record of union democracy, like the record of our nation's democracy, is not perfect. A few unions do not adequately,
in their constitutions, provide for these basic elements of democratic practice. A few unions do not practice or implement the
principles set forth in their constitutions. Finally, while the over-
whelming majority of American unions both preach and practice the
principles of democracy, in all too many instances the membership
by apathy and indifference have forfeited their rights of union citizenship.

The provisions of the Taft-Hartley Act have substantially
frustrated previously successful efforts by unions to ensure maximum attendance and participation by the membership in union meetings and affairs. The real corrective in this area is not so much
the establishment of new principles as the exercise of rights presently recognized and accorded. Just as eternal vigilance is the
price of liberty, so is the constant exercise of the rights of union
citizenship the price of union democracy.

It is valuable, nevertheless, to restate the principles which
should govern all free and democratic unions and to rededicate the
labor movement to the preservation of these principles.

The Committee on Ethical Practices has attempted to formulate in the following code the basic and elementary principles which
any affiliated union should achieve if it is to comply with the basic
principles and objects of the AFL-CIO Constitution. Necessarily,
since each union has grown up in its own tradition and with its own
background, forms and procedures may differ widely. Unions should

be free to determine their own governmental structure and to regulate their own affairs. But, whatever the form, the basic democratic rights set forth in the code should be guaranteed.

1.   Each member of a union should have the right to full
and free participation in union self-government. This should include the right (a) to vote periodically for his local and national
officers, either directly by referendum vote or through delegate
bodies, (b) to honest elections, (c) to stand for and to hold office,
subject only to fair qualifications uniformly imposed, (d) to voice
his views as to the method in which the union's affairs should be
conducted.
2.   Each member of a union should have the right to fair
treatment in the application of union rules and law. The general
principle applicable to union disciplinary procedures is that such
procedures should contain all the elements of fair play. No particular formality is required. No lawyers need be used. The essential
requirements of due process, however--notice, hearing, and judgment on the basis of the evidence--should be observed. A method
of appeal to a higher body should be provided to ensure that judgment at the local level is not the result of prejudice or bias.
3.   Each member of a union has the responsibility (a) fully
to exercise his rights of union citizenship and (b) loyally to support
his union. The right of an individual member to criticize the policies and personalities of his union officers does not include the right
to undermine the union as an institution, to advocate dual unionism,
to destroy or weaken the union as a collective bargaining agency, or
to carry on slander and libel.
4.   To safeguard the rights of the individual members and to
safeguard its democratic character, the AFL-CIO and each affiliated
national or international union should hold regular conventions at
stated intervals, which should be not more than four years. The
convention should be the supreme governing body of the union.
5.   Officers of the AFL-CIO and of each affiliated national or
international union should be elected, either by referendum vote or
by the vote of delegate bodies. Whichever method is used, election
should be free, fair and honest and adequate internal safeguards
should be provided to ensure the achievement of that objective.
6.   All general conventions of the AFL-CIO and of affiliated
national or international unions should be open to the public, except
for necessary executive sessions. Convention proceedings or an
accurate summary thereof should be published and be available to
the membership.
7.   The appropriate officials of the union and such bodies
which are given authority to govern a union's affairs between conventions should be elected, whether from the membership at large
or by appropriate divisions, either by referendum vote or by the
vote of delegate bodies. Such bodies shall abide by and enforce the
provisions of the union's constitution and carry out the decisions of
the convention.
8.   Membership meetings of local unions should be held periodically with proper notice of time and place.

9. Elections of local union officers should be democratic, conducted either by referendum or by vote of a delegate body which is itself elected by referendum or at union meetings.

10. The term of office of all union officials should be stated in the organization's constitution or by-laws and should be for a reasonable period, not to exceed four years.

11. To ensure democratic, responsible, and honest administration of its locals and other subordinate bodies, the AFL-CIO and affiliated national and international unions should have the power to institute disciplinary and corrective proceedings with respect to local unions and other subordinate bodies, including the power to establish trusteeships where necessary. Such powers should be exercised sparingly and only in accordance with the provisions of the union's constitution, and autonomy should be restored promptly upon correction of the abuses requiring trusteeship.

12. Where constitutional amendments or changes in internal administrative procedures are necessary to comply with the standards herein set forth such amendments and changes should be undertaken at the earliest practicable time.

PALEONTOLOGISTS

THE PALEONTOLOGICAL SOCIETY (PS)
   345 Middlefield Rd., Menlo Park, Cal. 94025
   Warren C. Addicott, Secretary

Membership: The Paleontological Society, founded in 1908 and with a present (1973) membership of over 1200, is an organization of paleontologists "associated with the Geological Society of America for the purpose of cooperation in annual meetings, publication, and in other ways for the furtherance of the science of Paleontology" (Constitution and Bylaws, Article I). Membership in the Society is open to both professional scientists and amateurs interested in the study of paleontology.

Code of Ethics: The Paleontological Society does not have a formal code of ethics.

Professional Insignia: The Paleontological Society has two emblems which appear on the organization letterhead. These designs are the two sides of the Paleontological Society Medal--an award given intermittently for exceptional service and outstanding scientific achievement in paleontology. The two circular designs are:

(1)   The Society monogram, "PS," entwined in the center,
       superimposed over two crossed geological picks; a globe
       at the lower left showing the American continent, the
       lamp of learning at the lower right; an open book at the
       bottom of the insignia, bearing the date of founding of
       the group, "1908"; the motto "Frango ut Patefaciam" ("I
       break to bring light")--indicating the process of dis-
       closing paleontological specimens--is given around the
       upper half of the design.

(2)   The other side of the medal, which was adopted about
       1961, shows three kinds of fossils--symbolizing the
       three fields of paleontology:
           Vertebrate--a fish (reconstruction of the Devonian
               fish Eusthenopteron);
           Invertebrate--a trilobite (Ceraurus of the Ordovician
               age);
           Plant--horsetail (Calamites of Pennsylvanian age).
       The trilobite is centered in the emblem, the fish below
       this symbol, and the plant sprays on either side of the
       centered trilobite. The organization name, "Paleontolog-
       ical Society," bands the upper half of the design.

Bibliography:
    Paleontological Society. Constitution and By-Laws. 1965. 4
        pages. (Reprint from Journal of Paleontology, 39:530-533
        May 1965).
    Includes purpose of the Society and membership requirements.
    Yochelson, E. L. "Paleontological Society." Geotimes, vol. 9,
        no. 7:10-12 1965.

PENOLOGISTS

AMERICAN CORRECTIONAL ASSOCIATION (ACA)
    4321 Hartwick Rd., Suite L208, College Park, Md. 20740
    E. Preston Sharp, Ph.D., Executive Director

Membership: The American Correctional Association, founded in
1870 and with a present (1973) membership of 10,000, is an association of individuals and institutions in correctional fields, including
correctional administrators, such as wardens and superintendents;
members of prison and parole boards; and other professional workers
in the field of detention and rehabilitation of delinquents and crim-
inals--psychiatrists, psychologists, sociologists, and parole and probation officers. Any person interested in correctional work is
eligible for membership in the Association.

Code of Ethics: The guide to professional conduct for ACA members is the Association's Declaration of Principles, which was
unanimously adopted by the Centennial Congress of the American
Correctional Association on October 15, 1970. This Declaration--
revising the Declaration of Principles of 1870, a landmark document in the field of correction, that was updated twice (in 1930 and
1960)--was prepared by a specially appointed ACA Committee.
This Committee developed the present Principles from a canvass of
officers and members of ACA, that included the opinions of scholars
and leaders in the field of criminal justice and the prevention of
crime and delinquency.

The "ideals and aspirations" of the Association are set forth in
the 31 principles covering the different aspects of prevention and
control of crime and delinquency, that include treatment of offenders,
organization of correctional agencies and their administration, and
probation and community-based correctional facilities. No procedures for enforcement of the Principles are reported.

Professional Insignia: The emblem of the American Correctional
Association is a pentagonal shield;
with an eagle to the right of the design;
the organization initials, "ACA, " in
the lower left of the shield, and the
date of the organization's founding,
"1870, " at the lower right of the design.   The color of the insignia is
shown variously--black printing and
border, with white eagle and base, on
a light blue background (letterhead,
publications); blue and gold--the official ACA colors--on publications.

Bibliography:
      American Correctional Association.   Declaration of Principles.
            1970.   3 pages. (Reprint from American Journal of Cor-
            rection, November/December 1970.)
      Thirty-one principles give ACA "ideals and aspirations" as
      a guide to corrections practice.
              .   Manual of Correctional Standards.   Revised edition,
            1966. $6.50.
      Institutional and service standards in correction, that will
      form the basis of ACA accrediting, to be undertaken in 1973.
      Chamber of Commerce of the United States.   Marshaling Citi-
            zen Power to Modernize Corrections. 1972.   Pamphlet.
            23 p. $1.
      Mentions (p. 18) the ACA accreditation plan for correctional
      institutions and services, based on their Manual of Correc-
      tional Standards.

"Declaration of Principles of the
American Correctional Association"

One of the many tasks of the Centennial Congress of Correction of the American Correctional Association was the centennial review of the Declaration of Principles of 1870--one of the
greatest documents of all times in the field of corrections. The
Declaration was updated twice: in 1930 and 1960.   The Association
felt that in entering its second century, it was appropriate to formulate a new statement, in the tradition of the document of 1870, but
with the sights set on the years ahead. The President of the
Association, Dr. George Beto, appointed a committee of three to
prepare the draft: Dr. Peter P. Lejins, chairman, Dr. George
G. Killinger, and H. G. Moeller. The Committee canvassed the
membership generally, the past presidents, the Board of Directors,
and the officers of the Association, as well as a selected group of
outstanding scholars and leaders in the field.   The Congress then
held a hearing on the draft thus prepared, and in its business meeting of October 15, 1970, unanimously adopted the Centennial Declaration.

Preamble. The Centennial Congress of Correction, to reaffirm the ideals and aspirations of its membership, to encourage
a more enlightened criminal justice in our society, to promote improved practices in the treatment of adult and juvenile offenders,
and to rededicate its membership to the high purposes stated by its
founding leaders in 1870, does adopt this Centennial Declaration of
Principles.

Principle 1. The prevention and control of crime and delinquency are urgent challenges to society. The growing body of
scientific knowledge, especially in the behavioral sciences, coupled
with the practical wisdom and skill of those professionally engaged
in society's struggle with the problem of crime, provides the sound-
est basis for effective action.

Principle II. The forces for the prevention and control of
crime and delinquency ultimately must find their strength in the constructive qualities of the society itself. Properly functioning basic
institutions--the family, the school and the church, as well as the
economic and political institutions--and a society united in the pursuit of worthwhile goals are the best guarantees against crime and
delinquency.

Principle III. Correction and punishment are the presently
recognized methods of preventing and controlling crime and delinquency. The strengthening and expansion of the correctional
methods should generally be the accepted goal.

Principle IV. In a democracy the success of any public
agency, including that of corrections, depends in the final analysis
on popular acceptance and support. An adequate financial base,

emphasis on the adequacy of personnel, and insistence on an alert and progressive administration is the responsibility of the public and a function of its enlightened concern about crime and delinquency problems. This places on corrections the all-important burden of preparing and disseminating objective information needed for public policy decisions at all jurisdictional levels.

Principle V. The length of the punitive sentence should properly be commensurate with the seriousness of the offense and the extent of the offender's participation. Inequality of sentences for the same or similar crimes is always interpreted as an injustice both by the offender and the society. On the other hand, the length of the correctional treatment given the offender for purposes of rehabilitation depends on the circumstances and characteristics of the particular offender and may have little relationship to the seriousness of the crime committed. In a correctionally oriented system of crime control, statutes providing maximum flexibility in the determination of the appropriate release date can assure the optimal benefits of correctional treatment.

Principle VI. No law, procedure or system of correction should deprive any offender of the hope and possibility of his ultimate return to full, responsible membership in society.

Principle VII. The correctional process has as its aim the reintegration of the offender into society as a law-abiding citizen. In the course of non-institutional treatment the offender continues as a member of the conventional community. In the course of his institutional stay, constructive community contacts should be encouraged and maintained. The success of the correctional process in all its stages can be greatly enhanced by energetic, resourceful and organized citizen participation.

Principle VIII. Corrections, comprising both institutional and community-based programs, should be planned and organized as an integrated system responsible for guiding, controlling, unifying and vitalizing the correctional process.

Principle IX. The variety of treatment methods corresponding to the varying needs of the offenders suggests a diversification of correctional effort, resulting in a system of specialized agencies, institutions and programs. These should be so planned and organized as to meet the differential needs of the offender. The spirit of continued experimentation with new types of programs which show promise of more effective results should be encouraged and supported.

Principle X. The organization and administration of correctional agencies and institutions is a complex area of public administration and management, which deals with one of the most involved of social problems. It is essential that the administration of the correctional agencies meet the highest standards of public service, and that all employees be selected in accordance with the best criteria and serve on the basis of merit and tenure systems.

Principle XI. The special and complex problems in understanding and dealing with criminal and delinquent behavior imply the
need for personnel possessing suitable personality traits and specialized skills and hence the need for special professional education
and training of a high standard, including pre-service and continued
in-service training at all levels. The potential contributions of ex-
offenders as correctional workers should be recognized.

Principle XII. The collection and publication of criminal
statistics designed to provide information on the extent and nature of
criminality and juvenile delinquency and on the various phases of the
correctional process is indispensable for the understanding of crime
and for the planning and evaluation of correctional and preventive
measures.
    Such statistics are necessary and should be developed on
national, state and local levels and should consist of statistics of
the offenses known to the police, arrest statistics, judicial statistics,
probation, institutional and parole statistics, as well as criminal
career records.

Principle XIII. Research and the scientific study of the problems of criminal behavior and of the methods of dealing with it are
essential prerequisites for progress. Through its educational and
research institutions, society should sponsor, finance and carry out
both basic and applied research in this area. The law enforcement
and correctional agencies and institutions should lend their support,
take initiative and engage in appropriate research as an indispensable
part of their effort to improve their performance.

Principle XIV. Correctional agencies and institutions can
best achieve their objectives by providing resources for the complete
study and evaluation of the offender. Decisions determining the
treatment design for the offender should be based on a full investigation of the social and personality factors. These investigations
may be made at different levels, so long as the essential information
is available at the proper step in the decision-making process.

Principle XV. To assure the eventual restoration of the offender as an economically self-sustaining member of the community,
the correctional program must make available to each inmate every
opportunity to raise his educational level, improve his vocational
competence and skills, and provide him with meaningful knowledge
about the world and the society in which he must live.

Principle XVI. Well-organized correctional programs will
actively seek opportunities to collaborate with other public and private
agencies to assure that the offender has access to a wide range of
services which will contribute to his stability in the community.

Principle XVII. The criminal justice system should, insofar
as possible, be relieved of responsibility for the care or treatment
of persons who are charged with offenses which have their origins

in the abuse of alcohol or drugs. Such persons are more appropriately the concern of community health and mental health services.

Principle XVIII. Community-based correctional programs are
essential elements in the continuum of services required to assure
the reintegration of the offender into the society. Probation, parole,
residential treatment centers and other forms of conditional freedom
such as work and study furlough programs provide important and
necessary alternatives to imprisonment.

Principle XIX. Probation is the most efficient and economical method of treatment for a great number of offenders. To enhance the achievement of the full potentialities of probation, mandatory exceptions to the use of probation with respect to specific crimes
or to types of offenders should be eliminated from the statutes.

Principle XX. All offenders should be released from correctional institutions under parole supervision, and parole should be
granted at the earliest date consistent with public safety and the
needs of the individual. Parole decisions should be made by a
professionally competent board. The type and degree of supervision
should fit the needs of the individual offender.

Principle XXI. Community-based correctional facilities, such
as community treatment centers and half-way houses, provide important alternatives to more formally organized institutions and
facilitate access to supportive community services.

Principle XXII. The transition of the offender from institutional life into the community should be facilitated wherever feasible
by measures which permit his participation in normal community
activities such as work and study furlough programs. Participants
should be carefully selected and supervised and their economic exploitation scrupulously avoided.

Principle XXIII. The principles of humanity and human dignity as well as the purposes of rehabilitation require that the offender, while under the jurisdiction of the law enforcement and
correctional agencies, be accorded acceptable standards of decent
living and human dignity.

Principle XXIV. The architecture and construction of penal
and correctional institutions should be functionally related to program
designs. The variety of existing programs, to be further expanded
in the future, indicates the need for similar variety and flexibility of
architectural design and construction. The building standards and
technological advances of the day should be reflected in these structures. The failure of large institutions indicates the desirability of
institutions of moderate size, lending themselves better to fulfillment
of the objectives of a good correctional program.

Principle XXV. New correctional institutions should be

located with ready access to community agencies which provide services, such as mental health centers, and educational training institutions--all of which provide support to correctional programs and contribute to continuing staff development.

Principle XXVI. Except in most unusual circumstances, provision should be made for the separate housing of persons charged with crime and detained for court action and convicted prisoners who are under sentence.

Principle XXVII. Every effort should be made to establish, maintain, and develop local correctional facilities and programs which are designed to meet the needs of short-term offenders or offenders who are soon to be released from long-term imprisonment. Such facilities should work closely with and use the resources of local human service agencies, both public and private.

Principle XXVIII. Some criminal law violators who are found by the courts to be criminally responsible, but who, from the point of view of modern psychiatry and psychology are abnormal, need psychotherapy. Diagnostic and treatment facilities for such offenders should be provided at appropriate stages of the correctional process.

Principle XXIX. Control and management of offenders should be by sound scientific methods, stressing moral values and organized persuasion, rather than primarily dependence upon physical force.

Principle XXX. All employable offenders in correctional institutions should be given the opportunity to engage in productive work, without in any way exploiting the labor of prisoners for financial gain, or unduly interfering with free enterprise. It is imperative that all governmental jurisdictions, industry and labor, give full cooperation to the establishment of productive work programs with a view to imparting acceptable skills, work habits, and attitudes conducive to later gainful employment.

Principle XXXI. Religion represents a rich resource for moral and spiritual regeneration. Specifically trained chaplains, organized religious instruction and counseling, together with adequate facilities for group worship of the inmate's own choice, are essential elements in the program of a correctional institution.

PERSONNEL WORKERS

AMERICAN SOCIETY FOR PERSONNEL ADMINISTRATION (ASPA)
    19 Church St., Berea, Ohio 44107
    L. R. Brice, Executive Vice President

Membership: The American Society for Personnel Administration,
founded in 1948 and with a present (1973) membership of over
11,000, is a "National Organization of Personnel and Industrial
Relations Administrators." In addition to the categories of membership for students and retired personnel administrators, the ASPA
professional membership qualifications for membership are:
> Regular Membership: Qualified persons responsibly engaged
> in human resource management, with three or more years
> of personnel experience or university equivalence.
> Associate Membership: Persons who do not qualify for regu-
> lar membership, but who have a bona-fide interest in per-
> sonnel work and in the purposes of the Society.

Although no voluntary licensing in the form of certification or accreditation is awarded by the Society, plans are now (1973) being
drawn and a program for such licensure should be in effect in the
near future.

Code of Ethics: The guide to professional conduct of ASPA members, is the Society Code of Ethics, developed by the organization
Board of Directors in 1949, and revised in 1971 to its current form.
This Code, which appears each month in the group's journal, Personnel Administrator, is in the form of a pledge, taken by all
members upon admission to membership. The conduct guide sets
forth in eleven general principles the obligations and responsibilities
of ASPA members. Under procedure for enforcement of the Code,
the By-Laws Committee receives complaints of infringements of the
Code, investigates alleged violations, and reports findings to the
Board of Directors, which may expel a member for unprofessional
conduct.

Professional Insignia: The emblem of the American Society for
Personnel Administration is its
official seal--circular in form,
the insignia bears the printed
initials of the organization,
"A.S.P.A.," superimposed on
a global map of the North
American continent; the society name, "American Society
for Personnel Administration,"
is shown in a bordering band.
The colors of the emblem (as
shown on the letterhead) are
gold globe on white ground,
gold Society name and outline
of bordering band; border and
group initials in dark blue.

Bibliography:
> American Society for Per-
> sonnel Administration.
> Code of Ethics. 1971.

This pledge of ethical practice sets forth eleven principles as professional conduct guides.

_____. Membership Brochure.
Includes a brief history and description of ASPA goals, organization, services, and activities.

"Code of Ethics"

In affiliating with THE AMERICAN SOCIETY FOR PERSONNEL ADMINISTRATION, I recognize and accept the responsibility incumbent upon me as a member of the Personnel and Industrial Relations Profession, I pledge myself to observe, practice and maintain the following ethical practices of the profession:

Advance all ethical personnel administration and labor relations concepts, methods and skills that contribute to productivity and profit ability of an enterprise.

Recognize and support the essential authority and responsibility of the management to manage.

Promote acceptance by line management of its primary responsibility for sound personnel administration and labor relations.

Respect and adhere to the principle of the staff and advisory nature of personnel administration.

Effectively and efficiently administer the personnel and labor relations functions and activities.

Periodically evaluate all personnel administration activities, and promptly take the necessary action to maintain an economically efficient operation.

Encourage and participate in continuous research for the development and advancement of new, improved personnel administration principles, methods, skills and practices; making all findings available to others; likewise, keeping abreast of the findings of others.

Demonstrate and persuade others to accept the values of recognizing the development and dignity of the individual human being as one of the essential factors for success in any enterprise and in the American way of life.

Develop and promote a spirit of cooperative teamwork among members of management, owners, employees, and those of the general public directly or indirectly connected with the enterprise.

Accept no remuneration or compensation from persons whose products or services I recommend or use in the performance of my functions and activities.

Never use the Society or its membership for purposes other than those for which they were designed.

INTERNATIONAL PERSONNEL MANAGEMENT ASSOCIATION (IPMA)
    1313 E. 60th St., Chicago, Illinois 60637
    Eugene F. Berrodin, Executive Director

Membership: The International Personnel Management Association
came into being on January 1, 1973 by consolidation of the Society
for Personnel Administration (founded in 1937 in Washington, D.C.)
and the Public Personnel Association (founded in 1906 in Chicago).
It is an organization for agencies and individuals in the public personnel field, in federal, state, provincial and local governments
throughout the United States, Canada, and elsewhere around the
world. Requirements for Individual Membership (Bylaws, Article
3) make eligible for such membership:
    "Any person who is either:
1. An official or staff member of a public personnel agency;
   or
2. Engaged in personnel work in a public agency; or
3. Engaged in teaching public personnel administration as a
   faculty member of a college or university; or
4. Providing consulting services in the field of public personnel administration; or
5. Employed by management in personnel work in private
   enterprise. "

Code of Ethics: The IPMA Code of Ethics is currently (1973) under
revision, but adheres mainly to the former Public Personnel Association's Statement of Principles for Members, which sets forth conduct guides as a credo and pledge. No procedures for enforcement
of the ethical guide are reported.

Professional Insignia: The emblem of the Association is its logo-
type--a globe, with the initials of the group, "IPMA," in a band
comprising the third lower quarter of the design; the group name,
"International Personnel Management Association," is printed around
the emblem in an unbanded
border. The colors of the
emblem are shown variously
--blue and gold (membership
certificate); white on gold,
with monogram in brown (letterhead); black and white (logotype).

Bibliography:
    International Personnel
        Management Associa-
        tion. Bylaws. Jan-
        uary 1, 1973.
    Includes membership
    requirements.
    _____. IPMA: The
    Agency Membership

Program. Pamphlet.
Association purposes, brief history, services.

"Statement of Principles for Members"

I believe in a system of responsible representative government. As a part of such a government, I will do everything within my power to uphold, defend, and protect it.

I believe that my stewardship in government is one of public trust. I will endeavor to perform my duties in a manner to bring honor and credit to my government, and in accordance with the highest moral and ethical standards.

I will ever be mindful of this public trust in the use of property and funds under my care, and by efficient operation and diligent economy I will protect and conserve them. I am committed to uphold the public interest as opposed to personal, individual, private, or group interest.

I believe that government should be served by the best--in skills and competence, in attitude and personal qualifications, and in loyalty.

I believe in competitive selection under a merit system.

I believe that public personnel practitioners, as a part of public management, have an obligation to the citizens, to the people's elected representatives, and to employees, and that a proper administration of a sound competitive merit system fulfills these obligations.

As a part of government management, I respect the operating needs and the ultimate responsibility of government. I recognize my responsibility to accept changes in government policies so that at all times the expressed will of the people is dominant.

I believe good personnel administration requires that I base my decisions and behavior on sound principles, on objective analysis, and on the recognized methods of the merit system.

I recognize my obligation to provide uniformity of treatment to all, to act with objectivity and impartiality, and to do nothing which would impair this standard.

I believe that I am obliged continually to perfect my knowledge of the disciplines of public administration and my skill in applying them.

I shall always conduct myself in accordance with these beliefs, commitments, and obligations.

PHARMACISTS

AMERICAN PHARMACEUTICAL ASSOCIATION (APhA)
    2215 Constitution Ave., N.W., Washington, D.C. 20037
    William S. Apple, Ph.D., Executive Director

Membership: The American Pharmaceutical Association, national professional association of pharmacists, was founded in 1852 and has a present (1973) membership of approximately 50,000. Active Members of the organization are required to be "Pharmacists"--defined by the APhA as individuals who hold a "license to practice pharmacy in the United States" or who hold earned degrees in pharmacy qualifying them for such licensure (Bylaws, Chapter I, Article II, Section A). Specialty interests in pharmacy are represented in Academies and Sections of the Association, and in national specialty affiliates, such as the American Society of Hospital Pharmacies, and the American College of Apothecaries.

Code of Ethics: The guide to professional conduct for association members is the APhA Code of Ethics, developed by a committee in the year of the group's founding--1852--and most recently revised, upon House of Delegate approval, in August 1969. This Code realizes an objective of the Association:

> "To develop, maintain, and enforce a Code of Ethics which will assure to the public the highest type of pharmaceutical services, safeguard the professional relations between medical practitioners, pharmacists, and patients, and develop interprofessional relations which will tend to uplift the profession scientifically, spiritually, and morally" (Constitution, Article II, Section f).

The Code, "established to guide the pharmacist in his relationship with patients, fellow practitioners, other health professionals, and the public" (Code of Ethics), consists of nine principles of professional conduct for pharmacists.

The APhA Judicial Board interprets and enforces this Code, following established procedures of receipt of written complaint of code violation, investigation, hearing, and appeal (Bylaws, Chapter VII). Discipline of a member for unprofessional conduct may include reprimand, suspension or expulsion from the Association (Bylaws, Chapter I, Article XIV). The Judicial Board--upon the written question on professional conduct by any member--renders "Interpretive Statements" of the principles of the Code of Ethics, and "Advisory Opinions." These are published in the official monthly magazine of the Association, Journal of the American Pharmaceutical Association, and in the Annual Report of the APhA Judicial Board at the Annual Meeting.

Professional Insignia: The emblem of the American Pharmaceutical Association is its official seal--a circular design, bearing in the

American Pharmaceutical Association

upper portion a shield, with a centered "Bowl of Hygeia" (symbol
of pharmacy) within the coils of an entwined serpent (symbol of
healing); the organization name, "American Pharmaceutical Association," is given in the lower section of the emblem. The official
color of the insignia is "pharmacy green" (a greyed yellow-green)
on white; it is also shown in black on white (publication, logotype);
and as an embossed design on white (letterhead). The design,
first developed when the organization was founded in 1852, was
revised by an individual artist in 1964 to produce the present emblem, approved by the Board of Trustees.

The insignia is used only on or by Association publications and
projects. It is also available for pharmacy members' display as a
decal or as a cloth sleeve emblem on pharmacists' jackets, with the
word, "Pharmacist," shown in white. The emblem may also be
worn by members as a sterling silver pin--lapel pin or tie tac--with
the Bowl of Hygeia in pharmacy green on the APhA shield in silver
over a pearl background, with the Association's name in raised lettering.

Other Identification of Professional Status: Another professional
insignia is pharmacy's Coat of Arms, developed by Dr. Robert A.
Hardt in 1957. In this emblem are the traditional symbols of pharmacy "employed by pharmacists since the Middle Ages." The shield
bears in its four quarters--from upper left to lower left:
> Mortar and Pestle--"most common and universally accepted
> symbol of Pharmacy";
> ℞   --the prescription symbol, "signifying 'Recipe: Take
> Thou' ";
> --the alchemical symbol signifying "to compound";
> --"Bowl of Hygeia," the symbol for pharmacy, used by
> "many pharmaceutical associations and most pharmaceutical
> journals in Europe and South America."

The crest--a closed helmet, facing left in profile, denotes "wisdom

and surety in defense," a person
of some importance (a member
of the peerage: the professional pharmacist); decorative
scarves appear at each side of
the crest. The supporters at
either side of the shield are
facing horses, designating
"medicinal contribution of hor-
mones and antitoxins from the
horse."

The group motto, in the
scroll at the bottom of the design, is "Secundum Artem"
("According to the Art" of Pharmacy)--"was once commonly
used on prescriptions." Official

colors of the Coat of Arms are black on white ground; with two additional colors in the shield--white figures on red ground in upper left
and lower right quadrant; green figures on white ground in upper
right and lower left quadrant.

Bibliography:
     American Pharmaceutical Association.   Background Information.
          Single page.
     Brief statement of APhA purpose, objectives, services.
          _____ .   Code of Ethics. August 1969. 1 page.
     Conduct guide for professional pharmacist in relationship
     with patients, colleagues, other health professionals, and
     the public.
          _____ .   Constitution and Bylaws. September 1971. 57 pages.
     APhA membership requirements; procedures for enforcement
     of the Code of Ethics.
     Hardt, Robert A., George B. Griffenhagen and Norman Vineis.
          History and Significance of Pharmacy's New Coat of Arms.
          1 page.
     Sources, symbolism and description of the Coat of Arms--
     shield, crest, supporters, and motto.
     Steib, Ernst W. "Symbols of Pharmacy." Journal of the Ameri-
          can Pharmaceutical Association. NS 2:206-209 April 1962.
     Traditional symbols of pharmacy pictured and described, in-
     cluding Mortar and Pestle, Show Globe, Prescription and other
     alchemical symbols; Bowl of Hygeia; The Gaper; The Sala-
     mander, Present Coat of Arms of APhA described.   Bibli-
     ography of 13 publications.

"Code of Ethics"

Preamble.   These principles of professional conduct for
pharmacists are established to guide the pharmacist in his relationship with patients, fellow practitioners, other health professionals
and the public.

Section 1.   A pharmacist should hold the health and safety
of patients to be of first consideration; he should render to each
patient the full measure of his ability as an essential health practitioner.

Section 2.   A pharmacist should never knowingly condone the
dispensing, promoting or distributing of drugs or medical devices,
or assist therein, which are not of good quality, which do not meet
standards required by law or which lack therapeutic value for the
patient.

Section 3.   A pharmacist should always strive to perfect
and enlarge his professional knowledge.   He should utilize and make
available this knowledge as may be required in accordance with his
best professional judgment.

Section 4.   A pharmacist has the duty to observe the law, to
uphold the dignity and honor of the profession, and to accept its
ethical principles.   He should not engage in any activity that will

bring discredit to the profession and should expose, without fear or favor, illegal or unethical conduct in the profession.

Section 5. A pharmacist should seek at all times only fair and reasonable remuneration for his services. He should never agree to, or participate in transactions with practitioners of other health professions or any other person under which fees are divided or which may cause financial or other exploitation in connection with the rendering of his professional services.

Section 6. A pharmacist should respect the confidential and personal nature of his professional records; except where the best interest of the patient requires or the law demands, he should not disclose such information to anyone without proper patient authorization.

Section 7. A pharmacist should not agree to practice under terms or conditions which tend to interfere with or impair the proper exercise of his professional judgment and skill, which tend to cause a deterioration of the quality of his service or which require him to consent to unethical conduct.

Section 8. A pharmacist should not solicit professional practice by means of advertising or by methods inconsistent with his opportunity to advance his professional reputation through service to patients and to society.

Section 9. A pharmacist should associate with organizations having for their objective the betterment of the profession of pharmacy; he should contribute of his time and funds to carry on the work of these organizations.

PHARMACOLOGISTS

AMERICAN SOCIETY FOR PHARMACOLOGY AND EXPERIMENTAL
    THERAPEUTICS, INC. (ASPET)
    9650 Rockville Pike, Bethesda, Md. 20014
    Ellsworth B. Cook, Ph. D., Executive Officer

Membership: The American Society for Pharmacology and Experimental Therapeutics, founded in 1908 and with a present (1973) membership of approximately 2000, is a professional organization of pharmacologists--engaged in investigating the effects of chemicals on living tissues. "Regular Members" of the Society are nominated for membership by two members as "qualified investigators," resident in the U. S. A., Canada, or Mexico, who have "conducted and published meritorious original investigation in pharmacology" (By-laws, Article II, Section 1). A category of "Affiliate Member" is open to "Persons who have contributed to the profession or science of pharmacology but who do not meet the requirements for regular membership (meritorious and independent research in pharmacology)."

<u>Code of Ethics</u>: No formalized Code of Ethics has been issued by
the Society. On rare occasions when the matter of ethical behavior
of a member has been raised (once in the last ten years), an ad
hoc committee, composed of senior members of the Society, was
convened to study the problem, and to make recommendations to
the Council for appropriate disciplinary action (<u>Bylaws,</u> Article II,
Section 3).

<u>Professional Insignia</u>: The emblem of the ASPET is its official seal
(pictured and described in the
organization's <u>Constitution,</u>
Article III)--circular in form,
the design shows the centered
legend, "Corporate 1933 Seal
Maryland"; in a bordering
band, marked by an inner
circle of dots and an outer
circle of short uniformly
slanted parallel marks, is the
association name, "The American Society for Pharmacology
and Experimental Therapeutics,
Inc." The color of this seal
is black on white.

<u>Bibliography</u>:
     American Society for
          Pharmacology and Experimental Therapeutics. <u>Constitu-</u>
          <u>tion.</u> April 17, 1969; <u>Bylaws</u>, July 1972.
          Includes membership requirements; pictures and describes
          emblem (corporate seal).

PHOTOGRAMMETRISTS

AMERICAN SOCIETY OF PHOTOGRAMMETRY (ASP)
     105 N. Virginia Ave., Falls Church, Va. 22036
     Lawrence P. Jacobs, B/Gen, USA (Ret), Executive Director

<u>Membership</u>: The American Society of Photogrammetry, founded
in 1934 and with a present (1973) membership of 6000, is a professional association of persons in industry, government, and the
educational community engaged in the measurement and interpretation of photographs. It includes such fields of science and technology
as aerial mapping, photogrammetric surveys, remote sensing, and
photographic interpretation. Any person interested in photogrammetry
and photographic interpretation is eligible for membership. Categories of membership are regular, student, honorary, and emeritus

(life). "Honorary Members" are selected for outstanding contributions to the field of photogrammetry.

Code of Ethics: The guide to professional conduct for photogrammetrists is in the process of being prepared.

Professional Insignia: The ASP emblem is the organization's official seal--a circular design, symbolizing the subject matter and techniques of photogrammetry; a centered globe shows the North and South American continents; the name of the organization, "American Society of Photogrammetry," is given in a bordering band around the globe; a crest, surmounting the globe, consists of a centered date of the group's founding, "1934," between two wings extending beyond the circular insignia by about half its diameter. The color of the emblem (letterhead) is turquoise blue on white ground.

PHOTOGRAPHERS

PROFESSIONAL PHOTOGRAPHERS OF AMERICA (PP of A)
        1090 Executive Way, Oak Leaf Commons,
        Des Plaines, Illinois 60018
        Frederick Quellmalz, Executive Vice President

Membership: The Professional Photographers of America, founded in 1880 and with a present (1973) membership of 13,500, is an association of photographers in all branches of that art--including individuals and firms. "Active Individual Members" qualify for membership by deriving the major portion of their earned income from photography. Various applications of photography are represented in the three divisions of the PP of A:
        Portraits;
        Commercial;
        Industrial;
and by the 44 specialty classification listings for the Membership Directory, including Aerial Photography and Aerial Mapping; and photographic specialization in Animals, Architecture, Biology, Criminal, Legal, Public Relations, Conventions, Theatrical; and in technical phases of photography, such as Direct Color and Processing,

Enlargements, Photo Engraving, Photostats, Photo Murals, and
Photo Finishing.

The Association recognizes "exceptional ability in photography
and exceptional services to the profession" or to the Association
"by awarding of Degrees to individual members" (Bylaws, Article
XIII). These awards--diploma, insignia, and professional desig-
nation--are:

> Honorary Master of Photography Degree (Hon. M. Photog.)--
> awarded to individuals who have rendered exceptional ser-
> vice to the photographic profession or to the PP of A;
> Master of Photography Degree (M. Photog.)--awarded to
> Association members of three or more years, who have
> 25 or more Merits, at least 13 of which must have been
> Exhibition Merits;
> Photographic Craftsman Degree (Cr. Photog.)--awarded to
> Association members of three or more years, who have
> 25 or more Achievement Merits, at least 13 of which must
> have been made for demonstrations or lectures on approved
> programs;
> Master of Photography and Photographic Craftsman (M. Pho-
> tog. Cr.)--combination of the immediately preceding two
> degrees, awarded for 50 or more merits, including at least
> 13 Exhibition Merits and at least 25 Achievement Merits,
> of which 13 have been for demonstrations or lectures.

The color of the neck ribbons holding the insignia for the various degrees is distinctive:

> Honorary Master of Photography--purple;
> Master of Photography--gold;
> Honorary Master of Photography and Master of Photography,
> or Photographic Craftsman--purple and gold;
> Master of Photography and Photographic Craftsman--blue and
> gold;
> Honorary Master of Photography, Master of Photography, and
> Photographic Craftsman--purple and gold ribbon on right
> side of neck, blue and gold ribbon on left.

A bar on the neck ribbon is used to indicate each additional 25 merits.

Code of Ethics: The professional guide, subscribed to by each member of the Professional Photographers of America, upon admission
to membership, is the Code of Ethics. This Code, developed by a
Committee of the National Council was adopted in 1915, and has been
revised a number of times since that date by the National Council, in
order to keep the professional guide up to date. The Code--in the
form of a pledge--sets forth seven obligations and responsibilities of
professional photographers. Interpretation and enforcement of the
Code is assigned to the Committee on Ethics and Standards, which--
after investigation of written complaint of a member's unethical con-
duct--recommends disciplinary action to the PP of A Council, through
the Board of Directors.

Other Guides to Professional Conduct: An additional conduct guide,
the Code of Ethics for Wedding Photography, was adopted by the
Professional Photographers of America in 1967, and is approved by
all major American religious denominations:
     National Council of Churches of Christ,
     Family Life Bureau of the National Catholic Welfare Con-
       ference, and
     Association of Boards of Rabbis.
This professional guide is directed "to assure brides, their families,
and the clergy of the highest professional standards" in bridal por-
traits, and "candid" and informal pictures of the wedding; and "to
help preserve the dignity of the wedding ceremony."

Professional Insignia: The emblem of the Professional Photographers

of America is its official seal--
which was developed by a Committee of the Board of Directors,
adopted about 1930, and revised
in 1969. The insignia is oval
in shape, shows a professional
camera with expanded lens in
rays of light; the name of the
organization, "Professional
Photographers of America,"
appears as an unbanded border.
Color of the emblem is shown
variously--black on white, or
brown on white (publications);
black and gold with white light
rays (decal); black camera and
lettering, gold rays of light on
red and white vertically striped
background (member card for
studio display).   The emblem is
available for wear by Active
and Life Members as a lapel
button.

Other Identification of Professional Status: As described above under
"Membership," special degrees are awarded by the Association to
qualified members to indicate professional competence through professional designation and emblem:
     Honorary Master of Photography--Hon. M. Photog.,
     Master of Photography--M. Photog.,
     Photographic Craftsman--Cr. Photog.,
     Master of Photography and Photographic Craftsman--M.
      Photog. Cr.

Bibliography:
     Professional Photographers of America.   Bylaws and Operating
       Rules and Procedures.   13 pages.   Pamphlet.
     Includes Code of Ethics; procedures for enforcement of Code;

membership qualifications; degrees awarded, with qualifications, special professional designations, and merit awards. Detailed index.

_____. Code of Ethics. 1 page.
Pledge of members, subscribed to upon admission to PP of A, with obligations and responsibilities of professional photographers.

_____. Code of Ethics for Wedding Photography. 1967.
Folder.
Professional responsibilities; accepted by major American religious denominations.

"Code of Ethics"

I, having been accepted into membership in the Professional Photographers of America, Inc., do hereby subscribe without reservation to this Code of Ethics, and do solemnly agree that:

1. I will endeavor to maintain a dignity of manner in my behavior, in the presentation of my photography and photographic services, in my appearance and that of my studio or place of business, and in all other forms of public contact.
2. I will observe the highest standard of honesty in all my transactions, avoiding the use of false, confusing, inaccurate and misleading terms, descriptions and claims.
3. I will at all times endeavor to produce photographs of a quality equal or superior to the samples I display, to apply my best efforts towards providing the best possible photographic services and to play my part in raising the general standard of photographic craftsmanship.
4. I will show a friendly spirit of cooperation to my fellow professional photographers and assist them whenever possible should they be in trouble or difficulty.
5. I will at all times avoid the use of unfair competitive practices as determined by any court of competent jurisdiction, the Federal anti-trust laws and related statutes.
6. I will assist my fellow photographers and share my knowledge with them and encourage them individually and collectively to achieve and maintain the highest standards of quality.
7. I will recognize the authority of this Association in all matters relating to the interpretation of this Code in accordance with the statutes of the United States and the various states and the decisions of courts and governmental agencies of competent jurisdiction.

In witness whereof I hereunto append my signature this _____ day of
_____ 19__.

                                              studio _____
                              signature _____   title

"Code of Ethics for Wedding Photography"

As a member of the Professional Photographers of America, Inc., I do hereby solemnly promise that:

I shall contact officiating clergymen to inform myself fully of prevailing customs and regulations in regard to taking photographs before, during and after the wedding ceremony.

I shall abide at all times by the rules established by each particular House of Worship.

I shall work in a dignified, professional and unobtrusive manner while recording this sacred and memorable ceremony.

I shall at no time, leave empty cartons, flash bulbs, or film pack tops on church property.

PHYSICAL THERAPISTS

AMERICAN PHYSICAL THERAPY ASSOCIATION (APTA)
1156 15th St., N.W., Washington, D.C. 20005
Royce P. Noldand, Executive Director

Membership: The American Physical Therapy Association, founded in 1921 and with a present (1973) membership of approximately 17,000 is the professional association of physical therapists. "Active Membership" in APTA requires graduation from a program approved by APTA and the Council on Medical Education of the American Medical Association. Similarly qualified foreign nationals, who are members of an organization belonging to the World Confederation for Physical Therapy, are also eligible for "Active Membership." The Members--who automatically become members of the state association where they practice--work in various settings, and their special interests are reflected in the six sections of the Association:

Education,   Self-Employed,
Public Health,   Administration,
Research,   State Licensure Boards.

Code of Ethics: The Code of Ethics of the Association, adopted in 1968 and amended in 1969, consists of ten principles setting forth the obligations and responsibilities of physical therapists. The Judicial Committee acts in monitoring, interpreting, and revising the Code, and their interpretations, opinions, decisions, and counsel have been formulated in a Guide for Professional Conduct, grouped in four sections:

1. Referral Relationships;
2. Professional Practice;
3. Compensation for Services;
4. Association Relationships.

Complaints of violations of these ethical standards may be made in writing either to a member's chapter or to the Judicial Committee, and a member may be disciplined for unethical action--following prescribed precedures--by expulsion from membership, or other action (<u>Bylaws</u>, Article IV, Section 5).

<u>Professional Insignia</u>:   The emblem of APTA is its official seal--a triangular design, with the caduceus between the initials, "PT, " in a centered inner triangle, and the association name, "American Physical Therapy Association, " spaced in the three sides of the bordering band. The color of the emblem is shown variously--black on white, or chartreuse on black, or dark blue on light blue (publications); gold on white (frameable <u>Code of Ethics</u>).   The insignia is available as membership emblem to members for their wear or display as shoulder patch, pin, lapel tack, tie bar or clip, and paper weight.

Bibliography:
    American Physical Therapy Association.   <u>American Physical</u>
            <u>Therapy Association</u>.   Folder.
    Informational brochure, including APTA membership require-
    ments, organization and activities.
            ____.   <u>Bylaws</u>.   1970 (Reprint from <u>Journal of the Ameri-</u>
            <u>can Physical Therapy Association</u>   50:1609-1618 November
            1970).
    Gives membership requirements; disciplinary action for vio-
    lations of the Code of Ethics.
            ____.   <u>Code of Ethics</u>.   July 1969.
    Obligations and responsibilities of physical therapists in ten
    principles of conduct.
            ____.   Judicial Committee.   <u>Guide for Professional Conduct</u>.
            September 1968.   4 pages.   Pamphlet.
    The Judicial Committee's interpretations, opinions, decisions,
    and counsel, based on the Code of Ethics.

<u>"Code of Ethics"</u>

        The physical therapist should respect the human dignity of each individual with whom he is associated in his profession, being guided at all times by his concern for the welfare of the patient and by his responsibilities to his associates and colleagues.
        The physical therapist should accept and seek full responsibility for the exercise of judgment within the area of his competence and should require referral by a physician or dentist in providing direct patient services.
        The physical therapist should comply with existing laws

governing the practice of physical therapy and should maintain acceptable standards of professional practice.

The physical therapist should respect the confidentiality of all privileged information and should voluntarily share such information only as it serves the welfare of the patient.

The physical therapist should accept responsibility for services to patients referred to him and is obligated to provide continuing supervision when any portion of the service is delegated to supportive personnel.   He should not delegate to a less qualified person any service which requires the skill and judgment of the physical therapist.

The physical therapist should not solicit patients, should avoid the use of advertisement or any form of self-aggrandizement, and should not seek to obtain more than just and professionally appropriate remuneration for his service.

The physical therapist should not permit his name to be used in connection with advertisement of products, and should not dispense or supply physical therapy equipment unless it is in the best interest of the patient.

The physical therapist should assume responsibility for the interpretation of his profession to all segments of society so that his services may be appropriately and effectively employed in meeting current health needs and to assure the future growth of the profession.

The physical therapist should accept responsibility for exposing incompetence and illegal or unethical conduct to the appropriate authority.

The physical therapist should give his loyalty and support to the American Physical Therapy Association in its efforts to attain its objectives.

PHYSICIANS

AMERICAN MEDICAL ASSOCIATION (AMA)
    535 N. Dearborn St., Chicago, Ill. 60610
    Ernest B. Howard, M.D., Executive Vice President

Membership: The American Medical Association, founded in 1847 and with a present (1973) membership of over 200,000, is a professional association of medical doctors, who are members in good standing of the 54 affiliated state, commonwealth, and territorial medical organizations.   The variety of interests of physician members of the AMA is shown in the 23 specialty sections of the Association, whose members subscribe to the ethical code of the American Medical Association, including such medical specialty groups as American Geriatrics Society, American Association of Ophthalmology, and American Proctologic Society.

Code of Ethics: "One of the paramount reasons for founding the
AMA was to develop an accepted code of ethical conduct for physicians.
The present AMA Principles of Ethics have been evolved through the
years by action of the House of Delegates, " the governing body of
the Association. "These Principles, which are 'not laws, but standards by which a physician may determine the propriety of his conduct
in his relationship with patients, with colleagues, with members of
allied professions and with the public, ' have been set down primarily
for the good of the public. They also serve as an inspiration to the
physician to remain true to his oath. "

       The Principles of Medical Ethics are augmented by the interpre-
tations of the AMA Judicial Council, often referred to as "medicine's Supreme Court. " These interpretations are published in the
weekly American Medical News, and are compiled from time to
time in the Opinions and Reports of the Judicial Council (AMA.   The
American Medical Association, p. 19-20).

       The Principles consist of ten numbered sections, each setting
forth a standard of medical ethics. These ethical guides are enforced by the county medical associations, affiliated with the state
medical associations which form the AMA federation.   The local
medical association receives complaints of alleged unprofessional
conduct, and--after investigation and appeal by the physician whose
conduct has allegedly violated the Principles--may reprimand, suspend, or expel a member.

Other Guides to Professional Conduct: Several other guides to the
physician's professional behavior are recognized by the AMA.   These
are:
       Oath of Hippocrates--The traditional pledge of service taken
              by doctors of medicine since the time of Hippocrates
              (famous physician of Greece in the fifth century B. C.,
              known as the "Father of Medicine") upon entering the
              medical profession.   Today--if taken at all--the oath is
              administered at the graduation ceremony of a medical
              school.
       Daily Prayer of Maimonides--a pledge of service and a guide
              to high ideals in healing--attributed to Maimonides, twelfth
              century physician to the Sultan of Egypt.

Professional Insignia: The emblem
of the American Medical Association is its seal--circular in design,
with a centered staff of Aesculapius
(Son of Apollo and God of Medicine)
--a clubbed staff with a single
coiled serpent--a traditional symbol of healing; the society's initials, "AMA, " appear at the top of
a bordering band, and the organization's name, "American Medical

Association," is shown around the lower portion of the band. The color of this insignia is shown variously--dark green on white (letterhead); black on white, or black on turquoise (publications).

Other Identification of Professional Status: The wand of Mercury (a god known to the Greeks as Hermes) is also used as an emblem by physicians to indicate their profession. This wand is available as an AMA automobile emblem (the "MD Caduceus"), where it is shown in the more conventional form of a winged staff with two entwined serpents. This symbol--widely known as identifying physicians and as the emblem of medicine--is also (since 1902) the insignia of the United States Army Medical Corps.

Bibliography:
    American Medical Association. The American Medical Association. 1972. 29 pages. Pamphlet.
        Description includes AMA membership requirements, organization, purpose, and enforcement procedure for code of ethics. Pictures insignia.
           . Daily Prayer of Maimonides. 1 page.
    Medical ideals of a famous 12th century physician.
           . Hippocratic Oath. 1 page.
    Traditional oath taken by physicians since the 5th century B.C., pledging high standards of service.
           . Principles of Medical Ethics. 1 page.
    Ten standards providing guide to professional conduct for physicians.
           . Judicial Council. Opinions and Reports. $1.
    Interpretations of the Principles of Medical Ethics, published in the weekly American Medical News; they are abstracted and annotated to the Principles and published at irregular intervals as a separate pamphlet.

"Principles of Medical Ethics"

Preamble: These principles are intended to aid physicians individually and collectively in maintaining a high level of ethical conduct. They are not laws but standards by which a physician may determine the propriety of his conduct in his relationship with patients, with colleagues, with members of allied professions, and with the public.

Section 1. The principal objective of the medical profession is to render service to humanity with full respect for the dignity of man. Physicians should merit the confidence of patients entrusted to their care, rendering to each a full measure of service and devotion.

Section 2. Physicians should strive continually to improve medical knowledge and skill, and should make available to their patients and colleagues the benefits of their professional attainments.

Section 3. A physician should practice a method of healing founded on a scientific basic; and he should not voluntarily associate professionally with anyone who violates this principle.

Section 4. The medical profession should safeguard the public and itself against physicians deficient in moral character or professional competence. Physicians should observe all laws, uphold the dignity and honor of the profession and accept its self-imposed disciplines. They should expose, without hesitation, illegal or unethical conduct of fellow members of the profession.

Section 5. A physician may choose whom he will serve. In an emergency, however, he should render service to the best of his ability. Having undertaken the care of a patient, he may not neglect him; and unless he has been discharged he may discontinue his services only after giving adequate notice. He should not solicit patients.

Section 6. A physician should not dispose of his services under terms or conditions which tend to interfere with or impair the free and complete exercise of his medical judgment and skill or tend to cause a deterioration of the quality of medical care.

Section 7. In the practice of medicine a physician should limit the source of his professional income to medical services actually rendered by him, or under his supervision, to his patients. His fee should be commensurate with the services rendered and the patient's ability to pay. He should neither pay nor receive a commission for referral of patients. Drugs, remedies or appliances may be dispensed or supplied by the physician provided it is in the best interests of the patient.

Section 8. A physician should seek consultation upon request; in doubtful or difficult cases; or whenever it appears that the quality of medical service may be enhanced thereby.

Section 9. A physician may not reveal the confidences entrusted to him in the course of medical attendance, or the deficiencies he may observe in the character of patients, unless he is required to do so by law or unless it becomes necessary in order to protect the welfare of the individual or of the community.

Section 10. The honored ideals of the medical profession imply that the responsibilities of the physician extend not only to the individual, but also to society where these responsibilities deserve his interest and participation in activities which have the purpose of improving both the health and the well-being of the individual and the community.

"Oath of Hippocrates"

I swear by Apollo, the Physician, and Aesculapius and health

and all-heal and all the Gods and Goddesses that, according to my
ability and judgment, I will keep this oath and stipulation:

To reckon him who taught me this art equally dear to me
as my parents, to share my substance with him and relieve his
necessities if required: to regard his offspring as on the same
footing with my own brothers, and to teach them this art if they
should wish to learn it, without fee or stipulation, and that by precept, lecture and every other mode of instruction, I will impart a
knowledge of the art to my own sons and to those of my teachers,
and to disciples bound by a stipulation and oath, according to the
law of medicine, but to none others.

I will follow that method of treatment which, according to my
ability and judgment, I consider for the benefit of my patients, and
abstain from whatever is deleterious and mischievous. I will give
no deadly medicine to anyone if asked, nor suggest any such counsel;
furthermore, I will not give to a woman an instrument to produce
abortion.

With Purity and with Holiness I will pass my life and practice my art. I will not cut a person who is suffering with a stone,
but will leave this to be done by practitioners of this work. Into
whatever houses I enter I will go into them for the benefit of the
sick and will abstain from every voluntary act of mischief and corruption; and further from the seduction of females or males, bond
or free.

Whatever, in connection with my professional practice, or
not in connection with it, I may see or hear in the lives of men
which ought not to be spoken abroad I will not divulge, as reckoning
that all such should be kept secret.

While I continue to keep this oath unviolated may it be granted
to me to enjoy life and the practice of the art, respected by all men
at all times but should I trespass and violate this oath, may the
reverse be my lot.

"Daily Prayer of Maimonides"

Almighty God, You have created the human body with infinite
wisdom. In Your Eternal Providence You have chosen me to watch
over the life and health of your creatures. I am now about to apply
myself to the duties of my profession. Support me in these great
labors that you may benefit mankind for without Your help not even
the least thing will succeed.

Inspire me with love for my art and for Your creatures.
Do not allow thirst for profit, ambition for renown and admiration
to interfere with my profession. For these are the enemies of
truth and can lead me astray in the great task of attending to the

welfare of Your creatures. Preserve the strength of my body and
soul that they may be ever ready to help rich and poor, good and
bad, enemy as well as friend. In the sufferer let me see only the
human being.

Enlighten my mind that it may recognize what presents itself
and that it may comprehend what is absent or hidden. Let it not
fail to see what is visible but do not permit it to arrogate to itself
the power to see what cannot be seen for delicate and indefinite are
the bounds of the great art of caring for the lives and health of
Your creatures. May no strange thoughts divert my attention at
the bedside of the sick or disturb my mind in its silent labors.

Grant that my patients may have confidence in me and my
art and follow my directions and my counsel. When those who are
wiser than I wish to instruct me, let my soul gratefully follow their
guidance for vast is the extent of our art. Imbue my soul with
gentleness and calmness. Let me be contented in everything except
in the great science of my profession. Never allow the thought to
arise in me that I have attained to sufficient knowledge but vouchsafe
to give me the strength and the ambition to extend my knowledge.
The art is great, but the mind of man is ever expanding.

Almighty God You have chosen me in Your mercy to watch
over the life and death of Your creatures. Support me in Your
great tasks so that it will benefit mankind, for without Your help
not even the least thing will succeed.

THE WORLD MEDICAL ASSOCIATION (WMA)
[L'Association Medicale Mondiale (AMM)]
[La Asociación Medica Mundial (AMM)]
   10 Columbus Circle, New York, N.Y. 10019
   Alberto Z. Romualdez, M.D., Secretary General
   Margaret L. Natwick, Executive Secretary

Membership: The World Medical Association, founded in 1947 and
with a present (1973) membership of 60 national medical associations,
is a federation of the national professional associations of medical
doctors in 60 countries throughout the world. There are over
700,000 physicians in the component national associations. The
WMA purpose is "to unite the profession throughout the world in a
single brotherhood."

Code of Ethics: The International Code of Medical Ethics, adopted
by the Third General Assembly of the World Medical Association in
October 1949, is a statement of principles providing a guide to
professional action for physicians. These guides are grouped under
three headings:

Duties of Doctors in General;
Duties of Doctors to the Sick;
Duties of Doctors to Each Other.
In addition to an English language text, the Code is available in the
two other official languages of WMA--French and Spanish. The Code
is "under review for updating with relation to advances in medical
science and other codes adopted by the WMA in the interim"--of
time since the date of adoption, 1949.

Other Guides to Professional Conduct: Several other Declarations
have been adopted by the Association as guides and standards.   The
Declaration of Geneva, adopted by the General Assembly of WMA at
Geneva, Switzerland in September 1948 (amended in 1968), is "a
modern restatement of the Oath of Hippocrates, " prepared as a vow
to be administered at the time a physician is admitted as a member
of the medical profession.   In some countries this pledge is taken
at the time of graduation from medical school, and in other countries
it is taken at the time of licensure as a physician.   The physician
takes an oath--in ten paragraph statements--to consecrate his life
to the service of humanity, and to carry on his profession with the
highest standards, including relations with patients and colleagues.
This Declaration--as is the Code of Ethics--is under review by the
WMA for possible revision.

Other WMA Declarations providing standards and guides are:
    Declaration of Helsinki--1964:   Guides for Doctors in Clinical
        Research;
    Declaration of Sidney--1968:   Statement on the Determination
        of the Time of Death;
    Declaration of Oslo--1970:   Statement on Therapeutic Abor-
        tion.

Professional Insignia: The World Medical Association emblem was
adopted by the Third World Medical Assembly in 1949.   The final

design--decided upon by the WMA
Council and incorporating features suggested by a number of WMA member
associations--consists of a globe on
which is superimposed the ancient insignia of medicine, a serpent entwined
on a forked stick; around the periphery,
of the globe at the top appears the
name of the WMA in Latin--"Societas
Mundi Medica"; and at the bottom is
the date of the Association's founding,
in Roman numerals--"A. D. MCMXLVII. "
The color of the emblem is blue on
white (letterhead, publication); black
on white (publication).   As a separate seal, the emblem background
is blue, the continents are white, and the caduceus and the band
bearing the printing are silver.

Bibliography:
World Medical Association. Declarations. 10 pages. Pamphlet.
Four Declarations adopted by the WMA: Declaration of
Geneva (modern Oath of Hippocrates); Declaration of Helsinki
(Guide in Clinical Research); Declaration of Sidney (Statement
on Determination of the Time of Death); Declaration of Oslo
(Statement on Therapeutic Abortion).
_____. International Code of Medical Ethics; Declaration of
Geneva. April 1956. 1 page.
Guides to professional conduct adopted by WMA.
_____. What in the World. 12 pages. Pamphlet.
Informational brochure describing WMA goals, activities, and
services.

"International Code of Medical Ethics"

DUTIES OF DOCTORS IN GENERAL

A doctor must always maintain the highest standards of professional conduct.

A doctor must practice his profession uninfluenced by motives of profit.

The following practices are deemed unethical:

a)   Any self advertisement except such as is expressly authorized by the national code of medical ethics.

b)   Collaborate in any form of medical service in which the doctor does not have professional independence.

c)   Receiving any money in connection with services rendered to a patient other than a proper professional fee, even with the knowledge of the patient.

Any act, or advice which could weaken physical or mental resistance of a human being may be used only in his interest.

A doctor is advised to use great caution in divulging discoveries or new techniques of treatment.

A doctor should certify or testify only to that which he has personally verified.

DUTIES OF DOCTORS TO THE SICK

A doctor must always bear in mind the obligation of preserving human life.

A doctor owes to his patient complete loyalty and all the resources of his science.   Whenever an examination or treatment is beyond his capacity he should summon another doctor who has the necessary ability.

A doctor shall preserve absolute secrecy on all he knows about his patient because of the confidence entrusted in him.

A doctor must give emergency care as a humanitarian duty unless he is assured that others are willing and able to give such care.

DUTIES OF DOCTORS TO EACH OTHER

A doctor ought to behave to his colleagues as he would have them behave to him.

A doctor must not entice patients from his colleagues.

A doctor must observe the principles of "The Declaration of Geneva" approved by The World Medical Association.

"Declaration of Geneva"

At the Time of Being Admitted as a
Member of the Medical Profession:

I solemnly pledge myself to consecrate my life to the service of humanity.

I will give to my teachers the respect and gratitude which is their due;

I will practice my profession with conscience and dignity;

The health of my patient will be my first consideration;

I will respect the secrets which are confided in me;

I will maintain by all the means in my power, the honor and the noble traditions of the medical profession;

My colleagues will be my brothers;

I will not permit considerations of religion, nationality, race, party politics or social standing to intervene between my duty and my patient.

I will maintain the utmost respect for human life, from the time of conception; even under threat, I will not use my medical knowledge contrary to the laws of humanity.

I make these promises solemnly, freely and upon my honor.

"Declaration of Helsinki"
(Recommendations Guiding Doctors in Clinical Research)

Introduction:

It is the mission of the doctor to safeguard the health of the people. His knowledge and conscience are dedicated to the fulfillment of this mission.

The Declaration of Geneva of The World Medical Association binds the doctor with the words: "The health of my patient will be my first consideration" and the International Code of Medical Ethics which declares that "Any act or advice which could weaken physical or mental resistance of a human being may be used only in his interest."

Because it is essential that the results of laboratory experiments be applied to human beings to further scientific knowledge and to help suffering humanity. The World Medical Association has prepared the following recommendations as a guide to each doctor in clinical research. It must be stressed that the standards as drafted

are only a guide to physicians all over the world.   Doctors are not
relieved from criminal, civil and ethical responsibilities under the
laws of their own countries.

In the field of clinical research a fundamental distinction
must be recognized between clinical research in which the aim is
essentially therapeutic for a patient, and the clinical research, the
essential object of which is purely scientific and without state of
medicine nor can any one technological procedure be substituted for
the overall judgment of the physician.   If transplantation of an organ
is involved, the decision that death exists should be made by two
or more physicians and the physicians determining the moment of
death should in no way be immediately concerned with the performance
of the transplantation.

Determination of the point of death of the person makes it
ethically permissible to cease attempts at resuscitation and in countries where the law permits, to remove organs from the cadaver
provided that prevailing legal requirements of consent have been
fulfilled.

"Declaration of Sydney"
(A Statement on Death)

The determination of the time of death is in most countries
the legal responsibility of the physician and should remain so.
Usually he will be able without special assistance to decide that
a person is dead, employing the classical criteria known to all
physicians.

Two modern practices in medicine, however, have made
it necessary to study the question of the time of death further:
(1) the ability to maintain by artificial means the circulation of
oxygenated blood through tissues of the body which may have been
irreversibly injured and (2) the use of cadaver organs such as
heart or kidneys for transplantation.

A complication is that death is a gradual process at the
cellular level with tissues varying in their ability to withstand depri-
vation of oxygen.   But clinical interest lies not in the state of
preservation of isolated cells but in the fate of a person.   Here the
point of death of the different cells and organs is not so important
as the certainty that the process has become irreversible by whatever techniques of resuscitation that may be employed.   This determination will be based on clinical judgment supplemented if necessary by a number of diagnostic aids of which the electroencephalo-
graph is currently the most helpful.   However, no single technological
criterion is entirely satisfactory in the present therapeutic value to
the person subjected to the research.

I.   Basic Principles.

1.   Clinical research must conform to the moral and scientific principles that justify medical research and should be based on
laboratory and animal experiments or other scientifically established
facts.

2.   Clinical research should be conducted only by scientifically qualified persons and under the supervision of a qualified medical man.

3.   Clinical research cannot legitimately be carried out unless the importance of the objective is in proportion to the inherent risk to the subject.

4.   Every clinical research project should be preceded by careful assessment of inherent risks in comparison to foreseeable benefits to the subject or to others.

5.   Special caution should be exercised by the doctor in performing clinical research in which the personality of the subject is liable to be altered by drugs or experimental procedure.

II.   Clinical Research Combined with Professional Care.

1.   In the treatment of the sick person, the doctor must be free to use a new therapeutic measure, if in his judgment it offers hope of saving life, reestablishing health, or alleviating suffering.

If at all possible, consistent with patient psychology, the doctor should obtain the patient's freely given consent after the patient has been given a full explanation.   In case of legal incapacity, consent should also be procured from the legal guardian; in case of physical incapacity the permission of the legal guardian replaces that of the patient.

2.   The doctor can combine clinical research with professional care, the objective being the acquisition of new medical knowledge, only to the extent that clinical research is justified by its therapeutic value for the patient.

III.   Non-Therapeutic Clinical Research.

1.   In the purely scientific application of clinical research carried out on a human being, it is the duty of the doctor to remain the protector of the life and health of that person on whom clinical research is being carried out.

2.   The nature, the purpose and the risk of clinical research must be explained to the subject by the doctor.

3a.   Clinical research on a human being cannot be undertaken without his free consent after he has been informed; if he is legally incompetent, the consent of the legal guardian should be procured.

3b.   The subject of clinical research should be in such a mental, physical and legal state as to be able to exercise fully his power of choice.

3c.   Consent should, as a rule, be obtained in writing.   However, the responsibility for clinical research always remains with the research worker; it never falls on the subject even after consent is obtained.

4a.   The investigator must respect the right of each individual to safeguard his personal integrity, especially if the subject is in a dependent relationship to the investigator.

4b.   At any time during the course of clinical research the subject or his guardian should be free to withdraw permission for research to be continued.

The investigator or the investigating team should discontinue the research if in his or their judgment, it may, if continued, be harmful to the individual.

"Declaration of Oslo"
(Statement on Therapeutic Abortion)

1. The first moral principle imposed upon the doctor is respect for human life as expressed in a clause of the Declaration of Geneva: "I will maintain the utmost respect for human life from the time of conception."

2. Circumstances which bring the vital interests of a mother into conflict with the vital interests of her unborn child create a dilemma and raise the question whether or not the pregnancy should be deliberately terminated.

3. Diversity of response to this situation results from the diversity of attitudes towards the life of the unborn child. This is a matter of individual conviction and conscience which must be respected.

4. It is not the role of the medical profession to determine the attitudes and rules of any particular state or community in this matter, but it is our duty to attempt both to ensure the protection of our patients and to safeguard the rights of the doctor within society.

5. Therefore, where the law allows therapeutic abortion to be performed, or legislation to that effect is contemplated, and this is not against the policy of the national medical association, and where the legislature desires or will accept the guidance of the medical profession, the following principles are approved:

(a) Abortion should be performed only as a therapeutic measure.

(b) A decision to terminate pregnancy should normally be approved in writing by at least two doctors chosen for their professional competence.

(c) The procedure should be performed by a doctor competent to do so in premises approved by the appropriate authority.

6. If the doctor considers that his convictions do not allow him to advise or perform an abortion, he may withdraw while ensuring the continuity of (medical) care by a qualified colleague.

7. This statement, while it is endorsed by the General Assembly of the World Medical Association, is not to be regarded as binding on any individual member association unless it is adopted by that member association.

PHYSICIANS--OSTEOPATHIC

AMERICAN OSTEOPATHIC ASSOCIATION (AOA)
    212 E. Ohio St., Chicago, Ill. 60601
    Edward P. Crowell, D.O., Executive Director

Membership: The American Osteopathic Association, founded in
1897 and with a present (1973) membership of over 10,000, is a
professional association of physicians and surgeons of osteopathic
medicine. "Osteopathic medicine"--according to the Association--
        "encompasses all phases of medicine but goes beyond general
        medicine in its recognition of the function of the musculo-
        skeletal system in health and disease."
"Regular Members" of the AOA are graduates of colleges of osteo-
pathy, approved by the AOA, and eligible for licensure as osteopathic
physicians and surgeons in their states of practice, or in a training
program approved by the Association. The diversity of practice of
members is demonstrated by the twelve certifying boards of the
Association, which certify specialists in areas ranging from Anes-
thesiology to Surgery.

Code of Ethics: The standards of professional conduct, established
by the American Osteopathic Association for the information and
guidance of its members (Bylaws, Article IV, Section 1), is the
Code of Ethics, which consists of 23 sections covering the duties of
physicians to patients, to other physicians and to the profession at
large, and responsibilities of the physician to the public. The present Code, in its July 1965 edition, may be amended by the House of
Delegates, and is enforced by the Committee on Membership (Bylaws, Article II, Section 3), which investigates complaints and holds
hearings as required, and by the Executive Committee, which takes
such disciplinary action as revocation or suspension of membership,
or placing a member on probation. The Board of Trustees reviews
such disciplinary action upon appeal of the member to be disciplined.

Professional Insignia: The American Osteopathic Association emblem is a square, divided into two rectangles; the left rectangle
bears the symbol of the Association--a modernized club-like staff of

Aesculapius, son of Apollo and god
of medicine, with the initials "D"
and "O" on either side of the serpent entwined on the staff; the
right rectangle contains the organization name, "American Osteopathic Association." The four
coils of the entwined serpent symbolize four elements generally
describing the human cycle: birth,
death, male, and female. The
association initials and name in the
insignia is in sans-serif typeface
(suggested type faces are specified
for use in the insignia). The official colors of AOA are green and
gold; and the emblem may be correctly shown in these official colors,

or in black and white. The insignia is used by the Association or
its chapters, and is available to association members, for use on
stationery, business forms, publications, exhibits and displays,
signs, and vehicle identification.

Bibliography:

American Osteopathic Association. The American Osteopathic
Association Trademark/Symbol: Guidelines and Basic
Usages. Folder.
Pictures and describes the AOA emblem; specifies acceptable
typefaces, color, usage, and variations.

_____. Constitution, Bylaws, Code of Ethics. Revised edi-
tion, July 1970. 18 pages. Pamphlet.
Includes membership requirements; Code of Ethics with interpreted sections of the Code; disciplinary procedures for enforcement of the Code.

_____. Factsheet AOA. October 1971. 1 sheet.
AOA purpose, definition of profession, licensure requirements.

"Code of Ethics"

Section 1. The physician shall keep in confidence whatever
he may learn about a patient in the discharge of professional duties.
Information shall be divulged by the physician when required by law
or when authorized by the patient.

Section 2. The physician shall give a candid account of the
patient's condition to the patient or to those responsible for the
patient's care.

Section 3. A physician-patient relationship must be founded
on mutual trust, cooperation, and respect. The patient, therefore,
must have complete freedom to choose his physician. The physician
must have complete freedom to choose patients whom he will serve.
In emergencies, a physician should make his services available.

Section 4. The physician shall give due notice to the patient
or to those responsible for the patient's care when he withdraws
from a case so that another physician may be summoned.

Section 5. A physician is never justified in abandoning a
patient.

Section 6. A physician shall practice in accordance with the
body of systematized knowledge related to the healing arts and shall
avoid professional association with individuals or organizations which
do not practice or conduct organization affairs in accordance with
such knowledge.

Section 7. A physician should join and actively support the
recognized local, state, and national bodies representing the osteopathic profession and should abide by the rules and regulations of
such bodies.

Section 8. A physician shall not solicit patients, commer-
cialize or advertise his services, or associate professionally with,
or aid in any manner, individuals or organizations which indulge in
such practices.

Section 9. A physician shall not be identified in any manner with testimonials for proprietary products or devices advertised or sold directly to the public.

Section 10. A physician shall not hold forth or indicate possession of any degree recognized as the basis for licensure to practice the healing art unless he is actually licensed on the basis of that degree in the state in which he practices.

Section 11. A physician shall not seek or acquire any healing arts degree from institutions not approved by the American Osteopathic Association or not approved by a body recognized for the purpose by the American Osteopathic Association.

Section 12. A physician shall designate his osteopathic school of practice in all professional uses of his name. Indications of specialty practice, membership in professional societies, and related matters shall be governed by rules promulgated by the Board of Trustees of the American Osteopathic Association.

Section 13. A physician shall obtain consultation whenever requested to do so by the patient. A physician should not hesitate to seek consultation whenever he himself believes it advisable.

Section 14. In any dispute between or among physicians involving ethical or organizational matters, the matter in controversy should be referred to the arbitrating bodies of the profession.

Section 15. In any dispute between or among physicians regarding the diagnosis and treatment of a patient, the attending physician has the responsibility for final decisions, consistent with any applicable osteopathic hospital rules or regulations.

Section 16. A physician shall not comment, directly, or indirectly, on professional services rendered by other physicians except before duly constituted professional bodies of inquiry or in public proceedings judicial in nature.

Section 17. Illegal, unethical, or incompetent conduct of physicians shall be revealed to the proper tribunals.

Section 18. A physician shall not assume treatment of a patient under the care of another physician except in emergencies and only during the time that the attending physician is not available.

Section 19. Any fee charged by a physician shall be reasonable and shall compensate the physician for services actually rendered.

Section 20. Division of any professional fees not based on actual services rendered is a violation which will not be tolerated within the membership of this Association.

Section 21. A physician shall not pay or receive compensation for referral of patients.

Section 22. The physician shall cooperate fully in complying with all laws and regulations pertaining to practice of the healing arts and protection of the public health.

Section 23. No code or set of rules can be framed which will particularize all ethical responsibilities of the physician in the various phases of his professional life. The enumeration of obligations in the Code of Ethics is not exhaustive and does not constitute a denial of the existence of other obligations, equally imperative, though not specifically mentioned.

PHYSICISTS

AMERICAN INSTITUTE OF PHYSICS (AIP)
    335 E. 45th St., New York, N.Y. 10017
    Wallace Waterfall, Director

Membership: The American Institute of Physics, founded in 1931, is a federation of leading societies in the field of physics, brought together in the AIP for the purpose of "advancement and diffusion of the knowledge of physics and its application to human welfare." There are 50,000 members (in unduplicated memberships) in the eight member societies:
    The American Physical Society,
    Optical Society of America,
    Acoustical Society of America,
    Society of Rheology,
    American Association of Physics Teachers,
    American Crystallographic Association,
    American Association of Physicists in Medicine.
Other member groups of the Institute are:
    Affiliated Societies--organizations in related scientific and
        technical disciplines, and local physics associations;
    Corporate Associate Members--100 corporations, institutions,
        and laboratories representing industries interested in
        physics; and
    Society of Physics Students--chapters in over 400 colleges,
        including collegiate chapters of Sigma Pi Sigma, the
        physics honor society.

Code of Ethics: No formal guide for ethical practice has been formulated by the American Institute of Physics, as it is a federation of scientific and educational institutions, rather than an organization of individuals or societies engaged in professional practice.

Professional Insignia: The emblem of the American Institute of Physics is its official seal --circular in form, with a centered design composed of common tools of physical measurement, signifying the subject matter of physics: a weight, resting on a ruler, is superimposed over a swinging pendulum; the organization name, "American Institute of Physics," is spaced around the upper border inside the circular

design, and the word, "Incorporated," appears at the bottom of the
circular emblem. The color of the insignia is shown variously--
gold on white (letterhead); maroon on white, and with central elements in grey, centered in a red outlined square (information brochure).

Bibliography:
    American Institute of Physics. American Institute of Physics,
        On Its 40th Anniversary: Purpose, Organization, Pro-
        gram. 1971. 20 pages.
    Includes listing of society and industry members.

PHYSIOLOGISTS

AMERICAN PHYSIOLOGICAL SOCIETY (APS)
    9650 Rockville Pike, Bethesda, Md. 20014
    Orr E. Reynolds, Executive Secretary-Treasurer

Membership: The American Physiological Society, founded in 1887
and with a present (1973) membership of approximately 4500, is
a professional organization of physiologists. Patterned on the
British Physiological Society, which was established in 1876, the
APS was organized "to promote the increase of physiological knowledge and its utilization." Since "meritorious research" is the prime
consideration for election to the American Physiological Society, its
requirements for "Regular Membership" are stated:
        "Any person who has conducted and published meritorious
        original research in physiology, who is presently engaged in
        physiological work, and who is a resident of North America."
    The American Physiological Society is a member of the Federa-
tion of American Societies for Experimental Biology and through
this Federation shares professional activities and meetings with the
other member societies: American Society of Biological Chemists;
American Society for Pharmacology and Experimental Therapeutics;
American Society for Experimental Pathology; American Institute of
Nutrition; American Association of Immunologists.

Code of Ethics: The American Physiological Society has issued a
statement of professional conduct pertaining to one phase of members' work: Guiding Principles in the Care and Use of Animals.
These principles set standards for the acquisition, care and use of
laboratory animals for research and study.

Professional Insignia: The emblem of the American Physiological
Society is its corporate seal (Bylaws, Article II), which was
adopted in 1958 from the design of Dr. W. F. Hamilton, Past-
President (1955) of the Society--a circular design with centered

monogram of entwined ini-
tials of the organization,
"APS"; the Society name,
"American Physiological
Society, " shown around the
top portion of a banding border; the date of incorporation,
"Founded 1887, " at the bottom of the design within the
border.   The color of the
emblem (publications, and
official documents) is black
and white.

Bibliography:
    American Physiological
        Society.   "Consti-
        tution and Bylaws. "   The Physiologist, vol. 11, no.
        3, 1968, pp. 140-146.
    Bylaws include specifications for corporate seal (insignia);
    membership requirements.
        _____.   "Brief History of the Society. "   The Physiologist,
        vol. 11, no. 3, 1968, pp. 147-150.
    Facts on founding and development of the APS, with list of
    original members, and published memento of 1938, issued
    to commemorate the 50th anniversary of the Society, with
    portraits of the founders (Dr. H. P. Bowditch, Dr. S. Weir
    Mitchell, and Dr. H. N. Martin); and representations of the
    seals of institutions associated with the founders and original
    members (Harvard University, Jefferson Medical College,
    University of Pennsylvania, and Johns Hopkins University).

"Guiding Principles in the Care and Use of Animals"

        Only animals that are lawfully acquired shall be used in this
laboratory, and their retention and use shall be in every case in
strict compliance with state and local laws and regulations.
        Animals in the laboratory must receive every consideration
for their bodily comfort; they must be kindly treated, properly fed,
and their surroundings kept in a sanitary condition.
        Appropriate anesthetics must be used to eliminate sensibility
to pain during operative procedures.   Where recovery from anesthesia is necessary during the study, acceptable technic to minimize
pain must be followed.   Curarizing agents are not anesthetics.
Where the study does not require recovery from anesthesia, the
animal must be killed in a humane manner at the conclusion of the
observations.
        The postoperative care of animals shall be such as to mini-
mize discomfort and pain, and in any case shall be equivalent to
accepted practices in schools of Veterinary Medicine.
        When animals are used by students for their education or the

advancement of science such work shall be under the direct supervision of an experienced teacher or investigator. The rules for the
care of such animals must be the same as for animals used for
research.

PLANNERS--URBAN AND REGIONAL

AMERICAN INSTITUTE OF PLANNERS (AIP)
   1776 Massachusetts Ave., N.W., Washington, D.C. 20036
   John R. Joyner, AIP, Executive Director

Membership: The American Institute of Planners, founded in 1917
and with a present (1973) membership of approximately 8000, is a
professional organization of planners who are engaged in planning
for the unified physical, social, and economic development of cities,
counties, regions, states, and the nation for the public interest.
According to the Institute definition of "Professional Planning Experience," such work must:
   "(1)   include analysis, projection, design or program develop-
          ment which specifically requires consideration and ex-
          pression of the interrelationships among resources,
          facilities, and activities of an area of jurisdiction ex-
          tended through time;
   (2)   show a specific relationship to the development of poli-
          cies and implementation programs, for public or pri-
          vate agencies or individuals, which are intended to di-
          rect or influence change in the public interest;
   (3)   show initiative, judgment, substantial involvement, and
          personal accountability for definition or preparation of
          significant substantive elements of a planning program."

     To qualify for full Membership in the AIP an applicant must
be currently engaged in professional planning, pass an examination,
and have a graduate degree in planning from an educational program
recognized by AIP and two years of professional planning experience, or have other specified combinations of education and experience. The required examination is an oral examination, of approximately one hour in length, conducted by three members of the AIP
Board of Examiners, and consisting of four basic questions.

Code of Ethics: The AIP Code of Professional Responsibility and
Rules of Procedure gives standards of professional conduct for
planners. This Code (Bylaws, Article IX, Section 1, 2), adopted
in April 1970 to replace the former Code of Professional Conduct,
was developed to provide "an administratively and legally usable
set of standards and procedures under which to expeditiously handle
alleged ethical violations." The standards consist of:

1. Code of Professional Responsibility--including Canons
      (five general rules of professional conduct); and
      Rules of Discipline (15 instances setting forth "mini-
      mum levels of acceptable planners' conduct");
2. Rules of Procedure--methods of filing complaints against,
      and discipline of, members alleged to have violated
      the ethical standards.
The Rules of Procedure provide for enforcement of the Code of Professional Responsibility by the Executive Director and the Executive
Committee of AIP, who receive and investigate complaints of unethical conduct, and--after hearing--may recommend to the Board
of Governors appropriate disciplinary action, including censure,
suspension, or expulsion from the Institute.

Other Guides to Professional Conduct: The AIP has also issued
Rules for Reference to Institute Membership, which provide a guide
for members referral to membership in the Institute to differentiate
between the different membership grades and to accurately represent members professional qualifications.

Professional Insignia: The emblem of the American Institute of
Planners is its logotype--a
stylized design of the association initials, "AIP," as an unbordered monogram, which
appears on official AIP documents, including stationery
and publications. The color
of the emblem is shown vari-
ously--black on white (logotype);
embossed (letterhead); combination of colors ("a" black,
"ip" brown--Newsletter May
1970).

Other Identification of Profes-
sional Status: A full Member of the AIP may use the letters indicating Institute membership with his name to designate professional
competence, "AIP."

Bibliography:
      American Institute of Planners. "Code of Professional Respon-
            sibility and Rules of Procedure." AIP Newsletter 5:2-3
            May 1970. (Reprint, single sheet, 1972).
      Ethical code and rules for enforcement (Bylaws, Article IX).
      _____. Examination Information Folder.
      _____. Membership Information Folder.
      Includes requirements for different categories of AIP mem-
            bership; definition of "Professional Planning Experience"; in-
            formation about examination content, form, and scheduling.
      _____. Rules for Reference to Institute Membership. Single
            page.

Written references to AIP membership, and use of "AIP" with name.

_____. The Social Responsibility of the Planner. Pamphlet.
    1973.
Guidelines for the planner in performance of his professional work--general, local areas, regional jurisdictions, and state and federal programs.

"Code of Professional Responsibility and Rules of Procedure"

Members shall be subject to the Code of Professional Responsibility. The Code is divided into two parts: Canons and Rules of Discipline. The standards of professional conduct are expressed in general terms in the Canons, while the Rules of Discipline establish the minimum level of professional conduct. Any member whose professional conduct violates the Rules of Discipline shall be subject to expulsion, suspension or censure in accordance with the Rules of Procedure established in Section 2.

SECTION 1--CODE OF PROFESSIONAL RESPONSIBILITY

The ultimate objective of the planning profession is the co-ordination, for the general welfare, of that use and development of community resources that are best designed to fulfill human needs and purposes, as more specifically expressed in Article II of these Bylaws. In view of this objective the professional endeavors of the planner demand the highest values of social consciousness and professional conduct.

The members of the American Institute of Planners subscribe to this Code of Professional Responsibility as their basic policy in relationships with the public, their clients and employers, both public and private, and with fellow members of their profession and related professions.

1.1 Canons

The following Canons are statements of axiomatic norms expressing in general terms the standards of professional conduct expected of planners.

(a) A planner serves the public interest primarily. He shall accept or continue employment only when he can insure accommodation of the client's or employer's interest with the public interest.

(b) A planner shall seek to expand choice and opportunity for all persons, recognizing a special responsibility to plan for the needs of disadvantaged groups and persons, and shall urge the alteration of policies, institutions and decisions which militate against such objectives.

(c) A planner shall exercise independent professional judgment on behalf of his client or employer and shall serve him in a competent manner.

(d)   A planner shall preserve the secrets and confidences of
a client or employer.

(e)   A planner shall assist in maintaining the integrity and
competence of the planning profession.

(f)   A planner shall avoid even the appearance of improper
professional conduct.

1.2 Rules of Discipline

The following Rules of Discipline express the minimum level
of conduct below which no member may fall without being subject
to disciplinary action.   The severity of action taken against a member found blameworthy of violating a Rule of Discipline shall be
determined by the character of the offense and the circumstances
surrounding it.

(a)   A planner shall not engage in conduct involving dishonesty, fraud, deceit or misrepresentation.

(b)   A planner shall not seek personal publicity, nor shall
he advertise in self-laudatory language calculated to attract clients,
or in any other manner derogatory to the dignity of the planning
profession.

(c)   A planner shall not give compensation in any form to
a person or organization to recommend or secure his employment
or as a reward for having made a recommendation resulting in his
employment.

(d)   Except with the consent of the client or employer after
full disclosure, or except as required by law, court or administrative order or subpoena, a planner shall not reveal, use to his personal advantage or to the advantage of a third person, information
gained in the professional relationship or employment that the client
or employer has requested be held inviolate or the disclosure of
which would be likely to be detrimental to the client or employer.

(e)   Except with the consent of the client after full disclosure,
a planner shall not accept or continue employment if the exercise
of his professional judgment on behalf of his client or employer
will be or reasonably may be adversely affected by his own financial, business, property or personal interests or his relationship
with another client or employer.

(f)   Except with the consent of his client after full disclosure, a planner shall not accept compensation for his planning services rendered a client or employer from one other than that client
or employer.

(g)   A planner shall not permit a person who recommends,
employs, or pays him to render planning services for another to
direct or regulate his professional judgment in rendering such services.

(h)   A planner shall not accept employment to perform
planning services which he is not competent to perform.

(i)   A planner shall not neglect planning services which he
has agreed to perform, nor shall he render services without research and preparation adequate in the circumstances.

(j)   A planner shall not give, lend or promise anything of value to a public official in order to influence or attempt to influence the official's judgment or actions.

(k)   A planner who holds public office or employment shall not use his position to obtain or attempt to obtain a special advantage in legislative or administrative matters for himself, a client or an employer under circumstances where he knows or it is obvious that such action is not in the public interest.

(l)   A planner who holds public office or employment shall not accept anything of value or the promise of anything of value, including prospective employment, from any person when the planner knows or it is obvious that the offer is for the purpose of influencing his action as a public official or employee.

(m)   A planner shall not state or imply that he is able to influence improperly any public official, legislative or administrative body.

(n)   A planner shall not attempt to displace another planner knowing that a firm commitment has been made toward the other's employment.

(o)   A planner shall not directly or indirectly discriminate against any person because of said person's race, color, creed, sex or national origin in any aspect of job recruitment, hiring, conditions of employment, training, advancement or termination of employment.

SECTION 2--RULES OF PROCEDURE

The Rules of Procedure provide the mechanism for filing complaints against members alleged to have violated a Rule of Discipline and for the determination of the merits of complaints and possible imposition of disciplinary action against offending members.

2.1   Any person may file a charge of misconduct against a member of the Institute by transmitting to the Executive Director a statement of the charge, including the facts upon which it is based, the precise Rule of Discipline allegedly violated and all relevant dates.   The Executive Director shall transmit copies of the charge and the name of the party who filed the charge to the accused member and to the Executive Committee.

2.2   If the Executive Director determines that the charge may be meritorious he shall diligently conduct an investigation which shall include an invitation to the accused member to respond to the charge and an opportunity for the person who filed the charge to reply to any new facts raised by the accused member in his response.   The investigation shall not be restricted to the precise facts stated in the charge, but may include other related conduct in possible violation of the Rules of Discipline.   In conducting the investigation the Executive Director may request the assistance of the Chapter to which the accused member belongs.

2.3   The Executive Director shall transmit to the Executive Committee a summary report of the investigation and the Executive Director's recommendations as to whether the charge should be dismissed or a complaint issued.

2. 4   The Executive Committee shall review the Executive Director's summary report and recommendations and direct either dismissal of the charge, or the issuance of a complaint.

2. 5   Upon the direction of the Executive Committee the Executive Director shall prepare a complaint and transmit copies thereof to the accused member ("the respondent"), the Executive Committee and the party who filed the charge against the member. Service upon the accused member shall be made by certified mail.

2. 6   Within thirty days from his receipt of the complaint the respondent shall file an answer to the complaint.   The answer shall follow the paragraphs of the complaint and each fact alleged shall be admitted or denied.   If the fact is denied, the answer may contain an affirmative statement of the respondent's version thereof. If the respondent fails to timely answer the complaint, the facts asserted in the complaint shall be deemed admitted, absent a showing by the respondent that his failure to timely answer was caused by extenuating circumstances warranting an extension of time for his answer.

2. 7   If the answer denies any facts alleged in the complaint the Executive Committee shall have authority to designate one or more of its members to examine witnesses and take testimony. The ordinary rules of evidence shall not apply to such examination of witnesses and taking of testimony; however, the substantive rights of the respondent shall at all times be preserved.   Upon request of either the Executive Committee or the respondent, the testimony shall be transcribed and a copy furnished the respondent at his expense.

2. 8   Following a hearing the Executive Committee member(s) who conducted the hearing shall issue findings of fact and transmit a copy thereof to the respondent.

2. 9   On the basis of findings of fact at the close of the hearing and/or on the basis of the facts admitted by the answer or failure to timely answer the complaint the Executive Committee shall issue and publish its opinion whether the facts complained of and proved or admitted violated the Rules of Discipline.   The name of a member determined to be blameworthy shall be omitted from the opinion.

2. 10   If the Executive Committee decides to recommend that the respondent be expelled, suspended or censured, the Committee shall transmit its recommendations in writing to the Board of Governors for its approval or disapproval.   A copy of the recommendation shall be transmitted to the respondent.

2. 11   The imposition of disciplinary action again.. a member and the official publication by the Institute of such action shall require the affirmative vote of a majority of the Board of Governors.

2. 12   The Secretary-Treasurer shall notify the respondent, the Executive Director and the President of the respondent's chapter of disciplinary action taken by the Board of Governors.

AMERICAN SOCIETY OF PLANNING OFFICIALS (ASPO)
    1313 E. 60th St., Chicago, Ill. 60637
    Israel Stollman, Executive Director

Membership: The American Society of Planning Officials, founded
in 1934 and with a present (1973) membership of over 9000, is an
organization of individuals interested in "working for better-planned
environments." Membership is open to any person interested, and
among the members are professional planners, citizens, citizen
members of planning boards and commissions, elected officials,
developers, students, and teachers.

Code of Ethics: The ASPO Code of Ethics in Planning--setting
standards for the actions of staff members of planning agencies,
and of the citizen members of planning commissions, urban renewal commissions, and zoning boards--was revised most recently
in 1972. It sets forth desirable planning goals under six headings:
        Conflict of Interest,
        Outside Employment of Planning Staff,
        Gifts and Favors,
        Treatment of Information,
        Respect for Professional Practice, and
        Political Activity.
The general provisions of the Code are not enforced by the American Society of Planning Officials, which specifies administrative
methods of ethical code enforcement, including character requirements for appointment of planning officials, staff rules of planning
agency operation, bylaws of planning boards and commissions, and
public evaluation of professional quality and fairness of planning
agency activities.

Professional Insignia: The emblem of the American Society of
 Planning Officials is its logo-
type--an unbordered monogram
of the Society, "ASPO," created by a graphics designer,
and in use since 1969 on official publications, and stationery.

Bibliography:
        American Society of Planning Officials. American Society of
            Planning Officials. 4 pages. Pamphlet.
        Informational brochure describing ASPO purposes, member-
        ship and services.
        _____. A Code of Ethics in Planning. 1972. 4 pages.
            Pamphlet.
        Includes Rules of Ethical Conduct in Planning, and state-
        ments regarding enforcement of the Code.

"A Code of Ethics in Planning"

Preamble

Ethical practice has special relevance to all people who are charged with responsibilities in public service. Planners, whose decisions and actions have long-range consequences for later generations, must be keenly concerned to adhere to ethical principles.

Codes of ethics, as commonly adopted, present a catalog of temptations that are prohibited. It cannot be an exhaustive catalog: human imagination is sufficiently rich to discover new variations of old temptations. The existence of a code simply puts a challenge, to some, to find a gap or loophole. Emphasis must be put not on the letter of prohibition but on the spirit of observance. A performance standard of ethical behavior will be superior to a specification standard.

Enforcement of an Ethical Code

Reliance upon criminal prosecution for the enforcement of an ethical code would allow ethical behavior to rest at a level just above the criminal. Administrative methods of enforcement are more effective for the higher level of behavior sought by the code here presented. These methods call for the use of this code (1) by appointing authorities in considering the character of those selected to become planning officials; (2) by planning executives in establishing staff rules for agency operations; (3) by boards and commissions in drafting by-laws; (4) by the public in judging the professional quality and fairness of planning agencies. Its most important use, however, will be as a guide to the conscience of the individual citizen or practitioner in the daily discharge of planning responsibilities.

This code is written primarily for the lay, citizen member of a planning commission or urban renewal commission or zoning board although individual provisions of this code govern the actions also of staff members of planning agencies. Both groups are equally concerned with the application of the entire code. The term "planning official" is used comprehensively to include any citizen or staff member of a public agency engaged in planning, urban renewal, zoning, or community development. It also includes a consultant and his staff who is under contract, or is negotiating a contract, with a public agency. This code applies to the professional planner in his role as a public official. (His professional society, the American Institute of Planners, has a Code of Professional Conduct dealing with additional professional matters.)

This code is not written for the regulation of behavior of elected officials, who are accountable for their ethical standards to the electorate.

Ethics and Membership in ASPO

ASPO invites active or associate membership of all persons

who wish to promote sound city and regional planning methods and
who wish to improve the efficacy of planning administration.

ASPO applies no test for membership. While a great many
members of ASPO are professional planners, ASPO is not an association of professionals only. Membership in ASPO, therefore,
does not in itself imply expertness in the field of planning. ASPO
members must not, therefore, use the fact of membership as a
badge of professional qualification in planning. ASPO does not undertake to police ethics in the planning profession or among its members. ASPO seeks to promote ethics in planning, including the distribution of this statement, public discussion of ethical practice,
and advising on problems involving the application of this code.

Rules of Ethical Conduct in Planning

Conflict of Interest. A person to whom some private benefit
may come as the result of some public action, should not be a participant in that action.

1.   The private benefit may be direct or indirect, create a
material, personal gain or provide an advantage to relations or to
friends or to groups and associations which hold some share of a
person's loyalty.

2.   The possibility, not the actuality, of a conflict of interest
should govern.   The question is not "Do I think I would be biased?"
but "Would a reasonable person think I could be biased?"

3.   In making appointments, there should be no attempt to
exclude whole categories of business or professional persons in an-
ticipation of conflict of interest problems. The service of competent
people of good character need not be sacrificed. Their withdrawal
from participation in planning matters is necessary only in those
specific cases in which a conflict arises.

4.   A person experiencing a conflict of interests should
declare his interest publicly, abstain from voting on the matter
should he have a vote, keep out of any deliberations on the matter,
and leave any chamber in which such deliberations are to take place.
He should not discuss the matter privately with any fellow official.

5.   No planning official should engage in any transaction in
which he has a financial interest, direct or indirect, with the agency
or jurisdiction that he serves unless the transaction is disclosed
publicly and determined to be lawful.

6.   No planning official should advise or assist anyone in any
action that is adverse to the jurisdiction he serves.

Outside Employment of Planning Staff. A full-time member
of a planning agency staff owes his loyalty, his energy and his
powers of mind to the service of its planning program.

1.   A planning staff member should take no employment outside of his official duties without explicit approval of the staff director or of the commission or comparable authority.

2.   No such outside employment should be undertaken if its
performance will reduce the quality or dispatch with which the staff
member can execute his primary responsibilities. The number of

hours and the scheduled times devoted to outside employment should not interrupt or interfere with the time that should be devoted to primary planning responsibilities.

3.   A staff member must never consider taking any outside employment if this outside work may deal with any matter that requires an action or recommendation of his full-time agency.

4.   A staff member must not have, as an outside employer, any person or organization who does business with his agency or with other agencies under the same jurisdiction. This limitation must apply even when the outside work deals with matters which will never be related to the official responsibilities of the employee.

5.   Public property should not be used for any private purpose, including performance of work for other public employers, without explicit approval by an appropriate authority.

6.   Upon leaving public employment, a staff member or consultant must not use information or associations gained while in public employ to bring special advantage or favor to any new employer, to himself, friends or relations.

Gifts and Favors. Gifts, favors or advantages must not be accepted if they are offered because the receiver holds a position of public responsibility.

1.   The value of a gift or advantage and the relation of the giver to public business should be considered in determining acceptability. Small gifts that come in the form of business lunches, calendars or office bric-a-brac are often, not always, acceptable. In cases of doubt, refuse. In cases of marginal doubt, refuse.

Treatment of Information. It is important to discriminate between planning information that belongs to the public and planning information that does not.

1.   Reports and official records of a public planning agency must be open on an equal basis to all inquirers. Planning advice should not be furnished to some unless it is available to all.

2.   Information of private affairs that is learned in the course of performing planning duties must be treated in confidence. Private affairs become public affairs when an official action--such as a change of zone classification or approval of a plat--is requested with respect to them. Only then is disclosure of relevant information proper.

3.   Information contained in studies that are in progress in a planning agency should not be divulged except in accordance with established agency policies on the release of its studies. A public planning agency is not required to do its thinking out loud in public.

4.   Boards and commissions holding public hearings on planning questions should permit the presentation of information on behalf of any party to a question only at the scheduled hearing, not in private, unofficially, or with other interested parties absent. Partisan information received in the mail, by telephone or other communication, should be made part of the public record.

Respect for Professional Practice. Officials should respect

the codes of professional conduct established by the planning profession and by the several professions related to the practice of
planning.

1. Professional codes commonly include provisions to protect the integrity of professional judgment, insure the selection of
a professional service on the basis of qualifications and experience,
maintain the confidential relationship of client and professional, and
establish professional standards. These provisions of professional
codes should be understood and observed by officials to the extent
that they are compatible with public laws and regulations.

2. A professional person should not undertake to provide
advice on questions which lie beyond the scope of his training and
experience and which require the qualifications of some other profession.

3. In contracting for the performance of professional planning
services, planning officials should not participate in any procedure
that requires the professional to compete or bid for work on the
basis of the fee to be charged, since such basis is professionally
unethical. Experience and qualifications for the work to be done
should be the basis of competition.

4. In recommending the employment of any professional
firm or person, a planning official must not allow his choice or
recommendation to be influenced by friendship, personal gain, or
political pressure. A planner must not seek to use these influences
in his own behalf.

Political Activity. Membership in a political party and contributions to its finances or activities are matters of individual
decision that should neither be required of, nor prohibited to,
planning officials.

1. The extent of participation in political activities should
be governed by professional judgment as well as limited by any applicable civil service laws or regulations.

2. The powers of planning officials must not be exercised,
nor their duties performed, in any way that will create special advantages for a political party. The special position of a commission or board member, or of a staff officer, should not be used to
obtain contribution or support for a political party and should not
be used to obtain partisan favors.

3. Partisan debate of a community's planning program, and
the consideration of planning in a party's platform is proper.
Planning officials should, however, give political parties equal access
to information.

PODIATRISTS

AMERICAN PODIATRY ASSOCIATION (APA)
   20 Chevy Chase Circle, NW, Washington, D.C. 20015
   Seward P. Nyman, D.P.M., Executive Director

Membership: The American Podiatry Association, founded in 1912
and with a present (1973) membership of almost 6000, is the professional association of podiatrists. Podiatrists, who are concerned
with the study and treatment of foot ailments, provide complete
foot care, or specialize in such areas as biomechanics (bone,
muscle, and joint disorders), podopediatrics (diseases of the feet
of children), or foot surgery. APA has component podiatry societies in every state, the District of Columbia, and Puerto Rico.
A podiatrist can become an Active Member of APA provided he is
licensed in his state of practice, and is a member in good standing
of one of the component state societies.

Code of Ethics: The professional conduct guide for podiatrists is
the American Podiatry Association Code of Ethics, in which general
principles of practice are grouped in thirteen sections. This code
may be revised by the House of Delegates, and it is enforced by
the component societies. An APA Board of Inquiry may be appointed
to consider alleged misconduct charges against any individual member, either upon referral or initiative. After investigating the
charges and holding hearings, the Board of Inquiry reports findings
and recommendations to the APA Board of Trustees, which trans-
mits the findings of the inquiry with its recommendations to the
Association House of Delegates for disciplinary action. This may
include suspension or expulsion from the Association (Bylaws, Chapter IX).

Professional Insignia: The emblem of the APA is its official seal--a
circular design, with centered
caduceus (Mercury's winged
staff with two entwined serpents), signifying medicine or
healing, upon which is superimposed the winged foot of
Mercury, indicating the treatment area of podiatry; the organization name, "American
Podiatry Association," circles
the design in a bordering band.
The color of the insignia is
black on white (logotype).
The insignia is used on official
documents of the APA, and its
publications.

Bibliography:
   American Podiatry Association. Desk Reference and Directory.
      Annual.
   Includes Constitution and Bylaws; Code of Ethics.

"Code of Ethics"

Preamble. These principles are intended to aid podiatrists individually and collectively in maintaining a high level of ethical conduct. They are not laws but standards by which a podiatrist may determine the propriety of his conduct and his relationship with patients, colleagues, members of allied health professions and with the public.

Section 1. The conduct of a practitioner of podiatry shall at all times be such as becomes a gentleman, and should be creditable to the profession of which he is a member. The principal objective of the podiatry profession is to render service to humanity with full respect for the dignity of man. Podiatrists should merit the confidence of patients entrusted to their care, rendering to each a full measure of service and devotion.

Section 2. Podiatrists should strive continually to improve their knowledge and skill, and should make available to their patients and colleagues the benefits of their professional attainments.

Section 3. A podiatrist should neither tender nor receive a commission for referral of patients.

Section 4. It is unethical for a podiatrist to enter into contracts or agreements which impose conditions that make it impossible to deal fairly with the public and fellow practitioners in the locality. A podiatrist should not dispose of his services under terms or conditions which tend to interfere with or impose the free and complete exercise of his judgment and skill or tend to cause deterioration of the quality of podiatric care.

Section 5. The confidence and knowledge which podiatrists receive, through their professional attendance upon patients, should be guarded with the most scrupulous care.

Section 6. The podiatrist has the obligation of not referring disparagingly in the presence of a patient to the services of another podiatrist or to those of members of other health professions. A lack of knowledge of conditions under which the services were afforded may lead to unjust criticism and to a lessening of the patient's confidence.

Section 7. A podiatrist should seek consultation upon request, in doubtful or difficult cases, or whenever it appears that the quality of podiatric service would be enhanced thereby.

Section 8. Every profession has the responsibility to regulate itself, to determine and judge its own members. Such regulation is achieved largely through the influence of professional societies, and every podiatrist has the dual obligation of making himself a part of a professional society and of observing its rules of ethics.

Section 9. Advertising reflects adversely on the podiatrist who employs it and lowers the public esteem of the podiatry profession. The podiatrist has the obligation of advancing his reputation for fidelity, judgment and skill solely through his professional services to his patients and to society. The use of advertising in any form to solicit patients is inconsistent with this obligation.

A podiatrist may properly utilize professional cards, announcement cards, notices to patients of record and letterheads when the style and text are consistent with the dignity of the profession and with the custom of other podiatrists in the community.

Announcement cards may be sent when there is a change in location or an alteration in the character of practice, but only to other podiatrists, to members of other health professions, and to patients of record.

A podiatrist may properly utilize office door lettering and signs provided that their style and text are consistent with the dignity of the profession and with the custom of other podiatrists in the community.

A podiatrist may use his title or degrees in connection with his name on cards, letterheads, office door signs and announcements. A podiatrist who has been certified by a specialty board or group for one of the specialties approved by the American Podiatry Association may use the appropriate term in connection with his specialty on his cards, letterheads and announcements if such usage is consistent with the custom of podiatrists of the community, and provided that he uses the designation of not more than one specialty organization.

Section 10. A podiatrist may properly participate in a program of health education of the public involving such media as the press, radio, television and lecture, provided that such programs are in keeping with the dignity of the profession and the custom of the podiatric profession of the community.

Section 11. The podiatrist has an obligation of prescribing and supervising the work of all auxiliary personnel in the interest of rendering the best service to the patient.

Section 12. Problems involving questions of ethics should be resolved, whenever possible, by the local society of which the podiatrist is a member. In appropriate cases, an appeal to a Board of Inquiry of the American Podiatry Association may be taken in accordance with the jurisdiction and procedure governing such Boards.

Section 13. A podiatrist must practice according to the highest ethical standards in his own community. Therefore, any violation of the Code of Ethics of the state where he practices shall automatically be construed as a violation of the Code of Ethics of the American Podiatry Association.

POLITICAL SCIENTISTS

AMERICAN POLITICAL SCIENCE ASSOCIATION (APSA)
    1527 New Hampshire Ave., N.W., Washington, D.C. 20036
    Evron M. Kirkpatrick, Executive Director

Membership: The American Political Science Association, organized
in 1903 and with a present (1973) membership of approximately
12,000, is an association of professional political scientists working
as scholars, educators, social engineers, and consultants. Any interested person may become a member of the Association. The
four major types of members are:
    Faculty Members,
    Graduate Students,
    Researchers in public and private organizations not affiliated
        with universities,
    Government Officials and Employees.

Code of Ethics: The guide for professional standards, responsibilities, and conduct of the American Political Science Association is
contained in its Rules of Conduct, proposed by the Committee of
Professional Standards and Responsibilities (also known as the Bernstein Committee, after the chairman, Marver H. Bernstein), consisting of ten academic political scientists, and several other non-
academic and younger academic members. The 21 rules of conduct,
recommended by the Committee and adopted by the APSA in 1968,
are focused "on the ethical problems of academic political scientists," and are grouped under four headings:
    Teacher-Student Relations,
    Conduct of Officers and Employees of the Association,
    Political Activity of Academic Political Scientists, and
    Freedom and Integrity of Research.
    The majority of the precepts are in the last category (rules 9
through 21), and cover such problems of paramount concern to
academic political scientists as:
    Special Problems of Research Overseas,
    Disclosure of Financial Support for Research,
    Instruments of Financial Sponsorship,
    Guidelines to Maintain Integrity of Scholarship, and
principles for funding agencies, individual researchers, and contract
research funded by the federal government.

    Following recommendations of the Committee on Professional
Standards and Responsibilities, a standing Committee on Professional Ethics was appointed in 1968 "to consider questions of professional ethics involving members of the American Political Science
Association." It acts in identifying and clarifying "specific rules of
conduct in the context of actual situations as they may arise," rather

than in receiving specific complaints of unethical professional conduct directed against an individual member. This Committee
renders advisory opinions--upon its own initiative or upon request of
individual members or component chapters. These opinions are reported (beginning in 1969) in PS, the quarterly professional newsletter of the Association. They are published as issued, from time
to time; and are also published as a cumulative set of advisory
opinions (most recently in 1970).

Professional Insignia: The American Political Science Association
has adopted no official emblem.

Bibliography:
    American Political Science Association. Ethical Problems of
        Academic Political Scientists. 1968. 28 pages (Reprint
        from PS 1, Summer 1968).
    Final report of the Committee on Professional Standards and
    Responsibilities, containing the 21 proposed rules of conduct
    for academic political scientists, adopted by APSA in 1968.
        _____. Committee on Professional Ethics. Reports. 1969-
        (Printed in PS).
    Advisory opinions of the Committee, identifying and clarifying
    specific rules of conduct.

From "Ethical Problems of Academic Political Scientists"

[PROPOSED] RULES OF CONDUCT

A.   Teacher-Student Relations

        Few, if any, academic political scientists would disagree
with general statements of proper ethics for scholars. For example, the teacher should not neglect his teaching duties, plagiarize,
deliberately withhold evidence, alter findings for reasons of personal advantage, financial or otherwise, or report his conclusions
and data in such a manner as to deceive the reader. What is portrayed as a product of scholarship should meet the standards of
scholarship and not those of special pleading.

        The Committee sees little need to dwell on the responsibility
of political scientists to follow the recognized canons of scholarship:
objectively gathering and reporting data, awareness of one's own
biases, recognition of the impact of selective perception, honesty of
statement and so on. Nor do we see any need to dwell on the
normal professional and civic obligations of the academic political
scientist to his students and to his department and university, including his willingness to devote a reasonable amount of time to
service on committees and participation in studies and in appropriate
meetings and discussions. We doubt that many political scientists
deliberately violate these canons.

However, the Committee proposes rules of conduct governing two potentially troublesome aspects of the teacher-student relationship.

Rule 1. A faculty member must not expropriate the academic work of his students. As a dissertation adviser, he is not entitled to claim joint authorship with a student of a thesis or dissertation. The teacher cannot represent himself as the author of independent student research; and research assistance, paid or unpaid, requires full acknowledgement.

Rule 2. The academic political scientist must be very careful not to impose his partisan views--conventional or otherwise--upon his students or colleagues.

B. Conduct of Officers and Employees of the Association

Officers and employees of the Association have special obligations to avoid confusion between their position as political scientists and their formal responsibilities within the Association. They should not engage in activities that are inconsistent with their duties to the Association, and they should not be permitted to engage in any activity involving a conflict of interest.

The following rules are proposed governing the conduct of officers and employees of the Association. The first of these rules also covers members of the Association.

Rule 3. When an officer, member, or employee of the Association speaks out on an issue of public policy, endorses a political candidate, or otherwise participates in political affairs, he should make it as clear as possible that he is not speaking on behalf of the Association unless he is so authorized by the Association, and he should not encourage any inference that he acts for the Association unless he is so authorized by the Association.

Rule 4. Officers and employees of the Association are free to engage in activities outside their obligations to the Association provided that such activities are consistent with their duties and responsibilities to the Association. When doubts arise about the activities of subordinate staff members, they should be resolved by the Executive Director in consultation with Executive Committee of the Association. Similarly when doubts arise about the activities of the Executive Director, they should be resolved by the Executive Committee.

Rule 5. An officer or employee of the Association should not knowingly participate in a transaction involving the Association in the consequences of which he has a substantial economic interest. In such event he should disqualify himself from participating in a transaction involving the Association when a violation of this rule would result. Procedures for such disqualification shall be established by the Executive Committee.

C.   Political Activity of Academic Political Scientists

A major concern within the profession currently is the political activity of academic political scientists, such as signing
statements for newspaper publication, making speeches open to
the public, holding office in a party, taking part in political cam-
paigns, and running for elective office. Difficult questions arise
when political scientists who take public positions on political issues
give the impression that their views are supported by the research
findings of political science.

All professionally trained people, and indeed intellectuals in
general, have special responsibilities correlative to their training,
capacities, and functions. The professor is put under exceptional
obligations by his special commitment and capacity to discover new
knowledge and to communicate it to others. This commitment and
capacity are a principal basis for his claim to academic freedom,
a privilege which exempts him from certain controls by his employer, especially over opinion and speech, to which employees in
other lines of work might legitimately be subject. Moreover, his
discoveries are not his private possessions, but must be made
publicly available. In the research that led to these discoveries,
he may have been moved entirely by curiosity and without regard
for social consequences. Still, we would agree that he has an
obligation to make his knowledge available.

When, however, we ask how far he may or ought to go in
trying to influence or persuade the public or to champion causes
and men, controversy arises. As a recent statement of an AAUP
Committee on professors and political activity notes, some colleges
and universities severely restrict the political activities of their
faculties. The AAUP Committee recommends the following governing standard: "The college or university faculty member is a citizen and, like other citizens, should be free to engage in political
activities so far as he is able to do so consistently with his obligations as a teacher and scholar." This means, for example, that
those restrictions are not legitimate which are based on such considerations as the fact that the institution is publicly supported, that
the political views of its professors may conflict with those of
donors or trustees, etc. It leaves open, however, the possibility of
restriction--whether enforced by individual conscience or institutional
regulation is not now the question--based upon the professor's obligations as teacher and scholar. A few of our colleagues may well
believe that these restrictions begin when the professor goes much
beyond talk in the classroom or publication in the scholarly journal
and certainly to bar him from any significant political activity.

The case for abstention from political activity is said to follow from the needs of scholarship, but the reply of the political
scientist may rest on the same grounds. He can argue that his
own understanding of political behavior will be enhanced by participation and even that such participation is necessary if he is fully to

appreciate the meaning attached to this behavior by the subjects of
his study.   Participation may enable him to get to the center of
decision-making where the mere observer would never be permitted.
But observation is not the essential point, which is that he will
never be able to interpret the inner life of politics--its passions,
commitments, and beliefs--unless he has himself in some degree
and at some time experienced such an inner life.

Where the democratic ethos is strong and the professor is
taken seriously--i. e., as a man with useful truth and not merely a
kind of Ichabod Crane--the impulse for some professors to get into
politics will be irresistible.   Certainly, in the U. S. since the rise
of the research university, the professor has been closely associated
with government service, whether in LaFollette's "university in the
service of the people" or Roosevelt's "brain trust."

It is no solution to the problem to say that the professor in
general, and the political scientist in particular, has all the rights
and duties of the ordinary citizen in a democracy.   One must at
least have the realism to recognize, as the AAUP statement does,
that special conditions are created by his "obligations as a teacher
and scholar. "   These obligations not only involve the needs of
scholarship but also the professor's relationship with the democratic
public.   In that relationship he is not just an ordinary citizen; on
the contrary, he has special capacities and functions and these impose special responsibilities upon him.   When, for instance, a political scientist signs a statement on foreign or domestic affairs
for publication in the New York Times, and adds his university
and disciplinary affiliation, does the little note at the bottom "for
identification only" mean that the affiliation is mentioned only to
avoid confusing him with other "ordinary citizens" who may have
the same name?   Obviously, it is there to show that he is a person
with special abilities whose opinion should be given special weight.
Presumably the public thinks that a professor is a man who is particularly skillful and particularly scrupulous in assessing the merits
of a question and who, moreover, depending on the issue, may have
some special knowledge of the subject being agitated.

If this is what the public thinks, it would seem that the pro-
fessor-signer is under the obligation to make such a skillful and
scrupulous assessment.   How far then must he have direct, professional knowledge of the question at issue?   How far, on the other
hand, may he give his assent simply because a colleague whose expertise he trusts, has assured him of the merits?

The example of signing a political advertisement raises considerations which apply along the whole spectrum of political activities,
from occasional polemical interventions to sustained activity on behalf of a party of candidate.   On the one hand, it may be argued in
the democratic vein that the professor has not only the right, but
in some degree a duty to bring to the democratic process his special
capacities.   These may be a field of special knowledge relevant to

public policy or they may be simply his presumably superior ability
for rational inquiry and communication.

At the same time, restraints are put on his activity by the
need to foster the professional development and use of these capacities. The professor may well feel some obligation to contribute
directly to the public good through political participation. Yet in
most cases surely the main contribution he can make is through his
professional activity as scholar and teacher. He must take care,
therefore, not to let political participation undermine his ability to
make such a professional contribution. Moreover, the fact that he
presumably has such special capacities and functions will arouse certain expectations among members of the public and these expectations themselves will impose special conditions on his conduct. No
one suggests that the rules of a political campaign are the same as
those of a seminar. Yet even when he is openly in the political
arena the professor may not entirely forget his professional standards
of skillful and scrupulous inquiry and rational utterance.

The following recommendations are made respecting the political activity of academic political scientists.

Rule 6. The college or university teacher is a citizen, and
like other citizens, he should be free to engage in political activities
insofar as he can do so consistently with his obligations as a teacher
and scholar. Effective service as a faculty member is often compatible with certain types of political activity, for example, holding
a part-time office in a political party or serving as a citizen of a
governmental advisory board. Where a professor engages in full-
time political activity, such as service in a state legislature, he
should, as a rule, seek a leave of absence from his institution.
Since political activity by academic political scientists is both legitimate and socially important, universities and colleges should have
institutional arrangements to permit such activity, including reduction in the faculty member's work-load or a leave of absence, subject to equitable adjustment of compensation when necessary.

Rule 7. A faculty member who seeks a leave to engage in
political activity should recognize that he has a primary obligation
to his institution and to his growth as a teacher and scholar. He
should consider the problems which a leave of absence may create
for his administration, colleagues and students, and he should not
abuse the privilege by asking for leaves too frequently, or too late,
or for too extended a period of time. A leave of absence incident
to political activity should not affect unfavorably the tenure status of
the faculty member.

Rule 8. Special problems arise if departments or schools
endorse or sponsor political activities or public policies in the name
of the entire faculty of the department or school. One of the purposes of tenure--to shelter unpopular or unorthodox teaching--is in
some degree vitiated if the majority of a departmental faculty

endorses or sponsors a particular political position in the name of
the faculty of the department.   The simple way out of this dilemma
is to adhere strictly to the rule that those faculty members who wish
to endorse or sponsor a political position or activity do so in their
own names without trying to bind their colleagues holding differing
views.   Departments as such should not endorse political positions.

D.   Freedom and Integrity of Research

The Paramount Concern.   In administering research funds
the paramount concern of a university and its faculty and research
staff should be to maintain an environment in which the freedom and
integrity of research can flourish.   The purpose of research is to
advance knowledge.   The ability of scholars to advance knowledge
will depend in no small measure on two factors: first, on their
freedom to seek and use all relevant evidence and to draw conclusions from it by the rigorous application of the methods of science
and the disciplines of humane learning; secondly, on the integrity of
their personal commitment to the spirit of free inquiry.   To the
extent to which the range of evidence open to them is narrowed or
their ability to draw unbiased conclusions from it is impaired either
by external pressures or by the infirmity of their scholarly purpose,
to that extent their research will be deficient in qualities which are
essential for the advancement of knowledge [1--see end of this sec-
tion].

In administering research funds entrusted directly to its care,
a university, together with its faculty, should do its best to ensure
that no restrictions are placed on the availability of evidence to
scholars or on their freedom to draw their own conclusions from the
evidence and to share their findings with others.   Having fulfilled
its responsibility to recruit good scholars to its faculty and research
staff and to foster honest and rigorous inquiry in its graduate students and undergraduates, a university should be scrupulous in assuring their right to engage in the pursuit of knowledge according to
the dictates of their individual consciences.   They, in turn, are personally accountable for the conditions of research which they accept
and for the integrity with which they examine and use evidence.   It
is, of course, assumed that they will conduct their research with
due consideration for the rights of those whom it affects.

The financing of research by public and private sponsors
highlights some of the most important issues of ethical conduct con-
fronting political scientists.   The external sponsorship of intellectual
endeavor is fraught with risks to the integrity of the scholar.   Problems arise not so much because a scholar is told by his sponsors
what to write but rather because a scholar may, wittingly or unwit-
tingly, condition his manuscript to the assumed or divined values of
his financial sponsors.

This issue is further complicated by the fact that whether or
not the scholar has been true to himself, the acceptance of research

funds from certain kinds of donors raises in the minds of peers and
of the public the question of the <u>possibility</u> of scholarly objectivity.
This is notably true in the United States in the case of money contributed by government intelligence agencies a part of whose functions are covert, and in the case of private firms and associations
with an obvious political or economic axe to grind. A study of "The
Administration of Farm Policy" conducted by a scholar with funds
provided by the American Farm Bureau Federation, or a study of
"Chinese Ambitions in Southeast Asia" conducted in the field with
funds provided by C. I. A., may represent unfettered scholarly research. The very nature of the sponsorship in each case would,
however, cast doubt upon the aims, methods, and objectivity of the
investigation. If such sponsors remain anonymous, the ethical
questions for the individual scholar, and for the profession he represents, are even more serious. For if the scholar purports to be
free, the very assignment of anonymity to his sponsor may be interpreted as an act of subservience. If the anonymity is subsequently
blown, the scholar may be faced with the charge of prostituting both
himself and his profession--drying further access for himself and for
other scholars in his particular professional field.

       And yet totally disinterested sponsors of social science re-
search are relatively scarce. The least corrupting research money
is probably that which has been homogenized and purified in the investment portfolios of colleges and universities. Next is money
from large and secure private foundations issued directly, or through
peer panels (e. g., Ford Foundation, Rockefeller Foundation, Carnegie Corporation, Social Science Research Council). Third are
funds from government agencies and sub-divisions specifically
charged with the subvention of general and basic research (e. g.,
N. S. F., N. I. H., the Bureau of Research in the U. S. Office of
Education). Many other public agencies at all levels provide research funds, and have a vested interest in the impartiality and objectivity of sponsored scholarship; but the more specific the mission
of the sponsoring agency, especially if it is politically insecure or
deals with politically sensitive issues, the more danger there is that
its research money will be, or will appear to be, wrapped in strings
and bound by conditions of preview and censorship.

       In the past twenty years the scholarly community in the
United States has been engaged in an effort of unprecedented scope
with the aim of understanding the forces at work in the modern
world--an effort directed toward problems that concern the fate of
mankind itself. The very size and vigor of the American academic
activities lie at the heart of many of the problems that have been
encountered in the foreign aspects of this research. Within the
United States, the problems created by programmed and individual
research on a large scale are difficult enough to plan, administer,
and finance within the existing institutional system. When this research effort is extended to other countries, it raises issues that
have not yet been fully understood or adequately handled.

602 Professional Ethics and Insignia

Special Problems of Research Overseas. The very magnitude
of this American effort, motivated though it is by the desire to extend the frontiers of knowledge in the interest of human welfare,
tends to arouse apprehensions on the part of officials and scholars
abroad. The number of American scholars abroad is large and
growing. In some countries it is larger than that of the native
scholars concerned with the study of their own society, culture,
and resources. Local sensitivities on this score are often aggra-
vated by differences in cultural heritage and political outlook. In
some countries the fear has been expressed that if American research plays too large a role in the study of their problems, it
will favor solutions alien to their way of life. Most countries welcome American scholarly assistance in the study of problems affecting them, but they wish this assistance to be in a reasonable proportion to their own research capacities.

A special dilemma surrounds research conducted in foreign
countries. Regardless of sponsorship, a political scientist conducting
research in alien cultures may be faced with the excruciating dilemma of retaining academic integrity at the price of the national interest or of denying to himself and his professional peers a continuing access to documents and interviews. The scholar must report
the truth as he perceives it, but truth has consequences. A fearless exposition of corruption in the administrative procedures of a
friendly, under-developed nation, might have local as well as international consequences of the most serious nature. If the research
were conducted with U. S. Government funds, the dimensions of the
exposition might be increased exponentially. Even within our own
nation, the content and timing of the publication of political science
research may have serious repercussions for individuals, agencies,
and programs.

The United States government plays an important, legitimate,
and valued role in the sponsorship of research abroad; and the research that it sponsors, whether it is administered directly, by universities, or by other institutions, normally conforms to the highest
standards of freedom and integrity. There may be exceptional and
regrettable cases, however, when agencies of the United States
government concerned primarily with foreign policy and national
security covertly support research abroad. On occasion, these
agencies might also supplement the support received by scholars
from a university, and without the knowledge of the latter. We
are opposed to such arrangements. It is difficult for officials and
scholars abroad to make clear distinctions between the policies of
the United States government in the political, economic, and military
spheres, and the objectives of the research sponsored by it. When
it becomes known or suspected that such research is covertly sponsored, the freedom and integrity of all research abroad by Ameri-
cans tends to be affected.

A scholar cannot divorce himself from these kinds of considerations; and yet he has to remain faithful to his basic commitment

to search for the truth and to report reality as he sees it.   To
state that this is one of the dilemmas of all social science research
may help to sensitize political scientists to the nature of ethical
paradox.

Disclosure of Financial Support for Research.   Perhaps the
issue that has aroused the most concern among political scientists
has to do with disclosure of financial support for research.   There
appears to be general agreement that a scholar should be what he
says he is and make known the sources of his support, and any fact
or circumstance that might be thought to limit his freedom to pursue
the truth.

But should we as an Association make it a rule of professional ethics that one must always disclose the sources of financial
support?   Should we make it a matter of ethical obligation to disclose any financial interest that might have an impact, or which
some might think might have an impact, for example, stock ownership in a publisher whose book is favorably mentioned, or stock
ownership in a company under study?

Furthermore, unless it is assumed that financial interests are
the only or the primary factor that might bias one's research, how
should such potential "biasing factors" as political affiliation, race,
religion, or national origins be treated?   Personal wealth, political
affiliation, or even the network of friendships, and a host of other
factors may be more relevant in attempting to assess biasing factors
than financial sponsorship.   Should we require the political scientist
to disclose any factor that the reader should know about that might
bias the outcome of the research?   In any case the primary protection against unethical, non-professional, or incompetent performance
remains the evaluation of the merits of a publication, judged independently of who writes it or who paid for it.

Even if the disclosure of financial support is placed in proper
perspective, the application of a simple rule of disclosure may be
confronted by difficulties.   The following questions may be suggestive:

a. Is disclosure enough?   Are some sources of support so tainted--
   or at least so suspect--that support from them must simply be
   rejected?   The answer is easy when the sponsor fixes conditions
   that restrict the freedom of the scholar to pursue the truth, but
   it is not easy when and if he gives the necessary assurances on
   this point.   The question is how credible the assurances are, and
   to whom.   Suppose that, with full publicity and with all necessary assurances given, a professor of political science is offered
   a grant or contract for research by a governmental or private
   agency.   Suppose, further that the individual professor is satisfied that the assurances of freedom of inquiry are reliable.
   Does this make an acceptable basis for proceeding?   Is it important for him to ask whether others will find it credible that
   he has been given adequate assurances?   Who are the others

whose attitudes are relevant? If the professor believes that the significant others within this country would approve his acceptance of the invitation, should he be deterred (e. g., in case of research for the C. I. A.) by the possibility that others abroad would take a different view? Suppose that the suspect agency is willing to channel its funds through an intermediary. What kind of intermediary, if any, might provide the necessary assurance that freedom is being accorded? Under what conditions, if any, is a university sufficiently reassuring as an intermediary?

b. Is disclosure mandatory even when a sponsor wants to remain anonymous for quite innocent reasons? For example, suppose that, though he is willing to support one project, he wants to avoid publicity that might lead to requests that he support others. Might the use of an intermediary (e. g., a university) solve this kind of problem acceptably? Would it be sufficient, in these circumstances, to disclose the character, but not the identity, of the sponsorship?

c. Is disclosure mandatory against the call of moral or patriotic duty? Suppose, for example, that a political scientist on a university faculty believes it to be his duty to serve the C. I. A. in some way, and suppose that disclosures would impair his effectiveness in one or another of his two roles. Does the nature of the covert activity affect the answer? One can imagine numerous possibilities: e. g., that the scholar pursues his scholarly work abroad in genuine fashion for his own purposes, but then on his return to the United States reports privately to the C. I. A. on a matter thought to be of interest to it; that the scholar uses his status as a cover in connection with the publication of material that the C. I. A. wants to appear for purposes of its own. Does the political scientist respond to the problem in one way in his capacity as a political scientist, and in another way in his capacity as a citizen?

d. What must be disclosed? Simply the fact of sponsorship? The precise nature of the work undertaken? The outcome, or the results achieved? If a political party wishes to retain a political science professor to make studies that are not to be published but are for its internal use only, is this acceptable? If so, is it also acceptable for a political science professor to make studies for the Department of Defense or the C. I. A. on the understanding that the results are to be classified? Is it acceptable to make studies for a sponsor who retains control over the results, and who may publish on a selective basis-- releasing such studies (or parts thereof?) as serve its purposes and withholding the rest?

Instruments of Financial Sponsorship. Research financing may take any of several forms, including a research contract, a grant, appointment as a consultant, and part-time or temporary employment. Private sponsors normally use the device of the grant; government

agencies make extensive use of all of the instruments noted, although
some agencies emphasize research contracts while other make
grants.

In recent years considerable controversy has developed over
the definition and use of contracts and grants by government agencies. Loosely speaking, a contract for research calls for specific
performance under terms set by the contractor. A grant is often--
but not always--regarded as a gift given in trust to an individual in
support of some general activity that the granting agency believes
to be desirable.

A critical aspect of these loose formulations relates to the
responsibility of the recipient. Under a contract, the government
agency carries a heavy responsibility for insuring proper and prudent
expenditure of government funds. Under a grant, some tend to
argue, the responsibility for lawful and effective expenditure of
government funds rests more heavily, if not exclusively, with the
recipient. It is not surprising that Congressional committees generally regard these distinctions as invalid and assert that a government agency "is equally responsible for the proper, efficient, and
economical use of public funds irrespective of the final instrument
employed. "[2]

The Committee on Science and Public Policy of the National
Academy of Sciences, in its report of 1965,[3] deplored the trend
toward more detailed reporting and accounting by grantees of the
use of grants and advised grant-aided researchers to recognize that
grants are trusts and not to spend grant money for purposes unrelated to the grant. In this context of continuing controversy, more
support has developed for the view that the supervisory role of the
grantee institution be strengthened. This in turn has highlighted
serious administrative weaknesses in universities and other grantee
institutions, a condition that leads some in Congress and elsewhere
to demand that government agencies exercise more control over the
universities. The response to these demands generally has been
the effort by universities to overcome their administrative weaknesses and to strengthen their supervisory effectiveness.

The distinction between contracts and grants has been blurred
also by government agency practice. Grants may sometimes be
made for purposes similar to or as specific as those set forth in
research contracts. Some research contracts may be as general in
setting forth the purposes and product of the contract as grants are
normally expected to be. An agency may prefer to avoid the administrative and legal complexities of the contractual instrument
and utilize the device of the consultant appointment or temporary
employment to achieve the same substantive result. The researcher,
in any case, has the obligation to utilize research funds, from whatever source derived, for the purposes set forth in the instrument.

Because of persisting ambiguities in the distinction between contracts and grants, the Committee has not proposed rules of professional conduct keyed in detail to the distinctions between these two types of instruments. Rather it proposes guidelines generally applicable to the financial sponsorship of research, public and private, supplemented by more specific rules for government contract research.

Guidelines to Maintain Integrity of Scholarship. The academic political scientist may be confronted by dangers to his scholarly integrity, whether his research is carried out in the United States or overseas, and whether it is financed by external sponsors--public or private--or by his university or his own personal resources. In recent years the more conspicuous dangers have tended to arise from federal funding.

The management of federal research funds by individual researchers and universities has received considerable attention in the past decade by Congress and agencies of the federal executive branch. [4] As federal academic research enterprise has expanded, some government agencies have tended to impose substantial controls on researchers and research administrators in the universities in consequence of perceived weaknesses in supervision within the universities. Political scientists must exercise honesty and prudence in their relations with federal funding agencies. They must not engage in practices that provide additional and justifiable grounds for the sharp criticism of federal support of political science research that has been expressed by members of appropriations subcommittees of Congress. [5]

While it is highly appropriate for the Association to stress the professional obligations of its members in a relationship with research sponsors, the relationship is many-sided. Funding agencies and universities administering external research funds also have major obligations to act in ways that protect and advance the freedom and integrity of scholarship. Accordingly the following sections set forth proposed principles and rules for the guidance of public and private funding agencies, universities, and political science researchers.

Principles for Funding Agencies: The Committee urges the Association to undertake vigorous efforts in cooperation with other interested academic and professional groups to seek the adoption of these principles by public and private financial sponsors of research in the United States and overseas.

Rule 9. Financial sponsors of research have the responsibility for avoiding actions that would call into question the integrity of American academic institutions as centers of independent teaching and research. [6] They should not sponsor research as a cover for intelligence activities.

Rule 10. Openness concerning material support of research

is a basic principle of scholarship. In making grants for research, government and non-government sponsors should openly acknowledge research support and require that the grantee indicate in any published research financed by their grants the relevant sources of financial support. Where anonymity is requested by a non-government grantor and does not endanger the integrity of research, the character of the sponsorship rather then the identity of the grantor should be noted.

Rule 11. Political science research supported by government grants should be unclassified.

Rule 12. After a research grant has been made, the grantor shall not impose any restriction on or require any clearance of research methods, procedures, or content.

Rule 13. The grantor assumes no responsibility for the findings and conclusions of the researcher and imposes no restrictions on and carries no responsibility for publication.

Principles for Universities: The Committee urges academic members of the Association to work within their Universities for the adoption of the following principles:

Rule 14. A university or college should not administer research funds derived from contracts or grants whose purpose and the character of whose sponsorship cannot be publicly disclosed.

Rule 15. A university or college that administers research funds provided through contracts and grants from public and/or private sources must act to assure that research funds are used prudently and honorably.

Rule 16. In administering research funds entrusted directly to its care, a university or college should do its best to ensure that no restrictions are placed on the availability of evidence to scholars or on their freedom to draw their own conclusions from the evidence and to share their findings with others.

Principles for Individual Researchers: The following rules are proposed for the guidance of academic political scientists in their relations with any governmental or private sponsor of research.

Rule 17. In applying for research funds, the individual researcher should:
    (a)   clearly state the reasons he is applying for support and not resort to strategems of ambiguity to make his research more acceptable to a funding agency;
    (b)   indicate clearly the actual amount of time he personally plans to spend on the research;
    (c)   indicate other sources of support of his research, if any; and

(d)   refuse to accept terms and conditions that he believes will
      undermine his freedom and integrity as a scholar.

Rule 18.   In conducting research so supported, the individual
(a)   bears sole responsibility for the procedures, methods, and
      content of research;
(b)   must avoid any deception or misrepresentation concerning
      his personal involvement or the involvement of respondents
      or subjects, or use research as a cover for intelligence
      work;
(c)   refrain from using his professional status to obtain data
      and research materials for purposes other than scholar-
      ship; and
(d)   with respect to research abroad, should not concurrently
      accept any additional support from agencies of the govern-
      ment for purposes that cannot be disclosed.

Rule 19.   In managing research funds, the individual researcher should:
(a)   carefully comply with the time, reporting, accounting, and
      other requirements set forth in the project instrument, and
      cooperate with university administrators in meeting these
      requirements; and
(b)   avoid commingling project funds with personal funds, or
      funds of one project with those of another.

Rule 20.   With respect to publication of the results of his
research, the individual researcher:
(a)   bears sole responsibility for publication;
(b)   should disclose relevant sources of financial support, but
      in cases where anonymity is justified and does not endanger
      the integrity of research, by noting the character of the
      sponsorship;
(c)   should indicate any material condition imposed by his finan-
      cial sponsors or others on his research and publication;
(d)   should conscientiously acknowledge any assistance he re-
      ceives in conducting research; and
(e)   should adhere strictly to the requirements, if any, of the
      funding agency.

Contract Research Funded by the Federal Government: Research by political scientists may be financed and sponsored by governmental agencies, private foundations, and other non-governmental
units.   While political scientists must be alert to dangers to maintaining the freedom and integrity of their research, whatever the
source of those dangers may be, the dominant threat emerging in
recent years lies in governmental influence over and control of research.

In the area of federal research contracts, the most constructive step to date has been taken by the Foreign Area Research Co-
ordination Group, a voluntary interagency body of the Federal

government. On December 5, 1967, the FAR Group adopted guidelines on government contracts with academic institutions for research in the behavioral and social sciences dealing with foreign areas and international relations. A primary objective of the guidelines is to end covert support of academic institutions for foreign area research and to recognize governmental responsibility for avoiding actions that call into question the integrity of academic institutions. The guidelines deal only with contracts with academic institutions and not with non-contractual research grants to an academic institution or an individual or consultant relations between an individual scholar and a government agency.

The Committee recommends that the American Political Science Association endorse and support these guidelines. They are reproduced below, together with an official introductory statement. Collectively they constitute proposed Rule 21.

Rule 21. Foreign Area Research Guidelines: The following guidelines have been adopted by the Foreign Area Research Coordination Group (FAR) to provide general guidance to the FAR agencies. These agencies of the United States Government--twenty one in number--seek through their voluntary association in FAR "the systematic coordination of government-sponsored foreign area and cross-cultural research in the social sciences. "

These guidelines deal with two sets of problems: A) Those that arise when a government agency contracts with an academic institution for behavioral and social science research dealing with foreign areas and international relations, and B) Those that arise when such contracts call for the conduct by academic personnel of some or all of the research in foreign countries.

It should be recognized that these guidelines have been formulated and adopted by government departments and agencies that have a variety of missions and a great diversity of programs for supporting research. Thus not every guideline will have equal applicability to all research programs of every member agency. The guidelines are meant to deal with what, from the point of view of government-academic relations, are usually perceived to be the most troublesome cases of foreign area and foreign affairs research involving the social and behavioral sciences. Typically, those cases involve a contractual relationship between a policy or operating department or agency of government and an academic institution in which the latter undertakes to conduct research which the former has determined is pertinent to its policy or action responsibilities in the foreign affairs field. Though they may have some applicability, the guidelines were not designed to deal with consultant relations between an individual scholar and a government agency or with non-contractual research grants made by a foundation-like government agency to academic institutions or individuals.

In formulating the first set of guidelines (section A below),

FAR members recognized the importance in an open society of
strong, independent universities.   FAR members worked from the
premise that the government, in carrying out various foreign affairs
missions on behalf of an open society, needs to seek contributions
from all sectors of American society, including the resources of
knowledge, analysis and insight available on university campuses.
The problem--in which the government, the universities, and society
at large all have a stake--is for government agencies to arrange to
draw upon university resources for this purpose without diminishing
either those resources or the status of the universities as centers
of independent teaching and research.   This problem takes on added
dimensions when scholars associated with American universities go
to foreign countries to carry out government-supported contract research.   Thus the second set of guidelines (section B below) is designed to reflect the desire of government agencies to avoid adverse
effects on foreign relations as well as concern with restrictions on
the access of American scholars overseas and increased difficulties
in carrying out many types of foreign area research.

Many of the factors behind these latter restrictions and difficulties are not amenable to government action, and certain of them
should not be.   Some stem from the cultural and political sensitivities
of other nations, especially newly independent ones.   Others derive
from the relative scope, size, sophistication, and affluence of American social science research, which have resulted in high concentra-
tion in certain countries and in high visibility of research personnel.
Still others result from the inadequate preparation of the researcher
himself or from his personal characteristics.   Insofar as these
problems lend themselves to solution, responsibility must ordinarily
lie with the academic profession itself.   Thus the government looks
to the academic community to formulate its own standards of conduct
in performing research overseas and welcomes the initiatives which
have already been taken in this regard.   However, the government
recognizes that its own research programs can sometimes affect
not only official U. S. foreign relations but also the overseas rela-
lationships and access of private scholars.   The role of the government is therefore significant and carries an obligation to ensure that
government-supported foreign area research is conducted in ways
that reflect favorably on the United States and on the integrity of
American scholarship.

FAR members hope through the promulgation of these guidelines to alleviate some of the difficulties encountered in government-
supported foreign area research and to participate with the academic
community in constructive and clarifying interaction.   Through the
FAR and similar mechanisms, government agencies concerned with
foreign area research will try to strengthen their liaison with the
scholarly community.   While the guidelines will neither solve every
problem of relations between government and the academic world nor
be applicable to every situation, the process of application by individual agencies and discussion with the academic community should
help to illuminate the interests and obligations of the parties concerned.

A. Guidelines for Research Contract Relations between Government and University

A1. The Government has the responsibility for avoiding actions that would call into question the integrity of American academic institutions as centers of independent teaching and research. A large portion of government-supported contract research carried out by American universities is long-range unclassified and of academic interest to the faculties concerned; it poses no more serious challenges to academic integrity than do public and private research grants. The issues of acknowledgment and classification may pose problems and are dealt with below in paragraphs A2 and A3. In addition, there are certain specialized research needs--sometimes involving foreign sensitivities--for which Government agencies should continue to use or develop their own capabilities or those of non-academic institutions in order, among other things, to avoid possible embarrassment to academic research personnel and institutions.

A2. The fact of Government research support should always be acknowledged by sponsor, university, and researcher. Covert support to institutions of higher education is contrary to national policy, 7 on the broad and vital principle that it runs contrary to the spirit of our institutions, and on the pragmatic basis that it may reduce the reliability and credibility of the research project's conclusions and eventually result in damage to the reputation of our scholarly community.

A3. Government-supported contract research should in process and results ideally be unclassified, but the practical needs of the nation in the modern world may require that some portion be subject to classification; the balance between making work public or classified should incline whenever possible toward making it public. The free flow of ideas is basic to our system of democracy and to academic freedom. There are other reasons why the government should make generally available the results of its contract research; to do so not only results in the advancement of learning and public enlightenment, but also subjects government-supported research to the closest possible professional scrutiny.

Nevertheless, other responsibilities of the government sometimes must prevail. Material which cannot be declassified must sometimes be used in research required for important purposes. There are other reasons why the use of confidential limitations is as legitimate a practice in the government as it is in the private sector, where the substance of information is sometimes withheld even when its existence is known. In exploring alternative courses of action, the government often needs research-based analysis and reflection which if made public, could produce serious misunderstandings and misapprehensions abroad about U.S. intentions. To abandon restrictions of these sorts altogether would impose serious limitations on the agencies' use of contract research.

However, to the maximum extent feasible, agencies should design projects in such ways that only those portions requiring restrictive treatment are so treated. If classification is necessary, the university is its own judge of whether or not it wishes to contract for research in this category. In any case, the researcher should always be notified in advance of entering into the contract if the project is to be classified or if the results will need to undergo final review for possible security classification or administrative control.

A4. As a general rule, agencies should encourage open publication of contract research results. Subject to the ordinary canons of confidentiality and good taste which pertain in responsible privately-supported academic research, and subject to paragraph 3 above, open publication of research results in government or private media serves the greatest general good, both at home and abroad. The best guarantee that government-supported research will be of high quality is to have its results exposed to peer-group judgment; open publication is the most effective means for this purpose. To assure maximum feasible publication of research results and to minimize the risk that research publications will be misconstrued as statements or indicators of public policy, government agencies should give careful attention to the language and places in which their support is acknowledged and their responsibility for accuracy, findings, interpretations, and conclusions asserted or disclaimed. The researcher should be given a clear understanding of the agency's position on these matters before entering into the contract.

A5. Government agencies that contract with university researchers should consider designing their projects so as to advance knowledge as well as to meet the immediate needs of policy or action. Few agencies have as their central mission the advancement of knowledge for its own sake or for its general utility. Most agencies that contract for research look to research--and rightfully so--for assistance in carrying out specific missions or tasks in policy or action, in short, for applications of scholarly knowledge. It is therefore often assumed that these agencies consume a tailored product and do not contribute to the nation's intellectual capital. Consumers they certainly are; however scholars, as they work on applied problems, may also collect new data and again new insights into the theoretical and methodological strengths and weaknesses of their scholarly fields; thus they generate as well as apply scholarly knowledge. Agencies should entertain research proposals and encourage research designs which permit such contributions to basic knowledge to the maximum degree consistent with the project's sensitivity and mission-related purpose.

A6. The government agency has the obligation of informing the potential researcher of the needs which the research should help meet, of any special conditions associated with the research contract, and generally of the agency's expectations concerning the research and the researcher. The researcher has a right to prior knowledge of the use to which the agency expects to put his research even though, as in the case of privately-supported research, no assurances can be given that it will in fact be used or that other uses will not also be made of it, by either the supporting agency or others.

Nothing is more conducive to bad relations between researcher and government agency than failure to establish mutual understanding in advance concerning a research project. The best research designs are often those that emerge from extensive discussion between potential contractor and supporting agency; if elements of the design cannot or should not be completed until the project is under way, this prospect should be explicitly acknowledged and provided for.

A7. The government should continue to seek research of the highest possible quality in its contract programs. As scholars have much to contribute in assessing the quality of research designs and the capabilities of colleagues, their advice should be sought at key stages in the formulation of projects. Advice can be obtained through consultants, advisory panels, independent review, or utilization of staff scientists.

B. Guidelines for the Conduct of Foreign Area Research Under Government Contract

B1. The government should take special steps to ensure that the parties with which its contracts have highest qualifications for carrying out research overseas. Some of the points to be considered in assessing qualifications are professional competence, area experience, language competence, and personal alertness to problems of foreign sensitivity. Scholars in the same field or discipline are usually in the best position to judge the qualifications of a given researcher. Whenever feasible, consultation with academic experts should be a part of the process of contracting for foreign area research.

B2. The government should work to avert or minimize adverse foreign reactions to its contract research programs conducted overseas. All other things being equal, government-supported projects are more likely than private ones to be misinterpreted by both government and nongovernment institutions in foreign countries. Sponsoring agencies should keep in mind that ordinarily research supported by government will be held abroad to have a very practical purpose--often a purpose more immediate and direct than the agency intended, or even imagined. Thus, some combinations of topic, place, time, and agency support result in sensitivity so great as to make pursuit of some research projects actually harmful. While the existing procedures for review of government-supported foreign area research projects in the social and behavioral sciences have clarified and alleviated many of the problems, the supporting agency should always be on the watch to ensure that its research projects do not adversely affect either U.S. foreign relations or the position of the private American scholar.

B3.   When a project involves research abroad it is particularly important that both the supporting agency and the researcher
openly acknowledge the auspices and financing of research projects.
(See paragraph A2 above) One source of difficulty for the scholar
overseas is the unfounded suspicion that all American researchers
are covertly supported by the U.S. Government. A policy of full
disclosure of support will help to eliminate the suspicion of all
American research--whether private or government, classified or
unclassified--and will allow that which is supported by the government to be judged on its own merits. If the research is of such a
character, as in opinion sampling, that the objectivity of its research techniques is substantially destroyed when respondents know
of the project's auspices, then it is doubly important that either the
host government or collaborating local researchers, or both, be
fully informed about the nature of the project.

B4.   The government should under certain circumstances
ascertain that the research is acceptable to the host government.
In most cases the open acknowledgment of auspices and financing
discussed in paragraph B3 is sufficient to satisfy the interest of the
host government in the research. In some cases it is desirable to
take specific steps to inform the host government. For example,
when the U.S. Government supports a classified research project
involving substantial field work abroad by scholars associated with
American universities, sufficient information about the project should
be communicated to the host government to convey a true picture of
the character and purpose of the project. Similar steps may often
be desirable for unclassified projects which either deal with very
sensitive matters or easily lend themselves to misunderstanding and
misrepresentation.

B5.   The government should encourage cooperation with
foreign scholars in its contract research programs. Cooperation
with local scholars not only adds valuable viewpoints to a foreign area
research project, but also goes far to remove antagonisms and sus-
picions. This cooperation must, in large part, be the responsibility
of the American scholars who carry on the projects, but the government should, where legislation permits, look favorably upon research
proposals that contain provisions for cooperative ventures and should
otherwise seek to facilitate and encourage these ventures within the
limits imposed by local resources and needs. The supporting agency
should encourage and assist American researchers to distribute to
those foreign colleagues who have cooperated in the research copies
of open publications arising from the project. The supporting
agency should also consider distribution of such publications to other
interested persons and institutions in the host country, either directly
through appropriate sections of the U.S. Embassy or by submitting
copies to the FAR Secretariat for transmittal to the Embassy.

B6.   Government agencies should continue to coordinate
their foreign area research programs to eliminate duplication and
overloading of any one geographic area. Agencies planning projects

will continue to make use of the various FAR facilities for information exchange and consultation in order to ascertain whether similar
projects have already been completed or are underway and in order
to coordinate with other agency plans where feasible.   Since the pro-
liferation of American researchers overseas has been one source of
irritation, government agencies should continue to ensure that their
programs do not arouse foreign sensitivities by concentrating too
many researchers and research projects in any one overseas area.

B7.   Government agencies should collaborate with academic
associations on problems of foreign area research. Professional
scholarly associations, both American and international, and especially those related to specific areas, have much experience with
the problems of research abroad, and they have an interest like that
of the government in ensuring that research relationships across
national boundaries flow smoothly.   Government agencies, through
such mechanisms as the FAR, should consult with these associations on the problems involved to arrive at mutually agreeable
procedures and solutions.

NOTES

1. Some of the material in this section has been adapted from a
   report on "Freedom and Integrity of Overseas Research,"
   adopted by the Faculty of Princeton University in May 1968.
2. U.S. Congress, House, Committee on Government Operations,
   Administration of Grants by the National Institutes of Health,
   Report of the Intergovernmental Relations Subcommittee,
   87th Congress, 2d Session, 1962, p. 15.
3. National Academy of Sciences, Committee on Science and Public
   Policy, Federal Support of Basic Research in Institutions of
   Higher Learning, 1965.
4. (See, e.g., U.S. Congress, House, House Committee on Government Operations, Health Research and Training: The Administration of Grants and Awards by the National Institutes of
   Health, Report of the Intergovernmental Relations Subcommittee, 87th Congress, 1st Session, 1961; The Administration of
   Grants by the National Institutes of Health, Hearings before
   the Intergovernmental Relations Subcommittee, 87th Congress,
   2nd Session, 1962; The Administration of Research Grants in
   the Public Health Service, Report of the Intergovernmental
   Relations Subcommittee, 90th Congress, 1st Session, 1967;
   National Academy of Sciences, Committee on Science and
   Public Policy, Federal Support of Basic Research in Insti-
   tutions of Higher Learning, 1965; Biomedical Science and Its
   Administration, Report to the President by the Office of
   Science and Technology, 1965; U.S. Bureau of the Budget,
   The Administration of Government Supported Research at
   Universities, 1966.)
5. (See e.g., U.S. Congress, House, Committee on Appropriations,
   Hearings on Independent Offices Appropriations for 1967,
   89th Congress, 2nd Session, 1966, pp. 144-145; D. S.

Greenberg, "NSF; Senator Warns Against Budget Lobbying, "
Science, Vol. 169, No. 3827 (May 3, 1968), p. 518, which
inter alia reports sharp criticism of NSF support of political
science research projects by Senator Warren G. Magnuson,
Chairman, Senate Independent Offices Appropriations Subcom-
mittee. See also James D. Carroll, "The Support of Political
Science Research Projects by the Division of Social Sciences
of the National Science Foundation, " U.S. Congress, House,
Committee on Government Operations, The Use of Social
Research in Federal Domestic Programs, 90th Congress, 1st
Session, 1967, Vol. IV (pp. 81-105).

6. This is identical with A1 of the Guidelines for Research Contract
Relations between Government and University (p. 611).

7. As stated in the report of the committee chaired by Under Secretary of State Katzenbach which was accepted by the President
on March 29, 1967. See The Department of State Bulletin,
April 24, 1967, p. 665.

PROCTOLOGISTS

AMERICAN PROCTOLOGIC SOCIETY (APS)
    320 W. Lafayette Ave., Detroit, Mich. 48226
    Miss Harriette Gibson, Administrative Secretary

Membership: The American Proctologic Society, founded in 1899
and with a present (1973) membership of 900, is a professional
society of physicians specializing in proctology--a branch of surgery
concerned with diagnosis and treatment of diseases of the colon,
rectum, and anus. In addition to the national society, there are
18 regional organizations throughout the United States. Qualified
specialists in this field of medicine are certified by the Board of
Colon and Rectal Surgery--one of the specialty boards organized to
designate medical doctors competent in a specialty, through specialized training and experience. Qualifications for the three main
classes of Society membership are:
    Affiliate Members--Candidates customarily apply for this
        category of membership; minimum qualifications include
        graduation from a medical school approved by the APS
        Executive Council; and licensure in state of practice;
    Associate Fellows--In addition to qualifications for Affiliate,
        must have demonstrated through education or training, a
        special interest in colon and rectal surgery;
    Fellows--Medical specialists who confine their practice to
        colon and rectal surgery, and are certified by either the
        American Board of Surgery or the American Board of
        Colon and Rectal Surgery.
Fellows of the Society may choose to indicate their membership by

using with their names the initials, "F. A. P. S." (Fellow, American Proctologic Society).

Code of Ethics: As proctologists are medical physicians practicing in a recognized specialty, the APS subscribes to the Principles of Medical Ethics of the American Medical Association.

Professional Insignia: The emblem of the American Proctologic Society is its official seal, adopted in 1947 at the time of the Society's incorporation. The design is circular, with a centered caduceus (winged staff entwined with two serpents); the date of society founding, "1899," appears at the top of the design; the organization's initials, "APS," are arranged about the caduceus; the group name, "American Proctologic Society," is spaced around the design, within a bordering band. The color of the emblem is black and white.

"Code of Ethics"

see page 564

PSYCHIATRIC TECHNICIANS

NATIONAL ASSOCIATION OF HUMAN SERVICES TECHNOLOGIES (NAHST)
1127 Eleventh St., Sacramento, Cal. 95814
William M. Grimm, Executive Director

Membership: The National Association of Human Services Technologies, founded in 1961 as the National Association of Psychiatric Technicians, assumed its present title in 1968. It is a professional organization of persons employed in the field of Human Services Technologies, defined by the Association as:
"therapeutic care of the Mentally Ill, Mentally Retarded, and the Emotionally Disturbed" (Bylaws, Article I, Section 2).
Among the present (1973) membership of over 6000, are "Professional Members," who are required to possess "the qualifications, as required by their state, to practice as a psychiatric technician or the equivalent" (Bylaws, Article III, Section 2).

Code of Ethics: The guide to professional conduct issued by the
Association is its Code of Ethics, which--following one of the purposes of the group (Bylaws, Article I, Section 3)--was developed by
a Committee and adopted by the NAHST in October 1970. Members
subscribe to 13 statements of professional obligation in the Code, including standards for relationships with patients, colleagues, and
the public. Complaints of violations of the code of ethics are received and investigated by the Professional Standards Committees
in local chapters of the Association, and the Board of Directors of
the national association (after hearing) may discipline a member by
dismissal from membership (Bylaws, Article IV).

Other Guides to Professional Conduct: Upon becoming a member,
each member of the Association takes the Pledge of the Psychiatric
Technician, which sets forth the ideals and goals of these workers
in mental health.

Professional Insignia: The emblem of the Association is a round
design, with a centered caduceus
(winged staff with two entwined
serpents), framed by sprays
of laurel at either lower side;
the name of the organization,
"National Association of Human Services Technologies,"
circles the design within a
bordering band. The color of
the emblem is black on white.

Bibliography:
    National Association of
        Human Services
        Technologies. By-
        laws. 1970. 16
        pages. Pamphlet.
    Gives purposes, membership requirements, disciplinary pro-
    cedures for alleged violations of the code of ethics, Pledge
    of the Psychiatric Technician (page 5).
    _____. Code of Ethics. 1970. Single sheet.
    Conduct guide enumerating 13 principles.

"Code of Ethics"

       The Psychiatric Technician's work is based on democratic
humanitarian ideals, dedication to service for the welfare of mankind, disciplined use of recognized body of knowledge about human
beings and their interactions and promotion of the well being of all
without discrimination.

       As a member of the National Association of Human Service
Technologies, we commit ourselves to conduct our professional

relationships in accord with this Code of Ethics and subscribe to the following statements:

1.   Precedence to our professional responsibility and personal interest.

2.   Responsibility for the quality and extent of the service we perform.

3.   Respect for the privacy of the people we serve.

4.   Responsible use of information gained in professional relationship.

5.   Respect for the findings, views and actions of colleagues and use of appropriate channels to express judgment on these matters.

6.   Practice of our profession within the recognized knowledge and competence of the profession.

7.   Acceptance of the responsibility to help protect the community against unethical practice by any individual or organization engaged in the Psychiatric Technician profession.

8.   Readiness to give appropriate professional service in public emergencies.

9.   Statements and actions in public as an individual must be clearly distinguished from those representing the organization.

10.   Support of the principle that professional practice requires professional education.

11.   Contribution of knowledge, skills, and support to programs of human welfare.

12.   Relations with others based on their qualities as individual human beings, without distinction as to race, creed or color, economic or social status.

13.   No invasion into the personal affairs of another individual without his consent, except when in an emergency we must act to prevent injury to him or others.

"Pledge of the Psychiatric Technician"

Having developed an awareness of the dignity encompassed in the field of psychiatric technology and of my responsibility because of specialized training in the therapeutic techniques utilized in the promotion of mental health,

I Pledge Myself:

To uphold the integrity and human dignity of those entrusted in my care and protect them against humiliation, insult or injury without regard to race, color or creed.

To inspire hope and confidence, giving assistance with understanding and friendliness, in finding realistic and meaningful living.

To continue my development of professional competence, complementing scientific study, improvement of therapeutic techniques and maintaining high standards of leadership in the field of Psychiatric Technology.

PSYCHIATRISTS

AMERICAN PSYCHIATRIC ASSOCIATION (APA)
    1700 18th St., N.W., Washington, D.C. 20009
    Walter E. Barton, M.D., Medical Director

Membership: The American Psychiatric Association, founded in
1844 and with a present (1973) membership of over 19,000, is a
professional organization of psychiatrists--medical doctors specializing in the diagnosis, treatment and prevention of mental illness.
The Association, the oldest national medical society in the United
States, was founded as the Association of Medical Superintendents
of American Institutions for the Insane.   In 1892 the name was
changed to the American Medico-Psychological Association, and the
present name of the organization was adopted in 1921.   Among the
major categories of membership are:
    Associate Members--physicians who have completed at least
        one year of training in psychiatry but who are not eligible
        for General Membership or Member-in-Training.
    General Membership--conferred upon those who have com-
        pleted their graduate residency training in an approved
        center and who have demonstrated basic competence and
        promise in the field.
    Members-in-Training--established in 1969, residents are
        eligible to apply at the end of their first year of training.
        They may retain this category of membership for no
        longer than five years.   They are transferred automatically
        to general membership status at the completion of their
        training, or--if they do not complete their training--they
        are made Associate Members.
    Fellowship--highest status of membership, conferred on gen-
        eral members who, over a period of at least five years,
        have proved a constructive influence in the Association and
        in the community they serve.   Ability in clinical work,
        administration, teaching and research, and certification by
        the American Board of Psychiatry and Neurology are among
        criteria considered in according fellowship.

Code of Ethics: As an association of physicians practicing in a
medical specialty, the American Psychiatric Association subscribes
to the principles of ethics of the American Medical Association, and
its Judicial Opinions and Reports that interpret ethics.

Professional Insignia: The emblem of the Association is its official
seal--a circular design with a centered drawing depicting the bust
of Dr. Benjamin Rush, Member of the Continental Congress and a
signer of the Declaration of Independence, who is considered the
founder of psychiatry in the United States.   His book, Medical

Inquiries and Observations upon
Diseases of the Mind (1812),
guided psychiatric thought in
America for nearly fifty years.
An inner bordering band shows
13 stars in the upper portion--
symbolizing the 13 colonies;
the portrait title, "Dr. Benjamin
Rush, " appears beneath the portrait; the organization name,
"American Psychiatric Association, " is printed around the top
of the outer bordering band, and
the date of the association founding "1844, " is given at the bottom of the design within the
border.   The color of the insignia is black on white (letterhead).

Bibliography:
    The American Psychiatric Association. The American Psychi-
        atric Association.   Pamphlet.
    Informational brochure includes brief history of the associa-
    tion; membership requirements.

"Code of Ethics"

see page 564

PSYCHOANALYSTS

AMERICAN PSYCHOANALYTIC ASSOCIATION (APA)
    1 East 57th St., New York, N.Y. 10022
    Miss Helen Fischer, Executive Secretary

Membership: The American Psychoanalytic Association, founded
in 1914 and with a present (1973) membership of 1350, is a professional society of psychoanalysts.   Psychoanalysis, a sub-specialty
of psychiatry, is the practice of a therapy as originally described
by Sigmund Freud.   An "Active Member" of the Association is required to have an M. D. degree, have completed a residency in
Psychiatry, and be a graduate of an Approved Institute.

Code of Ethics: The American Psychoanalytic Association is presently preparing a draft of a Code of Ethics, not yet available for
public distribution.

Professional Insignia: The Association has not adopted a professional emblem.

PSYCHOLOGISTS

AMERICAN BOARD OF PROFESSIONAL PSYCHOLOGY (ABPP)
    1300 Midtown Tower, Rochester, N. Y. 14606
    Mark H. Lewin, Ph. D. , Executive Secretary

Membership: The American Board of Professional Psychology, Inc. ,
originally incorporated as the American Board of Examiners in
Professional Psychology, was established in 1947 in order to:
    1)   grant, issue, and control the use of its diplomas of
         special competence in fields of professional psychology,
         and
    2)   to arrange, conduct and control investigations and ex-
         aminations to determine the qualifications of individuals
         who make voluntary application for such diplomas.
The Board now awards a diploma in professional psychology.   It
has previously granted diplomas in four professional psychology
specialties:
    Clinical Psychology,
    Counseling Psychology,
    Industrial and Organizational Psychology, and
    School Psychology.

    The Board encourages the pursuit of excellence through its
program of certification at an advanced professional level, and its
diploma signifies to the public and the profession the highest recognition of competence as judged by one's professional peers.   Psychologists, who are members of the American Psychological Association or--where appropriate--the Canadian Psychological Association, are eligible to apply for candidacy for the diploma if they
meet the following requirements:
    1.   A Ph. D. degree in psychology from a college or univer-
         sity acceptable to the American Psychological Association,
    2.   Five years of acceptable qualifying experience, four years
         of which must have been post-doctoral,
    3.   Present engagement in professional work in the field of
         specialization.

    After a careful credentials review to insure the psychologist
candidate meets the Board's standards in regard to basic training,
professional experience, special competence, and reputation among
professional colleagues, the candidate is eligible to meet with a committee of diplomate examiners.   This examining panel plans an oral
examination designed to judge competence at the Diplomate level in

the candidate's professional practice.   The examination covers the following interrelated areas:

1. The effectiveness of the candidate's efforts toward constructive intervention based on realistic assessment of the problem presented.
2. Awareness of the relevance of research and theory.
3. Sensitivity to the Ethical Implications of his Professional Practice.

Successful candidates are granted a Diploma of the Board and may use the designation, "Diplomate, " to signify their professional competence.

Code of Ethics: As members of the American Psychological Association, Diplomates subscribe to the APA Ethical Standards of Psychologists.

Professional Insignia: The insignia of the American Board of Professional Psychology is a rectangular design with a centered oval bearing an outlined "psi"--twenty-third letter of the Greek alphabet, used to designate "Psychology"--in the center of the oval, with the organization name, "American Board of Professional Psychology, Inc., " forming an unbanded border within the oval; the date, "Founded  1947, " beneath the "psi. "   The printing and Greek letter are in black in a blue rectangle on a lighter blue ground ("Directory of Diplomates").

Bibliography:

American Board of Professional Psychology.   The American Board of Professional Psychology.   Pamphlet.
Gives meaning of the ABPP Diploma, and Board purpose and aims, requirements for diplomate candidacy, description of oral examination.
_____.   Directory of Diplomates.   Annual.   Southern Illinois University, Carbondale, Illinois. $3.
Lists APA members holding the Diploma of the Board; gives standards for candidacy for Diploma, and brief description of examination required.

"Code of Ethics"

see page 625

AMERICAN PSYCHOLOGICAL ASSOCIATION (APA)
    1200 17th St., N.W., Washington, D.C. 20036
    Kenneth B. Little, Executive Officer

Membership: The American Psychological Association, founded in
1892 and with a present (1972) membership of more than 12,000, is
a professional association that includes "most of the qualified psychologists in the United States." The diversity of activity of
psychologists "is shown in the 30 Divisions of the Association,"
each of which "has its own membership requirements, for election
to the APA." Members of the APA--in such areas as teaching,
research, service functions, consultation, or administration--are
organized in state and local associations in major population areas
throughout the country. A fully professional "Member" of the association must have "a doctoral degree based in part upon a psychological dissertation and conferred by a graduate school of recognized
professional standing." The other major types of APA membership
are:
    Associate--(nonvoting) requiring "a master's degree in psy-
        chology from a recognized school, plus a year of accep-
        table experience; or two years of graduate work in psy-
        chology in a recognized graduate school; and
    Fellow--an honorary category of membership, requiring
        nomination by one of the 30 Divisions, conferred upon
        APA members of a year's standing, with a doctoral de-
        gree followed by five years acceptable experience, and
        "evidence of unusual and outstanding contribution or per-
        formances in the fields of psychology."

Code of Ethics: The guide to professional conduct for members of
the American Psychological Association is its Ethical Standards of
Psychologists, adopted in 1963. These Standards, after a general
statement of professional obligation, give 19 principles of professional conduct, including:

Responsibility of the Psychologist;   Interprofessional Relations;
Competence in Professional Ser-   Remuneration;
    vice;   Test Security, Test Interpreta-
Moral and Legal Standards;   tion, Test Publication;
Misrepresentation, Public State-   Publication Credit;
    ments and Confidentiality;   Responsibility Toward Organiza-
Client Welfare and Client Re-   tion;
    lationships;   Promotional Activities.
Impersonal Service;
Announcement of Services;

    This code is interpreted and enforced by the standing committee
of the association, the Committee on Scientific and Professional
Ethics and Conduct, which--upon investigation and hearing of a com-
plaint--may censure, suspend or expel a member. Interpretation

and application of ethical standards are reported in the published <u>Case-book on Ethical Standards of Psychologists</u> (1967).

<u>Other Standards of Professional Conduct:</u> "Criteria for Psychology as a Profession" enumerates 12 criteria of a good profession, to which professional psychologists subscribe and aspire.

<u>Professional Insignia:</u> The emblem of the American Psychological Association is "psi," the twenty-third letter of the Greek alphabet, a monogram--and in common use for a number of years in the profession--denoting "Psychology." This emblem appears unbordered, in black and white, on the monthly news bulletin of the APA, the <u>APA Monitor</u>.

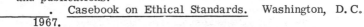

Bibliography:
> American Psychological Association. <u>About the American Psychological Association.</u> 1972. Folder. Informational brochure showing membership requirements, Divisions, and publications.
>
>   . <u>Casebook on Ethical Standards.</u> Washington, D. C. 1967.
> Interpretation and application of APA ethical code.
>
>   . <u>Ethical Standards of Psychologists.</u> 1963. 8 pages. (Reprint from <u>American Psychologist</u>, January 1963). Official conduct guide for professional psychologists.
>
>   . <u>Psychology as a Profession.</u> 1968. Pamphlet. 10 pages.
> Mentions code of ethics and its enforcement, lists Divisions, discusses standards of practice, and gives "Criteria for Psychology as a Profession."

"Ethical Standards of Psychologists"*

The psychologist believes in the dignity and worth of the individual human being. He is committed to increasing man's understanding of himself and others. While pursuing this endeavor,

---

*Reprinted (and edited) from the <u>American Psychologist</u>, January 1963. Copyrighted by the American Psychological Association, Inc., January 1963.

he protects the welfare of any person who may seek his service or of any subject, human or animal, that may be the object of his study. He does not use his professional position or relationships, nor does he knowingly permit his own services to be used by others, for purposes inconsistent with these values. While demanding for himself freedom of inquiry and communication, he accepts the responsibility this freedom confers: for competence where he claims it, for objectivity in the report of his findings, and for consideration of the best interests of his colleagues and of society.

SPECIFIC PRINCIPLES

Principle 1. Responsibility. The psychologist, * committed to increasing man's understanding of man, places high value on objectivity and integrity, and maintains the highest standards in the services he offers.

a. As a scientist, the psychologist believes that society will be best served when he investigates where his judgment indicates investigation is needed; he plans his research in such a way as to minimize the possibility that his findings will be misleading; and he publishes full reports of his work, never discarding without explanation data which may modify the interpretation of results.
b. As a teacher, the psychologist recognizes his primary obligation to help others acquire knowledge and skill, and to maintain high standards of scholarship.
c. As a practitioner, the psychologist knows that he bears a heavy social responsibility because his work may touch intimately the lives of others.

Principle 2. Competence. The maintenance of high standards of professional competence is a responsibility shared by all psychologists, in the interest of the public and of the profession as a whole.

a. Psychologists discourage the practice of psychology by unqualified persons and assist the public in identifying psychologists competent to give dependable professional service. When a psychologist or a person identifying himself as a psychologist violates ethical standards, psychologists who know firsthand of such activities attempt to rectify the situation. When such a situation cannot be dealt with informally, it is called to the attention of the appropriate local, state, or national committee on professional ethics, standards, and practices.
b. Psychologists regarded as qualified for independent practice are those who (a) have been awarded a Diploma by the American Board of Examiners in Professional Psychology, or (b) have been licensed or certified by state examining boards, or (c) have been certified by voluntary boards established by state psychological

---

*A student of psychology who assumes the role of psychologist shall be considered a psychologist for the purpose of this code of ethics.

associations. Psychologists who do not yet meet the qualifications recognized for independent practice should gain experience under qualified supervision.

c. The psychologist recognizes the boundaries of his competence and the limitations of his techniques and does not offer services or use techniques that fail to meet professional standards established in particular fields. The psychologist who engages in practice assists his client in obtaining professional help for all important aspects of his problem that fall outside the boundaries of his own competence. This principle requires, for example, that provision be made for the diagnosis and treatment of relevant medical problems and for referral to or consultation with other specialists.

d. The psychologist in clinical work recognizes that his effectiveness depends in good part upon his ability to maintain sound interpersonal relations, that temporary or more enduring aberrations in his own personality may interfere with this ability or distort his appraisals of others. There he refrains from undertaking any activity in which his personal problems are likely to result in inferior professional services or harm to a client; or, if he is already engaged in such an activity when he becomes aware of his personal problems, he seeks competent professional assistance to determine whether he should continue or terminate his services to his client.

Principle 3. Moral and Legal Standards. The psychologist in the practice of his profession shows sensible regard for the social codes and moral expectations of the community in which he works, recognizing that violations of accepted moral and legal standards on his part may involve his clients, students, or colleagues in damaging personal conflicts, and impugn his own name and the reputation of his profession.

Principle 4. Misrepresentation. The psychologist avoids misrepresentation of his own professional qualifications, affiliations, and purposes, and those of the institutions and organizations with which he is associated.

a. A psychologist does not claim either directly or by implication professional qualifications that differ from his actual qualifications, nor does he misrepresent his affiliation with any institution, organization, or individual, nor lead others to assume he has affiliations that he does not have. The psychologist is responsible for correcting others who misrepresent his professional qualifications or affiliations.

b. The psychologist does not misrepresent an institution or organization with which he is affiliated by ascribing to it characteristics that it does not have.

c. A psychologist does not use his affiliation with the American Psychological Association or its Divisions for purposes that are not consonant with the stated purposes of the Association.

d. A psychologist does not associate himself with or permit his name to be used in connection with any service or products in

such a way as to misrepresent them, the degree of his responsibility
for them, or the nature of his affiliation.

  Principle 5. Public Statements. Modesty, scientific caution,
and due regard for the limits of present knowledge characterize all
statements of psychologists who supply information to the public,
either directly or indirectly.

  a.   Psychologists who interpret the science of psychology or
the services of psychologists to clients or to the general public have
an obligation to report fairly and accurately. Exaggeration, sensationalism, superficiality, and other kinds of misrepresentation are
avoided.
  b.   When information about psychological procedures and techniques is given, care is taken to indicate that they should be used
only by persons adequately trained in their use.
  c.   A psychologist who engages in radio or television activities does not participate in commercial announcements recommending purchase or use of a product.

  Principle 6. Confidentiality. Safeguarding information about
an individual that has been obtained by the psychologist in the course
of his teaching, practice, or investigation is a primary obligation of
the psychologist.   Such information is not communicated to others
unless certain important conditions are met.

  a.   Information received in confidence is revealed only after
most careful deliberation and when there is clear and imminent
danger to an individual or to society, and then only to appropriate
professional workers or public authorities.
  b.   Information obtained in clinical or consulting relationships,
or evaluative data concerning children, students, employees, and
others are discussed only for professional purposes and only with
persons clearly concerned with the case.   Written and oral reports
should present only data germane to the purposes of the evaluation;
every effort should be made to avoid undue invasion of privacy.
  c.   Clinical and other materials are used in classroom teaching and writing only when the identity of the persons involved is
adequately disguised.
  d.   The confidentiality of professional communications about
individuals is maintained.   Only when the originator and other persons involved give their express permission is a confidential professional communication shown to the individual concerned.   The
psychologist is responsible for informing the client of the limits of
the confidentiality.
  e.   Only after explicit permission has been granted is the
identity of research subjects published.   When data have been published without permission for identification, the psychologist assumes responsibility for adequately disguising their sources.
  f.   The psychologist makes provisions for the maintenance of
confidentiality in the preservation and ultimate disposition of confidential records.

Principle 7. Client Welfare. The psychologist respects the integrity and protects the welfare of the person or group with whom he is working.

a. The psychologist in industry, education, and other situations in which conflicts of interest may arise among various parties, as between management and labor, or between the client and employer of the psychologist, defines for himself the nature and direction of his loyalties and responsibilities and keeps all parties concerned informed of these commitments.

b. When there is a conflict among professional workers, the psychologist is concerned primarily with the welfare of any client involved and only secondarily with the interest of his own professional group.

c. The psychologist attempts to terminate a clinical or consulting relationship when it is reasonably clear to the psychologist that the client is not benefiting from it.

d. The psychologist who asks that an individual reveal personal information in the course of interviewing, testing, or evaluation, or who allows such information to be divulged to him, does so only after making certain that the responsible person is fully aware of the purposes of the interview, testing, or evaluation and of the ways in which the information may be used.

e. In cases involving referral, the responsibility of the psychologist for the welfare of the client continues until this responsibility is assumed by the professional person to whom the client is referred or until the relationship with the psychologist making the referral has been terminated by mutual agreement. In situations where referral, consultation, or other changes in the conditions of the treatment are indicated and the client refuses referral, the psychologist carefully weighs the possible harm to the client, to himself, and to his profession that might ensue from continuing the relationship.

f. The psychologist who requires the taking of psychological tests for didactic, classification, or research purposes protects the examinees by insuring that the tests and test results are used in a professional manner.

g. When potentially disturbing subject matter is presented to students, it is discussed objectively, and efforts are made to handle constructively any difficulties that arise.

h. Care must be taken to insure an appropriate setting for clinical work to protect both client and psychologist from actual or imputed harm and the profession from censure.

i. In the use of accepted drugs for therapeutic purposes special care needs to be exercised by the psychologist to assure himself that the collaborating physician provides suitable safeguards for the client.

Principle 8. Client Relationship. The psychologist informs his prospective client of the important aspects of the potential relationship that might affect the client's decision to enter the relationship.

a.   Aspects of the relationship likely to affect the client's decision include the recording of an interview, the use of interview material for training purposes, and observation of an interview by other persons.

b.   When the client is not competent to evaluate the situation (as in the case of a child), the person responsible for the client is informed of the circumstances which may influence the relationship.

c.   The psychologist does not normally enter into a professional relationship with members of his own family, intimate friends, close associates, or others whose welfare might be jeopardized by such a dual relationship.

Principle 9.   Impersonal Services.   Psychological services for the purpose of diagnosis, treatment, or personalized advice are provided only in the context of a professional relationship, and are not given by means of public lectures or demonstrations, newspaper or magazine articles, radio or television programs, mail, or similar media.

a.   The preparation of personnel reports and recommendations based on test data secured solely by mail is unethical unless such appraisals are an integral part of a continuing client relationship with a company, as a result of which the consulting psychologist has intimate knowledge of the client's personnel situation and can be assured thereby that his written appraisals will be adequate to the purpose and will be properly interpreted by the client.   These reports must not be embellished with such detailed analyses of the subject's personality traits as would be appropriate only after intensive interviews with the subject.   The reports must not make specific recommendations as to employment or placement of the subject which go beyond the psychologist's knowledge of the job requirements of the company.   The reports must not purport to eliminate the company's need to carry on such other regular employment or personnel practices as appraisal of the work history, checking of references, past performance in the company.

Principle 10.   Announcement of Services.   A psychologist adheres to professional rather than commercial standards in making known his availability for professional services.

a.   A psychologist does not directly solicit clients for individual diagnosis or therapy.

b.   Individual listings in telephone directories are limited to name, highest relevant degree, certification status, address, and telephone number.   They may also include identification in a few words of the psychologist's major areas of practice; for example, child therapy, personnel selection, industrial psychology.   Agency listings are equally modest.

c.   Announcements of individual private practice are limited to a simple statement of the name, highest relevant degree, certification or diplomate status, address, telephone number, office hours, and a brief explanation of the types of services rendered.   Announce-

ments of agencies may list names of staff members with their qualifications. They conform in other particulars with the same standards as individual announcements, making certain that the true nature
of the organization is apparent.

d. A psychologist or agency announcing nonclinical professional services may use brochures that are descriptive of services
rendered but not evaluative. They may be sent to professional persons, schools, business firms, government agencies, and other
similar organizations.

e. The use in a brochure of "testimonials from satisfied
users" is unacceptable. The offer of a free trial of services is unacceptable if it operates to misrepresent in any way the nature or
the efficacy of the services rendered by the psychologist. Claims
that a psychologist has unique skills or unique devices not available
to others in the profession are made only if the special efficacy of
these unique skills or devices has been demonstrated by scientifically
acceptable evidence.

f. The psychologist must not encourage (nor, within his power, even allow) a client to have exaggerated ideas as to the efficacy
of services rendered. Claims made to clients about the efficacy
of his services must not go beyond those which the psychologist
would be willing to subject to professional scrutiny through publishing his results and his claims in a professional journal.

Principle 11. Interprofessional Relations. A psychologist
acts with integrity in regard to colleagues in psychology and in
other professions.

a. A psychologist does not normally offer professional services to a person receiving psychological assistance from another
professional worker except by agreement with the other worker or
after the termination of the client's relationship with the other professional worker.

b. The welfare of clients and colleagues requires that psychologists in joint practice or corporate activities make an orderly
and explicit arrangement regarding the conditions of their association and its possible termination. Psychologists who serve as employers of other psychologists have an obligation to make similar
appropriate arrangements.

Principle 12. Remuneration. Financial arrangements in
professional practice are in accord with professional standards that
safeguard the best interest of the client and the profession.

a. In establishing rates for professional services, the psychologist considers carefully both the ability of the client to meet
the financial burden and the charges made by other professional persons engaged in comparable work. He is willing to contribute a portion of his services to work for which he receives little or no financial return.

b. No commission or rebate or any other form of remuneration is given or received for referral of clients for professional services.

c. The psychologist in clinical or counseling practice does not use his relationships with clients to promote, for personal gain or the profit of an agency, commercial enterprises of any kind.

d. A psychologist does not accept a private fee or any other form of remuneration for professional work with a person who is entitled to his services through an institution or agency. The policies of a particular agency may make explicit provision for private work with its clients by members of its staff, and in such instances the client must be fully apprised of all policies affecting him.

Principle 13. Test Security. Psychological tests and other assessment devices, the value of which depends in part on the naivete of the subject, are not reproduced or described in popular publications in ways that might invalidate the techniques. Access to such devices is limited to persons with professional interests who will safeguard their use.

a. Sample items made up to resemble those of tests being discussed may be reproduced in popular articles and elsewhere, but scorable tests and actual test items are not reproduced except in professional publications.

b. The psychologist is responsible for the control of psychological tests and other devices and procedures used for instruction when their value might be damaged by revealing to the general public their specific contents or underlying principles.

Principle 14. Test Interpretation. Test scores, like test materials, are released only to persons who are qualified to interpret and use them properly.

a. Materials for reporting test scores to parents, or which are designed for self-appraisal purposes in schools, social agencies, or industry are closely supervised by qualified psychologists or counselors with provisions for referring and counseling individuals when needed.

b. Test results or other assessment data used for evaluation or classification are communicated to employers, relatives, or other appropriate persons in such a manner as to guard against misinterpretation or misuse. In the usual case, an interpretation of the test result rather than the score is communicated.

c. When test results are communicated directly to parents and students, they are accompanied by adequate interpretive aids or advice.

Principle 15. Test Publication. Psychological tests are offered for commercial publication only to publishers who present their tests in a professional way and distribute them only to qualified users.

a. A test manual, technical handbook, or other suitable report on the test is provided which describes the method of constructing and standardizing the test, and summarizes the validation research.

b. The populations for which the test has been developed and the purposes for which it is recommended are stated in the manual. Limitations upon the test's dependability, and aspects of its validity on which research is lacking or incomplete, are clearly stated. In particular, the manual contains a warning regarding interpretations likely to be made which have not yet been substantiated by research.

c. The catalog and manual indicate the training or professional qualifications required for sound interpretation of the test.

d. The test manual and supporting documents take into account the principles enunciated in the Standards for Educational and Psychological Tests and Manuals.

e. Test advertisements are factual and descriptive rather than emotional and persuasive.

Principle 16. Research Precautions. The psychologist assumes obligations for the welfare of his research subjects, both animal and human.

a. Only when a problem is of scientific significance and it is not practicable to investigate it in any other way is the psychologist justified in exposing research subjects, whether children or adults, to physical or emotional stress as part of an investigation.

b. When a reasonable possibility of injurious aftereffects exists, research is conducted only when the subjects or their responsible agents are fully informed of this possibility and agree to participate nevertheless.

c. The psychologist seriously considers the possibility of harmful aftereffects and avoids them, or removes them as soon as permitted by the design of the experiment.

d. A psychologist using animals in research adheres to the provisions of the Rules Regarding Animals, drawn up by the Committee on Precautions and Standards in Animal Experimentation and adopted by the American Psychological Association.

e. Investigations of human subjects using experimental drugs (for example: hallucinogenic, psychotomimetic, psychedelic, or similar substances) should be conducted only in such settings as clinics, hospitals, or research facilities maintaining appropriate safeguards for the subjects.

Principle 17. Publication Credit. Credit is assigned to those who have contributed to a publication, in proportion to their contribution, and only to these.

a. Major contributions of a professional character, made by several persons to a common project, are recognized by joint authorship. The experimenter or author who has made the principal contribution to a publication is identified as the first listed.

b. Minor contributions of a professional character, extensive clerical or similar non-professional assistance, and other minor contributions are acknowledged in footnotes or in an introductory statement.

c. Acknowledgment through specific citations is made for

unpublished as well as published material that has directly influenced the research or writing.

d. A psychologist who compiles and edits for publication the contributions of others publishes the symposium or report under the title of the committee or symposium, with his own name appearing as chairman or editor among those of the other contributors or committee members.

Principle 18. Responsibility toward Organization. A psychologist respects the rights and reputation of the institute or organization with which he is associated.

a. Materials prepared by a psychologist as a part of his regular work under specific direction of his organization are the property of that organization. Such materials are released for use or publication by a psychologist in accordance with policies of authorization, assignment of credit, and related matters which have been established by his organization.

b. Other material resulting incidentally from activity supported by any agency, and for which the psychologist rightly assumes individual responsibility, is published with disclaimer for any responsibility on the part of the supporting agency.

Principle 19. Promotional Activities. The psychologist associated with the development or promotion of psychological devices, books, or other products offered for commercial sale is responsible for ensuring that such devices, books, or products are presented in a professional and factual way.

a. Claims regarding performance, benefits, or results are supported by scientifically acceptable evidence.

b. The psychologist does not use professional journals for the commercial exploitation of psychological products, and the psychologist-editor guards against such misuse.

c. The psychologist with a financial interest in the sale or use of a psychological product is sensitive to possible conflict of interest in his promotion of such products and avoids compromise of his professional responsibilities and objectives.

"Rights and Responsibilities of a Profession"

As a profession, psychology in America is sensitive to its rights and responsibilities. In this concluding section, some principles and statements are presented which describe the Association's policies and points of view.

The Question of Rights

As a member of an autonomous profession, a psychologist rejects limitations upon his freedom of thought and action other than those imposed by his moral, legal, and social responsibilities. The Association is always prepared to provide appropriate assistance to any responsible member who becomes subjected to unreasonable limitations upon his opportunity to function as a practitioner, teacher, researcher, administrator, or consultant. The Association is always prepared to cooperate with any responsible professional organization in opposing any unreasonable limitations on the professional functions of the members of that organization.

This insistence upon professional autonomy has been upheld over the years by the affirmative actions of the courts and other public and private bodies in support of the right of the psychologist --and other professionals--to pursue those functions for which he is trained and qualified to perform.

Some Criteria for Psychology as a Profession

Psychologists share enough common values which yield a description of what they regard as criteria for a good profession. A combination of values which psychologists share and strive to protect is a respect for evidence combined with a recognition of the dignity of the human being. These give rise to the following characteristics of a good profession to which psychologists subscribe and aspire. As members of a good profession, psychologists:

1. Guide their practices and policies by a sense of social responsibility;

2. Devote more of their energies to serving the public interest than to "guild" functions and to building ingroup strength;

3. Represent accurately to the public their demonstrable competence;

4. Develop and enforce a code of ethics primarily to protect the client and only secondarily to protect themselves;

5. Identify their unique pattern of competencies and focus their efforts to carrying out those functions for which they are best equipped;

6. Engage in cooperative relations with other professions having related or overlapping competencies and common purposes;

7. Seek an adaptive balance among efforts devoted to research, teaching, and application;

8. Maintain open channels of communication among "discoverers," teachers, and appliers of knowledge;

9. Avoid nonfunctional entrance requirements into the profession, such as those based on race, nationality, creed, or arbitrary personality considerations;

10. Insure that their training is meaningfully related to the subsequent functions of the members of the profession;

11. Guard against premature espousal of any technique or theory as a final solution to substantive problems;

12. Strive to make their services accessible to all persons seeking such services, regardless of social and financial considerations.

PUBLIC OPINION RESEARCHERS

AMERICAN ASSOCIATION FOR PUBLIC OPINION RESEARCH
(AAPOR)
    817 Broadway, New York, N.Y. 10003
    Don Cahalan, Secretary-Treasurer
        Social Research Group, School of Public Health
        University of California
        1912 Bonita Ave., Berkeley, Cal. 94704

Membership: The American Association for Public Opinion Research, founded in 1947 and with a present (1973) membership of
over 700, is "a professional society of individuals engaged in or
interested in public opinion research and its allied fields." Members, professional public opinion poll takers and market researchers,
assess and study public opinion on major issues facing today's society to provide guides for business, industry, government, social
scientists, and political parties. "Any person professionally engaged or interested in the field of public opinion research or social
behavior" is eligible to join AAPOR, provided he is nominated by
two Association members.

"Public Opinion Research" is defined by the group as
    "studies in which the principal sources of information about
    individual beliefs, preferences, and behavior is a report
    given by the individual himself."
Over half the association members are "employees and executives
of commercial organizations doing market research and various
forms of attitude and opinion research for private corporations,
private research firms, advertising agencies, and trade associations."
The next largest group of members is "employed in the academic
world, especially in the fields of sociology, political science, psychology, and economics," and the remaining members (about 15
per cent of the total membership) "are employed by government,
foundations, and a variety of voluntary groups."

Code of Ethics: The professional conduct guide for AAPOR members is the organization's Code of Professional Ethics and Practices,
adopted in 1960, and most recently amended in June 1970. The
Code includes a general pledge "to maintain high standards of competence and integrity," and groups duties and obligations in public
opinion research under:
    Principles of Professional Practice in the Conduct of Our
        Work;
    Principles of Professional Responsibility in Our Dealings
        with People.
In enforcement of the Code, a member proved in violation of the
conduct guide is given adverse publicity, censured, or dropped

from membership in the Association, upon two-thirds vote of the
members.

Other Guides to Professional Conduct: In 1968, the AAPOR adopted
standards for evaluating public opinion polls, in order to assist
clients and the public in distinguishing between "surveys which are
conducted with a proper concern for professional competence and
those which reflect ignorance or willful unconcern with good research
practice" (Los Angeles Times 1:B May 12, 1968).   Standards for
Reporting Public Opinion Polls show the minimal essential information to be given when public opinion survey results are released to
"mass media." These include identity of the sponsor of the survey,
exact wording of questions asked, definition of population sampled,
type of interview (telephone, mail, or street corner), and interview
timing. In addition to these "minimal disclosure" essentials, the
Standards provide a list of essentials to be given to allow professional evaluation of a public opinion poll--"Illustrative Questions
for Full Disclosure": survey sampling, interviewing procedures,
and interview supervision and training.

Professional Insignia: The AAPOR reports no official emblem.

Bibliography:
      American Association for Public Opinion Research.   Code of
         Professional Ethics and Practices.   Amended to June
         1970.   2 pages.   (Reprint from Public Opinion Quarterly
         24:Fall 1960, with 1970 amendment.)
      Pledge and professional guidelines of AAPOR.
            .   Standards for Reporting Public Opinion Polls.   1969.
         4 pages.   Pamphlet.
      Includes Minimum Disclosure essentials for reporting a sur-
      vey to the mass media, and Full Disclosure--in the form of
      illustrative questions--for a detailed professional evaluation of
      a public opinion poll.
            .   What is AAPOR?   Folder.
      Gives membership requirements, and AAPOR composition, ob-
      jectives, organization, and activities.

"Code of Professional Ethics and Practices"*

We, the members of the American Association for Public
Opinion Research, subscribe to the principles expressed in the following code.   Our goal is to support sound practice in the profession of public opinion research.   (By public opinion research we
mean studies in which the principal source of information about individual beliefs, preferences, and behavior is a report given by the
individual himself.)
      We pledge ourselves to maintain high standards of scientific

*From The Public Opinion Quarterly, vol. 24 (Fall 1960) as amend-
ed June, 1970.

competence and integrity in our work, and in our relations both
with our clients and with the general public. We further pledge
ourselves to reject all tasks or assignments which would be inconsistent with the principles of this code.

THE CODE

I. Principles of Professional Practice in the Conduct of Our Work

A. We shall exercise due care in gathering and processing
data, taking all reasonable steps to assure the accuracy of results.

B. We shall exercise due care in the development of research designs and in the analysis of data.

1. We shall employ only research tools and methods of analysis
   which, in our professional judgment, are well suited to the
   research problem at hand.
2. We shall not select research tools and methods of analysis
   because of their special capacity to yield a desired conclusion.
3. We shall not knowingly make interpretations of research results, nor shall we tacitly permit interpretations, which are
   inconsistent with the data available.
4. We shall not knowingly imply that interpretations should be
   accorded greater confidence than the data actually warrant.

C. We shall describe our findings and methods accurately
and in appropriate detail in all research reports.

II. Principles of Professional Responsibility in Our Dealings with People

A. The Public:
1. We shall protect the anonymity of every respondent. We
   shall hold as privileged and confidential all information which
   tends to identify the respondent.
2. We shall cooperate with legally authorized representatives of
   the public by describing the methods used in our studies.
3. We shall withhold the use of our name in connection with the
   planned publication of research findings unless we have first
   examined and approved the material.

B. Clients or Sponsors:
1. We shall hold confidential all information obtained about the
   client's general business affairs and about the findings of
   research conducted for the client, except when the dissemination of such information is expressly authorized.
2. We shall be mindful of the limitations of our techniques and
   facilities and shall accept only those research assignments
   which can be accomplished within these limitations.

C. The Profession:
1. We shall not cite our membership in the Association as evidence of professional competence, since the Association does

not so certify any persons or organizations.

2. We recognize our responsibility to contribute to the science of public opinion research and to disseminate as freely as possible the ideas and findings which emerge from our research.

The following amendment, approved June 1970, replaces Section II, A, 3:

"We shall maintain the right to approve the release of our findings, whether or not ascribed to us. When misinterpretation appears, we shall publicly disclose what is required to correct it, notwithstanding our obligation for client confidentiality in all other respects."

"Standards for Reporting Public Opinion Polls"

Good professional practice imposes the obligation upon all survey research organizations...

1) to include, in any news release, essentials about how the survey was conducted; and

2) to inform their private clients in detail as to the elements of the research design and how it was implemented.

A proper concern for the public interest imposes the obligation upon the news media to inform themselves as to the credentials of any poll results that come to their attention and to report them in the light of such information.

Introduction

While it may appear easy to conduct some kind of a public opinion poll, it is not so easy to conduct one whose results would be acceptable to competent professionals. A compilation of street-corner interviews may provide useful insights but is not a substitute for a professionally designed and implemented poll of public opinion.

There are no "secrets" as to what is good research practice. The fundamentals are to be found in the standard statistics and survey research textbooks. Any properly trained person, if provided with certain kinds of information about a survey, can evaluate whether it reflects a proper awareness of and concern with the canons of survey research.

For this reason, the American Association for Public Opinion Research has prepared the following standards for releasing the results of surveys of public opinion to the news media:

Minimal Disclosure

The following minimum essentials for a professional

assessment of how a survey was conducted should be incorporated
in the text of any news release:

1. Identity of who sponsored the survey.
2. The exact wording of questions asked.
3. A definition of the population actually sampled.
4. Size of sample. For mail surveys, this should include the
   number of questionnaires mailed out and the number returned.
5. An indication of what allowance should be made for sampling
   error.
6. Which results are based on parts of the sample, rather
   than the total sample. (For example: likely voters only,
   those aware of an event, those who answered other questions
   in a certain way.)
7. Whether interviewing was done personally, by telephone,
   mail or on street-corners.
8. Timing of the interviewing in relation to relevant events.

We strongly urge the news media to ask for and to include ALL the
above information when preparing final copy for publication or broadcast. This should apply not only to polls conducted for publication
but also to "private polls" whose results are publicized.
       We strongly urge survey organizations that conduct polls for
the news media to prepare standard descriptions of their methods for
public distribution.
       We recommend that survey organizations use professional
journals and meetings to inform their colleagues in detail of their
activities and methods.
       We encourage the news media, and the professional staffs of
political parties, to use these professional sources of information to
become aware of what is accepted research practice.
       We wholeheartedly endorse the practice now adhered to by
many survey organizations of making their surveys available to
scholars for further analysis, and recommend its extension to confidential polls whenever possible.

Full Disclosure

       In the event that any question arises concerning the credi-
bility of a poll that is released to the public, detailed information
about how the survey was conducted would be needed. The availability of such information is essential if the acceptability of con-
tested poll results is to be professionally evaluated.
       For this reason, we have prepared an illustrative listing of
the kinds of questions that might be raised and discussed in a
detailed professional evaluation of a poll. All these questions
would not necessarily be raised in a specific case. But we believe
that all survey organizations should be willing to answer these kinds
of questions when raised in responsible inquiries.
       This would apply to any published poll, as well as to ques-
tions raised by clients who privately sponsor a poll.

Since answering questions such as those listed below can be time-consuming and can distract attention from on-going surveys, it is important that inquiries are made in a way that would not subject the survey organization to harassment. We particularly recommend the use of professional guidance whenever such inquiries are made.

ILLUSTRATIVE QUESTIONS FOR FULL DISCLOSURE

The Sample:

1. What is the precise definition of the population covered? (For example: all adults of voting age, all registered voters, city residents.)
2. What are the sampling procedures? (For example: sampling from telephone directories or membership lists, use of probability or quota methods, whether substitutions are permitted or callbacks made, completion rates.)
3. What is the size of the sample, and were there any weighting or statistical adjustments made?
4. What are the characteristics of the final sample? (For example: proportion of men and women, college educated persons, age distribution.)
5. What allowance should be made for sampling error and how was this calculated?
6. Which results are based on parts of the sample? (For example: "likely voters," those who are aware of an event, those who answered other questions in a certain way.)
7. Were special statistical or analytical procedures used in developing estimates of the split in public opinion on any issue or candidate for office?

Interviewing Procedures:

1. What is the exact wording of questions asked, or did interviewers word questions on the spot?
2. What was the sequence of questions?
3. How were people contacted? (For example: personal interview, telephone, mailed questionnaires, group interviews.)
4. Where were people contacted? (For example: at home, street corners, at work. Note: Street-corner interviews provide biased samples since they do not give every person a chance to be included in the sample.)
5. During what time of day were interviews conducted? (If interviews are conducted during the day only, employed persons are under-represented, while the ill and unemployed tend to be over-represented.)
6. What were the starting and ending dates of interviewing? (Intervening events can sometimes create major shifts in public opinion.)

Interviewer Supervision and Training:

    1.   Who were the interviewers? Were they members of the
        survey organization's own staff, were they recruited from
        local interviewing services, or were they untrained and
        possibly biased personnel such as volunteer party workers?
    2.   How are interviewers trained and instructed?
    3.   How are interviewers supervised and their work validated?

PUBLIC RELATIONS WORKERS

NATIONAL SCHOOL PUBLIC RELATIONS ASSOCIATION (NSPRA)
    1201 Sixteenth St., N.W., Washington, D.C. 20036
    Roy K. Wilson, Executive Director

Membership: The National School Public Relations Association,
founded in 1935 and with a present (1973) membership of 3000, is
an associated organization of the National Education Association.
Its members are engaged in Public relations in education organ-
izations--"school districts; community colleges; and national, regional, state, or local education associations and agencies."

Code of Ethics: The conduct guide for educators concerned with
public relations is the NSPRA Ethics for Educational Public Relations, developed and adopted by fourteen members of the Association
serving on a Task Force on Standards and on the Ethics Subcommittee of the Task Force, and on the Executive Committee of the
NSPRA. The conduct guide, adopted on March 28, 1970, "to promote and maintain the highest standards of personal and professional behavior and practice," includes a "Preamble" which outlines
"basic public relations principles to be followed by every person
in education"; and the Code of Ethics, which identifies guidelines
for the "public relations professional with major responsibility for
public relations" in an educational organization. No procedures for
enforcement of these ethical standards are reported.

Professional Insignia: The emblem of the National School Public
Relations Association is its logotype--a registered trademark in
the form of an unbordered design consisting of two school children
carrying books, a girl to the left, a boy to the right. This insignia is used on the organization letterhead and publications. The
color of the emblem is shown variously--gold on white (letterhead);
black on white (logotype).

Bibliography:
    National School Public Relations Association. Ethics for Edu-
        cational Public Relations. 1970. 8 pages. Pamphlet.

Includes "Preamble"--
public relations princi-
ples for all educators;
and "Code of Ethics"--
guidelines for public
relations professionals
in educational organiza-
tions.
_____. NSPRA Educa-
tional Public Rela-
tions Standards for
Programs.

"Ethics for Educational Public Relations"

Preamble

Every educational organization* has its many, varied publics
with which it must maintain effective relations. Public relations
must be an integral part of the total education enterprise, and everyone within that enterprise must recognize his public relations functions, responsibilities, and ethical obligations. Because all educational public relations must be founded upon certain basic precepts,
we believe public relations practices should reflect the high ethical
standards established by the National School Public Relations Association.

All persons in education, we believe, must accept a general
responsibility for the development of effective public relations. In
accordance with this general responsibility they must:

Seek continuously the improvement of educational opportunities
    for all children, youth, and adults.
Strive for professional growth and self-improvement.
Strive, within the area of their particular responsibilities,
    to enhance the communication concepts and expand the
    activities leading to more effective interpretation of the
    objectives, accomplishments, problems, and needs of
    education.
Utilize the growing number of resources and techniques of
    proven value in the field of public relations.
Be loyal to public relations ideals and practices and also
    to the best interests of the organization they serve,

_____

*An educational organization, as defined by the NSPRA Educational
Public Relations Standards for Programs, includes school districts;
community colleges; and national, regional, state, or local education associations and agencies.

striving constantly to harmonize the two loyalties.
Maintain high standards of personal and professional conduct,
   guided in all activities by truth, accuracy, fairness, and
   good taste.
Hold themselves accountable for the truth, accuracy, fairness, good taste, and general objectivity of their public
   utterances, both written and spoken.
Preserve the confidentiality of data which have been given
   under conditions of trust and promise.

Section I

   The public relations professional with all his publics shall
be guided constantly by truth, accuracy, good taste, and fairness.
   A.   He shall honor a system of fairness and good judgment
in the release of educational information to the news media.
   B.   He shall not intentionally disseminate misinformation.
The unintentional release of misinformation shall be immediately
rectified.
   C.   He shall do nothing to lessen the personal reputation
upon which his professional effectiveness rests.
   D.   He shall do nothing to lessen the reputation of the
organization.

Section II

   The public relations professional shall give his primary loyalty and support to the educational organization which employs him,
but he shall insist on the right to give advisory counsel in accordance
with public relations ideals and practices.
   A.   A public relations professional shall, whenever possible,
cooperate with other educational organizations or groups so long as
his association with such groups does not cause major continuing
conflict with his primary responsibility to his own organization.
   B.   The public relations professional shall notify his employer when policies or activities of the organization place him in
an untenable position and when his employment forces him to promote activities in opposition to the principles of this Code.

Section III

   The public relations professional shall be especially aware
of the influence he wields, and he shall neither promise nor grant
unprofessional advantages to those having special ties or relationships with him.
   A.   He shall be especially careful, as a member of a staff
with special skills and information, in providing services of a political nature for persons aspiring to elected educational positions.
   B.   The rights of a public relations professional to exercise
his privileges as a citizen and to use his special skills outside his
hours of employment, in ways not adverse to the special interest
of the employing agency, shall not be abridged.

C.   A public relations professional in a position to exercise influence on his own organization's policies and decisions shall refrain from accepting special gratuities.

D.   He shall not use for personal gain, except with the express permission of the employing organization, any of the facilities or materials which are provided for him in his employment.

E.   He shall avoid any derogatory acts or utterances designed to affect the employment of another professional.

Section IV

The public relations professional shall recognize that his effectiveness now and in the future is dependent in a large degree upon his own personal integrity and regard for the ideals of the profession as exemplified in this Code.

A.   He shall not misrepresent his professional qualifications.

B.   He shall in all of his activities faithfully observe copyright laws and shall give due credit to those individuals whose thoughts and words are borrowed and used.

C.   He shall cooperate with his professional colleagues to uphold and enforce this Code.

PUBLIC RELATIONS SOCIETY OF AMERICA (PRSA)
845 Third Ave., New York, N.Y. 10022
Mrs. Rea W. Smith, Vice President, Administration

Membership: The Public Relations Society of America, founded in 1948 and with a present (1973) membership of over 7000--grouped in local chapters in major cities throughout the United States--is a professional association of public relations workers. PRSA members work in business and industry, and in "public relations counseling firms, government agencies, educational institutions, trade and professional groups, and other non-profit organizations."

Education and experience requirements for the various Society membership classifications are:
    Pre-Associate Membership--Recent college graduates with
        less than one year of public relations experience, who as
        students, qualified for membership in the Public Relations
        Society of America.
    Associate Membership--Applicants with at least one year of
        experience in the practice or teaching of public relations.
    Accredited Membership--Applicants with at least five years
        of experience in the practice or teaching of public rela-
        tions, who complete the required written and oral examina-
        tions given by the Society. This classification replaced on
        January 1, 1969, the membership classification "Active
        Membership," which did not require passing an examination.

The Accreditation program "offers members an opportunity to take written and oral examinations to demonstrate their competence in the practice of public relations." Successful completion of these examinations entitles members to use the professional designation, "PRSA Accredited," and the use of the Accreditation Insignia.

The subject matter of the examination covers essentially:
"1.   the history, theory and fundamentals of public relations,
 2.   the techniques of public relations, and
 3.   the ethics of public relations."
The written examination is given in three parts requiring a total of five and one-half hours:
Part 1--multiple choice and true false questions testing
         general knowledge of public relations (1 1/2 hours);
Part 2--four discussion questions testing practical application
         of public relations principles in solving problems
         and in applying communications skills (1 hour);
Part 3--preparation of a complete and detailed plan for deal-
         ing with a public relations situation or problems
         (selected by the candidate from six different areas
         of practice) (3 hours).
The oral examination takes approximately 1 1/2-2 hours during which the candidate is asked a series of structured questions in discussion with a panel of three examiners.

Code of Ethics: The PRSA guide to professional conduct is its Declaration of Principles and Code of Professional Standards for the Practice of Public Relations, which was adopted in 1960 and most recently amended in 1963. This ethical guide, which enlarges and strengthens a similar Code of Professional Standards for the Practice of Public Relations in force since 1954, contains a Declaration of Principles--in the form of a pledge, and 17 Professional Standards--enumerating responsibilities in practice of public relations and relationships with clients, colleagues, and the public. Several of the Code paragraphs have been clarified by interpretations, which are published with the Code.

In enforcement of the Code, complaints from members, or the public, are received by the Grievance Board of the Society, which --since 1962--may also initiate allegations of unprofessional conduct against members. The Grievance Board through its Judicial Panels (one in each of the nine PRSA administrative districts throughout the United States) investigates conduct reported in violation of the professional code, may bring the accused member before a Judicial Panel, and recommends disciplinary action to the Society Board of Directors, in one of six forms: Warning, Admonishing, Reprimanding, Censuring, Suspension, Expulsion.

Other Guides to Professional Conduct: In 1963 the Society applied its ethical code to a specific aspect of public relations work, and issued:
An Official Interpretation of the PRSA Code of Professional

Standards for the Practice of Public Relations as it Applies to Financial Public Relations.
This area of public relations work, PRSA defined as:

"that area of public relations which relates to the dissemination of information that effects the understanding of stockholders and investors generally concerning the financial position and prospects of a company, and includes among its objectives the improvement of relations between corporations and their stockholders."

Responsibilities and duties are enumerated in ten subjects, and a violation of any of these points is "subject to the same procedure and penalties as a violation of the Code."

Professional Insignia: The emblem of the Society is "a reproduction of a sealing wax impression of the Society's initials," PRSA, in the form of an unbordered monogram. This insignia is used by the organization and its chapters on letterheads and publications, and by individual members on calling cards, letterheads, and other printed materials upon which the member's name appears, and on membership pins and tie bars. Color of the emblem is shown variously--black on white (logotype); white on turquoise (letterhead); turquoise on buff, red on buff, red on white, buff on grey, green on blue (publications).

Other Identification of Professional Status: PRSA members are authorized to identify themselves with the appropriate phrase of membership classification:

Member of the Public Relations Society of America,
Associate Member of the Public Relations Society of America,
Accredited Member of the Public Relations Society of America.
These designations--like the PRSA emblem--are correctly used to indicate an individual's membership, and are not shown with the firm or partnership names with which a member is associated.   Members meeting specified experience requirement and passing examinations, as described above under "Membership," are awarded the

professional designation to denote competence, "Accredited Member,"
and are authorized to use the Accreditation Insignia--the Society
emblem (its monogram) centered in a shield, with the word "Accredited" printed inside the top of the shield.

Bibliography:
        Decker, Francis K.   "PRSA's Code: How the Practitioner and
            the Public are Protected."   Public Relations Journal 25:
            26-29 March 1967.
            Review of cases brought before the Panels of the National
            Judicial Council concerning complaints of unprofessional con-
            duct under the code of professional standards.
        McKee, James E., Jr.   "The PRSA Grievance Board."   Public
            Relations Journal 27:18-21 June 1971
            Review of activity of the Board--number of cases heard, dis-
            position and comments on enforcement of the code of profession-
            al standards.   Comparison of PRSA disciplinary machinery with
            that in six other professional and trade associations.
        Public Relations Society of America.   Declaration of Principles and
            Code of Professional Standards for the Practice of Public Re-
            lations with Interpretations.   1963.   10 pages.   Pamphlet.
            Includes the PRSA code, with official interpretations and the in-
            terpretations of the Code as applied to financial public relations.
            _____.   PRSA Accreditation--What It Is and How to Prepare for
                It: A Study Guide.   1972.   17 pages.   Pamphlet.
            Information about qualifications for accreditation and the
            examination study guide, with books, periodicals and pam-
            phlets listed--basic texts keyed to study guide, and publica-
            tions for general reference.
            _____.   PRSA Membership--Hallmark of the Public Relations
                Professional.   Folder.
            Correct use of the PRSA identification of membership, desig-
            nations, and insignia.
            _____.   PRSA--Where the Action Is.   Folder.
            Informational brochure describing PRSA activities, member-
            ship qualifications, accreditation examinations.
            _____.   Rules of Procedure for Judicial Panels; Rules of
                Procedure for Grievance Board.   November 18, 1965,
                and April 7, 1967.
            Enforcement procedure for code of professional standards--
            complaint receipt and investigation of alleged violations of
            ethical guide.
            _____.   A Selected Public Relations Bibliography, 1972.   6
                pages.   Pamphlet.
            Annotated list of books and periodicals--General; Special;
            Directories, Bibliographies.
            _____.   Smith, Rea W.   "The PR Chronicle."   Public Rela-
                tions Journal 26:124-125 October 1970.
            History of professional organization in the public relations field.

                            "Declaration of Principles"

        Members [i.e., Active and Associate] of the Public Relations

Society of America acknowledge and publicly declare that the public relations profession in serving the legitimate interests of clients or employers is dedicated fundamentally to the goals of better mutual understanding and cooperation among the diverse individuals, groups, institutions and elements of our modern society.

In the performance of this mission, we pledge ourselves:

1. To conduct ourselves both privately and professionally in accord with the public welfare.

2. To be guided in all our activities by the generally accepted standards of truth, accuracy, fair dealing and good taste.

3. To support efforts designed to increase the proficiency of the profession by encouraging the continuous development of sound training and resourceful education in the practice of public relations.

4. To adhere faithfully to provisions of the duly adopted Code of Professional Standards for the Practice of Public Relations, a copy of which is in the possession of every member.

"Code of Professional Standards for the Practice of Public Relations"

This Code of Professional Standards for the Practice of Public Relations is adopted by the Public Relations Society of America to promote and maintain high standards of public service and conduct among its members in order that membership in the Society may be deemed a badge of ethical conduct; that Public Relations justly may be regarded as a profession; that the public may have increasing confidence in its integrity; and that the practice of Public Relations may best serve the public interest.

1. A member has a general duty of fair dealing towards his clients or employers, past and present, his fellow members and the general public.

2. A member shall conduct his professional life in accord with the public welfare.

3. A member has the affirmative duty of adhering to generally accepted standards of accuracy, truth and good taste.

4. A member shall not represent conflicting or competing interests without the express consent of those concerned, given after a full disclosure of the facts; nor shall he place himself in a position where his interest is or may be in conflict with his duty to his client, employer, another member or the public, without a full disclosure of such interests to all concerned.

5. A member shall safeguard the confidences of both present and former clients or employers and shall not accept retainers or employment which may involve the disclosure or use of these confidences to the disadvantage or prejudice of such clients or employers.

6. A member shall not engage in any practice which tends to corrupt the integrity of channels of public communication.

7. A member shall not intentionally disseminate false or

misleading information and is obligated to use ordinary care to avoid dissemination of false or misleading information.

8. A member shall be prepared to identify to the public the source of any communication for which he is responsible, including the name of the client or employer on whose behalf the communication is made.

9. A member shall not make use of any individual or organization purporting to serve or represent some announced cause, or purporting to be independent or unbiased, but actually serving an undisclosed special or private interest of a member or his client or his employer.

10. A member shall not intentionally injure the professional reputation or practice of another member. However, if a member has evidence that another member has been guilty of unethical, illegal or unfair practices, including practices in violation of this Code, he should present the information to the proper authorities of the Society for action in accordance with the procedure set forth in Article XIII of the Bylaws.

11. A member shall not employ methods tending to be derogatory of another member's client or employer or of the products, business or services of such client or employer.

12. In performing services for a client or employer a member shall not accept fees, commissions or any other valuable consideration in connection with those services from anyone other than his client or employer without the express consent of his client or employer, given after a full disclosure of the facts.

13. A member shall not propose to a prospective client or employer that the amount of his fee or other compensation be contingent on or measured by the achievement of specified results; nor shall he enter into any fee agreement to the same effect.

14. A member shall not encroach upon the professional employment of another member. Where there are two engagements, both must be assured that there is no conflict between them.

15. A member shall, as soon as possible, sever his relations with any organization when he knows or should know that his continued employment would require him to conduct himself contrary to the principles of this Code.

16. A member called as a witness in a proceeding for the enforcement of this Code shall be bound to appear unless, for sufficient reason, he shall be excused by the panel hearing the same.

17. A member shall co-operate with fellow members in upholding and enforcing this Code.

"Code Interpretations"

Interpretation of Code Paragraph 6 which reads, "A member shall not engage in any practice which tends to corrupt the integrity of the channels of public communication."

1. Practices prohibited by this Code paragraph are those which tend to place representatives of media under obligation to the

member or his company or his client, such as--

a. any form of payment or compensation to a media representative in order to obtain, and in exchange for which, preferential or guaranteed news or editorial coverage in the medium is promised, implied or delivered.

b. any retainer of a media employee which involves the use of his position as a media employee for the private purposes of the member or his client or employer where the circumstances of such retainer are not fully disclosed to and accepted by the media employer.

c. an agreement between a member and a media employee when such agreement includes a provision that the media employee will secure preferential or guaranteed coverage in the medium for the member, his firm or his client, or utilization by a member of such an agreement between his employer, his firm or his client and a media employee.

d. providing vacation trips to media representatives where no news assignment is involved.

e. any attempt by a member to lead his employer or client to believe that a member has obtained independent coverage for the employer or client in a medium over which the member has financial or editorial influence or control.

f. the use by a member of an investment made by the member, his firm or his client in a medium to obtain preferential or guaranteed coverage in the medium.

g. the use by a member of a loan of money made to a medium by the member, his firm or his client to obtain preferential or guaranteed coverage in the medium.

2. This Code paragraph does not prohibit entertaining media representatives at meals, cocktails or press parties, nor does it prohibit the bona fide press junket where media representatives are given an opportunity for on-the-spot viewing of a news event or product or service in which the media representative has a legitimate news interest, provided that independence of action is left to the media representative.

3. This Code paragraph does not prohibit the gift or loan of sample products or services to media representatives whose assignments indicate an interest in such products or services, if the sample products or services are manufactured, sold or rendered by the member's company or client and the sampling is a reasonable method of demonstrating the product or service.

4. This Code paragraph does not prohibit the giving of souvenirs or holiday gifts of nominal value as goodwill gestures to media representatives.

Interpretation of Code Paragraph 13 which reads, "A member shall not propose to a prospective client or employer that the amount of his fee or other compensation be contingent on or measured by the achievement of specified results; nor shall he enter into any fee agreement to the same effect."

1. This Code paragraph means that a member may take into consideration the following factors in determining compensation for his services:

a. the experience, judgment and skills required to handle the matter properly.
b. the characteristics and difficulty of the problems involved.
c. the time and labor required.
d. the effect on the member's employment by other clients or potential clients.
e. the customary or prevailing compensation for similar services.
f. the values involved in the matter and the benefits resulting to the client or employer from the services.
g. the duration and character of the employment, whether casual or for a continuing period.
h. the equipment or personnel investment required in order to perform the function.

2. This Code paragraph prohibits a member from entering into any agreement whereby the member's rate of compensation is determined or conditioned by the amount of newspaper or magazine lineage obtained for the member's company or client. This applies equally to radio and television coverage, or any form of exposure of a client's message. It applies further to any contingency fee based on increase in sales volume, increase in profit margins, increase in stock value or the attainment of specified political or legislative results. (See also paragraph 9, "Official Interpretation of the Code as it applies to Financial Public Relations")

3. This Code paragraph means that a member may guarantee to produce certain materials, such as films, feature articles, scripts, news releases, etc., and promise that these will be of high quality or specific type; but any guarantee that such materials, once produced, shall achieve a specified minimum use by media outlets, in other than paid time or space, and failing which use the fee or compensation will be reduced, is a practice prohibited by this Code paragraph.

Interpretation of Code Paragraph 14 which reads, "A member shall not encroach upon the professional employment of another member. Where there are two engagements, both must be assured that there is no conflict between them."

1. This Code paragraph is not designed to curb the freedom of a member to seek employment or business for his counseling firm by all approved and legitimate means. However, it is interpreted to mean that a member shall not invade or infringe upon the counselor-client or employee-employer relationship of another member.

2. A member would not violate this Code paragraph by--
a. sending copies of his resume and examples of his work to potential employers even if the employers currently employ members of the Society.

b. advertising his or his firm's qualifications in any publication he deems suitable.

c. mailing copies of advertisements, circulars or booklets describing his or his firm's services, or copies of speeches or articles to potential clients, provided any such mailing is not one of solicitation and provided the mailing contains no derogatory comment about another member.

d. furnishing, upon specific request, factual information about his firm, its principals, personnel and types of services rendered, including names of clients, provided such information contains no proposals to a client of another member.

3.   This Code paragraph prohibits a member from seeking individual professional employment by deprecating the character, ability or performance of another member.

4.   This Code paragraph requires that a counselor member--

a. before soliciting a prospective client, make all reasonable attempts to determine whether the prospective client has an existing relationship with another counselor member who would be replaced, and, if so, make no contact until the incumbent has been notified that his replacement is being considered or that the employment of the incumbent has been terminated.

b. after making an initial contact with a prospective client and subsequently learning that a counselor member-client relationship exists of which he was unaware, shall at that point make no further overtures nor conduct any negotiations with the prospective client until the incumbent has been notified that his replacement is being considered or that the employment of the incumbent has been terminated.

5.   Where a member is solicited by a prospective client to take over the functions currently performed by another member, he shall decline to consider the offer until the incumbent member has been advised that a replacement of his services is being considered. Upon specific request, the member may provide information of a factual nature about his firm and its services but shall make no proposals to the client of another member until he has determined that the incumbent has been notified of a possible change.

6.   Where a member is solicited by a prospective client to perform functions separate from those currently performed for the same client by another member, it is the responsibility of the solicited member to determine that the incumbent member has been informed, since both must be assured that there is no conflict between the two functions.

"An Official Interpretation of the PRSA Code
as It Applies to Financial Public Relations"

The Public Relations Society of America adopted a Code of

Professional Standards for the Practice of Public Relations in 1959
and later amended it in 1963.   These Standards replaced and
strengthened a similar Code previously in force since 1954.

In 1963 the PRSA Board of Directors approved the following
interpretation of this Code as it applies to financial public relations
practice which is defined as "that area of public relations which relates to the dissemination of information that affects the understanding of stockholders and investors generally concerning the financial
position and prospects of a company, and includes among its objectives the improvement of relations between corporations and their
stockholders. "

This interpretation which was prepared for the PRSA Board
by the Society's Legal Counsel, an Advisory Committee working with
the Securities and Exchange Commission and the PRSA Committee
on Standards of Professional Practice is rooted directly in the Code
and has the full force of the Code behind it.   A violation of any
one of the following ten points should be subject to the same procedures and penalties as a violation of the Code.

1.   It is the responsibility of the member practicing financial public relations to know and understand the rules and regulations of the SEC and the laws which it administers and the other
laws, rules and regulations affecting financial public relations and
to act in accordance with their letter and spirit.   (See paragraph 2
of the Code.)

2.   It shall be the objective of such member to follow the
policy of full disclosure of corporate information, except in such
instances where such information is of a confidential nature.   The
purpose of this objective is to enable the investing public to make
an accurate evaluation of the company and not to influence the price
of securities.   Such information should be accurate, clear and
understandable.   (See paragraphs 1 and 2 of the Code.)

3.   Such member shall observe the confidential nature of
certain of the information he has access to because of his employment and shall take every precaution to make sure this information
is not used in a manner detrimental to his client's or employer's
best interests.   (See paragraph 5 of the Code.)

4.   Such member shall disclose or release information both
favorable and unfavorable--promptly so as to avoid the possibility
of any use of the information by an insider or "tippee" for personal
gain or avoidance of loss.   In general, such member should make
every effort to comply with the spirit and intent of the "Timely
Disclosure" provisions of the company manuals of the New York
Stock Exchange.   Information deemed not confidential but which is
not subject to a formal release shall be available to all on an equal
basis.   (See paragraphs 1 and 2 of the Code.)

5. Such member shall exercise reasonable care to ascertain the facts correctly and to disseminate only information which he believes to be accurate and adequate. Such member shall use reasonable care to avoid the issuance or release of predictions or projections of financial or other matters lacking adequate basis in fact. (See paragraph 7 of the Code.)

6. Such member shall act promptly to correct false or misleading information or rumors concerning his client's or employer's securities or business whenever he has reason to believe such information or rumors exist. (See paragraphs 1, 2 and 7 of the Code.)

7. Such member shall clearly identify to the investing public the sources of any communication for which he is responsible, including the name of the client or employer on whose behalf the communication is made. (See paragraph 8 of the Code.)

8. Such member shall not exploit the information he has gained as an insider for personal gain. However, this is not intended to prohibit a member from making bona fide investments in his company's or client's securities in accordance with normal investment practices. (See paragraphs 1 and 4 of the Code.)

9. Such member shall not accept compensation which would place him in a position of conflict with his duty to his client, employer or the investing public. Specifically, such member shall not accept a contingent fee and he shall not accept a stock option from his client or employer unless part of an over-all plan in favor of corporate executives, nor shall he accept securities as compensation at a value substantially below market price. (See paragraphs 4 and 13 of the Code.)

10. Such member shall so act as to maintain the integrity of channels of public communication and to observe generally accepted standards of good taste. He shall as a minimum observe the publicly announced standards published by organizations representing the media of communications. (See paragraph 6 of the Code.)

PURCHASING AGENTS

NATIONAL ASSOCIATION OF PURCHASING MANAGEMENT (NAPM)
    11 Park Place, New York, N.Y. 10007
    G. W. Howard Ahl, Executive Vice President

<u>Membership:</u> The National Association of Purchasing Management

(known as the National Association of Purchasing Agents until June
1, 1968) founded in 1915 and with a present (1973) membership of
approximately 18,500, is a professional association of purchasing
agents, who are individual members of more than one hundred
affiliated city, state, or regional groups, organized into nine geographic districts throughout the United States.   Members, drawn
from widely diversified business interests, include purchasing
executives from "large and small units of industrial, educational,
governmental, utility, and distribution organizations." The variety
of membership interest is reflected in eleven national interest groups
in the Association, including purchasing agents and buyers for drug,
pharmaceutical and chemical companies; food, health and petroleum
industries; government, educational, and institutional units; office
supplies and equipment; public utilities; and editors of affiliated
association publications.

Purchasers are eligible for membership in NAPM if they perform or are assigned as one or more of the following:
"1.   Director or manager of a purchasing department.
2.   Assistant, supervisor, or buyer in a purchasing department.
3.   Member of a purchasing department having responsibility
for purchasing research, value analysis, inventory control or other activity or function, other than a routine
clerical or record-keeping function, which is directly
related to purchasing."
Salesmen engaged in the selling or solicitation of orders are not
eligible for membership in NAPM.

Code of Ethics: The guide for professional conduct of purchasing
managers is the NAPM Principles and Standards of Purchasing Practice, prepared by an Association committee and adopted in May 1923.
These ten principles form the basis of the professional standards of
purchasing practice.   No formal procedures have been established
for enforcement of these principles.

Other Guides to Professional Conduct: The NAPM Standards of Conduct adopted by the organization's Executive Committee on June 11,
1959, contain the Principles and Standards of Purchasing Practice
and two other codes of ethical purchasing practice:
Standards and Ethics of Buying and Selling--ten obligations
and conduct guides, with detailed elaboration of several
principles, such as "Gifts and Gratuities," "Outside Business Affiliations," and "Ethical Responsibility of Groups."
Standards of Practice of NAPM Editors' Group--seven principles of publication practice regarding content and purpose of printed materials, editorial pages and advertising.

Professional Insignia: The NAPM emblem is its official seal--a
design selected from drawings submitted by members, and adopted in
May 1919.   This insignia is an arrowhead, point down, with a centered triangle bearing the script initials of the organization, "NAPM";

and the name of the group, "The
National Association" (at the top
of the bordering band), "Purchasing" (at the left side in the band),
and "Management," (in the right
side of the band).   The color of
the emblem is shown variously--
blue on white; black on white
(publications).   This insignia is
authorized for use by affiliated
association and individual members, as well as by the national
association.

Bibliography:
       National Association of Pur-
              chasing Management.
              National Association of Purchasing Management.   1970.
              15 pages.   Pamphlet.
       Informational brochure including NAPM membership qualifi-
       cations.
              _____.   Standards of Conduct.   June 11, 1951.   4 pages.
       Text of Principles and Standards of Purchasing Practice,
       Standards and Ethics of Buying and Selling, and Standards of
       Practice of the NAPM Editors' Group.

"N. A. P. M. Standards of Conduct"

Foreword: "What Makes A Profession"

"If there is such a thing as a profession as a concept distinct from a vocation, it must consist in the ideals which
its members maintain, the dignity of character which they
bring to the performance of their duties, and the austerity
of the self-imposed ethical standards.   To constitute a
true profession, there must be ethical tradition so potent
as to bring into conformity members whose personal
standards of conduct are at a lower level, and to have an
elevating and ennobling effect on those members.   A profession cannot be created by resolution, or become such
overnight.   It requires many years for its development,
and they must be years of self-denial, years when success
by base means is scorned, years when no results bring
honor except those free from the taint of unworthy methods."

--Author Unknown

When a group of people engaged in the same profession get
together to form an Association, the aims and purposes are carefully outlined for all to heed and follow.   This brings about unity
of action and the results will be accumulative and reflect the ability

and accomplishments of the membership.   This is taken care of in
the Constitution and By-Laws.

If the Association is to prosper and receive the desired degree of respect by society, a Standards of Conduct is essential.
Just what does the phrase "Standards of Conduct" mean? Standards
of Conduct for those engaged in the field of purchasing are simply
a code of ethical behavior which practically all of us would live by
even if they were not in existence.   They are set up not because it
is assumed that we would act improperly without them, but primarily
to help us recognize an appropriate action from an inappropriate
one.   Since the decisions involved entail the use of judgment, a
Standards of Conduct Manual should help us as members of the National Association of Purchasing Management and the profession it
represents, to evaluate the factors in a similar manner and help
us arrive at uniform conclusions.   The underlying principles of
these standards are based on common sense, courtesy, and moral
codes that are essential for us to govern our official conduct in a
manner to reflect our profession in the most favorable manner to
society.

Purchasing people are engaged in activities which come under
the continuing scrutiny of our superiors, our associates, our suppliers and prospective suppliers, the public and the press.   In our
contacts with individuals, and the suppliers with whom we have business dealings, it is necessary for all of us to exercise a strict rule
of personal conduct to insure that relations of a compromising nature,
or even the appearance of such relations be scrupulously avoided.

How we ourselves judge our personal actions is essential to
us, but we must be ever mindful of the impression made on the
public, for it is by them our profession is judged.   Hard and fast
rules applicable to every incident and situation which may confront
us cannot be laid down.   Holding, as we all do, positions of trust
dictates that our actions must be governed by the highest standards
of conduct.

The National Association of Purchasing Management many years
ago established "Principles and Standards of Purchasing Practice"
and "Standards and Ethics of Buying and Selling" for the guidance
of all in our daily conduct.

"Principles and Standards of Purchasing Practice"

Loyalty to His Company
Justice to Those with Whom He Deals
Faith in His Profession

From these principles are derived the N. A. P. M.
standards of purchasing practice.

1. To consider, first, the interest of his company in all transactions and to carry out and believe in its established policies.

2. To be receptive to competent counsel for his colleagues and to be guided by such council without impairing the dignity and responsibility of his office.

3. To buy without prejudice, seeking to obtain the maximum ultimate value for each dollar of expenditure.

4. To strive consistently for knowledge of the materials and processes of manufacture, and to establish practical methods for the conduct of his office.

5. To subscribe to and work for honesty and truth in buying and selling, and to denounce all forms and manifestations of commercial bribery.

6. To accord a prompt and courteous reception, so far as conditions will permit, to all who call on a legitimate business mission.

7. To respect his obligations and to require that obligations to him and to his concern be respected, consistent with good business practice.

8. To avoid sharp practice.

9. To counsel and assist fellow purchasing agents in the performance of their duties, whenever occasion permits.

10. To co-operate with all organizations and individuals engaged in activities designed to enhance the development and standing of purchasing.

"Standards and Ethics of Buying and Selling"

Unnecessary sales and purchasing expense is an economic waste--a tax on legitimate industry. Its elimination will assure satisfactory profits to the producer, economy to the consumer, and greater efficiency in commercial relations.

We recognize that the concern which buys must also sell, that buying and selling are companionate functions, that sound commercial transactions must be mutually profitable, and that co-operation between buyer and seller will reduce the cost to purchasing, sales, and distribution with consequent benefits to industry as a whole.

In furtherance of these principles, we subscribe to the following standards in our buying and selling:

1. To buy and sell on the basis of value, recognizing that value represents that combination of quality, service, and price which assures greatest ultimate economy to the user.

2. To respect our obligations and neither expressly nor impliedly to promise a performance which we cannot reasonably expect to fulfill.

3. To avoid misrepresentation and sharp practice in our purchases and sales, recognizing that permanent business relations can be maintained only on a structure of honesty and fair dealing.

4. To be courteous and considerate of those with whom we

deal, to be prompt and business like in our appointments, and to
carry on negotiations with all reasonable expedition so as to avoid
trespassing on the rights of others to the time of buyers and salesmen.

5.   To avoid statements tending to injure or discredit a
legitimate competitor, and to divulge no information acquired in
confidence with the intent of giving or receiving an unfair advantage
in a competitive business transaction.

6.   To strive for simplification and standardization within the
bounds of utility and industrial economy, and to further the development of products and methods which will improve industrial efficiency.

7.   To recognize that character is the greatest asset in commerce, and to give it major consideration in the selection of customers and source of supply.

8.   To adjust claims and settle disputes on the basis of facts
and fairness, to submit the facts to arbitration if a mutual agreement cannot be reached, to abide by the decisions of the arbiters
and to resort to legal measures in commercial disputes only when
the preceding courses prove ineffective.

9.   To provide or accept no gifts or entertainment in the
guise of sales expense, where the intent or effect is to unduly prejudice the recipients in favor of the donor as against legitimate
competitors.

10.   To give or receive no bribes, in the form of money or
otherwise, in any commercial transaction and to expose commercial
bribery wherever encountered for the purpose of maintaining the
highest standard of ethics in industry.

In this manual we are going to elaborate on a few principles
which are mentioned rather briefly and which have come in for considerable discussion in Association meetings.   We believe we should
maintain our standards on an even higher plane than that generally
accepted by society.   This is the true test of greatness.

Gifts and Gratuities

This is a subject of increasing concern to all clear-thinking
purchasing people.   There is a lot of precedent involved and it is
difficult to reconcile the philosophy of a Purchasing Department
which does not desire to receive gifts with that of a Sales Department in the same company which makes it a regular practice to
present gifts.   However, a firm and understandable attitude on our
part will go a long way to attain the position of dignity and repute
for which we are striving.   Time and concerted action will eventually
bring about the desired results.

There is nothing that can undermine respect for the purchasing profession more than improper action on the part of its members
with regard to gifts, gratuities, favors, etc.   People engaged in
purchasing should not accept from any supplier or prospective supplier any money, gift or favor which might influence, or be suspected of influencing their buying decisions.   We must decline to

accept or must return any such gift or favor offered us or members of our immediate family. The declination of these gifts or favors must be done discreetly and courteously. Possible embarrassment resulting from refusals does not constitute a basis for an exception.

The term "Gifts, Gratuities and Favors" includes, but is not limited to, monies, credits, discounts, seasonal or special occasion presents (Christmas, birthday, weddings, etc.) edibles, drinks, household appliances and furnishings, clothing, loans of goods or money, tickets to sporting events, theaters, etc., dinners, parties, transportation, vacations, travel or hotel expenses and various forms of entertainment. In any case, where the return of a gift is impracticable because of its perishability, disposition may be made to a charitable institution, and the donor informed of the disposition.

Personal business transactions with suppliers or prospective suppliers should be scrupulously avoided. Personal loans must not be accepted from such companies on any basis. Offers of hospitality, business courtesies, or favors, no matter how innocent in appearance, can be a source of embarrassment to all parties concerned.

We should not allow ourselves to become involved in situations where unnecessary embarrassment may result from an offer or refusal of a hospitality or a business courtesy from our suppliers or potential suppliers. It is generally the best policy to decline any sort of favor, hospitality or entertainment, to insure that all relationships are above reproach at all times. Situations requiring common sense and good judgment will develop, such as a company-provided luncheon during the course of a visit to a supplier's plant located in some remote area. Another example is the case of a buyer or a purchasing expeditor-inspector accepting free company-provided automobile transportation on a temporary or emergency basis where other means are not available.

A purchasing man may ethically attend periodic meetings or dinners of trade associations, professional and technical societies or other industrial organizations as the guest of a supplier where the meetings are of an educational and informative nature and where it is considered to be in the best interest of buyer-seller relationships. The repeated appearance of an individual at such regularly scheduled meetings, as the guest of the same company, is the type of situation which should be tactfully avoided.

The simple casual luncheon or cocktail with a supplier's representative are merely normal expressions of a friendly business relationship or a time-saving expediency. It would be prudish to raise any serious question on this score. The purchasing man himself is in the best position to judge when this point has been exceeded. It is the time-saving expediency which makes up the great majority of such instances and, since the buyer's company prestige is also involved, there is every reason why an adequate expense

account should be available to the buyer. It is a small price for
maintaining a position free from any taint of obligation.

Mature purchasing people know that they are quickly classified among the sales' fraternity by the amount of entertainment
they expect or will accept. Salesmen usually speak with real respect of the buyer who pays his share of entertainment expenses.
The purchasing expense account is the most effective answer to this
ethical problem.

Outside Business Affiliations

Since we are engaged in the administration and expenditure of
funds of the company we represent, our conduct must necessarily be
subject to more restrictions and to higher standards not only on the
job, but in our outside activities as well. We should not be involved in purchasing transactions with any companies in which we,
our family or relatives are owners or have a substantial financial
interest. We should not engage in business and professional activities from which we might derive financial profit or other benefits
resulting from our employment as a buyer.

Ethical Responsibility of Groups

If we will concede that it is important for purchasing people
to conform to high ethical standards as individuals, then it will
inexorably follow that it is more important that purchasing people
in groups do so. The impact of group deviation from the highest
of ethical standards will be infinitely greater than deviations of a
single individual. And this is true if only for the fact that more
people are involved. A single person can be guilty of unethical conduct and this does not necessarily reflect discredit upon the organization nor upon purchasing generally. But, when a group commits
an error of this kind the charge can justifiably be made that someone in the group should have known better. And, the next step by
someone who is so inclined would very likely be to generalize and
say they're all alike.

It is quite possible for an individual who personally observes
the highest degree of ethical conduct to accede to the majority
opinion or remain silent when a questionable act is being considered
by a group. The individual may hide behind the cloak of anonymity
provided by the fact that action is being taken as a group. He may
also feel that criticism which might be justly directed toward an
individual act would be withheld in the case of a group. Lack of
respect and vocal criticism do not necessarily go hand in hand.
We can well have the former without the latter. And, if we are
to engender that respect for our profession which we so earnestly
desire then we must be extremely careful that group action is such
that the highest order of respect is commanded--that our actions
are above criticism.

In most organizations, there are developed over the years habits and patterns of action which tend to be taken for granted as being perfectly natural and in conformance with the aims and ideals of the group. Newcomers into the group and, particularly, newly appointed or elected officials of the group, tend to automatically continue these action patterns. Periodic scrutiny to determine conformance with current aims and ideals is minimized. Minor changes from year to year, although insignificant in themselves, can cumulatively distort the action pattern so that it no longer represents the ideals of the group.

It is necessary, therefore, to take stock periodically to see that programs are consistent with the high ideals for which we strive. Each element of the program should be subjected to a searching examination to determine whether it does or does not conform to the highest of standards. And, if it does not, it should be discontinued. It will probably be well to consider here some group actions which may be considered to be at least questionable. This is not to say that those practices discussed below are all-inclusive. Rather, it is the intent that they should be considered as examples.

There has grown up among groups of purchasing people and particularly local associations of the National Association of Purchasing Management, the custom of holding periodic joint meetings with sales organizations, such as local affiliates of the National Sales Executives' organization. This can be an estimable practice and can be beneficial to both groups. Quite frequently, a "hospitality hour" becomes part of the program. And, more than likely, the entire meeting can be enhanced by a custom of this kind. However, consideration should be given to each organization acting as host on an alternate basis. In this way, there is no obligation incurred by anyone and no one is penalized.

The temptations are many and sometimes the pressure is great to let a salesman's organization or a supplier company provide the cocktail party, the prizes for the Christmas party or the golf outing or the annual picnic. There is frequently the implied if not the direct offer to provide more than the proper degree of hospitality during a plant visit. But those in authority on the purchasing side of the coin will think twice before departing from the strictest interpretation of the highest standards of conduct.

Purchasing organizations which publish magazines or other periodicals containing advertising must be especially conscious of the proprieties. Here, again, the temptation (admittedly with only the good of the organization in mind) is great to subject the advertiser or prospective advertiser to pressure.

"Standards of Practice of NAPM Editors' Group"

In this area of association activities it is well to conform

to the "Standards of Practice" established by the Editors' Group of
the National Association of Purchasing Management, which are:

We, the publishers of magazines, published by, and/or for
Associations affiliated with the National Association of Purchasing Management, pledge ourselves to the following Standards of Practice:

1. To disseminate information relative to and to promote the
welfare of industry in general and the purchasing profession in particular.

2. To promote a better understanding of the ethics and functions of purchasing.

3. To decline any advertisement that has a tendency to mislead or that does not conform to business integrity.

4. To establish and maintain suitable contacts with Association members.

5. To establish contacts with, and arouse interest of prospective members in our local Associations and the National Association of Purchasing Management.

6. To maintain our editorial pages in accordance with the
highest journalistic practice ... to maintain balanced publications
... to publish nothing that will reflect upon the good name of an
individual, an association, a firm, or the purchasing profession.

7. To accept advertising solely upon the basis of value of
the medium to the advertiser ... to accept no advertising given as
a favor to any purchaser or group of purchasers ... to recognize
a definite responsibility to the advertiser ... to keep our reading
columns independent of advertising consideration.

Actions of all purchasing people on ethical questions must
not only be meticulous at all times and under all circumstances,
but must also be constant and consistent. Relations of a compromising nature, or even the appearance of such relations must be
scrupulously avoided.

QUALITY TECHNOLOGISTS

AMERICAN SOCIETY FOR QUALITY CONTROL (ASQC)
    161 W. Wisconsin Ave., Milwaukee, Wis. 53203
    Robert W. Shearman, Executive Director

Membership: The American Society for Quality Control, founded
in 1946 and with a present (1973) membership of 20,000, is a professional society of engineers working primarily in the field of
quality control. To qualify for one of the categories of membership
(other than "Honorary Member" and "Fellow"), an applicant must
meet specified education and experience requirements:

Senior Member--have been "engaged professionally in quality

control, quality engineering, or in allied field of industrial, administrative, or analytical control for 10 years."

Member--"a graduate in engineering, science, mathematics, or statistics curriculum, or equivalent attainments including six years of increasingly important experience in quality or inspection work or in statistical operations of a control or analytical nature."

Associate Member--"engaged or interested in inspection or quality engineering work."

"The ASQC Education and Training Institute has developed criteria establishing the essential areas of knowledge required of a quality or reliability engineer or technician. Rigorous examinations ... must be passed for ASQC certification of professional knowledge." This certification "serves as a benchmark of recognition by professional colleagues."

Code of Ethics: The guide for professional conduct of members is the ASQC Code of Ethics, consisting of four Fundamental Principles and twelve Canons, which generally follow the Engineers' Council for Professional Development ethical guide, Canons of Ethics of Engineers. Canons of the ASQC Code are grouped in three sections:
Relations with the Public,
Relations with Employers and Clients, and
Relations with Peers.
No enforcement procedures for the Code are reported.

Professional Insignia: The ASQC emblem is a circular design--a Greek sigma, with a centered line graph, representing a production control chart; the organization name, "American Society for Quality Control," is spaced around a bordering band. The color of the emblem is dark blue on white.

Bibliography:
Alger, Philip L. "Ethics and the ASQC." Quality Progress, pages 11-12, October 1968.
Background and application of the ASQC Code of Ethics.
American Society for Quality Control. Background Information on the American Society for Quality Control. Revised September 12, 1972.
Includes membership categories and requirements, certification awarded for professional knowledge.
_____. Code of Ethics. 1 page.
Principles and canons governing professional conduct of ASQC members.
Broffman, Morton H. "A New Concern for the Old Business Ethics." Quality Progress, page 12, September 1971.
Effect of changes in social values on business ethics.

"Code of Ethics"

Fundamental Principles

Each member of the Society, to uphold and advance the
honor and dignity of the profession, and in keeping with high
standards of ethical conduct:
I.   Will be honest and impartial, and serve with devotion his
employer, his clients and the public.
II.   Will strive to increase the competence and prestige of
the profession.
III.   Will use his knowledge and skill for the advancement
of human welfare, and in promoting the safety and reliability of
products for public use.
IV.   Will earnestly endeavor to aid the work of the Society.

Relations with the Public

1.1   Each Society member will do whatever he can to promote the reliability and safety of all products that come within his
jurisdiction.
1.2   He will endeavor to extend public knowledge of the
work of the Society and its members that relates to the public welfare.
1.3   He will be dignified and modest in explaining his work
and merit.
1.4   He will preface any public statements that he may
issue by clearly indicating on whose behalf they are made.

Relations with Employers and Clients

2.1   Each Society member will act in professional matters as
a faithful agent or trustee for each employer or client.
2.2   He will inform each client or employer of any business
connections, interests or affiliations which might influence his judgment or impair the equitable character of his services.
2.3   He will indicate to his employer or client the adverse
consequences to be expected if his professional judgment is overruled.
2.4   He will not disclose information concerning the business
affairs or technical processes of any present or former employer or
client without his consent.
2.5   He will not accept compensation from more than one
party for the same service without the consent of all parties.   If
employed, he will engage in supplementary employment of consulting
practice only with the consent of his employer.

Relations with Peers

3.1   Each member of the Society will take care that credit
for the work of others is given to those to whom it is due.
3.2   He will endeavor to aid the professional development

and advancement of those in his employ or under his supervision.
    3. 3   He will not compete unfairly with others.   He will extend his friendship and confidence to all associates and those with whom he has business relations.

RADIOLOGIC TECHNOLOGISTS

AMERICAN REGISTRY OF CLINICAL RADIOGRAPHY TECHNOLOGISTS (ARCRT)
    Bass Bldg., 9th Floor, Enid, Okla.   73701
    Charles G. Huddleston, Administrative Director

Membership: The American Registry of Clinical Radiography Technologists (also known as "ART"--"American Radiography Technologists"), founded in 1955 and with a present (1973) membership of about 6000, is a professional association of radiography technologists, who have been admitted to membership by passing a written examination prepared and administered by the registry.

    To qualify for examination, an applicant must have completed a two year course in Radiography Technology, in a hospital affiliated school approved by the Registry, or in a college or university offering an associate degree in Radiography Technology; college graduates with a Bachelor of Science degree also qualify to take the examination. Technologists are admitted to membership without examination if they are licensed in state of practice or are members of the American Registry of Radiologic Technologists.   When a technologist is admitted to ART membership, he is awarded as an indication of competence the professional designation, "Registered Radiography Technologist"--"R. T. (ART). "

Code of Ethics: The conduct guide of the American Radiography Technologists is its Code of Ethics, a pledge of service, practice, and dedication.   Members found in violation of the professional code may be disciplined by suspension of their certificate.

Professional Insignia: The official emblem of the Registry is a circular design, with a centered X-Ray Machine; a rectangle to the right with the word, "Registered, " below which is the name of the organization, "American Radiography Technologists"; a bordering

wreath shows at the bottom a scalloped tab, and at the top, the
framed word, "Member." This insignia is shown in black on white
(stationery; publications).

Other Identification of Professional Status: As described above
under "Membership," the title and letters of a professional designation are authorized for use by qualified members as an indication
of competence, "Registered Radiography Technologist"--"R.T. (ART)."

Bibliography:
    American Radiography Technologists. Code of Ethics. Single
        sheet.
    Conduct code in form of pledge.
    American Registry of Clinical Radiography Technologists.
        Minimum Requirements for Registry of Approved X-Ray
        Training Schools. April 1971. 8 pages. Pamphlet.
    Approval procedure and standards for hospital affiliated
    schools of X-Ray Technology.

                            "Code of Ethics"

    I, a registered X-Ray Technologist, pledge myself to the ser-
vice of mankind and to the alleviation of human suffering;
    I pledge myself to the service of the medical profession and
will provide para-medical services, within the limits of my capabilities as an x-ray technologist, only under the supervision of a
licensed practitioner of the healing arts;
    I pledge that I will utilize my best efforts and judgment to
assure that no word, act or deed of mine will adversely affect the
welfare of a patient entrusted to my care, the members of the
medical profession, or my colleagues in x-ray technology;
    I pledge that I will protect the confidential relationship which
exists between the patient and the physician, and will never reveal
or discuss information acquired by virtue of my position;
    I pledge to devote my life to the service of my God and my
Country;
    In the spirit of those who have contributed to the art and
science of radiation medicine, I dedicate myself;
    I so affirm....

AMERICAN REGISTRY OF RADIOLOGIC TECHNOLOGISTS (ARRT)
    2600 Wayzata Blvd., Minneapolis, Minn. 55405
    Roland C. McGowan, R.T. (ARRT), Executive Director

Membership: Founded in 1922 as the American Registry of X-Ray
Technicians by the joint efforts of the Radiological Society of North
America, the American Roentgen Ray Society, the Canadian

Association of Radiologists, and the American Society of X-Ray Technicians, the ARRT is a professional organization that conducts semi-annual examinations and authorizes certification designating qualified radiologic technologists. The Registry name was changed to the present title--American Registry of Radiologic Technologists-- in 1962, when its voluntary licensure program was expanded to include Nuclear Medicine Technicians, and Radiation Therapy Technicians, in addition to X-Ray Technicians.

The governing Board of Trustees of ARRT, which is appointed in equal number from the American College of Radiology and the American Society of Radiologic Technologists, issues a registration indicating professional competence in three categories:

(1) X-Ray Technology--"primarily concerned with demonstrations of portions of the human body on an x-ray film or fluoroscopic screen for diagnostic use of the radiologist. "
Education and Experience Requirement: Completion of a program of formal education in x-ray technology, approved by the Council on Medical Education of the American Medical Association. "
Written Examination: Subjects covered include: Radiographic Techniques; Standard Positioning; Anatomy and Physiology; X-Ray Physics and Electricity; The Darkroom; Special Procedures; Radiation Protection; Medical Terminology; Professional Ethics; and Related Nursing.

(2) Nuclear Medicine Technology--"uses radioactive isotopes to assist the physician in the diagnosis and/or treatment of illness or injury. "
Education and Experience Requirement: At least one year's education in a school of nuclear medicine technology accepted by the ARRT, and one of the following--
1--Graduation from an American Medical Association approved program in x-ray technology;
2--Certification as an x-ray technologist by ARRT;
3--Certification as a medical technologist by the Registry of Medical Technologists (American Society of Clinical Pathologists);
4--Registration as a professional nurse;
5--Baccalaureate degree from an accredited college. Substitution of required formal education by experience and education in nuclear medicine technology and a radioisotope laboratory accepted by ARRT is allowed.
Written Examination: Subjects covered include: Mathematics; Basic Radiation Physics; Interaction of Radiation with Matter and Physiological Systems; Radiation Units; Protection and Shielding; Instrumentation; Clinical Laboratory Equipment and Procedures; Specific Procedures; Records and Administrative Procedures.

(3)   Radiation Therapy Technology--"uses radiation producing
      device to administer therapeutic treatments as pre-
      scribed by the radiologist. "
      Education and Experience Requirement: At least one
          year's education in a school of radiation therapy tech-
          nology, with a curriculum equivalent to that prescribed
          by the American College of Radiology, American So-
          ciety of Radiologic Technologists, and the American
          Registry of Radiologic Technologists, and one of the
          following:
          1--Graduation from a two-year program in x-ray
             technology approved by the Council on Medical
             Education of the American Medical Association;
          2--Certification as an x-ray technologist by the ARRT;
          3--Certification as a nuclear medicine technologist
             by ARRT;
          4--Registration as a professional nurse.
          Effective July 1, 1974, only graduates of radiation
          therapy schools approved by the Council of Medical
          Education of the American Medical Association will
          be accepted for examination and certification in radia-
          tion therapy technology.

     Certification, which must be renewed annually, confers the right
to use the professional designation--the abbreviation, "R. T. (ARRT)"
--and, as appropriate, the title indicating competence in the specialty
of:
      X-Ray: "Registered X-Ray Technologist. "
      Nuclear Medicine: "Registered Nuclear Medicine Technologist. "
      Radiation Therapy: "Registered Radiation Therapy Tech-
         nologist. "

Code of Ethics: The ARRT guide to professional conduct is its
Code of Ethics, a pledge subscribed to at the time of application
for certification, and each year when the certificate authorized by
the Registry is renewed.   In this Code, a technologist pledges to
perform his duties "only under the supervision of a person whose
qualifications are acceptable" to the ARRT, to abide by rules and
regulations of the ARRT, and to conduct himself in a manner consistent with the principles of the Medical Ethics of the American
Medical Association.   The Code is identical for each of the certificate areas, with the exception of the title and the professional
designation, which varies with the subject of each of the three
certificates: X-Ray, Nuclear Medicine, Radiation Therapy.   The
ARRT Board of Trustees acts in enforcement of the Code of Ethics,
and may--after investigation and hearing of complaint of unprofessional conduct--revoke or refuse registration to a technologist who
has violated this conduct code.

Professional Insignia: The ARRT official emblem is circular in
design, with a centered x-ray tube, and the letters of the organization name, "ARRT, " spaced in a bordering band--left, top, right,

bottom--separated by radiation waves.
The color of the insignia is blue on
gold.   A pin is sold to registered technologists in gold, with the x-ray tube
in raised gold on a ground of blue
enamel.

Other Identification of Professional
Status: As described above under
"Membership," professional competence is indicated by the designation
authorized with registration, "R. T.
(ARRT)," in each of the three spe-
cialty fields.   A woven patch for wear on uniforms is gold on a
deep blue ground, with the border-
ing band in white.   A cloth shield
for uniform wear shows the centered insignia in gold on a blue
ground on a white shield; the title,
"X-Ray Technologist," is at the
top of the badge, and "Registered,"
at the bottom of the design, around
the centered circular insignia.

Bibliography:
American Registry of Radiologic Technologists.
ARRT.   12 pages.   Pam-
phlet.
Informational brochure with requirements in the three certification programs, subjects of examinations, Code of Ethics.

"Code of Ethics"

Applicants for certification in radiation therapy technology
must, at the time of application, and on subsequent occasions when
the certificate is renewed, agree to abide by the following code of
ethics:
"In consideration of the granting to me of a certificate of
registration, or the renewal thereof, and the attendant right to use
the title 'Registered Radiation Therapy Technologist' and its abbreviation, 'R. T. (ARRT),' in connection with my name, I do hereby
agree to perform the duties of a radiation therapy technologist only
under the supervision of a person whose qualifications are acceptable
to this Registry; and to abide by all the rules and regulations of the
American Registry of Radiologic Technologists as they apply to my
profession; and to conduct myself in a manner appropriate to the
dignity of my profession consistent with the Principles of Medical
Ethics of the American Medical Association. "

REAL ESTATE SALESMEN AND BROKERS

NATIONAL ASSOCIATION OF REALTORS
    155 E. Superior St., Chicago, Ill. 60611
    H. Jackson Pontius, Executive Vice President

Membership: The National Association of Realtors, founded in 1908 and with a present (1973) membership of approximately 110,000, is a trade association whose members belong to constituent local and state real estate boards. The Association defines its member "Realtors" as:

> "professionals in real estate who subscribe to a strict Code of Ethics as a member of local and state boards and of the National Association of Realtors."

Any person interested is eligible to become a member of a local real estate board. Beginning in 1974 (January 1) there will also be a membership category of "Associate Members."

Code of Ethics: The National Association of Realtors guide to ethical practice is its Code of Ethics, which includes a brief Preamble of obligations and responsibilities of the real estate salesman and broker, and 30 articles of standards, grouped in three sections:

> Relations to the Public,
> Relations to the Client,
> Relations to Fellow-Realtor.

This Code, adopted in 1913, has been amended through the years to keep it current with social changes. It was most recently revised in 1962, and is now under consideration for revisions, which it is anticipated will be completed in late 1973, or 1974.

Interpretations of the code of ethics are made by the Board of Directors, and have been assembled in the book, Interpretations of the Code of Ethics (5th edition, 1970), which gives the applications of the ethical guide in over 100 interpretations, and modifications which have been approved since 1970. Preparation of a new edition (6th edition) of the interpretations is in process. No enforcement procedures for the code of ethics are reported.

Other Guides to Professional Conduct: The I Am a Realtor Pledge, taken by each member upon admission to the association, provides another guide to ethical conduct for realtors.

Professional Insignia: The emblem of the National Association of Realtors is its logotype, adopted in May 1973. The design is a stylized "R," that stands for the term "Realtor," and symbolizes Real Estate, and "also Readiness, Responsibility, Reliability, Resourcefulness, Right and Responsiveness." The "R" logo is shown on a square colored background, with the word, "Realtor," printed

below the insignia. The colors
of the emblem are blue background and "Realtor," with
white "R."   Permissible use
of the symbol is given in the
Policy and Identification Manual.

Bibliography:
    National Association of
        Realtors.   Code of
        Ethics.   1962.
        Single sheet.
        Conduct guide for real-
        tors.
_____.   I Am a Realtor
        Pledge.   1 page.
        Responsibility and ser-
        vices statement sub-
        scribed to upon induction
        to the association.

REALTOR ®

_____.   Interpretations of the Code of Ethics.   5th edition,
    1970. $4.
Over 100 applications and expansions of the articles in the
Code of Ethics.   Supplemented by modifications approved
since 1970.
_____.   Realtor Headlines.   40:1 April 16, 1973.
Pictures and describes the new Association Symbol.

"Code of Ethics"

Preamble

        Under all is the land.   Upon its wise utilization and widely
allocated ownership depend the survival and growth of free institutions and of our civilization.   The Realtor is the instrumentality
through which the land resource of the nation reaches its highest
use and through which land ownership attains its widest distribution.
He is a creator of homes, a builder of cities, a developer of industries and productive farms.
        Such functions impose obligations beyond those of ordinary
commerce.   They impose grave social responsibility and a patriotic
duty to which the Realtor should dedicate himself, and for which
he should be diligent in preparing himself.   The Realtor, therefore, is zealous to maintain and improve the standards of his calling
and shares with his fellow-Realtors a common responsibility for its
integrity and honor.
        In the interpretation of his obligations, he can take no safer
guide than that which has been handed down through twenty centuries,
embodied in the Golden Rule:
        "Whatsoever ye would that men should do to you, do ye even
        so to them."

Accepting this standard as his own, every Realtor pledges himself to observe its spirit in all his activities and to conduct his business in accordance with the following Code of Ethics:

Part I. Relations to the Public

Article 1. The Realtor should keep himself informed as to movements affecting real estate in his community, state, and the nation, so that he may be able to contribute to public thinking on matters of taxation, legislation, land use, city planning, and other questions affecting property interests.

Article 2. It is the duty of the Realtor to be well informed on current market conditions in order to be in a position to advise his clients as to the fair market price.

Article 3. It is the duty of the Realtor to protect the public against fraud, misrepresentation or unethical practices in the real estate field.

He should endeavor to eliminate in his community any practices which could be damaging to the public or to the dignity and integrity of the real estate profession. The Realtor should assist the board or commission charged with regulating the practices of brokers and salesmen in his state.

Article 4. The Realtor should ascertain all pertinent facts concerning every property for which he accepts the agency, so that he may fulfill his obligation to avoid error, exaggeration, misrepresentation, or concealment of pertinent facts.

Article 5. The Realtor should not be instrumental in introducing into a neighborhood a character of property or use which will clearly be detrimental to property values in that neighborhood.

Article 6. The Realtor should not be a party to the naming of a false consideration in any document, unless it be the naming of an obviously nominal consideration.

Article 7. The Realtor should not engage in activities that constitute the practice of law and should recommend that title be examined and legal counsel be obtained when the interest of either party requires it.

Article 8. The Realtor should keep in a special bank account, separated from his own funds, monies coming into his possession in trust for other persons, such as escrows, trust funds, client's monies and other like items.

Article 9. The Realtor in his advertising should be especially careful to present a true picture and should neither advertise without disclosing his name, nor permit his salesmen to use individual names or telephone numbers, unless the salesman's connection with the Realtor is obvious in the advertisement.

Article 10. The Realtor, for the protection of all parties with whom he deals, should see that financial obligations and commitments regarding real estate transactions are in writing, expressing the exact agreement of the parties, and that copies of such agreements, at the time they are executed, are placed in the hands of all parties involved.

Part II. Relations to the Client

Article 11. In accepting employment as an agent, the Realtor pledges himself to protect and promote the interests of the client. This obligation of absolute fidelity to the client's interest is primary, but it does not relieve the Realtor from the obligation of dealing fairly with all parties to the transaction.

Article 12. In justice to those who place their interests in his care, the Realtor should endeavor always to be informed regarding laws, proposed legislation, governmental orders, and other essential information and public policies which affect those interests.

Article 13. Since the Realtor is representing one or another party to a transaction, he should not accept compensation from more than one party without the full knowledge of all parties to the transaction.

Article 14. The Realtor should not acquire an interest in or buy for himself, any member of his immediate family, his firm or any member thereof, or any entity in which he has a substantial ownership interest, property listed with him, or his firm, without making the true position known to the listing owner, and in selling property owned by him, or in which he has such interest, the facts should be revealed to the purchaser.

Article 15. The exclusive listing of property should be urged and practiced by the Realtor as a means of preventing dissention and misunderstanding and of assuring better service to the owner.

Article 16. When acting as agent in the management of property, the Realtor should not accept any commission, rebate or profit on expenditures made for an owner, without the owner's knowledge and consent.

Article 17. The Realtor should not undertake to make an appraisal that is outside the field of his experience unless he obtains the assistance of an authority on such types of property, or unless the facts are fully disclosed to the client. In such circumstances the authority so engaged should be so identified and his contribution to the assignment should be clearly set forth.

Article 18. When asked to make a formal appraisal of real property, the Realtor should not render an opinion without careful and thorough analysis and interpretation of all factors affecting the value of the property. His counsel constitutes a professional service.

The Realtor should not undertake to make an appraisal or render an opinion of value on any property where he has a present or contemplated interest unless such interest is specifically disclosed in the appraisal report. Under no circumstances should he undertake to make a formal appraisal when his employment or fee is contingent upon the amount of his appraisal.

Article 19. The Realtor should not submit or advertise property without authority, and in any offering, the price quoted should not be other than that agreed upon with the owners as the offering price.

Article 20. In the events that more than one formal written offer on a specific property is made before the owner has accepted

an offer, any other formal written offer presented to the Realtor,
whether by a prospective purchaser or another broker, should be
transmitted to the owner for his decision.

Part III.   Relations to His Fellow-Realtor

Article 21.   The Realtor should seek no unfair advantage over
his fellow-Realtors and should willingly share with them the lessons
of his experience and study.

Article 22.   The Realtor should so conduct his business as to
avoid controversies with his fellow-Realtors.   In the event of a controversy between Realtors who are members of the same local board,
such controversy should be arbitrated in accordance with regulations
of their board rather than litigated.

Article 23.   Controversies between Realtors who are not
members of the same local board should be submitted to an arbitration board consisting of one arbitrator chosen by each Realtor
from the real estate board to which he belongs or chosen in accordance with the regulations of the respective boards.   One other
member, or a sufficient number of members to make an odd number, should be selected by the arbitrators thus chosen.

Article 24.   When the Realtor is charged with unethical practice, he should place all pertinent facts before the proper tribunal
of the member board of which he is a member, for investigation and
judgment.

Article 25.   The Realtor should not voluntarily disparage the
business practice of a competitor, nor volunteer an opinion of a
competitor's transaction.   If his opinion is sought it should be rendered with strict professional integrity and courtesy.

Article 26.   The agency of a Realtor who holds an exclusive
listing should be respected.   A Realtor cooperating with a listing
broker should not invite the cooperation of a third broker without
the consent of the listing broker.

Article 27.   The Realtor should cooperate with other brokers
on property listed by him exclusively whenever it is in the interest
of the client, sharing commissions on a previously agreed basis.
Negotiations concerning property listed exclusively with one broker
should be carried on with the listing broker, not with the owner, except with the consent of the listing broker.

Article 28.   The Realtor should not solicit the services of an
employee or salesman in the organization of a fellow-Realtor without the knowledge of the employer.

Article 29.   Signs giving notice of property for sale, rent,
lease or exchange should not be placed on any property by more
than one Realtor, and then only if authorized by the owner, except
as the property is listed with and authorization given to more than
one Realtor.

Article 30.   In the best interest of society, of his associates
and of his own business, the Realtor should be loyal to the real
estate board of his community and active in its work.

Conclusion

The term Realtor has come to connote competence, fair dealing and high integrity resulting from adherence to a lofty ideal of
moral conduct in business relations. No inducement of profit and
no instructions from clients ever can justify departure from this
ideal, or from the injunctions of this Code.

NATIONAL INSTITUTE OF REAL ESTATE BROKERS (NIREB)
  of the National Association of Realtors
    155 E. Superior St., Chicago, Ill. 60611
    Jack W. Kleeman, Executive Vice President

Membership: The National Institute of Real Estate Brokers, founded
in 1923 and with a present (1973) membership of over 25,000, is a
trade association, composed of members of local Boards of Realtors
affiliated with the National Association of Realtors--of which the
Institute is an affiliate. The requirement for gaining entrance to
the Institute as a general member is affiliation with a local board of
realtors as either a broker or sales associate. The NIREB awards
designations to indicate competence as a real estate broker and
salesman to members who quality for such designations through
meeting "stringent requirements of education, experience, and
ethics."

Certificates are issued by the Institute to indicate competence
in the two main fields of real estate--Commercial-Investment and
Residential:
    Certified Commercial-Investment Member--CCIM: Required
        to have 200 "credits" in education, experience, and special
        training through:
            "Demonstration of academic competence,
            Documentation of ability by actual performance, and
            Elevation to prominence as determined by standards of
                experts in the field."
        Candidate must be at least 21 years of age, a member of
        NIREB's Commercial and Investment Division, a high
        school graduate (or equivalent), and have at least one
        year of full-time experience as a licensed real estate
        salesman or broker. Candidate must complete before his
        examinations given by NIREB a course of training, includ-
        ing buying, selling, exchanging, and leasing real estate
        (CID I, II, III, IV).
        Program begun in 1968.

    Certified Residential Broker--CRB: Required to have 200
        "credits" in education, experience, and special training
        through:

"Academic training, experience, NIREB courses, examination by NIREB. "
Candidate must be at least 25 years of age, a high school
graduate (or equivalent), have held a broker's license for
two years, and "have successfully passed an examination
based on a survey course covering the fundamentals of
effective real estate management. " Candidate must complete and pass examinations in NIREB Courses I through
IV, given by NIREB, and hold a GRI (Graduate Realtors
Institute) designation from the state in which he practices.
Program begun in 1968.
The examinations required in gaining certification are in the form of
written tests given at the conclusion of each course required for
certification, rather than a single comprehensive examination.   As
the final step in his candidacy for certification, each candidate must
take part in a personal interview.

Code of Ethics: NIREB, as an affiliate of the National Association
of Realtors, subscribes to the Realtors Code of Ethics.

Professional Insignia: The NIREB emblem is its seal--a shield
with a bar from lower left to upper right, bearing five stars; two
symbols of knowledge are shown on the shield--a quill pen before
an open book, at the upper left, and the lamp of learning, at the
lower right; a scroll at the top of the shield carries the Institute

initials, "NIREB. "   The official color of this insignia is blue on
white, with stars, quill pen and book, and lamp and initials in gold.
This emblem is used on the badges awarded to members as professionally competent:
Certified Commercial-Investment Member (CCIM)--Institute
emblem in lower part of a shield, with initials of the
professional designation, "CCIM, " across the top of the

shield. Color is gold on red.
<u>Certified Residential Broker (CRB)</u>--Institute emblem in
lower part of a shield, with initials of professional designation, "CRB," across the top of the shield. Color is
gold on green.

<u>Other Identification of Professional Status:</u> As described above
under "Membership," the two designations awarded as an indication
of competence by the National Institute of Real Estate Brokers are,
"Certified Commercial-Investment Member--CCIM"
"Certified Residential Broker--CRB."

<u>Bibliography:</u>
National Institute of Realtors. <u>Certified Commercial-Investment</u>
<u>Broker Directory.</u> Annual (July/Aug).
Gives requirements and significance of "CCIM," geographical
and alphabetical listings of members certified; Code of Ethics
of National Association of Realtors. Emblem pictured in
color on cover.
_____. <u>Certified Residential Broker Directory.</u> Annual
(July/August).
Gives requirements and significance of "CRB," geographical
and alphabetical listings of members; Code of Ethics of
National Association of Realtors. Emblem pictured in color
on cover.
_____. <u>Professional Designations of NIREB.</u> Sets of 2
sheets.
Course and other requirements for certification.

"Code of Ethics"

see page 673

RECREATION WORKERS

NATIONAL RECREATION AND PARK ASSOCIATION (NRPA)
1700 Pennsylvania Ave., N.W., Washington, D.C. 20006
Dwight F. Rettie, Executive Director

<u>Membership:</u> The National Recreation and Park Association, founded
in 1965 and with a present (1973) membership of 30,000, is an organization engaged in service, research, and education, directed to improving the "quality of life through effective utilization of natural and
human resources." More than 60 state and regional associations are
affiliated with the Association. Membership in NRPA is open to any
interested person, and among its members are professionals, laymen, friends, and organizations in the United States and Canada.

Diversity of membership interest is shown in the Association's
eight branch organizations:
    APRS--American Park and Recreation Society,
    AFRS--Armed Forces Recreation Society,
    NCSP--National Conference on State Parks,
    NTRS--National Therapeutic Recreation Society,
    SPRE--Society of Park and Recreation Educators,
    FRP--Friends of Recreation and Parks,
    CBM--Commissioners and Board Members,
    NSRPS--National Student Recreation and Parks Society.

One of the NRPA branches--the American Park and Recreation
Society--"serves members representing diversified park and recreation interests in federal, county, local and special district government and in private and voluntary agencies. Membership is available to professionals and associates at all levels of services." Individual membership categories of NRPA include:
    Professional--"Administrators, managers, supervisors,
        planners, specialists, leaders, park rangers, interpretive
        staff and educators employed full or part-time in public
        or private services in parks, recreation, leisure, con-
        servation and the environment or related fields. Open also
        to retired professionals."
    Associate--"Foremen, maintenance personnel, aides and at-
        tendants, and other support staff employed full- or part-
        time in parks and recreation, conservation or an allied
        field. Also open to non-active (former) board or com-
        mission members."

Code of Ethics: The conduct guide for recreation workers is the
American Park and Recreation Society's standards for professional
conduct given in its Code of Ethics. This Code contains the responsibilities and obligations of recreation workers and provisions for
enforcement and amendment of the Code in four parts:
    Declaration of Policy,
    Canons,
    Enforcement,
    Amendments.
According to the enforcement procedures of the professional guide
(Code, Part 3), the APRS Committee on Professional Ethics and
Grievances interprets the code and receives and investigates complaints of code violations. The Committee recommends appropriate
action to the Board of Directors for the disposition of complaints of
unprofessional conduct of members.

Professional Insignia: The emblem of the American Park and Recreation Society is its official seal--a circular design containing
the initials of the organization, "APRS." The color of the insignia
is black on white.

Other Identification of Professional Status: The National Therapeutic
Recreation Society is another branch of NRPA. It is composed

mainly of professional workers
and maintains a registry of
members, but issues no certification, registration, or
other form of voluntary licensure, and awards no professional designation.

Bibliography:
    American Park and Re-
        creation Society.
        Code of Ethics. 6
        pages. Pamphlet.
    Recreation workers pro-
        fessional conduct guide.
    National Recreation and
        Park Association.
        An Invitation to Join
        the National Recreation and Park Association. 16 pages.
        Pamphlet.
    Informational brochure giving NRPA services and publications;
    membership categories.

American Park and Recreation Society
"Code of Ethics"

Introduction

       This Code of Ethics establishes a set of rules, arranged in
an orderly manner so that they may be understood and used by the
members of the profession of parks and recreation.
       Its content is a part of the science and philosophy dealing
with moral conduct, duty and judgment. It establishes standards of
professional right and wrong conduct or behavior.

       THE CODE: Establishes desirable standards of relationships
to accomplish the declared purpose and objectives of the profession.
       Provides for a committee on professional ethics and griev-
ances.
       States the standards for professional relationships so that
the committee on ethics and grievances or other interested persons
or groups can express an opinion on a violation of any Canon of
Ethics contained herein.
       Provides a framework for advisory opinions for and against
members, bodies, and persons not members.
       Provides a plan for the accumulation of a body of decisions
based on opinions rendered by the Committee on Ethics and Grievances and on practical experiences.
       Provides a plan for additions, deletions, and amendments so
that the Code will remain a living document.

Part 1. Declaration of Policy

The American Park and Recreation Society, recognizing its obligations to its members and to those whom they serve, issues this Code of Professional Ethics which constitutes its standards.

Responsibility and Obligation

By the publication of these Canons, the American Park and Recreation Society assumes responsibility for:

The competence of its members.

The character of professional relationship among its several members.

The character of professional relationship between its several members and the publics which they serve.

The quality of performance expected by the several members of one another and by the publics whom they serve.

The prohibition of conduct which brings disrepute to the profession and the Society.

The conduct of recreation and management of parks in the interests of participants.

1.   Definition of Parks and Recreation

Parks and recreation provide the opportunities for leisure living which is satisfying, meaningful, and necessary for the purposeful fulfillment of life: mental, physical, emotional, social and cultural. They include the leadership, services, and facilities desirable to achieve such a quality of life.

2.   Professional Qualifications

Park and recreation professionals are career personnel qualified by education and experience to assume the professional responsibilities of park and recreation services.

Part 2.   Canons

These canons express desirable standards of duty, obligation, and conduct of professional members to one another, to groups, agencies, authorities, and participants in park and recreation services.

1.   Governing Authority Policies

1. 1   Governing Authority to the Administrator.
Governing authority:
1. 11   Represents the people served and constitutes the legally responsible body to determine policy and objectives, to manage parks and conduct recreation in an orderly and efficient manner and to evaluate achievements.
1. 12   Recognizes in its organizational structure that parks and recreation are essential and important services, necessary to human well-being.
1. 13   Recognizes that park and recreation services are varied

in nature and must be designed to serve interests and needs of all.

1. 14 Selects the park and recreation administrator on the basis of clearly defined personal and professional qualifications, specifies conditions of employment, assures freedom from political influence and other unrelated considerations, and retains him on this same basis.

1. 15 Delegates implementation of approved policies to the administrator, gives him the freedom to execute them, and holds him responsible for results.

1. 16 Observes and receives public reaction regarding the execution of policy as well as needs and demands for new services and keeps the administrator informed.

1. 5 Administrator to the Governing Authority.

The Administrator:

1. 51 Accepts and supports the statutes which bind the governing authority and executes its policies and decisions in an efficient manner.

1. 52 Keeps the governing authority fully, promptly, and objectively informed.

1. 53 Owes his loyalty to the governing authority in public and in private.

1. 54 Keeps informed and is alert to trends and needs in programs, finance, maintenance, facilities, and personnel. He provides professional information, advice, and recommendations on these matters to the governing authority.

2. Administration and Staff

2. 1 Administrator to Staff.

The administrator:

2. 11 Informs staff of the objectives, policies, and decisions of the governing authority.

2. 12 Provides the organizational structure, personnel policies, and operating procedures for the agency and communicates these to staff.

2. 13 Defines responsibilities and delegates authority commensurate therewith.

2. 14 Evaluates performances of staff members, providing continuing opportunities for professional growth.

2. 15 Recognizes staff members as human beings with feelings, problems, and ambitions within context of their relationships.

2. 16 Provides fair and objective procedures for consideration of personal concerns.

2. 17 Provides opportunities for the staff by democratic processes to share their professional competencies.

2. 18 Sets an example by his own high standard of personal and professional conduct.

2. 5 Staff to Administrator.

The staff:

2. 51   Respects the authority of the administrator and the importance of responsibilities of the position he holds.

2. 52   Conscientiously performs delegated duties.

2. 53   Owes to the administrator continuing personal and professional growth and creative performance of his duties.

2. 54   Contributes ideas and suggestions for improvements in park and recreation services, proposing procedures and methods for their implementation.

2. 8   Staff to Staff.

All staff members:

2. 81   Respect the professional competence of their colleagues and recognize that different techniques and philosophies may accomplish identical objectives.

2. 82   Contribute to staff morale by refraining from actions, words, or deeds which negate mutual respect, cooperation, and team work.

3.   Staff and Participants

3. 1   Staff to Participants.

The staff:

3. 11   Recognizes needs and interests of people in a service area, establishes goals, and provides for joint staff-participant planning, leadership, and conduct of program.

3. 13   Provides supporting information, equipment, facilities, instruction, and leadership to enable and encourage the participant to develop his potential qualities so that he may become self-sufficient in his own leisure time pursuits.

3. 14   Respects the dignity of the participants as a person and maintains relationships based on integrity and understanding.

3. 15   Seeks to improve personal and professional qualities to assure enthusiastic and imaginative performance and desired relationships.

3. 5   Participant to Staff.

The participant:

3. 51   Develops and uses his leadership qualities for growth and maintenance of parks and recreation in his community.

3. 52   Respects and protects the personal and property rights of others.

3. 53   Engages in activity for his own satisfaction and personal growth.

4.   Staff and Public

4. 1   Staff to Public.

The staff:

4. 11   Plans and works with self-organized and motivated specialized interest groups for enriching and increasing participation in their activities.

4. 12   Develops awareness of the importance of leisure time

opportunities for people of all ages on a year-round basis.

4.3 Public to Staff.
    The public:
    4.31 Shares skills, interests, and programs with others by
means of training, leadership, and sponsorship.
    4.32 Encourages actions which make possible the establish-
ment and maintenance of year-round programs and facilities for all
people.

4.5   Public and Voluntary Agencies

4.6 Public Agencies to Voluntary Agencies.
    The public agency is:
    4.61 Obligated to plan policies and coordinate services with
voluntary agencies, and to share information, facilities, and program responsibilities with them in order to provide leisure time
opportunities in the most economic and efficient manner.

    The voluntary agency is:
    4.81 Obligated to state its policies, objectives, areas of
service, and programs, and to join with the public agency in developing and providing information, facilities, and programming.
    4.82 Obligated to plan with the public agency for addition,
change, or curtailment of any park or recreation services which
might alter respective park or recreation responsibilities.

5.   Agency and Commercial Recreation

5.1 Agency to Commercial Recreation.
    The agency:
    5.11 Recognizes as necessary and desirable the role of com-
mercial interests as a means of providing adequate and desirable
leisure time opportunities to meet the demands of people.
    5.12 Plans and works with commercial interests in develop-
ment of skills, insights, and resources for leisure and in the
operation of desirable facilities and programs.

5.5 Commercial Recreation to Agency.
    Commercial recreation:
    5.51 Provides, operates and maintains specialized programs
and facilities with adequate and qualified leadership in an orderly
and efficient manner.
    5.52 Plans and works with the agency in development of
resources for leisure, skills, and operation of desirable programs
and facilities.
    5.53 Recogn'zes and appreciates the mental, physical, and
emotional objectives of park and recreation services and cooperates
and plans with other agencies to provide satisfying opportunities
for all.

6.   Agencies and Suppliers

6. 1   Agency to Supplier.
The agency:
6. 11   Recognizes economic implications of parks and recreation and their dynamic effect on the general economy.
6. 12   Informs potential suppliers of purchasing and accounting requirements and procedures and makes no exception in following ethical business practices in dealing with them.
6. 13   Respects supplier representatives as they communicate information about the benefits of their products and services as they relate to needs.
6. 14   Is aware of agency needs for goods and services and keeps informed about trends in products and services with regard to utility and availability.
6. 15   Permits no employee to transact business on behalf of the agency directly or indirectly with suppliers for personal gain.

6. 5   Suppliers to Agency.
The supplier:
6. 52   Encourages and supports agency consideration and evaluation of supplies, equipment and services, only on basis of quality, utility, and economy.
6. 53   Understands and respects existing laws, rules, and regulations regarding purchase of goods and services by the agency.
6. 54   Maintains high standards of quality in products with regard to safety, economy, and attractiveness, and works constantly to improve their products.
6. 55   Maintains high standards of competency and quality in consultants services.

7.   Profession and Institutions of Higher Education

7. 1   Profession to University.
The profession:
7. 11   Cooperates with colleges and universities in the recruitment of students who qualify for careers in parks and recreation in the development, supervision and conduct of field work; internship programs and research; and in financing of student assistance.
7. 12   Conveys to the college or university information about needs and requirements of parks and recreation program, personnel, qualifications, facilities, finance, and maintenance.

7. 5   University to the Profession.
The university:
7. 51   Offers a professional curriculum, broad in concept, high in academic standards, practical in content and imaginative in outlook, under the direction of a qualified instructional staff provided with adequate educational facilities, appropriately financed, and an independently administered curriculum.
7. 52   Provides for research and dissemination of information on problems that confront the profession.

8. Agency and the Communications Media

8. 1   Agency to Media.
The agency:
8. 11   Provides the media with a written agency public relations policy, outlining goals set, principles followed, means to be
used in carrying out policy, and information on the park and recreation staff and governing authority, and their respective responsibilities.
8. 12   Utilizes all media to inform the people.
8. 13   Must provide the media with continuing newsworthy information, adequate calendar scheduling, cooperation in coverage,
and evaluate facts descriptive of plans, performance, and achievement.
8. 14   Offers orientation to assist the media in the interpretation of significance of parks and recreation matters as to their
economic and social implications.

8. 5   Media to Agency.
Communication media:
8. 51   Should feel an obligation to tell the park and recreation
story on the basis of facts supplied, and on appropriate occasions,
interpret to the public the necessity for support, the rewards of
participation, the opportunities available and what they mean to the
public.

9. Profession and Society

9. 1   Profession to the Society.
9. 11   Qualified career park and recreation personnel should
be active members of the American Park and Recreation Society,
support the principles for which it stands, participate in its affairs,
and contribute personally to development and maintenance of professional standards.

9. 5   Society to the Profession.
The Society should:
9. 51   Provide mutual association for continuing growth and
professional excellence, cooperating and working with other organizations, groups, and individuals for the advancement of the
parks and recreation profession.

Part 3. Enforcement

1.   The American Park and Recreation Society, through its
committee on Professional Ethics and Grievances, will accept requests for decisions or opinions and complaints by any person or
body affected by the canons.
2.   The committee will advise any member of the Society,
or any person or body so requesting of its opinion as to whether
any source of professional conduct under stated circumstances is in
accord with the canons.
3.   Requests to the committee must set forth the facts in

writing in sufficient detail to provide a respondent with a fair opportunity to deny or disprove them. All requests must be signed.

4. Committee deliberations shall be conducted in a spirit of objectivity after ascertainment of the facts and full and free opportunity for hearing all concerned.

5. At least two-thirds of the committee members must concur in the decision. Opinions of the committee may be published by the American Park and Recreation Society, with deletion of personal names and agencies involved.

6. It will be the responsibility of the Society's Ethics and Grievances Committee to recommend appropriate action to the Board of Directors of the American Park and Recreation Society. Recommendations for action with regard to violations of the Code of Ethics may include reprimand, suspension, or expulsion from the Society.

Part 4. Amendments

Upon written request to the APRS Executive Secretary by five percent (5%) of the voting members, or by a majority vote of the Board of Directors, amendment(s) to this Code of Ethics are to be submitted by mail ballot to the voting membership of the Society.

A ballot listing the amendment(s) shall be mailed to each voting member at least thirty (30) days prior to the date ballots are tabulated.

REHABILITATION WORKERS

AMERICAN CORRECTIVE THERAPY ASSOCIATION (ACTA)
    1222 S. Ridgeland Ave., Berwyn, Ill. 60402
    Julian Vogel, Executive Director

Membership: The American Corrective Therapy Association, founded in 1946 and with a present (1973) membership of 500, is a professional association of corrective exercise therapists, working in the field of corrective therapy or adapted physical education. The Association, founded as the "Association of Physical and Mental Rehabilitation," and changing its name to the present designation in 1967, grew out of the great expansion in the fields of physical and mental rehabilitation in the Veterans Administration, and other United States Armed Forces institutions during and following World War II. Corrective therapy functions primarily within hospitals and centers for physical and mental restoration or rehabilitation, and adapted physical education is "an integral part of various educational levels," from elementary through university.

"Corrective Therapy" is defined by the ACTA as:

"The application of the principles, tools, techniques, and
psychology of medically oriented physical education to assist
the physician in the accomplishment of prescribed objectives. "
ACTA requirements for membership include:

Active Membership--"A bachelor's degree with a major in
    health and physical education and a 400-hour clinical
    training program in an approved hospital or institution. "
Professional Membership--Open to "persons with a degree
    in an allied field other than physical education. "

In order to designate qualified and competent corrective therapists,
a voluntary certification procedure was initiated in 1953.   The
agency administering this program is the American Board for Certification of Corrective Therapists.   It is composed of authorities
from the fields of medicine, psychiatry, and education, and gives
examinations, issues certificates allowing successful candidates who
pass the examination to use the professional designation, "Certified
Corrective Therapist" ("CCT"), and publishes a national register
of such certified therapists.

"Active Members" of ACTA are eligible for the certifying
examination, providing their undergraduate college training included
specified courses in applied sciences, psychology, health and physical education, corrective therapy and adapted physical education
and 400 hours of clinical training (160 hours of experience may
substitute for 160 hours of this required clinical training).

The examination for certification consists of a three and one-
half hour written and oral test, which includes a variety of question
forms--true-false, completion, multiple choice, essay, and definitions.   The examination, covering the total field of corrective therapy,
is administered by a testing panel composed of a physician and two
certified corrective therapists.   An applicant may prepare for the
examination by reviewing textbooks in kinesiology, anatomy, and
physiology, and the Introductory Handbook for Corrective and Adapted
Physical Education by Earl Mason and Harry B. Dando.   Each candidate for testing receives a sample of the examination questions prior
to taking the test.

Code of Ethics: The professional conduct guide for corrective therapists is the ACTA Code of Ethics (text in Bylaws, Article 1, Section 7a), which sets forth 14 standards of practice.   Regulations
(Bylaws) govern "the interpretation and application of the Code ...
which also provides action to be taken in event an Active Member
fails to observe any part of the Code. "

Professional Insignia: The insignia of the ACTA is an oval design,
with a centered caduceus (winged staff with two entwined serpents),
the name, "Corrective Therapy, " appears with one word above, and
one below, the caduceus.   The color of the emblem is shown vari-
ously--blue on white (letterhead); black on white (publications).
Cloth patches for attaching to uniforms are available in a modification of the Association emblem to show:

Corrective Therapist--Member badge with gold caduceus and
    oval outline, with "Corrective Therapist" above caduceus,
    in blue on white ground.
Certified Corrective Therapist--Identical to above, except
    the designation, "Certified," appears in blue letters below
    the caduceus.

Other Identification of Professional Status: As described above under
"Membership," the professional designation (title and initials) award-
ed to indicate professional competence is "Certified Corrective
Therapist" ("CCT").

Bibliography:
    American Corrective Therapy Association. American Correc-
        tive Therapy Association. 1970. 20 pages. Pamphlet.
    Descriptive brochure including definition of "corrective
    therapy," ACTA membership and certification requirements.
    _____. Code of Ethics (Bylaws, Article 1, Section 7a). 2
        pages.
    Fourteen Standards of Professional Conduct.
    Rhea, Kermit. "Perspective for Corrective Therapy and Adapted
        Physical Education." American Corrective Therapy Jour-
        nal 22:89-91 May/June 1968.
    Brief history of the occupation, the ACTA definition of "cor-
    rective therapy," and certification procedure.

"Code of Ethics"

        Active members of the American Corrective Therapy Associa-
tion, Inc. are required to observe the Code of Ethics set out in the
following fourteen rules. The regulations governing the interpretation and application of the Code are provided for in the Constitution
of the ACTA, which also provides action to be taken in the event an
Active Member fails to observe any part of the Code.

        An Active Member of the ACTA is hereafter referred to as
a "Member."

1. A Member shall comply with the Rules of the Constitution of the ACTA for the time being in force.

2. A Member shall not at any time, either in his professional capacity or otherwise, undertake to give, or accept responsibility for, any treatment unless under the supervision of a physician who is legally licensed to practice in his state or commonwealth.

3. A Member shall not at any time, either in his professional capacity or otherwise, undertake to give, or accept responsibility for, a form of treatment in which he does not hold a recognized qualification.

4. A Member shall not at any time, either in his professional capacity or otherwise, discuss with a patient, or within a patient's hearing, any treatment or other professional matter in such a way as may be calculated to bring doubt or discredit on the professional skill, knowledge, services or qualifications of any other registered medical auxiliary or professional colleague or any other person in the medical field.

5. A Member shall not, for the purposes of obtaining patients or work, or of promoting his own professional prestige, directly advertise himself in any manner not consistent with the ruling of the ACTA.

6. A Member shall at all times, in his professional capacity or otherwise, respect the status of, and show courtesy to, his medical seniors, his own departmental superiors or staff, and to his professional colleagues.

7. A Member shall at all times, in his professional capacity or otherwise, give the best of his skill and knowledge when treating any patient, without prejudice and irrespective of financial renumeration.

8. A Member shall report to the physician accurately, and with adequate frequency, the patient's progress and response to treatment. He shall report to the physician immediately, if or when, the patient exhibits responses which are not normally expected and shall report any accident which may occur in the course of treatment.

9. A Member shall, in his professional capacity, maintain a clean and tidy appearance, shall maintain identification with his profession, and shall wear a uniform which is acceptable to the institution in which he works.

10. A Member shall faithfully observe the conditions of his appointment with an employer, whether these conditions have been agreed upon verbally or in writing.

11. A Member shall hold any information coming to his attention regarding a patient as confidential and consider it "privileged communications." Such information will not be made available to anyone except those responsible for the patient's medical care.

12. A Member shall not at any time, either in his professional capacity or otherwise, act in such a manner as to bring discredit upon his colleagues or the ACTA. He shall maintain integrity and discipline in personal behavior so as to sustain and

enhance public confidence in his profession.

    13. A Member shall publish only information and opinions which can be reasonably expected to be a scientific contribution to the field of rehabilitation.

    14. A Member shall strive at all times to improve his professional knowledge, skill and efficiency and thereby increase the value of his contribution to the field of rehabilitation.

NATIONAL REHABILITATION COUNSELING ASSOCIATION (NRCA)
    1522 K St., N.W., Washington, D.C. 20005
    Fletcher R. Hall, Executive Director

Membership: The National Rehabilitation Counseling Association, founded in 1958 and with a present (1973) membership of 5000, is the largest professional division of the National Rehabilitation Association (NRA), a citizens' interest group association "dedicated to the rehabilitation of handicapped people." NRCA membership requirements include:

    Member--Minimum of a baccalaureate degree from an accredited college and employment in a rehabilitation counseling setting.

    Professional Member--A master's degree in rehabilitation counseling with a minimum of one year's experience in a rehabilitation counseling setting; or a master's degree appropriate for rehabilitation counseling and a minimum of two year's experience in a rehabilitation counseling setting.

A procedure to certificate rehabilitation counselors is being developed by the Association.

Code of Ethics: The professional conduct guide is the NRCA's Ethical Standards, developed over a three year period by the Ethics Sub-Committee, from "vignettes of compromising ethical situations" and courses of action taken, as reported by rehabilitation counselors. These "critical incident" applications of ethical principles were classified and incorporated in a "Draft of Proposed Ethical Standards for Rehabilitation Counselors." From these case studies an Ethical Standards Statement was prepared and adopted by the Delegate Assembly of the Association at their October 1972 meeting.

    The professional conduct guide groups acceptable rules of behavior for rehabilitation counselors in ten areas of relationship-- such as client and client's family, employer; fellow counselors and other professional colleagues; employers or supervisors; the community; and other programs, agencies and institutions; and research. Procedures for enforcement of the ethical standards are in the developmental stage.

Professional Insignia: The NRCA emblem is a circular design, formed by two laurel branches, with a shield centered, broken vertically in two halves, by a waving line; each half broken vertically into thirds by horizontal lines, with each of the six-parts of the shield alternately colored in solid and horizontal stripes, beginning in the upper left with a solid color; a right hand, with fingers extended and palm forward, is shown at the top of the shield above a horizontal six-linked chain; a scroll superimposed across the bottom of the design carries the organization name, "National Rehabilitation Counseling Association. "

The color of the emblem is gold on white, with blue chain, solid-color shield sixths, and scroll; the association name in white. The insignia is shown on publications in a simplified design--without the chain links and the association name (Journal of Applied Rehabilitation Counseling, cover).

The insignia of the National Rehabilitation Association-- of which NRCA is a professional branch--is an unbordered design--an outline human figure, arms outstretched in liberation or celebration, to the right, and the door of darkness (disability) from which the figure has emerged to the left. The emblem is shown in various colors--moss green figure, door colors (from left to right) moss green, grey, black, white, in vertical stripes (letterhead); figure and door outlined in black on white, with door colors (from left to right) white, dark grey, black, light grey, in vertical stripes (publication).

Bibliography:
National Rehabilitation Counseling Association.   Certification of
    Rehabilitation Counselors.   July 1972.   5 pages.
This Report of Joint Certification Committee proposes the
initiation of the full procedure of certification and examina-
tion by July 1, 1975.
_____. Certification Philosophy and Conclusions.   1 sheet.
Indicates the requirements in terms of education and experi-
ence for certification; and the information content of the ex-
amination for professional rehabilitation counselor certification.
_____. NRCA.   Folder.
NRCA background, goals, membership requirements.
Oberman, C. Esco.   "Preliminary Statement ... and Draft of
    Proposed Ethical Standards for Rehabilitation Counselors."
    Journal of Applied Rehabilitation Counseling 2:71-83 Sum-
    mer 1971.
Chairman of the NRCA Ethics Sub-Committee reports the
procedures used in the preparation of the draft of proposed
ethical standards for rehabilitation counselors, and gives
the standards in proposed rules of professional behavior.
Ethical Standards adopted September 25, 1972.

"Ethical Standards for Rehabilitation Counselors"

A rehabilitation counselor has a commitment to the effective
functioning of all human beings; his emphasis is on facilitating the
functioning or refunctioning of those persons who are at some disadvantage in the struggle to achieve viable goals.   While fulfilling
this commitment he interacts with many people, programs, institutions, demands and concepts, and in many different types of relationships.   In his endeavors he seeks to enhance the welfare of his
clients and of all others whose welfare his professional roles and
activities will affect.   He recognizes that both action and inaction
can be facilitating or debilitating and he accepts the responsibility
for his action and inaction.

The acceptable rules of behavior which the rehabilitation
counselor himself observes and which he urges his colleagues to
observe are in relationships with (1) his client, (2) his client's
family, (3) his client's employer or prospective employer, (4) his
fellow counselors, (5) his colleagues in other professions, (6) his
own employer or supervisor, (7) the community, (8) other programs,
agencies and institutions, (9) maintenance of his technical competency, and (10) research.   The ethical rules presented here are
organized to group specific rules or principles as they cluster about
these various relationships.

I.   Counselor--Client

The primary obligation of the rehabilitation counselor is to
his client.   In all his relationships he will protect the client's

welfare and will diligently seek to assist the client towards his goals.

A.   The rehabilitation counselor will keep confidential any information he acquires concerning the client, the divulgence of which might be inimical to the best interests of the client.

1. The rehabilitation counselor will persist in claiming the "privileged" status of confidential information concerning his clients in court proceedings.

2. Where there are conflicts between the client's interests and the interests and welfare of the community, the rehabilitation counselor will protect the client, unless by his doing so there is created a real and imminent danger to others.

    a. The counselor will try to persuade the client to report knowledge of crimes or planned crimes to the appropriate law enforcement authorities.

    b. The client will be warned that information acquired in the counseling relationship might have to be reported in court proceedings; that it might not be possible to withhold the information as "privileged."

3. Where illegal behavior of the client is destructive to himself as well as to the community, the rehabilitation counselor will report such behavior to the appropriate authorities, after advising the client that this must be done.

4. In situations where it is necessary to share information with others in order to advance the rehabilitation goals of the client, consent of the client or his guardian or parent will be secured before release of such information.

    a. Only information essential to advancing the goals of the client will be given to others.

    b. Only those persons for whom it is essential to have information about the client in order to advance his rehabilitation will be given information.

5. Only such information as the client requires to advance his rehabilitation will be given to him. The counselor will personally give and interpret information to the client that is within the scope of the rehabilitation counseling specialty to develop and establish.

6. Only information essential to advancing the goals of the client will be included in the records kept on the client.

7. Client records will be safeguarded to insure that unauthorized persons shall not have access to them.

    a. All nonprofessional persons who must have access to the client's records will be thoroughly briefed concerning the confidentiality standards to be observed. Compliance with these standards will be continuously monitored by the counselor and will be his responsibility.

    b. The counselor will insist on an administrative plan for retirement and destruction of client records that will afford satisfactory protection of the client's future interests and welfare.

B.   The rehabilitation counselor will maintain objective and professional standards in his personal relationships with the client.

1. He will refrain from urging the client's acceptance of values, life styles, plans, decisions and beliefs that represent only the counselor's personal judgments or values.
2. If he learns of criminal and destructive activities of the client, either current or planned, he will advise the client that this must be reported to law enforcement authorities.
3. He will refer to others for service those to whom he is not able to relate objectively, e.g., relatives, close friends, persons against whom he is prejudiced.
4. He will, in serving the client, function within the limits of his defined role, training, and technical competency. In discussing probable or hoped-for outcomes of services to be offered, he will refrain from promising greater results than can reasonably be expected. He will not misrepresent his role or his competency to the client or to others. He will refer the client to other specialists as the client's needs dictate. He will not discuss with the client any professional incompetency he might feel is characteristic of his colleagues or other professional persons or agencies involved in the client's rehabilitation plan.
5. He will know thoroughly the legal or regulatory limits or the extent of the services that he may offer. He will operate within these limits. He will brief his clients on these limits, as appropriate.
6. He will not exploit the client or the counselor-client relationship for agency or personal advantage.
7. He will assist the client in devising an integrated, individualized rehabilitation plan that he believes offers reasonable promise of success in reaching the stated goals.
   a. He will approve only those services that the client needs for his rehabilitation and which the client is capable of accepting in an effective way.
   b. He will persistently follow up on the client's rehabilitation plan to insure its continued viability and effectiveness.
8. He will act responsibly in the client's behalf in emergency situations.
9. A counselor not in private practice will accept no fee or gratuity from clients for services given.
10. He will not become involved with clients in any fiscal or business arrangements or commitments beyond those required for delivery of services.
11. He will recommend the client's employment in only such jobs and circumstances as fit the capabilities of the client, his welfare, and his needs.

II. Counselor--Client's Family

The rehabilitation counselor recognizes that the client's family is typically a very important factor in the client's rehabilitation. He will strive to enlist the understanding and involvement of the family as a positive resource in promoting the client's rehabili-

tation.   He will strive to enlist the understanding and involvement
of the family as a positive resource in promoting the client's rehabilitation plan and in enhancing his continued effective functioning.

A.   The rehabilitation counselor will promote the interest,
involvement, and cooperation of the client's family in his rehabilitation plan if the family is of sufficient significance to the client to
exert an impact on the plan.

B.   The counselor will communicate to the family such information as will facilitate the client's welfare and rehabilitation,
but will refrain from including information that would represent ~
violation of essential confidentiality.

C.   The counselor will refrain from becoming a partisan in
any intra-family conflict; he will try to resolve such conflicts where
they are interfering with the welfare and rehabilitation of the client.

III.   Counselor--Client's Employer or Prospective Employer

The rehabilitation counselor is obligated to protect the client-
employer relationship by adequately apprising the latter of the client's
capabilities and limitations.   He will not participate in placing a
client in a position that will result in damaging the interests and
welfare of either or both the employer and the client.

A.   The rehabilitation counselor will refrain from recommending a client to an employer for employment in work for which
the client is not properly qualified in terms of the job's requirements
and the standards set by the employer.

B.   The counselor will give a prospective employer only such
information about the client as is necessary to identify the client's
fitness for the job under consideration.   The counselor will secure
the consent of the client, or his parent or guardian, for the release
to employers of any information that might be considered confidential.

C.   The counselor will not collaborate in placing a client for
employment in a situation where the client is likely to be unfairly
exploited or where he is likely to experience management prejudice
or discrimination.

D.   If the client finds a job without the intervention of the
counselor or his agency, the counselor will supply information about
the client to the employer only if requested by the client.

E.   The counselor will not collaborate in placing a client in
a job where his functioning would be illegal or detrimental to his
health and welfare or a threat to the safety of his fellow workers.

F.   The counselor will recommend the client for only those
jobs that appear to be compatible with the client's rehabilitation
plan and long-term welfare.

IV.   Counselor--Counselor

The rehabilitation counselor will relate to his colleagues in
the profession so as to facilitate their ongoing technical effectiveness
as professional persons.

A.   The counselor will encourage his colleagues to observe
ethical rules and professional standards such as will protect clients

and the rehabilitation counseling profession.

    1. If defections from acceptable standards are observed, the counselor will discuss the behavior directly with the defector, reporting the problem to the local ethics committee only when direct discussion brings no corrective results.

    B.   The counselor will not knowingly withhold information from his colleagues that would enhance their effectiveness.

    C.   The counselor will not disseminate information about his colleagues that would tend to erode their professional status or effectiveness.

    D.   Clients will be accepted readily in transfer or will be transferred to a colleague whenever it is deemed to be in the best interest of the client.

    1. The counselor will not transfer a client to a colleague without the latter's consent.

    2. In transferring a client the counselor will refrain from committing the receiving counselor to any prescribed course of action in relation to the client and his problems. The receiving counselor will continue with the rehabilitation plan formulated by the transferring counselor unless the best interests of the client dictate a change in the plan.

    3. The transferring counselor will not disparagingly discuss with the client the receiving counselor's capabilities, deficiencies or methods.

    4. The receiving counselor will not discuss in a disparaging way with the client transferred to him the competencies of the transferring counselor or agency, the judgments made, the methods used, or the quality of the client's rehabilitation plan.

    5. The transferring counselor will withdraw from involvement in the case when a client has been transferred, except to act as a resource for the receiving counselor.

        a.   If the client is received on a temporary basis for continuation of services when the regular counselor cannot continue his relations to the client for a time, the receiving counselor will refrain from making basic changes in the client's rehabilitation plan without the prior approval of his colleague.

    E.   The counselor will refrain from public display or behavior and from expression of opinions, complaints or frustrations that might bring discredit to rehabilitation, to his profession, or his colleagues。

    F.   The counselor will give active support to his colleagues who experience administrative or other pressures because of observance of ethical and professional principles.

V.   Counselor--Other Professionals

    Typically, the implementation of a rehabilitation plan for a client is a multidisciplinary effort. The rehabilitation counselor will conduct himself in his interdisciplinary relationships in such a way as to facilitate the contribution of all the specialists involved for maximum benefit of the client and to bring credit to his own profession.

A.   The rehabilitation counselor will not abdicate his role in relation to the client by delegating his responsibilities to other specialists; he will accept and discharge his responsibilities to the client.   If necessary, he will request involved others to refrain from altering the client's rehabilitation plan for which he is responsible or committing him or his agency to giving services not prescribed by him.   He will insist on proper controls on confidential information made available to other professionals by himself or his agency.   If there is noncompliance with his requests, he will ask that the offending persons or agencies be withdrawn from participation in implementing the client's rehabilitation plan.

B.   If "team" decisions are involved in formulating procedures, he will abide by and help to implement those decisions even though he might not personally agree with them.

C.   The rehabilitation counselor will not waste the resources of his agency and of the client by requiring more other-professional services than are indicated for adequately serving the client.

D.   The rehabilitation counselor will request such other-professional examinations, data and advice as are indicated for adequately evaluating, counseling and otherwise serving the client.

E.   As far as possible, the rehabilitation counselor will defer to other specialists the responsibility of interpreting their findings to the client; he will ask for reports from these specialists for his own guidance in counseling the client.

F.   The counselor will defer to the other specialists involved in releasing information confidential to the client that is wholly within the scope of such specialists to develop and establish.

G.   The rehabilitation counselor will report his findings and conclusions to other involved specialists to the extent necessary for them to cooperate effectively in implementing the client's rehabilitation plan.

1. Reports will be made and requested promptly so that the client's progress will not be impeded.
2. Procedures and reports ("red tape") will not be permitted to inhibit the progress of the client in his rehabilitation plan.
3. Reports of findings, decisions and results will be made to referring agencies and individuals within proper limits of confidentiality.

H.   The rehabilitation counselor will avoid any economic advantage to himself resulting from referrals for evaluations, training, or opinions to other persons or agencies.

VI.   Counselor--His Employer, Agency, Supervisor

The rehabilitation counselor will be loyal to the agency that employs him and to the administrators and supervisors who supervise him.   He will refrain from speaking, writing, or acting in such a way as to bring discredit on his agency.

A.   The rehabilitation counselor will persistently try to have amended those regulatory and administrative conditions of his

employment that require him to act in an unethical or unprofessional
manner or that erode the effectiveness of his professional functioning.

    B.   The counselor will act at a professional and responsible
level by carrying his administrative and professional duties efficiently,
devoting the hours to his work as required by the conditions of his
employment.   When he decides upon resignation or separation from
his position, he will give his employer timely and adequate advance
notice and will leave his work in such condition that his successor
can continue effective services to clients.

    C.   When there are differences in opinions and values be-
tween the counselor and his agency, he will attempt to resolve these
differences through discussion and other communication with the
appropriate persons in the agency.   He will not carry his dissent to
persons and agencies outside his own agency.

    D.   The rehabilitation counselor will promptly inform his
supervisors of any situations in his work that might develop into
problems that would become difficult or embarrassing for the agency.

VII.   Counselor--Community

    The rehabilitation counselor will regard his professional
status as imposing on him the obligation to relate to the community
(the public) at levels of responsibility and morality that are higher
than are required for persons not classified as "professional." He
will use his specialized knowledge, his special abilities, and his
leadership position to promote understanding and the general welfare
of handicapped persons in the community, and to promote acceptance
of the viable concepts of rehabilitation and of rehabilitation counseling.

    A.   The rehabilitation counselor will not compromise the
professional and ethical correctness and quality of his functioning in
response to political or economic pressures.

    B.   The counselor will resist any arrangements or operations
that will result in exploitation of his clients by business or other
interests.

    C.   The counselor will resist situations where his relation-
ships with business or other activities might be interpreted in the
community as a "conflict of interest."

    D.   The counselor will refuse to participate in or apply any
policies that involve discrimination of any type.

VIII.   Counselor--Other Programs, Agencies, and Institutions

    In his relationships with other programs, agencies and institu-
tions that will participate in the rehabilitation plan of the client, the
rehabilitation counselor will follow procedures and insist on arrangements that will foster maximum mutual facilitation and effectiveness
of services for the benefit of the client.

    A.   The counselor will insure that there is full mutual un-
derstanding of the client's rehabilitation needs and plan on the part of
all agencies cooperating in the rehabilitation of the client.

    B.   If the counselor cannot concur in the rehabilitation plan for a client referred to him, he will resolve the differences between the plan and what he believes should be done.

    C.   The counselor will keep himself aware of the actions being taken by cooperating agencies on behalf of his client and act as an advocate of the client to insure services delivery and effectiveness. He will insist on discontinuance of any procedures that exploit the client or threaten his welfare.

    D.   The counselor will take action to correct a situation where the client is improperly exploiting the agencies involved in the client's rehabilitation.

    E.   The counselor will insure that there are defined policies and practices in the other agencies cooperating in serving his client that effectively protect information confidentiality and the general welfare of the client.

    1. All information necessary for the cooperating agencies to be effective in serving the client will be promptly supplied by the referring counselor.

    2. Information supplied to a cooperating agency will be limited to that which is necessary for effective delivery of service.

IX.   Counselor--Maintenance of Technical Competency

    The rehabilitation counselor is obligated to keep his technical competency at such a level that his clients receive the benefit of the highest quality of services the profession is capable of offering.

    A.   The counselor will continuously strive, through reading, attending professional meetings, and taking courses of instruction, to keep abreast of new developments in concepts and practices and will apply those that appear to be viable and effective for his practice.

    B.   The counselor will take the initiative to arrange for in-service instruction adequate for him to perform his assigned duties competently and efficiently. He will not permit himself to be placed in a situation where he must carry out his duties without understanding what he is to do, how he is to do it, and what effects his doing it will have on his clients.

    C.   If the agency provides "time off" training to enhance the professional status of the counselor, he will arrive at an understanding of his obligation to remain with the agency for a period of time following such training and he will honor any such obligation.

X.   Counselor--Research

    The rehabilitation counselor is obligated to assist in the efforts to expand the knowledge needed to serve handicapped persons with increasing effectiveness.

    A.   The counselor will cooperate in research efforts whenever it is feasible for him to do so without jeopardizing his primary obligations and responsibilities to his clients and his agency.

    B.   In supplying data for research, the counselor will insure that it meets rigid standards of validity, honesty and protection of confidentiality.

C. In cooperating with research projects, the counselor will
supply the data or action to which he commits himself, timely and in
a form usable in the projects.

RESPIRATORY THERAPISTS

AMERICAN ASSOCIATION FOR RESPIRATORY THERAPY (AART)
    7411 Hines Place, Dallas, Texas 75235
    Winfield S. Singletary, Executive Director

Membership: The American Association for Respiratory Therapy,
founded in 1947 and with a present (1973) membership of over
11, 000, is a professional association in the paramedical specialty of
respiratory therapy. Originally organized as the Inhalation Therapy
Association, the group was known as the American Association of
Inhalation Therapists from 1954 until 1967, and as the American
Association for Inhalation Therapy until 1973, when the present
name became official. As health specialists in the "new medicine, "
in the "frontiers of the healing arts, " workers in respiratory ther-
apy--according to the AART official definition of the field--are engaged "in the treatment, management, control and care of patients
with deficiencies and abnormalities associated with respiration. "

Respiratory therapy requires proficiency in a variety of diagnostic procedures, and in such therapeutic aids as "medical gases,
air, oxygen administration apparatus, environmental control systems;
humidification, aerosols, drugs, and medications; ventilatory assistance and control; postural drainage; chest physiotherapy and breathing exercises; respiratory rehabilitation; assistance with cardiopulmonary resuscitation; and maintenance of natural, artificial, and
mechanical airways. " Of the several categories of AART membership, "Active Member"--the fully professional level of membership
--qualifies for joining the Association with at least 1 1/2 years in
inhalation therapy related to patient care in a recognized institution
or organization.

In order to recognize professional achievement in its field,
AART conducts a certification program for Respiratory Therapy
Technician. Since November 1969, the organization has authorized
the use of the designation, "Certified Respiratory Therapy Technician"
("CRTT"), to members meeting the basic requirements of education
and experience in one of the three requirements:
    "(1) Have a high school education or its equivalent, plus two
         years of clinical experience under medical supervision.
    (2) Be a graduate of a qualified one year respiratory therapy
         training program, plus one year's respiratory therapy
         clinical experience under medical supervision.

(3) Be a graduate of an American Medical Association approved respiratory therapy program on the associate degree level. "

The certification program is administered by a special committee of AART--the Technician Certification Board (TCB), a 12-man group of six AART members and six physicians--one from each of six medical groups with a special interest in respiratory therapy. Applicants for certification must pass a three-hour written examination of multiple-choice questions, developed and administered by the Psychological Corporation. The subject matter of the examination is:

Basic and Applied Sciences (1/3 of the examination)--anatomy, physiology, physics, chemistry, mathematics, and pharmacology.

Clinical Applications (2/3 of the examination)--gas administration, humidity and Aerosol, positive pressure breathing treatments, assisted and controlled continuous mechanical ventilation, cardiopulmonary resuscitation, chest physical therapy, patient care, ethics, professional conduct, history, cleaning, decontamination and sterilization, and microbiology.

The AART also sponsors--along with the American College of Chest Physicians and the American Society of Anesthesiologists--another program of nongovernment agency licensure, the registration of AART members by the American Registry of Respiratory Therapists. Applicants who meet the education and experience requirements--basically, being the holder of an Association Degree from an American Medical Association approved (or provisionally approved) school in respiratory therapy, and passing a written and oral examination--are authorized to use the professional designation, "Registered Respiratory Therapist" ("ARRT"). Prior to issuance of registration, the candidate must have completed one full year of clinical experience under licensed medical supervision. Other combinations of education and licensure as a graduate nurse also qualify an applicant for registration examination, provided he or she has the required training for respiratory therapy.

The two parts of the examination for registration are:

Written Examination: About 150 multiple-choice questions to be completed in three hours, on such subjects as "Techniques, indications and response to general inhalation therapy; Department administration, ethics, and nursing arts; Anatomy, physiology, cardiopulmonary pathophysiology, physics, chemistry, microbiology and sterilization. "

Oral Examination: Two 20-minute performance tests, during which a physician and a registered therapist "evaluate the candidate with respect to his depth of knowledge of equipment, procedures, theory and clinical ability. "

Both registration and certification must be renewed annually, with proof of employment in respiratory therapy, and a roster is issued by the respective licensing agencies each year for Certified Technicians and Registered Therapists.

Code of Ethics: The conduct guide for members of AART is the organization's Code of Ethics, adopted and most recently revised November 13, 1967.   According to the Code, obligations of workers in this paramedical specialty of respiratory therapy are set forth in broad principles concerning relationships and responsibilities to:
    The Patient,
    The Physician,
    The Employer,
    Profession and Associates.
Both the American Association for Respiratory Therapy and the American Registry of Respiratory Therapists provide in their Bylaws for the enforcement of the code of ethics, through prescribed disciplinary procedure.

Professional Insignia: The emblem of AART is an unbordered design showing a banded square superimposed on the caduceus--winged staff with two entwined serpents--signifying healing; a torch tops the caduceus; the square bears a centered circle showing the center portion of the staff and entwined serpents on a dark ground; the organization initials, "AART, " are given--one letter in each corner of the square design, from upper left to right, lower left to right. The color of this emblem is shown variously--black on white (publication); green on white (stationery).

Other Identification of Professional Status: As described above under "Membership, " to indicate professional competence through education, experience, and examination, the professional designations are awarded, "CRTT"--"Certified Respiratory Therapy Technician"; and "ARRT"--"American Registry of Respiratory Therapists. "

Bibliography:
    American Association for Respiratory Therapy.   Candidate Handbook for the Certification Examination.   1972.   10 pages.
    Describes content of AART examination, gives examination requirements and testing location for Certified Respiratory Therapy Technician examinations.

_____. The Certification of Respiratory Therapy Technicians
of the AART. 8 pages.
Fact sheet issued by the Technician Certification Board.
_____. Code of Ethics. November 13, 1967. 3 pages; also
1973 edition, 1 page.
Professional conduct guide for Respiratory Therapy.
_____. Considering a Career in Respiratory Therapy?
Pamphlet.
Guidance brochure describing work as inhalation therapist,
professional identification and licensure.
_____. Essentials for Certified Respiratory Therapy Tech-
nician Training Program, with Guidelines. April 1971.
38 pages. $5.75.
"Detailed curricula, with course scopes, course outlines and
bibliography."
American Registry of Respiratory Therapists. General Informa-
tion. Pamphlet.
Describes registration procedures, giving qualifications and
examination required.

"Code of Ethics"

As Allied Health professionals engaged in the performance of
Respiratory Therapy, we realize we must individually and collectively
strive to maintain the highest obtainable level of ethical standards.

The principles set forth define the ethical and moral standards
to which each member of the American Association for Respiratory
Therapy should conform. This Code of Ethics shall be subject to
monitoring, interpretation, and timely revision by the Association's
Board of Directors, with the advice of the Board of Medical Advisors.

Each member of this Association shall conduct himself in such
a manner as to gain the respect and confidence of other Health Care
personnel, as well as respecting the human dignity of each of his
superiors, subordinates, and other associates.

Each member shall be responsible for the competent and efficient execution of his assigned duties, being guided at all times by
his concern for the welfare of the patient.

Each member shall be familiar with, and comply with existing
state and/or federal laws governing the practice of Respiratory
Therapy.

Each member shall keep in confidence any and all privileged
information concerning the patient. Inquiries regarding the dissemination of privileged personal or clinical information pertaining
to the patient by persons other than those members of the Health
Care team who are responsible for the care of the patient, shall
be referred to the physician in charge of the patient's medical care.

No member shall endeavor to extend his province beyond his
competence and the authority invested to him by a physician.

No member shall accept gratuities in the form of bribes or
tips for preferential consideration of the patient, or to supplement
professional income. The member must carefully guard against

conflicts of professional interest.

Each member shall accept responsibility for exposing incompetence and illegal or unethical conduct to the proper authorities and/or the Judicial Committee of this Association. Only through the integrity of each member can the highest purpose of the profession be served.

Each member shall adhere to the Bylaws of the Association and support the objectives and purposes contained therein.

SANITARIANS

INTERNATIONAL ASSOCIATION OF MILK, FOOD AND ENVIRON-MENTAL SANITARIANS (IAMFES)
Blue Ridge Rd., P. O. Box 437, Shelbyville, Ind. 46176
H. L. Thomasson, Executive Director

Membership: The International Association of Milk, Food and Environmental Sanitarians (formerly the International Association of Milk and Food Sanitarians), founded in 1911 and with a present (1973) membership of 4500, is a professional association of "milk, food and environmental sanitarians, food and drug officials, milk and food industry field men and technicians, laboratory workers, sanitary engineers, college and university extension members, research and teaching personnel, agriculture and military personnel."

Membership in the Association is open to "all persons who have a professional or business interest in advancing the field of environmental sanitation." Members are grouped in 25 affiliate associations in states and regions of the United States and Canada, and direct membership in foreign countries and in states not having affiliate associations.

Code of Ethics: No formal code of ethics has been formulated by the Association. The Bylaws (Article II, Section 5G) contain procedures for disciplinary action for a member found to have engaged in unprofessional conduct--the Executive Board may, by two-thirds vote, recommend expulsion from membership of a member "for cause," after written notice to the member in question and opportunity for hearing or written rebuttal of charges of unprofessional conduct.

Professional Insignia: The IAMFES emblem is its seal--a circular design with a centered "S" (for "Sanitarians"); with the organization name, "International Association" (top of design), "Sanitarians" (bottom of design); and "Milk, Food, & Environmental" (band superimposed upon the centered "S"). The color of the emblem is blue on white (publication). The insignia is also available to members

for display or wear, in the
same colors--blue on white
--as a decal, lapel button,
or tie tac and lapel pin combination.

Bibliography:
    International Association
        of Milk, Food and
        Environmental Sani-
        tarians. Constitu-
        tion and Bylaws.
        March 1964. (Re-
        print from Journal
        of Milk and Food
        Technology 27:352-
        356 November 1964).
    Includes membership
    requirements; disci-
    plinary procedures for unprofessional conduct.
    _____. International Association of Milk, Food and Environ-
        mental Sanitarians. Folder.
    Gives IAMFES categories of membership; lists affiliate asso-
    ciations.

NATIONAL ENVIRONMENTAL HEALTH ASSOCIATION
    1600 Pennsylvania Ave. , Denver, Colo. 80203
    Nicholas Pohlit, M. P. H. , R. S. , Executive Director

Membership: The National Environmental Health Association (formerly the National Association of Sanitarians), founded in 1937 and with
a present (1973) membership of about 6000, is a professional organization of "men and women engaged in environmental control. "
Among the members are administrators, technicians, educators and
other professional workers employed by federal, state, and local
governments, institutions (including schools, hospitals, and nursing
homes), private industry and business in "programs directed to
creating a safer, more healthful environment. "

    "Active Members" (professional members fully qualified to vote
and hold office in the Association) have met a requirement of graduation from an accredited college with a bachelor's degree including a
minimum of 30 semesters of academic work in physical, biological
and environmental sciences, and are full-time employees working as
"environmentalist"--in water pollution control, solid waste disposal,
vector control, housing, noise, industrial hygiene, community health
planning, environmental education, food sanitation, in related educational activities, or in military organization.

Code of Ethics: The Association conduct guide for its members is
the Code of Ethics, adopted in 1969.   This Code contains a brief
statement in the form of a credo, and an oath concerning obligations
and responsibilities to the field of public health, the public, and the
Association.

Professional Insignia: The emblem of the Association is in the form

of a shield--the organization
name, "National Environmental
Health Association," is printed
below a top band of the design;
and the two lower halves of
the shield (left to right) bear
a star on a dark ground, and
the legend, "Serving Mankind."
The color of the emblem is
black on white (membership
application).

Other Identification of Professional Status: The National
Environmental Health Association sponsors (with the other
professional association of
sanitarians--the International
Association of Milk, Food,
and Environmental Sanitarians--and the American Public Health
Association) a certification program for sanitarians.   The program is administered by the American Intersociety Academy for
Certification of Sanitarians (17309 Fletchall Drive, Toolesville,
Maryland 20837).

     By an examination program, founded in 1966, individuals meet-
ing the basic requirement of Master's degree in appropriate field
and registration in state of practice, are eligible to take a written
and oral examination--developed by the Professional Examination
Service of the American Public Health Association, and administered
by the Academy.   Successful candidates in the examination are
awarded a certificate as Diplomate of the Academy, and authorized
to use that professional designation, "Diplomate, American Intersociety Academy for Certification of Sanitarians."

Bibliography:
     National Environmental Health Association.   National Environ-
          mental Health Association Is....   Folder.
     Descriptive brochure, including membership requirements.

"Code of Ethics"

     As a member of the National Environmental Health Associa-
tion I acknowledge:

That I have an obligation to the sciences and arts for the advancement of public health. I will uphold the standards of my profession, continually search for truths, and disseminate my findings; and will strive to keep myself fully informed of the developments in the field of public health.

That I have an obligation to the public whose trust I hold and I will endeavor to the best of my ability to guard these interests honestly and wisely. I will be loyal to the governmental division or industry by which I am retained.

That the enjoyment of the highest attainable standard of health is one of the fundamental rights of every human being without distinction of race, religion, cultural background, economic or social condition.

That, being loyal to my profession, I will uphold the constitution and by-laws of National Environmental Health Assn. and will at all times conduct myself in a manner worthy of my profession. My signature hereon constitutes a realization of my personal responsibility to actively discharge these obligations.

SCHOOL ADMINISTRATORS

AMERICAN ASSOCIATION OF SCHOOL ADMINISTRATORS (AASA)
1801 N. Moore St., Arlington, Va. 22209
Paul B. Salmon, Executive Director

Membership: The American Association of School Administrators, founded in 1865 as the National Association of School Superintendents, and with a present (1973) membership of 19,000, is a professional organization of school administrators at all levels of public and private schools--elementary through university. The AASA became associated with the National Education Association--first as the Department of School Superintendence, and later (after the name of the group was changed to the present designation in 1937), beginning in 1969. In 1973 the Association severed all relationship with the NEA and became totally independent and autonomous.

Among Association members are educators qualified as "Active Members" by fulfilling one of the following position requirements:
"Administrative officers of local intermediate, or state boards of education; city, county, town, village, and local district superintendents, including central school principals, supervising principals, executive heads, and their professional staffs, and administrative officers of private and public schools and school systems.
Associate, assistant, and deputy superintendents or department heads who exercise administrative or supervisory functions in local, intermediate, and state school systems.

Presidents or heads of universities, colleges, teacher education institutions, junior colleges.
Heads of departments of colleges of education, professors of
educational administration, and placement officers of those
institutions.
Executive secretaries, and others with administrative responsibility in state and national education associations. State
and national educational administrative officers.
Principals of elementary schools, junior high schools, and
high schools. "

Code of Ethics: The professional conduct guide for school administrators is the AASA Policies to Govern the Ethical Professional Behavior of School Administrators. Under each of the nine Policies,
examples illustrative of policy applications are given. These ethical
Policies are "a definition of the ideals and responsibilities of school
administrators, " and "represent a creed which defines acceptable
standards of behavior. " The Principles constitute Part One of the
AASA Code of Ethics. Part Two of the Code of Ethics is Implementing Standards of Ethical Behavior for School Administrators,
"setting forth suggested procedures whereby AASA and state associations of school administrators could implement a code of ethical
behavior. " The Procedures for enforcement of the Policies are
given in Part Two of the Code of Ethics (Section F, and other
Sections).

Other Guides to Professional Conduct: Two other guides to the
professional conduct of school administrators have been issued by
the AASA:
Platform of the AASA--adopted on February 15, 1967, this
credo of school administrators as citizens of the United
States of America and as educators, includes means of
realizing the stated goals.
Report of the AASA Resolutions Committee--adopted on
February 20-21, 1971 and most recently amended February 28, 1973, this statement of AASA stand on 46 current
questions, includes the Association position on Race Relations, Administrative-Staff Relationships, Student Unrest,
Achieving Racial Balances, Citizenship, Environment,
Drug Use, Year-Round Schools.

Professional Insignia: The emblem of the AASA is its logotype,

consisting of a design of the organization's initials, "aasa, " in
lower case letters. The color of
the emblem is shown variously--
grey and white letters on dark
blue ground (publication); multi-
color letters (first two "a"'s red,
"s, " lavender, final "a, " yellow--
on black ground (publication).

Bibliography:
   American Association of School Administrators. AASA, 108
      Years of Service. 1973. Pamphlet.
   Informational brochure, including brief AASA history, goals,
   activities, and membership requirements.
   _____. AASA Code of Ethics. 1966. 68 pages. Pamphlet.
      $1.
   Includes Policies to Govern the Ethical Professional Behavior
   of School Administrators (Part One), and Promoting and Implementing Standards of Ethical Behavior for School Administrators (Part Two), which gives procedures for enforcement
   of the code.
   _____. AASA Resolutions, Platform, Constitution, Bylaws,
      Ethics. 1973. 38 pages. Pamphlet.
   Policies on 45 issues to govern ethical professional behavior
   of school administrators.

"Policies to Govern the Ethical Professional Behavior of School Administrators"

Preamble

Public education in America rests on firm commitments to
the dignity and worth of each individual, to the preeminence of enlightenment and reason over force and coercion, and to government
by the consent of the governed. Public schools prosper to the extent they merit the confidence of the people. In judging its schools,
society is influenced to a considerable degree by the character and
quality of their administration. To meet these challenges school
administrators have an obligation to exercise professional leadership.

Society demands that any group that claims the rights, privileges, and status of a profession prove itself worthy through the
establishment and maintenance of ethical policies governing the activities of its members. A professional society must demonstrate
the capacity and willingness to regulate itself and to set appropriate
guides for the ethical conduct of its members. Such obligations are
met largely by practitioners through action in a professional society
such as the American Association of School Administrators.

Every member of a profession carries a responsibility to
act in a manner becoming a professional person. This implies that
each school administrator has an inescapable obligation to abide by
the ethical standards of his profession. The behavior of each is the
concern of all. The conduct of any administrator influences the
attitude of the public toward the profession and education in general.

These policies of ethical behavior are designed to inspire a
quality of behavior that reflects honor and dignity on the profession
of school administration. They are not intended as inflexible rules
or unchangeable laws. They serve to measure the propriety of an
administrator's behavior in his working relationships. They encourage and emphasize those positive attributes of professional

conduct which characterize strong and effective administrative leadership.

(The term administrator, as used herein, refers to those persons who, regardless of title, serve as chief school administrators.)

Policy I

The professional school administrator constantly upholds the honor and dignity of his profession in all his actions and relations with pupils, colleagues, school board members, and the public.

The following examples illustrate but do not limit applications of this policy.

The professional school administrator--

A.   Is impartial in the execution of school policies and the enforcement of rules and regulations.   It is a breach of ethics to give preferential consideration to any individual or group because of their special status or position in the school system or community.

B.   Recognizes and respects fully the worth and dignity of each individual in all administrative procedures and leadership actions.

C.   Demonstrates professional courtesy and ethical behavior by informing a colleague in another system of his intention to consider for employment personnel from that system.

D.   Never submits official and confidential letters of appraisal for teachers or others which knowingly contain erroneous information or which knowingly fail to include pertinent data.

E.   Never fails to recommend those worthy of recommendation.

F.   Is alert to safeguard the public and his profession from those who might degrade public education or school administration.

G.   Seeks no self-aggrandizement.

H.   Refrains from making unwarranted claims, from inappropriate advertising, and from misinterpreting facts about his school system to further his own professional status.

I.   Never makes derogatory statements about a colleague or a school system unless he is compelled to state his opinion under oath or in official relationships where his professional opinion is required.

J.   Exhibits ethical behavior by explaining and giving reasons to individuals affected by demotions or terminations of employment.

Policy II

The professional school administrator obeys local, state, and national laws; holds himself to high ethical and moral standards; and gives loyalty to his country and to the cause of democracy and liberty.

The following examples illustrate but do not limit applications of this policy:

A.   A legal conviction for immorality, commission of a crime involving moral turpitude, or other public offense of similar degree shall be sufficient grounds for expelling a school administrator from membership in the American Association of School Administrators.

B.   Affiliation with organizations known to advocate the forcible overthrow of the government of the United States is evidence of unworthiness of public trust.   A person who is so affiliated shall not be permitted to become or to continue as a member of the American Association of School Administrators.

C.   A professional school administrator, in common with other citizens, has a right and in many instances an obligation to express his opinion about the wisdom or justice of a given law. An opinion questioning a law, however, does not justify failure to fulfill the requirements of that law.

D.   The ideals of his profession require a school administrator to resist ideological pressures that would contravene the fundamental principles of public education or would pervert or weaken public schools, their educational program, or their personnel.

E.   It is unethical to ignore or divert attention from laws which are incompatible with the best interests and purposes of the schools, as a way of avoiding controversy.   Rather, the professional school administrator will take the initiative to bring about the reconsideration, revision, or repeal of the statute.

F.   The professional school administrator will not withhold evidence or knowingly shield lawbreakers.

Policy III

The professional school administrator accepts the responsibility throughout his career to master and to contribute to the growing body of specialized knowledge, concepts, and skills which characterize school administration as a profession.

The following examples illustrate but do not limit applications of this policy:

A.   In addition to meeting the minimum standards required for legal certification in his state, the professional school administrator has a responsibility to satisfy the preparation standards recommended by his professional association and has an obligation to work toward the adoption of these professional standards by the appropriate certification authorities in his state.

B.   The school administrator has a professional obligation to attend conferences, seminars, and other learning activities which hold promise of contributing to his professional growth and development.

C.   It is in keeping with the highest ideals of the profession for the administrator to support local, state, and national

committees studying educational problems and to participate in such
activities whenever and wherever possible, consistent with his obligations to his district.

D.   The school administrator has a leadership responsibility
for the professional growth of his associates which requires encouragement of their attendance at appropriate professional meetings
and their participation in the work of local, state, and national committees and associations.

E.   Concern for improving his profession, and for education
generally, requires that the school administrator seek out promising
educational practices and relevant research findings and that he
share with others any significant practices and research from within
his own institution.

F.   The school administrator has a special obligation to contribute to the strengthening of his own state and national professional
association.

Policy IV

The professional school administrator strives to provide the
finest possible educational experiences and opportunities to all
persons in the district.

The following examples illustrate but do not limit applications
of this policy:

A.   The school administrator will base differentiation of
educational experiences on the differing needs and abilities of pupils,
giving no preference to factors such as social status or other un-
democratic or discriminating considerations.

B.   A school administrator has an obligation to inform the
board and the community of deficiencies in educational services
or opportunities.

C.   A school administrator resists all attempts by vested
interests to infringe upon the school program as a means of promoting their selfish purposes.

D.   A school administrator resists all attempts to exclude
from consideration as teaching personnel members of any particular
race or creed. He also resists pressures to employ teachers on
the basis of the political, marital, or economic status of the applicant. The ability and fitness of the candidates for teaching positions are the sole criteria for selection.

E.   A school administrator recognizes that the provisions
of equal educational opportunities for all pupils may require greater
or different resources for some than for others.

F.   A school administrator is professionally obligated to assume clear, articulate, and forceful leadership in defining the role
of the school in the community and pointing the way to achieve its
functions.

Policy V

The professional school administrator applying for a position or entering into contractual agreements seeks to preserve and enhance the prestige and status of his profession.

The following examples illustrate but do not limit applications of this policy:

A.   A school administrator is morally committed to honor employment contracts.   He shall refuse to enter into a new contractual agreement until termination of an existing contract is completed to the satisfaction of all concerned.

B.   A school administrator does not apply for positions indiscriminately nor for any position held by an administrator whose termination of employment is not a matter of record.

C.   Misrepresentations, use of political influence, pressure tactics, or undermining the professional status of a colleague is unethical practice and is inimical to his professional commitment.

D.   Advertising, either to solicit new school positions or to offer professional consultation services, is inconsistent with the ideals of the profession of school administration.

E.   A school administrator refrains from making disparaging comments about candidates competing for a position.

F.   A school administrator refuses to accept a position in which established principles of professional school administration must be seriously compromised or abandoned.

G.   A school administrator does not apply for or accept a position where a competent special professional investigating committee endorsed by the Association has declared working conditions unsatisfactory until such time as appropriate corrections in the situation have been made.

Policy VI

The professional school administrator carries out in good faith all policies duly adopted by the local board and the regulations of state authorities and renders professional service to the best of his ability.

The following examples illustrate but do not limit applications of this policy:

A.   Adoption of policies not in conformity with the administrator's recommendations or beliefs is not just cause for refusal by the administrator to support and execute them.

B.   It is improper for an administrator to refuse to work at his optimum level.

C.   A school administrator has an obligation to support publicly the school board and the instructional staff if either is unjustly accused.   He should not permit himself to become involved publicly in personal criticism of board or staff members.   He should be at liberty, however, to discuss differences of opinion on professional matters.

D.   If a situation develops whereby an administrator feels

that to retain his position would necessitate that he violate what he
and other members of the profession consider to be ethical conduct,
he should inform the board of the untenable position. In the event
of his imminent dismissal, the superintendent should request adequate reasons; and if they are not forthcoming or if the situation
is not resolved to his professional satisfaction, he should report
to the public.

Policy VII

The professional school administrator honors the public trust
of his position above any economic or social rewards.

The following examples illustrate but do not limit applications
of this policy:

A.   To resist, or to fail to support, clearly desirable approaches to improving and strengthening the schools is unbecoming
to a professional person and unethical conduct on the part of a
school administrator.
B.   The school administrator has a commitment to his position of public trust to resist unethical demands by special interest
or pressure groups. He refuses to allow strong and unscrupulous
individuals to seize or exercise powers and responsibilities which
are properly his own.
C.   The rank, popularity, position or social standing of any
member of the school staff should never cause the professional
school administrator to conceal, disregard, or seemingly condone
unethical conduct. Any and all efforts to disregard, overlook, or
cover up unethical practices should be vigorously resisted by a
school administrator.

Policy VIII

The professional school administrator does not permit considerations of private gain nor personal economic interest to
affect the discharge of his professional responsibilities.

The following examples illustrate but do not limit applications of this policy:

A.   A school administrator refuses to permit his relationship
with vendors primarily interested in seeling goods and services to
influence his administration of the school system he serves.
B.   It is improper for a school administrator to accept employment by any concern which publishes, manufactures, sells, or
in any way deals in goods or services which are or may be expected
to be purchased by the school system he serves.
C.   It is improper for a school administrator to be engaged
in private ventures if such endeavors cause him to give less than
full-time concern to his school system.
D.   This policy in no way precludes private investment of

personal funds of the school administrator in ventures not influenced by his position in a given school system provided his own professional obligations are not neglected.

E. During the time of his employment the school administrator shall have no personal interest in, nor receive any personal gain or profit from, school supplies, equipment, books, or other educational materials or facilities procured, dispensed, or sold to or in the school system he serves.

F. It is a breach of public trust for a school administrator to use confidential information concerning school affairs (such as the knowledge of the selection of specific school sites) for personal profit or to divulge such information to others who might so profit.

G. It is inappropriate for a school administrator to utilize unpublished materials developed in line of duty by staff members in a school system in order to produce a publication for personal profit, without the expressed permission of all contributors.

H. A school administrator must be wary of using free consultative services from a commercial concern which may in effect be a skillful technique for promoting the sale of instructional or other materials in which that concern has a pecuniary interest.

I. A school administrator does not publicly endorse goods or services provided for schools by commercial organizations.

J. The school administrator should not recommend the appointment of immediate relatives to positions under his jurisdiction.

Policy IX

The professional school administrator recognizes that the public schools are the public's business and seeks to keep the public fully and honestly informed about their schools.

The following examples illustrate but do not limit applications of this policy:

A. A school administrator has an obligation to interpret to the community the work and activities of the school system, revealing its weaknesses as well as its strengths. It is unethical for a school administrator to present only the favorable facts to the patrons of the district.

B. A school administrator maintains confidences or qualified privileged communications entrusted to him in the course of executing the affairs of the public schools. These confidences shall be revealed only as the law or courts may require or when the welfare of the school system is at stake.

C. It is proper for a school administrator to discuss confidential information with the board of education meeting in executive session.

D. A school administrator considers that those with whom he deals are innocent of any disparaging accusations until valid evidence is presented to substantiate any charges made.

Overview

High standards of ethical behavior for the professional school
administrator are essential and are compatible with his faith in
the power of public education and his commitment to leadership
in the preservation and strengthening of the public schools.

The true sense of high calling comes to the superintendent of
schools as he faces squarely such widely held beliefs as the following:

A.   The effectiveness of the schools and their programs is
inescapably the responsibility of the superintendent.
B.   Every act, or every failure to act, of the superintendent
has consequences in the schools and in the lives of people.
C.   In many situations and to many people in a community
the superintendent is the living symbol of their schools.
D.   The public entrusts both the day-by-day well-being and
the long-range welfare of its children and of its school system to
the superintendent and board of education.
E.   The ultimate test for a superintendent is the effort which
he makes to improve the quality of learning opportunity for every
child in the schools.
F.   In the long run, what happens in and to the public
schools of America happens to America.

SCIENTISTS

SOCIETY FOR SOCIAL RESPONSIBILITY IN SCIENCE (SSRS)
    221 Rock Hill Rd., Bala-Cynwyd, Pa. 19004
    J. Malvern Benjamin, Vice President

Membership: The Society for Social Responsibility in Science,
founded in 1949 and with a present (1973) membership of 750, is
"a body of scientific workers organized to foster throughout the
world a tradition of personal moral responsibility for the consequences to humanity of professional activity, with emphasis on constructive alternatives to militarism." The Society, with members
and subscribers in 45 countries--including seven Nobel Laureates,
sponsors discussion groups on ethics in science at universities and
population centers. "Full Membership" in SSRS is open to professional workers, "educated or working in fields of pure and applied
physical, biological, and social science, and also students in these
fields."

Code of Ethics: The SSRS has issued no formal code of ethics,
but each person joining the Society signs a personal pledge on his

application blank for membership, subscribing to the purposes of the Society for Social Responsibility in Science.

Other Guides to Professional Conduct: At the international conference of SSRS in Trondheim, Norway, in 1971, a Pledge for Engineers was prepared in draft, and was discussed, but not adopted.

Professional Insignia: The Society emblem is its logotype--the group's initials in a square monogram. The color of the insignia is grey on black (letterhead, publication).

Bibliography:
> "Society for Social Responsibility in Science." Science 118:3. 1953.
> Society for Social Responsibility in Science. Pledge for Engineers. Social responsibility of the scientists and technologists working as engineers.
> _____. SSRS. Folder. Informational brochure, including the Purposes of the Society, which applicants accept as a pledge.

"Pledge for Social Responsibility in Science"

"To meet by constructive means the central problem of our day: the survival of civilization itself in an age in which the destructive power of military weapons reaches ever more devastating proportions. In this context, SSRS calls upon every scientist and engineer

(1) to foresee, insofar as possible, the results of his professional work,
(2) to recognize his personal moral responsibility for the consequences of this work, irrespective of outside pressures,
(3) to seek work which seems to him of benefit to mankind and abstain from that which he judges to be injurious to it, and
(4) to use his scientific and technological knowledge guided by ethical judgment to aid government and layman in the intelligent and human use of the tools which science and technology provide."

SCULPTORS

NATIONAL SCULPTURE SOCIETY (NSS)
    250 E. 51st St., New York, N.Y. 10022
    Claire A. Stein, Executive Director

Membership: The National Sculpture Society, founded in 1893 and
with a present (1973) membership of about 350, is an organization
of artists who work in all types of sculptures. Any sculptor in
the United States is eligible for membership in the Society, provided
his work passes a Membership Committee, and then the full membership.

Code of Ethics: Several guides to ethical practices for sculptors
have been developed by the National Sculpture Society. These in-
clude: Contract Forms for Sculpture Commissions, A Suggested
Schedule of Payments for Large Commissions, A Guide for Running
Sculpture Competitions, A Price Charge Guide for Bronze Casting,
Stone Enlarging and Carving.

    One guide is directed to the craftsmen who assist sculptors in
the duplication, casting or carving of sculptured work. Such
assistants, engaged in technical services to professional sculptors,
subscribe to the NSS Code of Ethical Practices Governing the
Crafts and Services Associated with the Profession of Sculpture.
According to the principles of the Code, carvers and casters of
sculptured works agree to file with the National Sculpture Society
copies of their promotional materials (letters, circulars, folders),
and a sculptor member of the Society, who receives a commission
from a suggestion of a caster or carver, is expected to assign
casting or carving of the completed design to the individual or firm,
suggesting his name for the commission, and to allow such individual
or firm a commission fee not exceeding ten per cent of the total
sculptural fee.

Professional Insignia: The National Sculpture Society does not report any official emblem.

Bibliography:
    National Sculpture Society. Code of Ethical Practices Govern-
           ing the Crafts and Services Associated with the Profession
           of Sculpture. 2 pages.
    Business ethics for craftsmen serving professional sculptors,
    as through casting or carving.

"Code of Ethical Practices
Governing the Crafts and Services Associated with
the Practice of Sculpture"

The undersigned agrees to abide by the following code of business ethics in the sculptural field.

1.   It will not attempt to solicit business by means of agents, letters, circulars, advertisements or otherwise, which attempt to create the impression in the mind of any prospective customer that sculpture of any nature previously entrusted to the undersigned solely for technical services, such as casting or carving, was actually created by such firm through the employment of the services of the sculptor who created the model or design therefor, unless in fact such sculptor is a paid employee of the undersigned, or under retainer contract with it.

2.   It will not solicit business of any manner which will create the impression in the mind of any prospective customer that distinguished sculptors are in their employ, or are under retainer contract with them, or have prepared illustrative material for distribution by such firm, or are available for the creation, at the request of such firm, of memorials, tablets, etc., unless said sculptors of such distinction are actually employed by or are under retainer contract with such firm.

3.   It will, if approached by any individual, group, committee, municipality, etc., with respect to the designing, modeling, or fabrication of any sculpture, including memorials, tablets, etc., involving sculpture, either:
(a)   Suggest one or more sculptors qualified in its opinion to develop the project contemplated, and notify such sculptors of its recommendation; or
(b)   Request the National Sculpture Society to recommend sculptors qualified to undertake such project; or
(c)   Accept a contract for the execution of a sculptural project directly, but only where the design and modeling is to be entrusted to a sculptor already on the payroll of, or under written contract with, the undersigned, in which event the customer is to be promptly so advised and shown photographs and examples of the actual creative work of such sculptor.

4.   Unless the undersigned is the actual owner of a completed sculptural work, photographic reproductions of completed works will only be promulgated by the undersigned with the permission of the sculptor.   All such reproductions shall clearly indicate that said work is by the particular sculptor and that the undersigned was engaged to do the casting or carving thereof.

5.   The undersigned will file with the National Sculpture Society copies of all printed or otherwise duplicated matter, such as letters, circulars, folders, etc., issued by it to the public, dealing with sculpture.

6. The undersigned understands that the National Sculpture Society will recommend to its members that any sculptor commissioned as a result of the suggestion of the undersigned, entrust the casting or carving to the undersigned at prices similar to those asked by it for services of similar character, and pay the undersigned as motivating agent, such additional commission fee as may be mutually agreeable in an amount not exceeding ten per cent of the total sculptural fee.

_____(signature)_____

SECRETARIES

NATIONAL SECRETARIES ASSOCIATION [INTERNATIONAL] (NSA)
     616 E. 63rd St., Kansas City, Mo. 64110
     Mrs. Angeline Krout, CPS, President

Membership: The National Secretaries Association, founded in 1942 and with a present (1973) membership of 29,000, is a "professional organization of secretaries" in the United States and Canada. The members are grouped in about 570 chapters, throughout the United States, Canada, and other countries around the world. "Regular Members" qualify for NSA membership provided they
     "have had secretarial training and at least two years of
     secretarial experience, and are actively engaged as full-
     time secretaries or part-time secretaries not engaged in
     any other gainful employment at the time of admission to
     membership."

As part of its activities to accomplish the purpose of NSA-- "elevation of the standards of the secretarial profession"--the society in 1951 instituted a Certified Professional Secretary Program. The Institute for Certifying Secretaries, a department of NSA, administers the program, a basic part of which is a two-day, six-part examination. Candidates successfully completing all parts of the examination are awarded the designation, "CPS" ("Certified Professional Secretary"), to signify that they have attained a "recognized standard of proficiency in the secretarial profession." Candidates for the certification examination qualify for the test by being high school graduates and having three years of secretarial experience, or by other specified education and experience.

The examination, administered each year on the first Friday and Saturday in May, consists of multiple-choice questions in five written tests, and a performance test (Part V)--demonstrating in part transcription and composition skills. The tests of the examination--designed to measure "basic knowledge in economics, business organization, accounting and business law"; and "secretarial forms and procedures, office management and supervisory skills, principles of good human relations, with emphasis on judgment, understanding, and administrative ability gained through experience"--consists of six parts:

I. Environmental Relationships in Business--125 minutes.
II. Business and Public Policy--60 minutes.
III. Economics and Management--105 minutes.
IV. Financial Analysis and Mathematics for Business-- 150 minutes.
V. Communication and Decision Making--120 minutes.
VI. Office Procedures--75 minutes.

"A study outline and a bibliography of books and periodicals dealing with each of the parts of the examination are available without cost from the Institute for Certifying Secretaries."

Code of Ethics: The conduct guide of NSA is its Code of Ethics, adopted at the 1968 International Convention. This code is several paragraphs of brief statements, giving resolutions to establish, practice, and promote professional standards, and to follow ethical secretarial conduct, including loyalty and conscientiousness in business associations. No provisions for enforcement of the code are reported.

Other Guides to Professional Conduct: A Secretary's Credo, adopted by the National Secretaries Association on July 18, 1970, gives eight principles accepted by the professional secretary concerning the work of the secretary and management, and other business relationships.

Professional Insignia: The emblem of the National Secretaries

Association is the group's official seal--a quartered shield, bearing in the upper left and lower right quadrants, respectively, the letters "B" and "L," which stand for "Better Learning, Better Letters, Better Living." The other two quadrants with a horizontally striped ground show (the upper right) a globe with the map of the American Continent--signifying extent of the Association; and (the lower left) the lamp of learning; a scroll below the shield bears the initials of the group, "NSA." The colors of the emblem are black and white (letterhead). The NSA membership pin is a replica of the association emblem.

Other Identification of Professional Status: As described above under "Membership," candidates successful in the examination for

Certified Professional Secretary are authorized to use the designation, CPS ("Certified Professional Secretary"), with their names. This designation, "the recognized standard of proficiency in the secretarial profession," may also be worn as jewelry--a key (bordered rectangle with concave corners) bearing the letters "CPS."

Bibliography:
> Institute for Certifying Secretaries. Certified Professional Secretary Examination Bibliography. 6 pages. October 1970.
> List of books and periodical articles recommended for study for each of the six parts of the examination qualifying for CPS.
> _____. Study Outline for the Certified Professional Secretary Examination. 14 pages. October 1970.

Detailed outline of the subjects covered in each of the six parts of the examination for Certification as Professional Secretary.

National Secretaries Association. Announcement of the CPS Examination. 1970. Folder.
Purposes, qualifications required, costs, and content of the CPS examination.

_____. Code of Ethics, and A Secretary's Credo, from NSA International Bylaws, Standing Rules, and Procedures. 1971.
Conduct code and pledge.

_____. Development of the Certified Professional Secretary Program. 1966. 4 pages. (From Institute Manual).
History and development of the certified professional secretary examination and the CPS designation.

_____. NSA, The Professional Way. 1971. Folder.
Information about NSA membership, certification designation; pictures and describes emblem.

"Code of Ethics"

Recognizing the secretary's position of trust, we resolve in all of our activities to be guided by the highest ideals for which THE NATIONAL SECRETARIES ASSOCIATION stands; to establish, practice, and promote professional standards; and to be ethical and understanding in all of our business associations.

We resolve to promote the interest of the business in which we are employed; to exemplify loyalty and conscientiousness at all times; and to maintain dignity and poise under all circumstances.

We further resolve to share knowledge; to encourage ambition and inspire hope; and to sustain faith, knowing that the eternal laws of God are the ultimate laws under which we may truly succeed.

"A Secretary's Credo"

I believe that the philosophy of the secretarial profession embodies a foundation of logic and learning, ethics and integrity, courtesy and understanding, and a desire to be of benefit to others;
the principal obligation of a secretary is to function as a support to management and to increase the effectiveness of the executive;
a secretary occupies a position of confidence, trust, and responsibility and accepts this position as a privilege to guard carefully;
secretarial excellence requires comprehensive educational preparation;
a secretary strives for self-improvement through a program of continuing education;
the maintenance of high standards is essential to the continuing advancement of the secretarial profession;
the qualifications of a secretary are enhanced by a business-like demeanor and by friendliness, cooperation, good humor, and enthusiasm;
a secretary should assume responsibility for guiding qualified young people toward secretarial careers;
a secretarial career is both challenging and rewarding;

So believing, I therefore dedicate myself to preserve and to practice these principles and to uphold them at all times with dignity and honor.

SECURITIES DEALERS

NEW YORK STOCK EXCHANGE, INC. (NYSE)
    11 Wall St., New York, N.Y. 10005
    James J. Needham, Chairman of the Board of Directors

Membership: The New York Stock Exchange was founded in 1792. It has, at present, a fixed membership of 1366. The Exchange is a not-for-profit corporation--"an incorporated association of brokers whose principal purpose is to conduct the nation's largest marketplace for securities." Memberships, or "seats" as they are called, are bought and sold on a bid and asked basis. The Exchange is the world's foremost marketplace for the trading of listed securities. Only members are allowed to trade on the Exchange.

Several types of members are found on the trading floor.

These are:

Specialists--Dealers who specialize in "making a market" for
one or more stocks listed on the Exchange. The Specialist
is expected, insofar as reasonably practical, to maintain
continuously fair and orderly markets in the stocks assigned
to him. He also acts as a broker and executes certain
orders that may be left with him by other Exchange members.

Commission Brokers--Members affiliated with member organizations doing a securities business with the public.
They execute the orders to buy and sell which their organizations send to them on the floor. They transact
business among themselves or with the Specialists.

Independent Brokers (or $2 Brokers)--Members who execute
orders for other members who may be absent from the
floor or who may be extremely busy. They also execute
orders for member organizations who prefer to utilize the
services of their own Exchange members in other phases
of the securities business.

Odd-Lot Dealer or Broker--Executes orders of "odd-lots" of
stock. An odd-lot is generally less than 100 shares, as
opposed to a round-lot which is 100 shares or any multiple
of 100. Currently, there is only one odd-lot firm on the
Exchange.

Registered Trader--A member who trades for his own account.

Other categories of membership on the Exchange include:

Allied Members--Partners of member firms or principal
officers of member corporations. Allied members cannot
transact business on the Exchange trading floor.

Member Firms or Corporations--Firms or corporations trans-
acting business as a broker or dealer in securities, having
at least one general partner or officer who is a member of
the Exchange. The firm or corporation must be approved
by the Exchange Board of Directors.

Registered Representatives--Member organization employees
who do business with the public.

Listed Companies--Companies whose shares are traded on
the Exchange. Must meet specific listing standards established by the Exchange.

Supervisory Analysts--Employees of member firms or corporations. Plans, assigns and reviews stock and investment analyses produced by an organization.

Individuals who make up the Exchange are subject to strict rules,
regulations and laws established by the Exchange and by appropriate
federal and state government agencies. Exchange Members are required to meet minimum eligibility standards (such as age), and to
pass examinations and demonstrate the ability to function on the
trading floor. Specialists and other members and member organizations must meet specific capital requirements. Prospective Registered Representatives must meet the requirements of the Exchange.

To qualify as a Registered Representative, a training candidate without previous actual experience is required to have:

Six months' experience for Full Registration.

Three months' experience for Limited Registration.

For Full Registration via Limited Registration, must have eight months' experience.

The Exchange examination for Registered Representatives is designed to test the securities knowledge of the applicant, and consists of 175 questions covering a wide variety of securities and financial topics. A candidate must pass the examination before he is approved as Registered Representative, and those failing may retake the examination. To prepare candidates for examination, training programs are offered in New York City, Chicago, San Francisco, and Los Angeles. These programs are offered by private concerns, local universities and correspondence schools--not by the Exchange.

Code of Ethics: Exchange Members, Allied Members, Analysts, and Registered Representatives are subject to a comprehensive code of regulations in the Exchange's Constitution and Rules. There is continuous check for compliance with the rules and regulations. Each Registered Representative at the time the Exchange approves his application for Registration is required to sign a statement to comply with the Exchange Constitution and Rules.

Professional Insignia: The identification insignia of the Exchange is a new logotype, adopted in 1972. Since its founding in 1792, the Exchange has had a number of formal and informal emblems. Following World War II, its insignia was a circular design showing a sketch of the Exchange facade, superimposed over a map of the United States.

THE New York Stock
Exchange

The current logotype, which replaces this design, is made up from the words, "The New York Stock Exchange," with "The" and "Exchange" predominating. The new design was developed by the firm of Lippincott & Margulies, Inc., and "is based on a style of type called Helvetica, a sans-serif letter form." The symbol is used "in all forms of Exchange communications," including advertisements, booklets and other publications, signs, stationery, displays, and on "uniforms for Exchange staff members who work on the trading floor and guides in the visitors' gallery."

Bibliography:

New York Stock Exchange. Constitution and Rules. March 1,

1973. 5603 pages. Paperbound.
Includes definitions of work for which examinations are given
and registrations issued by the Exchange; gives Pledge of
Registered Representatives. Detailed index.
_____. Fact Book. Annual. Pamphlet.
Statistical picture of the Exchange for the current year, with
historical data.
_____. Understanding the New York Stock Exchange. June
1, 1971. 46 pages. Pamphlet.
Brief history and description of activities of the NYSE.

SOCIAL WORKERS

NATIONAL ASSOCIATION OF SOCIAL WORKERS (NASW)
  2 Park Ave., New York, N.Y. 10016
  Chauncey A. Alexander, ACSW, Executive Director

Membership: The National Association of Social Workers, founded
in 1955 and with a present (1973) membership of over 55, 000, is
the largest professional organization of social workers in the world.
This "single, unified organization in social work" was first organized
as a temporary council in 1950, when seven social work associations
--The American Association of Social Workers (which grew out of
the first formal organization of Social Workers, the National Social
Workers Exchange established in 1917) and six groups of social
workers in specialized areas of the profession (American Association
of Medical Social Workers, American Association of Psychiatric
Social Workers, American Association of Group Workers, Association for the Study of Community Organization, National Association
of School Social Workers, and Social Work Research Group)--com-
bined into one professional association.

     Members of NASW, who are organized in 173 local chapters
throughout the United States, qualify for professional membership
by holding a degree from an accredited school or program. Since
April 1970, social workers with bachelor's degrees, or with doctoral degrees in fields related to social work, may qualify for membership. In March 1972, membership was expanded to students in
undergraduate social work programs. Another membership category
is "ACSW, " the designation of regular members of the Association
who belong to the Academy of Certified Social Workers.

     The NASW administers the Academy of Certified Social Workers
(ACSW), which assesses the competence of individual social workers
for self-directed practice. Membership in the Academy is open to
NASW members with an MSW degree and two years professional
experience. Acceptance is based on the ACSW certification of

competence, which includes a written examination covering all fields
of social work practice, and a reference voucher system.

Code of Ethics: Carrying out one of the purposes of the NASW--
"to develop, promulgate, and enforce social work's Code of Ethics"
--the association membership developed the Code of Ethics as a
professional conduct guide. It was adopted October 12, 1960, and
amended April 11, 1967. This Code consists of an introductory
statement, and a pledge of standards to be followed in professional
relationships with "those served, " colleagues, employing agency,
other professions, and the community.

The Code is enforced by the NASW Committees on Inquiry, both
local and national, which handle complaints or grievances involving
unethical practice or alleged breaches of agency personnel policies,
or individual rights. There is a formal review process that involves the complainant, the NASW chapter, the national office--if
necessary--and the NASW Board of Directors. Penalties for complaints or grievances that are upheld include public and professional
sanction of an individual or agency, loss of NASW and ACSW membership, public notice in the press, and other actions. NASW publishes procedures for handling complaints and explaining the adjudication process.

Professional Insignia: The official emblem of the National Association of Social Workers is the organization monograph--the letters,
"NASW, " centered in a rectangle with a broken border band. The
color of the emblem is shown variously--blue on white (letterhead);
other colors (publications).

Other Identification of Professional Status: As described above
under "Membership, " a professional designation to denote competence in social work is issued
to indicate membership in the
Academy of Certified Social
Workers: "ACSW. "

Bibliography:
    National Association of Social
        Workers. Code of
        Ethics. 1967. Folder.
    Standards of behavior for
    social workers in profes-
    sional relationships.
        . A Profession in
        Action. 1970. Folder.
    Informational brochure
    mentions Code of Ethics
and its enforcement, and the designation of professional competence authorized by the Association, "ACSW. "

"Code of Ethics"

Social work is based on humanitarian, democratic ideals. Professional social workers are dedicated to service for the welfare of mankind; to the disciplined use of a recognized body of knowledge about human beings and their interactions; and to the marshaling of community resources to promote the well-being of all without discrimination.

Social work practice is a public trust that requires of its practitioners integrity, compassion, belief in the dignity and worth of human beings, respect for individual differences, a commitment to service, and a dedication to truth. It requires mastery of a body of knowledge and skill gained through professional education and experience. It requires also recognition of the limitations of present knowledge and skill and of the services we are now equipped to give. The end sought is the performance of a service with integrity and competence.

Each member of the profession carries responsibility to maintain and improve social work service; constantly to examine, use, and increase the knowledge upon which practice and social policy are based; and to develop further the philosophy and skills of the profession.

This Code of Ethics embodies certain standards of behavior for the social worker in his professional relationships with those he serves, with his colleagues, with his employing agency, with other professions, and with the community. In abiding by the code, the social worker views his obligations in as wide a context as the situation requires, takes all of the principles into consideration, and chooses a course of action consistent with the code's spirit and intent.

As a member of the National Association of Social Workers I commit myself to conduct my professional relationships in accord with the code and subscribe to the following statements:

I regard as my primary obligation the welfare of the individual or group served, which includes action for improving social conditions.

I will not discriminate because of race, color, religion, age, sex, or national ancestry, and in my job capacity will work to prevent and eliminate such discrimination in rendering service, in work assignments, and in employment practices.

I give precedence to my professional responsibility over my personal interests.

I hold myself responsible for the quality and extent of the service I perform.

I respect the privacy of the people I serve.

I use in a responsible manner information gained in professional relationships.

I treat with respect the findings, view, and actions of colleagues, and use appropriate channels to express judgment on these
matters.

I practice social work within the recognized knowledge and
competence of the profession.

I recognize my professional responsibility to add my ideas
and findings to the body of social work knowledge and practice.

I accept responsibility to help protect the community against
unethical practice by any individuals or organizations engaged in
social welfare activities.

I stand ready to give appropriate professional service in public emergencies.

I distinguish clearly, in public, between my statements and
actions as an individual and as a representative of an organization.

I support the principle that professional practice requires
professional education.

I accept responsibility for working toward the creation and
maintenance of conditions within agencies which enable social workers
to conduct themselves in keeping with this code.

I contribute my knowledge, skills, and support to programs
of human welfare.

SOCIOLOGISTS

AMERICAN SOCIOLOGICAL ASSOCIATION (ASA)
    1722 N St., N.W., Washington, D.C. 20036
    N. J. Demerath, Executive Officer

Membership: The American Sociological Association, founded in
1905 and with a present (1973) membership of approximately
14,000, is a professional association of sociologists. Any person
interested in sociology may join the Association. The category of
membership for professional sociologists, engaged in the scientific
study of society, is
    Member--Requires a PhD in sociology or in closely related
        fields or completion of at least three years of graduate
        study in such fields in good standing in accredited institu-
        tions; or persons lacking these qualifications providing
        they can present evidence of comparable professional com-
        petence and commitment to the field.
    Diversity of membership interest is shown in the Sections of the
ASA in special fields of sociology:
Social Psychology;   Theoretical Sociology;
Medical Sociology;   Sociology of Organizations and
Criminology;   Occupations;
Sociology of Education;   Sociology of Sex Roles;
Family;   Sociology of Language;

Methodology;   Community.
Undergraduate Education;

Code of Ethics: The guide to professional conduct of the American
Sociological Association is its Code of Ethics, developed by a committee of the Association, and adopted in 1970. The Code sets forth
14 standards to be followed in conducting sociological research, including objectivity and integrity of inquiry, research subjects' rights
and protection, confidentiality of research data, presentation of research findings, research collaboration and assistance, research
financial support sources. Section 14 of the Code of Ethics provides
for the appointment by the ASA Council of a Standing Committee on
Professional Ethics to interpret and enforce the Ethical Principles
of the Code. According to this provision--and the Rules of Procedure of the Standing Committee on Professional Ethics, effective
September 1, 1971--the Committee interprets the Code of Ethics,
recommends amendment or clarification of the Ethical Code, and
receives complaints of non-professional conduct, and recommends--
after investigation and (as appropriate) hearing--sanctions, including
reprimand, suspension, request for resignation from membership,
or termination of membership.

Professional Insignia: The
emblem of the American Sociological Association is its
logotype--a stylized monogram of the organization name,
"ASA." The color of the emblem is shown variously--em-
bossed (letterhead); black on
white (envelope); light green
on dark green (publication).

Bibliography:
        American Sociological
            Association. The
            American Sociological
            Association. Folder.
        Informational brochure,
        includes membership re-
quirements. Pictures emblem on cover.
        . Code of Ethics; Standing Committee on Professional
        Ethics Rules of Procedure. 1971. Folder.
Guides to professional conduct of sociologists in sociological
inquiry, with procedures for interpretation and enforcement
of these standards.

"Standards of Sociological Research"

"Preamble"

Sociological inquiry is often disturbing to many persons and

groups. Its results may challenge long-established beliefs and lead
to change in old taboos. In consequence such findings may create
demands for the suppression or control of this inquiry or for a dilu-
tion of the findings. Similarly, the results of sociological investigation may be of significant use to individuals in power--whether in
government, in the private sphere, or in the universities--because
such findings, suitably manipulated, may facilitate the misuse of
power. Knowledge is a form of power, and in a society increasingly
dependent on knowledge, the control of information creates the potential for political manipulation.

For these reasons, we affirm the autonomy of sociological
inquiry. The sociologist must be responsive, first and foremost,
to the truth of his investigation. Sociology must not be an instrument of any person or group who seeks to suppress or misuse knowledge. The fate of sociology as a science is dependent upon the fate
of free inquiry in an open society.

At the same time this search for social truths must itself
operate within constraints. Its limits arise when inquiry infringes
on the rights of individuals to be treated as persons, to be con-
sidered--in the renewable phrase of Kant--as ends and not as means.
Just as sociologists must not distort or manipulate truth to serve
untruthful ends, so too they must not manipulate persons to serve
their quest for truth. The study of society, being the study of human
beings, imposes the responsibility of respecting the integrity, promoting the dignity, and maintaining the autonomy of these persons.

To fulfill these responsibilities, we, the members of the
American Sociological Association, affirm the following Code of
Ethics:

"Code of Ethics"

1. Objectivity in Research
In his research the sociologist must maintain scientific objectivity.

2. Integrity in Research
The sociologist should recognize his own limitations and,
when appropriate, seek more expert assistance or decline to undertake research beyond his competence. He must not misrepresent
his own abilities, or the competence of his staff to conduct a particular research project.

3. Respect of the Research Subject's Rights to Privacy and Dignity
Every person is entitled to the right of privacy and dignity
of treatment. The sociologist must respect these rights.

4. Protection of Subjects from Personal Harm
All research should avoid causing personal harm to subjects
used in research.

5. Preservation of Confidentiality of Research Data
        Confidential information provided by a research subject must
be treated as such by the sociologist. Even though research information is not a privileged communication under the law, the
sociologist must, as far as possible, protect subjects and informants.
Any promises made to such persons must be honored. However,
provided that he respects the assurances he has given his subjects,
the sociologist has no obligation to withhold information of misconduct of individuals or organizations.
        If an informant or other subject should wish, however, he
can formally release the researcher of a promise of confidentiality.
The provisions of this section apply to all members of research
organizations (i.e., interviewers, coders, clerical staff, etc.), and
it is the responsibility of the chief investigators to see that they
are instructed in the necessity and importance of maintaining the
confidentiality of the data. The obligation of the sociologist includes
the use and storage of original data to which a subject's name is
attached. When requested, the identity of an organization or subject
must be adequately disguised in publication.

6. Presentation of Research Findings
        The sociologist must present his findings honestly and without
distortion. There should be no omission of data from a research
report which might significantly modify the interpretation of findings.

7. Misuse of Research Role
        The sociologist must not use his role as a cover to obtain
information for other than professional purposes.

8. Acknowledgment of Research Collaboration and Assistance
        The sociologist must acknowledge the professional contribu-
tions or assistance of all persons who collaborated in the research.

9. Disclosure of the Sources of Financial Support
        The sociologist must report fully all sources of financial sup-
port in his research publications and any special relations to the
sponsor that might affect the interpretation of the findings.

10. Distortion of Findings by Sponsor
        The sociologist is obliged to clarify publicly any distortion
by a sponsor or client of the findings of a research project in which
he has participated.

11. Disassociation from Unethical Research Arrangements
        The sociologist must not accept such grants, contracts, or
research assignments as appear likely to require violation of the
principles above, and must publicly terminate the work or formally
disassociate himself from the research if he discovers such a violation and is unable to achieve its correction.

12. Interpretation of Ethical Principles
        When the meaning and application of these principles are

unclear, the sociologist should seek the judgment of the relevant
agency or committee designated by the American Sociological Association. Such consultation, however, does not free the sociologist
from his individual responsibility for decisions or from his accountability to the profession.

13. Applicability of Principles

In the conduct of research the principles enunciated above
should apply to research in any area either within or outside the
United States of America.

14. Interpretation and Enforcement of Ethical Principles

The Standing Committee on Professional Ethics, appointed
by the Council of the Association, shall have primary responsibility
for the interpretation and enforcement of the Ethical Code. The
Committee shall

(a) Advise members of the Association of its interpretation
of the ethical propriety of professional conduct through formal
opinions of the Committee published from time to time in The American Sociologist, which opinions shall omit all references to the
names of individuals or institutions;

(b) Recommend amendments to or clarification of the Ethical
Code when they appear to be advisable;

(c) Receive complaints of violations of the Ethical Code by
members of the Association, endeavor to settle complaints privately,
and, if private settlement cannot be effected, investigate such complaints as the Committee shall determine to investigate, under Rules
of Procedure from time to time adopted by the Committee and approved by the Council and the membership of the Association. If
on the basis of its investigation the Committee by two-thirds majority
of all its members determines that an ethical violation has occurred,
the Committee shall communicate to the complainant and to the member charged with the violation the finding of the Committee, and it
shall impose one or more of the following sanctions:

(i) Reprimand the member;

(ii) Suspend the membership of the member for a period to
be determined by the Committee;

(iii) Request the resignation of the member; or

(iv) Terminate the membership of the member;
and

(d) Receive requests that sanctions imposed herein be modified or revoked after a period of time, and take such action, including modification or revocation of the said sanctions, as the Committee in its discretion shall determine.

The Council of the Association shall:

(a) Constitute from among its members a committee which
shall decide appeals from findings of ethical violations by the Standing Committee on Professional Ethics, on the record and without
further hearing.

(b) Receive reports from the Committee on the disposition
of complaints received by it, and approve the Committee's report to

the membership of the Association of the types of complaints that have been filed with the Committee. The report to the membership shall not disclose the name of any person or persons whose past or proposed professional conduct has been called into question.

"Rules of Procedure"

Under Rule 14 of the Ethical Code of the American Sociological Association, the Standing Committee on Professional Ethics of the American Sociological Association is instructed to establish rules governing its own procedures. The following are the rules and procedures under which the Committee operates.

1. Pursuant to Section 14(a) of the Ethical Code, the Committee will issue opinions with respect to the ethical propriety and conduct under the Ethical Code which the Committee determines to be of widespread interest.

    a.   All opinions shall be adopted at a called meeting at which a quorum of four members is present, by a majority vote of the members present and voting.

    b.   Opinions will not disclose the name of any person or persons whose past or proposed professional conduct has been called into question, and the Committee shall word its opinions to insure that the persons or institutions involved shall not be otherwise identifiable.

    c.   Opinions involving past conduct will be made on such assumed factual circumstances as are deemed relevant by the Committee. Accordingly, unless investigation has been undertaken under Rule 2 hereunder, the Committee need not conduct an investigation or look to outside sources to determine the precise factual nature of the conduct involved.

2. With respect to investigations under Article 14(c) of the Ethical Code, all complaints of violations of the Ethical Code received by members of the Council or at the Executive Office of the Association shall be immediately forwarded, without acknowledgment and without further communication, to the Chairman of the Committee.

    a.   The Committee shall recognize complaints received from both members and nonmembers of the Association. A member of the Committee may file a complaint if he is aware of a possible violation of the Ethical Code but no complaint has been filed with respect to the violation.

    b.   If the complaint does not involve a member of the Association, the Chairman of the Committee shall return the complaint to the complainant and advise him that no action on the complaint can be taken. If the complaint involves a member of the Association, the Chairman of the Committee shall acknowledge receipt of the complaint, shall send a copy of the Rules of Procedure of the Committee and advise the complainant that he will be notified of any action taken by the Committee. The Chairman may request elaboration and clarifiction when he deems it necessary. Anonymous complaints shall not be recognized, and are normally to be destroyed upon receipt.

c. After acknowledgment of the complaint and the receipt of specification of charges by the complainant, if any, the Chairman shall mail copies of the complaint and other documents received by him with respect to the complaint to all the members of the Committee. The Committee members shall, by simple majority vote at a meeting of the Committee or by mail ballot, determine whether the complaint should be investigated, or dropped, or whether further correspondence with the complainant is necessary before a decision whether or not to investigate the complaint could be undertaken or whether such private settlement efforts should be undertaken as may be deemed appropriate.

d. If the Committee decides that the complaint should be dropped, the complainant shall be so notified.

e. If the Committee decides that the complaint should be investigated, the Committee shall notify the member that a formal charge of violation of the Ethical Code is pending against him. It shall advise the complainant and the accused member that a hearing will be conducted by the Committee at a place within the county or city in which the member against whom the complaint is made resides, or, if the Committee so determines, at the place in which the alleged offense was committed. The accused member shall be served with a copy of the complaint and all other documents supplied to the Committee by the complainant, and advised that he has the right to introduce witnesses and evidence in his own behalf and to cross-examine witnesses. Prior to the hearing, all documentary evidence to be introduced by the complainant, and the names of all witnesses to be offered in support of the charges, shall be supplied to the accused member. If the accused member refuses to participate in the investigation, the Committee may continue its investigation of the complaint without his participation.

f. No fewer than four members of the Committee may conduct a hearing. Any member of the Committee may examine or cross-examine witnesses in any matter relevant to the complaint at any time, in the discretion of the presiding chairman. At the hearing, the evidence in support of the complaint shall be presented by a representative of the Standing Committee, and the member shall have full opportunity to answer the charges. The hearing may be adjourned as necessary, and the Committee may introduce rebuttal witnesses.

g. The Committee may employ a court reporter or stenographer to record, and, if necessary, to transcribe the proceedings of the hearing.

h.   The hearing of the complaint before the Committee shall
be private, and all persons shall be excluded except those necessary
for the conduct of the investigation, unless the accused member
specifically elects in writing to have a public hearing within ten
days prior to the hearing.

i.   Committee investigations need not be conducted strictly
in accordance with the procedure of a court in the trial of a criminal case.   However, functional rules of evidence followed in a court
of law will be generally employed.   The Committee shall be authorized to retain legal counsel to advise and assist in the Committee
investigation.

j.   At the conclusion of the introduction of all evidence, the
member against whom the complaint has been made, or his counsel,
or both, shall be permitted to argue matters in defense or mitigation
of the complaint.

k.   Thereafter, the full Committee shall discuss the matter
and conduct its further discussion in private, based upon the evidence
adduced at the hearing.   The quorum at a meeting to decide the case
shall consist of five members of the Committee, and any decision
to impose sanctions shall be by a two-thirds majority of all the
members of the Committee.   If the Committee concludes that no
disciplinary action is justified, it shall dismiss the complaint and
promptly advise the accused member of its action.   The Committee
may, under certain circumstances, find it necessary to defer decision for further study and investigation.   However, utmost diligence
should be used to complete the investigation on the date fixed for
the hearing.

l.   If the Committee concludes that disciplinary action is
merited, then it shall make a written report of the proceedings
and advise the complainant and the accused member of the sanction
imposed, and advise the member that he has a right to appeal within thirty days the finding of the Committee on the existing record
and without further hearing to such members of the Council as have
been designated by the President of the Association to hear such
appeals.   The member shall be advised that notification of appeal
should be filed with the Executive Officer of the Association.

m.   The Committee shall report to the Council all action
taken by the Committee, including findings of ethical violations and
sanctions imposed with respect to all complaints received by it, provided that the Committee shall not advise the Council of any finding
of ethical violation until the period for appeal to the Council has expired, or, if an appeal has been filed, until a decision on the appeal
has been rendered.   The Committee shall report to the membership
of the Association the types of complaints that have been filed with
the Committee, which report shall be approved by the Council.   The
report to the membership shall not disclose the name of any person
or persons whose past or proposed professional conduct has been
called into question.

3.   The effective date of these Rules of Procedure is September 1, 1971.

SPEECH PATHOLOGISTS AND AUDIOLOGISTS

AMERICAN SPEECH AND HEARING ASSOCIATION (ASHA)
    9030 Old Georgetown Rd., Washington, D. C. 20014
    Kenneth Johnson, Executive Director

<u>Membership</u>:   The American Speech and Hearing Association, founded in 1925 and with a present (1973) membership of more than 14, 000, is a professional association "for speech and language pathologists, audiologists, and speech and hearing scientists concerned with communication behavior and disorders." The organization was established as the American Academy of Speech Correction, later was known as the American Society for the Study of Disorders of Speech, and took its present name in 1947.   Professional members of the Association are required to
        "hold a graduate degree or the equivalent in speech pathology, audiology, or speech and hearing science; or hold a graduate degree in an allied discipline and have demonstrated an active interest in disorders of communication or speech and hearing science. "

In 1951 the ASHA initiated certification procedure and since 1965 the Association has issued a Certificate of Clinical Competence to members who qualify by having completed specified academic work during the five years of college study required for ASHA membership; have supervised clinical experience in communication disorders (275 clock hours) and a Clinical Fellowship Year (CFY) of "nine months' full-time professional employment pertinent to the certificate being sought"--in Audiology or in Speech Pathology; passed a comprehensive two-hour written examination testing knowledge of "normal development and use of speech, hearing, and language, " and of "disorders of human communication" related to the work of the Speech Pathologist or Audiologist.

The examination is developed and administered by the Educational Testing Service, in Princeton, New Jersey, as part of the National Teacher Examinations.   This National Examination in Speech Pathology (and in Audiology) "is designed to measure the candidate's academic preparation in and knowledge of the field." Certificates are issued to qualified candidates passing the examination by the ASHA agency, the American Boards of Examiners in Speech Pathology and Audiology (ABESPA), which was established in 1959.   Holders of the ASHA's Certificate of Clinical Competence use the following titles with their names:

"Certificate of Clinical Competence in Speech Pathology";
"Certificate of Clinical Competence in Audiology. "
Names of the Holders of the Certificates--some 10, 500--are listed
each year in the annual ASHA Directory.

Code of Ethics: The present guide to professional conduct issued
by the ASHA is its Code of Ethics, developed by a Committee on
Ethical Practices (currently known as the Ethical Practices Board),
adopted in 1951, and most recently revised on January 1, 1971.
The Code gives standards of professional integrity and practice, including relations with clients, colleagues, and the public. It is
interpreted and enforced by the Ethical Practices Board, which receives complaints of unprofessional conduct, and may discipline
members--after investigation and hearing--by revocation of membership.

Professional Insignia: There are two official logotypes of the ASHA.
One is the Association monogram--the four letters, "ASHA. " The
other logotype shows the monogram in an elipse, with the organization name, "American Speech and Hearing Association, " printed
around the design within a bordering band; the group's date of founding, "1925, " at the bottom of the emblem within the bordering band.

These logotypes are shown in various colors on Association publications.

Other Identification of Professional Status: As described above
under "Membership, " professional designations are used by holders
of the ASHA Certificate of Clinical Competence.

Bibliography:
    American Speech and Hearing Association. Code of Ethics.
        1971. 2 pages. (Reprint from ASHA Directory).
        Standards of professional practice in Speech Pathology and
        Audiology, most recently revised January 1, 1971.
                . Information About ASHA. 1971. Folder.
        Descriptive brochure includes membership requirements and
        certifications issued.
                . Requirements for the Certificate of Clinical Compe-
            tence. 4 pages. (Reprint from ASHA Directory).
        Requirements of academic training, supervised experience,

and written examination.
Educational Testing Service. National Teacher Examinations:
   The Examination in Audiology;... ; The Examination in
   Speech Pathology. 1970. 2 pamphlets. 6 pages each.
Booklets giving rationale, content and scope of examinations,
and samples of multiple choice questions used in examination.
National Teacher Examinations, Educational Testing Service,
Box 911, Princeton, New Jersey 08540.

"Code of Ethics"

Preamble

The preservation of the highest standards of integrity and
ethical principles is vital to the successful discharge of the responsibilities of all Members. This Code of Ethics has been promulgated by the Association in an effort to highlight the fundamental
rules considered essential to this basic purpose. The failure to
specify any particular responsibility or practice in this Code of
Ethics should not be construed as denial of the existence of other
responsibilities or practices that are equally important. Any act
that is in violation of the spirit and purpose of this Code of Ethics
shall be unethical practice. It is the responsibility of each Member
to advise the Committee on Ethical Practice of instances of violation of the principles incorporated in this Code.

Section A

The ethical responsibilities of the Member require that the
welfare of the person he serves professionally be considered paramount.

1.   The Member who engaged in clinical work must possess
appropriate qualifications. Measures of such qualifications are provided by the Association's program for certification of the clinical
competence of Members.
   (a)   The Member must not provide services for which he
has not been properly trained, i.e., had the necessary course work
and supervised practicum.
   (b)   The Member who has not completed his professional
preparation must not provide speech or hearing services except in
a supervised clinical practicum situation as a part of his training.
A person holding a full-time clinical position and taking part-time
graduate work is not, for the purpose of this section, regarded as
a student in training.
   (c)   The Member must not accept remuneration for providing
services until he has completed the necessary course work and
clinical practicum to meet certification requirements. The Member
who is uncertified must not engage in private practice.

2.   The Member must follow acceptable patterns of

professional conduct in his relations with the persons he serves.

(a)   He must not guarantee the results of any speech or hearing consultative or therapeutic procedure. A guarantee of any sort, expressed or implied, oral or written, is contrary to professional ethics. A reasonable statement of prognosis may be made, but successful results are dependent on many uncontrollable factors, hence, any warranty is deceptive and unethical.

(b)   He must not diagnose or treat individual speech or hearing disorders by correspondence. This does not preclude follow-up by correspondence of individuals previously seen, nor does it preclude providing the persons served professionally with general information of an educational nature.

(c)   He must not reveal to unauthorized persons any confidential information obtained from the individual he serves professionally without his permission.

(d)   He must not exploit persons he serves professionally: (1) by accepting them for treatment where benefit cannot reasonably be expected to accrue; (2) by continuing treatment unnecessarily; (3) by charging exorbitant fees.

3.   The Member must use every resource available, including referral to other specialists as needed, to effect as great improvement as possible in the persons he serves.

4.   The Member must take every precaution to avoid injury to the persons he serves professionally.

Section B

The duties owed by the Member to other professional workers are many.

1.   He should seek the freest professional discussion of all theoretical and practical issues but avoid personal invective directed toward professional colleagues or members of allied professions.

2.   He should establish harmonious relations with members of other professions. He should endeavor to inform others concerning the services that can be rendered by members of the speech and hearing profession and in turn should seek information from members of related professions. He should strive to increase knowledge within the field of speech and hearing.

3.   He must not accept fees, gifts, or other forms of gratuity for serving as a sponsor of applicants for clinical certification by the American Speech and Hearing Association.

Section C

The ASHA Member has other special responsibilities.

1.   He must guard against conflicts of professional interest.

(a)   He must not accept compensation in any form from a manufacturer or a dealer in prosthetic or other devices for recommending any particular product.

(b)   The Member in private practice must not advertise.   It is permissible only to employ a business card or similar announcement, and to list one's name, highest academic degree, type of services, and location in the classified section of the telephone directory in the manner customarily followed by physicians and attorneys.   He may state that he holds the Certificate of Clinical Competence in the appropriate area (speech or hearing) issued by the American Speech and Hearing Association.

(c)   He must not engage in commercial activities that conflict with his responsibilities to the persons he serves professionally or to his colleagues.   He must not permit his professional titles or accomplishments to be used in the sale or promotion of any product related to his professional field.   He must not perform clinical services or promotional activity for any profit-making organization that is engaged in the retail sales of equipment, publications, or other materials.   He may be employed by a manufacturer or publisher, provided that his duties are consultative, scientific, or educational in nature.

2.   He should help in the education of the public regarding speech and hearing problems and other matters lying within his professional competence.

3.   He should seek to provide and expand services to persons with speech and hearing handicaps, and to assist in establishing high professional standards for such programs.

4.   He must not discriminate on the basis of race, religion, or sex in his professional relationships with his colleagues or clients.

STATISTICIANS

AMERICAN STATISTICAL ASSOCIATION (ASA)
806 15th St., N.W., Washington, D.C. 20005
John W. Lehman, Executive Director

Membership: The American Statistical Association, founded in 1839 and with a present (1973) membership of approximately 10,000, is a professional association of statisticians.   Its members are grouped in 52 local chapters throughout the United States and Canada, most in larger cities and college communities.   Any person with an interest in applied or theoretical statistics may join ASA.

Code of Ethics: The American Statistical Association reports that
it has no formal code of ethics.

Professional Insignia: The official emblem of the Association is
the organization seal--an oval design, with a centered eagle on a

column, standing with out-
spread wings, looking back to
left over right shoulder; two
serpents extend--one on each
side of the eagle--from bottom
of design to the eagle's wings;
on the outside of a beaded
bordering band the legend
"American Statistical Association, Founded 1839," appears.
This insignia came into use
early in this century, probably before 1909. The color
of the emblem is shown vari-
ously--black on white (letterhead); rust on tan (publication).

Bibliography:
American Statistical Asso-
ciation. American
Statistical Association:
What It Is; What It
Does; What It Offers; How to Join. Pamphlet.
Informational brochure; pictures emblem on cover.

SURGEONS--NEUROLOGICAL

THE AMERICAN ASSOCIATION OF NEUROLOGICAL SURGEONS
(AANS)
c/o Michael O'Connor, Exec. Sec.
428 E. Preston St., Baltimore, Md. 21202

Membership: The American Association of Neurological Surgeons,
founded in 1931 as The Harvey Cushing Society and with a present
(1973) membership of over 1300, is a professional association of
medical doctors specializing in neurological surgery. The organization, originally named after Harvey Cushing (1869-1939), American
pioneer in neurological survey who was the first general surgeon to
apply himself exclusively to surgery of the nervous system, changed
its name to the present designation five years ago, to reflect the
national, and international, character of its membership and interest.
Members are required to have specialized education, training, and

experience, in addition to graduation from an approved medical
school and licensure as physician in state of practice.   An examination is required for certification by the American Board of Neurological Surgery.

Code of Ethics: As a group of physicians specializing in neurological surgery,   the American Association of Neurological Surgeons
subscribes to the American Medical Association Principles of Medical Ethics.

Professional Insignia: The official emblem of the American Associa-

tion of Neurological Surgeons
is its insignia--a circular design, with a centered, right-
facing profile of Harvey Cushing, with the legend of the
original name of the society
and date of founding on two
lines below the portrait,
"Harvey Cushing Society 1931";
the present name of the group,
"American Association of
Neurological Surgeons," is
shown in a bordering band
around the design.   The
color of this emblem, as it
appears on the letterhead, is
black on white.

"Code of Ethics"

see page 564

SURVEYORS

AMERICAN CONGRESS ON SURVEYING AND MAPPING (ACSM)
    430 Woodward Bldg. ,   733 15th St. ,   N. W. ,   Washington,   D. C.
    20005
Robert E. Herndon,   Executive Director

Membership: The American Congress on Surveying and Mapping,
founded in 1941 and with a present (1973) membership of approximately 6000, is a professional society in the field of surveying and
mapping.   Members, grouped in over 25 local sections and some
30 affiliated state surveyor associations throughout the United States,
qualify for professional membership (that is, Corporate Member) in
the Congress by meeting the following education and experience requirements:

Cartography--Qualifications for professional position in mapping or charting through
   (1)   Graduation from an accredited college, with a bachelor's or higher degree in an area of study related to cartography; or
   (2)   Eight years' experience in mapping or charting, including at least four years in "recognized professional activities." Up to four years of higher education may be substituted year for year for the required experience.

Control Surveys--Qualification "in the mathematical, physical, or applied sciences or engineering arts, with specialist interests in control surveys, geodetic or precise plan surveys, geodesy, geophysics, optical or radio astronomy, earth environmental or space physics, specialized precision measurements and related adjustments and computations, or the development of optical electromagnetic, mechanical, photogrammetric or other appropriate means of metrology," acquired through
   (1)   Graduation from an accredited college with a bachelor's or higher degree related to one of the above fields; or
   (2)   Licensure as Professional Engineer, Land Surveyor, Photogrammetric Engineer, or Planner, "competent and experienced" in one of the above fields; or
   (3)   Eight years' experience in one of the above fields. Up to four years of higher education may be substituted year for year for the required experience.

Land Surveys--Qualification through
   (1)   Licensure as Land Surveyor or Engineer; or
   (2)   Eight years' experience as "practicing Land Surveyor" (defined as, in "responsible charge"). Up to four years of higher education may be substituted year for year for the required experience.
An honorary membership as "Fellow" may be awarded Corporate Members, who have belonged to ACSM for eight or more years, and are otherwise qualified for this honor.

Code of Ethics: The guide to professional conduct of the ACSM is its Code of Ethics for Professional Practitioners, adopted by the Property Surveys Division of the American Congress on Surveying and Mapping in January 1959, and endorsed by the ACSM Board of Directors. This Code includes enumeration of eight types of activity considered unprofessional in performance of duty and in relations with clients, employers, and colleagues; and pledge to perform work on conformance with the two standards issued by the Congress: Technical Standards for Property Surveys, June 28, 1946; Equitable Fees for Property Surveys, 1949.
No procedures for enforcement of the Code are reported.

Other Guides to Professional Conduct: The ACSM has also issued a Statement of Principles, which in seven paragraphs sets forth professional responsibilities and ideals of service, methods, and standards in surveying.

Professional Insignia: The official ACSM emblem is the organization seal--a circular design with a centered circle, showing the points of a compass, bearing map of the American continent; four bordering bands and lines bound this central area; the association name and founding date, "American Congress on Surveying and Mapping 1941, " appears in the third border. The color of this emblem is blue on white or blue on gray--with the first band bordering the central design, stippled (dotted). The emblem may be displayed by members to indicate affiliation with ACSM. In this instance, the word "Member" is printed on top of the design, and the colors of the emblem are gold on blue, with the first band bordering the central circle in white.

Bibliography:
> American Congress on Surveying and Mapping. Code of Ethics for Professional Practitioners. 1959. 1 page.
> Guide to professional conduct and work standards.
> _____. Equitable Fees for Property Surveys. 1949. 1 page.
> Statement of Principles adopted by ACSM.
> _____. Statement of Principles. 1 page.
> Goals and ideals of survey work.
> _____. Technical Standards for Property Surveys. 1946. 4 pages. Pamphlet. (Reprint from Surveying and Mapping, v. 6, July-September 1946).
> Standards for Land Titles and Location, Maps, Coordinate Surveys and Base Triangulation Systems, Measurements, Monuments, Planning and Design.

"Code of Ethics for Professional Practitioners"

A. It shall be considered unprofessional and inconsistent with honorable and dignified bearing for any professional practitioner:
1. To act for his client, or employer, in professional matters otherwise than as a faithful agent or trustee, or to accept any remuneration other than his stated recompense for services rendered.
2. To attempt to injure falsely or maliciously, directly or indirectly, the professional reputation, prospects, or business of anyone.

3.   To attempt to supplant another fellow professional practitioner after definite steps have been taken toward his employment.

4.   To compete with another fellow practitioner for employment by the use of unethical practices.

5.   To review the work of another fellow practitioner for
the same client, except with the knowledge of such practitioner or
unless the connection of such practitioner with the work has terminated.

6.   To attempt to obtain or render technical services or
assistance without fair and just compensation commensurate with
the services rendered.

7.   To advertise in self-laudatory language or any other
manner derogatory to the dignity of the profession.

8.   To attempt to practice in any professional field in which
the registrant is not proficient.

B.   All land survey work shall be done in conformity with
the "Technical Standards for Property Surveys" as compiled by the
American Congress on Surveying and Mapping and adopted by the
ACSM on June 28, 1946 (and as it may be further properly amended
by ACSM).

C.   The "Statement of Principles" as outlined in the document entitled "Equitable Fees for Property Surveys" as compiled
and adopted by the American Congress on Surveying and Mapping in
1949 (and as it may be further properly amended by ACSM), shall
be considered as a statement for proper ethical practice herein.

"Statement of Principles"

A.   Property surveying is a profession of ancient origin.   It
has not only survived the centuries, but its requirements have continually increased both in scope and in the application of technical
knowledge.

B.   As an occupation, it demands an adherence to the rules
of good business conduct.   As a profession, it owes responsibility
to itself and to the public which it serves.

C.   These responsibilities demand adherence to those Codes
of Ethics and Standards established and recognized by the profession.
They also demand a character and scope of work which includes,
not only those services properly requested by the client, but also
those that a broad professional experience would indicate as a necessary and logical part of the work to be performed.

D.   The best service to the client and to the public can be
assured only when the surveyor receives an adequate fee for his
work.   That fee should cover all expenses and salaries applicable
to the job, plus those expenses that are created by the necessities
of continued and sustained practice, plus a fair compensation to the

surveyor for his time, knowledge, advice and responsibility. Such compensation should be commensurate with that of other professional men of similar training and responsibility, operating under similar conditions.

E. Again the best service to the client and to the public can be assured only when competent employees are engaged in the various classifications of the work. Adequate compensation to such employees is a prerequisite for their continued interest and performance. This compensation should be commensurate with that of other men of similar training, experience and responsibility.

F. The methods used and the standards of accuracy required for property surveys are, in a great measure, determined by local conditions. Variations in methods and standards occur because of such factors as the diversity of laws controlling the interpretation of deeds and documents, history of the community, customs, and topography. Except for the more simple property surveys, conditions are usually such that it is not possible to predict all of the elements that will affect the time and cost of a survey.

G. Fixed fees, however just and equitable, may subject a profession to accusations of price fixing or unethical conduct. The standard by which to determine an equitable fee should be based on the following minimum requirement: The minimum fee for a property survey is that which is necessary for the proper performance of the particular service on a recognized professional level.

TEACHERS

NATIONAL EDUCATION ASSOCIATION OF THE UNITED STATES (NEA)
    1201 16th St., N.W., Washington, D.C. 20036
    Sam M. Lambert, Executive Secretary

Membership: The National Education Association, founded in 1857 and with a present (1973) membership of over 1,000,000, is the prof.ssional association of educators. Its members, grouped in state societies throughout the United States, and in some 60 affiliated associations and councils, are engaged in all aspects of public education--classroom teachers, principals and other school administrators, deans and counselors, school nurses, school librarians, and school secretaries. Groups of subject specialists-- in such areas as mathematics; science; industrial arts; health, physical education and recreation; home economics; music; journalism--are affiliated with the NEA as Departments of the Association, as are groups of educators at all school levels, from Elementary-

Kindergarten-Nursery School through Secondary School, to Higher
Education and Community and Junior Colleges. Members of component groups are required to meet legal requirements of education
and experience in the state where they work, evidenced--in many
instances--by state licensure.

Code of Ethics: The guide to conduct for professional educators in
the NEA is the Association's Code of Ethics of the Education Profession, adopted in its current form July 1968, and most recently
amended July 1970. The present Code has grown through the years,
since NEA adopted its first official statement of ethics in 1929, to
expand its application to "educators," rather than limit its conduct
guide to "teachers," and is directed to standards of behavior, as
distinct from standards of competence "relating to knowledges,
skills, and attitudes."

The Code includes ideals of conduct in a "Preamble," and under
four principles, which give the general Commitment of the Professional Educator to the Student, the Public, the Profession, and Professional Employment Practices, and set forth standards of acceptable professional behavior. Adherence to the Code is required of
all NEA members (Bylaws, Article I, Section 13). A permanent
Committee on Professional Ethics interprets the conduct guide, upon
written request, and periodically reviews and recommends revisions
of the Code. Current ethics opinions are published in the NEA
Journal, and are assembled from time to time in published form
(Opinions of the Committee on Professional Ethics).

Enforcement of the Code is carried out in the State and local
associations affiliated with NEA. According to prescribed procedures (Enforcement of the Code of Ethics of the Education Profession, 1969), the NEA National Committee on Professional Ethics
conducts hearings on cases in its original jurisdiction--as when the
NEA or a local affiliated organization is a party to an ethical com-
plaint--and considers appeals referred to it by local associations.
Discipline of members, where complaints of unethical conduct are
substantiated, may include censure, suspension, or expulsion of a
member, subject to review by the NEA Executive Committee.

Professional Insignia: The
official emblem of the NEA is
a triangular insignia, with
curved sides; a centered Greek
letter "pi," written in script,
transfixed by an arrowhead.
This central symbol was in
use in 1962 (Fraser, Dorothy
M. Current Curriculum
Studies in Academic Subjects,
Washington, D.C., NEA, 1962,
reverse of title page) as the
symbol of the Project on Instruction, and was defined at

that time as a symbol which combined "a legacy of the past (π for $\pi\alpha\iota\delta\epsilon\iota\alpha$, the ancient Greek word for education) with direction for the future (➤──)." The color of the emblem is shown variously on publications--dark blue triangle, light gray "pi," with darker grey arrowhead; dark blue triangle, with white "pi," and red arrowhead.

Bibliography:
    National Education Association. Committee on Professional
        Ethics. Code of Ethics of the Education Profession. Re-
        vised edition, 1970. 4 pages. Pamphlet.
    Guide for professional educators' behavior, with general Pre-
    amble, Principles, and standards of conduct under each of
    four Principles.
    _____. Enforcement of the Code of Ethics of the Education
        Profession. 1969. 19 pages.
    Procedures for national enforcement of the Code of Ethics,
    with pertinent sections of the NEA Bylaws.
    _____. Opinions. Revised edition, 1969. 113 pages. $1.
    Includes history and development of the Code, text of the an-
    notated Code, and 53 Opinions. Index.

"Code of Ethics"

Preamble

      The educator believes in the worth and dignity of man. He recognizes the supreme importance of the pursuit of truth, devotion to excellence, and the nurture of democratic citizenship. He regards as essential to these goals the protection of freedom to learn and to teach and the guarantee of equal educational opportunity for all. The educator accepts his responsibility to practice his profession according to the highest ethical standards.

      The educator recognizes the magnitude of the responsibility he has accepted in choosing a career in education, and engages himself, individually and collectively with other educators, to judge his colleagues, and to be judged by them, in accordance with the provisions of this code.

Principle I--Commitment to the Student

      The educator measures his success by the progress of each student toward realization of his potential as a worthy and effective citizen. The educator therefore works to stimulate the spirit of inquiry, the acquisition of knowledge and understanding, and the thoughtful formulation of worthy goals.

      In fulfilling his obligation to the student, the educator--
      1. Shall not without just cause restrain the student from independent action in his pursuit of learning, and shall not without just

cause deny the student access to varying points of view.

2.   Shall not deliberately suppress or distort subject matter for which he bears responsibility.

3.   Shall make reasonable effort to protect the student from conditions harmful to learning or to health and safety.

4.   Shall conduct professional business in such a way that he does not expose the student to unnecessary embarrassment or disparagement.

5.   Shall not on the ground of race, color, creed, or national origin exclude any student from participation in or deny him benefits under any program, nor grant any discriminatory consideration or advantage.

6.   Shall not use professional relationships with students for private advantage.

7.   Shall keep in confidence information that has been obtained in the course of professional service, unless disclosure serves professional purposes or is required by law.

8.   Shall not tutor for remuneration students assigned to his classes, unless no other qualified teacher is reasonably available.

Principle II--Commitment to the Public

The educator believes that patriotism in its highest form requires dedication to the principles of our democratic heritage. He shares with all other citizens the responsibility for the development of sound public policy and assumes full political and citizenship responsibilities.   The educator bears particular responsibility for the development of policy relating to the extension of educational opportunities for all and for interpreting educational programs and policies to the public.

In fulfilling his obligation to the public, the educator--

1.   Shall not misrepresent an institution or organization with which he is affiliated, and shall take adequate precautions to distinguish between his personal and institutional or organizational views.

2.   Shall not knowingly distort or misrepresent the facts concerning educational matters in direct and indirect public expressions.

3.   Shall not interfere with a colleague's exercise of political and citizenship rights and responsibilities.

4.   Shall not use institutional privileges for private gain or to promote political candidates or partisan political activities.

5.   Shall accept no gratuities, gifts, or favors that might impair or appear to impair professional judgment, nor offer any favor, service, or thing of value to obtain special advantage.

Principle III--Commitment to the Profession

The educator believes that the quality of the services of the education profession directly influences the nation and its citizens. He therefore exerts every effort to raise professional standards, to improve his service, to promote a climate in which the exercise of professional judgment is encouraged, and to achieve conditions which

attract persons worthy of the trust to careers in education. Aware
of the value of united effort, he contributes actively to the support,
planning, and programs of professional organizations.

In fulfilling his obligation to the profession, the educator--
1.   Shall not discriminate on the ground of race, color, creed,
or national origin for membership in professional organizations, nor
interfere with the free participation of colleagues in the affairs of
their association.
2.   Shall accord just and equitable treatment to all members
of the profession in the exercise of their professional rights and
responsibilities.
3.   Shall not use coercive means or promise special treatment in order to influence professional decisions of colleagues.
4.   Shall withhold and safeguard information acquired about
colleagues in the course of employment, unless disclosure serves
professional purposes.
5.   Shall not refuse to participate in a professional inquiry
when requested by an appropriate professional association.
6.   Shall provide upon the request of the aggrieved party a
written statement of specific reason for recommendations that lead
to the denial of increments, significant changes in employment, or
termination of employment.
7.   Shall not misrepresent his professional qualifications.
8.   Shall not knowingly distort evaluations of colleagues.

Principle IV--Commitment to Professional Employment Practices

The educator regards the employment agreement as a pledge
to be executed both in spirit and in fact in a manner consistent with
the highest ideals of professional service. He believes that sound
professional personnel relationships with governing boards are built
upon personal integrity, dignity, and mutual respect.   The educator
discourages the practice of his profession by unqualified persons.

In fulfilling his obligation to professional employment practices, the educator--
1.   Shall apply for, accept, offer, or assign a position or
responsibility on the basis of professional preparation and legal
qualifications.
2.   Shall apply for a specific position only when it is known
to be vacant, and shall refrain from underbidding or commenting adversely about other candidates.
3.   Shall not knowingly withhold information regarding a position from an applicant or misrepresent an assignment or conditions
of employment.
4.   Shall give prompt notice to the employing agency of any
change in availability of service, and the employing agent shall
give prompt notice of change in availability or nature of a position.
5.   Shall adhere to the terms of a contract or appointment,
unless these terms have been legally terminated, falsely represented,
or substantially altered by unilateral action of the employing agency.

6.   Shall conduct professional business through channels, when available, that have been jointly approved by the professional organization and the employing agency.

7.   Shall not delegate assigned tasks to unqualified personnel.

8.   Shall permit no commercial exploitation of his professional position.

9.   Shall use time granted for the purpose for which it is intended.

["Bylaws, National Education Association":]

Article I, Section 13.   Adherence to the Code of Ethics adopted by the Association shall be a condition of membership.   The Committee on Professional Ethics shall after due notice and hearing have power to censure, suspend, or expel any member for violation of the Code subject to review by the Executive Committee.   A member may within sixty days after a decision by the Ethics Committee file an appeal of the decision with the Executive Secretary.

["Provisions for National Enforcement":]

Code Development--It shall be the duty of the Committee to maintain a continuous review of the Code of Ethics of the Education Profession.   Amendments or revision of the Code shall be presented for approval to the Representative Assembly.

Interpretations of the Code of Ethics of the Education Profession--A request for interpretation of the Code shall be in writing and shall describe the matter to be interpreted in sufficient detail to enable the members of the Committee on Professional Ethics to evaluate the request in all its aspects.

Disciplinary Action--In addition to the provisions of Article I, Section 13, the Committee on Professional Ethics will consider disciplinary action against a member when written charges are preferred by the official governing body of the NEA affiliated state or local education association or NEA Department of which the person in question is a member.

If charges are based on a hearing held by any of the groups authorized to prefer charges, a record of the hearing shall be submitted to the Committee on Professional Ethics.   Disciplinary action will only be considered as resulting from a fair hearing or a proper hearing record.   A member will have an opportunity to show cause why such action should not be taken.

TEACHERS--READING

INTERNATIONAL READING ASSOCIATION (IRA)
    6 Tyre Ave., Newark, Del. 19711
    Ralph C. Staiger, Executive Secretary-Treasurer

Membership: The International Reading Association, formed through
a merger of the International Council for the Improvement of Reading Instruction and the National Association of Remedial Teaching in
1955, began to function as a professional organization on January 1,
1956. Membership in the IRA, "open to any individual concerned
with the improvement of reading," includes among professional members teachers, psychologists, librarians, and school administrators
concerned with all phases of the school reading program. Over 800
local councils in the United States and Canada, "interested in the
teaching of reading," are affiliated with the IRA.

Code of Ethics: As part of its activities in establishing standards
for professionals in the IRA, the Professional Standards and Ethics
Committee of the association prepared, in the 1950's, a conduct
guide for "members of the International Reading Association who are
concerned with the teaching of reading." In this Code of Ethics
standards are grouped under two headings--four under "Ethical
Standards in Professional Relationships," and five under "Ethical
Standards in Reading Services." Breaches of the Code of Ethics,
reported to IRA headquarters, are referred to the Committee on
Professional Standards and Ethics. Complaints that warrant investigation and hearings, if substantiated, may result in the dismissal of
a member from membership in the association.

Professional Insignia: The
emblem of the IRA is its col-
lophon--a monogram of the
name, showing the stylized
initials, "IRA." This emblem is used on the association stationery and publications,
and member groups are authorized to identify themselves
with the design.

Bibliography:
    International Reading As-
        sociation. Interna-
        tional Reading Asso-
        ciation. 1971.
        Folder.
    Informational brochure giving purpose and activities of IRA,
        membership information and insignia.
    International Reading Association. Reading Specialists. Folder.
        Standards for special teachers of reading and clinicians, con-
        sultants, and supervisors of reading in terms of (1) definition
        of their work and qualifications, and (2) standards of conduct
        to be followed as expressed in the Code of Ethics.

"Code of Ethics"

The members of the International Reading Association who are concerned with the teaching of reading form a group of professional persons, obligated to society and devoted to the service and welfare of individuals through teaching, clinical services, research, and publication. The members of this group are committed to values which are the foundation of a democratic society--freedom to teach, write, and study in an atmosphere conducive to the best interests of the profession. The welfare of the public, the profession, and the individuals concerned should be of primary consideration in recommending candidates for degrees, positions, advancements, the recognition of professional activity, and for certification in those areas where certification exists.

Ethical Standards in Professional Relationships:

1. It is the obligation of all members of the International Reading Association to observe the Code of Ethics of the organization and to act accordingly so as to advance the status and prestige of the Association and of the profession as a whole. Members should assist in establishing the highest professional standards for reading programs and services, and should enlist support for these through dissemination of pertinent information to the public.

2. It is the obligation of all members to maintain relationships with other professional persons, striving for harmony, avoiding personal controversy, encouraging cooperative effort, and making known the obligations and services rendered by the reading specialist.

3. It is the obligation of members to report results of research and other developments in reading.

4. Members should not claim nor advertise affiliation with the International Reading Association as evidence of their competence in reading.

Ethical Standards in Reading Services:

1. Reading specialists must possess suitable qualifications (see Minimum Standards for Professional Training of Reading Specialists) for engaging in consulting, clinical, or remedial work. Unqualified persons should not engage in such activities except under the direct supervision of one who is properly qualified. Professional intent and the welfare of the person seeking the services of the reading specialist should govern all consulting or clinical activities such as counseling, administering diagnostic tests, or providing remediation. It is the duty of the reading specialist to keep relationships with clients and interested persons on a professional level.

2. Information derived from consulting and/or clinical services should be regarded as confidential. Expressed consent of

persons involved should be secured before releasing information to outside agencies.

3.   Reading specialists should recognize the boundaries of their competence and should not offer services which fail to meet professional standards established by other disciplines.   They should be free, however, to give assistance in other areas in which they are qualified.

4.   Referral should be made to specialists in allied fields as needed.   When such referral is made, pertinent information should be made available to consulting specialists.

5.   Reading clinics and/or reading specialists offering professional services should refrain from guaranteeing easy solutions or favorable outcomes as a result of their work, and their advertising should be consistent with that of allied professions.   They should not accept for remediation any persons who are unlikely to benefit from their instruction, and they should work to accomplish the greatest possible improvement in the shortest time.   Fees, if charged, should be agreed on in advance and should be charged in accordance with an established set of rates commensurate with that of other professions.

TEACHERS--UNIVERSITY

AMERICAN ASSOCIATION OF UNIVERSITY PROFESSORS (AAUP)
    One Dupont Circle, Suite 500, Washington, D. C. 20036
    Bertram H. Davis, General Secretary

Membership: The American Association of University Professors, founded in January 1915 and with a present (1973) membership of approximately 100, 000, is the professional association of academic faculty--teachers in colleges and universities in the United States. Professional membership in the association is open to teachers and research scholars on the faculties of approved colleges and universities--"those on the accredited or 'candidate for accreditation' lists of the established regional or professional accrediting agencies. " An academic employee is eligible as an "Active Member, " if he is employed in an approved institution with "at least a one-year appointment to a position of at least half-time teaching and/or research, with the rank of instructor or its equivalent, " "or other acceptable evidence of faculty status. "   AAUP chapters are organized in institutions where there are at least seven members, and chapters throughout the United States now number approximately 1300.

Code of Ethics: Since its inception, the American Association of University Professors has been concerned with the promulgation and enforcement of a code of ethics (Metzger:233). The Association's ethical standard, Statement on Professional Ethics, was developed by its Committee B (on Professional Ethics) in 1965, and--after modification by the Council and the membership that same year-- was adopted in 1966. This Statement consists of five principles setting standards of conduct for professors, and giving special obligations of academic employees in their performance as academician, teacher, colleague, member of an educational institution, and member of a community.

The Committee on Professional Ethics (Committee B) applies this code to specific problems, and develops and reports on current policies and procedures. These reports are published in the official journal of the organization, the quarterly AAUP Bulletin. An example of such statements of the ethics committee is the 1968 Report from Committee B: Late Resignations and Professional Ethics, which amplifies and clarifies an ethical area of the conduct standards. The Committee acts on complaints from academic institutions of a professor's departure from these late resignation standards, and--after investigation--may address "an appropriate letter of disapprobation to individuals who have significantly departed from these standards." Generally, the enforcement of ethical standards for the academic profession is handled within the employing institution by referral of questions of propriety of conduct to an appropriate faculty committee.

Other Guides to Professional Conduct: The Association's major document--from which the ethical code and other standards of conduct are derived--is its 1949 Statement of Principles and Interpretive Comments. Special responsibilities of teachers concerning academic freedom and tenure are given in the original statement (1940), and in the comments made nearly thirty years later (1969).

Subsequent application and expansions of the principles of this basic guide are the Association's Statement on Professional Ethics (1966), the Report ... on Late Resignations and Professional Ethics (1968), which--together with two other documents, Statement on Recruitment and Resignation of Faculty Members (endorsed by the AAUP in 1961 and approved by the Association of American Colleges, with modifying preamble, that same year) and the Council statement Freedom and Responsibility (1970) on academic freedom--"constitute the basic philosophy and guidelines" for ethical conduct of teachers in higher education.

Professional Insignia: The AAUP reports no official emblem for the Association or for its members.

Bibliography:
American Association of University Professors. Constitution. Amended edition, 1967. 3 pages. (Reprint from AAUP

Bulletin 54:442-444 Winter 1968).
Includes membership requirements.

_____. Policy Documents and Reports.   1971.   79 pages.
$2.

The AAUP major policy document, 1940 Statement of Principles and Interpretive Comments, and subsequent conduct
guides, including the Statement on Professional Ethics.

Joughlin, Louis.   Academic Freedom and Tenure.   Madison,
University of Wisconsin Press, 1969.   374 pages. $7.50;
paper $2.50.

Metzger, Walter P.   Origins of the Association.   1965.   9
pages.   (Reprint from AAUP Bulletin 51:229-237 Summer
1965).

Brief history of the AAUP, and its code of ethics.

"Statement on Professional Ethics"*

Introduction

From its inception, the American Association of University
Professors has recognized that membership in the academic profession carries with it special responsibilities.   The Association has
consistently affirmed these responsibilities in major policy statements, providing guidance to the professor in his utterances as a
citizen, in the exercise of his responsibilities to students, and in
his conduct when resigning from his institution or when undertaking
government-sponsored research. † The Statement on Professional
Ethics that follows, necessarily presented in terms of the ideal,
sets forth those general standards that serve as a reminder of the
variety of obligations assumed by all members of the profession.
For the purpose of more detailed guidance, the Association, through
its Committee B on Professional Ethics, intends to issue from time
to time supplemental statements on specific problems.

In the enforcement of ethical standards, the academic profession differs from those of law and medicine, whose associations
act to assure the integrity of members engaged in private practice.
In the academic profession the individual institution of higher learning provides this assurance and so should normally handle questions
concerning propriety of conduct within its own framework by reference to a faculty group.   The Association supports such local action
and stands ready, through the General Secretary and Committee B,
to counsel with any faculty member or administrator concerning
questions of professional ethics and to inquire into complaints when
local consideration is impossible or inappropriate.   If the alleged
offense is deemed sufficiently serious to raise the possibility of
dismissal, the procedures should be in accordance with the 1940
Statement of Principles on Academic Freedom and Tenure and the
1958 Statement on Procedural Standards in Faculty Dismissal Proceedings.

The Statement

I.   The professor, guided by a deep conviction of the worth and dignity of the advancement of knowledge, recognizes the special responsibilities placed upon him.   His primary responsibility to his subject is to seek and to state the truth as he sees it.   To this end he devotes his energies to developing and improving his scholarly competence.   He accepts the obligation to exercise critical self-discipline and judgment in using, extending, and transmitting knowledge.   He practices intellectual honesty.   Although he may follow subsidiary interests, these interests must never seriously hamper or compromise his freedom of inquiry.

II.   As a teacher, the professor encourages the free pursuit of learning in his students.   He holds before them the best scholarly standards of his discipline.   He demonstrates respect for the student as an individual, and adheres to his proper role as intellectual guide and counselor.   He makes every reasonable effort to foster honest academic conduct and to assure that his evaluation of students reflects their true merit.   He respects the confidential nature of the relationship between professor and student.   He avoids any exploitation of students for his private advantage and acknowledges significant assistance from them.   He protects their academic freedom.

III.   As a colleague, the professor has obligations that derive from common membership in the community of scholars.   He respects and defends the free inquiry of his associates.   In the exchange of criticism and ideas he shows due respect for the opinions of others.   He acknowledges his academic debts and strives to be objective in his professional judgment of colleagues.   He accepts his share of faculty responsibilities for the governance of his institution.

IV.   As a member of his institution, the professor seeks above all to be an effective teacher and scholar.   Although he observes the stated regulations of the institution, provided they do not contravene academic freedom, he maintains his right to criticize and seek revision.   He determines the amount and character of the work he does outside his institution with due regard to his paramount responsibilities within it.   When considering the interruption or termination of his service, he recognizes the effect of his decision upon the program of the institution and gives due notice of his intentions.

V.   As a member of his community, the professor has the rights and obligations of any citizen.   He measures the urgency of these obligations in the light of his responsibilities to his subject, to his students, to his profession, and to his institution.   When he speaks or acts as a private person he avoids creating the impression that he speaks or acts for his college or university.   As a citizen engaged in a profession that depends upon freedom for its health and integrity, the professor has a particular obligation to promote conditions of free inquiry and to further pı ɔlic understanding of academic freedom.

NOTES

*Reprinted from the Spring 1969 AAUP Bulletin.
†1964 Committee A Statement on Extra Mural Utterances (Clarification of sec. 1c of the 1940 Statement of Principles on Academic Freedom and Tenure)
1968 Joint Statement on Rights and Freedoms of Students
1961 Statement on Recruitment and Resignation of Faculty Members
1964 On Preventing Conflicts of Interest in Government-Sponsored Research
1966 Statement on Government of Colleges and Universities

TELEVISION AND ELECTRONIC REPAIR TECHNICIANS

NATIONAL ALLIANCE OF TELEVISION AND ELECTRONIC SERVICE ASSOCIATIONS (NATESA)
    5906 S. Troy St., Chicago, Ill. 60629
    Frank J. Moch, Executive Director

Membership: The National Alliance of Television and Electronic Service Associations, founded in 1950 and with a present (1973) membership of 7500, is a trade association of "independently owned television-radio-home electronics service businesses." The owner of any such business servicing and repairing television, radio, high fidelity, and office or home electronics equipment is eligible for membership in NATESA. Among the projects of the association is its certification program, begun in 1951. Certificates are awarded for:
    Electronics Technician--requires passing of a two-hour examination, consisting of multiple choice questions "designed to determine the technician's capability to relate symptoms to cause."
    Safe Servicer--requires passing of a special test, written questions on the various aspects of electronic repair, including "adjustment of color television set high voltage to meet factory specifications on x-ray radiation."

Code of Ethics: The guide to ethical practice issued by the NATESA is its Code of Ethics, adopted in 1950. This Code enumerates 16 standards of conduct, including the employment of qualified repairmen, ethical advertising and guarantees, and details of service procedure, such as promptness, use of adequate test equipment, returning replaced parts to customers, itemization of bills, provision of estimates of repair cost. The association, through local grievance committees, "investigates every complaint charged against its members, and guarantees the public that it will be treated fairly." Substantiated complaints may result in need to recompense the investigator's service call. Expulsion from membership may be the penalty for serious offenses or repeated violations of the ethical code.

Professional Insignia: The NATESA official emblem is oval in shape, with a centered television rectangular picture tube, viewed obliquely from the left; on the tube face is a map of the United States on which is superimposed the initials of the organization,

"NATESA"; a bordering band bears the group's name, "National Alliance of Television and Electronic Service Associations"; the first three words of the name at the top of the design are separated from the remaining five words of the name by a stylized circuit tube, in the border, at the left and right.

The color of the emblem is shown variously--black on white (publication); dark blue on white, with red map (certificate of membership); turquoise blue on white, with dotted red map and oval background outside the centered picture tube (letterhead). This emblem is used on association stationery, publications, and news releases. It is authorized for display by members on business store fronts, vehicles and stationery.

Bibliography:
    National Alliance of Television and Electronic Service Associa-
        tions. Joy of Electronic Living. 1970. 15 pages.
        Pamphlet.
    Informational brochure for public, includes code of ethics
    and emblem.
        _____. NATESA. Pamphlet.
    Membership brochure gives specific services of the associa-
    tion.

"Code of Ethics"

1. Employ qualified personnel to assure proper service. No student shall be passed off as a technician.
2. Make proper arrangements for protection of reserve funds on contracts.
3. Carry adequate insurance coverage.
4. Avoid trick advertising which offers to service or deliver materials under conditions which are questionable or unfair to the set owner or your fellow members.
5. Employ professional methods of doing installations and maintenance.
6. Issue a standard guarantee.

7. Have available sufficient and proper test equipment to assure a good job.

8. Maintain an adequate service data library.

9. Render service without undue delay.

10. Install only parts as are really necessary. Use only new parts of a quality at least equal to original.

11. Leave with, or return to customer, all parts replaced, when requested, (except where impractical).

12. Issue an itemized bill.

13. Furnish estimates upon request.

14. Service sets in home whenever possible.

15. Be honest, courteous and treat each client in a professional manner.

16. Observe the Golden Rule.

TRAVEL AGENTS

AMERICAN SOCIETY OF TRAVEL AGENTS (ASTA)
360 Lexington Ave., New York, N.Y. 10017
George L. Fichtenbaum, Executive Vice President

Membership: The American Society of Travel Agents, founded in 1931 and with a present (1973) membership of over 10,000, is a trade association of the travel industry, whose "Active Members" are year-round tour operators and travel agents. The "Allied Members" of the organization include "airline and steamship companies, railroads, bus lines, car rental firms, hotels, resorts, government tourist offices and other organizations regularly engaged with the travel industry or associated industries." Members are grouped in 24 chapters located through the United States and Canada, and nearly 1000 travel agents are "international members," working in many countries of Europe, the Orient, Middle East, Africa, and Latin America. ASTA--originally organized as the American Steamship and Tourist Agents' Association--adopted its present name in 1944.

Code of Ethics: Carrying out one of the purposes of the association--"to promote ethical practices in the travel industry"--the Society first published its guide to ethical standards, Code of Professional Conduct, in 1963. The most recent edition of the ethical code, Principles of Professional Conduct and Ethics, adopted in May 1971, enumerates 24 standards for "the travel agent's proper relations with public, with airlines, hotels, and other travel organizations and with fellow travel agents."

Grievances or complaints against an ASTA member, charging violation of the principles of professional conduct, are usually handled locally at the chapter level, and disciplinary action may include censure, suspension, or expulsion of a member (Bylaws, Article VIII). The Grievance and Ethics Committee of the local chapter submits a copy of each complaint letter to the National Chairman and to the national Grievance Department, who may decide that the complaint is of industry-wide importance so that it should be considered at the national level. The Grievance Department also acts on complaints referred by a local chapter, because they "cannot be disposed of within a reasonable time and after diligent effort."

Professional Insignia: The official emblem of ASTA is an oval design, with a centered globe which shows seven latitude and eight

longitude lines, and bears the centered organization initials, "ASTA"; the name of the association, "American Society of Travel Agents," forms an unbordered border to the design. The color of the insignia is shown variously--black on white (display sign); black on white on a blue rectangle, and without bordering organization name (letterhead); blue on white, white on blue (publications). The ASTA emblem is used on publications and letterheads of the national headquarters and chapters, and is available to members in the form of a business display card.

Bibliography:
American Society of Travel Agents. Fact Sheet. 8 pages. Mimeographed.
Includes membership requirements, grievance and ethics procedures, and a directory of the Board of Directors, Area Directors, and Chapter Presidents.
_____. Principles of Professional Conduct and Ethics. 1971. 16 pages. Pamphlet.
ASTA code of ethics; enforcement of ethical code procedures (Bylaws, Article VIII); instructions for processing grievances.

"Principles of Professional Conduct and Ethics"

Part I.   Relations with the Public

1. It is the duty of the ASTA Member to protect the public against any fraud, misrepresentation or unethical practices in the Travel Agency Industry. He should endeavor to eliminate any practices which could be damaging to the public or to the dignity and integrity of the Travel Agent's profession. The ASTA Member shall report in writing any alleged unethical practices of fellow members

which come to his attention accompanied by such evidence as will, in his opinion, support the allegations to the Grievance and Ethics Committee.

2. It is the duty of the ASTA Member to keep himself and his staff fully informed on all phases of domestic and international travel in order to be in a position to give clients truly professional travel advice and to secure for them the best possible travel services and accommodations.

3. The ASTA Member should ascertain all pertinent facts concerning every tour, transportation, accommodation or other travel service offered to the public, for which he accepts the agency, so that he may fulfill his obligation to inform his clients accurately about the services he sells and the costs involved.

4. ASTA Members shall consider every transaction with a client to be strictly confidential unless the client specifically authorizes disclosure.

5. At the time initial payment is made for any booking ASTA Members must advise their clients in writing whether the client will be required to pay a cancellation fee or charge in the event the booking is changed or cancelled.

6. ASTA Members should use advertising materials to acquaint the public with the advantages to be gained through the use of the ASTA Travel Agent. Every effort shall be made to inform the public that the ASTA insignia is the hallmark of dependable travel service. The ASTA insignia should be used on entrance doors, display windows, cases, etc., and all office forms including checks, billheads, letterheads, envelopes, etc., as permitted in the Rules on Use of Insignia. The imprint of an ASTA Member on any brochure or on any newspaper advertisement should always include the ASTA insignia. On tour folders, the insignia shall not be used in the space reserved for the imprinting of an agent's name to avoid the possibility of misleading the public to believe the Travel Agent imprinting his name in this space is an ASTA Member, if in fact he is not.

7. The ASTA Member in his advertising should avoid misleading statements and doubtful superlatives. Such phrases as "our services are free" or "it costs no more" or words of similar import shall not be used. Specific mention of particular services for which no charge is made is permissible providing that the nature of such services is clearly stated.

Part II. Relations with Carriers, Hotels, and Other Principals

8. ASTA Members shall, at all times, follow the best traditions of salesmanship and fair dealing by according all carriers, hotels and agencies which they represent fair and impartial representation.

9.   ASTA Members shall adhere to all valid rules and regulations of carriers and carrier conferences.

10.   ASTA Members shall make themselves thoroughly conversant with conference agreements and with tariff rules and regulations; they shall be certain that their sales employees know of these agreements and rules, have access to them and understand them.

11.   ASTA Members shall not divide any commission allowed them by any carrier or hotel with the passenger or any other individual not regularly in its employ, either directly or indirectly or use any similar subterfuge to effect the sale of tickets or coupons. Nothing in this clause shall be construed to regulate any arrangement that an Active Member may have with persons regularly employed by it, which employees devote their entire business activities to the interests of it, nor with individual organizers engaged in stimulating group movements.

12.   ASTA Members shall not improperly attempt in any manner to influence the employees of carriers, hotels, tour operators or other organizations for the purpose of securing preferential consideration in the assignment of space or for any other purpose.

13.   ASTA Members, to ease space availability problems of the carriers, shall release promptly all unsold space and return cancelled accommodations with a minimum of delay.   Members shall refrain from suggesting and/or making duplicate bookings for clients.

14.   Orders placed by ASTA Members for accommodations or services, written or oral, are binding and, if not required, shall be cancelled.   When vouchers and exchange orders are presented for accommodations or services they shall be honored without delay.

15.   ASTA Members shall adhere to the standards of truth and good taste when called on to give an opinion of a carrier, hotel, tour operator or other travel organization.

16.   In the event of a complaint or grievance by a client against any carrier, hotel or other principal, ASTA Members shall give the principal an opportunity to make a full investigation before taking any action against the principal.

Part III.   Relations with Fellow ASTA Members and Other Travel Agents

17.   The ASTA Member should seek no unfair advantage over his fellow Travel Agent and should willingly share with him the lessons of his experience and study.

18. An ASTA Member should so conduct his business as to avoid controversies with his fellow Travel Agents. In the event of a controversy between ASTA Members, such controversy should be submitted to the Grievance and Ethics Committee rather than initially resort to litigation.

19. An ASTA Member should not disparage the business practices of a competitor, nor volunteer an opinion of a competitor's transaction. If his opinion is sought it should be rendered with strict professional integrity and courtesy.

20. ASTA Members shall not willfully interfere with or induce the cancellation of a definite sale made by another Travel Agent.

21. ASTA Members shall not solicit the services of an employee or salesman in the organization of another Travel Agent without the knowledge of that Agent.

22. ASTA Members shall not imitate, simulate or copy any name design, style mark or pattern used by another ASTA Member, agent, hotel or common carrier without specific permission.

23. When an ASTA Member is charged with an alleged unethical practice, he should willingly place all pertinent facts before the Grievance and Ethics Committee for investigation.

24. ASTA Members are not justified in violating any provision of these Principles of Professional Conduct and Ethics on the ground that some other Travel Agent may be doing so.

Conclusion

The ASTA insignia is recognized throughout the world as the "Hallmark of Dependable Travel" and signifies competence, fair dealing and high integrity resulting from strict adherence to a lofty ideal but nevertheless realistic practice of moral conduct in business relations. Every ASTA Member pledges that no promise of profit or instruction from client or principal will ever induce him to depart from the ASTA ideal or to disobey the injunctions of this creed.

INSTITUTE OF CERTIFIED TRAVEL AGENTS (ICTA)
610 RCA Bldg., 1901 N. Moore St., Arlington, Va. 22209
James Poynter, Administrative Director

Membership: The Institute of Certified Travel Agents, founded in 1964 and with a present membership of over 550, is a professional

organization of travel agents, who have met the Institute requirements for "Certified Travel Counselor." The Institute reports that
it is an "educational institution, not an association." Institute members who have had at least five years' experience with a travel
agency in the United States or Canada may qualify for certification
by successfully completing the required examinations, which have
been developed by the Institute, and by preparing an original research report in the field of travel counseling. Travel agents meeting the requirements for certification are awarded the professional
designation--title and letters--as an indication of competency,
"Certified Travel Counselor" ("CTC").

Code of Ethics: The guide for conduct of the ICTA is the Certified
Travel Counselor's Code of Ethics, adopted on August 15, 1966.
This code sets forth "basic standards of conduct and principles" in
travel counseling. The conduct guide considers obligations and re-
sponsibilities of travel agents in four sections:
      Responsibility to the Public,
      Responsibility to Clients and Employers,
      Responsibility to Association,
      Responsibility to Principals.
No procedures for enforcement of the code are reported.

Professional Insignia: The official emblem of the ICTA is an oval

design--with a world map
showing the western hemisphere,
surmounted by centered initials
of the Institute's certification
designation, "CTC": a bordering band bears the organization name, "Institute of Certified Travel Agents," printed
around the design, and--at
the bottom within the border,
the Institute monogram, "ICTA."
The color of the emblem is
black on white. The insignia
appears on ICTA letterheads
and publications.

Other Designations of Professional Status: As described above under
"Membership," the professional designation is authorized for use by
members on their business cards, stationery, and display poster (but
may only be used after the name(s) of individuals certified), "Certified Travel Counselor" ("CTC").

Bibliography:
    Institute of Certified Travel Agents. Bulletin. 1972.
        Includes sample certification examination questions; books
        recommended for examination study (p. 17-18); information
        about required original research report (p. 16).
        _____. Code of Ethics. 1966. 1 page.

Basic standards of conduct and principles for travel counselors.
_____. Original Research Reports Submitted in Requirement
for "Certified Travel Counselor. " $5.
List of qualifying papers submitted by candidates for CTC.

"Certified Travel Counselor's Code of Ethics"

Whereas, the profession of travel counseling has developed
because of the enormous growth of tourism and travel, both domestic
and international, bringing about an increasing need for truly competent, trustworthy advice and expert assistance; and

Whereas, the Travel Agents engaged in this profession have
incorporated an organization known as the Institute of Certified
Travel Agents; and

Whereas, although there is a recognized substantial diversity
of activities and types of businesses interested in travel counseling,
nevertheless, certain basic standards of conduct and principles are
common to all engaged in this profession;

Now, therefore, we, the members of the Board of Trustees
of the Institute of Certified Travel Agents, DO, this 15th day of
August, 1966, adopt this Professional Code of Ethics representing
the high principles guiding those who have been designated as
Certified Travel Counselors.

I.   Responsibility to the Public

From the Certified Travel Counselor the general public has
the right to expect professional competence and ability, the maintaining of a high degree of knowledge by keeping up to date on industry developments, accuracy, honesty and a high degree of integrity, objectivity in opinions expressed, and avoidance of exaggeration and misrepresentation.   In the solicitation of business, a
Certified Travel Counselor not only does not resort to improper
sales techniques nor misleading advertising which are illegal under
federal or state law, but he avoids all methods and advertising
which are other than candid and in good taste.

II.   Responsibility to Clients and Employers

Clients or employers of a CTC should expect and receive
strict, undivided fidelity and loyalty to their individual interests;
maintenance of complete confidence respecting their private affairs;
and diligent and judicious effort in the handling of their arrangements.   If requested, clients should receive a clear explanation of
the several sources of compensation received by the CTC or his
organization in connection with services rendered to them.   The
CTC will not enter into any business arrangement which might impair his ability to render unbiased and objective advice.

III.   Responsibility to Associates

The travel industry is entitled to expect of each CTC a high

standard of professional conduct in all matters pertaining to competition with colleagues and others in the travel field; relations with
professional organizations; use of material; and terms and conditions
of employment within his own organization. Every effort is to be
exerted to maintain unimpaired the professional status of the CTC
in all aspects of his business relationships, and to uphold the honor
and maintain the dignity of the profession.

IV. Responsibility to Principals

Just as the Certified Travel Counselor exercises due care
and discrimination in the choice of principals whose services and
facilities he will offer to the public, and just as he expects these
principals to grant him the status of fully recognized sales and
service representative, he should bind himself to adhere to his
principals' rates and procedures, their properly issued instructions,
and the conference regulations to which they themselves are bound.

VETERINARIANS

AMERICAN VETERINARY MEDICAL ASSOCIATION (AVMA)
    600 S. Michigan Ave. , Chicago, Ill. 60605
    D. A. Price, D. V. M. , Executive Vice President

Membership: The American Veterinary Medical Association, founded
in 1863 and with a present (1973) membership of over 21, 000, is a
professional association of veterinarians. "Active Members, " who
must be "graduates of colleges and schools of veterinary medicine, "
are organized in constituent associations of the AVMA--state groups
and the National Association of Federal Veterinarians. Members
practice in all aspects of veterinary medicine: activities related to
public health--including meat and milk inspection--and agriculture,
and in general and specialty areas, such as Large Animals, Small
Animals, Poultry, Veterinary Research, Regulatory Veterinary
Medicine, Laboratory Animal Medicine.

The AVMA recognizes seven specialty boards in Veterinary
Medicine, each of which issues a Diploma and authorizes the use
of the professional designation, "Diplomate, " as an indication of
competence, to veterinarians meeting requirements of specialized
training and experience.

Code of Ethics: The AVMA guide to professional conduct is its
Principles of Veterinary Medical Ethics, first adopted in 1940, and
most recently revised in its present 1970 edition. This ethical
code--after a general statement of professional responsibility--
gives, in six sections, broad principles of veterinary medical ethics.

The Judicial Council of AVMA, at the time the code of ethics was published, "prepared an abstract of previous rulings and interpretations" of the ethical principles "to serve as a practical reference document for the guidance of the individual and the profession." This Judicial Council interprets and enforces the ethical code (Bylaws, Article V, Section 2). While complaints of violations of the ethical guide are generally considered at the local level in constituent association, the Council may recommend the appointment of an investigating jury and a prosecutor, who receive, investigate, and prosecute complaints of unethical conduct. After hearing, the Council may admonish, suspend, or expel a member found guilty of violating the ethical guide.

Other Guides to Professional Conduct: The AVMA Veterinarian's Oath is a brief acceptance of social responsibility and ethical practice.

Professional Insignia: The official emblem of the AVMA is a circular design, with a centered
staff of Aesculapius (single
entwined serpent facing left)
signifying healing or medicine; a "V," Veterinary monogram, superimposed on the
lower portion of the centered
design; the organization name,
"American Veterinary Medical Association," forms a
circle within a bordering
band. No color is specified
for this insignia, and the
emblem is shown variously
--blue centered emblem with
black letters and border on
a white ground (letterhead);
gold staff and border, green
ground with "V" and printed
Association name in white
(Veterinarian's Oath; decal); black on white; white on black.

Bibliography:
        American Veterinary Medical Association.   Constitution and
            Bylaws.   1970.
        Includes membership requirements, Judicial Council inter-
        pretations and enforcement of ethical principles.
                    .   Principles of Veterinary Medical Ethics.   1970.
            (Reprint from AVMA Journal, May 1, 1971).
        Annotated professional ethical code for veterinarians, with
        introductory statement by AVMA Judicial Council.
                    .   Veterinarian's Oath.   Single sheet.
        AVMA pledge of service for veterinarians.

"Principles of Veterinary Medical Ethics"

Preamble

The honor and dignity of our profession lies in our obedience to a just and reasonable code of ethics set forth as a guide to the members. The purpose of this code is far-reaching because exemplary professional conduct not only upholds honor and dignity, but also enlarges our sphere of usefulness, exalts our social standards, and promotes the science we cultivate.

Briefly stated, our code of ethics is the foundation of our individual and collective efforts.

It is based on the Golden Rule.

Section I

The principal objectives of the veterinary profession are to render service to society, to conserve our livestock resources, and to relieve suffering of animals. A veterinarian should conduct himself in relation to the public, his colleagues and their patients, and the allied professions, so as to merit their full confidence and respect.

Section II

A veterinarian may choose whom he will serve. Once he has undertaken care of a patient he must not neglect him. In an emergency, however, he should render service to the best of his ability. He should not solicit clients.

Section III

A veterinarian should not employ his professional knowledge and attainments nor dispose of his services under terms and conditions which tend to interfere with the free exercise of his judgment and skill or tend to cause a deterioration of the quality of veterinary service.

Section IV

A veterinarian should strive continually to improve veterinary knowledge and skill, making available to his colleagues the benefit of his professional attainments, and seeking, through consultation, assistance of others when it appears that the quality of veterinary service may be enhanced thereby.

Section V

The veterinary profession should safeguard the public and itself against veterinarians deficient in moral character or professional competence. Veterinarians should observe all laws, uphold the honor and dignity of the profession, and accept its self-imposed discipline.

Section VI

The responsibilities of the veterinary profession extend not only to the patient but also to society. The health of the community as well as the patient deserves his interest and participation in non-professional activities and organizations.

"Veterinarian's Oath"

Being admitted to the profession of veterinary medicine,
I solemnly swear to use my scientific knowledge and skills
for the benefit of society through the protection of animal health,
the relief of animal suffering, the conservation of livestock resources, the promotion of public health, and the advancement of
medical knowledge.

I will practice my profession conscientiously, with dignity,
and in keeping with the principles of veterinary medical ethics.

I accept as a lifelong obligation the continual improvement of
my professional knowledge and competence.

WATCHMAKER/CLOCKMAKER REPAIRMEN

AMERICAN WATCHMAKERS INSTITUTE (AWI)
    3810 Harrison Ave., P.O. Box 11011, Cincinnati, Ohio 45211
    Milton C. Stevens, Executive Director

Membership: The American Watchmakers Institute, founded in
1960--upon the merger of the Horological Institute of America and
the United Horological Association of America--and with a present
(1973) membership of approximately 4000, is a trade association of
watch and clock repairmen, open to any person interested in repair
work on timekeeping mechanisms. The AWI conducts a certification
program in which it awards a certificate and a designation of competence to members who meet specified experience requirements,
and pass the AWI's proficiency examinations in horology. The Institute "recognizes certification granted by its two founding organiza-
tions--The Horological Institute of America and the United Horological Association of America. Those certified by either of these organizations are granted AWI CMW certification on request. "

The certification examinations consist of a written test and a
practical examination in bench work. Examinations are open to
practicing watchmakers and clockmakers, graduates of horological
schools, and lay persons interested in horology. Designations--
titles and initials--awarded by the AWI to denote a competent and
skilled craftsman in watch or clock repair are:
    "Certified Watchmaker" ("CW"),
    "Certified Master Watchmaker" ("CMW-AWI"),
    "Certified Clockmaker" ("CC"),
    "Certified Master Clockmaker" ("CMC-AWI").

Code of Ethics: The conduct guide of the AWI, developed by a committee in 1960, is its Code of Ethics, six general principles in the
form of a pledge, to be followed in timekeeping mechanical repair.

No procedures for enforcement of the Code are reported.

Professional Insignia: The official emblem of the American Watch-

makers Institute, developed by a group in 1960, is its seal-- a circular design with a centered map of North America, on which is superimposed the monogram of the Institute, "AWI"; at the top of the bordering band of the design is the name of the group, "American Watchmakers Institute," with three stars at the bottom of the design within the border. The insignia is shown on Institute stationery and publications, and is available to Institute members for wear as a lapel pin, for display as a poster in place of business, or for use in advertising and other promotional materials. The color of the emblem is shown variously--black on yellow; red on green; red on white; black on white (publications).

Bibliography:

American Watchmakers Institute. Code of Ethics. Single sheet. Guide to conduct for watch and clock repairmen.

———. Information on Clock Certification. 12 pages. Pamphlet.

Outlines examinations for Certified Clockmaker and Certified Master Clockmaker. Gives sample questions and books and other publications recommended for examination preparation.

———. Information on Certification. 1971. 12 pages. Pamphlet.

Outlines examinations for Certified Watchmaker and Certified Master Watchmaker. Gives sample questions and books and other publications recommended for examination preparation.

———. You and the American Watchmakers Institute. Folder.

Informational brochure mentioning AWI activities, including technical certification of competence for qualified watch and clock repairmen.

"Code of Ethics"

I will not knowingly mislead, deceive or defraud the public.

I will not advertise in any manner that is untruthful or misleading.

I will not knowingly represent a watch to have been overhauled unless it has been properly cleaned and regulated.

I will not knowingly represent to the public that certain parts are required for a watch which are actually unnecessary in the repair to be performed.

I agree that it is unethical to perform any unworkmanlike or unskilled watch repairs.

I agree to conduct myself in my business and private life in such a manner as will reflect credit to myself, the American Watchmakers Institute, my fellow professionals and the entire industry.

WILDLIFE MANAGERS

WILDLIFE SOCIETY (WS)
   Suite S 176, 3900 Wisconsin Ave., N.W., Washington, D.C.
   20016
   Dr. Fred G. Evenden, Executive Director

Membership: The Wildlife Society, established in 1937 (growing out of the Society of Wildlife Specialists organized the previous year) and with a present (1973) membership of approximately 6000, is a professional association in the wildlife field.   Among the Society's objectives is the establishment and maintenance of the highest possible professional standards in wildlife management.   Membership in the WS is open to "all those with a serious interest in wildlife conservation and management," including of course, professional workers.   The diversity of work among the professional members, who reside in over 60 countries, is shown by the range of disciplines represented--game managers, "embracing the practical ecology of all vertebrates and their plant and animal associates"; administrators; educators; enforcement officers; information specialists; and research workers.

Code of Ethics: The conduct guide for members of the Wildlife Society is the Code of Ethics, adopted in 1963.   This Code (Bylaws, Article II) sets forth in brief paragraphs the professional goals of wildlife managers. The conduct guide is enforced by the President of the Society, who

may "with the approval of the Council appoint a Board of Inquiry to
review any reported breach of the Code by a Society member. " If
the charge is substantiated, a member "may be denied future membership" in the Society.

Professional Insignia: The official emblem of the Wildlife Society,
adopted in 1937, is a rectangular design with four horizontal lines
of Egyptian hieroglyphics, symbolizing the subject matter of the wildlife manager--mammals, birds, fishes, and flowering plants; a line
border encloses the inscription. The color of the design is shown
variously--red on grey (letterhead); black on white; brown on yellow
(publications).

Bibliography:
    Kalmbach, R. R. , W. L. McAtee, and Tracy L. Storer. "The
        Wildlife Society: Its First Quarter Century. " Journal of
        Wildlife Management 26:39-306 [3] 1962.
    Complete history of the first twenty-five years of the Wild-
    life Society.
    Wildlife Society. Bylaws. April 19, 1971.
    Includes membership classes and Code of Ethics (Bylaws,
    Article II)--text and enforcement procedure.
    _____. The Wildlife Society: A Brief History. Pamphlet.
        9 pages.
    Informational brochure giving in addition to history, member-
    ship composition, activities, publications, awards.

"Code of Ethics"

Section 1. Code of Ethics. --Members of The Wildlife Society
have a responsibility for contributing to an understanding of man's
proper relationship with natural resources, and, in particular, for
determining the role of wildlife in satisfying human needs.

Each member will strive to meet this obligation by subscribing to the highest standards of integrity and conduct and to
the following professional goals: He recognizes the conservation
and wise management of wildlife species as the primary goal of his
profession.

He will support research to improve wildlife conservation
programs, and he will encourage the exchange of information among
members of his profession and the interested public. He will strive
for public understanding of the need for the wise use of wildlife
resources.

He will increase his knowledge and utilize his skills to advance the practice of wildlife management; he will encourage professional competence by supporting high standards of education, employment, and performance. He will discharge his professional
responsibilities in an objective manner, and he will base decisions
on sound biological and management principles.

He will act in such manner and engage in those practices
that will bring credit to his profession, employer, and community.

Section 2. Enforcement. --The President shall, with the
approval of the Council, appoint a Board of Inquiry to review any
reported breach of this Code by a Society member, and said member may be denied future membership if such is both recommended
by the Board of Inquiry and approved by the Council.

WRITERS

P. E. N. American Center
    156 Fifth Ave. , New York, N. Y. 10010
    Mrs. Kirsten Michalski, Executive Secretary

Membership: P. E. N. , founded in London in 1921 by John Gals-
worthy and established in an American Center in 1922, with Booth
Tarkington as its first president, is a world association of writers.
In the American Center there are currently (1973) 1200 members,
including poets, essayists, and novelists (whose initials give the
name, "P. E. N. "), and also editors, playwrights, and translators.
P. E. N. "membership is by invitation of the Membership Committee,
extended to published writers of demonstrated accomplishment, or
by recommendation of writers of distinction who are already members. "

Code of Ethics: P. E. N. has issued no formal code of ethics, but
the Charter of International P. E. N. , adopted in its present form at
the 1948 Congress held in Copenhagen, "pledges that members of
P. E. N. do their utmost to dispel race, class, and national hatreds,
and to champion the ideal of peace in one world. "

Professional Insignia: The emblem of P. E. N. is a crossed sword
and pen (signifying the non-political ac-
tion of the group in defending free literature, the exchange of ideas, freedom
of expression and good will); the initials of the organization--comprising
its name, "P. E. N. "--are placed one
in each quadrant of the central design,
clockwise beginning in the left quadrant. The color of the insignia is black
on white (letterhead); or in various
colors (publications).

Bibliography:
    Chute, Marchette. P. E. N. American Center: A History of
        the First Fifty Years. P. E. N. , American Center, 1972.

P. E. N.   P. E. N. --What It Is ... What It Does.   4 pages.
        P. E. N. , American Center, 1970.
Describes P. E. N. organization, goals, activities, membership requirements and gives principles affirmed in International P. E. N. Charter.

"Charter of International P. E. N. "

International P. E. N. affirms that:
    1.   Literature, national though it be in origin, knows no
frontiers, and should remain common currency between nations in
spite of political or international upheavals.

    2.   In all circumstances, and particularly in time of war,
works of art, the patrimony of humanity at large, should be left
untouched by national or political passion.

    3.   Members of the P. E. N. should at all times use what in-
fluence they have in favour of good understanding and mutual respect
between nations; they pledge themselves to do their utmost to dispel
race, class and national hatreds and to champion the ideal of one
humanity living in peace in one world.

    4.   The P. E. N. stands for the principle of unhampered
transmission of thought within each nation and between all nations,
and members pledge themselves to oppose any form of suppression
of freedom of expression in the country and community to which
they belong.   The P. E. N. declares for a free press and opposes
arbitrary censorship in time of peace.   It believes that the necessary advance of the world towards a more highly organized political
and economic order renders a free criticism of governments, ad-
ministrations and institutions imperative.   And since freedom implies voluntary restraint, members pledge themselves to oppose
such evils of a free press as mendacious publication, deliberate
falsehood and distortion of facts for political and personal ends.

SOCIETY FOR TECHNICAL COMMUNICATION (STC)
        1010 Vermont Ave. , N. W. , Suite 421, Washington, D. C. 20005
        Curtis T. Youngblood, Executive Director

Membership: The Society for Technical Communication, founded in
1953 and with a present (1973) membership of approximately 4000,
is a professional association in the field of technical communication
in all media.   The diversity of interests and activities of members
is shown in the many aspects of technical communication in which
they are engaged; in addition to technical writers, editors, publishers, members are technical writers and draftsmen, designers,

educators, engineers, copywriters, documentation specialists, researchers in information science, illustrators, book designers, and audio-visual specialists. The Society grew from two organizations, both founded in 1953 (Society of Technical Writers and Association of Technical Writers and Editors), which merged in 1957 to form the Society of Technical Writers and Editors. This group, in turn, merged in 1960 with the Technical Publishing Society (organized in 1954) to form the Society of Technical Writers and Publishers. The group's name was changed in 1970 to the present "Society for Technical Communication. "

Members are organized in 50 autonomous chapters and branches throughout the United States and Eastern Canada, and one branch in Israel. There are several grades of membership, including the entrance membership grades of:
> Member--professionals;
> Affiliate Member--nonprofessionals interested in the art;
> Student Member--enrolled in training course;
> Sustaining Member--companies interested in technical communication.

Qualifications for professional members are:
> Member--"must be actively engaged full-time in some phase of technical communications and have at least one year's such experience"; and "must be able to perform complex and important work with only moderate supervision";
> Senior Member--may be applied for after two years in the grade of Member. Applicant "must have 7 years of active technical communication experience, three of which involved primary responsibility for directing major tasks or programs. "

The Society has two distinguished member grades, Associate Fellow and Fellow. Application may not be made for these grades. They are selective grades, based on a member's professional attainments and contributions and ten years membership in STC.

Code of Ethics: No formal code of ethics has been published by the Society for Technical Communication. Bylaws of the Society "provide for discipline, suspension, or expulsion of members whose conduct and activities are considered to be inimical to the Society's purpose. "

Professional Insignia: The official emblem of the STC is its logotype--the monogram of the organization, "STC, " in a rectangular design. The color of the insignia is shown variously --black on white, white on black, white on red. The emblem appears on stationery and publications of the national group and of its chapters and branches. Members are

authorized to wear the insignia on jewelry denoting various membership grades and offices held in the Society. Categories of membership distinguished in the jewelry include:
> Member and Affiliate--Sterling silver, white enamel;
> Senior Member--10-karat gold, blue enamel;
> Associate Fellow--10-karat gold, red enamel with 1.4 pt
>   diamond;
> Fellow--10-karat gold, red enamel with 2.4 pt diamonds.

Bibliography:
> Society for Technical Communication. An Introduction to STC.
>   Pamphlet.
> Informational brochure giving membership classes and re-
> quirements, group history and activities.

ZOOLOGISTS

INTERNATIONAL COMMISSION ON ZOOLOGICAL NOMENCLATURE (ICZN)

> c/o British Museum (Natural Science)
> Cromwell Rd., London, S.W. 7, England
> R. V. Melville, Executive Secretary

Membership: The International Commission on Zoological Nomenclature, organized in 1895 and with a present (1973) membership of
26, is an association of taxonomists in the field of zoology.   Publications of the Commission are distributed by the
> International Trust for Zoological Nomenclature
> Francis J. Griffin, O. B. E., Managing Dir. and Sec.
> 14 Belgrave Square, London, S.W. 1.x 8PS, England
and include the International Code of Zoological Nomenclature (2nd
ed., 1964), as well as Official lists of generic, specific, and
family-group names in zoology, and rejected and invalid names.
Current proposals on zoological nomenclature submitted to the Commission for deliberation and decision are reported in the Bulletin
of Zoological Nomenclature.

Code of Ethics: The professional conduct guide for zoologists
issued by the Commission concerns zoological nomenclature, and
this Code of Ethics is included in the International Code of Zoological Nomenclature, 1964 (page 93).

Other Guides to Professional Conduct: An additional guide to the
responsibility of the zoologist in questions of zoological nomenclature
is the "Monaco Resolution, " adopted at Monaco by the Ninth International Congress of Zoology, 1913.   It defines the obligation of the
zoologist who notices "that the generic or specific name published

by any living author as new is in reality a homonym. "

Professional Insignia: No official emblem is reported by the International Commission on Zoological Nomenclature.

Bibliography:
> International Code of Zoological Nomenclature, adopted by the XV International Congress of Zoology. [2d. ed.], London. Published by the International Trust for Zoological Nomenclature, 1964. 115 p. $3.
> Includes the Code of Ethics (page 93).
> "Monaco Resolution. " Bulletin of Zoological Nomenclature. 14:xxvii (Introductory Part) June 27, 1958.
> Ethical guide in specific instances of zoological nomenclature --generic or specific name published as new by living author, but in reality a homonym.

"Code of Ethics"

1. Zoologists publishing new names should observe the following principles, which together constitute a "Code of Ethics. "

2. A zoologist should not himself establish a new taxon if he has reason to believe that another zoologist has already recognized the same taxon and is on the point of establishing it (or that the taxon is to be named in a posthumous work). He should communicate with the other zoologist (or his representatives) and consider himself free to establish the new taxon only if the other zoologist (or his representatives) fails to do so in a reasonable period (not less than a year).

3. A zoologist should not publish a new replacement name for a junior homonym during the lifetime of its author without informing the latter of the homonymy and allowing him a reasonable interval, of at least a year, in which to publish a replacement name.

4. The period of time specified in 2 and 3 above may be reduced in exceptional circumstances, for example when in a work of revision a new generic name is urgently required as the basis of a familyname.

5. No zoologist should propose a name that, to his knowledge, gives offence on any grounds.

6. Intemperate language should not be used in the discussion of zoological nomenclature, which should be debated in a courteous and friendly manner. Difficult problems are most readily and quickly solved by respecting the rules of courtesy in discussing the views of others.

7.   Editors and others responsible for the publication of zoological papers should avoid publishing any paper that seems to them to contain a breach of the above principles.

8.   The observation of these principles is a matter for the proper feelings of individual zoologists, and the Commission is not authorized to investigate or pass judgment upon alleged breaches of them.

"Monaco Resolution"

Without presuming to be the arbiter of points of general ethics, the Commission is persuaded that there is one phase of this subject upon which it is competent to speak, and in reference to this point it suggests to the Congress the adoption of the following resolution:

Whereas--experience has shown that authors, not infrequently, inadvertently publish as new designations of genera or species, names that are preoccupied, and

Whereas--experience has also shown that some other authors, discovering the homonymy, have published new names for the later homonyms in question, be it therefore

Resolved--That when it is noticed by any zoologist that the generic or specific name published by any living author as new is in reality a homonym, and therefore unavailable under Articles 34 and 36 of the Rules on Nomenclature, the proper action, from a standpoint of professional etiquette, is for said person to notify said author of the facts of the case, and to give said author ample opportunity to propose a substitute name.

BIBLIOGRAPHY

1 American Management Association. Business Ethics for Trade
and Professional Associations. June 1962. 39 pages.
A collection of representative documents, compiled by
the Research and information Service, from 14 trade and
professional associations, prepared for the guidance of
AMA members: Codes of Ethics, Statements of Principles, Standards of Practice. Samples of "wide range of
scope and style in which standards of ethical conduct
may be expressed." Assembled as part of the cooperation of the AMA with the Business Ethics Advisory
Council, formed by Secretary of Commerce Luther H.
Hodges.

2 Angel, Juvenal L. Directory of Professional and Occupational
Licensing in the United States. New York: World Trade
Academy Press; dist. by Simon & Schuster, 1970. 755 p.
State licenses or certificates issued for about 1000 occupations. Occupations are keyed to the Dictionary of Occupational Titles (Government Printing Office, 1949, 2nd
ed). One section, arranged by state, gives names and
addresses of licensing agencies.

3 Annals of the American Academy of Political and Social Science.
Over a period of years have provided surveys, reports
and evaluations of professional ethics:

> 1922 King, Clyde L., ed. "The Ethics of the Profes-
> sions and Business." v. 101, May 1922.
> Includes: The significance of the ethical
> codes for the professions. --The ethical codes
> of lawyers. --The ethics of the medical pro-
> fession. --The ethical codes of the engineers.
> --The ethics of the architects. --Ethical
> standards for teachers, librarians, ministers
> and social workers. --Ethical standards for
> journalists. --The ethical code of accountants.
> --Ethics and business.

1952 Callender, Clarence E., and James C. Charles-
      worth, eds. "Ethical Standards in American
      Public Life." v. 280, March 1952.
      Special articles discuss ethics in American
      business, American labor, and in public em-
      ployment--legislative and judicial chambers,
      and executive departments. Includes one
      essay by Paul H. Douglas, "Improvement of
      Ethical Standards in the Federal Government:
      Problems and Proposals."

1955 Landis, Benson Y., ed. "Ethical Standards and
      Professional Conduct." v. 297, January 1955.
      "In large part a revision of some of the sub-
      ject matter appearing in The Annals of May
      1922"--"contains a symposium on the formu-
      lation of ethical standards of practice within
      specific professional groups." The first
      part--dealing with development of codes of
      conduct within particular professions--includes:
        Carey, John L. The ethics of public ac-
          counting;
        Cummings, George Bain. Standards of
          professional practice in architecture.
        Fitts, William T., and Barbara Fitts.
          Ethical standards of the medical profes-
          sion;
        Drinker, Henry S. Legal ethics;
        Wagner, H. A. Principles of professional
          conduct in engineering;
        Perry, Cyrus C. A code of ethics for
          public school teachers;
        Eby, Kermit. Organized labor and Amer-
          ican ethics;
        Stahl, O. Glenn. Democracy and public
          employee morality;
        Monypenny, Philip. The control of ethical
          standards in the public service.
      The second part of the issue consists of
      three articles--defining a profession, busi-
      ness management becoming a profession,
      and (a reprint from the 1922 volume) R. M.
      McIver's article, "The Social Significance
      of Professional Ethics."

1962 Miller, Arthur S., ed. "The Ethics of Business
      Enterprise." v. 343, September 1962. In-
      cludes: Leys, Wayne A. R. Ethics and the
      rule of law.

1966 Charlesworth, James C., ed. "Ethics in America:
      Norms and Deviations." v. 363, January 1966.

Includes articles on ethics in government
and business--Congress, public administration, politics, judiciary, ombudsman, law,
medicine, religion, journalism, public entertainment, business, insurance merchandising
and advertising, organized labor.

<u>1968</u>   Leys, Wayne A. R.   "Ethics in American Business
and Government; the Confused Issues." 378:
34-44, July 1968.

4   Association of the Bar of the City of New York.   Special Committee on Congressional Ethics.   <u>Congress and the Public</u>
<u>Trust.</u>   New York: Atheneum, 1970.   351 p.
"Constructive analysis of both houses, what their problems were and how they might be solved."   Recommendations given throughout 6 chapters.   Chapter VII, "Congressional Self-Discipline," gives activities and code
texts of the Senate Ethics Committee and Code of Ethics,
and the House Ethics Committee and Code of Ethics.

5   Bain, George Sayers.   <u>The Growth of White-Collar Unionism.</u>
Oxford: Clarendon Press, 1970.   233 p.
Study of the major factors which determined the growth
of white-color unions in England, particularly of workers
employed in the manufacturing industry.   Includes bibliography.

6   Ben-David, Joseph.   "Professions in the Class System of
Present-Day Societies: A Trend Report and Bibliography."
<u>Current Sociology</u> 12, no. 3, 1963-1964.
Discusses explicit or implicit codes of behavior, in dis-
cussions of "The Sociological Study of the Professions;
Social Mobility and the Professions; and The Growth of
the Professions and the Class System."

7   Bennion, Francis A. R.   <u>Professional Ethics.</u>   London: C.
Knight, 1969.   278 p.
First publication to analyze and evaluate the codes of
conduct in English "consultant professions" (those carried
on in private practice and offering public consultancy) in
the fields of health rights and property--such as law,
medicine, accountancy, architecture, surveying.

8   Blum, Albert A.   <u>White-Collar Workers.</u>   New York: Random
House, 1971.   225 p.
Relationships between white-collar workers and the unions
in the United States, in five occupational areas: the
office employee, retail clerks, engineers, teachers, and
the federal service.

9   Braemer, Richard J.   "Disciplinary Procedures for Trade and

Professional Associations. " Association Management 21:
46-52 September 1969.
An attorney "examines the legal steps which can guarantee
fairness in disciplinary actions" of professional associations. Reprinted from Business Lawyer, v. 23, July,
1968.

10 Cabot, Richard Clarke. Adventures in the Borderlands of Ethics.
New York: Harper, 1926. 152 p.
Explains the growth of professional codes (1920-1924) in
the United States, as a result of the Federal Trade Commission's requesting each occupation to set forth "unfair
methods of competition" (p. 77). Reports--in reprints
from the Survey Graphic--professional ethics and codes
of ethics in theology, medicine, business, teaching,
social work. Tabulates (p. 80-83) the principles underlying 198 codes of ethics, as these codes are reproduced
in the book, Heermance, Codes of Ethics, 1924.

11 Carmody, James. Ethical Issues in Health Services, A Report
and Annotated Bibliography. National Center for Public
Health Services Research and Development (Report HSRD
70...32, November 1970), Department of Health, Education
and Welfare, Public Health Services. 43 p. Rockville,
Md. , Health Services and Mental Health Administration.

12 Carr-Saunders, Alexander M. , and P. A. Wilson. The Professions. Oxford: Clarendon Press, 1933 (reprint 1973,
Humanities). 536 p.
History, organization and functioning of the professions
in England, with discussion of professional constitutions,
education, entry into profession, professional discipline
and conduct, economic problems of professional associations, professions and the public. Appendix IV includes
samples of four professional codes: General Medical
Council (G. M. C.); Rules to Ethics of Medical Consultation, British Medical Association (B. M. A.); Ethical
Rules of the Institution of Civil Engineers; Royal Institute
of British Architects (R. I. B. A.).

13 Christian, Portia. Ethics in Business Conduct. Detroit: Gale
Research, 1970. 156 p.
Source book reflecting changes which have occurred in
the standards of ethics and conduct in American business
since 1900. Consists of citations to sources--arranged
chronologically by decade, most recent first--in the form
of annotations and excerpts "to show the pressures, problems, and attempted solutions in each period. "

14 Council of State Governments. Occupations and Professions
Licensed by the States, Puerto Rico and the Virgin Islands.
Chicago: Council of State Governments, December 1968.
Pamphlet. 9 p.

Identifies 67 occupations which are licensed by five or
more jurisdictions in the United States.

15 Crawford, Nelson Antrim. The Ethics of Journalism. New
York: Knopf, 1924 (reprint 1973, Johnson). 264 p.
Ethics of publishing, editing and journalism, with several
codes of ethics adopted by newspapers and groups of
journalists (Appendix A, pages 183-240), such as Canons
of Journalism of the American Society of Newspaper
Editors; Journalist's Creed by Walter Williams.

16 Currie, James, ed. Professional Organizations in the Commonwealth. Published for The Commonwealth Foundation by
Hutchinson of London, 1970. 511 p.
Describes how each profession and professional body is
organized throughout the British commonwealth. Gives
details of over 1000 professional societies, including
qualifications required and examinations.

17 Daedalus. Professions in America. Edited by Kenneth S. Lynn.
Boston: Houghton Mifflin, 1965. 273 p.
A collective portrait of professions in the United States,
through essays by experts. Appeared as articles in
Daedalus (Fall 1963), plus three supplemental studies
added.

18 Dubin, Samuel S. Professional Obsolescence. Lexington, Mass.:
Lexington Books, 1972. 128 p.
Problems of updating professional knowledge, with description of motivational factors influencing obsolescence
reeducation, through reeducation and continuous education
programs.

19 Durkheim, Emile. Professional Ethics and Civic Morals. New
York: Free Press, 1958. 228 p.
Sociologist's theory on how rules of professional conduct
were established, and the way they operate in society.

20 Elliott, Philip. The Sociology of the Professions. New York:
Herder and Herder, 1972. 180 p.
English author reviews and analyzes "the historical shift
from traditional status professionalism to the occupational
professionalism of modern industry and commerce."

21 Encyclopedia of Associations: A Guide to National and International Organizations. (v. 1. National Organizations of the
United States.) 8th ed. Detroit: Gale Research, 1973.
Published since 1956, this edition includes more than
17,000 associations in the United States, with a few international and foreign groups. Gives identifying information and brief facts (membership, history, purposes,
publications) for each.

22   Etzioni, Amitai. The Semi-Professions and Their Organization:
     Teachers, Nurses, Social Workers. New York: Free
     Press, 1969.   328 p.
         Six sociologists analyze "the situation and its dynamics"
         of a "group of new professions. "

23   Fox-Davies, Arthur Charles.   The Book of Public Arms.   Lon-
     don: Jack, 1915.   (Reprint, Gale Research Co.)   876 p.
         Pictures and describes the arms of a number of occupa-
         tional societies in England, some dating from the 16th
         century.   Includes arms (shown in color) and blazons
         for haberdashers, wrights, barbers and surgeons,
         scriviners, pharmaceutical society, makers of playing
         cards.

24   Fulmer, Robert M.   "Ethical Activities of Associations. "
     Association Management 19:24-27, November 1967.
         A study of 90 leading national trade and professional
         associations shows that 60% of the groups had adopted
         some type of ethical code.   Reports that standards of
         conduct must be kept up-to-date by review and revision,
         and must be enforced with regard to discipline for in-
         fractions (according to 52% of the associations).

25   Gilb, Corinne L.   Hidden Hierarchies: The Professions and
     Government.   New York: Harper, 1966.   307 p.
         This report by a political scientist on the history of the
         development of professions and professional associations
         in the United States and their relations to government,
         uses the occupational groups in order "to illuminate this
         development of the American System as a whole and the
         relationship between its various parts. "

26   Gross, Ronald, and Paul Osterman.   New Professionals.   New
     York: Simon & Schuster, 1972.   316 p.
         The "New Professionals" are young "Militant to Moderate"
         students, professionals, consumers, who in these essays
         "espouse three basic ideas about professions: to emphasize
         furthering the well-being of people and de-emphasize self-
         aggrandizement of 'loyalty' to the profession; to insist upon
         accountability to the client; to abolish the credential sys-
         tem which tends to license and exclusive monopoly. "

27   Gusfield, Joseph R. , and Michael Schwartz.   "The Meanings of
     Occupational Prestige: Reconsiderations of the NORC Scale. "
     American Sociological Review 28:265-271, April 1963.
         Examines the National Opinion Research Center survey of
         occupational prestige.

28   Hansen, David A.   Police Ethics.   Springfield, Ill. :   Thomas,
     1973.   96 p.
         Discussion of the police code of ethics, with applications
         to law enforcement and professionalism.

29 Hawver, Carl. "Association Accreditation Programs Today."
    Association Management. 20:13-18, November 1968.
    Many associations grant certificates and registration to
    qualified members or as prerequisite to membership.
    The purposes of accreditation of association members--
    in programs which have developed within professional
    groups over the past 20 years--include: "Membership
    Recognition, Self-Regulation, Professional Upgrading,
    and Member Recruitment."

30 Heermance, Edgar Laing. Codes of Ethics: A Handbook.
    Burlington, Vt.: Free Press Printing Co., 1924. 525 p.
    A pioneering collection of 130 codes of ethics from a
    variety of professions, industries, and trades in the
    United States.

31 Hendrix, John, ed. Invitation to Dialogue: The Professional
    World, A Symposium on Professional Ethics. Nashville:
    Broadman, 1970. 126 p.
    A spokesman for each of 9 professions--under the aus-
    pices of the Church Training Department of the Baptist
    Sunday School Board--presents the ethical code of his
    professional group: Churches, Education, Medicine,
    Psychiatry and Counseling, Law, Politics, Business,
    Military, Sports. Includes "adaptations of ethical codes."

32 Jackson, John A., ed. Professions and Professionalization.
    Cambridge, Eng.: Cambridge University Press, 1970.
    226 p. (Sociological Studies 3.)
    Six international authorities in different countries ex-
    amine the sociological concepts of the professional
    status of certain occupations.

33 Landis, Benson Young. Professional Codes: A Sociological
    Analysis to Determine Applications to the Educational Pro-
    fession. New York: Teachers College, Columbia Univer-
    sity, 1927. (Teachers College, Columbia University.
    Contributions to Education, no. 267.) Also, published as
    a Ph.D. thesis, Columbia University, 1927 (reprint 1973,
    AMS Press). 108 p.
    Survey of the codes of ethics of 200 organizations, in-
    cluding the form, content, and effectiveness of the con-
    duct guides.

34 Leeson, R. A. United We Stand: An Illustrated Account of
    Trade Union Emblems. Bath, Eng.: Adams & Dart, 1971.
    72 p.
    Well-known artists (such as William Morris, Walter
    Crane, and Alexander Gos) were among the designers
    of these emblems of 19th and early 20th century unions
    in England. The badges of membership were worn in
    the lapel, shown on the contribution card, and displayed
    in the home as a framed insignia.

35 Lieberman, Jethro K. The Tyranny of the Experts. New York:
      Walker, 1970. 318 p.
      In a critical review of expansion of professionalism and
      the control of work by professions, discusses Codes of
      Ethics (Chapter 5, "Ethics and Profits," p. 69-84).

36 Millerson, Geoffrey. The Qualifying Associations: A Study of
      Professionalization. London: Routledge, 1964. 320 p.
      Describes typical structures of associations in England,
      showing how they gradually evolve a code of professional
      conduct. Lists over 100 associations (appendix)--the
      majority of which hold their own examinations and publish
      a journal.

37 Moore, Wilbert E. The Professions: Roles and Rules. New
      York: Russell Sage Foundation, 1970. 303 p.
      A recent and comprehensive account of the professions
      in the United States by an authority. Includes comments
      on the development of codes of conduct, as "one promi-
      nent way in which professional associations operate as
      agencies of self-regulation" (p. 116-120).

38 Nader, Ralph, and others, eds. Whistle Blowing: The Report
      of the Conference on Professional Responsibility. New
      York: Grossman, 1972. 302 p.
      Popularly written handbook on how to blow the whistle,
      with examples in short accounts of successful citizen or
      public reporting of unprofessional conduct--C-5 over-
      runs (A. E. Fitzgerald), cyclamates (Verrett), atomic
      radiation dangers (Gofmann). Gives prescriptions for
      change and corrective action. Appendices include pro-
      fessional ethical codes.

39 National Academy of Sciences. Scientific, Technical and Re-
      lated Societies of the United States. 9th ed. Washington,
      D. C.: National Academy of Sciences, 1971.
      Listing of "membership societies devoted to a particular
      scientific or technical discipline (or group of disciplines)
      and primarily committed to the study, development, and
      dissemination of knowledge in the discipline represented."

40 National Trade and Professional Associations of the United
      States and Labor Unions. 1973. Washington, D. C.: Colum-
      bia Books, 1973.
      This annual directory lists over 4, 000 organizations.
      Each issue includes articles, such as 1971: Lamb, George
      P., and Carrington Shields, "Trade Association Law and
      Practice, 1970," which discusses Codes of Ethics (p. 31-
      32).

41 Nimer, Gilda. Professions and Professionalism: A Biblio-
      graphic Overview. (Newsletter, no. 2, Manpower Research

Project, University of Maryland School of Library and Information Services.)   July 1968.   19 p.
A classified, annotated bibliography "selected on the
basis of inferred relevance to librarianship." Limited
to publications of the "past ten years," and landmark
works, referring "to the American Scene."

42 Occupational Outlook Handbook.   1972-1973 ed.   U.S. Department of Labor, Bureau of Labor Statistics.   (Bulletin 1700.)
Washington, D.C.:   Gov. Print. Off., 1972.
"Discusses the nature of work in more than 800 different
occupations as well as earnings, job prospects during the
1970's, and education and training requirements."

43 Parsons, Talcott.   "Professional Ethics." In: International
Encyclopedia of Social Sciences, v. 12.   New York: Macmillan and Free Press, 1968.   p. 536-547.
Sociologist considers professions and professional codes
--"The development and increasing strategic importance
of the professions probably constitutes the most important change that has occurred in the occupational
system of modern societies."

44 Pennell, Maryland Y., and others.   Accreditation and Certification in Relation to Allied Health Manpower.   U.S. Department of Health, Education and Welfare, Public Health
Service, National Institute of Health, Bureau of Health Manpower Education.   Washington, D.C.:   Gov. Print. Off.,
1971.   43 p.
Role of professional associations in raising the performance standards of individuals in health professions,
through accreditation of education programs and certification on a voluntary basis of qualified personnel. Includes selected information on 16 allied health occupa-
tions--designations of certification or registration of
health manpower by nongovernmental agencies in 1970.
Bibliography, p. 16-17.

45 Pirsig, Maynard E.   Cases and Materials on Professional Responsibility.   2nd ed.   St. Paul, Minn.:   West Pub. Co.,
1972.   447 p.   (American Casebook Series.)

46 Priestly, Barbara, ed.   British Qualifications: A Comprehensive Guide to Educational, Technical, Professional and
Academic Qualifications in Britain.   2nd ed.   London: Ko-
gan Page Ltd., 1970.   1278 p.
Provides information about the occupational requirements
current in the United Kingdom.   Includes an Index of
Abbreviations and Designatory Letters (p. 17-61).

47 Reader, William J.   Professional Men: The Rise of the Professional Classes in Nineteenth-Century England.   New York:

Basic Books, 1966.
How professions in England developed with the middle
class. "The new professional man brought one scale of
values--the gentleman's--to bear upon the other--the
tradesman's--and produced a specialized variety of business morality which came to be known as 'professional
ethics' " (p. 159).

48 Reed, Alfred Z. "Learned Professions and Their Organization." In: Review of Legal Education in the United States
and Canada for the Year 1933. New York: Carnegie
Foundation for the Advancement of Teaching, 1933. p. 3-
28.
An expert history.

49 Reynolds, Neil B. "Job Ranking on an Ethics Scale." Educational Record 39:192-193, April 1958.
A brief report of a survey by General Electric to find
out how 1827 undergraduates on the campuses of 20
universities and colleges in the United States regarded
occupations on an ethics scale. The occupation reported
as requiring least compromise with personal beliefs (most
ethics)--college teaching; that requiring most compro-
mise--politics.

50 Schouten, Jan. The Rod and the Serpent of Asklepios: Symbol
of Medicine. Amsterdam: Elsevier, 1967. 260 p.
A history of the symbol of medicine, with numerous illustrations.

51 Taeusch, Carl F. Professional and Business Ethics. New
York: Holt, 1926. 370 p.
In this early study of professional ethics in the United
States, chapters are devoted to discussions of ethical
codes of six occupations (law, engineering, education,
medicine, business, labor unions, farmers' cooperatives).
Also, distinguishes between law, morals, and ethics
(p. 74-99).

52 _____. "Professional Ethics." In: Encyclopedia of the
Social Sciences. v. 12. New York: Macmillan, 1930-1935.
p. 472-476.
The professional code of ethics--"ideals or standards of
behavior"--carries out the immediate objective of professional service and ethics: "The welfare of the client
or patient."

53 United States Government Printing Office. Seals and Other Devices in Use in the Government Printing Office. Washington,
D.C., June 1965. 72 p.
Seals officially approved by 50 United States departments
and agencies as their emblem. All seals reproduced

represent art on file in the Division of Typography and
Design of the United States Government Printing Office
"for making reproducibles in the sizes available in the
Printing Office."

54 United States National Institutes of Health. Equivalency and Proficiency Testing: A Survey of Existing Testing Programs
in Allied Health and Other Health Fields. Department of
Health, Education and Welfare, Public Health Service.
Washington, D. C.: Gov. Print. Off., 1971. 83 p.
Discusses problems of certification, licensure and pro-
ficiency/equivalency examinations by diverse licensing
agencies--federal and state government, armed services,
professional organizations--in a variety of health fields.
Annotated bibliography, p. 61-83.

55 _____. Report on Licensure and Related Health Personnel
Credentialing. U. S. Department of Health, Education and
Welfare, Public Health Service. Washington, D. C.: Gov.
Print. Off., 1971. 154 p.
Examines the major problems associated with licensure,
certification, and accreditation for practice or employment of health personnel. Gives certification or registration of individuals in 16 selected health occupations, by
nongovernmental agencies, including professional organizations.

56 Vollmer, Howard M., and Donald L. Mills, eds. Professionalization. Englewood Cliffs, N. J.: Prentice-Hall, 1966.
365 p.
Book of readings on the process of professionalization--
57 selections on 27 occupations. Considers "Codes of
Conduct" (Chapter 4, Professional Controls, p. 129-144).

57 Wilensky, Harold. "The Professionalization of Everyone?"
American Journal of Sociology. 70:137-158, September
1964.

58 Zald, Mayer N. Occupations and Organizations in American
Society: The Organization Dominated Man? Chicago:
Markham Pub. Co., 1971. 108 p.
Occupational strictures in contemporary technological
society. Includes bibliographies.

AAA (Amer Academy of Allergy) 40
AAA (Amer Anthropological Assn) 46
AAA (Amer Arbitration Assn) 76
AAAE (Amer Assn of Airport Executives) 38
AACE (Amer Assn of Cost Engineers) 277
A. A. E. (Accredited Airport Exutive) 38
AAE (Accredited Assessment Evaluator) 102
AAEA (Amer Agricultural Economics Assn) 31
AAEE (Amer Academy of Environmental Engineers) 281
AAF (Amer Advertising Federation) 26
A. A. G. O. 475
AAM (Amer Academy of Microbiology) 444
AAM (Amer Assn of Museums) 455
AAMFC (Amer Assn of Marriage & Family Counselors) 428
AANA (Amer Assn of Nurse Anesthetists) 42
AANS (Amer Assn of Neurological Surgeons) 744
AAO (Amer Assn of Opthalmology) 502
AAPOR (Amer Assn for Public Opinion Research) 636
AART (Amer Assn for Respiratory Therapy) 702

AAS (Amer Astronomical Soc) 109
AASA (Amer Assn of School Administrators) 709
AAUP (Amer Assn of University Professors) 757
AAUP Bulletin 758
ABA (Amer Bar Assn) 391; 408
ABESPA (Amer Board of Examiners in Speech Pathology & Audiology) 739
ABHD (Amer Board of Hypnosis in Dentistry) 363
ABHP (Amer Board of Health Physics) 341
ABMH (Amer Board of Medical Hypnosis) 363
ABO (Amer Board of Opticianry) 503
ABPH (Amer Board of Psychological Hypnosis) 363
ABPP (Amer Board of Professional Psychology) 363; 622
ACA (Amer Chiropractic Assn) 157
ACA (Amer Correctional Assn) 540
ACAS (Associate, Casualty Actuarial Society) 18, 19
ACHA (Amer College of Hospital Administrators) 355
ACME (Assn of Consulting Management Engineers) 271
ACNHA (Amer College of Nursing Home Administrators) 495
ACNM (Amer College of Nurse-Midwives) 450
ACS (Amer Chemical Soc) 154

Amer Arbitration Assn　76
Federal Mediation & Concilia-
tion Service　80
ARCHAEOLOGISTS　84-87
Soc for Amer Archaeology
ARCHITECTS　87-93
Amer Inst of Architects
ARCHIVISTS　93-96
Natl Archives & Records
Service　93
Soc of Amer Archivists　95
The Archivist's Code　94-95
Arenberg, Gerald S.　402
Armed Forces Recreation Soc
680
Arms see Genealogists;
Heralds
Army see Government Em-
ployees--Military
Arnold, Harvey　510
"Ars Vertus Caritas"　496
The Art Directors Club　98
Arthritis & Rheumatism Reme-
dies　120
ARTISTS　96-101
Artists Equity Assn　96
Joint Ethics Committee　98
ARTISTS EQUITY ASSN　96-98
Code of Ethics　97-98
Insignia　96
The Artists Guild, Inc. of N.Y.
98
ASSESSORS　101-106
Internatl Assn of Assessing
Officers
Associate see Professional
Designations
ASSOCIATED GENERAL CON-
TRACTORS OF AMERICA
195-201
Code of Ethical Conduct
197-201
Insignia　196
Motto　196
ASSOCIATION EXECUTIVES
106-109
Amer Soc of Association
Executives
Assn for Counselor Education
& Supervision　202
Assn for Measurement & Evalu-
ation in Guidance　202

Assn for the Study of Asthma &
Allied Conditions　40
Assn for the Study of Community
Organization　728
Assn of Better Business Bureaus
Internatl　27
Assn of Boards of Rabbis　558
ASSN OF CONSULTING MANAGE-
MENT ENGINEERS　271-277
Insignia　272
Standards of Professional Con-
duct & Practice　272-277
Assn of Labor Mediation Agencies
80
Assn of Medical Superintendents
of Amer Institutions for the
Insane　620
Assn of Operating Room Nurses
500
ASSN OF OPERATING ROOM
TECHNICIANS　500-502
Code of Ethics　502
Examination　500-501
Insignia　501
Professional Designation　500
Assn of Physical & Mental Re-
habilitation　688
Assn of Technical Writers &
Editors　779
Associations
Criteria for listing in sample
in this book　1
ASTRONOMERS　109
Amer Astronomical Soc
Attorneys　408-415
AUCTIONEERS　109-112
Natl Auctioneers Assn
Audiologists　739
AUDITORS　113-116
Inst of Internal Auditors
"Australian Eye"　510-511
Australian Optometric Assn　510
Authors　473
Automotive Engineers　259-260
Automotive Service Industry Assn
118
AUTOMOTIVE SERVICE TECH-
NICIANS　116-119
Independent Garage Owners of
America　116
Natl Automotive Technicians
Certification Board　118

Society of America 18
CASUALTY ACTUARIAL SOC
17-22
Examination 18
Guides to Professional Conduct 19-22
Professional Designations
18, 19
Casualty Underwriters 378
Ceramic Engineering 260
Certificate as Registered
Microbiologist 446
Certificate in Data Processing
214
Certificate of Clinical Competence in Audiology 740
Certificate of Clinical Competence in Speech Pathology
740
Certificate of Membership
(Amer Inst of Certified Public Accountants) 6
Certification of Automotive Technicians 116, 118-119
Certified Amer Lineage Specialist 320
Certified Assessment Evaluator
102
Certified Association Executive
106
Certified Clockmaker 773
Certified Commercial Investment Member 677
Certified Corrective Therapist
689
Certified Dental Assistant 218
Certified Documentary Specialist 308
Certified Genealogical Record
Searcher 320
Certified Genealogist 320
Certified Health Physicist 341
Certified Hearing Aid Audiologist 343
Certified Internatl Executive
308
Certified Laboratory Assistant
438
Certified Master Clockmaker
773
Certified Master Watchmaker
773
Certified Member 369

Certified Nurse-Midwife 451
Certified Occupational Therapy
Assistant 498
Certified Operating Room Technician 500
Certified Optician 504
Certified Personalty Evaluator
102
Certified Professional Secretary
722
Certified Public Accountants 5-
13
Certified Registered Nurse Anesthetist 42
Certified Respiratory Therapy
Technician 702
Certified Residential Broker 677-
678
Certified Technician 435
Certified Travel Counselor 768
Certified Watchmaker 773
Ch. M. 475
Chamber of Commerce of the
U. S. Marshaling Citizen Power to Modernize Corrections
541
Chamberlain, Mildred 354
Charter of Internatl P. E. N. 778
Chartered Assn Executive 107
Chartered Financial Analyst 302
Chartered Life Underwriter 373-
374
Chartered Property & Casualty
Underwriter 378
Charting 746
Chemical Engineers 262
CHEMISTS 154-156
Amer Chemical Soc
Chemists Creed 156
Chiefs of Police 404-406
Children's Premiums & Offers
120
Children's TV Advertising Statement of Principles 146-147
Chiropodists 591
CHIROPRACTORS 157-166
Amer Chiropractic Assn
Choir Master 474; 475
Christensen, Wayne C. 300
Church Musicians 474
Chute, Marchette. P. E. N. Amer
Center 777
Citizen Assns

Insignia 768
Professional Designation 768
INST OF CHARTERED FINAN-
CIAL ANALYSTS 302-304
Examination 302, 303
Insignia 303
Professional Designation 302
INST OF ELECTRICAL & ELEC-
TRONICS ENGINEERS 279-
281
Insignia 280
Professional Designation 281
Inst of Environmental Engineers
240
INST OF ENVIRONMENTAL SCI-
ENCES 240-241
Insignia 241
Professional Designation 240
INST OF INTERNAL AUDITORS
113-116
Code of Ethics 114-116
Insignia 114
Motto 114
Statement of Responsibilities
of the Internal Auditor 113
Insurance--Foreign Trade 309
INSURANCE AGENTS & BROK-
ERS 371-380
Natl Assn of Insurance Agents
Insurance Inst of America 378
INSURANCE UNDERWRITERS--
LIFE 373-378
Amer Soc of Chartered Life
Underwriters 373
Natl Assn of Life Under-
writers 376
INSURANCE UNDERWRITERS--
PROPERTY & CASUALTY
378-380
Soc of Chartered Property
& Casualty Underwriters
"Integritas Professionis" 15
INTERIOR DESIGNERS & DECO-
RATORS 380-389
Amer Inst of Interior Design-
ers 381
Natl Soc of Interior Designers
385
Intermediate Heraldry Certifi-
cate 352
Internatl Associates 408
INTERNATL ASSN OF ASSESS-
ING OFFICERS 101-106

Code of Ethics 103-104
Insignia 102
Professional Designation 102
Standards of Professional Con-
duct 104-105
INTERNATL ASSN OF CHIEFS OF
POLICE 404-406
Insignia 405
Law Enforcement Code of Ethics
406
INTERNATL ASSN OF FIRE
CHIEFS 307-308
Insignia 307
Internatl Assn of Milk & Food
Sanitarians 706
INTERNATL ASSN OF MILK,
FOOD, & ENVIRONMENTAL
SANITARIANS 706-707
Insignia 707
INTERNATL BAR ASSN 2; 412-
415
Insignia 412
Internatl Code of Ethics 413-
415
INTERNATL CITY MANAGEMENT
ASSN 166-169
City Management Code of Eth-
ics 168-169
Insignia 167
Internatl Code of Ethics for the
Legal Profession 413-415
Internatl Code of Medical Ethics
569-570
Internatl Code of Zoological No-
menclature 780, 781
INTERNATL COMMISSION ON
ZOOLOGICAL NOMENCLATURE
2; 780-782
Code of Ethics 781-782
Monaco Resolution 782
Internatl Council for the Improve-
ment of Reading 755
Internatl Film Importers & Dis-
tributors of America 452
Internatl Marketing 425
INTERNATL PERSONNEL MAN-
AGEMENT ASSN 549-550
Insignia 549
Statement of Principles for
Members 550
INTERNATL READING ASSN
755-757
Code of Ethics 756-757

"Let Them Live" 451
Lewin, Mark H. 622
Lewis, Charles 202
"Lex et Ordo" 404
LIBRARIANS 416-421
 Amer Library Assn 416
 Special Libraries Assn 419
Library of Congress 329, 330
Licenses
 Coast Guard 339
 Merchant Marine Officer 339
Licensing Assns & Agencies
 see also Occupational Desig-
 nations; Professional Designa-
 tions; and names of individual
 Professional Assns
 Amer Board for Certification
 of Corrective Therapists
 689
 Amer Board of Clinical Hyp-
 nosis 362
 Amer Board of Examiners
 in Speech Pathology &
 Audiology 739
 Amer Board of Health Phys-
 ics 341
 Amer Board of Hypnosis in
 Dentistry 362
 Amer Board of Medical Hyp-
 nosis 362
 Amer Board of Opticianry
 503
 Amer Board of Psychological
 Hypnosis 362
 Amer Medical Technologists
 435
 Amer Registry of Radiologic
 Technologists 668
 Amer Registry of Respira-
 tory Technicians 703
 Board for Certification of
 Genealogists 320
 Board for Registry of Med-
 ical Technologists 438
 Inst of Certified Travel
 Agents 767
 Inst of Chartered Financial
 Analysts 302
 Internatl Soc of Clinical Lab-
 oratory Technologists 439
 Intersociety Academy for
 Certification of Sanitarians
 708

 Technician Certification Board
 703
Life Insurance Underwriters 373-
 378
Lilley, Theodore I. 302
Linton, Bruce A. Self-Regula-
 tion in Broadcasting 122
"Littera Scripta Manet" 94
Little, Kenneth B. 624
Lobbying 329, 330
Lovett, George 483
Low, James P. 106
Lucas, Ferris E. 406
Lund, Sir Thomas 412
 Professional Ethics 413
Lutes, J. Dewey 356
Lyricists 473

MAA (Mathematical Assn of Amer-
 ica) 434
M. ASCE 266
M. D. Caduceus 564
MENC (Music Educators Natl
 Conference) 462
M. L. in Immunology 445
M. L. in Microbiology 445
M. L. in Mycology 445
M. L. in Parasitology 445
M. L. in Virology 445
M. L. T. 435
MLT (ASCP) 438
MOO 504
MPAA (Motion Picture Assn of
 America) 452
M. Photog. 557
M. Photog Cr. 557
M. T. 435
MT (ASCP) 438
MTNA (Music Teachers Natl Assn)
 466
McAtee, W. L. 776
MacBride, Dexter D. 55
McGowan, Roland C. 668
McGrath, Kyran M. 455
McKee, James E. 648
McKenna, F. E. 419
McKenzie, John F. 393
McMahon, G. J. 412
Maers & Paul. Dictionary of
 Color 299
Magonigle, N. Van Buren 88
Maimonides 563; 566-567